THIRTY FAMOUS
ONE-ACT PLAYS

THIRTY FAMOUS

One-Act Plays

>>

EDITED BY

BENNETT CERF *and* VAN H. CARTMELL

WITH AN INTRODUCTION BY

RICHARD WATTS, JR.

THE MODERN LIBRARY

NEW YORK

ACKNOWLEDGMENTS

For permission to include the following plays (in the order of their appearance in this volume), acknowledgment is here made to the authors of the plays and the publishers under whose imprint they were issued:

The Man Who Married a Dumb Wife by Anatole France. Copyright, 1915, by Dodd, Mead and Company, Inc.

Miss Julie by August Strindberg. Reprinted by permission of the Modern Library.

Salomé by Oscar Wilde. Reprinted by permission of the Modern Library.

The Rising of the Moon by Lady Gregory. Reprinted by permission of G. P. Putnam's Sons.

The Boor by Anton Chekov. Copyright, 1915, by Barrett H. Clark.

The Twelve-Pound Look by J. M. Barrie. Copyright, 1914, by Charles Scribner's Sons.

The Green Cockatoo by Arthur Schnitzler. Copyright, 1932, by Samuel French.

A *Miracle of Saint Antony* by Maurice Maeterlinck. Reprinted by permission of the Modern Library.

The Monkey's Paw by W. W. Jacobs. Copyright, 1910, by Samuel French, Ltd. Copyright, 1937 in renewal, by Louis N. Parker.

The Little Man by John Galsworthy. Copyright, 1915, by Charles Scribner's Sons. Copyright, 1943 in renewal, by Ada Galsworthy.

Riders to the Sea by J. M. Synge. Reprinted by permission of Random House, Inc.

FOREWORD

This is the fourth of a series of modern play anthologies by the same editors.

The first of the series was entitled *Sixteen Famous American Plays*, published in 1941. It contained the following plays:

Life with Father; The Time of Your Life; The Man Who Came to Dinner; The Little Foxes; Our Town; Having Wonderful Time; The Women; Boy Meets Girl; Waiting for Lefty; Dead End; The Petrified Forest; Ah, Wilderness!; The Front Page; Biography; The Green Pastures; They Knew What They Wanted.

The second in the series was entitled *Sixteen Famous British Plays*, published in 1942. It contained the following plays:

The Second Mrs. Tanqueray; The Green Bay Tree; Journey's End; Milestones; The Circle; Cavalcade; The Green Goddess; Dangerous Corner; Mr. Pim Passes By; The Barretts of Wimpole Street; Outward Bound; The Importance of Being Earnest; The Corn Is Green; What Every Woman Knows; Loyalties; Victoria Regina.

The third in the series was entitled *Sixteen Famous European Plays*, published in 1943. It contained the following plays:

The Wild Duck; The Weavers; The Sea Gull; Cyrano de Bergerac; The Lower Depths; The Playboy of the Western World; Anatol; The Cradle Song; Six Characters in Search of an Author; R.U.R.; The Dybbuk; Liliom; Grand Hotel; Tovarich; Shadow and Substance; Amphitryon 38.

In making these selections we confined ourselves almost entirely to modern plays, the great majority, in fact, being comparatively recent. We included only one play by any one author, and the prime requisite was the endorsement of a successful presentation in this country. We furthermore sought, we hope successfully, to achieve a wide variety in type and treatment.

The problems with which we were faced in the preparation of this volume were somewhat different. Since the days of the old vaudeville circuits the professional one-act play has become something of a rarity. It is chiefly to the vast number of little-theater groups throughout the country that the one-act play owes its prosperous survival. Only after the most careful study of the successful amateur productions all over the country have we ventured to make the present selection. We have allowed ourselves considerable latitude in our choice, including two plays that have more than one scene, but these are both short plays and may properly be considered to fall within the present category. Our range of playwrights in this case has been international, and the character and treatment shows even a wider scope than heretofore, a point that need not be labored when one considers the truly global stretch from Strindberg to Kaufman.

We have again limited ourselves to only a single play by a given author, although in some cases, notably O'Neill and Coward, this was hard discipline.

In the matter of successful presentation in this country we have found checking difficult, but we may confidently say that whether or not each play has been enthusiastically received, we are quite safe in asserting that each has been enthusiastically and frequently produced. We have been fortunate in being able to acquire a number of plays that are not easily accessible, and many that have never before appeared in any anthology. There are, of course, a few familiar selections which are definite "musts" for any such collection as this. We have not, however, relied on a few outstanding plays to carry the book. There is ground for suspicion that some anthologists have been content to present a few highlights or "plums" to entice the customer and then filled out their volume with less consequential material. Possibly, the success of this whole new series of play selections is due to the fact that the editors have endeavored to present tables of contents that have included *nothing but* highlights and spared neither effort nor expense to do so. Considerable patience and persistence have been required to track down permission to reprint all the selections in this anthology. A discouraging variety of difficulties was met with, but eventually only one play which we wished to include proved unobtainable.

Certain readers and critics will question the judgment that governed our selections, but the choices necessarily represent personal opinions, and we found that getting each other to agree on thirty plays was tough enough without undertaking completely to satisfy a wide public. As has been the case in the earlier books, the gentleman who has been kind enough to write our introduction has assumed no responsibility for the contents of the book. Messrs. Atkinson, John Mason Brown and John Anderson, who performed this service for the earlier volumes, did not concur in every instance with our selection, and we imagine Mr. Richard Watts, Jr., will have similar reservations.

For the first time in this series we have included, in an appendix, brief biographical data on the various authors. Here again, if any critical color has crept in, it is purely personal prejudice and enthusiasm on the part of the editors, who hereby accept the responsibility and at the same time express gratitude to the authors, agents and original publishers whose gracious permissions made this volume possible.

BENNETT CERF
VAN H. CARTMELL

CONTENTS

The plays are printed in chronological order of the authors' birth dates.

INTRODUCTION

By Richard Watts, Jr.

It is my great fear that I am going to be a disappointment to the Messrs. Cerf and Cartmell, the editors of this volume. Being combative gentlemen, these worthies are happiest when the critics whom they have selected to introduce their play anthologies are sniping at them scornfully, calling bitter attention to their various sins of commission and omission. Apparently it cheers them to be told that their taste in the drama is faulty and a trifle idiotic and upsets them immeasurably to be agreed with by their presiding critic—which may indicate their general attitude toward professional dramatic criticism. Anyway, it can hardly be said that the Hollywood vice of the yes-man has reached them.

It pains me, therefore, to contemplate their consternation when they find that I am in general agreement with them and think that their selections are fine. I have some dissents here and there, and I can think of some plays which I feel should have found a place in this collection—my professional pride, if nothing else, would insist on that—but I congratulate the two editors on the wisdom and the completeness of their choice. The plays herein presented make excellent reading as well as excellent acting; they represent a splendid range in subject, treatment, manner and setting; and they offer an admirable general view of the nature and quality of the one-act drama.

One virtue of this collection, and a considerable virtue it is, too, is that it is fun to read. On the whole I think there is more sheer pleasure in reading a one-act play than is to be found in perusing full-length dramas. It is a form which tends to set free the imagination and the spirit of the playwright and to send it bounding through time and space, ignoring the customary fetters of convention and of length. Almost any playwright can say what he wants to say in less time than the full-length play requires, and the one-act work is joyously free of the usual padding. It is a sprightly form and a splendidly easygoing one, and it is no chance that the Irish, who—as dramatists, at least—are inclined to be eloquent and original in their flights of the imagination, and not too formal, are particularly triumphant in it.

In fact, if I were determined to be disapproving of the Messrs. Cerf and Cartmell, one of my chief criticisms would be that they had included too few Irish plays in their collection. It is my dogmatic opinion that Synge's *Riders to the Sea* is not only the finest drama in this volume, but is the most eloquently powerful one-act play that has ever been written. Lady Gregory's *The Rising of the Moon* is a delightful little play and I am glad that it has been included, but I wish that space could likewise have been found for the selfsame Lady Gregory's *The Gaol Gate* and possibly for her *Spreading the News;* certainly for W. B. Yeats's stirring *Cathleen ni Houlihan.* I am a bit dubious about including St. John Ervine among the Irish playwrights, but I wish there had been room for his short work called *The Magnanimous Lover.*

Obviously it has been impossible to include in the space of one volume all of the works which should have been included, but even within these limits I would have made a few changes. For example, Eugene O'Neill's *The Moon of the Caribbees* is the best one-act play that I know of in America and is certainly the superior of the same author's effective but somewhat obvious and mechanical *In the Zone.* As for the inclusion of George S. Kaufman's *If Men Played Cards as Women Do,* it seems to me absurd to present it as the representative of American hilarity when such a wonderful work as Ring Lardner's magnificently insane *The Tridget of Greva* is omitted.

In fact if I wanted to include a short Kaufman work it

would have been the tale of a casual fire department called *The Still Alarm.* I think, though, that, despite my great admiration for Mr. Kaufman as collaborator and stage director, I would leave him out of my compilation and would, after substituting *The Tridget of Greva,* try to find a place for either Marc Connelly's saga of a traveler making epic preparations for a journey 'way up to 125th Street or, if too great a delicacy didn't interfere, perhaps Mr. Connelly's tale of a hapless gentleman who was forced to listen to tales of waterfalls, etc., upon a trying occasion.

Possibly at this point it may seem that, after rather grandly expressing great approval for the Messrs. Cerf and Cartmell at the outset, I am now determined to tear them apart. This, however, is not the case. While I would have preferred the suggestions I have set down and have a few other reservations here and there I find almost all of the plays herein included of interest for varying reasons. In truth, the only serious plays in the volume which strike me as completely without merit are Maeterlinck's *A Miracle of St. Antony* and Stanley Houghton's *The Dear Departed,* and I suppose that the fame of the Maeterlinck work warrants its inclusion, despite its hollowness.

In several other cases, even when I do not care particularly for the play, I can see why it was included and I hail the inclusion. For example, *The Drums of Oude* is certainly one of the worst melodramas ever written, and yet I have heard of it for so many years and it has achieved so widespread a reputation—in great part, of course, because its use of the native drums off stage foreshadowed the justly more celebrated employment of the tomtom in O'Neill's *The Emperor Jones*—that I am glad of the chance to read it here. I doubt, though, if I will ever bother to read it again.

Likewise I think the publishers were right when they included Oscar Wilde's *Salomé.* Certainly this is one of the most unhealthy and decadent dramas in the world and I doubt whether there is a line in this volume or even in all of world dramatic literature with which the reader will find himself in such utter accord as Herod's final "Kill that woman!" I dislike *Salomé* with great heartiness, yet there is no escaping its morbid fascination, even its touches of evil beauty, and I suspect that this volume would be incomplete without it.

At this point it might be well for me to turn to some of the plays I particularly admire. As I have said, *Riders to the Sea* seems to me the most eloquent one-act play ever written. And there are few short plays finer and more moving than William Saroyan's *Hello Out There*. In the most simple and heartbreaking terms Saroyan proves that he can be just as effective, if not more so, when he is writing directly and without eccentricities as when he is being just a bit studiously perverse. *Hello Out There* and the full-length *The Time of Your Life* offer between them complete evidence that the recluse from Fresno is a true dramatist and one of the glories of the American theatre.

One of my favorites in this collection is *A Sunny Morning* by the Quintero brothers. There is in this little story of ancient sweethearts a true sunniness of the heart, a gay spirit, a romantic graciousness and a gently ironic humor that make it thoroughly enchanting. In general, I am no great enthusiast for the drama of unhappy Spain, but this work is a delight.

After so many years it is pleasant to go back to Anatole France's *The Man Who Married a Dumb Wife* and find that it still maintains its playful manner and its air of humorous improvisation. In turning from the urbane and amused irony of cynical old Anatole to the savage, neurotic bitterness of Strindberg's *Miss Julie* one gets some idea of the range of plays included in this compilation. I find *Miss Julie* tiresome, overwrought and a little silly, but it still has a certain strange power about it and there is something undeniably fascinating about the black, humorless depths of its hatred. Anatole France's distaste for the human race is infinitely more adult and intelligent but somehow less disturbing in its pathological overtones.

As a writer of short plays Chekov is considerably less interesting and important than he is in his full-length dramas or his stories. *The Boor,* however, is a pleasant little comedy, a sort of brief Muscovite *Taming of the Shrew,* and if there is anyone still alive who holds to the one-time popular belief that the Russians are a humorless people, given exclusively to melancholia, it may possibly disabuse him of so fantastic an idea. The fact is, of course, that the Russians, like that curiously similar nationality, the Irish, are mercurial in temperament and are thus able to rush back and forth precipitously between the heights of merriment and the depths of despondency while indulging in either quality with a fine completeness which makes it at the time seem their exclusive preoccupation. It is one of the racial traits which makes the drama of both countries so vigorously emotional and, in a strange sort of way, so alike.

Sir James M. Barrie's *The Twelve-Pound Look* will be remembered by veteran theatregoers chiefly as a vehicle for Ethel Barrymore, who used to have a wonderful time playing its heroine and bringing the magic of her voice and her gracious humor to bear on it. It is an amiable little vaudeville, pleasant enough to see or to read, but I am afraid that anyone reading it today will be struck chiefly by the annoying whimsicality of the stage directions and of Sir James's coy little asides to the reader. If you think that the Barrie quaintness is offensive in *The Twelve-Pound Look,* however, you should examine the author's pixy annotations in *A Kiss for Cinderella,* and, anyway, this characteristic weakness of the playwright shouldn't altogether blind one to the effective if obvious quality of the comedy.

Schnitzler's *The Green Cockatoo* is still fun to read and, in a skillful production, would be entertaining to watch. Its romantic artificiality is well maintained, and while its irony is pretty obvious it does possess a true theatrical effectiveness. It is no *Anatole,* but it doesn't pretend to be, and we may continue to enjoy it for its debonair style and its sheer delight in the pleasant but now usually neglected business of using the theatre theatrically in frank and unashamed joyousness over the fact that it is being theatrical. Only the Lunts in our current drama seem to carry on this sheer relish for the theatre as theatre.

There are two famous and excellent horror plays in this volume, Lord Dunsany's *A Night at an Inn* and Louis N. Parker's dramatization of W. W. Jacob's *The Monkey's Paw.* Both of them are more effective in the theatre than in the library, but if you read them with any sense of the possibilities of staging and acting in such matters I think you will enjoy both of them. Dunsany, incidentally, seems to be pretty much forgotten these days. I saw him in Ireland recently, a massive, gray-bearded figure with the air of an old Celtic hero exiled from the company of Finn and his peers and uncomfortably thrust into modern evening clothes. I am afraid he is aware of the critical and popular neglect into which he has fallen these days and I hope the inclusion of his play here will recall to playgoers what a great man of the theatre he was just a couple of decades ago. I also wish there had been room in this volume for two other grand works of his, *King Argimenes and the Unknown Warrior* and *The Queen's Enemies.*

Perhaps the first thing that strikes a reader of Galsworthy's *The Little Man* is the absurd jargon that is allotted to the somewhat discreditable American of the brief morality play. When even so expert an observer as John Galsworthy can go so wrong, it is not surprising that the speech attributed to Americans in the plays and novels of lesser men should be so fantastically ridiculous. It might be hoped that one result of the war and the presence of so many American soldiers in England and so many English here would be to give our Allies at least a slightly more accurate picture of how we talk, but I am by no means optimistic. I saw a play by an Englishman about life in Kansas City in London last season, a weird and fantastic thing called *No Orchids for Miss Blandish,* and in it the playwright even thought Kansas City newspapermen drank pink gin. Anyway, despite a character Galsworthy fondly thought to be American, *The Little Man,* is a rather entertaining comedy about idealism called upon to go into action.

If Philip Moeller's *Helena's Husband* seems a trifle outmoded these days, it will be remembered that this is a natural fate of pioneers, even in the drama. *Helena's Husband,* like John Erskine's novel, *The Private Life of Helen of Troy,* was regarded as pretty fresh in its viewpoint and treatment when it began mocking the ancient legends back in the now-forgotten days of "debunking." To that same period in life and letters belong Susan Glaspell's *Suppressed Desires,* which made excellent fun of psychoanalysis, and Lawrence Langner's *Another Way Out,* which laughed at moral emancipation in Greenwich Village. All of these works possess, among their other interests, a value for the social historian of that fascinating if somewhat repulsive era in the national annals.

In Kenneth Sawyer Goodman's *A Game of Chess,* Holworthy Hall's and Robert Middlemass's *The Valiant* and Lewis Beach's *The Clod* we turn to three entertaining melodramas. To me the otherwise effective *A Game of Chess* ends in disappointment because its climax is so unsatisfactory. Endeavoring for a change to be a constructive critic, whatever that is, I would suggest that the work would have been improved had the remarkably inexpert villain unexpectedly turned the tables on his triumphant and self-satisfied antagonist. *The Valiant,* which has been so successful in vaudeville, is pat and mechanical in story and treatment but in a shameless sort of way it does get its effect. The most striking of the trio is Mr. Beach's Civil War incident, *The Clod,* which is still a play of power and merit.

The chief interest of *Lithuania* lies in matters which have nothing to do with its dramatic qualities. It seems to have been the only play written by Rupert Brooke and it represents one of the first emergences of a tale that used to come out of Eastern Europe with great regularity in the days immediately following the First World War until it became one of the favorite legends of the late Alexander Woollcott. In its own right, it is not without its interest as a horror play. Another poet, Miss Millay, is represented by her anti-war work, *Aria da Capo,* which belongs distinctly to a post-war period. It strikes me as considerably more dramatic and effective than her belligerent narrative poem, *Lidice.* Alice Gerstenberg's *Overtones* has been described as a sort of forerunner of O'Neill's *Strange Interlude,* although that is true only in the sense in which it can be said that *The Drums of Oude* foreshadowed *The Emperor Jones.*

Had I been selecting a Noel Coward play for inclusion in this volume I would have picked either the hilarious *Hands Across the Sea* or the touching *Still Life,* instead of *Fumed Oak,* but that does not prevent me from recognizing the effectiveness and skill of the comedy chosen. As for Mr. Odets's *Waiting for Lefty* it is obviously a required work for any collection of one-act plays. It is dramatic and exciting; it is filled with the sort of simple prose poetry which is Odets at his best and it is one of the finest of social protest dramas, long or short. I have already noted that Saroyan's *Hello Out There* seems to me a masterpiece.

Last of all comes Irwin Shaw's *Bury the Dead,* a striking anti-war play which has been the most-praised of its author's various contributions to the theatre. One of the best writers of short stories in America, Mr. Shaw has been unfortunate in the drama in that his stage works are better in their parts than as a whole and that the dramas continue to be those of a man of promise rather than of achievement. I think that *Bury the Dead* suffers from these characteristic defects and never quite comes off, but it does have its flashes of power.

The important thing about the accompanying collection is that, despite any complaints and objections that may be leveled against various entries in it—and despite my seeming querulousness I insist that my own complaints and objections are minor ones—it is interesting to read and gives the reader an excellent survey of the range and history of the one-act play. As for the current status of one-act playwriting, it is not encouraging, now that Mr. Saroyan is in the Army, the Irish talent for this particular form is undergoing a lapse characteristic of the present state of the Irish drama in general and a Southwestern newspaperman named Noel Houston, who wrote an excellent short play called *According to Law*, a couple of years ago, seems to have returned to his silence.

New York
September, 1943

The Man Who Married a Dumb Wife

A COMEDY IN TWO SCENES

BY ANATOLE FRANCE

TRANSLATED BY
CURTIS HIDDEN PAGE

CHARACTERS

MASTER LEONARD BOTAL, *judge*
MASTER ADAM FUMÉE, *lawyer*
MASTER SIMON COLLINE, *doctor*
MASTER JEAN MAUGIER, *surgeon*
MASTER SERAFIN DULAURIER, *apothecary*
GILES BOISCOURTIER, *secretary*
A BLIND FIDDLER
CATHERINE, *Botal's wife*
ALISON, *Botal's servant*
MADEMOISELLE DE LA GARANDIÈRE
MADAME DE LA BRUINE
THE CHICKWEED MAN
THE WATERCRESS MAN
THE CANDLE MAN
PAGE TO MADEMOISELLE DE LA GARANDIÈRE
FOOTMAN TO MADAME DE LA BRUINE
FIRST DOCTOR'S ATTENDANT
SECOND DOCTOR'S ATTENDANT
A CHIMNEY SWEEP
FIRST APOTHECARY'S BOY
SECOND APOTHECARY'S BOY

THE MAN WHO MARRIED
A DUMB WIFE

SCENE ONE

A large room in JUDGE LEONARD BOTAL'S *house at Paris.*

Left: Main entrance, from the rue Dauphine; when the door is open, vista to the Pont-Neuf.

Right: Door to the kitchen.

At the rear of the stage: A wooden stairway, leading to the upper rooms.

On the walls are portraits of magistrates, in gown and wig, and along the walls, great cabinets, or cupboards, full of books, papers, parchments, and bags of legal documents, with more piled on top of the cabinets. There is a double step-ladder on castors, with flat steps on each side, used to reach the top of the cabinets.

A writing-table, small chairs, upholstered arm-chairs, and a spinning-wheel.

(In Mr. Granville Barker's production the street is shown in front of the house, instead of being concealed behind it; so that the chimneysweep, the chickweed-seller, the candle-man, etc., pass across the front of the stage.)

The street door of the house opens on a hallway, from which a door leads off to the kitchen, and a short stairway leads up, in a direction parallel with the front of the stage, past a double lattice window open to the street, to an upper room in which most of the action takes place.

This room has a large balcony and window-seat, and stands entirely open to the street. The writing-table, book-case (instead of cabinets), and step-ladder are seen within it. There is a bench or form, long enough to seat two or three people, in front of the table. A door at the right rear corner of the room is supposed to open on a stairway leading to the rooms above.

(GILES *is discovered sitting on a small form in front of the table; on the rise of the curtain he turns to the audience, bows in flamboyant style, and then sits down again, with his back to the audience.)*

The CHICKWEED MAN *goes by, calling:* "Chickweed! Chickweed! Good birdseed, good birdseed, good bird-seed for saäle!"

(Enter ALISON, *with a large basket under each arm. She curtsies to the audience.* GILES, *as soon as he spies her, runs to the street door and stands quiet beside it, so that she does not notice him. As she starts to enter the house, he jumps at her and snatches a bottle from one of the baskets.)*

ALISON. Holy Mary, don't you know better than to jump at anybody like a bogie-man, here in a public place?

5

GILES (*pulling a bottle of wine out of the other basket*). Don't scream, you little goose. Nobody's going to pluck you. You're not worth it. (*Enter* MASTER ADAM FUMÉE. *He bows to the audience.*)

ALISON. Will you let the Judge's wine alone, you rascal! (*She sets down her baskets, snatches back one of the bottles, cuffs the secretary, picks up her baskets, and goes off to the kitchen. The kitchen fireplace is seen through the half-open door.*)

MASTER ADAM (*slightly formal in manner and speech at first*). Is this the dwelling of Mr. Leonard Botal, Judge in civil and criminal cases?

GILES (*with bottle behind his back, and bowing*). Yes, sir; it's here, sir; and I'm his secretary, Giles Boiscourtier, at your service, sir.

MASTER ADAM. Then, boy, go tell him his old school-fellow, Master Adam Fumée, lawyer, wishes to see him on business.

GILES. Here he comes now, sir. (LEONARD BOTAL *comes down the stairs.* GILES *goes off into the kitchen.*)

MASTER ADAM. Good day, Master Leonard Botal, I am delighted to see you again.

LEONARD. Good morning, Master Adam Fumée, how have you been this long time that I haven't set eyes on you?

MASTER ADAM. Well, very well. And I hope I find you the same, your Honor.

LEONARD. Fairly so, fairly so. And what good wind wafts you hither, Master Adam Fumée? (*They come forward in the room.*)

MASTER ADAM. I've come from Chartres on purpose to put in your own hands a statement on behalf of a young orphan girl . . .

LEONARD. Master Adam Fumée, do you remember the days when we were law students together at Orleans University?

MASTER ADAM. Yes, yes; we used to play the flute together, and take the ladies out to picnics, and dance from morning to night. . . . But I've come, your Honor, my dear old school-fellow, to hand you a statement on behalf of a young orphan girl whose case is now pending before you.

LEONARD. Will she give good fees?

MASTER ADAM. She is a young orphan girl. . . .

LEONARD. Yes, yes, I know. But, will she give good fees?

MASTER ADAM. She is a young orphan girl, who's been robbed by her guardian, and he left her nothing but her eyes to weep with. But if she wins her suit, she will be rich again, and will give plentiful proof of her gratitude.

LEONARD (*taking the statement which* MASTER ADAM *hands him*). We will look into the matter.

MASTER ADAM. I thank you, your Honor, my dear old school-fellow.

LEONARD. We will look into it, without fear or favor.

MASTER ADAM. That goes without saying. . . . But, tell me: Is everything going smoothly with you? You seem worried. And yet, you are well placed here . . . the judgeship's a good one?

LEONARD. I paid enough for it to be a good one—and I didn't get cheated.

MASTER ADAM. Perhaps you are lonely. Why don't you get married?

LEONARD. What, what! Don't you know, Master Adam, that I *have* just been married? (*They sit down on the form in front of the table*) Yes, only last month, to a girl from one of our best country families, young and handsome, Catherine Momichel, the seventh daughter of the Criminal Court Judge at Salency. But alas! she is dumb. Now you know my affliction.

MASTER ADAM. Your wife is dumb?

LEONARD. Alas, yes.

MASTER ADAM. Quite, quite dumb?

LEONARD. As a fish.

MASTER ADAM. And you didn't notice it till after you'd married her?

LEONARD. Oh, I couldn't help noticing it, of course, but it didn't seem to make so much difference to me then as it does now. I considered her beauty, and her property, and thought of nothing but the advantages of the match and the happiness I should have with her. But now these matters seem less important, and I do wish she could talk; that would be a real intellectual pleasure for me, and, what's more, a practical advantage for the household. What does a Judge need most in his house? Why, a good-looking wife, to receive the suitors pleasantly, and, by subtle suggestions, gently bring them to the point of making proper presents, so that their cases may receive—more careful attention. People need to be encouraged to make proper presents. A woman, by clever speech and prudent action, can get a good ham from one, and a roll of cloth from another; and make still another give poultry or wine. But this poor dumb thing Catherine gets nothing at all. While my fellow-judges have their kitchens and cellars and stables and store-rooms running over with good things, all thanks to their wives, I hardly get wherewithal to keep the pot boiling. You see, Master Adam Fumée, what I lose by having a dumb wife. I'm not worth half as much. . . . And the worst of it is, I'm losing my spirits, and almost my wits, with it all.

MASTER ADAM. There's no reason in that, now, your Honor. Just consider the thing closely, and you will find some advantages in your case as it stands, and no mean ones neither.

LEONARD. No, no, Master Adam; you don't understand. Think!— When I hold my wife in my arms— a woman as beautiful as the finest carved statue, at least so I think— and quite as silent, that I'm sure of —it makes me feel queer and uncanny; I even ask myself if I'm holding a graven image or a mechanical toy, or a magic doll made by a sorcerer, not a real human child of our Father in Heaven; sometimes, in the morning, I am tempted to jump out of bed to escape from be-witchment.

MASTER ADAM. What notions!

LEONARD. Worse yet! What with having a dumb wife, I'm going dumb myself. Sometimes I catch myself using signs, as she does. The other day, on the Bench, I even pronounced judgment in pantomime, and condemned a man to the galleys, just by dumb show and gesticulation.

MASTER ADAM. Enough! Say no more! I can see that a dumb wife may be a pretty poor conversationalist! There's not much fun in talking yourself, when you get no response.

LEONARD. Now you know the reason why I'm in low spirits.

MASTER ADAM. I won't contradict you; I admit that your reason is full and sufficient. But perhaps there's a remedy. Tell me: Is your wife deaf as well as dumb?

LEONARD. Catherine is no more deaf than you and I are; even less, I might say. She can hear the very grass growing.

MASTER ADAM. Then the case is not hopeless. When the doctors and surgeons and apothecaries succeed in making the deaf-and-dumb speak, their utterance is as poor as their ears; for they can't hear what they say themselves, any more than what's said to them. But it's quite different with the dumb who can hear. 'Tis but child's play for a doctor to untie their tongues. The operation is so simple that it's done every day to puppies that can't learn to bark. Must a countryman like me come to town to tell you that there's a famous doctor, just around the corner from your own house, in Buci Square, at the Sign of the Dragon, Master Simon Colline, who has made a reputation for loosing the tongues of the ladies of Paris? In a turn of the hand, he'll draw from your wife's lips a full flood of mellifluous speech, just as you'd turn on a spigot and let the water run forth like a sweet-purling brook.

LEONARD. Is this true, Master Adam? Aren't you deceiving me? Aren't you speaking as a lawyer in court?

MASTER ADAM. I'm speaking as a friend, and telling you the plain truth.

LEONARD. Then I'll send for this famous doctor—and that right away.

MASTER ADAM. As you please. . . . But before you call him in, you must reflect soberly, and consider what it's really best to do. For, take it all in all, though there are some disadvantages in having a dumb wife, there are some advantages, too. . . . Well, good day, your Honor, my dear old school-fellow. (*They go together to the street door*) Remember, I'm truly your friend—and read over my statement, I beg you. If you give your just judgment in favor of the orphan girl robbed by her grasping guardian, you will have no cause to regret it.

LEONARD. Be back this afternoon, Master Adam Fumée; I will have my decision ready. (*They bow low to each other. Exit* MASTER ADAM.)

LEONARD (*at the door, calling*). Giles! Giles! . . . The rogue never hears me; he is in the kitchen, as usual, upsetting the soup and the servant. He's a knave and a scoundrel. Giles! . . . Giles! . . . Here, you rapscallion! You reprobate! . . .

GILES (*entering*). Present, your Honor.

LEONARD (*taking him by the ear*). Sirrah! Go straight to the famous doctor, Master Simon Colline, who lives in Buci Square, at the Sign of the Dragon, and tell him to come to my house at once, to treat a dumb woman. . . .

GILES. Yes, your Honor. (GILES *starts off, running, to the right.*)

LEONARD. Go the nearest way, not round by the New Bridge, to watch the jugglers. I know you, you slow-poke; there's not such another cheat and loafer in ten counties.
(GILES *comes back, slowly, across stage, and stops.*)

GILES. Sir, you wrong me. . . .

LEONARD. Be off! and bring the famous doctor back with you.

GILES (*bolting off to the left*). Yes, your Honor.

LEONARD (*going up and sitting down at the table, which is loaded with brief-bags*). I have fourteen verdicts to render today, besides the decree in the case of Master Adam Fumée's ward. And that is no small labor, because a decree, to do credit to the Judge, must be cleverly worded, subtle, elegant, and adorned with all the ornaments both of style and of thought. The ideas must be pleasingly conceived and playfully expressed. Where should one show one's wit, if not in a verdict?
(*The* WATERCRESS MAN *enters from the right and crosses to the left singing:* "Good watercress, fresh from the spring! Keeps you healthy and hearty! Six farthings a bunch. Six farthings a bunch." *When the* WATERCRESS MAN *is well on, enter the* CANDLE MAN *from left to right, singing:* "Candles! Cotton-wick candles! Burn bright as the stars!" *While he is passing,* CATHERINE *enters from the upper stairway door; she curtsies to the audience and then sits on the window-seat, embroidering. As the street-cries die away* LEONARD *looks up from his work at the table, and seeing* CATHERINE, *goes to her and kisses her as she rises to meet him. She makes a curtsy, kisses him in return, and listens with pleased attention.*)
Good morning, my love. . . . I didn't even hear you come down. You are like the fairy forms in the stories, that seem to glide upon air; or like the dreams which the gods, as poets tell, send down to happy mortals. (CATHERINE *shows her pleasure in his compliments*) My love, you are a marvel of nature, and a triumph of art; you have all charms but speech. (CATHERINE *turns away sobbing slightly*) Shouldn't you be glad to have that, too? (*She turns back, intensely interested*) Shouldn't you be happy to let your lips utter all the pretty thoughts I can read in your eyes? Shouldn't you be pleased to show your wit? (*She waves her handkerchief in glee*) Shouldn't you like to tell your husband how you love him? Wouldn't it be delightful to call him your treasure and sweetheart? Yes, surely! . . . (*They rise.* CATHERINE *is full of pleased animation.*)

Well, I've a piece of good news for you, my love. . . . A great doctor is coming here presently, who can make you talk. . . . (CATHERINE *shows her satisfaction, dancing gracefully up and down*) He will untie your tongue and never hurt you a bit.

(CATHERINE'S *movements express charming and joyous impatience. A* BLIND MAN *goes by in the street playing a lively old-fashioned country dance. He stops and calls out in a doleful voice:* "Charity, for the love of God, good gentlemen and ladies." LEONARD *motions him away, but* CATHERINE *pleads for him by her gestures, indicating that he is blind.* LEONARD *yields and goes back to his writing-table. She stands at the window listening while the* BLIND MAN *sings.*)

The BLIND MAN.

There's lots of good fish in the sea,
    La dee ra, la dee ra;
Now who will come and fish with
    me?
    La dee ra, la dee ra;
Now who'll with me a-fishing go?
My dainty, dainty damsel, O!
Come fish the livelong day with me,
    La dee ra, la dee ra,
And who will then be caught?—
    we'll see!
    La dee ra, dee ra, day.

(*Toward the end of the verse* CATHERINE *glances at* LEONARD *and sees that she is unobserved; she steals to the street door as the* BLIND MAN *begins the second verse there; during this verse she dances to him and frolics around the stage as he sings.*)

The BLIND MAN.

Along the rippling river's bank,
    La dee ra, la dee ra,

Along the wimpling water's bank,
    La dee ra, la dee ra,
Along the bank so shady O
I met the miller's lady, O
And danced with her the livelong
    day
    La dee ra, la dee ra,
And oh! I danced my heart away!
    La dee ra, dee ra, day.

(*The* BLIND MAN *stops playing and singing, and says, in a hollow and terrifying voice:* "Charity, for the love of God, good gentlemen and ladies.")

LEONARD (*who has been buried in his documents and noticed nothing, now drives the* BLIND MAN *off the stage with objurgations*). Vagabond, robber, ruffian! (*And throws a lot of brief-bags and books at his head; then speaks to* CATHERINE, *who has gone back to her place*) My love, since you came downstairs, I haven't been wasting my time; I have sentenced fourteen men and six women to the pillory; and distributed, among seventeen different people— (*He counts up*)—six, twenty-four, thirty-two, forty-four, forty-seven; and nine, fifty-six; and eleven, sixty-seven; and ten, seventy-seven; and eight, eighty-five; and twenty, a hundred and five—a hundred and five years in the galleys. Doesn't that make you realize the great power of a judge? How can I help feeling some pride in it?

(CATHERINE, *who has stopped her work, leans on the table, and smilingly watches her husband. Then she sits down on the table, which is covered with brief-bags.*)

LEONARD (*making as if to pull the bags from under her*). My love, you are hiding great criminals from my justice. Thieves and murderers. But

1 will not pursue them, their place of refuge is sacred.

(A CHIMNEY SWEEP *passes in the street, calling:* "Sweep your chimneys, my ladies; sweep them clear and clean.")

(LEONARD *and* CATHERINE *kiss across the table. But, seeing the* DOCTORS *arriving,* CATHERINE *runs off up the stairs. Enter, in formal procession,* GILES, *leading the line and imitating a trumpeter, then the two* DOCTORS' ATTENDANTS, *then* MASTER SIMON *and* MASTER JEAN. *The* ATTENDANTS, *one carrying the case of instruments, take their stand on either side of the door. The* DOCTOR *and* SURGEON *bow formally to the audience.*)

GILES. Your Honor, here's the great doctor you sent for.

MASTER SIMON (*bowing*). Yes, I am Master Simon Colline himself. . . . And this is Master Jean Maugier, surgeon. You called for our services?

LEONARD. Yes, sir, to make a dumb woman speak.

MASTER SIMON. Good! We must wait for Master Serafin Dulaurier, apothecary. As soon as he comes we will proceed to operate according to our knowledge and understanding.

LEONARD. Ah! You really need an apothecary to make a dumb woman speak?

MASTER SIMON. Yes, sir; to doubt it is to show total ignorance of the relations of the organs to each other, and of their mutual interdependence. Master Serafin Dulaurier will soon be here.

MASTER JEAN MAUGIER (*suddenly bellowing out in stentorian tones*). Oh! how grateful we should be to learnèd doctors like Master Simon Colline, who labor to preserve us in health and comfort us in sickness. Oh! how worthy of praise and of blessings are these noble doctors who follow in their profession the rules of scientific theory and of long practice.

MASTER SIMON (*bowing slightly*). You are much too kind, Master Jean Maugier.

LEONARD. While we are waiting for the apothecary, won't you take some light refreshment, gentlemen?

MASTER SIMON. Most happy.

MASTER JEAN. Delighted.

LEONARD. Alison! . . . So then, Master Simon Colline, you will perform a slight operation and make my wife speak?

MASTER SIMON. Say, rather, I shall order the operation. I command, Master Jean Maugier executes. . . . Have you your instruments with you, Master Jean?

MASTER JEAN. Yes, Master. (*He claps his hands; the* ATTENDANTS *run forward into the room, and, each holding one side, they unfold the large cloth case of instruments and hold it up, disclosing a huge saw with two-inch teeth, and knives, pincers, scissors, a skewer, a bit-stock, an enormous bit, etc.*)

LEONARD. I hope, sirs, you don't intend to use all those?

MASTER SIMON. One must never be caught unarmed by a patient.

(The ATTENDANTS *fold up the case and give it to* MASTER JEAN; *then run back to their positions by the door, as* ALISON, *with a large tray, bottles, and glasses, enters from the kitchen.)*

LEONARD. Will you drink, gentlemen?

(COLLINE *and* MAUGIER *take glasses from* ALISON *and drink, after* ALISON *has kissed* COLLINE's *glass.)*

MASTER SIMON. This light wine of yours is not half bad.

LEONARD. Very kind of you to say so. It's from my own vineyard.

MASTER SIMON. You shall send me a cask of it.

LEONARD (*to* GILES, *who has poured himself a glass full to the brim*). I didn't tell you to drink, you reprobate.

MASTER JEAN (*looking out of the window*). Here is Master Serafin Dulaurier, the apothecary.

(*Enter* MASTER SERAFIN. *He trots across the stage, stopping to bow to the audience.)*

MASTER SIMON (*peering into the street*). And here is his mule! . . . Or no—'tis Master Serafin himself. You never can tell them apart. (MASTER SERAFIN *joins the group in the room*) Drink, Master Serafin. It is fresh from the cellar.

MASTER SERAFIN. Your good health, my Masters!

MASTER SIMON (*to* ALISON). Pour freely, fair Hebe. Pour right, pour left, pour here, pour there. Whichever way she turns, she shows new charms. Are you not proud, my girl, of your trim figure?

ALISON. For all the good it does me, there is no reason to be proud of it. Charms are not worth much unless they are hidden in silk and brocade.

MASTER SERAFIN. Your good health, my Masters! (*They* ALL *drink, and make* ALISON *drink with them.)*

ALISON. You like to fool with us. But free gratis for nothing.

MASTER SIMON. Now we are all here, shall we go see the patient?

LEONARD. I will show you the way, gentlemen.

MASTER SIMON. After you, Master Maugier, you go first.

MASTER MAUGIER (*glass in one hand, case of instruments in the other*). I'll go first, since the place of honor is the rear. (*He crosses to the left, and goes behind the table toward the door, following* BOTAL.)

MASTER SIMON. After you, Master Serafin Dulaurier.

(MASTER SERAFIN *follows* MAUGIER, *bottle in hand.* MASTER SIMON, *after stuffing a bottle into each pocket of his gown, and kissing the servant,* ALISON, *goes up stage, singing.)*

Then drink! and drink! and drink again!
Drink shall drown our care and pain.
Good friends must drink before they part,
To warm the cockles of the heart!
(ALISON, *after cuffing* GILES, *who was trying to kiss her, goes up last.)*
(ALL *sing in chorus as they go out by the right upper door.)*
Then drink! and drink! and drink again!

CURTAIN

SCENE TWO

SCENE:—*the same. Four or five hours have elapsed.*

MASTER ADAM. Good afternoon, your Honor. How are you this afternoon?

LEONARD. Well, fairly well. And how are you?

MASTER ADAM. Well as can be. Excuse my besieging you, your Honor, my dear comrade. Have you looked into the case of my young ward who's been robbed by her guardian?

LEONARD. Not yet, Master Adam Fumée. . . . But what's that you say? You've been robbing your ward?

MASTER ADAM. No, no, never think it, your Honor. I said "my" out of pure interest in her. But I am not her guardian, thank God! I'm her lawyer. And, if she gets back her estate, which is no small estate neither, then I shall be her husband; yes, I've had the foresight to make her fall in love with me already. And so, I shall be greatly obliged to you if you'll examine her case at the earliest possible moment. All you have to do is to read the statement I gave you; that contains everything you need to know about the case.

LEONARD. Your statement is there, Master Adam, on my table. I should have looked through it already, if I hadn't been so besieged. But I've been entertaining the flower of the medical faculty here. (*Suddenly seizing him by the shoulders and shaking him*) 'Twas your advice brought this trouble upon me.

MASTER ADAM. Why, what do you mean?

LEONARD. I sent for the famous doctor you told me about, Master Simon Colline. He came, with a surgeon and an apothecary; he examined my wife, Catherine, from head to foot, to see if she was dumb. Then, the surgeon cut my dear Catherine's tongue-ligament, the apothecary gave her a pill—and she spoke.

MASTER ADAM. She spoke? Did she need a pill, to speak?

LEONARD. Yes, because of the interdependence of the organs.

MASTER ADAM. Oh! Ah! . . . Anyhow, the main point is, she spoke. And what did she say?

LEONARD. She said: "Bring me my looking-glass!" And, seeing me quite overcome by my feelings, she added, "You old goose, you shall give me a new satin gown and a velvet-trimmed cape for my birthday."

MASTER ADAM. And she kept on talking?

LEONARD. She hasn't stopped yet.

MASTER ADAM. And yet you don't

thank me for my advice; you don't thank me for having sent you to that wonderful doctor? Aren't you overjoyed to hear your wife speak?

LEONARD (*sourly*). Yes, certainly. I thank you with all my heart, Master Adam Fumée, and I am overjoyed to hear my wife speak.

MASTER ADAM. No! You do not show as much satisfaction as you ought to. There is something you are keeping back—something that's worrying you.

LEONARD. Where did you get such a notion?

MASTER ADAM. From your face. . . . What is bothering you? Isn't your wife's speech clear?

LEONARD. Yes, it's clear—and abundant. I must admit, its abundance would be a trial to me if it kept up at the rate which it started at.

MASTER ADAM. Ah! . . . I feared *that* beforehand, your Honor. But you mustn't be cast down too soon. Perhaps this flood of words will ebb. It is the first overflow of a spring too long bottled up. . . . My best congratulations, your Honor. My ward's name is Ermeline de la Garandière. Don't forget her name; show her favor, and you will find proper gratitude. I will be back later in the day.

LEONARD. Master Adam Fumée, I will look into your case at once. (*Exit* MASTER ADAM FUMÉE. CATHERINE *is heard off stage singing the* BLIND MAN'S *song;* LEONARD *starts, shakes his head, hurries to his writing-table, and sits down to work.* CATHERINE, *still singing, enters gaily, and goes to him at the table.*)

LEONARD (*reading*). "Statement, on behalf of Ermeline-Jacinthe-Marthe de la Garandière, gentlewoman."

CATHERINE (*standing behind his chair, and first finishing her song:* "La dee ra, dee ra, day," *then speaking with great volubility*).What are you doing, my dear? You seem busy. You work too much. (*She goes to the window-seat and takes up her embroidery*) Aren't you afraid it will make you ill? You must rest once in a while. Why don't you tell me what you are doing, dear?

LEONARD. My love, I . . .

CATHERINE. Is it such a great secret? Can't I know about it?

LEONARD. My love, I . . .

CATHERINE. If it's a secret, don't tell me.

LEONARD. Won't you give me a chance to answer? I am examining a case and preparing to draw up a verdict on it.

CATHERINE. Is drawing up a verdict so very important?

LEONARD. Most certainly it is. (CATHERINE *sits at the window singing and humming to herself, and looking out*) In the first place, people's honor, their liberty, and sometimes even their life, may depend on it; and furthermore, the Judge must show therein both the depth of his thought and the finish of his style.

CATHERINE. Then examine your case and prepare your verdict, my dear. I'll be silent.

LEONARD. That's right. . . . "Er-

meline-Jacinthe-Marthe de la Garandière, gentlewoman . . ."

CATHERINE. My dear, which do you
think would be more becoming to
me, a damask gown, or a velvet suit
with a Turkish skirt?

LEONARD. I don't know, I . . .

CATHERINE. I think a flowered satin
would suit my age best, especially a
light-colored one, with a *small*
flower pattern.

LEONARD. Perhaps so. But . . .

CATHERINE. And don't you think,
my dear, that it is quite improper to
have a hoop-skirt very full? Of
course, a skirt must have *some* full-
ness . . . or else you don't seem
dressed at all; so, we mustn't let it
be scanty. But, my dear, you
wouldn't want me to have room
enough to hide a pair of lovers under
my hoops, now would you? That
fashion won't last, I'm sure; some
day the court ladies will give it up,
and then every woman in town will
make haste to follow their example.
Don't you think so?

LEONARD. Yes! Yes! But . . .

CATHERINE. Now, about high heels.
. . . They must be made just right.
A woman is judged by her foot-gear
—you can always tell a real fine
lady by her shoes. You agree with
me, don't you, dear?

LEONARD. Yes, yes, *yes,* but . . .

CATHERINE. Then write out your
verdict. I shan't say another word.

LEONARD. That's right. (*Reading,
and making notes*) "Now, the guard-

ian of the said young lady, namely,
Hugo Thomas of Piédeloup, gentleman, stole from the said young lady
her—"

CATHERINE. My dear, if one were to
believe the wife of the Chief Justice
of Montbadon, the world has grown
very corrupt; it is going to the bad;
young men nowadays don't marry;
they prefer to hang about rich old
ladies; and meanwhile the poor girls
are left to wither on their maiden
stalks. Do you think it's as bad as all
that? Do answer me, dear.

LEONARD. My darling, won't you
please be silent one moment? Or go
and talk somewhere else? I'm all at
sea.

CATHERINE. There, there, dear;
don't worry. I shan't say another
word! Not a word!

LEONARD. Good! (*Writing*) "The
said Piédeloup, gentleman, counting
both hay crops and apple crops . . ."

CATHERINE. My dear, we shall have
for supper tonight some minced
mutton and what's left of that goose
one of your suitors gave us. Tell me,
is that enough? Shall you be satisfied with it? I hate being mean, and
like to set a good table, but what's
the use of serving courses which will
only be sent back to the pantry untouched? The cost of living is getting higher all the time. Chickens,
and salads, and meats, and fruit
have all gone up so, it will soon be
cheaper to order dinner sent in by a
caterer.

LEONARD. I beg you . . . (*Writing*)
"An orphan by birth . . ."

CATHERINE. Yes, that's what we're

coming to. No home life any more. You'll see. Why, a capon, or a partridge, or a hare, cost less all stuffed and roasted than if you buy them alive at the market. That is because the cook-shops buy in large quantities and get a big discount; so they can sell to us at a profit. I don't say we ought to get our regular meals from the cook-shop. We can do our everyday plain cooking at home, and it's better to; but when we invite people in, or give a formal dinner party, then it saves time and money to have the dinner sent in. Why, at less than an hour's notice, the cook-shops and cake-shops will get you up a dinner for a dozen, or twenty, or fifty people; the cook-shop will send in meat and poultry, the caterer will send galantines and sauces and relishes, the pastry-cook will send pies and tarts and sweets and desserts; and it's all so convenient. Now, don't you think so yourself, Leonard.

LEONARD. Please! please!
(LEONARD *tries to write through the following speech, murmuring:* "An orphan by birth, a capon by birth, an olla podrida," *etc.*)

CATHERINE. It's no wonder everything goes up. People are getting more extravagant everv day. If they are entertaining a friend, or even a relative, they don't think they can do with only three courses, soup, meat, and dessert. No, they have to have meats in five or six different styles, with so many sauces, or dressings, or pasties, that it's a regular olla podrida. Now, don't you think that is going too far, my dear? For my part I just cannot understand how people can take pleasure in stuffing themselves with so many kinds of food. Not that I despise a

good table; why, I'm even a bit of an epicure myself. "Not too plenty, but dainty," suits *my* taste. Now, what I like best of all is capons' kidneys with artichoke hearts. But you, Leonard, I suspect you have a weakness for tripe and sausages. Oh, fie! Oh, fie! How can anyone enjoy sausages?

LEONARD. (*his head in his hands*). I shall go mad! I know I shall go mad.

CATHERINE (*running to the table behind him*). My dear, I just shan't say another word—not a single word. For I can see that my chattering *might* possibly disturb your work.

LEONARD. If you would only do as you say!

CATHERINE (*returning to her place*). I shan't even open my lips.

LEONARD. Splendid!

CATHERINE (*busily embroidering*). You see, dear, I'm not saying another word.

LEONARD. Yes.

CATHERINE. I'm letting you work in perfect peace and quiet.

LEONARD. Yes.

CATHERINE. And write out your verdict quite undisturbed. Is it almost done?

LEONARD. It never will be—if you don't keep still. (*Writing*) "Item, One hundred twenty pounds a year, which the said unworthy guardian stole from the poor orphan girl . . ."

CATHERINE. Listen! Ssh-sh! Listen! Didn't you hear a cry of fire? (LEONARD *runs to the window, looks out, and then shakes his head at* CATHERINE) I thought I did. But perhaps I may have been mistaken. Is there anything so terrifying as a fire? Fire is even worse than water. Last year I saw the houses on Exchange Bridge burn up. What confusion! What havoc! The people threw their furniture into the river, and jumped out of the windows. They didn't know what they were about; you see, fear drove them out of their senses.

LEONARD. Lord, have mercy upon me!

CATHERINE. Oh! What makes you groan so, dear? *Tell* me, tell me what is the matter?

LEONARD. I can't endure it another minute.

CATHERINE. You must rest, Leonard. You mustn't work so hard. It isn't reasonable. You have no right to . . .

LEONARD. Will you never be still?

CATHERINE. Now, don't be cross, dear. I'm not saying a word.

LEONARD. Would to Heaven! (MADAME DE LA BRUINE, *followed by her* FOOTMAN, *crosses the stage during the following speech.*)

CATHERINE (*looking out of the window*). Oh! Here comes Madame de la Bruine, the attorney's wife! She's got on a silk-lined hood and a heavy puce-colored cape over her brocade gown. And she has a lackey with a face like a smoked herring. Leonard, she's looking this way; I believe she's coming to call. Hurry and arrange the chairs and bring up an armchair for her; we must show people proper respect according to their rank and station. She is stopping at our door. No, she's going on. She's gone on. Perhaps I was mistaken. Perhaps it was somebody else. You can't be sure about recognizing people. But if it wasn't she, it was somebody like her, and even very much like her. Now I think of it, I'm sure it was she, there simply couldn't be another woman in Paris so like Madame de la Bruine. My dear. . . . My dear. . . . Would you have liked to have Madame de la Bruine call on us? (*She sits down on his table*) I know you don't like rattle-tongued women; it's lucky for you that you didn't marry *her*; she jabbers like a magpie; she does nothing but gabble from morning to night. What a chatterbox! And sometimes she tells stories which are not to her credit. (LEONARD, *driven beyond endurance, climbs upon his step-ladder and sits down on one of the middle steps, and tries to write there*) In the first place, she always gives you a list of all the presents her husband has received. It's a dreadful bore to hear her tell them over. (*She climbs up on the other side of the double step-ladder and sits down opposite* LEONARD) What is it to us, if the Attorney de la Bruine receives presents of game, or flour, or fresh fish, or even a sugar-loaf? But Madame de la Bruine takes good care *not* to tell you that one day her husband received a great Amiens pasty, and when he opened it he found nothing but an enormous pair of horns.

LEONARD. My head will burst! (*He takes refuge on top of one of the cabinets, with his writing-case and papers.*)

CATHERINE (*at the top of the ladder*). And did you see my fine lady, who's really no lady at all, wearing an embroidered cape, just like any princess? Don't you think it's ridiculous! But there! Nowadays everybody dresses above his station, men as well as women. Your court secretaries try to pass for gentlemen; they wear gold chains and jewelry, and feathers in their hats; all the same, anyone can tell what they are.

LEONARD. (*on top of his cupboard*). I've got to the point where I can't answer for the consequences; I feel capable of committing any crime. (*Calling*) Giles! Giles! Giles! The scoundrel! Giles! Alison! Giles! Giles! (*Enter* GILES) Go quick and find the famous Doctor in Buci Square, Master Simon Colline, and tell him to come back here at once for a matter far more needful and urgent than before.

GILES. Yes, your Honor. (*Exit.*)

CATHERINE. What's the matter, my dear? You seem excited. Perhaps the air is close. No? It's the east wind, then, don't you think?—or the fish you ate for dinner?

LEONARD (*frantically gesticulating on top of his cupboard*). *Non omnia possumus omnes.* It is the office of servants to clean crockery, of mercers to measure ribbon, of monks to beg, of birds to drop dirt around everywhere, and of women to cackle and chatter like mad. Oh! How I regret, you saucy baggage, that I had your tongue loosed. Don't you worry, though—the famous doctor shall soon make you more dumb

than ever you were. (*He catches up armfuls of the brief-bags which are piled on his cupboard of refuge, and throws them at* CATHERINE'S *head; she jumps nimbly down from the ladder and runs off in terror, crying.*)

CATHERINE. Help! Murder! My husband's gone mad! Help! help!

LEONARD. Alison! Alison! (*Enter* ALISON.)

ALISON. What a life! Sir, have you turned murderer?

LEONARD. Alison, follow her, stay by her, and don't let her come down. As you value your life, Alison, don't let her come down. For if I hear another word from her, I shall go raving mad, and God knows what I might do to her—and to you. Go! Off with you!

(ALISON *goes upstairs. Enter* MASTER ADAM, MLLE. DE LA GARANDIÈRE, *and a* LACKEY *carrying a basket.* LEONARD *is still on top of the cabinet or book-case.* MASTER ADAM *and* MLLE. DE LA GARANDIÈRE *climb up on each side of the step-ladder. The* LACKEY, *with an enormous basket on his head, kneels in front, center.*)

MASTER ADAM. Permit me, your Honor, with the object of softening your heart and arousing your pity, to present before you this young orphan girl, despoiled by a grasping guardian, who implores you for justice. Her eyes will speak to your heart more eloquently than my voice. Mlle. de la Garandière brings you her prayers and her tears: she adds thereunto one ham, two duck pies, a goose, and two goslings. She ventures to hope in exchange for a favoring verdict.

LEONARD. Mademoiselle, you arouse my interest. . . . Have you anything to add in defense of your case?

MLLE. DE LA GARANDIÈRE. You are only too kind, sir; I must rest my case on what my lawyer has just said.

LEONARD. That is all?

MLLE. DE LA GARANDIÈRE. Yes, sir.

LEONARD. She knows how to speak —and to stop. The poor orphan touches my heart. (*To the* LACKEY) carry that package to the pantry. (*Exit* LACKEY. *To* MASTER ADAM) Master Adam, when you came in, I was just drawing up the decree which I shall presently render in this young lady's case. (*He starts to come down from his cabinet.*)

MASTER ADAM. What, up on that cupboard?

LEONARD. I don't know where I am; my head is going round and round. Do you want to hear the decree? I need to read it over myself. (*Reading*) "Whereas, Mlle. de la Garandière, spinster, and an orphan by birth, did fraudulently, deceitfully, and with injurious intent, steal, filch, and subtract from her lawful guardian, Squire Piédeloup, gentleman, ten loads of hay and eighty pounds of fresh-water fish, and whereas, there is nothing so terrifying as a fire, and whereas, the State's Attorney did receive an Amiens pasty in which were two great horns . . ."

MASTER ADAM. What in Heaven's name are you reading?

LEONARD. Don't ask me. I don't know myself. I think my brains have been brayed in a mortar, for two hours running, by the very devil himself for a pestle. (*He breaks down and weeps on their shoulders*) I'm a driveling idiot. . . . And all your fault, too, Master Adam Fumée. . . . If that fine doctor of yours hadn't restored my wife's speech . . .

MASTER ADAM. Don't blame me, Master Leonard. I forewarned you. I told you right enough, that you must think twice before untying a woman's tongue.

LEONARD. Ah, Master Adam Fumée, how I long for the time when my Catherine was dumb. No! Nature has no scourge more fearsome than a rattle-tongued female. . . . But I count on the doctors to recall their cruel gift. I have sent for them. Here's the surgeon now.
(*Enter* MASTER JEAN MAUGIER.)

MASTER JEAN MAUGIER. Your Honor, I bid you good day. Here is Master Simon Colline coming forward upon his mule, followed by Master Serafin Dulaurier, apothecary. About him crowds the adoring populace: chambermaids, trussing up their petticoats, and scullions with hampers on their heads form his escort of honor. (*Enter* MASTER SIMON COLLINE *and* MASTER SERAFIN DULAURIER *followed by the* TWO APOTHECARY'S BOYS) Oh! how justly does Master Simon Colline command the admiration of the people when he goes through the city clad in his doctor's robe, his square cap, his cassock and bands. Oh! how grateful we should be to those noble doctors who labor to preserve us in health and comfort us in sickness. Ohhhh! how . . .

MASTER SIMON (*to* MASTER JEAN MAUGIER). Have done; 'tis enough.

LEONARD. Master Simon Colline, I was in haste to see you. I urgently beg for your services.

MASTER SIMON. For yourself? What is your disease? Where is the pain?

LEONARD. No! for my wife; the one who was dumb.

MASTER SIMON. Has she any trouble now?

LEONARD. None at all. I have all the trouble now.

MASTER SIMON. What? The trouble is with you, and it's your wife you want cured?

LEONARD. Master Simon Colline, she talks too much. You should have given her speech, but not so much speech. Since you've cured her of her dumbness, she drives me mad. I cannot bear another word from her. I've called you in to make her dumb again.

MASTER SIMON. 'Tis impossible!

LEONARD. What's that? You can't take away the power of speech which you gave her?

MASTER SIMON. No! That I cannot do. My skill is great, but it stops short of that.
(LEONARD *in despair turns to each of them in succession.*)

MASTER JEAN MAUGIER. We cannot do it.

MASTER SERAFIN. Our greatest efforts would have not the slightest result.

MASTER SIMON. We have medicines to make women speak; we have none to make them keep silence.

LEONARD. You haven't? Is that your last word? You drive me to despair.

MASTER SIMON. Alas, your Honor! (*He advances to the center, claps his hands for attention, and declaims*) There is no elixir, balm, magisterium, opiate, unguent, ointment, local application, electuary, nor panacea, that can cure the excess of glottal activity in woman. Treacle and orvietano would be without virtue, and all the herbs described by Dioscorides would have no effect.

LEONARD. Can this be true?

MASTER SIMON. Sir, you dare not so offend me as to doubt it.

LEONARD. Then I am a ruined man. There's nothing left for me to do but tie a stone around my neck and jump into the Seine. (*He rushes to the window and tries to jump out, but is held back by the* DOCTORS) I cannot live in this hubbub. (*The* DOCTORS *drag him back, set him down, and, with* MASTER ADAM, *stand in a circle in front of him*) If you don't want me to drown myself straightway, then you doctors must find me some cure.

MASTER SIMON. There is none, I tell you, for your wife. But there might be one for you, if you would consent to take it.

LEONARD. You give me a little hope. Explain it, for Heaven's sake.

MASTER SIMON. For the clack of a wife, there's but one cure in life. Let her husband be deaf. 'Tis the only relief.

LEONARD. What do you mean?

MASTER SIMON. Just what I say.

MASTER ADAM. Don't you understand? That's the finest discovery yet. Since he can't make your wife dumb, this great doctor offers to make you deaf.

LEONARD. Make me really deaf? Oh! . . . (*He starts to rise, but is pushed back by* MASTER SIMON, *who stands directly in front of him.*)

MASTER SIMON. Certainly. I can cure you at once, and for all time, of your wife's verbal hypertrophy, by means of cophosis.

LEONARD. By cophosis? What is cophosis?

MASTER SIMON. 'Tis what is vulgarly called deafness. Do you see any disadvantages in becoming deaf?

LEONARD. Certainly I do!

MASTER JEAN MAUGIER. You think so?

MASTER SERAFIN. For instance?

MASTER SIMON. You are a Judge. What disadvantage is there in a Judge's being deaf?

MASTER ADAM. None at all. Believe me; I am a practicing lawyer. There is none at all.

MASTER SIMON. What harm could come to justice thereby?

MASTER ADAM. No harm at all.

Quite the contrary. Master Leonard Botal could then hear neither lawyers nor prosecutors, and so would run no risk of being deceived by a lot of lies.

LEONARD. That's true.

MASTER ADAM. He will judge all the better.

LEONARD. May be so.

MASTER ADAM. Never doubt it.

LEONARD. But how do you perform this . . .

MASTER JEAN MAUGIER. This cure.

MASTER SIMON. Cophosis, vulgarly called deafness, may be brought about in several ways. It is produced either by otorrhœa, or by sclerosis of the ear, or by otitis, or else by anchylosis of the ossicles. But these various means are long and painful.

LEONARD. I reject them! . . . I reject them absolutely.

MASTER SIMON. You are right. It is far better to induce cophosis by means of a certain white powder which I have in my medicine-case; a pinch of it, placed in the ear, is enough to make you as deaf as Heaven when it's angry, or as deaf as a post.

LEONARD. Many thanks, Master Simon Colline; keep your powder. I will not be made deaf.

MASTER SIMON. What? You won't be made deaf? What? You refuse cophosis? You decline the cure which you begged for just now? Ah, 'tis a case but too common, and one calculated to make a judicious physician grieve, to see a recalcitrant patient refuse the salutary medicament . . .

MASTER JEAN MAUGIER. And flee from the care, which would cure all his ailments . . .

MASTER SERAFIN. And decline to be healed. Oh!

MASTER ADAM. Do not decide too quickly, Master Leonard Botal; do not deliberately reject this slight affliction which will save you from far greater torment.

LEONARD. No! I will not be deaf; I'll have none of your powder.

ALISON (*rushes in from the stairs, stopping her ears*). I can't stand it. My head will burst. No human creature can stay and listen to such a clatter. There's no stopping her. I feel as if I'd been caught in the millwheel for two mortal hours.
(CATHERINE *is heard off stage singing the* BLIND MAN's *song*.)

LEONARD. Wretch! Don't let her come down. Alison! Giles! Lock her in.

MASTER ADAM. Oh! Sir!

MLLE. DE LA GARANDIÈRE. Oh! Sir, can your heart be so cruel as to want to lock the poor lady up all alone? (CATHERINE *is heard singing again.* LEONARD *starts for the ladder, and climbs it as she enters.*)

CATHERINE. What a fine large assembly! I am your humble servant, gentlemen. (*She curtsies.*)

MASTER SIMON COLLINE. Well, madam? Aren't you pleased with us? Didn't we do our work well in loosing your tongue?

CATHERINE. Fairly well, sirs; and I'm truly grateful to you. At first, to be sure, I could speak but haltingly, and bring out only a few words; now, however, I have some degree of facility; but I use it with great moderation, for a garrulous wife is a scourge in the house. Yes, gentlemen, I should be in despair if you could so much as suspect me of loquacity, or if you think for a moment that any undue desire to talk could get hold on me. (LEONARD, *on top of the cabinet, laughs wildly*) And so, I beg you to let me justify myself here and now in the eyes of my husband, who, for some inconceivable reason, has become prejudiced against me, and taken it into his head that my conversation bothered him while he was drawing up a decree. . . . Yes, a decree in favor of an orphan girl deprived of her father and mother in the flower of her youth. But no matter for that. (*She crosses to the ladder and starts to go up one side of it.* LEONARD *climbs down the other side, goes first to one doctor, then to another, and finally sits down on the bench in front of the table*) I was sitting beside him and hardly saying a single word to him. My only speech was my presence. Can a husband object to that? Can he take it ill when his wife stays with him and seeks to enjoy his company, as she ought? (*She goes to her husband and sits down beside him. During the rest of the speech all those present, one after another, sink down in exhaustion at listening to her*) The more I think of it, the less I can understand your impatience. What can have caused it? You must stop pretending it was my talkativeness. That idea won't hold water one moment. My dear, you must have some grievance against me which I know nothing about; I *beg* you to tell me what it is. You *owe* me an explanation, and as soon as I find out what displeased you I will see to it that you have no reason to complain of the same thing again—if only you'll tell me what it is. For I am eager to save you from the slightest reason for dissatisfaction. My mother used to say: "Between husband and wife, there should be no secrets." And she was quite right. Married people have only too often brought down terrible catastrophes on themselves or their households just because they didn't tell each other everything. That is what happened to the Chief Justice of Beaupréau's wife. To give her husband a pleasant surprise, she shut up a little sucking pig in a chest in her room. Her husband heard it squealing, and thought it was a lover, so he out with his sword and ran his wife through the heart, without even waiting to hear the poor lady's explanation. You can imagine his surprise and despair when he opened the chest. And that shows you must never have secrets, even for good reasons. My dear, you can speak freely before these gentlemen. I know I have done nothing wrong, so whatever you say can only prove the more clearly how innocent I am.

LEONARD (*who has for some time been trying in vain by gestures and exclamations to stop* CATHERINE'S *flow of words, and has been showing signs of extreme impatience*). The powder! Give me the powder! Master Simon Colline, your powder —your white powder, for God's sake!

MASTER SIMON. Never was a deafness-producing powder more needed, that's sure. Be so kind as to sit down, your Honor. Master Serafin Dulaurier will inject the cophosis powder in your ears.
(*The* DOCTORS *crowd about* LEONARD, *and inject the powder first in one ear and then in the other.*)

MASTER SERAFIN. Gladly, sir, gladly.

MASTER SIMON. There! 'Tis done.

CATHERINE (*to* MASTER ADAM FUMÉE). Master Adam, you are a lawyer. Make my husband hear reason. Tell him that he must listen to me, that it's unheard of to condemn a wife without letting her state her case; tell him it's not right to throw brief-bags at your wife's head—yes, he threw brief-bags at my head—unless you are forced to it by some very strong feeling or reason. . . . Or no!—no, I'll tell him myself. (*To* LEONARD) My dear, answer me, have I ever failed you in anything? Am I a naughty woman? Am I a bad wife? No, I have been faithful to my duty; I may even say I have loved my duty . . .

LEONARD (*his face expressing beatitude, as he calmly twirls his thumbs*). 'Tis delicious. I can't hear a thing.

CATHERINE. Listen to me, Leonard, I love you tenderly. I will open my heart to you. I am not one of those light, frivolous women who are afflicted or consoled by airy nothings, and amused by trifles. (*She puts her arms about him and they rock back and forth,* LEONARD *grinning from ear to ear*) I need companion-ship. I need to be understood. That is my nature—I was born so. When I was only seven years old I had a little dog, a little yellow dog. . . . But you're not listening to me . . .

MASTER SIMON. Madam, he can't lis-ten to you, or to anyone else. He can't hear.

CATHERINE. What do you mean he can't hear?

MASTER SIMON. I mean just that. He can't hear, as the result of a cure he has just taken.
(*The* BLIND MAN *is heard again, playing the same air.*)

MASTER SERAFIN. A cure which has produced in him a sweet and pleas-ant cophosis.

CATHERINE. I'll make him hear, I tell you.

MASTER SIMON. No, you won't, mad-am; it can't be done.

CATHERINE. You shall see. (*To her husband, affectionately*) My dear, my beloved, my pretty one, my sweetheart, my better-half. . . . You don't hear me? (*She shakes him*) You monster, you Herod, you Blue-beard, you old cuckold.

LEONARD. I can't hear her with my ears, but I hear her only too well with my arms, and with my shoul-ders and back.

MASTER SIMON. She is going mad.

MASTER MAUGIER. She has gone mad! Stark staring mad!

LEONARD. Oh! How can I get away? (CATHERINE *bites his neck*) Oh! She has bitten me, I feel myself going mad, too.

(*The* BLIND MAN *has come forward, playing and singing the first verse of his song. Meanwhile* CATHERINE *and* LEONARD *go singing and danc-ing about, and bite the others, who likewise go mad and sing and dance wildly, all at the front of the stage. The other characters of the play come in—the* CANDLE MAN, CHIM-NEY SWEEP, MADAME DE LA BRUINE, *etc.; all are caught and bitten, and join in the song and the dance, which resolves itself into the old-fashioned country "right and left," as they sing the second verse.*)

ALL.
    Along the rippling river's bank,
      La dee ra, la dee ra,
    Along the wimpling water's bank,
      La dee ra, la dee ra,
    Along the bank so shady O
    I met the miller's lady O
    And danced with her the livelong
      day,
      La dee ra, la dee ra,
    And oh! I danced my heart away,
      La dee ra, dee ra, day.

(*As* LEONARD BOTAL *reaches the center of the front stage, the dance stops a moment for him to say to the audience.*)

LEONARD. Good gentlemen and la-dies, we pray you to forgive the author all his faults.
(*The dance re-commences, and as the curtain falls all dance off left or right, singing the refrain.*)

ALL (*diminuendo*).
    I danced with her the livelong
      day,
      La dee ra, la dee ra,
    And oh! I danced my heart away.
      La dee ra, dee ra, day.

CURTAIN

Miss Julie

BY AUGUST STRINDBERG

CHARACTERS

MISS JULIE, *aged twenty-five.*
JOHN, *a servant, aged thirty.*
CHRISTINE. *a cook, aged thirty-five.*

MISS JULIE

The action of the play takes place on Midsummer Night, in the Count's kitchen.
    CHRISTINE *stands on the left, by the hearth, and fries something in a pan. She has on a light blouse and a kitchen apron.* JOHN *comes in through the glass door in livery. He holds in his hand a pair of big riding boots with spurs, which he places on the floor at the back, in a visible position.*

JOHN. Miss Julie is mad again to-night—absolutely mad!

CHRISTINE. Oh! And so you're here, are you?

JOHN. I accompanied the Count to the station, and when I passed the barn on my way back I went in to have a dance. At that time Miss Julie was dancing with that man Forster. When she noticed me, she made straight for me and asked me to be her partner in the waltz, and from that moment she danced in a way such as I've never seen anything of the kind before. She is simply crazy.

CHRISTINE. She's always been that, but never as much as in the last fortnight, since the engagement was broken off.

JOHN. Yes; what an affair that was, to be sure. The man was certainly a fine fellow, even though he didn't have much cash. Well, to be sure, they have so many whims and fancies. (*He sits down at the right by the table*) In any case, it's strange that the young lady should prefer to stay at home with the servants rather than to accompany her father to her relations', isn't it?

CHRISTINE. Yes. The odds are that she feels herself a little embarrassed after the affair with her young man.

JOHN. Maybe; but at any rate he was a good chap. Do you know, Christine, how it came about? I saw the whole show, though I didn't let them see that I noticed anything.

CHRISTINE. What! You saw it?

JOHN. Yes, that I did. They were one evening down there in the stable, and the young lady was "training" him, as she called it. What do you think she was doing? She made him jump over the riding whip like a dog which one is teaching to hop. He jumped over twice, and each time he got a cut, but the third time he snatched her riding whip out of her hand, smashed it into smithereens and—cleared out.

CHRISTINE. Was that it? No, you can't mean it?

JOHN. Yes, that was how it happened. Can't you give me something nice to eat now, Christine?

CHRISTINE (*takes up the pan and puts it before* JOHN). Well, there's only a little bit of liver, which I've cut off the joint.

JOHN (*sniffs the food*). Ah, very

nice, that's my special dish. (*He feels the plate*) But you might have warmed up the plate.

CHRISTINE. Why, you're even more particular than the Count himself, once you get going. (*She draws her fingers caressingly through his hair.*)

JOHN (*wickedly*). Ugh, you mustn't excite me like that, you know jolly well how sensitive I am.

CHRISTINE. There, there now, it was only because I love you.

JOHN (*eats. CHRISTINE gets out a bottle of beer*). Beer on Midsummer's Night! Not for me, thank you. I can go one better than that myself. (*He opens the sideboard and takes out a bottle of red wine with a yellow label*) Yellow label, do you see, dear? Just give me a glass. A wineglass, of course, when a fellow's going to drink neat wine.

CHRISTINE (*turns again toward the fireplace and puts a small saucepan on*). God pity the woman who ever gets you for a husband, a growler like you!

JOHN. Oh, don't jaw! You'd be only too pleased if you only got a fellow like me, and I don't think for a minute that you're in any way put out by my being called your best boy. (*Tastes the wine*) Ah! very nice, very nice. Not quite mellowed enough though, that's the only thing. (*He warms the glass with his hand*) We bought this at Dijon. It came to four francs the liter, without the glass, and then there was the duty as well. What are you cooking there now? It makes the most infernal stink?

CHRISTINE. Oh, that's just some assafœtida, which Miss Julie wants to have for Diana.

JOHN. You ought to express yourself a little more prettily, Christine. Why have you got to get up on a holiday evening and cook for the brute? Is it ill, eh?

CHRISTINE. Yes, it is. It slunk out to the dog in the courtyard, and there it played the fool, and the young lady doesn't want to know anything about it, do you see?

JOHN. Yes, in one respect the young lady is too proud, and in another not proud enough. Just like the Countess was when she was alive. She felt most at home in the kitchen, and in the stable, but she would never ride a horse; she'd go about with dirty cuffs, but insisted on having the Count's coronet on the buttons. The young lady, so far now as she is concerned, doesn't take enough trouble about either herself or her person; in a manner of speaking, she is not refined. Why, only just now, when she was dancing in the barn, she snatched Forster away from Anna, and asked him to dance with herself. We wouldn't behave like that; but that's what happens when the gentry make themselves cheap. Then they are cheap, and no mistake about it. But she is real stately! Superb! Whew! What shoulders, what a bust and——

CHRISTINE. Ye-e-s; but she makes up a good bit, too. I know what Clara says, who helps her to dress.

JOHN. Oh, Clara! You women are always envious of each other. I've been out with her and seen her ride, and then how she dances!

CHRISTINE. I say, John, won't you dance with me when I'm ready?

JOHN. Of course I will.

CHRISTINE. Promise me?

JOHN. Promise? If I say I'll do a thing, then I always do it. Anyway, thanks very much for the food; it was damned good. (*He puts the cork back into the bottle. The young lady, at the glass door, speaks to people outside*) I'll be back in a minute. (*He conceals the bottle of wine in a napkin, and stands up respectfully.*)

JULIE (*enters and goes to* CHRISTINE *by the fireplace*). Well, is it ready?

(CHRISTINE *intimates to her by signs that* JOHN *is present.*)

JOHN (*gallantly*). Do the ladies want to talk secrets?

JULIE (*strikes him in the face with her handkerchief*). Is he inquisitive?

JOHN. Ah! what a nice smell of violets.

JULIE (*coquettishly*). Impudent person! Is the fellow then an expert in perfumes? (*She goes behind the table.*)

JOHN (*with gentle affection*). Have you ladies then been brewing a magic potion this Midsummer Night? Something so as to be able to read one's fortunes in the stars, so that you get a sight of the future?

JULIE (*sharply*). Yes, if he manages to see that, he must have very good eyes. (*To* CHRISTINE) Pour it into a half bottle and cork it securely. Let the man come now and dance the schottische with me. John? (*She lets her handkerchief fall on the table.*)

JOHN (*hesitating*). I don't want to be disobliging to anybody, but I promised Christine this dance.

JULIE. Oh, well, she can get somebody else. (*She goes to* CHRISTINE) What do you say, Christine? Won't you lend me John?

CHRISTINE. I haven't got any say in the matter. If you are so condescending, Miss, it wouldn't at all do for him to refuse. You just go and be grateful for such an honor.

JOHN. Speaking frankly, and without meaning any offence, do you think it's quite wise, Miss Julie, to dance twice in succession with the same gentleman, particularly as the people here are only too ready to draw all kinds of conclusions?

JULIE (*explodes*). What do you mean? What conclusion? What does the man mean?

JOHN (*evasively*). As you won't understand me, Miss, I must express myself more clearly. It doesn't look well to prefer one of your inferiors to others who expect the same exceptional honor.

JULIE. Prefer? What idea is the man getting into his head? I am absolutely astonished. I, the mistress of the house, honor my servants' dance with my presence, and if I actually want to dance I want to do it with a man who can steer, so that I haven't got the bore of being laughed at.

JOHN. I await your orders, Miss; I am at your service.

JULIE (*softly*). Don't talk now of orders; this evening we're simply merry men and women at a revel, and we lay aside all rank. Give me your arm; don't be uneasy, Christine, I'm not going to entice your treasure away from you.
(JOHN *offers her his arm and leads her through the glass door.* CHRISTINE *alone. Faint violin music at some distance to schottische time.* CHRISTINE *keeps time with the music, clears the table where* JOHN *had been eating, washes the plate at the side-table, dries it and puts it in the cupboard. She then takes off her kitchen apron, takes a small mirror out of the table drawer, puts it opposite the basket of lilacs, lights a taper, heats a hairpin, with which she curls her front hair; then she goes to the glass door and washes, comes back to the table, finds the young lady's handkerchief, which she has forgotten, takes it and smells it; she then pensively spreads it out, stretches it flat and folds it in four.* JOHN *comes back alone through the glass door.*)

JOHN. Yes, she is mad, to dance like that; and everybody stands by the door and grins at her. What do you say about it, Christine?

CHRISTINE. Ah, it's just her time, and then she always takes on so strange. But won't you come now and dance with me?

JOHN. You aren't offended with me that I cut your last dance?

CHRISTINE. No, not the least bit; you know that well enough, and I know my place besides.

JOHN (*puts his hand round her waist*). You're a sensible girl, Christine, and you'd make an excellent housekeeper.

JULIE (*comes in through the glass door. She is disagreeably surprised. With forced humor*). Charming cavalier you are, to be sure, to run away from your partner.

JOHN. On the contrary, Miss Julie, I've been hurrying all I know, as you see, to find the girl I left behind me.

JULIE. Do you know, none of the others dance like you do. But why do you go about in livery on a holiday evening? Take it off at once.

JOHN. In that case, Miss, I must ask you to leave me for a moment, because my black coat hangs up here. (*He goes with a corresponding gesture toward the right.*)

JULIE. Is he bashful on my account? Just about changing a coat! Is he going into his room and coming back again? So far as I am concerned he can stay here; I'll turn round.

JOHN. By your leave, Miss. (*He goes to the left, his arm is visible when he changes his coat.*)

JULIE (*to* CHRISTINE). I say, Christine, is John your sweetheart, that he's so thick with you?

CHRISTINE (*going toward the fireplace*). My sweetheart? Yes, if you like. We call it that.

JULIE. Call it?

CHRISTINE. Well, you yourself, Miss, had a sweetheart and——

JULIE. Yes, we were properly engaged.

CHRISTINE. But nothing at all came of it. (*She sits down and gradually goes to sleep.*)

(JOHN *in a black coat and with a black hat.*)

JULIE. Très gentil, Monsieur Jean; très gentil!

JOHN. Vous voulez plaisanter, madame!

JULIE. Et vous voulez parler Français? And where did you pick that up?

JOHN. In Switzerland, when I was a waiter in one of the best hotels in Lucerne.

JULIE. But you look quite like a gentleman in that coat. Charming. (*She sits down on the right, by the table.*)

JOHN. Ah! you're flattering me.

JULIE (*offended*). Flatter? You?

JOHN. My natural modesty won't allow me to imagine that you're paying true compliments to a man like me, so I took the liberty of supposing that you're exaggerating or, in a manner of speaking, flattering.

JULIE. Where did you learn to string your words together like that? You must have been to the theater a great deal?

JOHN. Quite right. I've been to no end of places.

JULIE. But you were born here in this neighborhood.

JOHN. My father was odd man to the State attorney of this parish, and I saw you, Miss, when you were a child, although you didn't notice me.

JULIE. Really?

JOHN. Yes, and I remember one incident in particular. Um, yes—I mustn't speak about that.

JULIE. Oh, yes—you tell me. What? Just to please me.

JOHN. No, really I can't now. Perhaps some other time.

JULIE. Some other time means never. Come, is it then so dangerous to tell me now?

JOHN. It's not dangerous, but it's much best to leave it alone. Just look at her over there. (*He points to* CHRISTINE, *who has gone to sleep in a chair by the fireplace.*)

JULIE. She'll make a cheerful wife. Perhaps she snores as well.

JOHN. She doesn't do that—she speaks in her sleep.

JULIE. How do you know that she speaks in her sleep?

JOHN. I've heard it.
(*Pause—in which they look at each other.*)

JULIE. Why don't you sit down?

JOHN. I shouldn't take such a liberty in your presence.

JULIE. And if I order you to——

JOHN. Then I obey.

JULIE. Sit down; but, wait a moment, can't you give me something to drink?

JOHN. I don't know what's in the refrigerator. I don't think there's anything except beer.

JULIE. That's not to be sniffed at. Personally I'm so simple in my tastes that I prefer it to wine.

JOHN (takes a bottle out of the refrigerator and draws the cork; he looks in the cupboard for a glass and plate, on which he serves the beer). May I offer you some?

JULIE. Thanks. Won't you have some as well?

JOHN. I'm not what you might call keen on beer, but if you order me, Miss——

JULIE. Order? It seems to me that as a courteous cavalier you might keep your partner company.

JOHN. A very sound observation. (He opens another bottle and takes a glass.)

JULIE. Drink my health! (JOHN hesitates) I believe the old duffer is bashful.

JOHN (on his knees, mock heroically, lifts up his glass). The health of my mistress!

JULIE. Bravo! Now, as a finishing touch, you must kiss my shoe. (JOHN hesitates, then catches sharply hold of her foot and kisses it lightly) First rate! You should have gone on the stage.

JOHN (gets up). This kind of thing mustn't go any further, Miss. Anybody might come in and see us.

JULIE. What would it matter?

JOHN. People would talk, and make no bones about what they said either, and if you knew, Miss, how their tongues have already been wagging, then——

JULIE. What did they say then? Tell me, but sit down.

JOHN (sits down). I don't want to hurt you, but you made use of expressions—which pointed to innuendoes of such a kind—yes, you'll understand this perfectly well yourself. You're not a child any more, and, if a lady is seen to drink alone with a man—even if it's only a servant, tête-à-tête at night—then——

JULIE. What then? And, besides, we're not alone: Christine is here.

JOHN. Yes, asleep.

JULIE. Then I'll wake her up. (She gets up) Christine, are you asleep?

CHRISTINE (in her sleep). Bla—bla—bla—bla.

JULIE. Christine! The woman can go on sleeping.

CHRISTINE (in her sleep). The Count's boots are already done—put the coffee out—at once, at once, at once—oh, oh—ah!

JULIE (takes hold of her by the nose). Wake up, will you?

JOHN (harshly). You mustn't disturb a person who's asleep.

JULIE (sharply). What?

JOHN. A person who's been on her legs all day by the fireplace will naturally be tired when night comes; and sleep should be respected.

JULIE (*in another tone*). That's a pretty thought, and does you credit —thank you. (*She holds her hand out to* JOHN) Come out now and pick some clover for me.
(*During the subsequent dialogue* CHRISTINE *wakes up, and exits in a dazed condition to the right, to go to bed.*)

JOHN. With you, Miss?

JULIE. With me.

JOHN. It's impossible, absolutely impossible.

JULIE. I don't understand what you mean. Can it be possible that you imagine such a thing for a single minute?

JOHN. Me—no, but the people— yes.

JULIE. What! That I should be in love with a servant?

JOHN. I'm not by any means an educated man, but there have been cases, and nothing is sacred to the people.

JULIE. I do believe the man is an aristocrat.

JOHN. Yes; that I am.

JULIE. And I'm on the down path.

JOHN. Don't go down, Miss. Take my advice, nobody will believe that you went down of your own free will. People will always say you fell.

JULIE. I have a better opinion of people than you have. Come and try. Come. (*She challenges him with her eyes.*)

JOHN. You are strange, you know.

JULIE. Perhaps I am, but so are you. Besides, everything is strange. Life, men, the whole thing is simply an iceberg which is driven out on the water until it sinks—sinks. I have a dream which comes up now and again, and now it haunts me. I am sitting on the top of a high pillar and can't see any possibility of getting down; I feel dizzy when I look down, but I have to get down all the same. I haven't got the pluck to throw myself off. I can't keep my balance and I want to fall over, but I don't fall. And I don't get a moment's peace until I'm down below. No rest until I've got to the ground, and when I've got down to the ground I want to get right into the earth. Have you ever felt anything like that?

JOHN. No; I usually dream I'm lying under a high tree in a gloomy forest. I want to get up right to the top and look round at the light landscape where the sun shines, and plunder the birds' nests where the golden eggs lie, and I climb and climb, but the trunk is so thick and so smooth, and it's such a long way to the first branch; but I know, if only I can get to the first branch, I can climb to the top, as though it were a ladder. I haven't got there yet, but I must get there, even though it were only in my dreams.

JULIE. And here I am now standing chattering to you. Come along now, just out into the park. (*She offers him her arm and they go.*)

JOHN. We must sleep tonight on nine Midsummer Night herbs, then our dreams will come true.

(*Both turn round in the doorway.* JOHN *holds his hand before one of his eyes.*)

JULIE. Let me see what's got into your eye.

JOHN. Oh, nothing, only a bit of dust—it'll be all right in a minute.

JULIE. It was the sleeve of my dress that grazed you. Just sit down and I'll help you get it out. (*She takes him by the arm and makes him sit down on the table. She then takes his head and presses it down, and tries to get the dust out with the corner of her handkerchief*) Be quite still, quite still! (*She strikes him on the hand*) There! Will he be obedient now? I do believe the great strong man's trembling. (*She feels his arm*) With arms like that!

JOHN (*warningly*). Miss Julie.

JULIE. Yes, Monsieur Jean.

JOHN. Attention! Je ne suis qu'un homme!

JULIE. Won't he sit still? See! It's out now! Let him kiss my hand and thank me.

JOHN (*stands up*). Miss Julie, listen to me. Christine has cleared out and gone to bed. Won't you listen to me?

JULIE. Kiss my hand first.

JOHN. Listen to me.

JULIE. Kiss my hand first.

JOHN. All right, but you must be responsible for the consequences.

JULIE. What consequences?

JOHN. What consequences? Don't you know it's dangerous to play with fire?

JULIE. Not for me. I am insured!

JOHN (*sharply*). No, you're not! And even if you were, there's inflammable material pretty close.

JULIE. Do you mean yourself?

JOHN. Yes. Not that I'm particularly dangerous, but I'm just a young man!

JULIE. With an excellent appearance—what incredible vanity! Don Juan, I suppose, or a Joseph. I believe, on my honor, the man's a Joseph!

JOHN. Do you believe that?

JULIE. I almost fear it. (JOHN *goes brutally toward and tries to embrace her, so as to kiss her.* JULIE *boxes his ears*) Hands off.

JOHN. Are you serious or joking?

JULIE. Serious.

JOHN. In that case, what took place before was also serious. You're taking the game much too seriously, and that's dangerous. But I'm tired of the game now, so would you please excuse me so that I can go back to my work? (*He goes to the back of the stage, to the boots*) The Count must have his boots early, and midnight is long past. (*He takes up the boots.*)

JULIE. Leave the boots alone.

JOHN. No. It's my duty, and I'm bound to do it, but I didn't take on the job of being your playmate. Besides, the thing is out of the question, as I consider myself much too good for that kind of thing.

JULIE. You're proud.

JOHN. In some cases, not in others.

JULIE. Have you ever loved?

JOHN. We people don't use that word. But I've liked many girls, and once it made me quite ill not to be able to get the girl I wanted, as ill, mind you, as the princes in "The Arabian Nights," who are unable to eat or drink out of pure love. (*He takes up the boots again.*)

JULIE. Who was it?
(JOHN *is silent.*)

JOHN. You can't compel me to tell you.

JULIE. If I ask you as an equal, as —a friend? Who was it?

JOHN. You!

JULIE (*sits down*). How funny!

JOHN. And if you want to hear the story, here goes! It was humorous. This is the tale, mind you, which I would not tell you before, but I'll tell you right enough now. Do you know how the world looks from down below? No, of course you don't. Like hawks and eagles, whose backs a man can scarcely ever see because they're always flying in the air. I grew up in my father's hovel along with seven sisters and—a pig

—out there on the bare gray field, where there wasn't a single tree growing, and I could look out from the window on to the walls of the Count's parks, with its apple-trees. That was my Garden of Eden, and many angels stood there with a flaming sword and guarded it, but all the same I, and other boys, found my way to the Tree of Life—Do you despise me?

JULIE. Oh, well—stealing apples? All boys do that.

JOHN. That's what you say, but you despise me all the same. Well, what's the odds! Once I went with my mother inside the garden, to weed out the onion bed. Close by the garden wall there stood a Turkish pavilion, shaded by jasmine and surrounded by wild roses. I had no idea what it was used for, but I'd never seen so fine a building. People went in and out, and one day the door stood open. I sneaked in, and saw the walls covered with pictures of queens and emperors, and red curtains with fringes were in front of the windows—now you know what I mean. I—— (*He takes a lilac branch and holds it under the young lady's nose*) I'd never been in the Abbey, and I'd never seen anything else but the church—but this was much finer, and wherever my thoughts roamed they always came back again to it, and then little by little the desire sprang up in me to get to know, some time, all this magnificence. *Enfin,* I sneaked in, saw and wondered, but then somebody came. There was, of course, only one way out for the gentry, but I found another one, and, again, I had no choice. (JULIE, *who has taken up the lilac branch, lets it fall on the table*) So I flew, and rushed through a lilac bush, clambered over a garden bed and came out by a terrace of roses. I there saw a light dress and a pair of white stockings —that was you. I laid down under a heap of herbage, right under them. Can you imagine it?—under thistles which stung me and wet earth which stank, and I looked at you where you came between the roses, and I thought if it is true that a murderer can get into the kingdom of heaven, and remain among the angels, it is strange if here, on God's own earth, poor lad like me can't get into the Abbey park and play with the Count's daughter.

JULIE (*sentimentally*). Don't you think that all poor children under similar circumstances have had the same thoughts?

JOHN (*at first hesitating, then in a tone of conviction*). That all poor children—yes—of course. Certainly.

JULIE. Being poor must be an infinite misfortune.

JOHN (*with deep pain*). Oh, Miss Julie. Oh! A dog can lie on the Count's sofa, a horse can be petted by a lady's hand, on its muzzle, but a boy! (*With a change of tone*) Yes, yes; a man of individuality here and there may have enough stuff in him to come to the top, but how often is that the case? What do you think I did then?—I jumped into the mill-stream, clothes and all, but was fished out and given a thrashing. But the next Sunday, when father and all of the people at home went to grandmother's, I managed to work it that I stayed at home, and I then had a wash with soap and warm water, put on my Sunday clothes and went to church, where

I could get a sight of you. I saw you and went home determined to die, but I wanted to die in a fine and agreeable way, without pain, and I then got the idea that it was dangerous to sleep under a lilac bush. We had one which at that time was in full bloom. I picked all the blooms which it had and then lay down in the oat bin. Have you ever noticed how smooth the oats are? As soft to the hand as human skin. I then shut the lid, and at last went to sleep and woke up really very ill; but I didn't die, as you see. I don't know what I really wanted; there was no earthly possibility of winning you. But you were a proof for me of the utter hopelessness of escaping from the circle in which I'd been born.

JULIE. You tell a story charmingly, don't you know. Have you been to school?

JOHN. A little, but I've read a lot of novels, and been a lot to the theater. Besides, I've heard refined people talk, and I've learned most from them.

JULIE. Do you listen, then, to what we say?

JOHN. Yes, that's right; and I've picked up a great deal when I've sat on the coachman's box or been rowing the boat. I once heard you, Miss, and a young lady friend of yours.

JULIE. Really? What did you hear then?

JOHN. Well, that I can't tell you, but I was really somewhat surprised, and I couldn't understand where you'd learned all the words from.

Perhaps at bottom there isn't so great a difference between class and class as one thinks.

JULIE. Oh, you ought to be ashamed of yourself! We are not like you are, and we have someone whom we love best.

JOHN (*fixes her with his eyes*). Are you so sure of that? You needn't make yourself out so innocent, Miss, on my account.

JULIE. The man to whom I gave my love was a scoundrel.

JOHN. Girls always say that—afterward.

JULIE. Always?

JOHN. Always, I think. I've certainly already heard the phrase on several previous occasions, in similar circumstances.

JULIE. What circumstances?

JOHN. The last time——

JULIE. Stop! I won't hear any more.

JOHN. She wouldn't either—it's remarkable. Oh, well, will you excuse me if I go to bed?

JULIE (*tartly*). Go to bed on Midsummer Night?

JOHN. Yes. Dance out there with the riff-raff, that doesn't amuse me the least bit.

JULIE. Take the key of the boathouse and row me out on the lake. I want to see the sun rise.

JOHN. Is that sensible?

JULIE. It seems you're concerned about your reputation.

JOHN. Why not? I'm not keen on making myself look ridiculous, nor on being kicked out without a reference, if I want to set up on my own, and it seems to me I have certain obligations to Christine.

JULIE. Oh, indeed! So it's Christine again?

JOHN. Yes; but it's on your account as well. Take my advice and go up and go to bed.

JULIE. Shall I obey you?

JOHN. This once for your own sake, I ask you; it's late at night, sleepiness makes one dazed, and one's blood boils. You go and lie down. Besides, if I can believe my ears, people are coming to find me, and if we are found here you are lost. (*Chorus is heard in the distance and gets nearer.*)

"She pleases me like one o'clock,
   My pretty young lidee,
For thoughts of her my bosom
      block,
   Her servant must I be,
For she delights my heart,
   Tiritidi—ralla, tiritidi—ra!"

"And now I've won the match,
   For which I've long been try-
      ing,
   The other swains go flying,
But she comes up to scratch,
   My pretty young lidee,
   Tiritidi—ralla—la—la!"

JULIE. I know our people, and I like them—just in the same way that they like me. Just let them come, then you'll see.

JOHN. No, Miss Julie. The folks don't love you. They eat your bread, but they make fun of you behind your back. You take it from me. Listen, just listen, to what they're singing. No, you'd better not listen.

JULIE (*listens*). What are they singing?

JOHN. It's some nasty lines about you and me.

JULIE. Horrible! Ugh, what sneaks they are!

JOHN. The riff-raff is always cowardly, and in the fight it's best to fly.

JULIE. Fly? But where to? We can't go out, and we can't go up to Christine's room either.

JOHN. Then come into my room. Necessity knows no law, and you can rely on my being your real, sincere and respectful friend.

JULIE. But just think, would they look for you there?

JOHN. I'll bolt the door, and if they try to break it in I'll shoot. Come. (*On his knees*) Come!

JULIE (*significantly*). Promise me.

JOHN. On my oath!
(JULIE *rushes off on the left.* JOHN *follows her in a state of excitement. Pantomime. Wedding party in holiday clothes, with flowers round their hats and a violin player at their head, come in through the glass door. Barrel of small beer and a keg of brandy wreathed with laurel are placed on the table. They take up glasses, they then drink, they then make a ring and a dance is sung and* executed. *Then they go out, singing again, through the glass door.* JULIE *comes in alone from the left, observes the disorder in the kitchen and claps her hands; she then takes out a powder puff and powders her face.* JOHN *follows after the young woman from the left, in a state of exaltation.*)

JOHN. There, do you see, you've seen it for yourself now. You think it possible to go on staying here?

JULIE. No, I don't any more. But what's to be done?

JOHN. Run away—travel, far away from here.

JULIE. Travel? Yes, but where?

JOHN. Sweden—the Italian lakes, you've never been there, have you?

JULIE. No; is it nice there?

JOHN. Oh! A perpetual summer—oranges, laurels. Whew!

JULIE. What are we to start doing afterward?

JOHN. We shall start a first-class hotel there, with first-class visitors.

JULIE. An hotel?

JOHN. That's a life, to be sure, you take it from me—an endless succession of new sights, new languages; not a minute to spare for sulking or brooding; no looking for work, for the work comes of its own. The bell goes on ringing day and night, the train puffs, the omnibus comes and goes, while the gold pieces roll into the till. That's a life, to be sure!

JULIE. Yes, that's what *you* call life; but what about me?

JOHN. The mistress of the house, the ornament of the firm, with your appearance and your manners—oh! success is certain. Splendid! You sit like a queen in the counting house, and set all your slaves in motion, with a single touch of your electric bell; the visitors pass in procession by your throne, lay their treasure respectfully on your table; you've got no idea how men tremble when they take a bill up in their hand—I'll touch up the bills, and you must sugar them with your sweetest laugh. Ah, let's get away from here. (*He takes a time-table out of his pocket*) Right away by the next train, by six-thirty we're at Malmo; at eight-forty in the morning at Hamburg; Frankfort—one day in Basle and in Como by the St. Gothard Tunnel in—let's see—three days. Only three days.

JULIE. That all sounds very nice, but, John, you must give me courage, dear. Tell me that you love me, dear; come and take me in your arms.

JOHN (*hesitating*). I should like to --but I dare not—not here in the house. I love you, no doubt about it—can you have any real doubt about it, Miss?

JULIE (*with real feminine shame*). Miss? Say "Dear." There are no longer any barriers between us— say "Dear."

JOHN (*in a hurt tone*). I can't. There are still barriers between us so long as we remain in this house: there is the past—there is my master the Count; I never met a man

whom I've respected so much—I've only got to see his gloves lying on a chair and straight away I feel quite small; I've only got to hear the bell up there and I dash away like a startled horse and—I've only got to see his boots standing there, so proud and upright, and I've got a pain inside. (*He pushes the boots with his feet*) Superstition, prejudice, which have been inoculated into us since our childhood, but which one can't get rid of. But only come to another country, to a republic, and I'll make people go on their knees before my porter's livery—on their knees, do you hear? You'll see. But not me: I'm not made to go on my knees, for I've got grit in me, character, and, once I get on to the first branch, you'll see me climb right up. Today I'm a servant, but next year I shall be the proprietor of a hotel; in ten years I shall be independent; then I'll take a trip to Roumania and get myself decorated, and may—note that I say, may—finish up as a count.

JULIE. Good! Good!

JOHN. Oh, yes, the title of Count is to be bought in Roumania, and then you will be a countess—my countess.

JULIE. Tell me that you love me, dear; if you don't—why, what am I, if you don't?

JOHN. I'll tell you a thousand times later on, but not here. And above all, no sentimentalism, if everything isn't to go smash. We must look at the matter quietly, like sensible people. (*He takes out a cigar, cuts off the end, and lights it*) You sit there, I'll sit here; then we'll have a little chat just as though nothing had happened.

JULIE. O my God! have you no feeling then?

JOHN. Me? There's no man who has more feeling than I have; but I can control myself.

JULIE. A short time back you could kiss my shoe—and now?

JOHN (brutally). Yes, a little while ago, but now we've got something else to think of.

JULIE. Don't talk brutally to me.

JOHN. No, but I'll talk sense. We've made fools of ourselves once, don't let's do it again. The Count may turn up any minute and we've got to map out our lives in advance. What do you think of my plans for the future? Do you agree?

JULIE. They seem quite nice, but one question—you need large capital for so great an undertaking—have you got it?

JOHN (going on smoking). Have I got it? Of course I have. I've got my special knowledge, my exceptional experience, my knowledge of languages, that's a capital which is worth something, seems to me.

JULIE. But we can't buy a single railway ticket with all that.

JOHN. That's true enough, and so I'll look for somebody who can put up the money.

JULIE. Where can you find a man like that all at once?

JOHN. Then you'll have to find him, if you're going to be my companion.

JULIE. I can't do that, and I've got nothing myself. (Pause.)

JOHN. In that case the whole scheme collapses.

JULIE. And?

JOHN. Things remain as they are now.

JULIE. Do you think I'll go on staying any longer under this roof as your mistress? Do you think I will let the people point their finger at me? Do you think that after this I can look my father in the face? No! Take me away from here, from all this humiliation and dishonor! O my God! What have I done! O my God! My God! (She cries.)

JOHN. Ho—ho! So that's the game —what have you done? Just the same as a thousand other people like you.

JULIE (screams as though in a paroxysm). And now you despise me? I'm falling, I'm falling!

JOHN. Fall down to my level and then I'll lift you up again afterward.

JULIE. What awful power dragged me down to you, the power which draws the weak to the strong?— which draws him who falls to him who rises? Or was it love?—love— this! Do you know what love is?

JOHN. I? Do you really suggest that I meant that? Don't you think I'd have felt it already long ago?

JULIE. What phrases, to be sure, and what thoughts!

JOHN. That's what I learned and that's what I am. But just keep your nerve and don't play the fine lady. We've got into a mess and we've got to get out of it. Look here, my girl. Come here, I'll give you an extra glass, my dear. (*He opens the sideboard, takes out the bottle of wine and fills two of the dirty glasses.*)

JULIE. Where did you get the wine from?

JOHN. The cellar.

JULIE. My father's Burgundy!

JOHN. Is it too good for his son-in-law? I don't think!

JULIE. And I've been drinking beer!

JOHN. That only shows that you've got worse taste than me.

JULIE. Thief!

JOHN. Want to blab?

JULIE. Oh, oh! the accomplice of a house-thief. I drank too much last night and I did things in my dream. Midsummer Night, the feast of innocent joys.

JOHN. Innocent! Hm!

JULIE (*walks up and down*). Is there at this moment a human being as unhappy as I am?

JOHN. Why are you? After such a fine conquest. Just think of Christine in there, don't you think she's got feelings as well?

JULIE. I used to think so before, but I don't think so any more—no, a servant's a servant——

JOHN. And a whore's a whore.

JULIE. O God in heaven! Take my

miserable life! Take me out of this filth in which I'm sinking. Save me, save me!

JOHN. I can't gainsay but that you make me feel sorry. Once upon a time when I lay in the onion bed and saw you in the rose garden then —I'll tell you straight—I had the same dirty thoughts as all youngsters.

JULIE. And then you wanted to die for me!

JOHN. In the oat bin? That was mere gas.

JULIE. Lies, you mean.

JOHN (*begins to get sleepy*). Near enough. I read the story once in the paper about a chimney-sweep who laid down in a chest full of lilac because he was ordered to take additional nourishment.

JULIE. Yes—so you are——

JOHN. What other idea should I have thought of? One's always got to capture a gal with flatteries.

JULIE. Scoundrel!

JOHN. Whore!

JULIE. So I must be the first branch, must I?

JOHN. But the branch was rotten.

JULIE. I've got to be the notice board of the hotel, have I?

JOHN. I'm going to be the hotel.

JULIE. Sit in your office, decoy your customers, fake your bills.

JOHN. I'll see to that myself.

JULIE. To think that a human being can be so thoroughly dirty!

JOHN. Wash yourself clean.

JULIE. Lackey! Menial! Stand up— you, when I'm speaking!

JOHN. You wench of a menial! Hold your jaw and clear out! Is it for you to come ragging me that I'm rough? No one in my station of life could have made herself so cheap as the way you carried on tonight, my girl. Do you think that a clean-minded girl excites men in the way that you do? Have you ever seen a girl in my position offer herself in the way you did?

JULIE (*humiliated*). That's right, strike me, trample on me! I haven't deserved anything better. I'm a wretched woman. But help me! Help me to get away, if there's any chance of it.

JOHN (*more gently*). I don't want to deny my share in the honor of having seduced you, but do you think that a person in my position would have dared to have raised his eyes to you if you yourself hadn't invited him to do it? I'm still quite amazed.

JULIE. And proud.

JOHN. Why not? Although I must acknowledge that the victory was too easy to make me get a swelled head over it.

JULIE. Strike me once more!

JOHN (*he gets up*). No, I'd rather ask you to forgive me what I've al-ready said. I don't hit a defenseless person, and least of all a girl. I can't deny that from one point of view I enjoyed seeing that it was not gold but glitter which dazzled us all down below; to have seen that the back of the hawk was only drab, and that there was powder on those dainty cheeks, and that those mani-cured nails could have grimy tips, that the handkerchief was dirty, even though it did smell of scent! But it pained me, on the other hand, to have seen that the thing I'd been striving for was not something higher, something sounder; it pains me to have seen you sink so deep that you are far beneath your own cook; it pains me to see that the au-tumn flowers have crumpled up in the rain and turned into a mess.

JULIE. You're talking as though you were already my superior.

JOHN. I am; look here, I could change you into a countess, but you could never make me into a count!

JULIE. But I am bred from a count, and that you can never be.

JOHN. That's true, but I could pro-duce counts myself if——

JULIE. But you're a thief, and I'm not.

JOHN. There are worse things than being a thief; that's not the worst; besides, if I'm serving in a house-hold, I look upon myself in a man-ner of speaking as one of the family, as a child of the house, and it isn't regarded as stealing if a child picks a berry from a large bunch. (*His passion wakes up afresh*) Miss Julie, you're a magnificent woman, much too good for the likes of me. You've been the prey of a mad fit and you want to cover up your mistake, and that's why you've got it into your head you love me, but you don't. Of course, it may be that only my personal charms attract you—and in that case your love is not a bit better than mine; but I can never be satisfied with being nothing more to you than a mere beast, and I can't get your love.

JULIE. Are you sure of it?

JOHN. You mean it might come about? I might love you? Yes, no doubt about it, you're pretty, you're refined. (*He approaches her and takes her hand*) Nice, when you want to be, and when you have roused desire in a man the odds are that it will never be extinguished. (*He embraces her*) You are like burning wine, with strong herbs in it, and a kiss from you—— (*He tries to lead her on to the left, but she struggles free.*)

JULIE. Let me alone! That's not the way to win me!

JOHN. In what way then? Not in that way? Not with caresses and pretty words—not with forethought for the future, escape from disgrace? In what way then?

JULIE. In what way? In what way? I don't know—I have no idea. I loathe you like vermin, but I can't be without you.

JOHN. Run away with me.

JULIE (*adjusts her dress*). Run away? Yes, of course we'll run away. But I'm so tired. Give me a glass of wine. (JOHN *pours out the wine.* JULIE *looks at her watch*) But we

must talk first; we've still a little time to spare. (*She drinks up the glass and holds it out for some more.*)

JOHN. Don't drink to such excess— you'll get drunk!

JULIE. What does it matter?

JOHN. What does it matter? It's cheap to get drunk. What do you want to say to me then?

JULIE. We'll run away, but we'll talk first, that means I will talk, because up to now you've done all the talking yourself. You've told me about your life; now I'll tell you about mine. Then we shall know each other thoroughly, before we start on our joint wanderings.

JOHN. One moment. Excuse me, just think if you won't be sorry afterward for giving away all the secrets of your life.

JULIE. Aren't you my friend?

JOHN. Yes, for a short time. Don't trust me.

JULIE. You don't mean what you say. Besides, everybody knows my secrets. Look here, my mother was not of noble birth, but quite simple; she was brought up in the theories of her period about the equality and freedom of woman and all the rest of it. Then she had a distinct aversion to marriage. When my father proposed to her, she answered that she would never become his wife, but—she did. I came into the world —against the wish of my mother so far as I could understand. The next was, that I was brought up by my mother to lead what she called a child's natural life, and to do that, I had to learn everything that a boy has to learn, so that I could be a living example of her theory that a woman is as good as a man. I could go about in boys' clothes. I learned to groom horses, but I wasn't allowed to go into the dairy. I had to scrub and harness horses and go hunting. Yes, and at times I had actually to try and learn farm work, and at home the men were given women's work and the women were given men's work—the result was that the property began to go down and we became the laughing-stock of the whole neighborhood. At last my father appears to have wakened up out of his trance and to have rebelled; then everything was altered to suit his wishes. My mother became ill. I don't know what the illness was, but she often suffered from seizures, hid herself in the grounds and in the garden, and remained in the open air the whole night. Then came the great fire, which you must have heard about. House, farm buildings and stables all were burnt, and under circumstances, mind you, which gave a suspicion of arson, because the accident happened the day after the expiration of the quarterly payment of the insurance installment, and the premiums which my father had sent were delayed through the carelessness of the messenger, so that they did not get there in time. (*She fills her glass and drinks.*)

JOHN. Don't drink any more.

JULIE. Oh, what does it matter? We were without shelter and had to sleep in the carriage. My father didn't know where he was to get the money to build a house again. Then my mother advised him to approach

a friend of her youth for a loan, a tile manufacturer in the neighborhood. Father got the loan, but didn't have to pay any interest, which made him quite surprised, and then the house was built. (*She drinks again*) You know who set fire to the house?

JOHN. My lady your mother.

JULIE. Do you know who the tile manufacturer was?

JOHN. Your mother's lover.

JULIE. Do you know whose the money was?

JOHN. Wait a minute. No, that I don't know.

JULIE. My mother's.

JOHN. The Count's then?—unless they were living with separate estates?

JULIE. They weren't doing that. My mother had a small fortune, which she didn't allow my father to handle, and she invested it with—the friend.

JOHN. Who banked it.

JULIE. Quite right. This all came to my father's ears, but he could not take any legal steps; he couldn't pay his wife's lover; he couldn't prove that it was his wife's money. That was my mother's revenge for his using force against her at home. He then made up his mind to shoot himself. The report went about that he had wanted to do it, but hadn't succeeded. He remained alive then, and my mother had to settle for what she'd done. That was a bad time for me, as you can imagine. I sympathized with my father, but I sided with my mother, as I didn't understand the position. I learnt from her to mistrust and hate men, for, so far as I could hear, she always hated men—and I swore to her that I would never be a man's slave.

JOHN. And then you became engaged to Kronvogt?

JULIE. For the simple reason that he was to have been my slave.

JOHN. And he wouldn't have it?

JULIE. He was willing enough, but nothing came of it. I got sick of him.

JOHN. I saw it, in the stable.

JULIE. What did you see?

JOHN. I saw how he broke off the engagement.

JULIE. That's a lie. It was I who broke off the engagement. Did he say that he did it? The scoundrel!

JOHN. No, he wasn't a scoundrel at all. You hate the men, Miss.

JULIE. Yes—usually, but at times, when my weak fit comes on—ugh!

JOHN. So you hate me as well?

JULIE. Infinitely. I could have you killed like a beast.

JOHN. The criminal is condemned to hard labor, but the beast is killed.

JULIE. Quite right.

JOHN. But there's no beast here—

and no prosecutor either. What are we going to do?

JULIE. Travel.

JOHN. To torture each other to death?

JULIE. No—have a good time for two, three years, or as long as we can—and then die.

JOHN. Die? What nonsense! I'm all for starting a hotel.

JULIE (*without listening to him*). By the Lake of Como, where the sun is always shining, where the laurel-trees are green at Christmas and the oranges glow.

JOHN. The Lake of Como is a rainy hole. I didn't see any oranges there, except in the vegetable shops; but it's a good place for visitors, because there are a lot of villas which can be let to honeymooning couples, and that's a very profitable industry. I'll tell you why. They take a six months' lease—and travel away after three weeks.

JULIE (*naively*). Why after three weeks?

JOHN. They quarrel, of course; but the rent's got to be paid all the same, and then we let again, and so it goes on one after the other, for love goes on to all eternity—even though it doesn't keep quite so long.

JULIE. Then you won't die with me?

JOHN. I won't die at all just yet, thank you. In the first place, because I still enjoy life, and, besides, because I look upon suicide as a sin against providence, which has given us life.

JULIE. Do you believe in God—you?

JOHN. Yes, I certainly do, and I go to church every other Sunday. But, speaking frankly, I'm tired of all this, and I'm going to bed now.

JULIE. You are, are you? And you think that I'm satisfied with that? Do you know what a man owes to the woman he has dishonored?

JOHN (*takes out his purse and throws a silver coin on the table*). If you don't mind, I don't like being in anybody's debt.

JULIE (*as though she had not noticed the insult*). Do you know what the law provides?

JOHN. Unfortunately, the law does not provide any penalty for the woman who seduces a man.

JULIE (*as before*). Can you find any other way out than that we should travel, marry and then get divorced again?

JOHN. And if I refused to take on the *mésalliance?*

JULIE. *Mésalliance?*

JOHN. Yes, for me. I've got better ancestors than you have: I haven't got any incendiaries in my pedigree.

JULIE. How do you know?

JOHN. At any rate, you can't prove the contrary, for we have no other pedigree than what you can see in the registry. But I read in a book on the drawing-room table about your pedigree. Do you know what the founder of your line was? A miller with whose wife the king spent a night during the Danish war. I don't run to ancestors like that. I've got no ancestors at all, as a matter of fact, but I can be an ancestor myself.

JULIE. This is what I get for opening my heart to a cad, for giving away my family honor.

JOHN. Family shame, you mean. But, look here, I told you so; people shouldn't drink, because then people talk nonsense, and people shouldn't talk nonsense.

JULIE. Oh, how I wish it undone, how I wish it undone! And if you only loved me!

JOHN. For the last time—what do you want? Do you want me to cry, do you want me to jump over your riding whip, do you want me to kiss you, or tempt you away for three weeks by the Lake of Como, and then, what am I to do?—what do you want? The thing's beginning to be a nuisance, but that's what one gets for meddling in the private affairs of the fair sex. Miss Julie, I see you're unhappy, I know that you suffer, but I can't understand you. People like us don't go in for such fairy tales; we don't hate each other either. We take love as a game, when our work gives us time off, but we haven't got the whole day and the whole night to devote to it. Let me look at you. You are ill; you are certainly ill!

JULIE. You must be kind to me, and now talk like a man. Help me! Help me! Tell me what I must do—what course I shall take.

JOHN. My Christ! If I only knew myself!

JULIE. I am raving, I have been mad! But isn't there any way by which I can be saved?

JOHN. Stay here and keep quiet. Nobody knows anything.

JULIE. Impossible! The servants know it; and Christine knows it.

JOHN. They don't know and they would never believe anything of the kind.

JULIE (*slowly*). It might happen again.

JOHN. That's true.

JULIE. And the results?

JOHN. The results? Where was I wool-gathering not to have thought about it? Yes, there's only one thing to do—to clear out at once. I won't go with you, because then it's all up, but you must travel alone—away— anywhere you like.

JULIE. Alone? Where? I can't do it.

JOHN. You must. And before the Count comes back too. If you stay, then you know what will be the result. If one has taken the first step, then one goes on with it, because one's already in for the disgrace, and then one gets bolder and bolder —at last you get copped—so you must travel. Write later on to the Count and confess everything except that it was me, and he'll never guess that. I don't think either that he'd be very pleased if he did find out.

JULIE. I'll travel, if you'll come with me.

JOHN. Are you mad, Miss? Do you want to elope with your servant? It'll all be in the papers the next morning, and the Count would never get over it.

JULIE. I can't travel, I can't stay. Help me! I am so tired, so infinitely tired—give me orders, put life into me again or I can't think any more, and I can't do any more.

JOHN. See here, now, what a wretched creature you are! Why do you strut about and turn up your nose as though you were the lord of creation? Well, then, I will give you orders; you go and change your clothes, get some money to travel with and come down here again.

JULIE (*sotto voce*). Come up with me.

JOHN. To your room? Now you're mad again. (*He hesitates for a moment*) No, you go at once. (*He takes her by the hand and leads her to the glass door.*)

JULIE (*as she goes*). Please speak kindly to me, John.

JOHN. An order always has an unkind sound. Just feel it now for yourself, just feel it. (*Exeunt both.*)

(JOHN *comes back, gives a sigh of relief, sits down at the table by the right, and takes out his notebook, now and again he counts aloud; pantomime.* CHRISTINE *comes in with a white shirt-front and a white necktie in her hand.*)

CHRISTINE. Good Lord! What does the man look like! What's happened here?

JOHN. Oh, Miss Julie called in the

servants. Were you so sound asleep that you didn't hear it?

CHRISTINE. I slept like a log.

JOHN. And dressed all ready for church?

CHRISTINE. Yes. You know you promised, dear, to come to Communion with me today.

JOHN. Yes, that's true, and you've already got some of my togs for me. Well, come here. (*He sits down on the right.* CHRISTINE *gives him the white front and necktie and helps him to put them on. Pause. Sleepily*) What gospel is it today?

CHRISTINE. I've got an idea it's about the beheading of John the Baptist.

JOHN. That's certain to last an awful time! Ugh! You're hurting me. Oh, I'm so sleepy, so sleepy!

CHRISTINE. Yes, what have you been doing all night? You look absolutely washed out.

JOHN. I've been sitting here chatting with Miss Julie.

CHRISTINE. She doesn't know what's decent. My God! she doesn't. (*Pause.*)

JOHN. I say, Christine dear.

CHRISTINE. Well?

JOHN. It's awfully strange when one comes to think it over.

CHRISTINE. What's so strange about her?

JOHN. Everything. (*Pause.*)

CHRISTINE (*looks at the glass which stands half empty on the table*). Did you drink together as well?

JOHN. Yes.

CHRISTINE. Ugh! Look me in the face.

JOHN. Yes.

CHRISTINE. Is it possible? Is it possible?

JOHN (*after reflecting for a short time*). Yes, it is.

CHRISTINE. Crikey! I'd never have thought it, that I wouldn't. No. Ugh! Ugh!

JOHN. I take it you're not jealous of her?

CHRISTINE. No, not of her; if it had been Clara or Sophie, yes, I should have been. Poor girl! Now, I tell you what. I won't stay any longer in this house, where one can't keep any respect for the gentry.

JOHN. Why should one respect them?

CHRISTINE. Yes, and you, who are as sly as they're made, ask me that. But will you serve people who carry on so improper? Why, one lowers oneself by doing it, it seems to me.

JOHN. Yes, but it's certainly a consolation for us that the others are no better than we are.

CHRISTINE. No, I don't find that; because if they're not better it's not worth while trying to be like our betters, and think of the Count, think of him; he's had so much trouble all his life long. No, I won't stay any longer in this house. And with the likes of you! If it had been even Kronvogt; if it had been a better man.

JOHN. What do you mean?

CHRISTINE. Yes, yes, you're quite a good fellow, I know, but there's always a difference between people and people—and I can never forget it. A young lady who was so proud, so haughty to the men that one could never imagine that she would ever give herself to a man—and then the likes of you! Her, who wanted to have the poor Diana shot dead at once, because she ran after a dog in the courtyard. Yes, I must say that; but I won't stay here any longer, and on the 24th of October I go my way.

JOHN. And then?

CHRISTINE. Well, as we're on the subject, it would be about time for you to look out for another job, as we want to get married.

JOHN. Yes, what kind of a job am I to look out for? I can't get as good a place as this, if I'm married.

CHRISTINE. Of course, you can't, but you must try to get a place as porter, or see if you can get a situation as a servant in some public institution. The victuals are few but certain, and then the wife and children get a pension.

JOHN (with a grimace). That's all very fine, but it's not quite my line of country to start off about thinking of dying for wife and child. I must confess that I've higher views.

CHRISTINE. Your views, to be sure! But you've also got obligations. Just think of her.

JOHN. You mustn't nag me by talking about my obligations. I know quite well what I've got to do. (He listens for a sound outside) But we've got time enough to think about all this. Go in, and get ready, and then we'll go to church.

CHRISTINE. Who's walking about upstairs?

JOHN. I don't know—perhaps Clara.

CHRISTINE (goes). I suppose it can't be the Count who's come back without anyone having heard him?

JOHN (nervously). No, I don't think so, because then he'd have rung already.

CHRISTINE. Yes. God knows. I've gone through the likes of this before. (Exit to the right. The sun has risen in the meanwhile and gradually illuminates the tops of the trees outside, the light grows gradually deeper till it falls slanting on the window. JOHN goes to the glass door and makes a sign.)

JULIE (comes in in traveling dress, with a small bird cage covered with a handkerchief, and places it on a chair). I'm ready now.

JOHN. Hush! Christine is awake.

JULIE (extremely excited in the following scene). Did she have any idea?

JOHN. She knows nothing. But, my God! what a sight you look.

JULIE. What! How do I look?

JOHN. You're as white as a corpse and, pardon my saying it, your face is dirty.

JULIE. Then give me some water to wash—all right. (*She goes to the washing-stand and washes her face and hands*) Give me a towel. Ah! the sun has risen.

JOHN. And then the hobgoblin flies away.

JULIE. Yes, a goblin has really been at work last night. Listen to me. Come with me. I've got the needful, John.

JOHN (*hesitating*). Enough?

JULIE. Enough to start on. Come with me; I can't travel alone today. Just think of it. Midsummer Day in a stuffy train, stuck in among a lot of people who stare at one; waiting about at stations when one wants to fly. No; I can't do it! I can't do it! And then all my memories, my memories of Midsummer's Day when I was a child, with the church decorated with flowers—birch and lilac; the midday meal at a splendidly covered table; relatives and friends; the afternoon in the park; dancing and music, flowers and games. Ah! you can run away and run away, but your memories, your repentance and your pangs of conscience follow on in the luggage van.

JOHN. I'll come with you, but right away, before it's too late. Now. Immediately.

JULIE. Then get ready. (*She takes up the bird cage.*)

JOHN. But no luggage. In that case we're lost.

JULIE. No, no luggage, only what we can take with us in the compartment.

JOHN (*has taken a hat*). What have you got there then? What is it?

JULIE. It's only my little canary. I don't want to leave it behind.

JOHN. Come, I say! Have we got to cart along a bird cage with us? How absolutely mad! Leave the bird there!

JULIE. The only thing I'm taking with me from home! The only living creature that likes me, after Diana was faithless to me! Don't be cruel. Let me take it with me!

JOHN. Leave it there, I tell you—and don't talk so loud. Christine might hear us.

JULIE. No, I won't leave it behind among strangers. I'd rather you killed it.

JOHN. Then give me the little thing; I'll twist its neck for it.

JULIE. Yes, but don't hurt it, don't! No, I can't!

JOHN. Hand it over—I'll do the trick.

JULIE (*takes the bird out of the cage and kisses it*). Oh, my dicky bird! Must you die by the hand of your own mistress?

JOHN. Be good enough not to make any scene; your life and well-being are at stake. That's right, quick! (*He snatches the bird out of her hand, carries it to the chopping block, and takes the kitchen knife.* JULIE *turns round*) You should have learned to kill fowls instead of shooting with your revolver. (*Chops*) And then you wouldn't have fainted at the sight of a drop of blood.

JULIE (*shrieking*). Kill me too, kill me! If you can kill an innocent animal without your hand shaking! Oh, I hate and loathe you! There is blood between us! I curse the hour in which I saw you! I curse the hour in which I was born!

JOHN. Now, what's the good of your cursing? Let's go!

JULIE. (*approaches the chopping block as though attracted to it against her will*). No, I won't go yet, I can't—I must see. Hush! there's a wagon outside. (*She listens, while her eyes are riveted in a stare on the chopping block and the knife*) Do you think I can't look at any blood? Do you think I'm so weak? Oh! I'd just like to see your blood and your brains on the chopping block. I'd like to see your whole stock swimming in a lake, like the one there. I believe I could drink out of your skull! I could wash my feet in your chest! I could eat your heart roasted! You think I am weak! You think I love you! You think I mean to carry your spawn under my heart and feed it with my own blood; bear your child and give it your name! I say, you, what is your name? I've never heard your surname—you haven't got any, I should think. I shall be Mrs. Head Waiter, or Madame Chimney Sweeper. You hound! You, who wear my livery, you menial, who wear my arms on your buttons—I've got to go shares with my cook, have I?—to compete with my own servant? Oh! oh! oh! You think I'm

a coward and want to run away? No, now I'm going to stay, and then the storm can burst. My father comes home—he finds his secretary broken open and his money stolen —then he rings the bell twice—for his servant—and then he sends for the police—and then I shall tell him everything. Everything! Oh, it's fine to make an end of the thing—if it would only have an end. And then he gets a stroke, and dies—and that's the end of the whole story. And then comes peace and quiet— eternal peace. And then the escutcheon is broken over the coffin: the noble race is extinct—and the servant's brat grows up in a foundling hospital—and wins his spurs in the gutter, and finishes up in a prison. (CHRISTINE, *dressed for church, enters on the right, hymn book in hand.* JULIE *rushes to her and falls into her arms, as though seeking protection*) Help me, Christine; help me against this man!

CHRISTINE (*immobile and cold*). What a pretty sight for a holiday morning! (*She looks at the chopping block*) And what a dirty mess you've been making here! What can it all mean? How you're shrieking and——

JULIE. Christine, you're a woman, and my friend. Beware of this scoundrel.

JOHN (*slightly shy and embarrassed*). If you ladies want to have an argument, I'll go in and have a shave. (*He sneaks away to the right.*)

JULIE. You will understand me, and you must do what I tell you.

CHRISTINE. No, I certainly don't

understand such carryings-on. Where are you going to in your traveling dress? And he's got his hat on. What's it all mean?

JULIE. Listen to me, Christine; listen to me; then I'll tell you everything.

CHRISTINE. I don't want to know anything.

JULIE. You must listen to me.

CHRISTINE. What is it, then? Your tomfoolery with John? Look here; I don't care anything about that, because it had nothing to do with me, but if you think you're going to tempt him to elope with you, then we'll put a very fine spoke in your little wheel.

JULIE (*extremely excited*). Try to be calm, Christine, and listen to me! I can't stay here, and John can't stay here, so we must travel.

CHRISTINE. Hm, hm!

JULIE (*with sudden inspiration*). But, look here. I've got an idea now. How about if we all three went—abroad—to Switzerland and started a hotel together? I've got money. (*She shows it*) You see; and John and I will look after the whole thing, and you, I thought, could take over the kitchen. Isn't it nice? Just say yes, and come with us, and all is fixed up. Just say yes. (*She embraces* CHRISTINE *and hugs her tenderly.*)

CHRISTINE (*cold and contemplative*). Hm, hm!

JULIE (*quicker*). You've never been out and traveled, Christine—you must come out in the world and look round; you can have no idea how jolly it is to travel on a railway—to be always seeing new people—new countries. And then we get to Hamburg and take a trip through the Zoological Gardens. What do you think of it? And then we'll go to the theater and hear the opera—and when we get to Munich we've got the museums, and there are Rubenses and Raphaels—pictures by the two great painters, you see. You've heard people talk of Munich, where King Ludwig used to live—the king, you know, who went mad—and then we'll go over his castles—he has castles which are got up just like fairy tales—and it's not far from there to Switzerland—with the Alps. Ugh! just think of the Alps covered with snow in the middle of summer; and tangerines and laurel trees grow there which are in bloom the whole year round. (JOHN *appears on the right, sharpening his razor on a strop, which he holds with his teeth and his left hand. He listens with pleasure to her speech, and now and again nods assent. Extremely quickly*) And then we take a hotel—and I sit in the bureau while John stands up and receives the visitors—goes out and does business—writes letters. That's a life, you take it from me; then the train puffs, the omnibus comes, the bells ring in the hotel itself, the bell rings in the restaurant—and then I make out the bills—and I'll touch them up—you can have no idea how shy travelers are when they've got to pay their bill. And you—you're installed as mistress in the kitchen. Of course, you haven't yourself got to stand by the fireplace, and you've got to have nice pretty dresses when you have to appear before the visitors—and a girl with an appearance like you—no, I'm not flattering you —you can get a husband perhaps some fine day, some rich Englishman; you see, people are so easy to catch. (*She commences to speak more slowly*) And then we shall get rich—and we'll build a villa by Lake Como—of course it rains there now and then, but (*in a less tense tone*) there's certain to be a great deal of sun—even though there's gloomy weather as well—and— then—then we can travel home again—and come back (*pause*) here—or anywhere else.

CHRISTINE. Look here, Miss; do you believe in all this yourself?

JULIE (*crushed*). Do I believe in it myself?

CHRISTINE. Yes.

JULIE (*tired*). I don't know. I don't really believe in anything any more. (*She sits down on the seat and lays her head on the table between her arms*) In anything, in anything at all.

CHRISTINE (*turns to the left, where* JOHN *is standing*). So you thought you'd elope, did you?

JOHN (*shamefaced, puts his razor on the table*). Elope? Come, that's a big word—you heard Miss Julie's plan; and although she's tired now, from having been up all night, the scheme can still be put through.

CHRISTINE. I say, did you mean that I should be cook there, for her?

JOHN (*sharply*). Be so kind as to speak more refined when you're talking of your mistress. Understand?

CHRISTINE. Mistress?

JOHN. Yes.

CHRISTINE. No. I say, I say there——

JOHN. Yes, listen to me. It is much better for you if you do, and don't gabble so much. Miss Julie is your mistress, and you ought to despise yourself for the same reason that you despise her.

CHRISTINE. I have always had so much self-respect——

JOHN. That you can despise others.

CHRISTINE. That I have never low-ered myself below my place. Just say, if you can, that the Count's cook had anything to do with the cattleman or the swineherd. You just try it on!

JOHN. Quite so. You had a little something on with a nice fellow, and very lucky for you, too.

CHRISTINE. A nice fellow, to be sure, who sells the Count's oats out of the stable.

JOHN. You're a nice one to talk; you get commissions from the vegetable man and ain't above being squared by the butcher.

CHRISTINE. What?

JOHN. And so it's you that can't respect your mistress any more! You —you—I don't think!

CHRISTINE. Come along to church now. A good sermon'll do you a lot of good after the way you've been carrying on.

JOHN. No fear, I'm not going to church today. You go alone, and confess your own sins.

CHRISTINE. Yes, that I will, and I'll come home with forgiveness, and for you too; the Redeemer suffered and died on the cross for all our sins, and if we go to Him with faith and a contrite spirit then He will take all our guilt on Himself.

JULIE. Do you believe that, Christine?

CHRISTINE. That's my living faith, as true as I stand here, and that's my faith from a child, that I've kept ever since I was young, and where sin overflows there grace overflows as well.

JULIE. Ah, if I had your faith! Ah, if——

CHRISTINE. Mark you, one can't just go and get it.

JULIE. Who gets it, then?

CHRISTINE. That's the great secret of grace, Miss, mark you, and God is no respecter of persons, but the first shall be last.

JULIE. Yes, but then He is a respecter of persons—the last.

CHRISTINE (continues). And it is easier for a camel to go through the eye of a needle than for a rich man to get into the kingdom of heaven. Mark you that's what it is, Miss Julie. Well, I'm off—alone, and on the way I'll tell the stable boy not to let out any horses, in case anybody wants to travel, before the Count comes home. Adieu! (*Exit through the glass door.*)

JOHN. What a devil! And all that fuss about a canary.

JULIE (*limply*). Leave the canary out of it. Can you see a way out of all this?—an end for the whole thing?

JOHN (*ponders*). No.

JULIE. What would you do in my position?

JOHN. In your position? Just wait a minute, will you? As a girl of good birth, as a woman—as a fallen woman? I don't know. Ah! I've got it!

JULIE (*takes up the razor and makes a movement*). That?

JOHN. Yes, but I wouldn't do it— note that well; that's the difference between us.

JULIE. Because you're a man and I'm a woman? What difference does that make?

JOHN. The same difference—as between men and women.

JULIE (*with the razor in her hand*). I want to, but I can't do it. My father couldn't do it either—the time when he ought to have.

JOHN. No; he shouldn't have done it—his first duty was to revenge himself.

JULIE. And now my mother avenges herself again through me.

JOHN. Have you never loved your father, Miss Julie?

JULIE. Yes, infinitely—but I'm sure

that I've hated him as well. I must have done it without having noticed it myself, but he brought me up to despise my own sex, to be half a woman and half a man. Who is to blame for what has happened? My father, my mother, I myself? I myself? I haven't got a self at all, I haven't got a thought which I don't get from my father, I haven't got a passion which I don't get from my mother, and the latest phase—the equality of men and women—that I got from my *fiancé*, whom I called a scoundrel for his pains. How then can it be my own fault? To shove the blame on Jesus as Christine does—no, I've got too much pride and too much common sense for that—thanks to my father's teaching. And as for a rich man not being able to get into the kingdom of heaven, that's a lie. Christine has got money in the savings bank. Certainly she won't get in. Who is responsible for the wrong? What does it matter to us who is? I know I've got to put up with the blame and the consequences.

JOHN. Yes—but—— (*There are two loud rings in succession.* JULIE *starts;* JOHN *quickly changes his coat, on the left*) The Count's at home—just think if Christine—— (*He goes to the speaking tube at the back, whistles, and listens.*)

JULIE. He must have already gone to his secretary by now.

JOHN. It's John, my lord. (*He listens. What the Count says is inaudible*) Yes, my lord. (*He listens*) Yes, my lord. At once. (*He listens*) Very well, my lord. (*He listens*) Yes, in half-an-hour.

JULIE (*extremely nervous*). What did he say? My God! what did he say?

JOHN. He asked for his boots and his coffee in half-an-hour.

JULIE. In half-an-hour then. Oh, I'm so tired, I can't do anything; I can't repent, I can't run away, I can't stay, I can't live, I can't die. Help me now! Give me orders and I'll obey like a dog. Do me this last service! Save my honor—save my name! You know what I ought to will, but don't will. Do you will it and order me to accomplish it.

JOHN. I don't know—but now I can't either. I can't make it out myself—it's just as though it were the result of this coat I've just put on, but I can't give you any orders. And now, after the Count has spoken to me, I can't explain it properly—but —ah! it's the livery which I've got on my back. I believe if the Count were to come in now and order me to cut my throat I'd do it on the spot.

JULIE. Then just do as though you were he, and I were you. You could imagine it quite well a minute ago, when you were before me on your knees. Then you were a knight. Have you ever been to the theater and seen the mesmerist? (JOHN *makes a gesture of assent*) He says to the medium, "Take the broom"; he takes it; he says "Sweep," and he sweeps.

JOHN. But in that case the medium must be asleep.

JULIE (*exalted*). I am already asleep. The whole room looks as though it were full of smoke—and you look like an iron furnace—

which is like a man in black clothes and top hat—and your eyes glow like coals when the fire goes out—and your face is a white blur like cinders. (*The sunlight has now reached the floor and streams over* JOHN) It's so warm and fine. (*She rubs her hands as though she were warming them by a fire*) And then it's so light—and so quiet.

JOHN (*takes the razor and puts it in her hand*). There is the broom; go, now that it's light, outside into the barn—and—— (*He whispers something in her ear.*)

JULIE (*awake*). Thank you. Now I'm going to have peace, but tell me now that the first shall have their share of grace too. Tell me that, even though you don't believe it.

JOHN. The first? No, I can't do that; but, one minute, Miss Julie—I've got it, you don't belong any longer to the first—you are beneath the last.

JULIE. That's true—I am beneath the very last; I am the last myself. Oh—but now I can't go. Tell me again that I must go.

JOHN. No, I can't do that again now either. I can't.

JULIE. And the first shall be last.

JOHN. Don't think, don't think. You rob me of all my strength and make a coward of me. What? I believe the clock was moving. No—shall we put paper in? To be so funky of the sound of a clock! But it's something more than a clock—there's something that sits behind it—a hand puts it in motion, and something else sets the hand in motion—just put your fingers to your ears, and then it strikes worse again. It strikes until you give an answer and then it's too late, and then come the police—and then—— (*Two loud rings in succession.* JOHN *starts, then he pulls himself together*) It's awful, but there's no other way out. Go! (JULIE *goes with a firm step outside the door.*)

CURTAIN

Salomé

BY OSCAR WILDE

CHARACTERS

SALOMÉ
JOKANAAN
HEROD
HERODIAS
TIGELLINUS
THE CAPPADOCIAN
THE YOUNG SYRIAN
THE NUBIAN
PAGE OF HERODIAS
A SADDUCEE
A PHARISEE
SOLDIERS, SLAVES, NAZARENES, JEWS

SALOMÉ

SCENE.—*A great terrace in the Palace of* HEROD, *set above the banqueting-hall. Some soldiers are leaning over the balcony. To the right there is a gigantic staircase, to the left, at the back, an old cistern surrounded by a wall of green bronze. The moon is shining very brightly.*

THE YOUNG SYRIAN. How beautiful is the Princess Salomé tonight!

THE PAGE OF HERODIAS. Look at the moon. How strange the moon seems! She is like a woman rising from a tomb. She is like a dead woman. One might fancy she was looking for dead things.

THE YOUNG SYRIAN. She has a strange look. She is like a little princess who wears a yellow veil, and whose feet are of silver. She is like a princess who has little white doves for feet. One might fancy she was dancing.

THE PAGE OF HERODIAS. She is like a woman who is dead. She moves very slowly. (*Noise in the banqueting-hall.*)

FIRST SOLDIER. What an uproar! Who are those wild beasts howling?

SECOND SOLDIER. The Jews. They are always like that. They are disputing about their religion.

FIRST SOLDIER. Why do they dispute about their religion?

SECOND SOLDIER. I cannot tell. They are always doing it. The Pharisees, for instance, say that there are angels, and the Sadducees declare that angels do not exist.

FIRST SOLDIER. I think it is ridiculous to dispute about such things.

THE YOUNG SYRIAN. How beautiful is the Princess Salomé tonight!

THE PAGE OF HERODIAS. You are always looking at her. You look at her too much. It is dangerous to look at people in such fashion. Something terrible may happen.

THE YOUNG SYRIAN. She is very beautiful tonight.

FIRST SOLDIER. The Tetrarch has a somber aspect.

SECOND SOLDIER. Yes; he has a somber aspect.

FIRST SOLDIER. He is looking at something.

SECOND SOLDIER. He is looking at someone.

FIRST SOLDIER. At whom is he looking?

SECOND SOLDIER. I cannot tell.

THE YOUNG SYRIAN. How pale the Princess is! Never have I seen her so pale. She is like the shadow of a white rose in a mirror of silver.

THE PAGE OF HERODIAS. You must not look at her. You look too much at her.

FIRST SOLDIER. Herodias has filled the cup of the Tetrarch.

THE CAPPADOCIAN. Is that the Queen Herodias, she who wears a black mitre sewed with pearls, and whose hair is powdered with blue dust?

FIRST SOLDIER. Yes; that is Herodias, the Tetrarch's wife.

SECOND SOLDIER. The Tetrarch is very fond of wine. He has wine of three sorts. One which is brought from the Island of Samothrace, and is purple like the cloak of Cæsar.

THE CAPPADOCIAN. I have never seen Cæsar.

SECOND SOLDIER. Another that comes from a town called Cyprus, and is as yellow as gold.

THE CAPPADOCIAN. I love gold.

SECOND SOLDIER. And the third is a wine of Sicily. That wine is red as blood.

THE NUBIAN. The gods of my country are very fond. Twice in the year we sacrifice to them young men and maidens; fifty young men and a hundred maidens. But I am afraid that we never give them quite enough, for they are very harsh to us.

THE CAPPADOCIAN. In my country there are no gods left. The Romans have driven them out. There are some who say that they have hidden themselves in the mountains, but I do not believe it. Three nights I have been on the mountains seeking them everywhere. I did not find them. And at last I called them by their names, and they did not come. I think they are dead.

FIRST SOLDIER. The Jews worship a God that one cannot see.

THE CAPPADOCIAN. I cannot understand that.

FIRST SOLDIER. In fact, they only believe in things that one cannot see.

THE CAPPADOCIAN. That seems to me altogether ridiculous.

THE VOICE OF JOKANAAN. After me shall come another mightier than I. I am not worthy so much as to unloose the latchet of his shoes. When he cometh, the solitary places shall be glad. They shall blossom like the rose. The eyes of the blind shall see the day, and the ears of the deaf shall be opened. The suckling child shall put his hand upon the dragon's lair, he shall lead the lions by their manes.

SECOND SOLDIER. Make him be silent. He is always saying ridiculous things.

FIRST SOLDIER. No, no. He is a holy man. He is very gentle, too. Every day, when I give him to eat he thanks me.

THE CAPPADOCIAN. Who is he?

FIRST SOLDIER. A prophet.

THE CAPPADOCIAN. What is his name?

FIRST SOLDIER. Jokanaan.

THE CAPPADOCIAN. Whence comes he?

FIRST SOLDIER. From the desert where he fed on locusts and wild honey. He was clothed in camel's hair, and round his loins he had a leathern belt. He was very terrible to look upon. A great multitude used to follow him. He even had disciples

THE CAPPADOCIAN. What is he talking of?

FIRST SOLDIER. We can never tell. Sometimes he says things that affright one, but it is impossible to understand what he says.

THE CAPPADOCIAN. May one see him?

FIRST SOLDIER. No. The Tetrarch has forbidden it.

THE YOUNG SYRIAN. The Princess has hidden her face behind her fan! Her little white hands are fluttering like doves that fly to their dovecotes. They are like white butterflies. They are just like white butterflies.

THE PAGE OF HERODIAS. What is that to you? Why do you look at her? You must not look at her. . . . Something terrible may happen.

THE CAPPADOCIAN (*pointing to the cistern*). What a strange prison!

SECOND SOLDIER. It is an old cistern.

THE CAPPADOCIAN. An old cistern! That must be a poisonous place in which to dwell!

SECOND SOLDIER. Oh, no! For instance, the Tetrarch's brother, his elder brother, the first husband of Herodias the Queen, was imprisoned there for twelve years. It did not kill him. At the end of the twelve years he had to be strangled.

THE CAPPADOCIAN. Strangled? Who dared to do that?

SECOND SOLDIER (*pointing to the Executioner, a huge Negro*). That man yonder, Naaman.

THE CAPPADOCIAN. He was not afraid?

SECOND SOLDIER. Oh, no! The Tetrarch sent him the ring.

THE CAPPADOCIAN. What ring?

SECOND SOLDIER. The death-ring. So he was not afraid.

THE CAPPADOCIAN. Yet it is a terrible thing to strangle a king.

FIRST SOLDIER. Why? Kings have but one neck, like other folk.

THE CAPPADOCIAN. I think it terrible.

THE YOUNG SYRIAN. The Princess is getting up! She is leaving the table! She looks very troubled. Ah, she is coming this way. Yes, she is coming toward us. How pale she is! Never have I seen her so pale.

THE PAGE OF HERODIAS. I pray you not to look at her.

THE YOUNG SYRIAN. She is like a dove that has strayed. . . . She is like a narcissus trembling in the wind. . . . She is like a silver flower.
(*Enter* SALOMÉ.)

SALOMÉ. I will not stay. I cannot stay. Why does the Tetrarch look at me all the while with his mole's eyes under his shaking eyelids? It is strange that the husband of my mother looks at me like that. I know not what it means. Of a truth I know it too well.

THE YOUNG SYRIAN. You have left the feast, Princess?

SALOMÉ. How sweet is the air here! I can breathe here! Within there are Jews from Jerusalem who are tearing each other in pieces over their foolish ceremonies, and barbarians who drink and drink, and spill their wine on the pavement, and Greeks from Smyrna with painted eyes and painted cheeks, and frizzed hair curled in columns, and Egyptians silent and subtle, with long nails of jade and russet cloaks, and Romans brutal and coarse, with their uncouth jargon. Ah! how I loathe the Romans! They are rough and common, and they give themselves the airs of noble lords.

THE YOUNG SYRIAN. Will you be seated, Princess?

THE PAGE OF HERODIAS. Why do you speak to her? Oh! something terrible will happen. Why do you look at her?

SALOMÉ. How good to see the moon! She is like a little piece of money, a little silver flower. She is cold and chaste. I am sure she is a virgin. Yes, she is a virgin. She has never defiled herself. She has never abandoned herself to men, like the other goddesses.

THE VOICE OF JOKANAAN. Behold! the Lord hath come. The son of man is at hand. The centaurs have hidden themselves in the rivers, and the nymphs have left the rivers, and are lying beneath the leaves of the forest.

SALOMÉ. Who was that who cried out?

SECOND SOLDIER. The prophet, Princess.

SALOMÉ. Ah, the prophet! He of whom the Tetrarch is afraid?

SECOND SOLDIER. We know nothing of that, Princess. It was the prophet Jokanaan who cried out.

THE YOUNG SYRIAN. Is it your pleasure that I bid them bring your litter, Princess? The night is fair in the garden.

SALOMÉ. He says terrible things about my mother, does he not?

SECOND SOLDIER. We never understand what he says, Princess.

SALOMÉ. Yes; he says terrible things about her.
(*Enter a* SLAVE.)

THE SLAVE. Princess, the Tetrarch prays you to return to the feast.

THE YOUNG SYRIAN. Pardon me, Princess, but if you return not some misfortune may happen.

SALOMÉ. Is he an old man, this prophet?

THE YOUNG SYRIAN. Princess, it were better to return. Suffer me to lead you in.

SALOMÉ. This prophet . . . is he an old man?

FIRST SOLDIER. No, Princess, he is quite young.

SECOND SOLDIER. One cannot be sure. There are those who say he is Elias.

SALOMÉ. Who is Elias?

SECOND SOLDIER. A prophet of this country in bygone days, Princess.

THE SLAVE. What answer may I give the Tetrarch from the Princess?

THE VOICE OF JOKANAAN. Rejoice not, O land of Palestine, because the rod of him who smote thee is broken. For from the seed of the serpent shall come a basilisk, and that which is born of it shall devour the birds.

SALOMÉ. What a strange voice! I would speak with him.

FIRST SOLDIER. I fear it may not be, Princess. The Tetrarch does not suffer anyone to speak with him. He has even forbidden the high priest to speak with him.

SALOMÉ. I desire to speak with him.

FIRST SOLDIER. It is impossible, Princess.

SALOMÉ. I will speak with him.

THE YOUNG SYRIAN. Would it not be better to return to the banquet?

SALOMÉ. Bring forth this prophet. (*Exit the* SLAVE.)

FIRST SOLDIER. We dare not, Princess.

SALOMÉ (*approaching the cistern and looking down into it*). How black it is, down there! It must be terrible to be in so black a hole! It is like a tomb. . . . (*To the* SOLDIERS) Did you not hear me? Bring out the prophet. I would look on him.

SECOND SOLDIER. Princess, I beg you do not require this of us.

SALOMÉ. You are making me wait upon your pleasure.

FIRST SOLDIER. Princess, our lives belong to you, but we cannot do what you have asked of us. And indeed, it is not of us that you should ask this thing.

SALOMÉ (*looking at* THE YOUNG SYRIAN). Ah!

THE PAGE OF HERODIAS. Oh! what is going to happen? I am sure that something terrible will happen.

SALOMÉ (*going up to* THE YOUNG SYRIAN). Thou wilt do this thing for me, wilt thou not, Narraboth? Thou wilt do this thing for me. I have ever been kind towards thee. Thou wilt do it for me. I would but look at him, this strange prophet. Men have talked so much of him. Often I have heard the Tetrarch talk of him. I think he is afraid of him, the Tetrarch. Art thou, even thou, also afraid of him, Narraboth?

THE YOUNG SYRIAN. I fear him not, Princess; there is no man I fear. But the Tetrarch has formally forbidden that any man should raise the cover of this well.

SALOMÉ. Thou wilt do this thing for me, Narraboth, and tomorrow when I pass in my litter beneath the gateway of the idol-sellers I will let fall for thee a little flower, a little green flower.

THE YOUNG SYRIAN. Princess, I cannot, I cannot.

SALOMÉ (*smiling*). Thou wilt do this thing for me, Narraboth. Thou knowest that thou wilt do this thing for me. And on the morrow when I pass in my litter by the bridge of the idol-buyers, I will look at thee through the muslin veils, I will look at thee, Narraboth, it may be I will smile at thee. Look at me, Narraboth, look at me. Ah! thou knowest that thou wilt do what I ask of thee. Thou knowest it. . . . I know that thou wilt do this thing.

THE YOUNG SYRIAN (*signing to the* THIRD SOLDIER). Let the prophet come forth. . . . The Princess Salomé desires to see him.

SALOMÉ. Ah!

THE PAGE OF HERODIAS. Oh! How strange the moon looks. Like the hand of a dead woman who is seeking to cover herself with a shroud.

THE YOUNG SYRIAN. She has a strange aspect! She is like a little princess, whose eyes are eyes of amber. Through the clouds of muslin she is smiling like a little princess. (*The prophet comes out of the cistern.* SALOMÉ *looks at him and steps slowly back.*)

JOKANAAN. Where is he whose cup of abominations is now full? Where is he, who in a robe of silver shall one day die in the face of all the people? Bid him come forth, that he may hear the voice of him who hath cried in the waste places and in the houses of kings.

SALOMÉ. Of whom is he speaking?

THE YOUNG SYRIAN. No one can tell, Princess.

JOKANAAN. Where is she who saw the images of men painted on the walls, even the images of the Chaldeans painted with colors, and gave herself up unto the lust of her eyes, and sent ambassadors into the land of Chaldea?

SALOMÉ. It is of my mother that he is speaking?

THE YOUNG SYRIAN. Oh, no, Princess.

SALOMÉ. Yes; it is of my mother that he is speaking.

JOKANAAN. Where is she who gave herself unto the Captains of Assyria, who have baldricks on their loins, and crowns of many colors on their heads? Where is she who hath given herself to the young men of the Egyptians, who are clothed in fine linen and hyacinth, whose shields are of gold, whose helmets are of silver, whose bodies are mighty? Go, bid her rise up from the bed of her abominations, from the bed of her incestuousness, that she may hear the words of him who prepareth the way of the Lord, that she may repent her of her iniquities. Though she will not repent, but will stick fast in her abominations; go, bid her come, for the fan of the Lord is in His hand.

SALOMÉ. Ah, but he is terrible, he is terrible!

THE YOUNG SYRIAN. Do not stay here, Princess, I beseech you.

SALOMÉ. It is his eyes above all that are terrible. They are like black holes burned by torches in a tapestry of Tyre. They are like the black caverns of Egypt in which the dragons make their lairs. They are like black lakes troubled by fantastic moons. . . . Do you think he will speak again?

THE YOUNG SYRIAN. Do not stay here, Princess. I pray you do not stay here.

SALOMÉ. How wasted he is! He is like a thin ivory statue. He is like an image of silver. I am sure he is chaste as the moon is. He is like a moonbeam, like a shaft of silver. I would look closer at him. I must look at him closer.

THE YOUNG SYRIAN. Princess! Princess!

JOKANAAN. Who is this woman who is looking at me? I will not have her look at me. Wherefore doth she look at me with her golden eyes, under her gilded eyelids? I know not who she is. I do not desire to know who she is. Bid her begone. It is not to her that I would speak.

SALOMÉ. I am Salomé, daughter of Herodias, Princess of Judæa.

JOKANAAN. Back! daughter of Babylon! Come not near the chosen of the Lord. Thy mother hath filled the earth with the wine of her iniquities, and the cry of her sinning hath come up even to the ears of God.

SALOMÉ. Speak again, Jokanaan. Thy voice is as music to mine ear.

THE YOUNG SYRIAN. Princess! Princess! Princess!

SALOMÉ. Speak again! Speak again, Jokanaan, and tell me what I must do.

JOKANAAN. Daughter of Sodom, come not near me! But cover thy face with a veil, and scatter ashes upon thine head, and get thee to the desert and seek out the Son of Man.

SALOMÉ. Who is he, the Son of Man? Is he as beautiful as thou art, Jokanaan?

JOKANAAN. Get thee behind me! I hear in the palace the beating of the wings of the angel of death.

THE YOUNG SYRIAN. Princess, I beseech thee to go within.

JOKANAAN. Angel of the Lord God, what dost thou here with thy sword? Whom seekest thou in this palace? The day of him who shall die in a robe of silver has not yet come.

SALOMÉ. Jokanaan!

JOKANAAN. Who speaketh?

SALOMÉ. I am amorous of thy body, Jokanaan! Thy body is white like the lilies of a field that the mower hath never mowed. Thy body is white like the snows that lie on the mountains of Judæa, and come down into the valleys. The roses in the garden of the Queen of Arabia are not so white as thy body. Neither the roses of the garden of the Queen of Arabia, the garden of spices of the Queen of Arabia, nor the feet of the dawn when they light on the leaves, nor the breast of the moon when she lies on the breast of the sea. . . . There is nothing in the world so white as thy body. Suffer me to touch thy body.

JOKANAAN. Back! daughter of Babylon! By woman came evil into the world. Speak not to me. I will not listen to thee. I listen but to the voice of the Lord God.

SALOMÉ. Thy body is hideous. It is like the body of a leper. It is like a plastered wall where vipers have crawled; like a plastered wall where the scorpions have made their nest. It is like a whitened sepulchre full of loathsome things. It is horrible, thy body is horrible. It is thy hair that I am enamoured of, Jokanaan. Thy hair is like clusters of grapes, like the clusters of black grapes that hang from the vine-trees of Edom in the land of the Edomites. Thy hair is like the cedars of Lebanon, like the great cedars of Lebanon that give their shade to the lions and to the robbers who would hide them by day. The long black nights, when the moon hides her face, when the stars are afraid, are not so black as thy hair. The silence that dwells in the forest is not so black. There is nothing in the world that is so black as thy hair. . . . Suffer me to touch thy hair.

JOKANAAN. Back, daughter of Sodom! Touch me not. Profane not the temple of the Lord God.

SALOMÉ. Thy hair is horrible. It is covered with mire and dust. It is like a knot of serpents coiled round thy neck. I love not thy hair. . . . It is thy mouth that I desire, Jokanaan. Thy mouth is like a band of scarlet on a tower of ivory. It is like a pomegranate cut in twain with a knife of ivory. The pomegranate-flowers that blossom in the gardens of Tyre, and are redder than roses, are not so red. The red blasts of trumpets that herald the approach of kings, and make afraid the enemy, are not so red. Thy mouth is redder than the feet of the doves who inhabit the temples and are fed by the priests. It is redder than the feet of him who cometh from a forest where he hath slain a lion, and seen gilded tigers. Thy mouth is like a branch of coral that fishers have found in the twilight of the sea, the coral that they keep for the kings! . . . It is like the vermilion that the Moabites find in the mines of Moab, the vermilion that the kings take from them. It is like the bow of the King of the Persians, that is painted with vermilion, and is tipped with coral. There is nothing in the world so red as thy mouth. . . . Suffer me to kiss thy mouth.

JOKANAAN. Never! daughter of Babylon! Daughter of Sodom! Never.

SALOMÉ. I will kiss thy mouth, Jokanaan. I will kiss thy mouth.

THE YOUNG SYRIAN. Princess, Princess, thou are like a garden of myrrh, thou who art the dove of all doves, look not at this man, look not at him! Do not speak such words to him. I cannot endure it. . . . Princess, do not speak these things.

SALOMÉ. I will kiss thy mouth, Jokanaan.

THE YOUNG SYRIAN. Ah! (*He kills himself and falls between* SALOMÉ *and* JOKANAAN.)

THE PAGE OF HERODIAS. The young Syrian has slain himself! The young captain has slain himself! He has slain himself who was my friend! I gave him a little box of perfumes and ear-rings wrought in silver, and now he has killed himself! Ah, did he not say that some misfortune would happen? I, too, said it, and it has come to pass. Well I knew that the moon was seeking a dead thing, but I knew not that it was he whom she sought. Ah! why did I not hide him from the moon? If I had hidden him in a cavern she would not have seen him.

FIRST SOLDIER. Princess, the young captain has just slain himself.

SALOMÉ. Suffer me to kiss thy mouth, Jokanaan.

JOKANAAN. Art thou not afraid, daughter of Herodias? Did I not tell thee that I had heard in the palace the beating of the wings of the angel of death, and hath he not come, the angel of death?

SALOMÉ. Suffer me to kiss thy mouth.

JOKANAAN. Daughter of adultery, there is but one who can save thee, it is He of whom I spake. Go seek Him. He is in a boat on the sea of Galilee, and He talketh with His disciples. Kneel down on the shore of the sea, and call unto Him by His name. When He cometh to thee (and to all who call on Him He cometh), bow thyself at His feet and ask of Him the remissions of thy sins.

SALOMÉ. Suffer me to kiss thy mouth.

JOKANAAN. Cursed be thou! daughter of an incestuous mother, be thou accursed!

SALOMÉ. I will kiss thy mouth, Jokanaan.

JOKANAAN. I will not look at thee, thou art accursed, Salomé, thou art accursed. (*He goes down into the cistern.*)

SALOMÉ. I will kiss thy mouth, Jokanaan; I will kiss thy mouth.

FIRST SOLDIER. We must bear away the body to another place. The Tetrarch does not care to see dead bodies, save the bodies of those whom he himself has slain.

THE PAGE OF HERODIAS. He was my brother, and nearer to me than a brother. I gave him a little box full of perfumes, and a ring of agate that he wore always on his hand. In the evening we were wont to walk by the river, and among the almond trees, and he used to tell me of the things of his country. He spake ever very low. The sound of his voice was like the sound of the flute, of one who playeth upon the flute. Also he had much joy to gaze at himself in the river. I used to reproach him for that.

SECOND SOLDIER. You are right; we must hide the body. The Tetrarch must not see it.

FIRST SOLDIER. The Tetrarch will not come to this place. He never comes on the terrace. He is too much afraid of the prophet.
(*Enter* HEROD, HERODIAS, *and all the Court.*)

HEROD. Where is Salomé? Where is the Princess? Why did she not return to the banquet as I commanded her? Ah! there she is!

HERODIAS. You must not look at her! You are always looking at her!

HEROD. The moon has a strange look tonight. Has she not a strange look? She is like a mad woman who is seeking everywhere for lovers. She is naked, too. She is quite naked. The clouds are seeking to clothe her nakedness, but she will not let them. She shows herself naked in the sky. She reels through the clouds like a drunken woman. . . . I am sure she is looking for lovers. Does she not reel like a drunken woman? She is like a mad woman, is she not?

HERODIAS. No; the moon is like the moon, that is all. Let us go within. . . . We have nothing to do here.

HEROD. I will stay here! Manasseh, lay carpets there. Light torches, bring forth the ivory table, and the tables of jasper. The air here is sweet. I will drink more wine with my guests. We must show all honors to the ambassadors of Cæsar.

HERODIAS. It is not because of them that you remain.

HEROD. Yes; the air is very sweet. Come, Herodias, our guests await us. Ah! I have slipped! I have slipped in blood! It is an ill omen. Wherefore is there blood here? . . . and this body, what does this body here? Think you I am like the King of Egypt, who gives no feast to his guests but that he shows them a corpse? Whose is it? I will not look on it.

FIRST SOLDIER. It is our captain, sire. He is the young Syrian whom you made captain of the guard but three days gone.

HEROD. I issued no order that he should be slain.

SECOND SOLDIER. He slew himself, sire.

HEROD. For what reason? I had made him captain of my guard.

SECOND SOLDIER. We do not know, sire. But with his own hand he slew himself.

HEROD. That seems strange to me. I had thought it was but the Roman philosophers who slew themselves. Is it not true, Tigellinus, that the philosophers at Rome slay themselves?

TIGELLINUS. There may be some who slay themselves, sire. They are the Stoics. The Stoics are people of no cultivation. They are ridiculous people. I myself regard them as being perfectly ridiculous.

HEROD. I also. It is ridiculous to kill oneself.

TIGELLINUS. Everybody at Rome laughs at them. The Emperor has written a satire against them. It is recited everywhere.

HEROD. Ah! he has written a satire against them? Cæsar is wonderful. He can do everything. . . . It is strange that the young Syrian has slain himself. I am sorry he has slain himself. I am very sorry; for he was fair to look upon. He was even very fair. He had very languorous eyes. I remember that I saw that he looked languorously at Salomé. Truly, I thought he looked too much at her.

HERODIAS. There are others who look too much at her.

HEROD. His father was a king. I drove him from his kingdom. And of his mother, who was a queen, you made a slave—Herodias. So he was here as my guest, as it were, and for that reason I made him my captain. I am sorry he is dead. Ho! why have you left the body here? I will not look at it—away with it! (*They take away the body*) It is cold here. There is a wind blowing. Is there not a wind blowing?

HERODIAS. No; there is no wind.

HEROD. I tell you there is a wind that blows. . . . And I hear in the air something that is like the beating of wings, like the beating of vast wings. Do you not hear it?

HERODIAS. I hear nothing.

HEROD. I hear it no longer. But I heard it. It was the blowing of the wind. It has passed away. But no, I hear it again. Do you not hear it? It is just like the beating of wings.

HERODIAS. I tell you there is nothing. You are ill. Let us go within.

HEROD. I am not ill. It is your daughter who is sick to death. Never have I seen her so pale.

HERODIAS. I have told you not to look at her.

HEROD. Pour me forth wine. (*Wine is brought*) Salomé, come drink a little wine with me. I have here a wine that is exquisite. Cæsar himself sent it me. Dip into it thy little red lips, that I may drain the cup.

SALOMÉ. I am not thirsty, Tetrarch.

HEROD. You hear how she answers me, this daughter of yours?

HERODIAS. She does right. Why are you always gazing at her?

HEROD. Bring me ripe fruits. (*Fruits are brought*) Salomé, come and eat fruits with me. I love to see in a fruit the mark of thy little teeth. Bite but a little of this fruit that I may eat what is left.

SALOMÉ. I am not hungry, Tetrarch.

HEROD (*to* HERODIAS). You see how you have brought up this daughter of yours.

HERODIAS. My daughter and I come of a royal race. As for thee, thy father was a camel driver! He was a thief and a robber to boot!

HEROD. Thou liest!

HERODIAS. Thou knowest well that it is true.

HEROD. Salomé, come and sit next to me. I will give thee the throne of thy mother.

SALOMÉ. I am not tired, Tetrarch.

HERODIAS. You see in what regard she holds you.

HEROD. Bring me—what is it that I desire? I forget. Ah! ah! I remember.

THE VOICE OF JOKANAAN. Behold the time is come! That which I foretold has come to pass. The day that I spoke of is at hand.

HERODIAS. Bid him be silent. I will not listen to his voice. This man is for ever hurling insults against me.

HEROD. He has said nothing against you. Besides, he is a very great prophet.

HERODIAS. I do not believe in prophets. Can a man tell what will come to pass? No man knows it. Also he is for ever insulting me. But I think you are afraid of him. . . . I know well that you are afraid of him.

HEROD. I am not afraid of him. I am afraid of no man.

HERODIAS. I tell you, you are afraid of him. If you are not afraid of him why do you not deliver him to the Jews who for these six months past have been clamoring for him?

A JEW. Truly, my lord, it were better to deliver him into our hands.

HEROD. Enough on this subject. I have already given you my answer. I will not deliver him into your hands. He is a holy man. He is a man who has seen God.

A JEW. That cannot be. There is no man who hath seen God since the prophet Elias. He is the last man who saw God face to face. In these days God doth not show Himself. God hideth Himself. Therefore great evils have come upon the land.

ANOTHER JEW. Verily, no man knoweth if Elias the prophet did indeed see God. Peradventure it was but the shadow of God that he saw.

A THIRD JEW. God is at no time hidden. He showeth Himself at all times and in all places. God is in what is evil even as He is in what is good.

A FOURTH JEW. Thou shouldst not say that. It is a very dangerous doctrine. It is a doctrine that cometh from Alexandria, where men teach the philosophy of the Greeks. And the Greeks are Gentiles. They are not even circumcised.

A FIFTH JEW. No one can tell how God worketh. His ways are very dark. It may be that the things which we call evil are good, and that the things which we call good are evil. There is no knowledge of any thing. We can but bow our heads to His will, for God is very strong. He breaketh in pieces the strong together with the weak, for He regardeth not any man.

FIRST JEW. Thou speakest truly. Verily God is terrible. He breaketh in pieces the strong and the weak as a man breaks corn in a mortar. But as for man, he hath never seen God. No man hath seen God since the prophet Elias.

HERODIAS. Make them be silent. They weary me.

HEROD. But I have heard it said that Jokanaan is in very truth your prophet Elias.

THE JEW. That cannot be. It is more than three hundred years since the days of the prophet Elias.

HEROD. There be some who say that this man is Elias the prophet.

A NAZARENE. I am sure that he is Elias the prophet.

THE JEW. Nay, but he is not Elias the prophet.

THE VOICE OF JOKANAAN. Behold the day is at hand, the day of the Lord, and I heard upon the mountains the feet of Him who shall be the Saviour of the world.

HEROD. What does that mean? The Saviour of the world?

TIGELLINUS. It is a title that Cæsar adopts.

HEROD. But Cæsar is not coming into Judæa. Only yesterday I received letters from Rome. They contained nothing concerning this matter. And you, Tigellinus. who were at Rome during the winter, you heard nothing concerning this matter, did you?

TIGELLINUS. Sire, I heard nothing concerning the matter. I was explaining the title. It is one of Cæsar's titles.

HEROD. But Cæsar cannot come. He is too gouty. They say that his feet are like the feet of an elephant. Also there are reasons of State. He who leaves Rome loses Rome. He will not come. Howbeit, Cæsar is lord, he will come if such be his pleasure. Nevertheless, I think he will not come.

FIRST NAZARENE. It was not concerning Cæsar that the prophet spake these words, sire.

HEROD. How?—it was not concerning Cæsar?

FIRST NAZARENE. No, my lord.

HEROD. Concerning whom then did he speak?

FIRST NAZARENE. Concerning the Messiah who has come.

A JEW. The Messiah hath not come.

FIRST NAZARENE. He hath come, and everywhere He worketh miracles.

HERODIAS. Ho! ho! miracles! I do not believe in miracles. I have seen too many. (To the PAGE) My fan.

FIRST NAZARENE. This man worketh true miracles. Thus, at a marriage which took place in a little town of Galilee, a town of some importance, He changed water into wine. Cer-

tain persons who were present related it to me. Also He healed two lepers that were seated before the Gate of Capernaum simply by touching them.

SECOND NAZARENE. Nay; it was blind men that He healed at Capernaum.

FIRST NAZARENE. Nay; they were lepers. But He hath healed blind people also, and He was seen on a mountain talking with angels.

A SADDUCEE. Angels do not exist.

A PHARISEE. Angels exist, but I do not believe that this Man has talked with them.

FIRST NAZARENE. He was seen by a great multitude of people talking with angels.

HERODIAS. How these men worry me! They are ridiculous! (To the PAGE) Well! my fan! (The PAGE gives her the fan) You have a dreamer's look; you must not dream. It is only sick people who dream. (She strikes the PAGE with her fan.)

SECOND NAZARENE. There is also the miracle of the daughter of Jairus.

FIRST NAZARENE. Yea, that is sure. No man can gainsay it.

HERODIAS. These men are mad. They have looked too long on the moon. Command them to be silent.

HEROD. What is this miracle of the daughter of Jairus?

FIRST NAZARENE. The daughter of Jairus was dead. This Man raised her from the dead.

HEROD. How! He raises people from the dead?

FIRST NAZARENE. Yea, sire, He raiseth the dead.

HEROD. I do not wish Him to do that. I forbid Him to do that. I suffer no man to raise the dead. This Man must be found and told that I forbid Him to raise the dead. Where is this Man at present?

SECOND NAZARENE. He is in every place, my lord, but it is hard to find Him.

FIRST NAZARENE. It is said that He is now in Samaria.

A JEW. It is easy to see that this is not the Messiah, if He is in Samaria. It is not to the Samaritans that the Messiah shall come. The Samaritans are accursed. They bring no offerings to the Temple.

SECOND NAZARENE. He left Samaria a few days since. I think that at the present moment He is in the neighborhood of Jerusalem.

FIRST NAZARENE. No; He is not there. I have just come from Jerusalem. For two months they have had no tidings of Him.

HEROD. No matter! But let them find Him, and tell Him, thus saith Herod the King, "I will not suffer Thee to raise the dead!" To change water into wine, to heal the lepers and the blind. . . . He may do these things if He will. I say nothing against these things. In truth I hold it a kindly deed to heal a leper. But no man shall raise the dead. It would be terrible if the dead came back.

THE VOICE OF JOKANAAN. Ah! the wanton one! The harlot! Ah! the daughter of Babylon with her golden eyes and her gilded eyelids! Thus saith the Lord God, Let there come up against her a multitude of men. Let the people take stones and stone her. . . .

HERODIAS. Command him to be silent.

THE VOICE OF JOKANAAN. Let the captains of the hosts pierce her with their swords, let them crush her beneath their shields.

HERODIAS. Nay, but it is infamous.

THE VOICE OF JOKANAAN. It is thus that I will wipe out all wickedness from the earth, and that all women shall learn not to imitate her abominations.

HERODIAS. You hear what he says against me? You suffer him to revile her who is your wife?

HEROD. He did not speak your name.

HERODIAS. What does that matter? You know well that it is I whom he seeks to revile. And I am your wife, am I not?

HEROD. Of a truth, dear and noble Herodias, you are my wife, and before that you were the wife of my brother.

HERODIAS. It was thou didst snatch me from his arms.

HEROD. Of a truth I was stronger than he was. . . . But let us not talk of that matter. I do not desire to talk of it. It is the cause of the terrible words that the prophet has spoken. Peradventure on account of it a misfortune will come. Let us not speak of this matter. Noble Herodias, we are not mindful of our guests. Fill thou my cup, my well-beloved. Ho! fill with wine the great goblets of silver, and the great goblets of glass. I will drink to Cæsar. There are Romans here, we must drink to Cæsar.

ALL. Cæsar! Cæsar!

HEROD. Do you not see your daughter, how pale she is?

HERODIAS. What is that to you if she be pale or not?

HEROD. Never have I seen her so pale.

HERODIAS. You must not look at her.

THE VOICE OF JOKANAAN. In that day the sun shall become black like sackcloth of hair, and the moon shall become like blood, and the stars of the heavens shall fall upon the earth like unripe figs that fall from the fig-tree, and the kings of the earth shall be afraid.

HERODIAS. Ah! Ah! I should like to see that day of which he speaks, when the moon shall become like blood, and when the stars shall fall upon the earth like unripe figs. This prophet talks like a drunken man . . . but I cannot suffer the sound of his voice. I hate his voice. Command him to be silent.

HEROD. I will not. I cannot understand what it is that he saith, but it may be an omen.

HERODIAS. I do not believe in omens. He speaks like a drunken man.

HEROD. It may be he is drunk with the wine of God.

HERODIAS. What wine is that, the wine of God? From what vineyards is it gathered? In what wine-press may one find it?

HEROD (from this point he looks all the while at SALOMÉ). Tigellinus, when you were at Rome of late, did the Emperor speak with you on the subject of . . . ?

TIGELLINUS. On what subject, my lord?

HEROD. On what subject? Ah! I asked you a question, did I not? I have forgotten what I would have asked you.

HERODIAS. You are looking again at my daughter. You must not look at her. I have already said so.

HEROD. You say nothing else.

HERODIAS. I say it again.

HEROD. And that restoration of the Temple about which they have talked so much, will anything be done? They say the veil of the sanctuary has disappeared, do they not?

HERODIAS. It was thyself didst steal it. Thou speakest at random and without wit. I will not stay here. Let us go within.

HEROD. Dance for me, Salomé.

HERODIAS. I will not have her dance.

SALOMÉ. I have no desire to dance, Tetrarch.

HEROD. Salomé, daughter of Herodias, dance for me.

HERODIAS. Peace! let her alone.

HEROD. I command thee to dance, Salomé.

SALOMÉ. I will not dance, Tetrarch.

HERODIAS (*laughing*). You see how she obeys you.

HEROD. What is it to me whether she dance or not? It is naught to me. Tonight I am happy, I am exceeding happy. Never have I been so happy.

FIRST SOLDIER. The Tetrarch has a somber look. Has he not a somber look?

SECOND SOLDIER. Yes, he has a somber look.

HEROD. Wherefore should I not be happy? Cæsar, who is lord of the world, Cæsar, who is lord of all things, loves me well. He has just sent me most precious gifts. Also he has promised me to summon to Rome the King of Cappadocia, who is my enemy. It may be that at Rome he will crucify him, for he is able to do all things that he has a mind to. Verily, Cæsar is lord. Therefore I do well to be happy. There is nothing in the world that can mar my happiness.

THE VOICE OF JOKANAAN. He shall be seated on his throne. He shall be clothed in scarlet and purple. In his hand he shall bear a golden cup full of his blasphemies. And the angel of the Lord shall smite him. He shall be eaten of worms.

HERODIAS. You hear what he says about you. He says that you will be eaten of worms.

HEROD. It is not of me that he speaks. He speaks never against me. It is of the King of Cappadocia that he speaks; the King of Cappadocia who is mine enemy. It is he who shall be eaten of worms. It is not I. Never has he spoken word against me, this prophet, save that I sinned in taking to wife the wife of my brother. It may be he is right. For, of a truth, you are sterile.

HERODIAS. I am sterile, I? You say that, you that are ever looking at my daughter, you that would have her dance for your pleasure? You speak as a fool. I have borne a child. You have gotten no child, no, not on one of your slaves. It is you who are sterile, not I.

HEROD. Peace, woman! I say that you are sterile. You have borne me no child, and the prophet says that our marriage is not a true marriage. He says that it is a marriage of incest, a marriage that will bring evils. . . . I fear he is right; I am sure that he is right. I would be happy at this. Of a truth, I am happy. There is nothing I lack.

HERODIAS. I am glad you are of so fair a humor tonight. It is not your custom. But it is late. Let us go within. Do not forget that we hunt at sunrise. All honors must be shown to Cæsar's ambassadors, must they not?

SECOND SOLDIER. The Tetrarch has a somber look.

FIRST SOLDIER. Yes, he has a somber look.

HEROD. Salomé, Salomé, dance for me. I pray thee dance for me. I am sad tonight. Yes; I am passing sad tonight. When I came hither I slipped in blood, which is an evil omen; also I heard in the air a beating of wings, a beating of giant wings. I cannot tell what they mean. . . . I am sad tonight. Therefore dance for me. Dance for me, Salomé, I beseech thee. If thou dancest for me thou mayest ask of me what thou wilt, and I will give it thee, even unto the half of my kingdom.

SALOMÉ (*rising*). Will you indeed give me whatsoever I shall ask of thee, Tetrarch?

HERODIAS. Do not dance, my daughter.

HEROD. Whatsoever thou shalt ask of me, even unto the half of my kingdom.

SALOMÉ. You swear it, Tetrarch?

HEROD. I swear it, Salomé.

HERODIAS. Do not dance, my daughter.

SALOMÉ. By what will you swear this thing, Tetrarch?

HEROD. By my life, by my crown, by my gods. Whatsoever thou shalt desire I will give it thee, even to the half of my kingdom, if thou wilt but dance for me. O Salomé, Salomé, dance for me!

SALOMÉ. You have sworn an oath, Tetrarch.

HEROD. I have sworn an oath.

HERODIAS. My daughter, do not dance.

HEROD. Even to the half of my king-

dom. Thou wilt be passing fair as a queen, Salomé, if it please thee to ask for half of my kingdom. Will she not be fair as a queen? Ah! it is cold here! There is an icy wind, and I hear . . . wherefore do I hear in the air this beating of wings? Ah! one might fancy a huge black bird that hovers over the terrace. Why can I not see it, this bird? The beat of its wings is terrible. The breath of the wind of its wings is terrible. It is a chill wind. Nay, but it is not cold, it is hot. I am choking. Pour water on my hands. Give me snow to eat. Loosen my mantle. Quick! quick! loosen my mantle. Nay, but leave it. It is my garland that hurts me, my garland of roses. The flowers are like fire. They have burned my forehead. (*He tears the wreath from his head and throws it on the table*) Ah! I can breathe now. How red those petals are! They are like stains of blood on the cloth. That does not matter. It is not wise to find symbols in everything that one sees. It makes life too full of terrors. It were better to say that stains of blood are as lovely as rose petals. It were better far to say that. . . . But we will not speak of this. Now I am happy. I am passing happy. Have I not the right to be happy? Your daughter is going to dance for me. Wilt thou not dance for me, Salomé? Thou hast promised to dance for me.

HERODIAS. I will not have her dance.

SALOMÉ. I will dance for you, Tetrarch.

HEROD. You hear what your daughter says. She is going to dance for me. Thou doest well to dance for me, Salomé. And when thou hast danced for me, forget not to ask of me whatsoever thou hast a mind to ask. Whatsoever thou shalt desire I will give it thee, even to the half of my kingdom. I have sworn it, have I not?

SALOMÉ. Thou hast sworn it, Tetrarch.

HEROD. And I have never broken my word. I am not of those who break their oaths. I know not how to lie. I am the slave of my word, and my word is the word of a king. The King of Cappadocia had ever a lying tongue, but he is no true king. He is a coward. Also he owes me money that he will not repay. He has even insulted my ambassadors. He has spoken words that were wounding. But Cæsar will crucify him when he comes to Rome. I know that Cæsar will crucify him. And if he crucify him not, yet will he die, being eaten of worms. The prophet has prophesied it. Well! wherefore dost thou tarry, Salomé?

SALOMÉ. I am waiting until my slaves bring perfumes to me and the seven veils, and take from off my feet my sandals.
(Slaves bring perfumes and the seven veils, and take off the sandals of SALOMÉ.)

HEROD. Ah, thou art to dance with naked feet. 'Tis well! 'Tis well. Thy little feet will be like white doves. They will be like little white flowers that dance upon the trees. . . . No, no, she is going to dance on blood. There is blood spilt on the ground. She must not dance on blood. It were an evil omen.

HERODIAS. What is it to thee if she dance on blood? Thou hast waded deep enough in it. . . .

HEROD. What is it to me? Ah! look at the moon! She has become red. She has become red as blood. Ah! the prophet prophesied truly. He prophesied that the moon would become as blood. Did he not prophesy it? All of ye heard him prophesying it. And now the moon has become as blood. Do ye not see it?

HERODIAS. Oh, yes, I see it well, and the stars are falling like unripe figs, are they not? and the sun is becoming black like sackcloth of hair, and the kings of the earth are afraid. That at least one can see. The prophet is justified of his words in that at least, for truly the kings of the earth are afraid. . . . Let us go within. You are sick. They will say at Rome that you are mad. Let us go within, I tell you.

THE VOICE OF JOKANAAN. Who is this who cometh from Edom, who is this who cometh from Bozra, whose raiment is dyed with purple, who shineth in the beauty of his garments, who walketh mighty in his greatness? Wherefore is thy raiment stained with scarlet?

HERODIAS. Let us go within. The voice of that man maddens me. I will not have my daughter dance while he is continually crying out. I will not have her dance while you look at her in this fashion. In a word, I will not have her dance.

HEROD. Do not rise, my wife, my queen, it will avail thee nothing. I will not go within till she hath danced. Dance, Salomé, dance for me.

HERODIAS. Do not dance, my daughter.

SALOMÉ. I am ready, Tetrarch. (SALOMÉ *dances the dance of the seven veils.*)

HEROD. Ah! wonderful! wonderful! You see that she has danced for me, your daughter. Come near, Salomé, come near, that I may give thee thy fee. Ah! I pay a royal price to those who dance for my pleasure. I will pay thee royally. I will give thee whatsoever thy soul desireth. What wouldst thou have? Speak.

SALOMÉ (*kneeling*). I would that they presently bring me in a silver charger . . .

HEROD (*laughing*). In a silver charger? Surely yes, in a silver charger. She is charming, is she not? What is it thou wouldst have in a silver charger, O sweet and fair Salomé, thou art fairer than all the daughters of Judæa? What wouldst thou have them bring thee in a silver charger? Tell me. Whatsoever it may be, thou shalt receive it. My treasures belong to thee. What is it that thou wouldst have, Salomé?

SALOMÉ (*rising*). The head of Jokanaan.

HERODIAS. Ah! that is well said, my daughter.

HEROD. No, no!

HERODIAS. That is well said, my daughter.

HEROD. No, no, Salomé. It is not that thou desirest. Do not listen to thy mother's voice. She is ever giving thee evil counsel. Do not heed her.

SALOMÉ. It is not my mother's voice that I heed. It is for mine own pleas-

ure that I ask the head of Jokanaan in a silver charger. You have sworn an oath, Herod. Forget not that you have sworn an oath.

HEROD. I know it. I have sworn an oath by my gods. I know it well. But I pray thee, Salomé, ask of me something else. Ask of me the half of my kingdom, and I will give it thee. But ask not of me what thy lips have asked.

SALOMÉ. I ask of you the head of Jokanaan.

HEROD. No, no, I will not give it thee.

SALOMÉ. You have sworn an oath, Herod.

HERODIAS. Yes, you have sworn an oath. Everybody heard you. You swore it before everybody.

HEROD. Peace, woman! It is not to you I speak.

HERODIAS. My daughter has done well to ask the head of Jokanaan. He has covered me with insults. He has said unspeakable things against me. One can see that she loves her mother well. Do not yield, my daughter. He has sworn an oath, he has sworn an oath.

HEROD. Peace! Speak not to me! . . Salomé, I pray thee be not stubborn. I have ever been kind toward thee. I have ever loved thee. . . . It may be that I have loved thee too much. Therefore ask not this thing of me. This is a terrible thing, an awful thing to ask of me. Surely, I think thou art jesting. The head of a man that is cut from his body is ill to look upon, is it not? It is not meet that the eyes of a virgin should look upon such a thing. What pleasure couldst thou have in it? There is no pleasure that thou couldst have in it. No, no, it is not that thou desirest. Hearken to me. I have an emerald, a great emerald, thou canst see that which passeth afar off. Cæsar himself carries such an emerald when he goes to the circus. But my emerald is the larger. I know well that it is the larger. It is the largest emerald in the whole world. Thou wilt take that, wilt thou not? Ask it of me, and I will give it thee.

SALOMÉ. I demand the head of Jokanaan.

HEROD. Thou art not listening. Thou art not listening. Suffer me to speak, Salomé.

SALOMÉ. The head of Jokanaan.

HEROD. No, no, thou wouldst not have that. Thou sayest that but to trouble me, because I have looked at thee and ceased not this night. It is true, I have looked at thee and ceased not this night. Thy beauty has troubled me. Thy beauty has grievously troubled me, and I have looked at thee over-much. Nay, but I will look at thee no more. One should not look at anything. Neither at things, nor at people should one look. Only in mirrors is it well to look, for mirrors do but show us masks. Oh! oh! bring wine! I thirst. . . . Salomé, Salomé, let us be as friends. Bethink thee. . . . Ah! what would I say? What was't? Ah! I remember it! . . . Salomé—nay but come nearer to me; I fear thou wilt not hear my words—Salomé, thou knowest my white peacocks, my beautiful white peacocks, that walk in the garden between the myrtles and the tall cypress trees. Their beaks are gilded with gold and the grains that they eat are smeared with gold, and their feet are stained with purple. When they cry out the rain comes, and the moon shows herself in the heavens when they spread their tails. Two by two they walk between the cypress trees and the black myrtles, and each has a slave to tend it. Sometimes they fly across the trees, and anon they crouch in the grass, and round the pools of the water. There are not in all the world birds so wonderful. I know that Cæsar himself has no birds so fair as my birds. I will give thee fifty of my peacocks. They will follow thee whithersoever thou goest, and in the midst of them thou wilt be like unto the moon in the midst of a great white cloud. . . . I will give them to thee all. I have but a hundred, and in the whole world there is no king who has peacocks like unto my peacocks. But I will give them all to thee. Only thou must loose me from my oath, and must not ask of me that which thy lips have asked of me. (*He empties the cup of wine.*)

SALOMÉ. Give me the head of Jokanaan.

HERODIAS. Well said, my daughter! As for you, you are ridiculous with your peacocks.

HEROD. Ah! thou art not listening to me. Be calm. As for me, am I not calm? I am altogether calm. Listen. I have jewels hidden in this palace—jewels that thy mother even has never seen; jewels that are marvellous to look at. I have a collar of pearls, set in four rows. They are like unto moons chained with rays of silver. They are even as half a hundred moons caught in a golden net. On the ivory breast of a queen they have rested. Thou shalt be as fair as a queen when thou wearest them. I have amethysts of two kinds, one that is black like wine, and one that is red like wine that one has colored with water. I have topazes, yellow as are the eyes of tigers, and topazes that are pink as the eyes of a wood-pigeon, and green topazes that are as the eyes of cats. I have opals that burn always, with a flame that is cold as ice, opals that make sad men's minds, and are afraid of the shadows. I have onyxes like the eyeballs of a dead woman. I have moonstones that change when the moon changes, and are wan when they see the sun. I have sapphires big like eggs, and as blue as blue flowers. The sea wanders within them and the moon comes never to trouble the blue of their waves. I have chrysolites and beryls and chrysoprases and rubies. I have sardonyx and hyacinth stones, and stones of chalcedony, and I will give them all unto thee, all, and other things will I add to them. The King of the Indies has but even now sent me four fans fashioned from the feathers of parrots, and the King of Numidia a garment of ostrich feathers. I have a crystal, into which it is not lawful for a woman to look, nor may young men behold it until they have been beaten with rods. In a coffer of nacre I have three wondrous turquoises. He who wears them on his forehead can imagine things which are not, and he who carries them in his hand can turn the fruitful woman into a woman that is barren. These are great treasures above all price. But this is not all. In an ebony coffer I have two cups, amber, that are like apples of pure gold. If an enemy pour poison into these cups they become like apples of silver. In a coffer incrusted with amber I have sandals incrusted with glass. I have mantles that have been brought from the land of the Seres, and bracelets decked about with carbuncles and with jade that come from the city of Euphrates. . . . What desirest thou more than this, Salomé! Tell me the thing that thou desirest, and I will give it thee. All that thou askest I will give thee, save one thing only. I will give thee all that is mine, save only the head of one man. I will give thee the mantle of the high priest. I will give thee the veil of the sanctuary

THE JEWS. Oh! oh!

SALOMÉ. Give me the head of Jokanaan.

HEROD (*sinking back in his seat*). Let her be given what she asks! Of a truth she is her mother's child! (*The* FIRST SOLDIER *approaches.* HERODIAS *draws from the hand of the Tetrarch the ring of death, and gives it to the* SOLDIER, *who straightway bears it to the* EXECUTIONER. *The* EXECUTIONER *looks scared*) Who has taken my ring? There was a ring on my right hand. Who has drunk my wine? There was wine in my cup. It was full of wine. Some one has drunk it! Oh! surely some evil will befall some one. (*The* EXECUTIONER *goes down into the cistern*) Ah! Wherefore did I give my oath? Hereafter, let no king swear an oath. If he keep it not, it is terrible, and if he keep it, it is terrible also.

HERODIAS. My daughter has done well.

HEROD. I am sure that some misfortune will happen.

SALOMÉ (*she leans over the cistern and listens*). There is no sound. I hear nothing. Why does he not cry out, this man? Ah! if any man sought to kill me, I would cry out, I would struggle, I would not suffer. . . . Strike, strike, Naaman, strike. I tell you. . . . No, I hear nothing. There is a silence, a terrible silence. Ah! something has fallen upon the ground. I heard something fall. He is afraid, this slave. He is a coward, this slave! Let soldiers be sent. (*She sees the* PAGE *of* HERODIAS *and addresses him*) Come hither, thou wert the friend of him who is dead, wert thou not? Well, I tell thee, there are not dead men enough. Go to the soldiers and bid them go down and bring me the thing I ask, the thing the Tetrarch has promised me, the thing that is mine. (*The* PAGE *recoils. She turns to the* SOLDIERS) Hither, ye soldiers. Get ye down into this cistern and bring me the head of this man. Tetrarch, Tetrarch, command your soldiers that they bring me the head of Jokanaan. (*A huge black arm, the arm of the* EXECUTIONER, *comes forth from the cistern, bearing on a silver shield the head of* JOKANAAN. SALOMÉ *seizes it.* HEROD *hides his face with his cloak.* HERODIAS *smiles and fans herself. The* NAZARENES *fall on their knees and begin to pray*) Ah! thou wouldst not suffer me to kiss thy mouth, Jokanaan. Well, I will kiss it now. I will bite it with my teeth as one bites a ripe fruit. Yes, I will kiss thy mouth, Jokanaan. I said it; did I not say it? I said it. Ah! I will kiss it now. . . . But, wherefore dost thou not look at me, Jokanaan? Thine eyes that were so terrible, so full of rage and scorn, are shut now. Wherefore are they shut? Open thine eyes! Lift up thine eyelids, Jokanaan! Wherefore dost

thou not look at me? Art thou afraid of me, Jokanaan, that thou wilt not look at me? . . . And thy tongue, that was like a red snake darting poison, it moves no more, it speaks no words, Jokanaan, that scarlet viper that spat its venom upon me. It is strange, is it not? How is it that the red viper stirs no longer? . . . Thou wouldst have none of me, Jokanaan. Thou rejectedst me. Thou didst speak evil words against me. Thou didst bear thyself toward me as to a harlot, as to a woman that is a wanton, to me, Salomé, daughter of Herodias, Princess of Judæa! Well, I still live, but thou art dead, and thy head belongs to me. I can do with it what I will. I can throw it to the dogs and to the birds of the air. That which the dogs leave, the birds of the air shall devour. . . . Ah, Jokanaan, thou wert the man that I loved alone among men. All other men were hateful to me. But thou wert beautiful! Thy body was a column of ivory set upon feet of silver. It was a garden full of doves and lilies of silver. It was a tower of silver decked with shields of ivory. There was nothing in the world so white as thy body. There was nothing in the world so black as thy hair. In the whole world there was nothing so red as thy mouth. Thy voice was a censer that scattered strange perfumes, and when I looked on thee I heard a strange music. Ah! wherefore didst thou not look at me, Jokanaan? With the cloak of thine hands and with the cloak of thy blasphemies thou didst hide thy face. Thou didst put upon thine eyes the covering of him who would see his God. Well, thou hast seen thy God, Jokanaan, but me, me, thou didst never see. If thou hadst seen me thou hadst loved me. I saw thee, and I loved thee. Oh, how I loved thee! I love thee yet, Jokanaan, I love only thee. . . . I am athirst for thy beauty; I am hungry for thy body; and neither wine nor apples can appease my desire. What shall I do now, Jokanaan? Neither the floods nor the great waters can quench my passion. I was a princess, and thou didst scorn me. I was a virgin, and thou didst take my virginity from me. I was chaste, and thou didst fill my veins with fire. . . . Ah! ah! wherefore didst thou not look at me? If thou hadst looked at me thou hadst loved me. Well I know that thou wouldst have loved me, and the mystery of love is greater than the mystery of death.

HEROD. She is monstrous, thy daughter, I tell thee she is monstrous. In truth, what she has done is a great crime. I am sure that it is. A crime against some unknown God.

HERODIAS. I am well pleased with my daughter. She has done well. And I would stay here now.

HEROD (rising). Ah! There speaks my brother's wife! Come! I will not stay in this place. Come, I tell thee. Surely some terrible thing will befall. Manasseh, Issadar, Zias, put out the torches. I will not look at things, I will not suffer things to look at me. Put out the torches! Hide the moon! Hide the stars! Let us hide ourselves in our palace, Herodias. I begin to be afraid.

(The slaves put out the torches. The stars disappear. A great cloud crosses the moon and conceals it completely. The stage becomes quite dark. The Tetrarch begins to climb the staircase.)

THE VOICE OF SALOMÉ. Ah! I have kissed thy mouth, Jokanaan, I have kissed thy mouth. There was a bitter taste on my lips. Was it the taste of blood? . . . Nay; but perchance it was the taste of love. . . . They say that love hath a bitter taste. . . . But what matter? What matter? I have kissed thy mouth.

HEROD (turning round and seeing SALOMÉ). Kill that woman!

(The soldiers rush forward and crush beneath their shields SALOMÉ, daughter of HERODIAS, Princess of Judæa.)

CURTAIN

The Rising of the Moon

BY LADY GREGORY

SAMUEL FRENCH, INC.
25 WEST 45TH STREET
NEW YORK CITY

CHARACTERS

Sergeant
Policeman X
Policeman B
A Ragged Man

THE RISING OF THE MOON

Scene: Side of a quay in a seaport town. Some posts and chains. A large barrel. Enter three policemen. Moonlight.

SERGEANT, *who is older than the others, crosses the stage to right and looks down steps. The others put down a pastepot and unroll a bundle of placards.*

POLICEMAN B. I think this would be a good place to put up a notice. (*He points to barrel.*)

POLICEMAN X. Better ask him. (*Calls to* SERGEANT) Will this be a good place for a placard? (*No answer.*)

POLICEMAN B. Will we put up a notice here on the barrel? (*No answer.*)

SERGEANT. There's a flight of steps here that leads to the water. This is a place that should be minded well. If he got down here, his friends might have a boat to meet him; they might send it in here from outside.

POLICEMAN B. Would the barrel be a good place to put a notice up?

SERGEANT. It might; you can put it there. (*They paste the notice up.*)

SERGEANT (*reading it*). Dark hair—dark eyes, smooth face, height five feet five—there's not much to take hold of in that—It's a pity I had no chance of seeing him before he broke out of gaol. They say he's a wonder, that it's he makes all the plans for the whole organization. There isn't another man in Ireland would have broken gaol the way he did. He must have some friends among the gaolers.

POLICEMAN B. A hundred pounds is little enough for the Government to offer for him. You may be sure any man in the force that takes him will get promotion.

SERGEANT. I'll mind this place myself. I wouldn't wonder at all if he came this way. He might come slipping along there (*points to side of quay*), and his friends might be waiting for him there (*points down steps*), and once he got away it's little chance we'd have of finding him; it's maybe under a load of kelp he'd be in a fishing boat, and not one to help a married man that wants it to the reward.

POLICEMAN X. And if we get him itself, nothing but abuse on our heads for it from the people, and maybe from our own relations.

SERGEANT. Well, we have to do our duty in the force. Haven't we the whole country depending on us to keep law and order? It's those that are down would be up and those that are up would be down, if it wasn't for us. Well, hurry on, you have plenty of other places to placard yet, and come back here then to me. You can take the lantern. Don't be too long now. It's very lonesome here with nothing but the moon.

91

POLICEMAN B. It's a pity we can't stop with you. The Government should have brought more police into the town, with *him* in gaol, and at assize time too. Well, good luck to your watch. (*They go out.*)

SERGEANT (*walks up and down once or twice and looks at placard*). A hundred pounds and promotion sure. There must be a great deal of spending in a hundred pounds. It's a pity some honest man not to be the better of that.
(*A ragged man appears at left and tries to slip past.* SERGEANT *suddenly turns.*)

SERGEANT. Where are you going?

MAN. I'm a poor ballad-singer, your honor. I thought to sell some of these (*holds out bundle of ballads*) to the sailors. (*He goes on.*)

SERGEANT. Stop! Didn't I tell you to stop? You can't go on there.

MAN. Oh, very well. It's a hard thing to be poor. All the world's against the poor!

SERGEANT. Who are you?

MAN. You'd be as wise as myself if I told you, but I don't mind. I'm one Jimmy Walsh, a ballad-singer.

SERGEANT. Jimmy Walsh? I don't know that name.

MAN. Ah, sure, they know it well enough in Ennis. Were you ever in Ennis, Sergeant?

SERGEANT. What brought you here?

MAN. Sure, it's to the assizes I came, thinking I might make a few shil-lings here or there. It's in the one train with the judges I came.

SERGEANT. Well, if you came so far, you may as well go farther, for you'll walk out of this.

MAN. I will, I will; I'll just go on where I was going. (*Goes toward steps.*)

SERGEANT. Come back from those steps; no one has leave to pass down them tonight.

MAN. I'll just sit on the top of the steps till I see will some sailor buy a ballad off me that would give me my supper. They do be late going back to the ship. It's often I saw them in Cork carried down the quay in a hand-cart.

SERGEANT. Move on, I tell you. I won't have any one lingering about the quay tonight.

MAN. Well, I'll go. It's the poor have the hard life! Maybe yourself might like one, Sergeant. Here's a good sheet now. (*Turns one over*) "Content and a pipe"—that's not much. "The Peeler and the Goat"—you wouldn't like that. "Johnny Hart"—that's a lovely song.

SERGEANT. Move on.

MAN. Ah, wait till you hear it. (*Sings.*)
> There was a rich farmer's daugh-ter lived near the town of Ross;
> She courted a Highland soldier, his name was Johnny Hart;
> Says the mother to her daughter, "I'll go distracted mad
> If you marry that Highland sol-dier dressed up in Highland plaid."

SERGEANT. Stop that noise.

(MAN *wraps up his ballads and shuffles toward the steps.*)

SERGEANT. Where are you going?

MAN. Sure you told me to be going, and I am going.

SERGEANT. Don't be a fool. I didn't tell you to go that way; I told you to go back to the town.

MAN. Back to the town, is it?

SERGEANT (*taking him by the shoulder and shoving him before him*). Here, I'll show you the way. Be off with you. What are you stopping for?

MAN (*who has been keeping his eye on the notice, points to it*). I think I know what you're waiting for, Sergeant.

SERGEANT. What's that to you?

MAN. And I know well the man you're waiting for—I know him well —I'll be going. (*He shuffles on.*)

SERGEANT. You know him? Come back here. What sort is he?

MAN. Come back is it, Sergeant? Do you want to have me killed?

SERGEANT. Why do you say that?

MAN. Never mind. I'm going. I wouldn't be in your shoes if the reward was ten times as much. (*Goes on off stage to left*) Not if it was ten times as much.

SERGEANT (*rushing after him*). Come back here, come back. (*Drags him back*) What sort is he? Where did you see him?

MAN. I saw him in my own place, in the County Clare. I tell you you wouldn't like to be looking at him. You'd be afraid to be in the one place with him. There isn't a weapon he doesn't know the use of, and as to strength, his muscles are as hard as that board. (*Slaps barrel.*)

SERGEANT. Is he as bad as that?

MAN. He is then.

SERGEANT. Do you tell me so?

MAN. There was a poor man in our place, a sergeant from Ballyvaughan.—It was with a lump of stone he did it.

SERGEANT. I never heard of that.

MAN. And you wouldn't, Sergeant. It's not everything that happens gets into the papers. And there was a policeman in plain clothes, too . . . It is in Limerick he was. . . . It was after the time of the attack on the police barrack at Kilmallock. . . . Moonlight . . . just like this . . . waterside. . . . Nothing was known for certain.

SERGEANT. Do you say so? It's a terrible county to belong to.

MAN. That's so, indeed! You might be standing there, looking out that way, thinking you saw him coming up this side of the quay (*points*), and he might be coming up this other side (*points*), and he'd be on you before you knew where you were.

SERGEANT. It's a whole troop of police they ought to put here to stop a man like that.

MAN. But if you'd like me to stop with you, I could be looking down this side. I could be sitting up here on this barrel.

SERGEANT. And you know him well, too?

MAN. I'd know him a mile off, Sergeant.

SERGEANT. But you wouldn't want to share the reward?

MAN. Is it a poor man like me, that has to be going the roads and singing in fairs, to have the name on him that he took a reward? But you don't want me. I'll be safer in the town.

SERGEANT. Well, you can stop.

MAN (getting up on barrel). All right, Sergeant. I wonder, now, you're not tired out, Sergeant, walking up and down the way you are.

SERGEANT. If I'm tired I'm used to it.

MAN. You might have hard work before you tonight yet. Take it easy while you can. There's plenty of room up here on the barrel, and you see farther when you're higher up.

SERGEANT. Maybe so. (Gets up beside him on barrel, facing right. They sit back to back, looking different ways) You made me feel a bit queer with the way you talked.

MAN. Give me a match, Sergeant (he gives it and MAN lights pipe); take a draw yourself? It'll quiet you. Wait now till I give you a light, but you needn't turn round. Don't take your eye off the quay for the life of you.

SERGEANT. Never fear, I won't. (Lights pipe. They both smoke) Indeed it's a hard thing to be in the force, out at night and no thanks for it, for all the danger we're in. And it's little we get but abuse from the people, and no choice but to obey our orders, and never asked when a man is sent into danger, if you are a married man with a family.

MAN (sings).
As through the hills I walked to view the hills and shamrock plain,
I stood awhile where nature smiles to view the rocks and streams,
On a matron fair I fixed my eyes beneath a fertile vale,
As she sang her song it was on the wrong of poor old Granuaile.

SERGEANT. Stop that; that's no song to be singing in these times.

MAN. Ah, Sergeant, I was only singing to keep my heart up. It sinks when I think of him. To think of us two sitting here, and he creeping up the quay, maybe, to get to us.

SERGEANT. Are you keeping a good lookout?

MAN I am; and for no reward too. Amn't I the foolish man? But when I saw a man in trouble, I never could help trying to get him out of it. What's that? Did something hit me? (Rubs his heart.)

SERGEANT (patting him on the shoulder). You will get your reward in heaven.

MAN. I know that, I know that, Sergeant, but life is precious.

SERGEANT. Well, you can sing if it gives you more courage.

MAN (*sings*).
Her head was bare, her hands and feet with iron bands were bound,
Her pensive strain and plaintive wail mingles with the evening gale,
And the song she sang with mournful air, I am old Granuaile.
Her lips so sweet that monarchs kissed . . .

SERGEANT. That's not it. . . . "Her gown she wore was stained with gore." . . . That's it—you missed that.

MAN. You're right, Sergeant, so it is; I missed it. (*Repeats line*) But to think of a man like you knowing a song like that.

SERGEANT. There's many a thing a man might know and might not have any wish for.

MAN. Now, I daresay, Sergeant, in your youth, you used to be sitting up on a wall, the way you are sitting up on this barrel now, and the other lads beside you, and you singing "Granuaile"? . . .

SERGEANT. I did then.

MAN. And the "Shan Bhean Bhocht"? . . .

SERGEANT. I did then.

MAN. And the "Green on the Cape?"

SERGEANT. That was one of them.

MAN. And maybe the man you are watching for tonight used to be sitting on the wall, when he was young, and singing those same songs. . . . It's a queer world.

SERGEANT. Whisht! . . . I think I see something coming. . . . It's only a dog.

MAN. And isn't it a queer world? . . . Maybe it's one of the boys you used to be singing with that time you will be arresting today or tomorrow, and sending into the dock.

SERGEANT. That's true inded.

MAN. And maybe one night, after you had been singing, if the other boys had told you some plan they had, some plan to free the country, you might have joined with them . . . and maybe it is you might be in trouble now.

SERGEANT. Well, who knows but I might? I had a great spirit in those days.

MAN. It's a queer world, Sergeant, and it's little any mother knows when she sees her child creeping on the floor what might happen to it before it has gone through its life, or who will be who in the end.

SERGEANT. That's a queer thought now, and a true thought. Wait now till I think it out. . . . If it wasn't for the sense I have, and for my wife and family, and for me joining the force the time I did, it might be myself now would be after breaking gaol and hiding in the dark, and it might be him that's hiding in the dark and that got out of gaol would be sitting up where I am on this barrel. . . . And it might be myself would be creeping up trying to make my escape from himself, and it might be himself would be keeping the law, and myself would be breaking it, and myself would be trying maybe to put a bullet in his head, or to take up a lump of a stone the way you said he did . . . no, that myself did. . . . Oh! (*Gasps. After a pause*) What's that? (*Grasps* MAN'S *arm.*)

MAN (*jumps off barrel and listens, looking out over water*). It's nothing, Sergeant.

SERGEANT. I thought it might be a boat. I had a notion there might be friends of his coming about the quays with a boat.

MAN. Sergeant, I am thinking it was with the people you were, and not with the law you were, when you were a young man.

SERGEANT. Well, if I was foolish then, that time's gone.

MAN. Maybe, Sergeant, it comes into your head sometimes, in spite of your belt and your tunic, that it might have been as well for you to have followed Granuaile.

SERGEANT. It's no business of yours what I think.

MAN. Maybe, Sergeant, you'll be on the side of the country yet.

SERGEANT (*gets off barrel*). Don't talk to me like that. I have my duties and I know them. (*Looks round*) That was a boat; I hear the oars. (*Goes to the steps and looks down.*)

MAN (*sings*).
   O, then, tell me, Shawn O'Farrell,

   Where the gathering is to be.
  In the old spot by the river
   Right well known to you and me!

SERGEANT. Stop that! Stop that, I tell you!

MAN (*sings louder*).
   One word more, for signal token,
    Whistle up the marching tune,
  With your pike upon your shoulder,
   At the Rising of the Moon.

SERGEANT. If you don't stop that, I'll arrest you.
(*A whistle from below answers, repeating the air.*)

SERGEANT. That's a signal. (*Stands between him and steps*) You must not pass this way. . . . Step farther back. . . . Who are you? You are no ballad-singer.

MAN. You needn't ask who I am; that placard will tell you. (*Points to placard.*)

SERGEANT. You are the man I am looking for.

MAN (*takes off hat and wig.* SERGEANT *seizes them*). I am. There's a hundred pounds on my head. There is a friend of mine below in a boat. He knows a safe place to bring me to.

SERGEANT (*looking still at hat and wig*). It's a pity! It's a pity. You deceived me. You deceived me well.

MAN. I am a friend of Granuaile. There is a hundred pounds on my head.

SERGEANT. It's a pity, it's a pity!

MAN. Will you let me pass, or must I make you let me?

SERGEANT. I am in the force. I will not let you pass.

MAN. I thought to do it with my tongue. (*Puts hand in breast*) What is that?

(*Voice of* POLICEMAN X *outside.*) Here, this is where we left him.

SERGEANT. It's my comrades coming.

MAN. You won't betray me . . . the friend of Granuaile. (*Slips behind barrel.*)

(*Voice of* POLICEMAN B.) That was the last of the placards.

POLICEMAN X (*as they come in*). If he makes his escape it won't be unknown he'll make it.
(SERGEANT *puts hat and wig behind his back.*)

POLICEMAN B. Did any one come this way?

SERGEANT (*after a pause*). No one.

POLICEMAN B. No one at all?

SERGEANT. No one at all

POLICEMAN B. We had no orders to go back to the station; we can stop along with you.

SERGEANT. I don't want you. There is nothing for you to do here.

POLICEMAN B. You bade us to come back here and keep watch with you.

SERGEANT. I'd sooner be alone.

Would any man come this way and you making all that talk? It is better the place to be quiet.

POLICEMAN B. Well, we'll leave you the lantern anyhow. (*Hands it to him.*)

SERGEANT. I don't want it. Bring it with you.

POLICEMAN B. You might want it. There are clouds coming up and you have the darkness of the night before you yet. I'll leave it over here on the barrel. (*Goes to barrel.*)

SERGEANT. Bring it with you I tell you. No more talk.

POLICEMAN B. Well, I thought it might be a comfort to you. I often think when I have it in my hand and can be flashing it about into every dark corner (*doing so*) that it's the same as being beside the fire at home, and the bits of bogwood blazing up now and again. (*Flashes it about, now on the barrel, now on* SERGEANT.)

SERGEANT (*furious*). Be off the two of you, yourselves and your lantern! (*They go out.* MAN *comes from behind barrel. He and* SERGEANT *stand looking at one another.*)

SERGEANT. What are you waiting for?

MAN. For my hat, of course, and my wig. You wouldn't wish me to get my death of cold? (SERGEANT *gives them.*)

MAN (*going toward steps*). Well, good night, comrade, and thank you. You did me a good turn tonight, and I'm obliged to you.

Maybe I'll be able to do as much for you when the small rise up and the big fall down . . . when we all change places at the Rising (*waves his hand and disappears*) of the Moon.

SERGEANT (*turning his back to audience and reading placard*). A hundred pounds reward! A hundred pounds! (*Turns toward audience*) I wonder, now, am I as great a too, as I think I am?

CURTAIN

The Boor

A COMEDY IN ONE ACT

BY ANTON CHEKOV

TRANSLATED BY HILMAR BAUKHAGE

CHARACTERS

HELENA IVANOVNA POPOV, *a young widow, mistress of a country estate*
GRIGORI STEPANOVITCH SMIRNOV, *proprietor of a country estate*
LUKA, *servant of* MRS. POPOV
A gardener
A coacnman
Several workmen

> SCENE: The estate of Mrs. Popov.
> TIME: The present.

THE BOOR

SCENE—*A well-furnished reception-room in* MRS. POPOV's *home.*
MRS. POPOV *is discovered in deep mourning, sitting upon a sofa, gazing steadfastly at a photograph.* LUKA *is also present.*

LUKA. It isn't right, ma'am. You're wearing yourself out! The maid and the cook have gone looking for berries; everything that breathes is enjoying life, even the cat knows how to be happy—slips about the courtyard and catches birds—but you hide yourself here in the house as though you were in a cloister. Yes, truly, by actual reckoning you haven't left this house for a whole year.

MRS. POPOV. And I shall never leave it—why should I? My life is over. He lies in his grave, and I have buried myself within these four walls. We are both dead.

LUKA. There you are again! It's too awful to listen to, so it is! Nikolai Michailovitch is dead; it was the will of the Lord, and the Lord has given him eternal peace. You have grieved over it and that ought to be enough. Now it's time to stop. One can't weep and wear mourning forever! My wife died a few years ago. I grieved for her, I wept a whole month—and then it was over. Must one be forever singing lamentations? That would be more than your husband was worth! (*He sighs*) You have forgotten all your neighbors. You don't go out and you receive no one. We live—you'll pardon me—like the spiders, and the good light of day we never see. All the livery is eaten by the mice —as though there weren't any more nice people in the world! But the whole neighborhood is full of gentlefolk. The regiment is stationed in Riblov—officers—simply beautiful! One can't see enough of them! Every Friday a ball, and military music every day. Oh, my dear, dear ma'am, young and pretty as you are, if you'd only let your spirits live—! Beauty can't last forever. When ten short years are over, you'll be glad enough to go out a bit and meet the officers—and then it'll be too late.

MRS. POPOV (*resolutely*). Please don't speak of these things again. You know very well that since the death of Nikolai Michailovitch my life is absolutely nothing to me. You think I live, but it only seems so. Do you understand? Oh, that his departed soul may see how I love him! I know, it's no secret to you; he was often unjust toward me, cruel, and —he wasn't faithful, but I shall be faithful to the grave and prove to him how I can love. There, in the Beyond, he'll find me the same as I was until his death.

LUKA. What is the use of all these words, when you'd so much rather go walking in the garden or order Tobby or Welikan harnessed to the trap, and visit the neighbors?

MRS. POPOV (*weeping*). Oh!

LUKA. Madam, dear Madam, what is it? In Heaven's name!

MRS. POPOV. He loved Tobby so! He always drove him to the Kortschagins or the Vlassovs. What a wonderful horseman he was! How fine he looked when he pulled at the reins with all his might! Tobby, Tobby—give him an extra measure of oats today!

LUKA. Yes, ma'am.
(A bell rings loudly.)

MRS. POPOV (shudders). What's that? I am at home to no one.

LUKA. Yes, ma'am. (He goes out, Center.)

MRS. POPOV (gazing at the photograph). You shall see, Nikolai, how I can love and forgive! My love will die only with me—when my poor heart stops beating. (She smiles through her tears) And aren't you ashamed? I have been a good, true wife, I have imprisoned myself and I shall remain true until death, and you—you—you're not ashamed of yourself, my dear monster! You quarrelled with me, left me alone for weeks——
(LUKA enters in great excitement.)

LUKA. Oh, ma'am, someone is asking for you, insists on seeing you——

MRS POPOV. You told him that since my husband's death I receive no one?

LUKA. I said so, but he won't listen, he says it is a pressing matter.

MRS. POPOV. I receive no one!

LUKA. I told him that, but he's a wildman, he swore and pushed himself into the room; he's in the dining-room now.

MRS. POPOV (excitedly). Good Show him in. The impudent—!
(LUKA goes out, Center.)

MRS. POPOV. What a bore people are! What can they want with me? Why do they disturb my peace? (She sighs) Yes, it is clear I must enter a convent. (Meditatively) Yes, a convent.
(SMIRNOV enters, followed by LUKA.)

SMIRNOV (to LUKA). Fool, you make too much noise! You're an ass! (Discovering MRS. POPOV—politely) Madam, I have the honor to introduce myself: Lieutenant in the Artillery, retired, country gentleman, Grigori Stepanovitch Smirnov! I'm compelled to bother you about an exceedingly important matter.

MRS. POPOV (without offering her hand). What is it you wish?

SMIRNOV. Your deceased husband, with whom I had the honor to be acquainted, left me two notes amounting to about twelve hundred rubles. Inasmuch as I have to pay the interest tomorrow on a loan from the Agrarian Bank, I should like to request, madam, that you pay me the money today.

MRS. POPOV. Twelve hundred—and for what was my husband indebted to you?

SMIRNOV. He bought oats from me.

MRS. POPOV (with a sigh, to LUKA). Don't forget to give Tobby an extra measure of oats.
(LUKA goes out.)

MRS. POPOV (to SMIRNOV). If Nikolai Michailovitch is indebted to you,

I shall of course pay you, but I am sorry, I haven't the money today. Tomorrow my manager will return from the city and I shall notify him to pay you what is due you, but until then I cannot satisfy your request. Furthermore, today it is just seven months since the death of my husband and I am not in a mood to discuss money matters.

SMIRNOV. And I am in the mood to fly up the chimney with my feet in the air if I can't lay hands on that interest tomorrow. They'll seize my estate!

MRS. POPOV. Day after tomorrow you will receive the money.

SMIRNOV. I don't need the money day after tomorrow, I need it today.

MRS. POPOV. I'm sorry I can't pay you today.

SMIRNOV. And I can't wait until day after tomorrow.

MRS. POPOV. But what can I do if I haven't it?

SMIRNOV. So you can't pay?

MRS. POPOV. I cannot.

SMIRNOV. Hm! Is that your last word?

MRS. POPOV. My last.

SMIRNOV. Absolutely?

MRS. POPOV. Absolutely.

SMIRNOV. Thank you. (*He shrugs his shoulders*) And they expect me to stand for all that. The toll-gatherer just now met me in the road and asked me why I was always worrying? Why in Heaven's name shouldn't I worry? I need money. I feel the knife at my throat. Yesterday morning I left my house in the early dawn and called on all my debtors. If even one of them had paid his debt! I worked the skin off my fingers! The devil knows in what sort of Jew-inn I slept: in a room with a barrel of brandy! And now at last I come here, seventy versts from home, hope for a little money and all you give me is moods! Why shouldn't I worry?

MRS. POPOV. I thought I made it plain to you that my manager will return from town, and then you will get your money?

SMIRNOV. I did not come to see the manager, I came to see you. What the devil—pardon the language—do I care for your manager?

MRS. POPOV. Really, sir, I am not used to such language or such manners. I shan't listen to you any further. (*She goes out, left.*)

SMIRNOV. What can one say to that? Moods! Seven months since her husband died! Do I have to pay the interest or not? I repeat the question, have I to pay the interest or not? The husband is dead and all that; the manager is—the devil with him! —traveling somewhere. Now, tell me, what am I to do? Shall I run away from my creditors in a balloon? Or knock my head against a stone wall? If I call on Grusdev he chooses to be "not at home," Iroschevitch has simply hidden himself, I have quarrelled with Kurzin and came near throwing him out of the window, Masutov is ill and this woman has—moods! Not one of them will pay up! And all because I've spoiled them, because I'm an old whiner, dish-rag! I'm too tender-hearted with them. But wait! I allow nobody to play tricks with me, the devil with 'em all! I'll stay here and not budge until she pays! Brr! How angry I am, how terribly angry I am! Every tendon is trembling with anger and I can hardly breathe! I'm even growing ill! (*He calls out*) Servant!

(LUKA *enters.*)

LUKA. What is it you wish?

SMIRNOV. Bring me Kvas or water! (LUKA *goes out*) Well, what can we do? She hasn't it on hand? What sort of logic is that? A fellow stands with the knife at his throat, he needs money, he is on the point of hanging himself, and she won't pay because she isn't in the mood to discuss money matters. Woman's logic! That's why I never liked to talk to women and why I dislike doing it now. I would rather sit on a powder barrel than talk with a woman. Brr! —I'm getting cold as ice, this affair has made me so angry. I need only to see such a romantic creature from a distance to get so angry that I have cramps in the calves! It's enough to make one yell for help! (*Enter* LUKA.)

LUKA (*hands him water*). Madam is ill and is not receiving.

SMIRNOV. March! (LUKA *goes out*) Ill and isn't receiving! All right, it isn't necessary. I won't receive, either! I'll sit here and stay until you bring that money. If you're ill a week, I'll sit here a week. If you're ill a year, I'll sit here a year. As Heaven is my witness, I'll get the money. You don't disturb me with

your mourning—or with your dimples. We know these dimples! (*He calls out the window*) Simon, unharness! We aren't going to leave right away. I am going to stay here. Tell them in the stable to give the horses some oats. The left horse has twisted the bridle again. (*Imitating him*) Stop! I'll show you how. Stop! (*Leaves window*) It's awful. Unbearable heat, no money, didn't sleep last night and now—mourning-dresses with moods. My head aches; perhaps I ought to have a drink. Ye-s, I must have a drink. (*Calling*) Servant!

LUKA. What do you wish?

SMIRNOV. Something to drink! (LUKA *goes out.* SMIRNOV *sits down and looks at his clothes*) Ugh, a fine figure! No use denying that. Dust, dirty boots, unwashed, uncombed, straw on my vest—the lady probably took me for a highwayman. (*He yawns*) It was a little impolite to come into a reception room with such clothes. Oh, well, no harm done. I'm not here as a guest. I'm a creditor. And there is no special costume for creditors.

LUKA (*entering with glass*). You take great liberty, sir.

SMIRNOV (*angrily*). What?

LUKA. I—I—I just——

SMIRNOV. Whom are you talking to? Keep quiet.

LUKA (*angrily*). Nice mess! This fellow won't leave! (*He goes out.*)

SMIRNOV. Lord, how angry I am! Angry enough to throw mud at the whole world! I even feel ill! Servant!

(MRS. POPOV *comes in with downcast eyes.*)

MRS. POPOV. Sir, in my solitude I have become unaccustomed to the human voice and I cannot stand the sound of loud talking. I beg you, please to cease disturbing my rest.

SMIRNOV. Pay me my money and I'll leave.

MRS. POPOV. I told you once, plainly, in your native tongue, that I haven't the money at hand; wait until day after tomorrow.

SMIRNOV. And I also had the honor of informing you in your native tongue that I need the money, not day after tomorrow, but today. If you don't pay me today I shall have to hang myself tomorrow.

MRS. POPOV. But what can I do if I haven't the money?

SMIRNOV. So you are not going to pay immediately? You're not?

MRS. POPOV. I cannot.

SMIRNOV. Then I'll sit here until I get the money. (*He sits down*) You will pay day after tomorrow? Excellent! Here I stay until day after tomorrow. (*Jumps up*) I ask you, do I have to pay that interest tomorrow or not? Or do you think I'm joking?

MRS. POPOV. Sir, I beg of you, don't scream! This is not a stable.

SMIRNOV. I'm not talking about stables, I'm asking you whether I have to pay that interest tomorrow or not?

MRS. POPOV. You have no idea how to treat a lady.

SMIRNOV. Oh, yes, I have.

MRS. POPOV. No, you have not. You are an ill-bred, vulgar person! Respectable people don't speak so to ladies.

SMIRNOV. How remarkable! How do you want one to speak to you? In French, perhaps! Madame, je vous prie! Pardon me for having disturbed you. What beautiful weather we are having today! And how this mourning becomes you! (*He makes a low bow with mock ceremony.*)

MRS. POPOV. Not at all funny! I think it vulgar!

SMIRNOV (*imitating her*). Not at all funny—vulgar! I don't understand how to behave in the company of ladies. Madam, in the course of my life I have seen more women than you have sparrows. Three times have I fought duels for women, twelve I jilted and nine jilted me. There was a time when I played the fool, used honeyed language, bowed and scraped. I loved, suffered, sighed to the moon, melted in love's torments. I loved passionately, I loved to madness, loved in every key, chattered like a magpie on emancipation, sacrificed half my fortune in the tender passion, until now the devil knows I've had enough of it. Your obedient servant will let you lead him around by the nose no more. Enough! Black eyes, passionate eyes, coral lips, dimples in cheeks, moonlight whispers, soft, modest sighs—for all that, madam, I wouldn't pay a kopeck! I am not speaking of present company, but of women in general; from the tiniest to the greatest, they are conceited, hypocritical, chattering, odious, deceitful from top to toe; vain, petty, cruel with a maddening logic and *(he strikes his forehead)* in this respect, please excuse my frankness, but one sparrow is worth ten of the aforementioned petticoat-philosophers. When one sees one of the romantic creatures before him he imagines he is looking at some holy being, so wonderful that its one breath could dissolve him in a sea of a thousand charms and delights; but if one looks into the soul—it's nothing but a common crocodile. *(He seizes the arm-chair and breaks it in two)* But the worst of all is that this crocodile imagines it is a masterpiece of creation, and that it has a monopoly on all the tender passions. May the devil hang me upside down if there is anything to love about a woman! When she is in love, all she knows is how to complain and shed tears. If the man suffers and makes sacrifices she swings her train about and tries to lead him by the nose. You have the misfortune to be a woman, and naturally you know woman's nature; tell me on your honor, have you ever in your life seen a woman who was really true and faithful? Never! Only the old and the deformed are true and faithful. It's easier to find a cat with horns or a white woodcock, than a faithful woman.

MRS. POPOV. But allow me to ask, who is true and faithful in love? The man, perhaps?

SMIRNOV. Yes, indeed! The man!

MRS. POPOV. The man! *(She laughs sarcastically)* The man true and faithful in love! Well, that is something new! *(Bitterly)* How can you make such a statement? Men true and faithful! So long as we have gone thus far, I may as well say that of all the men I have known, my husband was the best; I loved him passionately with all my soul, as only a young, sensible woman may love; I gave him my youth, my happiness, my fortune, my life. I worshipped him like a heathen. And what happened? This best of men betrayed me in every possible way. After his death I found his desk filled with love-letters. While he was alive he left me alone for months—it is horrible even to think about it—he made love to other women in my very presence, he wasted my money and made fun of my feelings—and in spite of everything, I trusted him and was true to him. And more than that: he is dead and I am still true to him. I have buried myself within these four walls and I shall wear this mourning to my grave.

SMIRNOV *(laughing disrespectfully)*. Mourning! What on earth do you take me for? As if I didn't know why you wore this black domino and why you buried yourself within these four walls. Such a secret! So romantic! Some knight will pass the castle, gaze up at the windows and think to himself: "Here dwells the mysterious Tamara who, for love of her husband, has buried herself within four walls." Oh, I understand the art!

MRS. POPOV *(springing up)*. What? What do you mean by saying such things to me?

SMIRNOV. You have buried yourself alive, but meanwhile you have not forgotten to powder your nose!

MRS. POPOV. How dare you speak so?

SMIRNOV. Don't scream at me, please, I'm not the manager. Allow me to call things by their right names. I am not a woman, and I am accustomed to speak out what I think. So please don't scream.

MRS. POPOV. I'm not screaming. It is you who are screaming. Please leave me, I beg of you.

SMIRNOV. Pay me my money and I'll leave.

MRS. POPOV. I won't give you the money.

SMIRNOV. You won't? You won't give me my money?

MRS. POPOV. I don't care what you do. You won't get a kopeck! Leave me!

SMIRNOV. As I haven't the pleasure of being either your husband or your fiancé please don't make a scene. (*He sits down*) I can't stand it.

MRS. POPOV (*breathing hard*). You are going to sit down?

SMIRNOV. I already have.

MRS. POPOV. Kindly leave the house!

SMIRNOV. Give me the money.

MRS. POPOV. I don't care to speak with impudent men. Leave! (*Pause*) You aren't going?

SMIRNOV. No.

MRS. POPOV. No?

SMIRNOV. No.

MRS. POPOV. Very well. (*She rings the bell.*)
(*Enter* LUKA.)

MRS. POPOV. Luka, show the gentleman out.

LUKA (*going to* SMIRNOV). Sir, why don't you leave when you are ordered? What do you want?

SMIRNOV (*jumping up*). Whom do you think you are talking to? I'll grind you to powder.

LUKA (*puts his hand to his heart*). Good Lord! (*He drops into a chair*) Oh, I'm ill, I can't breathe!

MRS. POPOV. Where is Dascha? (*Calling*) Dascha! Pelageja! Dascha! (*She rings.*)

LUKA. They're all gone! I'm ill! Water!

MRS. POPOV (*to* SMIRNOV). Leave! Get out!

SMIRNOV. Kindly be a little more polite!

MRS. POPOV (*striking her fists and stamping her feet*). You are vulgar! You're a boor! A monster!

SMIRNOV. What did you say!

MRS. POPOV. I said you were a boor, a monster!

SMIRNOV (*steps toward her quickly*). Permit me to ask what right you have to insult me?

MRS. POPOV. What of it? Do you think I am afraid of you?

SMIRNOV. And you think that because you are a romantic creature you can insult me without being punished? I challenge you!

LUKA. Merciful heaven! Water!

SMIRNOV. We'll have a duel.

MRS. POPOV. Do you think because you have big fists and a steer's neck I am afraid of you?

SMIRNOV. I allow no one to insult me, and I make no exception because you are a woman, one of the "weaker sex!"

MRS. POPOV (*trying to cry him down*). Boor, boor, boor!

SMIRNOV. It is high time to do away with the old superstition that it is only the man who is forced to give satisfaction. If there is equity at all let there be equity in all things. There's a limit!

MRS. POPOV. You wish to fight a duel? Very well..

SMIRNOV. Immediately.

MRS. POPOV. Immediately. My husband had pistols. I'll bring them. (*She hurries away, then turns*) Oh, what a pleasure it will be to put a bullet in your impudent head. The devil take you! (*She goes out.*)

SMIRNOV. I'll shoot her down! I'm no fledgling, no sentimental young puppy. For me, there is no weaker sex!

LUKA. Oh, sir! (*Falls to his knees*) Have mercy on me, an old man, and go away. You have frightened me to death already, and now you want to fight a duel.

SMIRNOV (*paying no attention*). A duel. That's equity, emancipation. That way the sexes are made equal. I'll shoot her down as a matter of principle. What can a person say to such a woman? (*Imitating her*) "The devil take you. I'll put a bullet in your impudent head." What can one say to that? She was angry, her eyes blazed, she accepted the challenge. On my honor, it's the first time in my life that I ever saw such a woman.

LUKA. Oh, sir. Go away. Go away!

SMIRNOV. That *is* a woman. I can understand her. A real woman. No shilly-shallying, but fire, powder, and noise! It would be a pity to shoot a woman like that.

LUKA (*weeping*). Oh, sir, go away. (*Enter* MRS. POPOV.)

MRS. POPOV. Here are the pistols. But before we have our duel please show me how to shoot. I have never had a pistol in my hand before!

LUKA. God be merciful and have pity upon us! I'll go and get the gardener and the coachman. Why has this horror come to us? (*He goes out.*)

SMIRNOV (*looking at the pistols*). You see, there are different kinds. There are special duelling pistols with cap and ball. But these are revolvers, Smith & Wesson, with ejectors; fine pistols! A pair like that cost at least ninety rubles. This is the way to hold a revolver. (*Aside*) Those eyes, those eyes! A real woman!

MRS. POPOV. Like this?

SMIRNOV. Yes, that way. Then you pull the hammer back—so—then you aim—put your head back a little. Just stretch your arm out, please. So—then press your finger on the thing like that, and that is all. The chief thing is this: don't get excited, don't hurry your aim, and take care that your hand doesn't tremble.

MRS. POPOV. It isn't well to shoot inside; let's go into the garden.

SMIRNOV. Yes. I'll tell you now, I am going to shoot into the air.

MRS. POPOV. That is too much! Why?

SMIRNOV. Because—because. That's my business.

MRS. POPOV. You are afraid. Yes. A-h-h-h. No, no, my dear sir, no flinching! Please follow me. I won't rest until I've made a hole in that head I hate so much. Are your afraid?

SMIRNOV. Yes, I'm afraid.

MRS. POPOV. You are lying. Why won't you fight?

SMIRNOV. Because—because—I— like you.

MRS. POPOV (with an angry laugh). You like me! He dares to say he likes me! (She points to the door) Go.

SMIRNOV (laying the revolver silently on the table, takes his hat and starts. At the door he stops a moment gazing at her silently, then he approaches her, hesitating). Listen! Are you still angry? I was mad as the devil, but please understand me—how can I express myself? The thing is like this—such things are— (He raises his voice) Now, is it my fault that you owe me money? (Grasps the back of the chair, which breaks) The devil knows what breakable furniture you have! I like you! Do you understand? I—I'm almost in love!

MRS. POPOV. Leave! I hate you.

SMIRNOV. Lord! What a woman! I never in my life met one like her. I'm lost, ruined! I've been caught like a mouse in a trap.

MRS. POPOV. Go, or I'll shoot.

SMIRNOV. Shoot! You have no idea what happiness it would be to die in sight of those beautiful eyes, to die from the revolver in this little velvet hand! I'm mad! Consider it and decide immediately, for if I go now, we shall never see each other again. Decide—speak—I am a noble, a respectable man, have an income of ten thousand, can shoot a coin thrown into the air. I own some fine horses. Will you be my wife?

MRS. POPOV (swings the revolver angrily). I'll shoot!

SMIRNOV. My mind is not clear—I can't understand. Servant—water! I have fallen in love like any young man. (He takes her hand and she cries with pain) I love you! (He kneels) I love you as I have never loved before. Twelve women I jilted, nine jilted me, but not one of them all have I loved as I love you. I am conquered, lost, I lie at your feet like a fool and beg for your hand. Shame and disgrace! For five years I haven't been in love; I thanked the Lord for it, and now I am caught, like a carriage tongue in another carriage. I beg for your hand! Yes, or no? Will you?—Good! (*He gets up and goes quickly to the door.*)

MRS. POPOV. Wait a moment!

SMIRNOV (*stopping*). Well?

MRS. POPOV. Nothing. You may go. But—wait a moment. No, go on, go on. I hate you. Or—no: don't go. Oh, if you knew how angry I was, how angry! (*She throws the revolver into the chair*) My finger is swollen from this thing. (*She angrily tears her handkerchief*) What are you standing there for? Get out!

SMIRNOV. Farewell!

MRS. POPOV. Yes, go. (*Cries out*) Why are you going? Wait—no, go!! Oh, how angry I am! Don't come too near, don't come too near—er— come—no nearer.

SMIRNOV (*approaching her*). How angry I am with myself! Fall in love like a school-boy, throw myself on my knees. I've got a chill! (*Strongly*) I love you. This is fine—all I needed was to fall in love. Tomorrow I have to pay my interest, the hay harvest has begun, and then you appear! (*He takes her in his arms*) I can never forgive myself.

MRS. POPOV. Go away! Take your hands off me! I hate you—you—this is— (*A long kiss.*)

(*Enter LUKA with an ax, the gardener with a rake, the coachman with a pitch-fork, and workmen with poles.*)

LUKA (*staring at the pair*). Merciful Heavens! (*A long pause.*)

MRS. POPOV (*dropping her eyes*). Tell them in the stable that Tobby isn't to have any oats.

CURTAIN

The Twelve-Pound Look

BY JAMES M. BARRIE

THE TWELVE-POUND LOOK

·ᵗ quite convenient (as they say about cheques) you are to conceive that the scene is laid in your own house, and that HARRY SIMS *is you. Perhaps the ornamentation of the house is a trifle ostentatious, but if you cavil at that we are willing to re-decorate: you don't get out of being* HARRY SIMS *on a mere matter of plush and dados. It pleases us to make him a city man, but (rather than lose you) he can be turned with a scrape of the pen into a K.C., fashionable doctor, Secretary of State, or what you will. We conceive him of a pleasant rotundity with a thick red neck, but we shall waive that point if you know him to be thin.*

It is that day in your career when everything went wrong just when everything seemed to be superlatively right.

In HARRY'S *case it was a woman who did the mischief. She came to him in his great hour and told him she did not admire him. Of course he turned her out of the house and was soon himself again, but it spoilt the morning for him. This is the subject of the play, and quite enough too.*

HARRY *is to receive the honor of knighthood in a few days, and we discover him in the sumptuous "snuggery" of his home in Kensington (or is it Westminster?), rehearsing the ceremony with his wife. They have been at it all the morning, a pleasing occupation.* MRS. SIMS *(as we may call her for the last time, as it were, and strictly as a good-natured joke) is wearing her presentation gown, and personates the august one who is about to dub her* HARRY *knight. She is seated regally. Her jewelled shoulders proclaim aloud her husband's generosity. She must be an extraordinarily proud and happy woman, yet she has a drawn face and shrinking ways as if there were someone near her of whom she is afraid. She claps her hands, as the signal to* HARRY. *He enters bowing, and with a graceful swerve of the leg. He is only partly in costume, the sword and the real stockings not having arrived yet. With a gliding motion that is only delayed while one leg makes up on the other, he reaches his wife, and, going on one knee, raises her hand superbly to his lips. She taps him on the shoulder with a paper-knife and says huskily, "Rise, Sir Harry." He rises, bows, and glides about the room, going on his knees to various articles of furniture, and rises from each a knight. It is a radiant domestic scene, and* HARRY *is as dignified as if he knew that royalty was rehearsing it at the other end.*

SIR HARRY (*complacently*). Did that seem all right, eh?

LADY SIMS (*much relieved*). I think perfect.

SIR HARRY. But was it dignified?

LADY SIMS. Oh, very. And it will be still more so when you have the sword.

SIR HARRY. The sword will lend it an air. There are really the five moments—(*suiting the action to the word*)—the glide—the dip—the kiss—the tap—and you back out a knight. It's short, but it's a very beautiful ceremony. (*Kindly*) Anything you can suggest?

LADY SIMS. No—oh no. (*Nervously, seeing him pause to kiss the tassel of a cushion.*) You don't think you have practised till you know what to do almost too well?

(*He has been in a blissful temper, but such niggling criticism would try any man.*)

SIR HARRY. I do not. Don't talk nonsense. Wait till your opinion is asked for.

LADY SIMS (*abashed*). I'm sorry, Harry. (*A perfect butler appears and presents a card*) "The Flora Type-Writing Agency."

SIR HARRY. Ah, yes. I telephoned them to send someone. A woman, I suppose, Tombes?

TOMBES. Yes, Sir Harry.

SIR HARRY. Show her in here. (*He has very lately become a stickler for etiquette*) And, Tombes, strictly speaking, you know, I am not Sir Harry till Thursday.

TOMBES. Beg pardon, sir, but it is such a satisfaction to us.

SIR HARRY (*good-naturedly*). Ah, they like it downstairs, do they?

TOMBES (*unbending*). Especially the females, Sir Harry.

SIR HARRY. Exactly. You can show her in, Tombes. (*The butler departs on his mighty task*) You can tell the woman what she is wanted for, Emmy, while I change. (*He is too modest to boast about himself, and prefers to keep a wife in the house for that purpose*) You can tell her the sort of things about me that will come better from you. (*Smiling happily*) You heard what Tombes said, "Especially the females." And

he is right. Success! The women like it even better than the men. And rightly. For they share. *You* share, Lady Sims. Not a woman will see that gown without being sick with envy of it. I know them. Have all our lady friends in to see it. It will make them ill for a week.

(*These sentiments carry him off lightheartedly, and presently the disturbing element is shown in. She is a mere typist, dressed in uncommonly good taste, but at contemptibly small expense, and she is carrying her typewriter in a friendly way rather than as a badge of slavery, as of course it is. Her eye is clear; and in odd contrast to* LADY SIMS, *she is self-reliant and serene.*)

KATE (*respectfully, but she should have waited to be spoken to*). Good morning, madam.

LADY SIMS (*in her nervous way, and scarcely noticing that the typist is a little too ready with her tongue*). Good morning. (*As a first impression she rather likes the woman, and the woman, though it is scarcely worth mentioning, rather likes her.* LADY SIMS *has a maid for buttoning and unbuttoning her, and probably another for waiting on the maid, and she gazes with a little envy perhaps at a woman who does things for herself*) Is that the type-writing machine?

KATE (*who is getting it ready for use*). Yes (*not "Yes, madam," as it ought to be*). I suppose if I am to work here I may take this off. I get on better without it. (*She is referring to her hat.*)

LADY SIMS. Certainly. (*But the hat is already off*) I ought to apologise for my gown. I am to be presented this week, and I was trying it on. (*Her tone is not really apologetic. She is rather clinging to the glory of her gown, wistfully, as if not absolutely certain, you know, that it is a glory.*)

KATE. It is beautiful, if I may presume to say so. (*She frankly admires it. She probably has a best, and a second best of her own: that sort of thing.*)

LADY SIMS (*with a flush of pride in the gown*). Yes, it is very beautiful. (*The beauty of it gives her courage*) Sit down, please.

KATE (*the sort of woman who would have sat down in any case*). I suppose it is some copying you want done? I got no particulars. I was told to come to this address. but that was all.

LADY SIMS (*almost with the humility of a servant*). Oh, it is not work for me, it is for my husband, and what he needs is not exactly copying. (*Swelling, for she is proud of* HARRY) He wants a number of letters answered—hundreds of them —letters and telegrams of congratulation.

KATE (*as if it were all in the day's work*). Yes?

LADY SIMS (*remembering that* HARRY *expects every wife to do her duty*). My husband is a remarkable man. He is about to be knighted. (*Pause, but* KATE *does not fall to the floor*) He is to be knighted for his services to—(*on reflection*)—for his services. (*She is conscious that she is not doing* HARRY *justice*) He can explain it so much better than I can.

KATE (*in her business-like way*). And I am to answer the congratulations?

LADY SIMS (*afraid that it will be a hard task*). Yes.

KATE (*blithely*). It is work I have had some experience of. (*She proceeds to type.*)

LADY SIMS. But you can't begin till you know what he wants to say.

KATE. Only a specimen letter. Won't it be the usual thing?

LADY SIMS (*to whom this is a new idea*). Is there a usual thing?

KATE. Oh, yes. (*She continues to type, and* LADY SIMS, *half-mesmerised, gazes at her nimble fingers. The useless woman watches the useful one, and she sighs, she could not tell why.*)

LADY SIMS. How quickly you do it! It must be delightful to be able to do something, and to do it well.

KATE (*thankfully*). Yes, it is delightful.

LADY SIMS (*again remembering the source of all her greatness*). But, excuse me, I don't think that will be any use. My husband wants me to explain to you that his is an exceptional case. He did not try to get this honor in any way. It was a complete surprise to him——

KATE (*who is a practical Kate and no dealer in sarcasm*). That is what I have written.

LADY SIMS (*in whom sarcasm would meet a dead wall*). But how could you know?

KATE. I only guessed.

LADY SIMS. Is that the usual thing?

KATE. Oh, yes.

LADY SIMS. They don't try to get it?

KATE. I don't know. That is what we are told to say in the letters. (*To her at present the only important thing about the letters is that they are ten shillings the hundred.*)

LADY SIMS (*returning to surer ground*). I should explain that my husband is not a man who cares for honors. So long as he does his duty——

KATE. Yes, I have been putting that in.

LADY SIMS. Have you? But he particularly wants it to be known that he would have declined a title were it not——

KATE. I have got it here.

LADY SIMS. What have you got?

KATE (*reading*). "Indeed, I would have asked to be allowed to decline had it not been that I want to please my wife."

LADY SIMS (*heavily*). But how could you know it was that?

KATE. Is it?

LADY SIMS (*who after all is the one with the right to ask questions*). Do they all accept it for that reason?

KATE. That is what we are told to say in the letters.

LADY SIMS (*thoughtlessly*). It is quite as if you knew my husband.

KATE. I assure you, I don't even know his name.

LADY SIMS (*suddenly showing that she knows him*). Oh, he wouldn't like that!
(*And it is here that* HARRY *re-enters in his city garments, looking so gay, feeling so jolly that we bleed for him. However, the annoying* KATHERINE *is to get a shock also.*)

LADY SIMS. This is the lady, Harry.

SIR HARRY (*shooting his cuffs*). Yes, yes. Good morning, my dear.
(*Then they see each other, and their mouths open, but not for words. After the first surprise* KATE *seems to find some humor in the situation, but* HARRY *lowers like a thundercloud.*)

LADY SIMS (*who has seen nothing*). I have been trying to explain to her——

SIR HARRY. Eh—what? (*He controls himself*) Leave it to me, Emmy; I'll attend to her.
(LADY SIMS *goes, with a dread fear that somehow she has vexed her lord, and then* HARRY *attends to the intruder.*)

SIR HARRY (*with concentrated scorn*). You!

KATE (*as if agreeing with him*). Yes, it's funny.

SIR HARRY. The shamelessness of your daring to come here.

KATE. Believe me, it is not less a surprise to me than it is to you. I was sent here in the ordinary way of business. I was given only the number of the house. I was not told the name.

SIR HARRY (*withering her*). The ordinary way of business! This is what you have fallen to—a typist!

KATE (*unwithered*). Think of it!

SIR HARRY. After going through worse straits, I'll be bound.

KATE (*with some grim memories*). Much worse straits.

SIR HARRY (*alas, laughing coarsely*). My congratulations!

KATE. Thank you, Harry.

SIR HARRY (*who is annoyed, as any man would be, not to find her abject*). Eh? What was that you called me, madam?

KATE. Isn't it Harry? On my soul, I almost forget.

SIR HARRY. It isn't Harry to you. My name is Sims, if you please.

KATE. Yes, I had not forgotten that. It was my name, too, you see.

SIR HARRY (*in his best manner*). It was your name till you forfeited the right to bear it.

KATE. Exactly.

SIR HARRY (*gloating*). I was furious to find you here, but on second thoughts it pleases me. (*From the depths of his moral nature*) There is a grim justice in this.

KATE (*sympathetically*). Tell me?

SIR HARRY. Do you know what you were brought here to do?

KATE. I have just been learning. You have been made a knight, and I was summoned to answer the messages of congratulation.

SIR HARRY. That's it, that's it. You come on this day as my servant!

KATE. I, who might have been Lady Sims.

SIR HARRY. And you are her typist instead. And she has four men-servants. Oh, I am glad you saw her in her presentation gown.

KATE. I wonder if she would let me do her washing, Sir Harry?
(*Her want of taste disgusts him.*)

SIR HARRY (*with dignity*). You can go. The mere thought that only a few flights of stairs separates such as you from my innocent children——
(*He will never know why a new light has come into her face.*)

KATE (*slowly*). You have children?

SIR HARRY (*inflated*). Two. (*He wonders why she is so long in answering.*)

KATE (*resorting to impertinence*). Such a nice number.

SIR HARRY (*with an extra turn of the screw*). Both boys.

KATE. Successful in everything. Are they like you, Sir Harry?

SIR HARRY (*expanding*). They are very like me.

KATE. That's nice. (*Even on such a subject as this she can be ribald.*)

SIR HARRY. Will you please to go.

KATE. Heigho! What shall I say to my employer?

SIR HARRY. That is no affair of mine.

KATE. What will you say to Lady Sims?

SIR HARRY. I flatter myself that whatever I say, Lady Sims will accept without comment. (*She smiles, heaven knows why, unless her next remark explains it.*)

KATE. Still the same Harry.

SIR HARRY. What do you mean?

KATE. Only that you have the old confidence in your profound knowledge of the sex.

SIR HARRY (*beginning to think as little of her intellect as of her morals*). I suppose I know my wife.

KATE (*hopelessly dense*). I suppose so. I was only remembering that you used to think you knew her in the days when I was the lady. (*He is merely wasting his time on her, and he indicates the door. She is not sufficiently the lady to retire worsted.*) Well, good-bye, Sir Harry. Won't you ring, and the four men-servants will show me out? (*But he hesitates.*)

SIR HARRY (*in spite of himself*). As you are here, there is something I want to get out of you. (*Wishing he could ask it less eagerly.*) Tell me, who was the man?

ιThe strange woman—it is evident now that she has always been strange to him—smiles tolerantly.)

KATE. You never found out?

SIR HARRY. I could never be sure.

KATE (*reflectively*). I thought that would worry you.

SIR HARRY (*sneering*). It's plain that he soon left you.

KATE. Very soon.

SIR HARRY. As I could have told you. (*But still she surveys him with the smile of Mona Lisa. The badgered man has to entreat.*) Who was he? It was fourteen years ago, and cannot matter to any of us now. Kate, tell me who he was? (*It is his first youthful moment, and perhaps because of that she does not wish to hurt him.*)

KATE (*shaking a motherly head*). Better not ask.

SIR HARRY. I do ask. Tell me.

KATE. It is kinder not to tell you.

SIR HARRY (*violently*). Then, by James, it was one of my own pals. Was it Bernard Roche? (*She shakes her head*) It may have been some one who comes to my house still.

KATE. I think not. (*Reflecting*) Fourteen years! You found my letter that night when you went home?

SIR HARRY (*impatient*). Yes.

KATE. I propped it against the decanters. I thought you would be sure to see it there. It was a room not unlike this, and the furniture was arranged in the same attractive way. How it all comes back to me. Don't you see me, Harry, in hat and cloak, putting the letter there, taking a last look round, and then stealing out into the night to meet——

SIR HARRY. Whom?

KATE. Him. Hours pass, no sound in the room but the tick-tack of the clock, and then about midnight you return alone. You take——

SIR HARRY (*gruffly*). I wasn't alone.

KATE (*the picture spoilt*). No? oh. (*Plaintively*) Here have I all these years been conceiving it wrongly. (*She studies his face*) I believe something interesting happened?

SIR HARRY (*growling*). Something confoundedly annoying.

KATE (*coaxing*). Do tell me.

SIR HARRY. We won't go into that. Who was the man? Surely a husband has a right to know with whom his wife bolted.

KATE (*who is detestably ready with her tongue*). Surely the wife has a right to know how he took it. (*The woman's love of bargaining comes to her aid*) A fair exchange. You tell me what happened, and I will tell you who he was.

SIR HARRY. You will? Very well. (*It is the first point on which they have agreed, and, forgetting himself, he takes a place beside her on the fireseat. He is thinking only of what he is to tell her, but she, womanlike, is conscious of their proximity.*)

KATE (*tastelessly*). Quite like old times. (*He moves away from her indignantly*) Go on, Harry.

SIR HARRY (*who has a manful shrinking from saying anything that is to his disadvantage*). Well, as you know, I was dining at the club that night.

KATE. Yes.

SIR HARRY. Jack Lamb drove me home. Mabbett Green was with us, and I asked them to come in for a few minutes.

KATE. Jack Lamb, Mabbett Green? I think I remember them. Jack was in Parliament.

SIR HARRY. No, that was Mabbett. They came into the house with me and—(*with sudden horror*)—was it him?

KATE (*bewildered*). Who?

SIR HARRY. Mabbett?

KATE. What?

SIR HARRY. The man?

KATE. What man? (*Understanding*) Oh no. I thought you said he came into the house with you.

SIR HARRY. It might have been a blind.

KATE. Well, it wasn't. Go on.

SIR HARRY. They came in to finish a talk we had been having at the club.

KATE. An interesting talk, evidently.

SIR HARRY. The papers had been full that evening of the elopement of some countess woman with a fiddler. What was her name?

KATE. Does it matter?

SIR HARRY. No. (*Thus ends the countess*) We had been discussing the thing and—(*he pulls a wry face*)—and I had been rather warm——

KATE (*with horrid relish*). I begin to see. You had been saying it served the husband right, that the man who could not look after his wife deserved to lose her. It was one of your favorite subjects. Oh, Harry, say it was that!

SIR HARRY (*sourly*). It may have been something like that.

KATE. And all the time the letter was there, waiting; and none of you knew except the clock. Harry, it is sweet of you to tell me. (*His face is not sweet. The illiterate woman has used the wrong adjective*) I forget what I said precisely in the letter.

SIR HARRY (*pulverizing her*). So do I. But I have it still.

KATE (*not pulverized*). Do let me see it again. (*She has observed his eye wandering to the desk.*)

SIR HARRY. You are welcome to it as a gift. (*The fateful letter, a poor little dead thing, is brought to light from a locked drawer.*)

KATE (*taking it*). Yes, this is it. Harry, how you did crumple it! (*She reads, not without curiosity*) "Dear husband—I call you that for the last time—I am off. I am what you call making a bolt of it. I won't try to excuse myself nor to explain, for you would not accept the excuses nor understand the explanation. It will be a little shock to you,

but only to your pride; what will astound you is that any woman could be such a fool as to leave such a man as you. I am taking nothing with me that belongs to you. May you be very happy.—Your ungrateful KATE. P.S.—You need not try to find out who he is. You will try, but you won't succeed." (*She folds the nasty little thing up*) I may really have it for my very own?

SIR HARRY. You really may.

KATE (*impudently*). If you would care for a typed copy——?

SIR HARRY (*in a voice with which he used to frighten his grandmother*). None of your sauce! (*Wincing*) I had to let them see it in the end.

KATE. I can picture Jack Lamb eating it.

SIR HARRY. A penniless parson's daughter.

KATE. That is all I was.

SIR HARRY. We searched for the two of you high and low.

KATE. Private detectives?

SIR HARRY. They couldn't get on the track of you.

KATE (*smiling*). No?

SIR HARRY. But at last the courts let me serve the papers by advertisement on a man unknown, and I got my freedom.

KATE. So I saw. It was the last I heard of you.

SIR HARRY (*each word a blow for*

her). And I married again just as soon as ever I could.

KATE. They say that is always a compliment to the first wife.

SIR HARRY (*violently*). I showed them.

KATE. You soon let them see that if one woman was a fool, you still had the pick of the basket to choose from.

SIR HARRY. By James, I did.

KATE (*bringing him to earth again*). But still, you wondered who he was.

SIR HARRY. I suspected everybody —even my pals. I felt like jumping at their throats and crying, "It's you!"

KATE. You had been so admirable to me, an instinct told you that I was sure to choose another of the same.

SIR HARRY. I thought, it can't be money, so it must be looks. Some dolly face. (*He stares at her in perplexity.*) He must have had something wonderful about him to make you willing to give up all that you had with me.

KATE (*as if he was the stupid one*). Poor Harry.

SIR HARRY. And it couldn't have been going on for long, for I would have noticed the change in you.

KATE. Would you?

SIR HARRY. I knew you so well.

KATE. You amazing man.

SIR HARRY. So who was he? Out with it.

KATE. You are determined to know?

SIR HARRY. Your promise. You gave your word.

KATE. If I must—— (*She is the villain of the piece, but it must be conceded that in this matter she is reluctant to pain him*) I am sorry I promised. (*Looking at him steadily*) There was no one, Harry; no one at all.

SIR HARRY (*rising*). If you think you can play with me——

KATE. I told you that you wouldn't like it.

SIR HARRY (*rasping*). It is unbelievable.

KATE. I suppose it is; but it is true.

SIR HARRY. Your letter itself gives you the lie.

KATE. That was intentional. I saw that if the truth were known you might have a difficulty in getting your freedom; and as I was getting mine it seemed fair that you should have yours also. So I wrote my good-bye in words that would be taken to mean what you thought they meant, and I knew the law would back you in your opinion. For the law, like you, Harry, has a profound understanding of women.

SIR HARRY (*trying to straighten himself*). I don't believe you yet.

KATE (*looking not unkindly into the soul of this man*). Perhaps that is the best way to take it. It is less unflattering than the truth. But you were the only one. (*Summing up her life*) You sufficed.

SIR HARRY. Then what mad impulse——

KATE. It was no impulse, Harry. I had thought it out for a year.

SIR HARRY. A year? (*Dazed*) One would think to hear you that I hadn't been a good husband to you.

KATE (*with a sad smile*). You were a good husband according to your lights.

SIR HARRY (*stoutly*). I think so.

KATE. And a moral man, and chatty, and quite the philanthropist.

SIR HARRY (*on sure ground*). All women envied you.

KATE. How you loved me to be envied.

SIR HARRY. I swaddled you in luxury.

KATE (*making her great revelation*). That was it.

SIR HARRY (*blankly*). What?

KATE (*who can be serene because it is all over*). How you beamed at me when I sat at the head of your fat dinners in my fat jewellery, surrounded by our fat friends.

SIR HARRY (*aggrieved*). They weren't so fat.

KATE (*a side issue*). All except those who were so thin. Have you ever noticed, Harry, that many

jewels make women either incredibly fat or incredibly thin?

SIR HARRY (*shouting*). I have not. (*Is it worth while to argue with her any longer?*) We had all the most interesting society of the day. It wasn't only business men. There were politicians, painters, writers——

KATE. Only the glorious, dazzling successes. Oh, the fat talk while we ate too much—about who had made a hit and who was slipping back, and what the noo house cost and the noo motor and the gold soup-plates, and who was to be the noo knight.

SIR HARRY (*who it will be observed is unanswerable from first to last*). Was anybody getting on better than me, and consequently you?

KATE. Consequently me! Oh, Harry, you and your sublime religion.

SIR HARRY (*honest heart*). My religion? I never was one to talk about religion, but——

KATE. Pooh, Harry, you don't even know what your religion was and is and will be till the day of your expensive funeral. (*And here is the lesson that life has taught her*) One's religion is whatever he is most interested in, and yours is Success.

SIR HARRY (*quoting from his morning paper*). Ambition—it is the last infirmity of noble minds.

KATE. Noble minds!

SIR HARRY (*at last grasping what she is talking about*). You are not saying that you left me because of my success?

KATE. Yes, that was it. (*And now she stands revealed to him*) I couldn't endure it. If a failure had come now and then—but your success was suffocating me. (*She is rigid with emotion*) The passionate craving I had to be done with it, to find myself among people who had not got on.

SIR HARRY (*with proper spirit*). There are plenty of them.

KATE. There were none in our set. When they began to go down-hill they rolled out of our sight.

SIR HARRY. (*clinching it*). I tell you I am worth a quarter of a million.

KATE (*unabashed*). That is what you are worth to yourself. I'll tell you what you are worth to me: exactly twelve pounds. For I made up my mind that I could launch myself on the world alone if I first proved my mettle by earning twelve pounds; and as soon as I had earned it I left you.

SIR HARRY (*in the scales*). Twelve pounds!

KATE. That is your value to a woman. If she can't make it she has to stick to you.

SIR HARRY (*remembering perhaps a rectory garden*). You valued me at more than that when you married me.

KATE (*seeing it also*). Ah, I didn't know you then. If only you had been a man, Harry.

SIR HARRY. A man? What do you mean by a man?

KATE (*leaving the garden*). Haven't you heard of them? They are something fine; and every woman is loathe to admit to herself that her husband is not one. When she marries, even though she has been a very trivial person, there is in her some vague stirring toward a worthy life, as well as a fear of her capacity for evil. She knows her chance lies in him. If there is something good in him, what is good in her finds it, and they join forces against the baser parts. So I didn't give you up willingly, Harry. I invented all sorts of theories to explain you. Your hardness—I said it was a fine want of maukishness. Your coarseness—I said it goes with strength. Your contempt for the weak—I called it virility. Your want of ideals was clear-sightedness. Your ignoble views of women—I tried to think them funny. Oh, I clung to you to save myself. But I had to let go; you had only the one quality, Harry, success; you had it so strong that it swallowed all the others.

SIR HARRY (*not to be diverted from the main issue*). How did you earn that twelve pounds?

KATE. It took me nearly six months; but I earned it fairly. (*She presses her hand on the typewriter as lovingly as many a woman has pressed a rose*) I learned this. I hired it and taught myself. I got some work through a friend, and with my first twelve pounds I paid for my machine. Then I considered that I was free to go, and I went.

SIR HARRY. All this going on in my house while you were living in the lap of luxury! (*She nods*) By God you were determined.

KATE (*briefly*). By God, I was.

SIR HARRY (*staring*). How you must have hated me.

KATE (*smiling at the childish word*). Not a bit—after I saw that there was a way out. From that hour you amused me, Harry; I was even sorry for you, for I saw that you couldn't help yourself. Success is just a fatal gift.

SIR HARRY. Oh, thank you.

KATE (*thinking, dear friends in front, of you and me perhaps*). Yes, and some of your most successful friends knew it. One or two of them used to look very sad at times, as if they thought they might have come to something if they hadn't got on.

SIR HARRY (*who has a horror of sacrilege*). The battered crew you live among now—what are they but folk who have tried to succeed and failed?

KATE. That's it; they try, but they fail.

SIR HARRY. And always will fail.

KATE. Always. Poor souls—I say of them. Poor soul—they say of me. It keeps us human. That is why I never tire of them.

SIR HARRY (*comprehensively*). Bah! Kate, I tell you I'll be worth half a million yet.

KATE. I'm sure you will. You're getting stout, Harry.

SIR HARRY. No, I'm not.

KATE. What was the name of that fat old fellow who used to fall asleep at our dinner-parties?

SIR HARRY. If you mean Sir William Crackley——

KATE. That was the man. Sir William was to me a perfect picture of the grand success. He had got on so well that he was very, very stout, and when he sat on a chair it was thus (*her hands meeting in front of her*)—as if he were holding his success together. That is what you are working for, Harry. You will have that and the half million about the same time.

SIR HARRY (*who has surely been very patient*). Will you please to leave my house.

KATE (*putting on her gloves, soiled things*). But don't let us part in anger. How do you think I am looking, Harry, compared to the dull, inert thing that used to roll round in your padded carriages?

SIR HARRY (*in masterly fashion*). I forget what you were like. I'm very sure you never could have held a candle to the present Lady Sims.

KATE. That is a picture of her, is it not?

SIR HARRY (*seizing his chance again*). In her wedding-gown. Painted by an R.A.

KATE (*wickedly*). A knight?

SIR HARRY (*deceived*). Yes.

KATE (*who likes LADY SIMS: a piece of presumption on her part*). It is a very pretty face.

SIR HARRY (*with the pride of possession*). Acknowledged to be a beauty everywhere.

KATE. There is a merry look in the eyes, and character in the chin.

SIR HARRY (*like an auctioneer*). Noted for her wit.

KATE. All her life before her when that was painted. It is a *spirituelle* face too. (*Suddenly she turns on him with anger, for the first and only time in the play*) Oh, Harry, you brute!

SIR HARRY (*staggered*). Eh? What?

KATE. That dear creature capable of becoming a noble wife and mother —she is the spiritless woman of no account that I saw here a few minutes ago. I forgive you for myself, for I escaped, but that poor lost soul, oh, Harry, Harry.

SIR HARRY (*waving her to the door*). I'll thank you— If ever there was a woman proud of her husband and happy in her married life, that woman is Lady Sims.

KATE. I wonder.

SIR HARRY. Then you needn't wonder.

KATE (*slowly*). If I was a husband —it is my advice to all of them—I would often watch my wife quietly to see whether the twelve-pound look was not coming into her eyes. Two boys, did you say, and both like you?

SIR HARRY. What is that to you?

KATE (*with glistening eyes*). I was only thinking that somewhere there are two little girls who, when they grow up—the dear, pretty girls who are all meant for the men that don't get on! Well, good-bye, Sir Harry.

SIR HARRY (*showing a little human weakness, it is to be feared*). Say first that you're sorry.

KATE. For what?

SIR HARRY. That you left me. Say you regret it bitterly. You know you do. (*She smiles and shakes her head. He is pettish. He makes a terrible announcement*) You have spoilt the day for me.

KATE (*to hearten him*). I am sorry for that; but it is only a pin-prick, Harry. I suppose it is a little jarring in the moment of your triumph to find that there is—one old friend— who does not think you a success; but you will soon forget it. Who cares what a typist thinks?

SIR HARRY (*heartened*). Nobody. A typist at eighteen shillings a week!

KATE (*proudly*). Not a bit of it, Harry. I double that.

SIR HARRY (*neatly*). Magnificent! (*There is a timid knock at the door.*)

LADY SIMS. May I come in?

SIR HARRY (*rather appealingly*). It is Lady Sims.

KATE. I won't tell. She is afraid to come into her husband's room without knocking!

SIR HARRY. She is not. (*Uxoriously*) Come in, dearest.

(*Dearest enters carrying the sword. She might have had the sense not to bring it in while this annoying person is here.*)

LADY SIMS (*thinking she has brought her welcome with her*). Harry, the sword has come.

SIR HARRY (*who will dote on it presently*). Oh, all right.

LADY SIMS. But I thought you were so eager to practice with it.
(*The person smiles at this. He wishes he had not looked to see if she was smiling.*)

SIR HARRY (*sharply*). Put it down. (LADY SIMS *flushes a little as she lays the sword aside.*)

KATE (*with her confounded courtesy*). It is a beautiful sword, if I may say so.

LADY SIMS (*helped*). Yes.
(*The person thinks she can put him in the wrong, does she? He'll show her.*)

SIR HARRY (*with one eye on* KATE). Emmy, the one thing your neck needs is more jewels.

LADY SIMS (*faltering*). More!

SIR HARRY. Some ropes of pearls. I'll see to it. It's a bagatelle to me. (KATE *conceals her chagrin, so she had better be shown the door. He rings*) I won't detain you any longer, miss.

KATE. Thank you.

LADY SIMS. Going already? You have been very quick.

SIR HARRY. The person doesn't suit, Emmy.

LADY SIMS. I'm sorry.

KATE. So am I, madam, but it can't be helped. Good-bye, your ladyship —good-bye, Sir Harry. (*There is a suspicion of an impertinent curtsey, and she is escorted off the premises by* TOMBES. *The air of the room is purified by her going.* SIR HARRY *notices it at once.*)

LADY SIMS (*whose tendency is to say the wrong thing*). She seemed such a capable woman.

SIR HARRY (*on his hearth*). I don't like her style at all.

LADY SIMS (*meekly*). Of course you know best. (*This is the right kind of woman.*)

SIR HARRY (*rather anxious for corroboration*). Lord, how she winced when I said I was to give you those ropes of pearls.

LADY SIMS. Did she? I didn't notice. I suppose so.

SIR HARRY (*frowning*). Suppose? Surely I know enough about women to know that.

LADY SIMS. Yes, oh yes.

SIR HARRY (*odd that so confident a man should ask this*). Emmy, I know you well, don't I? I can read you like a book, eh?

LADY SIMS (*nervously*). Yes, Harry.

SIR HARRY (*jovially, but with an inquiring eye*). What a different existence yours is from that poor lonely wretch's.

LADY SIMS. Yes, but she has a very contented face.

SIR HARRY (*with a stamp of his foot*). All put on. What?

LADY SIMS (*timidly*). I didn't say anything.

SIR HARRY (*snapping*). One would think you envied her.

LADY SIMS. Envied? Oh no—but I thought she looked so alive. It was while she was working the machine.

SIR HARRY. Alive! That's no life. It **is** you that are alive. (*Curtly*) I'm busy, Emmy. (*He sits at his writing-table.*)

LADY SIMS (*dutifully*). I'm sorry; I'll go, Harry. (*inconsequentially*) Are they very expensive?

SIR HARRY. What?

LADY SIMS. Those machines?
(*When she has gone the possible meaning of her question startles him. The curtain hides him from us, but we may be sure that he will soon be bland again. We have a comfortable feeling, you and I, that there is nothing of* HARRY SIMS *in us.*)

The Green Cockatoo

A GROTESQUE IN ONE ACT

BY ARTHUR SCHNITZLER

TRANSLATED FROM THE GERMAN
BY ETHEL VAN DER VEER

CHARACTERS

EMILE, *Duc de Cadignan*
FRANCOIS, *Viccmte de Nogeant*
ALBIN, *Chevalier de la Tremouille*
MARQUIS DE LANSAC
SÉVERINE, *his wife*
ROLLIN, *a poet*
PROSPÈRE, *host of "The Green Cockatoo," formerly manager of a theater*
HENRI ⎫
BALTHASAR ⎪
GUILLAUME ⎪
SCAEVOLA ⎪
JULES ⎬ *Prospère's troupe*
ETIENNE ⎪
MAURICE ⎪
GEORGETTE ⎪
MICHETTE ⎪
FLIPOTTE ⎭
LÉOCADIE, *an actress, Henri's wife*
GRASSET, *a philosopher*
LEBRÊT, *a tailor*
GRAIN, *a tramp*
A SERGENT DE VILLE
ARISTOCRATS, ACTORS *and* ACTRESSES, *and* CITIZENS

The action occurs in Paris on the 14th of July, 1789, in the tap-room of
"The Green Cockatoo."

THE GREEN COCKATOO

SCENE—*The tap-room of The Green Cockatoo. A not large cellar-room. Up right, a flight of seven steps, closed off at the top by a door, leads to the street. There is a second door up left, which is hardly visible. Almost the entire floor space is occupied by plain wooden tables surrounded by chairs. Left, is a kind of service bar, behind which are a number of casks, with spigots for drawing off wine. The room is lighted by oil lamps which hang from the ceiling. The proprietor,* PROSPÈRE, *is on the scene.*

(*Enter* GRASSET.)

GRASSET (*on the steps*). In here, Lebrêt. I know this place. My old friend the proprietor will have a barrel of wine hidden somewhere, even though the whole of Paris is dry.

(LEBRÊT *comes in.*)

PROSPÈRE. Good evening, Grasset. I'm glad you've shown up at last. Gone sour on Philosophy? Looking for another engagement with me?

GRASSET. To be sure. But for the moment I am the guest and you are the host. So bring us some wine.

PROSPÈRE. Wine? Now where should I get wine, Grasset? Last night they emptied all the wine-shops in Paris. And I'll wager you were mixed up in it, too.

GRASSET. Bring on the wine. Because the mob will follow us in an hour. (*Listening*) Do you hear anything, Lebrêt?

LEBRÊT. A rumble—like soft thunder.

GRASSET. Good—citizens of Paris. . . . (*To* PROSPÈRE) You have plenty for the mob. Bring some for us. My friend and admirer the Citi-zen Lebrêt, tailor of the Rue St. Honoré, will pay for everything.

LEBRÊT. Yes, certainly I'll pay. (PROSPÈRE *hesitates.*)

GRASSET. Show him you have some money, Lebrêt. (LEBRÊT *displays his purse.*)

PROSPÈRE. Well, I'll see if I— (*He fills two glasses from a spigot*) Where do you come from, Grasset? From the Palais Royal?

GRASSET. But yes, I just made a speech there. My friend, I'm in the running now. Can you imagine after whom I spoke?

PROSPÈRE. Well?

GRASSET. After Camille Desmoulins! Yes, I actually took the risk. And tell me, Lebrêt, who received the greater applause, Desmoulins or I?

LEBRÊT. You did—undoubtedly.

GRASSET. And how did I do?

LEBRÊT. Splendidly.

GRASSET. You hear that, Prospère? I climbed on the table . . . I looked as impressive as a monument . . . and thousands—five thousand, ten thousand, surrounded me—just as they did Camille Desmoulins . . . and how they applauded me!

LEBRÊT. It was a big demonstration.

GRASSET. And a very loud one. But they have heeded my words and have gone to the Bastile. And I promise you that before the night is over it will fall.

PROSPÈRE. If your speech could crumble the walls—

GRASSET. My speech indeed! Are you deaf? They are making an end of it. Our brave soldiers are with us. They will use their God-given courage on that damn prison. You know that behind those walls their fathers and brothers are confined. But they wouldn't have shot—if we hadn't talked. My dear Prospère, the power of the spirit is invincible. (*To* LEBRÊT) Where are the papers?

LEBRÊT (*producing them*). Here.

GRASSET. Here are the latest pamphlets, which are now being distributed in the Palais Royal. Here is one from my friend Cerutti: RECORDS FOR THE PEOPLE OF PARIS. Here is one from Desmoulins, without doubt a better orator than a writer: FRANCE FREED.

PROSPÈRE. When is your own pamphlet going to appear, the one you are always talking about?

GRASSET. We don't need any more. The time has come for deeds. The man who sits at home these days is a coward. The real men are on the streets.

PROSPÈRE. Bravo! Bravo!

GRASSET. In Toulon they killed the Mayor. In Brignolles they have plundered a hundred houses. Only the Parisians have been sluggards and allowed themselves to remain passive.

PROSPÈRE. That can no longer be said.

LEBRÊT (*who has been drinking steadily*). Rise, comrades! On to freedom!

GRASSET. Right! . . . Close up your shop, Prospère, and come along with us.

PROSPÈRE. I'll come freely, when the time is ripe.

GRASSET. Of course—when the danger is over.

PROSPÈRE. My dear friend, I love freedom as much as you do. But first I have my business to think about.

GRASSET. From now on there is only one business for the citizens of Paris; to set your brothers free.

PROSPÈRE. That's all very well for those who have nothing else to do.

LEBRÊT. What does he say? . . . He is making fun of us!

PROSPÈRE. That never would occur to me. But get along now. My performance is about to begin. And I can't use you in that.

LEBRÊT. What kind of a performance? Is this a theater?

PROSPÈRE. Certainly it's a theater. Your friend here played with us for a fortnight.

LEBRÊT. You played here, Grasset? And do you let this fellow poke fun at you without punishing him for it?

GRASSET. Keep quiet . . . it's true. I have played here. But this is not a wineshop . . . it's a criminal rendezvous. Come along.

PROSPÈRE. But first you'll have to pay.

LEBRÊT. If it's true that this is a criminal's hang-out, I'll not pay you a sou.

PROSPÈRE (to GRASSET). Explain to your friend the kind of place he is in.

GRASSET. It's a remarkable place. People come here who play at being criminals, and also others who really are criminals and don't know it.

LEBRÊT. So—?

GRASSET. I should like to call your attention to the fact that what I just said was exceedingly witty. It could have been made the hit of an entire speech.

LEBRÊT. I fail to understand you.

GRASSET. I have told you that Prospère was once my manager. He now directs his comedies in a quite original manner. My old colleagues sit around here and act as if they were criminals. Do you understand? They tell hair-raising tales of lives they never lived, of crimes they never committed. . . . And the public that haunts this place feels the agreeable thrill of contact with the most dangerous characters of Paris —with thieves and crooks and murderers—and—

LEBRÊT. What kind of a public?

PROSPÈRE. The aristocrats of Paris.

GRASSET. Nobility . . .

PROSPÈRE. The Gentlemen of the Court—

LEBRÊT. Down with them!

GRASSET. This is the very thing for them. A sauce for their sated palates, a thrill for their blasé nerves. It was here my own aims began, Lebrêt. Here I made my first speech—in the manner of a jest. . . . And here is where I first began to hate the aristos, with their beautiful clothes, their perfumes and full stomachs. . . . And I am very glad, my good Lebrêt, to ha   you see the place where the greatness of your friend first began to take shape. . . . (In another tone) Say, Prospère, suppose this whole affair were to go up in smoke.

PROSPÈRE. Which affair?

GRASSET. My great political career. . . . Would you reengage me?

PROSPÈRE. Not for the world.

GRASSET (lightly). Why not? Isn't there possibly a chance for anyone besides your Henri?

PROSPÈRE. Perhaps, but in your case —I have always feared you would some day forget yourself and do an injury to one of my paying guests. You might sometime, under the excitement of the moment, let yourself go.

GRASSET (flattered). Well, that would be possible.

PROSPÈRE. Yes. I have to use great restraint, myself. . . .

GRASSET. Truly, Prospère, I could admire your self-control—if I didn't know that you were a coward.

PROSPÈRE. Ah, my friend, I am satisfied with the opportunities afforded by my profession. It gives me much gratification to tell those people exactly what I think of them, straight to their faces. I bawl them out to my heart's content, while they regard it as a joke. It is an art to find an outlet for one's rancor. (*He draws a dagger and allows the lights to play upon it.*)

LEBRÊT. Citizen Prospère, what does that mean?

GRASSET. Have no fear. I bet you that dagger isn't even sharpened.

PROSPÈRE. You might lose, my friend. Some day it may be that a joke will turn out to be deadly serious. And for that time I am prepared.

GRASSET. That day is near. We are living in great times. Come, Citizen Lebrêt, we must join our comrades. (*To* PROSPÈRE) Good-bye. You'll see me come back as a great man— or—never.

LEBRÊT (*at the steps*). As a great man . . . or . . . never.
(*They go out.* PROSPÈRE *sits on a table, opens a pamphlet and begins to read aloud.*)

PROSPÈRE. "Now the beast is in the noose—strangle it!" Hmm—he doesn't write badly, this little Desmoulins. "Never has richer booty been offered for the taking. Forty thousand palaces and castles, two fifths of all the wealth of France, will be the reward of valor. The ones who believe themselves in power will be overthrown. The nation will be born anew."
(*A* SERGENT DE VILLE *enters.*)

PROSPÈRE (*looking him over*). Hmm—the rabble appears early tonight.

SERGENT. Spare me your wit, my dear Prospère. I am now the officer of your district.

PROSPÈRE. And what can I do for you?

SERGENT. I am ordered to attend your performance this evening.

PROSPÈRE. I am much honored.

SERGENT. That is not the intention. The authorities wish to know exactly what occurs here. During the last few weeks—

PROSPÈRE. This is a place of amusement, Mr. Sergent, nothing more.

SERGENT. Let me continue. For some weeks this place has been the scene of vile orgies.

PROSPÈRE. You've been misinformed, Mr. Officer. We just have a little fun, and that's all there is to it.

SERGENT. It may begin so, but my information goes further. You were once an actor?

PROSPÈRE. Director. Manager of an admirable company which last played in St. Denis.

SERGENT. That's immaterial. You came into a small inheritance?

PROSPÈRE. But not worth mentioning.

SERGENT. Your troupe was dispersed?

PROSPÈRE. Also the inheritance.

SERGENT. Good. So you opened this wine-room.

PROSPÈRE. It paid very little.

SERGENT. And then you got hold of an idea—which I must say was rather original.

PROSPÈRE. You make me very proud, Mr. Sergent.

SERGENT. No matter. You collected your troupe of actors and let them give a performance which I'm told is peculiar—and even questionable.

PROSPÈRE. Questionable? If it were, I could not hold my audiences—the finest audiences in Paris. The Vicomte de Nogeant is my daily guest. The Marquis de Lansac comes frequently, and the Duc de Cadignan, Mr. Sergent, is a warm admirer of my leading actor, the celebrated Henri Baston.

SERGENT. And he also admires the art—or the arts—of your actresses?

PROSPÈRE. Were you to see my little actresses, you couldn't blame any one for admiring them.

SERGENT. Enough. It is reported that the amusement offered by your —what shall I say—?

PROSPÈRE. The word "artists" would do.

SERGENT. I shall use the word "hirelings." The amusement offered by your hirelings goes far beyond what is permissible. We are told that your people make speeches here that are —what does my report say? (*He reads from a notebook:*) "that are not only immoral"—which would bother us very little—"but also seditious and inciting"—and in times like these—the State cannot wink at them.

PROSPÈRE. Mr. Officer, I answer these accusations only by a most polite invitation to attend the performance. You will then see for yourself that nothing seditious goes on here. Also that my audience is not one which would be susceptible to sedition. We give a theatrical performance, and that is all.

SERGENT. Naturally I cannot accept your invitation, as I must remain here in my official capacity.

PROSPÈRE. I believe I can give you excellent entertainment, Mr. Sergent. But you'll permit the advice that you remove your insignia and appear in civilian clothes? The presence of a police-officer, were it known to them, would make my actors self-conscious, and the mood of my audience would also suffer.

SERGENT. You are quite right. I will disappear for a while and return as a young man of fashion.

PROSPÈRE. Which should be easy for you, Mr. Officer. But even as a vagabond you would not attract attention. Only as an officer of the law.

SERGENT. Good-bye—for the moment.

PROSPÈRE (*bows ironically after him*). When the blessed day arrives, when I see you and your like— (GRAIN *comes in. He is a tramp, ragged and dirty, and looks alarmed at seeing a policeman. The* SERGENT DE VILLE *looks him over, then smiles.*)

SERGENT (*to* PROSPÈRE). One of your artists arriving? (*Goes out.*)

GRAIN (*whiningly, pathetically*). Good evening.

PROSPÈRE (*after a long scrutiny*). If you are one of my players, then I certainly must compliment you, for I don't recognize you.

GRAIN. What do you mean?

PROSPÈRE. Stop your fooling and take off your wig. I want to know who you are. (*He tugs at* GRAIN's *hair.*)

GRAIN. Ouch!

PROSPÈRE. By thunder . . . it's real hair . . . who the devil are you? You seem to be a genuine tramp.

GRAIN. But yes.

PROSPÈRE. What do you want, then?

GRAIN. I have the honor of speaking to the landlord of The Green Cockatoo?

PROSPÈRE. I am he.

GRAIN. My name is Grain . . . sometimes Carniche . . . some call me Whining Brimstone. But I was in prison under the name of Grain, so that's the most real to me.

PROSPÈRE. Ah—I understand. You wish me to engage you, so you at once begin to enact your part. Very good. Continue.

GRAIN. Citizen Prospère, please don't take me for a swindler. I am a man of honor. When I tell you that I have been in prison, that's the plain truth. (PROSPÈRE *regards him sceptically.*)

GRAIN (*taking a paper from his pocket*). Look at this, Citizen Prospère. It will show you that I was released yesterday afternoon at four o'clock.

PROSPÈRE (*looking at the paper*). After two years of imprisonment. . . . by thunder, this is genuine.

GRAIN. Were you still in doubt?

PROSPÈRE. What did you do, that they locked you up for two years?

GRAIN. They would have hanged me, but happily I was still half a child when I murdered my poor aunt.

PROSPÈRE. Man alive! How could any one murder his aunt?

GRAIN. Citizen Prospère, I wouldn't have done it if my aunt had not been false to me, and with my best friend.

PROSPÈRE. Your aunt?

GRAIN. Yes. We were more to each other than is usual between aunts and nephews. Our family relationships were peculiar. . . . I was embittered, highly embittered. Shall I tell you about it?

PROSPÈRE. Go right ahead. Tell me

the rest, and perhaps we can come to an agreement.

GRAIN. My sister was no more than half a child when she ran away from home. Could you guess with whom?

PROSPÈRE. I've no idea.

GRAIN. With her uncle. Then he left her in the lurch—with a child.

PROSPÈRE. With a whole child—I hope?

GRAIN. It is indelicate of you, Citizen Prospère, to make light of such matters.

PROSPÈRE. Let me tell you something, you Whining Brimstone. Your family affairs bore me. Do you think I'm here to listen to every chance ragamuffin's story of his murders? What is it to me? I take it you want something—

GRAIN. Yes indeed, Citizen Prospère. I've come to ask you for work.

PROSPÈRE (loftily). Let me call your attention to the fact that this is a pleasure resort. There are no aunts to be murdered here.

GRAIN. Oh, one was enough for me. I wish to become an upright man. I was sent to you.

PROSPÈRE. By whom?

GRAIN. A most kindly young man who shared my cell with me for the last three days. Now he is there alone. His name is Gaston, and you know him.

PROSPÈRE. Gaston! Now I know why he hasn't shown up for three nights.

He is one of my best men for the pickpocket act. Such stories as he can tell—they bring down the house.

GRAIN. Yes, yes. But now they have caught him.

PROSPÈRE. How could they catch him, when he has never really stolen?

GRAIN. But he has. Though it must have been for the first time, for he was incredibly clumsy. Imagine— (Lamentingly) on the Boulevard des Capucines—he simply ripped open a lady's pocket and pulled out her purse. A rank amateur. You've inspired me with confidence, so I'll confess to you that there was a time when I also was up to little tricks like that. But never without my dear father. It was in my childhood days, and we all lived together, and my poor aunt was still alive—

PROSPÈRE. What are you lamenting? I think it very poor taste. Didn't you kill her yourself?

GRAIN. Too late. But the reason I came to ask you to take me on— I'll be just the opposite to Gaston. He first played the thief and then became one. While I—

PROSPÈRE. You look the part. I'll try you out. Then, at a given moment, you simply tell the whole story about your aunt. Just as it was. Some one will lead the way with a question.

GRAIN. I thank you, Citizen Prospère. And about my salary—

PROSPÈRE. Tonight you'll be playing on trial. For that I cannot pay.

But you'll get plenty to eat and plenty to drink, and I'll hand you a couple of francs for your night's lodging.

GRAIN. I thank you. And you'll introduce me to your company as a visitor from the provinces?

PROSPÈRE. Oh no. I shall tell them at once that you are a real murderer. They will be delighted.

GRAIN. Excuse me—of course I want to put my best foot forward—but I don't exactly understand—

PROSPÈRE. You'll understand better after you've worked with them a little while. (SCAEVOLA and JULES enter.)

SCAEVOLA. Good evening, director!

PROSPÈRE. Host, if you please. How often must I tell you that if you address me as director, the whole show will be ruined.

SCAEVOLA. Whatever you say. But I don't believe we will play tonight.

PROSPÈRE. Why not?

SCAEVOLA. The people won't be in the mood. There is a terrific racket going on in the streets, and the mob in front of the Bastile is screaming with frenzy.

PROSPÈRE. What is that to us? For two months the noise has been going on, and our audience has never failed us. They enjoy themselves as always.

SCAEVOLA. Yes. Like the gaiety of people who are about to be hanged.

PROSPÈRE. Oh, that I may live to see it!

SCAEVOLA. Meanwhile, give us something to drink, to put us in the right mood. I haven't been in the right mood all day.

PROSPÈRE. That is frequently the case, my friend. I want to tell you that you were not very satisfactory last evening.

SCAEVOLA. In what way, may I ask?

PROSPÈRE. Your story of the burglary was utter piffle.

SCAEVOLA. Piffle!

PROSPÈRE. Precisely. It was absolutely unconvincing. Ranting alone is insufficient.

SCAEVOLA. I never rant!

PROSPÈRE. You always do. I'll have to rehearse these things with you. I can't depend on your inspiration, as I do with Henri—

SCAEVOLA. Henri! Always Henri! Henri is nothing but a stage-hand compared with me. My burglary was a masterpiece. Henri couldn't equal it in a lifetime. If I am not satisfactory to you, my friend, I'll go to a regular theater. This place is only a blot, a smear. (He sees GRAIN) Ah! Who is this? Not one of us. Have you already engaged a new performer, Prospère? What sort of a make-up does he think that is?

PROSPÈRE. Don't get uneasy, he's not a professional actor, but a real murderer.

SCAEVOLA. Indeed! (*Goes to* GRAIN) Delighted to make your acquaintance. My name is Scaevola.

GRAIN. I am called Grain. (JULES *has all the while been walking back and forth in the tap-room, occasionally halting, like a man greatly disturbed in mind.*)

PROSPÈRE. What's the matter with you, Jules?

JULES. I am rehearsing.

PROSPÈRE. As what?

JULES. A conscience-stricken soul. Tonight you will see me as a man writhing under the pangs of conscience. Look at me—look at my furrowed brow. Isn't it effective? Don't I look as if the furies of hell were after me? . . . (*He paces back and forth.*)

SCAEVOLA (*yells*). Wine! Wine here!

PROSPÈRE. Keep quiet! The audience is not yet here.
(HENRI *and* LÉOCADIE *enter.*)

HENRI. Good evening! (*With a light gesture of greeting*) Good evening, gentlemen.

PROSPÈRE. Good evening, Henri! What's this I see? You have Léocadie with you?

GRAIN (*who has been looking at* LÉOCADIE; *to* SCAEVOLA). I know her . . . (*He goes on talking with* SCAEVOLA.)

LÉOCADIE. Yes, my dear Prospère, it is I.

PROSPÈRE. Why, I haven't seen you

for a year. Let me greet you. (*Makes to kiss her.*)

HENRI. Here! Cut that out! (*His eyes rest on* LÉOCADIE *with pride, wistfulness, and a certain anxiety.*)

PROSPÈRE. But Henri . . . when we're such old friends . . . and your former manager, Léocadie!

LÉOCADIE. Ah, those were the days, Prospère! . . .

PROSPÈRE. Why sigh about it— when you've made your way so well since? To be sure, a beautiful young woman always has it easier than—

HENRI (*sharply*). Cut that out!

PROSPÈRE. Why do you flare up like that—when she's come here with you?

HENRI. Be still! . . . Since yesterday she has been my wife.

PROSPÈRE. Your wife! . . . (*To* LÉOCADIE) Is this a joke?

LÉOCADIE. No, he has really married me.

PROSPÈRE. Congratulations! . . . Here, Scaevola, Jules . . . Henri is married.

SCAEVOLA (*going to them*). My best wishes.
(JULES *shakes hands with her.*)

GRAIN (*to* PROSPÈRE). How strange! I saw this woman . . . just a few minutes after I was set free.

PROSPÈRE. How was that?

GRAIN. She was the first beautiful

woman I had seen in two years. I was greatly thrilled. But there was another gentleman with her— (*He goes on conversing with* PROSPÈRE.)

HENRI (*in an ecstatic, high-pitched tone, which must not be declamatory*). Léocadie, my beloved, my wife! . . . All that has been is now forgotten. In a moment like this, the past exists no more. (SCAEVOLA *and* JULES *have dropped back.* PROSPÈRE *comes forward.*)

PROSPÈRE. What moment?

HENRI. We have been united by the Holy Sacrament. That is stronger than human vows. Now God is watching over us, we have forgotten all that went before. A new day has dawned. Léocadie, everything between us is holy. Our kisses—once so passionate—from this day are sanctified. Léocadie, my beloved wife. (*He regards her glowingly*) Does she not look different, Prospère? Unlike when you knew her? Is her brow not purer, more serene? All that was is now no more. Is that not so, Léocadie?

LÉOCADIE. Of course, Henri.

HENRI. And all is well. Tomorrow we leave Paris. Léocadie is playing tonight for the last time at the Porte St. Martin. And for the last time, also, I play here with you.

PROSPÈRE. Have you gone crazy, Henri? You can't think of leaving me. And surely the manager of the Porte St. Martin won't let Léocadie go. She is his greatest attraction. The young men, they say, go in streams to see her.

HENRI. Be still! Léocadie is going

with me, and will never leave me. (*Brutally*) Tell them that you'll never leave me, Léocadie.

LÉOCADIE. I will never leave you.

HENRI. If you did, I should— (*Pause*) I'm weary of this life. I want rest—and rest I will have.

PROSPÈRE. But what will you do with yourself, Henri? It's ridiculous. I'll make you a proposition. Withdraw Léocadie from the Porte St. Martin—but let her come here with me. I can use an actress of talent.

HENRI. My mind is made up, Prospère. My decision is made. We leave the city. We go to the country.

PROSPÈRE. To the country? Where?

HENRI. To my old father, who lives alone in his poor village. I haven't seen him for seven years. He must have given up all hope of seeing his lost son. He'll receive us joyfully.

PROSPÈRE. And how are you going to support yourself and Léocadie? All over the land the people are dying of starvation. They are a thousand times worse off than we in the city. And don't think for a moment that you are the kind of man to labor in the fields.

HENRI. You'll find out that I am.

PROSPÈRE. There's hardly any wheat growing anywhere in France. You are going into certain misery.

HENRI. We are going into unimaginable happiness, Prospère. Isn't that so, Léocadie? Often we have dreamt about it. I look forward to the peace of the wide horizons. Yes,

Prospère, in my dreams I see myself with her, walking over lush fields, in the stillness of eventide, the starry heavens above. We are escaping from this terrible and dangerous city, and great peace will enfold us. Isn't that so, Léocadie? Have we not often dreamt of it?

LÈOCADIE. Yes, we have often dreamt about it.

PROSPÈRE. Listen to me, Henri. You must think this over well. I will gladly increase your salary. And I will pay Léocadie the same as I pay you.

LÉOCADIE. Do you hear that, Henri?

PROSPÈRE. I really can't imagine who would take your place here. No one has such clever ideas as you. No one has ever been so loved by our audiences. . . . Don't go—

HENRI. I realize, of course, that no one could take my place.

PROSPÈRE. Stay with us, Henri. (*A glance at* LÉOCADIE *informs him that she is in accord with him.*)

HENRI. The parting will be more painful for you than for me, I promise you. The regrets will all be yours. For tonight I have prepared the most dramatic of scenes, something that will cause everybody to shudder. There will be a presagement of the end of their world . . . for the end of their world is near at hand. We will hear of it from afar, Léocadie. They will tell us of it many days after it has occurred. But tonight you will all say only: Henri has never played so well before.

PROSPÈRE. What are you going to play? Do you know, Léocadie?

LÉOCADIE. Oh, I never know anything.

HENRI. Does any one realize the genius that is mine?

PROSPÈRE. We do, every one of us. That's why I insist it would be a sin to bury yourself in the country— with talents such as yours.

HENRI. I crave rest and serenity. You cannot understand that, Prospère. You've never loved—

PROSPÈRE. Oh—?

HENRI. As I love! I feel that I must be alone with her. . . . Léocadie, only in that way can we forget, and thus find peace. . . . And never before will two people have been so happy. We shall have babies. You'll make a good mother, Léocadie, and a splendid wife. Everything unlovely will have vanished. (*A long pause.*)

LÉOCADIE. It's growing late. I'm due at the theater. Good-bye, Prospère. I'm delighted to have seen your famous place, where Henri has achieved so many triumphs.

PROSPÈRE. And why have you never come before?

LÉOCADIE. Henri was not willing— on account of the young men with whom I should have to sit.

HENRI (*who has drawn near to* SCAEVOLA). Give me a swallow of that, Scaevola.

PROSPÈRE (*in a low tone, to* LÉOCADIE). A perfect fool, this Henri. If always you were only sitting with them—

LÉOCADIE. I won't let you speak to me so.

PROSPÈRE. Have a care, you little canaille— . . . Some day he'll kill you.

LÉOCADIE. What's the matter with you?

PROSPÈRE. Only yesterday you were seen with one of your fellows—

LÉOCADIE. That was no fellow, you dumbhead, that was—

HENRI (*turning to them suddenly*). What's going on here? No monkey-business, please. And no more secrets. She's my wife.

PROSPÈRE. What did you give her as a wedding present?

LÉOCADIE. Oh, Henri doesn't think about things like that.

HENRI. Well, you'll have it this very evening.

LÉOCADIE. What will it be?

SCAEVOLA *and* JULES (*simultaneously*). What are you going to give her?

HENRI (*very seriously, to* LÉOCADIE). After you shall have finished your scene at the Porte St. Martin, I shall allow you to come here and see me act. (*The* OTHERS *laugh*) Never did a bride receive a more practical gift. Come, Léocadie. So long, Prospère, I will return shortly.
(HENRI *and* LÉOCADIE *go out*. FRAN-COIS, *the* VICOMTE DE NOGEANT *and* ALBIN, CHEVALIER DE LA TREM-OUILLE *enter*.)

SCAEVOLA. What an insufferable braggart!

PROSPÈRE (*as the guests appear*). Good evening, you swine.
(ALBIN *draws back*.)

FRANCOIS (*ignoring it*). Wasn't that the little Léocadie of the Porte St. Martin who just left with Henri?

PROSPÈRE. Surely it was. And I suppose that if she took the trouble, she could make you remember that you're something of a man?

FRANCOIS (*laughing*). Possibly. It seems we have arrived rather early.

PROSPÈRE. Meantime you can amuse yourself with your country-bumpkin.
(ALBIN *rises*.)

FRANCOIS. Let him alone. I've told you of the sort of thing that goes on here. (*To* PROSPÈRE) Good host, fetch us some wine.

PROSPÈRE. I will. But the time will come when you will be thankful to have water from the Seine.

FRANCOIS. Of course, of course. But today I want wine, and of the best. (PROSPÈRE *goes to the service-bar*.)

ALBIN. What a dreadful person!

FRANCOIS. You should bear in mind that it's all a joke. But there are other places where you might hear similar things spoken in earnest.

ALBIN. Is it not frowned upon?

FRANCOIS (*laughs*). It's clear that you are fresh from the provinces.

ALBIN. Down our way things are almost as bad, nowadays. The peasants are becoming very insolent. But what is to be done about it?

FRANCOIS. What do you expect. The poor devils are hungry, and that's the whole trouble.

ALBIN. How can I help it? How can my great uncle help it?

FRANCOIS. Why do you mention your great uncle?

ALBIN. In our village they held a meeting—quite openly—where they actually called my great uncle, the Comte de la Tremouille, a grain-usurer.

FRANCOIS. Is that all!

ALBIN. Well, I should think—

FRANCOIS. Tomorrow we will go to the Palais Royal. There you'll hear the monstrous speeches made by the mob. But we let them talk, it is better so. They are good fellows at heart, and that is the safest vent for their feelings.

ALBIN (indicating SCAEVOLA and JULES). What suspicious characters! Look how they are staring at us. (He feels for his rapier.)

FRANCOIS. Don't make yourself ridiculous. (To the OTHERS) You needn't begin yet. The performance may wait until more of an audience has arrived. (To ALBIN) They are the nicest people in the world, these actors. I warrant you have often sat at table with many worse knaves.

ALBIN. But they were better dressed. (PROSPÈRE brings the wine. MICHETTE and FLIPOTTE enter.)

FRANCOIS. Bless you, my little pigeons, come over here and sit down.

MICHETTE. Come along, Flipotte. She is still so shy.

FLIPOTTE. Good evening, young gentlemen.

ALBIN. Good evening, ladies.

MICHETTE. He's a nice little dear. (Sits on ALBIN's lap.)

ALBIN. Please tell me, Francois, are these respectable women?

MICHETTE. What is he saying?

FRANCOIS. That is not quite the word. The ladies who come here . . . good heavens, Albin, but you are dense.

PROSPÈRE. What shall I bring for the duchesses?

MICHETTE. Sweet wine for me.

FRANCOIS (indicating FLIPOTTE). A friend of yours?

MICHETTE. We live together. We have only one bed between us.

FLIPOTTE (blushing). Would you mind that, when you come to see her? (Sits on FRANCOIS's lap.)

ALBIN. I wouldn't exactly call her shy—

SCAEVOLA (rises, comes threateningly to the table. To MICHETTE). So I've found you at last! (To ALBIN) And you, you miserable seducer—she is mine. (PROSPÈRE is looking on.)

FRANCOIS (*to* ALBIN). It's only a joke.

ALBIN. She isn't his—

MICHETTE. Go away. I shall sit where I like. {SCAEVOLA *stands with clenched fists.*)

PROSPÈRE (*behind*). Easy there.

SCAEVOLA. Ha, ha!

PROSPÈRE. Ha, ha! (*To* SCAEVOLA, *privately*) You haven't a sou's worth of talent. Roaring—that's all you do.

MICHETTE (*to* FRANCOIS). He used to do it much better.

SCAEVOLA (*to* PROSPÈRE). I'm not in the right mood yet. I'll do better when there are more people present. You see, Prospère, I need an audience. (*The* DUC DE CADIGNAN *comes in.*)

DUC. Already in full swing? (MICHETTE *and* FLIPOTTE *go up to him.*)

MICHETTE. My sweet duke.

FRANCOIS. Good evening, Emile. (*Introducing*) My young friend Albin, Chevalier de la Tremouille— the Duc de Cadignan.

DUC. I am charmed to meet you. (*To the girls, who are hanging on to him*) Let go of me, children. (*To* ALBIN) You've come to have a look at this queer wine-room?

ALBIN. It quite bewilders me.

FRANCOIS (*explaining*). The Chevalier has but recently come to Paris.

DUC (*laughingly*). You've chosen a good time.

ALBIN. What do you mean?

MICHETTE. He still has that delicious perfume. No other man in Paris smells so sweet.

DUC. She's comparing me with the seven or eight hundred other men she knows as well as she does me.

FLIPOTTE. May I play with your sword? (*She draws his sword from its sheath and holds it so that it reflects the light.*)

GRAIN (*to* PROSPÈRE). That's the man—the man I saw her with—. (*He talks further to* PROSPÈRE, *who seems astonished.*)

DUC. Henri not here yet? (*To* ALBIN) If you see Henri, you will not regret having come.

PROSPÈRE (*to the* DUC). So you've turned up again, have you? I'm glad, because we won't have that pleasure much longer.

DUC. Why not? I find it very pleasant here.

PROSEÈRE. I believe that. But it's quite likely that you'll be one of the first to go. . . .

ALBIN. What does that mean?

PROSPÈRE. You understand me well enough. The most fortunate will become the most unfortunate. (*Returns to the service-bar.*)

DUC. If I were the king I would make him my court jester.

ALBIN. What did he mean by saying you were too fortunate?

DUC. He means, Chevalier—

ALBIN. Oh please don't call me Chevalier. Everybody calls me Albin . . . simply Albin, because I look so young.

DUC (*smiling*). Very good. But then you must call me Emile.

ALBIN. With your permission, Emile.

DUC. They have a sinister wit, these folk.

FRANCOIS. Why sinister? To me, it's very reassuring. So long as the populace remains in jesting mood, nothing serious can happen.

DUC. Their jests have a curious twist. Only today I learned of something that gives food for thought.

FRANCOIS. Tell us.

FLIPOTTE *and* MICHETTE. Yes, tell us, sweet Duke.

DUC. Do you know Lalange?

FRANCOIS. The village? Surely. The Marquis de Montferrat has one of his finest game preserves there.

DUC. Quite so. My brother is visiting him at his castle and has just written me of the affair. In Lalange they have a mayor who is very unpopular.

FRANCOIS. Can you name one that isn't?

DUC. Now listen. The women of the village paraded around the Mayor's house, carrying a coffin.

FLIPOTTE. Carrying a coffin! Oh, I wouldn't carry a coffin for anything.

FRANCOIS. Be still! Nobody wishes you to carry a coffin. (*To the* DUC) Well?

DUC. Some of the women entered the house and told the Mayor that it was necessary he should die, but that they would give him the honor of being buried.

FRANCOIS. And did they really kill him?

DUC. No, or at least my brother did not say so.

FRANCOIS. You see! . . . Blusterers, show-offs, clowns, nothing worse. Today they are shrieking at the Bastile for a change—though they have done so half a dozen times before.

DUC. Well, if I were king I would have put a stop to it—long ago.

ALBIN. Is it true that the king is so kind and tolerant?

DUC. Have you not yet been presented to His Majesty?

FRANCOIS. The Chevalier is in Paris for the first time.

DUC. Yes, you are unbelievably young. May I ask your age?

ALBIN. It's only that I look young. I'm already seventeen.

DUC. Seventeen! How much is still before you. I have reached twenty-four and I begin already to regret how much of my youth I have squandered.

FRANCOIS. That is delicious, Duke —coming from you, who count that day as lost in which you have not won a woman or killed a man.

DUC. The pity is, one never wins the right woman, and always kills the wrong man. And so is youth wasted —just as Rollin says—

FRANCOIS. What does Rollin say?

DUC. I was thinking of his new piece they are giving at the Comédie—of that pretty simile—do you recall it?

FRANCOIS. I have no memory for verse.

DUC. Nor I, alas. I remember only the sense. He says that youth which is not enjoyed is like a feather ball left lying in the sand, instead of being tossed in the air.

ALBIN (*sagely*). Quite true.

DUC. Is it not? The feathers gradually lose their color and fall out. Far better that it should drop into a bush, where it cannot be seen.

ALBIN. What should I understand by that, Emile?

DUC. It's more a matter of feeling. Could I only repeat the verse, you'd understand at once.

ALBIN. I believe you could write verse, Emile, if you tried.

DUC. What makes you think that?

ALBIN. Since you came in, all life has seemed to flame up.

DUC (*with a smile*). Yes? Is life flaming up for you?
(*Meanwhile two more noblemen have entered and taken a distant table, where* PROSPÈRE *seems to be doing his best to insult them.*)

FRANCOIS (*to the* DUC). Won't you sit down with us?

DUC. I can't stop now. I will return later.

MICHETTE. Stay with us.

FLIPOTTE. Take me with you. (*They try to hold him.*)

PROSPÈRE (*joining them*). Leave him alone. You are not nearly bad enough to suit him. He's going out now to meet some trollop of the streets.

DUC (*ignoring him*). I can't stay now, but will surely be back in time to see Henri.

FRANCOIS. When we came in, Henri was just leaving with Léocadie.

DUC. He has married her. Did you know that?

FRANCOIS. Married, eh! What will the others say to that?

ALBIN. What others?

FRANCOIS. She is a general favorite, you know.

DUC. And he wants to take her away from Paris, or so I've been told.

PROSPÈRE (*meaningly*). So you've been told?

DUC. It's very foolish. Léocadie was created to be a great courtezan. .

FRANCOIS. As every one knows.

DUC. And could anything be more unreasonable than to take people away from their true vocation? (FRANCOIS *laughs*) I'm not jesting. Like poets and conquerors, good courtezans are born, not made.

FRANCOIS. That is paradoxical.

DUC. I'm sorry for her—and for Henri. He should stay here—no, not here. I would put him in the Comédie—though there also, no one would appreciate him as I do. But then, I often have that feeling concerning artists. If I were not the Duc de Cadignan, I should love to be an actor, a conqueror—

FRANCOIS. Like Alexander the Great.

DUC (*smiling*). Like Henri—or Alexander. (*To* FLIPOTTE) Give me my sword. (*He returns it to its scabbard. Slowly*) It is the choicest way to make sport of the world. He who can portray whatever he pleases is greater than the rest of us. (*As* ALBIN *regards him with astonishment*) Don't pay any attention to what I've said. It's true only at the moment. Good-bye.

MICHETTE. Give me a kiss before you go.

FLIPOTTE. Me, too. (*They cling to him. The* DUC *kisses them both at once and takes his leave.*)

ALBIN. A wonderful man.

FRANCOIS. Surely—in his way. But the fact that such men exist offers sufficient reason not to marry.

ALBIN. But who are these women?

FRANCOIS. Actresses—members of Prospère's troupe—
(GUILLAUME *rushes in breathlessly, goes to the table where the actors are sitting and theatrically puts his hand to his heart, apparently scarcely able to stand.*)

GUILLAUME. Saved! I'm saved!

SCAEVOLA. What's happened? What ails you?

ALBIN. What's the matter with the man?

FRANCOIS. That's only play-acting. Now watch.

ALBIN. Ah—!

MICHETTE *and* FLIPOTTE (*running to* GUILLAUME). What is it? What's the matter?

SCAEVOLA. Have a swallow—

GUILLAUME. More! More wine, Prospère! My tongue cleaves to my mouth. I've been running. They were at my heels!

JULES (*starts*). Hush! They're ever at our heels!

PROSPÈRE. Come, tell us what happened. (*Coaching the actors*) More movement—livelier, there!

GUILLAUME. Women here—where are the women? Ah—! (*An arm about* FLIPOTTE) that gives me new life. (*To* ALBIN, *who is highly impressed*) The devil take me, my boy, if I thought I should ever see you again. (*Listening*) They are coming! They are coming! (*Runs to the steps*) No, it's nothing—they—

ALBIN. How strange! There really is a noise outside, as if throngs were hurrying past. Is that just part of the stage-effects?

SCAEVOLA (*to* JULES). He does that trick every time. Silly realism.

PROSPÈRE. Now tell us why they are after you.

GUILLAUME. Nothing special—but if they get me—it will cost me my head. I set fire to a house—
(*During this scene, two more young noblemen drift in and sit at tables.*)

PROSPÈRE (*coaching* GUILLAUME). Go on—go on!

GUILLAUME. Go on? Isn't setting fire to a house sufficient?

FRANCOIS. You haven't told us why you set fire to the house.

GUILLAUME. Because the president of the Supreme Court lives in it. We chose him first—to show Parisian house-holders the danger of harboring tenants who have the power to send us poor devils to jail.

GRAIN. Good; that's very good.

GUILLAUME (*looks at* GRAIN *in surprise*). All such houses must be burned. Three more men like me, and there won't be a judge left in Paris.

GRAIN. Death to the judges!

JULES. Yes . . . but there is perhaps one Judge whom we cannot do away with.

GUILLAUME. Who is that?

JULES. The Judge that dwells within us.

PROSPÈRE. That stuff is vapid. Come, Scaevola, roar! Now is the moment.

SCAEVOLA. Bring wine, Prospère, that we may drink to the death of all the judges of France.
(*During the last words, the* MARQUIS DE LANSAC, *with his wife,* SÉVERINE, *and* ROLLIN, *the poet, have come in.*)

SCAEVOLA. Down with all those now in power! Down with them!

MARQUIS. You see, Séverine, this is the way they greet us.

ROLLIN. Marquis, I warn you.

SÉVERINE. But why?

FRANCOIS. Upon my word—the Marquise . . . allow me to kiss your hand. Good evening, Marquis. God bless you, Rollin. . . . Do you venture here, Marquise?

SÉVERINE. I've heard so much about this place. And besides, this is a day of adventure—isn't it, Rollin?

MARQUIS. Where do you suppose we've been? Yes, Vicomte, we've been to the Bastile.

FRANCOIS. Is the hullabaloo still going on there?

SÉVERINE. It looks as if they meant to storm the place.

ROLLIN (*declaims*).
It is like a river that washes away its own banks,
Like a flood that beats against the shore

In wrath that its own child, the earth,
Should dare resist its might.

SÉVERINE (*to* FRANCOIS). We drove quite close and watched it from our carriage. It was very spectacular. Great crowds are so magnificent.

FRANCOIS. Yes, if only they didn't smell so vilely.

MARQUIS. And then my wife insisted that we bring her here.

SÉVERINE. What is there so remarkable about this place?

PROSPÈRE (*to the* MARQUIS). So you're here, too, you dried-up old scoundrel! Did you bring your wife because you didn't think it safe to leave her alone at home?

MARQUISE (*forcing a smile*). He is at least original.

PROSPÈRE. Be careful you don't lose her here. These fine ladies often get an urge to find out what a real rogue is like.

ROLLIN. I suffer unspeakably, Séverine.

MARQUIS. Dear child, I warned you —but there's still time to go.

SÉVERINE. What is troubling you? I think it quite charming. Let us sit down.

FRANCOIS. Permit me, Marquise, to present the Chevalier de la Tremouille, also here for the first time. Marquis de Lansac; Rollin, our distinguished poet.
(*They exchange compliments and sit down.*)

ALBIN (*in an undertone to* FRANCOIS). Is she one of the players? It's a little confusing.

FRANCOIS. Shake up your wits, Albin. That is the real wife of the Marquis—a lady of rank.

ROLLIN (*to* SÉVERINE). Tell me that you love me.

SÉVERINE. Yes, yes, but don't ask me every few minutes.

MARQUIS. Have we missed anything?

FRANCOIS. Nothing much. That fellow over there is playing an incendiary.

SÉVERINE. Chevalier, are you not the cousin of the little Lydia de la Tremouille who was married today?

ALBIN. Yes, Marquise. That was one of my reasons for coming to Paris.

SÉVERINE. I recall now, having seen you at the church.

ALBIN (*self-consciously*). I am flattered, Marquise.

SÉVERINE (*to* ROLLIN). What a nice boy.

ROLLIN. Ah, Séverine, you never yet met a man you thought unpleasing.

SÉVERINE. Oh yes—but I married him at once.

ROLLIN. Yet I have a constant fear, Séverine, that there are moments when it is not safe for you to be with him.

PROSPÈRE (*bringing wine*). Here's

your wine. I wish it were poison, but at present I am not allowed to give you that.

FRANCOIS. That time will soon come, Prospère.

SÉVERINE (*to* ROLLIN). What's the matter with those two pretty girls, that they haven't come to our table? Now that I'm here, I want to be in everything that's going on. Thus far it has been offensively dull.

MARQUIS. Just have a little patience, Séverine.

SÉVERINE. I think that nowadays the streets are more diverting. (*To* FRANCOIS) Did you hear what happened to us yesterday when we went for a drive down the Promenade de Longchamps?

MARQUIS. I beg of you, my dear Séverine. . . .

SÉVERINE. One fellow jumped on the step of our carriage and shouted in our faces: Next year you will walk behind your coach, while we shall be riding in it.

FRANCOIS. That's rather strong.

MARQUIS. I think it indiscreet to mention these things. Paris is a little feverish—but that will soon pass.

GUILLAUME (*suddenly*). I see flames — everywhere flames — whichever way I look—red, leaping flames.

PROSPÈRE (*in low-voiced protest*). You're playing a madman, not a criminal.

SÉVERINE. He sees flames?

PROSPÈRE. This is only a prelude, Madame la Marquise.

ALBIN. I can't tell you how bewildered I feel.

MICHETTE (*goes to the* MARQUIS). I haven't greeted you yet, my sweet old pig.

MARQUIS (*embarrassed*). She is just being playful, dear Séverine.

SÉVERINE. I doubt it. Tell me, little one, how many love affairs have you had so far?

MARQUIS (*to* FRANCOIS). It's remarkable how my wife enters into the mood of this place.

ROLLIN. Quite.

MICHETTE (*to the* MARQUISE). Could you count yours?

MARQUISE. When I was your age . . . but yes, certainly.

ALBIN (*to* ROLLIN). Tell me, Monsieur Rollin, is the Marquise just acting—or is she really—? . . . I can't make it out.

ROLLIN. Reality . . . acting . . . can you always define the difference, Chevalier?

ALBIN. Why, I think so.

ROLLIN. I can't. And what I think so fascinating about this place, is that all apparent differences seem to be eliminated. Reality blends into illusion—illusion into actuality. Just look at the Marquise now, chatting with those creatures as if she were one of them. Yet she is—

ALBIN. Something entirely different.

ROLLIN I thank you, Chevalier.

PROSPÈRE (to GRAIN). How did it happen?

GRAIN. What?

PROSPÈRE. The story of your aunt, for whom you spent two years in the penitentiary.

GRAIN. I told you, I strangled her.

FRANCOIS. This fellow is weak. He must be an amateur. I've never seen him before.
(GEORGETTE comes in hastily, dressed as a prostitute of the lowest grade.)

GEORGETTE. Good evening, friends! . . . Is my Balthasar here?

SCAEVOLA. Georgette, come and sit with me. Your Balthasar will show up soon. He will have settled his affair.

GEORGETTE. If he is not here within ten minutes, he won't come.

FRANCOIS. Watch her, Marquise. She is the real wife of this Balthasar who is about to come in. She represents a common street-walker, while Balthasar is her bully. But she's actually the most faithful wife in Paris.
(BALTHASAR arrives. GEORGETTE runs to him with an embrace.)

GEORGETTE. My Balthasar! (Smiling she puts her arms about him.)

BALTHASAR. The matter is attended to. (The OTHERS listen) It was not worth the trouble—I felt almost sorry for him. You should size up your customers better, Georgette. I am sick of killing promising young men for the sake of a few francs.

FRANCOIS. Fine!

ALBIN. What—?

FRANCOIS. He gets his points over. (The SERGENT DE VILLE returns in disguise; sits at a table.)

PROSPÈRE (to the SERGENT). You arrive at an excellent time, Monsieur le Sergent. This is one of my cleverest performers.

BALTHASAR. I'm going to look for another kind of a job. I'm not without courage, but on my soul, this is a hazardous way of earning a living.

SCAEVOLA. I believe you.

GEORGETTE (to BALTHASAR). There's something else on your mind.

BALTHASAR. I'll tell you, Georgette. You are a little too nice to the young gentlemen.

GEORGETTE (to the OTHERS). You see how childish he is? I have to be nice to them, to inspire confidence.

ROLLIN. Her words are profoundly true.

BALTHASAR (to GEORGETTE). If I thought you had any feeling—

GEORGETTE. His silly jealousy will land him in his grave.

BALTHASAR. I heard a sigh, Georgette, at a moment when there already was plenty of confidence.

GEORGETTE. Of course, you can't stop pretending all of a sudden.

BALTHASAR. Beware, Georgette— the Seine is deep. (*Wildly*) You are deceiving me—

GEORGETTE. Never! I swear it!

ALBIN. I don't understand this at all.

SÉVERINE (*to* ROLLIN). She has the right idea.

ROLLIN. You think so?

MARQUISE. We can still go, Séverine.

SÉVERINE. But why? I am beginning to enjoy it.

GEORGETTE (*her arms about him*). My Balthasar, I adore you.

FRANCOIS. Bravo! Bravo!

BALTHASAR. What imbecile is that?

SERGENT. This is going too far . . . it is . . .
(MAURICE *and* ETIENNE *appear, dressed as noblemen, but the shabbiness of their costumes is not observed.*)

THE PLAYERS. Who are they?

SCAEVOLA. Devil take me if it isn't Maurice and Etienne.

GEORGETTE. As I live, it is.

BALTHASAR. Georgette!

SÉVERINE. What handsome young men!

ROLLIN. It is painful, Séverine, that every handsome face excites you so.

SÉVERINE. What do you think I came here for?

ROLLIN. At least you might tell me that you love me.

SÉVERINE (*with a look*). You have a short memory.

ETIENNE. Where do you suppose we've been today?

FRANCOIS. Pay attention, Marquis, these youths are very clever.

MAURICE. We've come from a wedding . . .

ETIENNE. You have to dress for that. Otherwise the confounded secret police are after you.

SCAEVOLA. Did you make a good haul?

PROSPÈRE. Let's see.

MAURICE (*taking several watches from his pocket*). What am I offered for these?

PROSPÈRE. For that one, a gold louis.

MAURICE. You would.

SCAEVOLA. I'd pay more. It's worth more to me.

MICHETTE. That's a woman's watch. Give it to me, Maurice.

MAURICE. What do you offer me for it?

MICHETTE. You may look at me.

MAURICE. My dear child, that is not enough.

SÉVERINE (*in a low voice*). I'll swear this is not just acting.

ROLLIN. There is an undercurrent—that's what makes it so fascinating—bits of the real flashing through.

SCAEVOLA. What wedding was it?

MAURICE. That of Mademoiselle de la Tremouille. She married the Comte de Bonville.

ALBIN. You hear that, Francois? I assure you they are real thieves.

FRANCOIS. Don't worry, Albin, I know this pair. I've seen them play a dozen times. They make a specialty of being pickpockets. (MAURICE *extracts some purses from his coat.*)

SCAEVOLA. You've done well by yourselves. Why not do well by us?

ETIENNE. It was a brilliant wedding. The entire nobility of France was there. Even the king was represented.

ALBIN (*excited*). That is all true!

MAURICE (*throws gold pieces about upon the actor's table*). That's for you, my friends, to show our loyalty.

FRANCOIS. Stage money, my dear Albin. (*He rises and picks up a few coins*) We can have some of it.

PROSPÈRE. Yes, take it—you never earned anything so honestly.

MAURICE (*holds aloft a garter set with diamonds*). To whom shall I give this? (GEORGETTE, MICHETTE *and* FLIPOTTE *hasten to him and reach for it*) Patience, my sweet mice. We'll talk it over. . . . I'll give it to the one who invents a new caress.

SÉVERINE (*to* ROLLIN). Would you allow me to compete with them?

ROLLIN. Séverine, you drive me mad.

MARQUIS. I think it is time for us to go.

SÉVERINE. By no means. I'm enjoying myself vastly. (*To* ROLLIN) I'm just getting into the spirit of it.

MICHETTE. How did you get that garter?

MAURICE. There was a great crowd in the church—and she thought I was making overtures . . .

(*All laugh. Meanwhile,* GRAIN *has "lifted"* FRANCOIS' *purse.*)

FRANCOIS (*showing the money to* ALBIN). All bogus—imitation money . . .
(GRAIN *is anxious to get out.*)

PROSPÈRE (*follows him and says softly*). Give me the purse you just took from that young man.

GRAIN. I?

PROSPÈRE. Be quick—or I'll have you set upon—

GRAIN. You needn't be rude about it. (*Gives him the purse.*)

PROSPÈRE. I have no time to search you now, and dear knows what else you've pocketed. Go back to your place.

FLIPOTTE. I know I'll win that garter.

PROSPÈRE (*to* FRANCOIS, *throwing him the purse*). There's your purse —you lost it out of your pocket.

FRANCOIS. Thanks, Prospère. (*To* ALBIN) You see how honest they are. (HENRI, *who has come in and has been sitting in the rear unobserved for some time, now rises.*)

ROLLIN. Henri! . . . Look, there's Henri!

SÉVERINE. The artist you told me about?

MARQUIS. He's the main attraction here—the reason for our coming. (HENRI *strides forward in majestic silence.*)

THE PLAYERS. What's wrong, Henri? What's the matter?

ROLLIN. Watch his expression . . . a world of suffering. He is playing the rôle of one who has committed a crime through soul-torment.

SÉVERINE. Splendid!

ALBIN. Why doesn't he commence?

ROLLIN. He's superb—watch him. . . . He's stunned by his own emotions.

FRANCOIS. But he overacts a little— seems to be preparing for a monologue.

PROSPÈRE. Henri, Henri, where have you been?

HENRI. I have just killed a man.

ROLLIN. What did I say!

PROSPÈRE. Who?

HENRI. My wife's lover.

(PROSPÈRE *looks at him and it dawns on him that it may be true.*)

HENRI (*looks up*). Yes, I've done it. Why do you stare at me so? It's the truth. It is so unexpected? You know what my wife is. It was bound to come.

PROSPÈRE. And she? Where is she?

FRANCOIS. You see, Prospère gives him his cue. How natural it all seems.
(*Noise outside, not too loud.*)

JULES. What is that noise out there?

MARQUIS. You hear it, Séverine?

ROLLIN. It sounds like troops marching by.

FRANCOIS. Oh no, it's our beloved Parisian populace—growling. (*Uneasiness in the cellar-room until the noise dies away.*)

FRANCOIS. Go on, Henri, go on.

PROSPÈRE. Tell us, Henri, where is your wife? Where did you leave her?

HENRI. Oh, I'm not worried about her. She won't die of it. This one or that one—what do these women care? There are a thousand good-looking men in Paris. What matter whether this one or that one—

BALTHASAR. May the same fate take all men who take our women—

SCAEVOLA. All who take what belongs to us!

SERGENT (*to* PROSPÈRE). These are inciting speeches.

ALBIN. It's frightful—these people are serious—mean every word they utter.

SCAEVOLA. Down with all the parasites of France. I'll wager that fellow he caught with his wife was one of the beasts who rob us of our bread.

ALBIN. I suggest that we go.

SÉVERINE. Henri! Henri!

MARQUIS. But Marquise, Séverine—!

SÉVERINE. Please, my dear Marquis, will you ask that man how he caught his wife? Or shall I ask him?

MARQUIS (unwillingly). Will you tell us, Henri, how you succeeded in catching those two?

HENRI (who has been deep in thought). Do you know my wife? She is the most beautiful and the most depraved being under the sun —and I love her. We have known each other for seven years . . . but only yesterday did she become my wife. In all those seven years, there was not one day that she did not lie to me. For everything about her lied —her eyes and her lips, her kisses and her smiles.

FRANCOIS. He overdoes it a trifle.

HENRI. Every young one and every old one—every one who attracted her, and every one who paid her— even every one who desired her— could have her . . . and I knew it.

SÉVERINE. Not every man could say as much.

HENRI. Yet nevertheless, my friends, she loved me. Can you understand that? From every one of those others, she came back to me. From the handsome ones and the ill-favored ones—from the clever ones and the stupid ones, from tramps, vagabonds, rapscallions and from cavaliers—always she came back to me.

SÉVERINE (to ROLLIN). Now if you could only understand that this coming back is the only real love . . .

HENRI. What I suffered . . . tortures . . . tortures!

ROLLIN. It gives you the shivers.

HENRI. And yesterday I married her. We dreamed—I dreamed—of our going away together, to the solitude, the infinite peace of the open country. We dreamed too of having a child.

ROLLIN (tenderly). Séverine! . . .

SÉVERINE. Yes, it's very good.

ALBIN. Francois, this man speaks the truth.

FRANCOIS. Of course, the love-story is true enough, but the murder—

HENRI. I had thought a new life had opened. But there was one man she had not yet forgotten. Today, I returned unexpectedly and found them together. Now he is no more.

THE PLAYERS. Who? . . . Who? How did it happen? . . . Where is he? . . . Are they after you? . . . How did it happen? . . . Where is she?

HENRI (always erect; in crescendo).

I had left her at the theater—it was to be her last appearance. She was on her way to her dressing room and I left her without a misgiving. But no more than a hundred steps away it began—a terrible unrest. It was as if something were compelling my return. And I did start back to the theater, then I was ashamed and walked away again. But once more, after about a hundred steps, it pulled at me again—irresistibly. Her scene is soon over—she has only to stand for a moment on the stage, half-naked—then she is through. I waited before her dressing room . . . I held my ear to the door and heard whispers—I couldn't make out the words. The whispering ceased. I forced open the door . . . (*With a cry like a wild animal*) It was the Duc le Cadignan—and I killed him!

PROSPÈRE (*fearing this is the truth*). Crazy fool!
(HENRI *gazes fixedly at him.*)

SÉVERINE. Bravo! Bravo!

ROLLIN. What are you doing, Marquise? The moment you call Bravo! the illusion is lost and all the exquisite shivers are gone.

MARQUIS. I can't say I find the shivers so agreeable. Let us applaud, friends, so that we can shake off this unpleasant feeling.
(*A murmur of Bravos! increasing in volume when all applaud.*)

PROSPÈRE (*to* HENRI). Save yourself, Henri! Go!

HENRI. What . . . what?

PROSPÈRE. That will be enough—go, make haste!

FRANCOIS. Quiet! Let's hear what Prospère says.

PROSPÈRE (*after a brief reflection*). I tell him he must flee, before the watch at the city gates are warned. (*To* HENRI) The handsome duke was a favorite of the king. He will break you on the wheel. Why didn't you put an end to that worthless wife of yours, instead?

FRANCOIS. What marvelous teamwork . . . magnificent!

HENRI. Prospère, is it you that is crazy—or I? (*He tries to read* PROSPÈRE'S *eyes.*)

ROLLIN. It's extraordinary! We all know that he is acting. And yet, if at this moment the Duc de Cadignan should walk in, we would take him for a ghost.
(*The tumult in the street has been growing in volume. Shouts and yells are heard, as the door bursts open and people press in, headed by* GRASSET, *with* LEBRÊT *following. Cries of "Vive la liberté!" outside.*)

GRASSET. Here we are, boys—in here.

ALBIN. What is this? Part of the programme?

FRANCOIS. No—I fear not.

MARQUIS. What is the meaning of this?

SÉVERINE. Who are the people?

GRASSET. Come in, children. My good friend Prospère always has a barrel of wine in reserve—and tonight we have earned it. (*Hullabaloo in the street*) Friends, brothers,

we have taken it! We have taken it!
(*Shouts of* "Vive la liberté!" *outside.*)

SÉVERINE. What is happening?

MARQUIS. Let us go! Let us go! The mob is pouring in.

ROLLIN. How do you think we can get out?

GRASSET. It has fallen—the Bastile has fallen!

PROSPÈRE. What's that you're saying? Is that true?

GRASSET. Don't you hear?
(ALBIN *would draw his sword.*)

FRANCOIS. Leave it where it is—or we are all lost.

GRASSET (*reeling down the stairs*). And if you hurry out, you'll see a merry sight. You'll see the head of our dear Delaunay stuck on the end of a pike.

MARQUIS. Is the fellow mad?

THE CROWD. Vive la liberté!

GRASSET. We lopped off the heads of a dozen of them. The Bastile is ours —the prisoners are free! Paris belongs to the people.

PROSPÈRE. Hear you—hear! Paris is ours!

GRASSET. Look how he gains courage! Yell if you like, Prospère, it can't harm you now.

PROSPÈRE (*to the* NOBLEMEN). What do you say to that, you swine? The play is ended. The joke is over.

ALBIN. Didn't I tell you?

SERGENT. Silence! (*Laughter*) I prohibit the continuance of this performance.

PROSPÈRE. He has gone mad. What is that to you now? You killed him— there's nothing more you can do.

FRANCOIS. For God's sake—is this true or not?

PROSPÈRE. Yes, it is true.

GRASSET. Henri, from now on you'll be my friend. Vive la liberté! Vive la liberté!

FRANCOIS. Henri, do speak!

HENRI. She was his mistress—the Duke's mistress. And I never knew it. And he lives . . . he still lives. (*There is a stir among the bystanders: intense interest.*)

SÉVERINE (*to the* OTHERS). Well, what is the truth?

ALBIN. For heaven's sake—
(*The* DUC DE CADIGNAN *forces his way through the crowd on the stairs.*)

SÉVERINE (*the first to observe him*). The Duke!

THE OTHERS. The Duke! The Duke!

DUC. Why yes, but what of it?

PROSPÈRE. It's a ghost.

DUC. Not so far as I know. Let me get in there.

ROLLIN. I'm positive all this was prearranged. The mob out there belong to Prospère's troupe. Bravo! Prospère, you've done it well.

DUC. How is this? You don't mean you are still dawdling here, while outside . . . don't you know, then, what is going on? . . . I have seen the head of Delaunay go past me on the end of a pole. Why do you look at me that way? (*He steps down into the room*) Henri—

FRANCOIS. Watch out for Henri! (HENRI *throws himself insanely upon the* DUC *and thrusts a dagger into his throat.*)

SERGENT (*rises*). That is going too far.

ALBIN. He is bleeding.

ROLLIN. A murder has been committed.

SÉVERINE. He is dying.

MARQUIS. I am distraught . . . dear Séverine, at having brought you to this place, and today of all days.

SÉVERINE (*a little unsteadily*). Why? I think it's thrilling. It isn't every day that you can see a real duke really murdered.

ROLLIN. I don't understand it yet. It's bewildering.

SERGENT. Quiet! No one is to leave this room.

GRASSET. What does *he* want?

SERGENT (*going to* HENRI). I arrest this man, in the name of the law.

GRASSET (*laughs*). We make the laws now, simpleton. He who wipes

out a duke is a friend of the people. Vive la liberté!

ALBIN (*with drawn sword*). Out of the way, there! . . . Follow me, my friends.
(LÉOCADIE *elbows her way in and down the stairs.*)

VOICES FROM THE CROWD. Léocadie!

OTHERS. His wife!

LÉOCADIE. Let me in! . . . I want to reach my husband. (*She runs forward, sees the* DUKE's *body and screams*) Who did this? . . . Henri! (HENRI *looks at her*) Henri—why did you do this?

HENRI. Why? . . .

LÉOCADIE. But yes, I don't have to be told—it was for my sake—and I —I am not worth it.

GRASSET (*beginning a speech*). Citizens of Paris! We wish to celebrate our victory. Chance has led us through the streets of Paris to this welcome resort. It couldn't have been a better one. Nowhere can the cry of Vive la liberté! sound more appropriate than over the dead body of a duke.
(VOICES FROM THE CROWD *call:* "Vive la liberté!")

FRANCOIS. I think we had best go. The people are mad. Let's go at once.

ALBIN. Are we going to leave the duke's body—

SÉVERINE. Vive la liberté!

MARQUIS. Are you out of your head? Have you lost your wits?

(CITIZENS, *including* PLAYERS, *shout:* "Vive la liberté!")

SÉVERINE. Rollin, wait for me tonight in front of the house. I'll throw a key down as before. I feel greatly exhilarated.

LEBRÊT. Stop these people—they are running away from us.

GRASSET. Let them go . . . for today. Let them go . . . they will not escape us.

CURTAIN

A Miracle of Saint Antony

A SATIRIC LEGEND

BY MAURICE MAETERLINCK

TRANSLATED FROM THE FRENCH
BY RALPH ROEDER

CHARACTERS

BLESSED SAINT ANTONY
GUSTAVUS
ACHILLES
THE DOCTOR
THE PASTOR
JOSEPH
A SERGEANT OF POLICE
THE MAIDEN LADY HORTENSIA
VIRGINIA
VALENTINE
AN OLD LADY
A GUEST
ANOTHER GUEST
ANOTHER GUEST
ANOTHER GUEST

The action passes at the present day in a small provincial town in the Low Countries.

A MIRACLE OF SAINT ANTONY

SCENE ONE

FIRST SCENE—*The entrance-hall of an old and spacious middle-class home-stead in a small town in the provinces. On the left the front door, giving onto the street. In the rear a small flight of steps leading up to a glass door, through which one enters the house. On the right another door. Against the walls leather-covered benches, a couple of wooden stoves and a clothes rack, on which are hats, a cape and wraps. As the curtain rises, the old drudge* VIRGINIA, *her skirts trussed up and her legs bare, stands with her feet in wooden clogs amid pails and mops, whisks and brooms, washing away the tracks on the vestibule floor. From time to time she breaks off to blow her nose voluminously and to wipe a tear away with the corner of her blue apron. There is a ring at the house door;* VIRGINIA *goes to open it, and on the sill appears, bare-headed and bare-footed, the tall and emaciated form of an old man, with scrubby beard and hair, clothed in a soiled, sack-like, faded and much dirtied cowl.*

VIRGINIA (*opening the door cautiously*). Well, what is it? God bless us! Another beggar! What are you after?

ST. ANTONY. Let me in.

VIRGINIA. No, you're too muddy. Stay out there. What do you want?

ST. ANTONY. To enter.

VIRGINIA. What for?

ST. ANTONY. To restore Miss Hortensia to life.

VIRGINIA. To restore Miss Hortensia to life? Go along! Who are you?

ST. ANTONY. Blessed Saint Antony.

VIRGINIA. Of Padua?

ST. ANTONY. The same. (*His halo glows and brightens.*)

VIRGINIA. Jesus! Jesus! And His Mother Mary! Well! Well! (*She swings the door wide open, falls on her knees and begins to pray rapidly, running through the Angelic Salutation, her hands folded on her broomstick. Then she kisses the hem of the Saint's robe and resumes mechanically and without thinking*) Blessed Saint Antony, have pity on us! Pray for us, Blessed Saint Antony! . . . Pray for us!

ST. ANTONY. Let me in and close the door.

VIRGINIA (*getting up crossly*). Well, wipe your feet there on the mat.

ST. ANTONY (*obeying her awkwardly*). She is laid out in there.

VIRGINIA (*bewildered but pleased*). How did you know that? Sure enough, she is laid out in the parlor! Oh, sir, the poor old lady! Just

169

turned seventy-seven—that ain't much, is it?—and wasn't she the God-fearing creature; you don't know the savings she laid by . . . And the money owing to her! She was rich, sure enough. She's left a neat two millions behind her. Two millions is a heap of money, ain't it?

ST. ANTONY. Yes, indeed.

VIRGINIA. And it all goes to her two nephews, Mr. Gus and Mr. Achilles and their children. Mr. Gus gets the house too. And she left a sum to the pastor and to the church and to the sexton and the sacristan and to the poor and to the Vicar and to fourteen Jesuits and to all her domestics, according to how long they was in her service. It's me that gets the most of that: I was 33 years in her service. I'm down for 3,300 francs. That's a handsome sum!

ST. ANTONY. So it is.

VIRGINIA. She paid me my just wages regular. You can say what you please . . . there ain't many a master would treat you that way, after they're dead. Oh! She was a God-fearing soul! And they're burying her today. Everybody has sent flowers. You ought to see the parlor. On the bed, on the table, on the chairs—the arm chairs—the piano —everywhere flowers! And all white, it's so pretty! We don't know where to put all the wreaths. (*There is a ring. She opens the door and comes back with two wreaths*) Here are two more. (*She scrutinizes the wreaths and weighs them in her hand*) They're fine-looking, ain't they? Just hold them a minute till I get through this washing up. (*She gives the wreaths to* SAINT ANTONY, *who takes one in each hand oblig-*

ingly) This afternoon she'll be taken to the cathedral! Everything's got to be in order and I've no more than time.

ST. ANTONY. Lead me to the corpse.

VIRGINIA. Lead you to the corpse? Now?

ST. ANTONY. Yes.

VIRGINIA. No!—no, sir! You'll have to wait awhile; they're still at table.

ST. ANTONY. God has enjoined haste; it is time to restore her to life.

VIRGINIA. You don't mean to raise her up from the dead?

ST. ANTONY. Yes.

VIRGINIA. But she's three days dead; she's stale . . .

ST. ANTONY. Therefore, on the third day, I shall raise her.

VIRGINIA. For her to live again like she used to?

ST. ANTONY. Yes.

VIRGINIA. Then we ain't to inheri' nothing?

ST. ANTONY. No.

VIRGINIA. But what'll Mr. Gus say to that?

ST. ANTONY. I don't know.

VIRGINIA. And my three thousand, three hundred francs—now, that's too bad.

ST. ANTONY. Haven't you laid by anything, Virginia?

VIRGINIA. Not a farthing . . . I've a sick sister takes every penny I earn.

ST. ANTONY. Well, if you are afraid you'll lose three thousand francs.

VIRGINIA. Three thousand, three hundred francs!

ST. ANTONY. If you're afraid you'll lose them, I shall not resurrect Miss Hortensia.

VIRGINIA. Couldn't you arrange it so she could live just the same and I needn't lose the money?

ST. ANTONY. No, one thing or the other. I have heard your prayers and returned to earth, Virginia, and now you must choose . . .

VIRGINIA (after brief reflection). Well, then . . . resurrect her. (The halo glows again) What's the matter with you now?

ST. ANTONY. You have made me happy.

VIRGINIA. And when I do that, does your thing, your lantern there, begin to shine?

ST. ANTONY. Yes;—all by itself . . .

VIRGINIA. That's queer. Don't stand so near the curtains; you'll set them on fire.

ST. ANTONY. Don't be afraid, the flame is heavenly. Lead me to the corpse.

VIRGINIA. I told you before, you must wait. I can't be disturbing them now. Can't you see they're all at table?

ST. ANTONY. Who?

VIRGINIA. Why, who do you think? The whole family! Her two nephews, Mr. Gustavus and Mr. Achilles with his wife and their children and Mr. George and Mr. Alberic and Mr. Alphonse and Mr. Desiré, and our cousins and their ladies, and the Pastor and the Doctor, and I don't know who all besides. Friends and relatives we never see before, and some from way away! They're all rich people!

ST. ANTONY. Well, well.

VIRGINIA. You see the street, coming in, didn't you?

ST. ANTONY. What street?

VIRGINIA. What street? Jesus Christ! Our street! In front of our house.

ST. ANTONY. Yes.

VIRGINIA. A grand street. Well, all the houses on the left side—except the first—you know that little one where the baker lives—they all belong to my mistress. All the houses on the right side of the street belong to Mr. Gus, twenty-two of them in all. That's a neat sum!

ST. ANTONY. Yes, indeed.

VIRGINIA (pointing to the halo). Look, your thing there; your lantern's going out.

ST. ANTONY (feeling for his halo). Yes, I'm afraid.

VIRGINIA. It don't burn very long somehow, does it?

ST. ANTONY. It depends, Virginia, on the thoughts it encounters.

VIRGINIA. Hm! . . . Well, they own woods and farms and houses, too. Mr. Gus has a big starch factory— "Gustavus's Starch, Ltd."—you heard of it, I'm sure. Yes, it's a mighty good and a mighty rich family. Four independent gentlemen in it as never did a stroke of work! They're all come to the burial, and some from way away. There's one of 'em had to travel two days in the night to be here prompt. I'll show him to you, he's got a beard. They're all at table still. We can't be disturbing them now. I tell you, it's a right big lunch; twenty-four covers. I see the bill of fare: oysters, two soups, three entrées, lobster jelly and trout à la Schubert . . . Do you know what that is?

ST. ANTONY. No.

VIRGINIA. Well, no more do I; it's something good, but not for the likes of you and me. There's no champagne on account of the mourning, but all other kinds of wine. My mistress had the best cellar in town! I'll try to sneak you out a good glass if they leave us anything. Just you wait here, I'll see what they are doing now. (*She goes up the stairs, draws the curtains aside and looks through the glass doors*) I think it's that trout—that trout à la Schubert! Oh, there's Joseph. He's just taking the pineapple off. They've a good two hours ahead of them. You'd better sit down. No, no, not on the leather there, you are too dirty; here, on this stool. I must hurry and clean up now . . . (ST. ANTONY *sits down on the stool,* VIRGINIA *goes back to her work and looks for a pail*) Look out, look out. Lift up your feet! I'm pouring the water. No! No! get out of that, you're in my way there! Sit

down in that corner! Put the stool up against the wall. (ST. ANTONY *does as he is told*) There now: you won't get wet. Ain't you hungry?

ST. ANTONY. No, thank you, but I am in a hurry; so go and tell your masters.

VIRGINIA. You're in a hurry? What have you got to do?

ST. ANTONY. A few miracles.

VIRGINIA. Well, I can't be disturbing them at table. We must wait till coffee is served. Mr. Gus might be very angry. I don't know what he'll say to you, sir: he ain't for having poor people come into his house. And you don't look over-prosperous . . .

ST. ANTONY. Saints are never prosperous.

VIRGINIA. But you get a good bit given away to you . . .

ST. ANTONY. Not everything that is given reaches Heaven, Virginia.

VIRGINIA. Don't it? And it's the priests take what we give you, is it? I've heard say that, but I wouldn't have believed it! Jesus Christ!— Listen to me!

ST. ANTONY. Well?

VIRGINIA. Do you see up there behind you—that brass tap?

ST. ANTONY. Yes.

VIRGINIA. Where the water's dribbling out—there's an empty pail behind you; suppose you was to fill it now.

ST. ANTONY. Certainly.

VIRGINIA. I'll never get this all clean if some one don't lend me a hand. And not a soul helps me; they're all off their heads. When a body dies, it's too much trouble! But I guess I know all about that! Lucky it don't happen every day, ain't it? This ain't what you'd call an easy job. I've still got the copper to shine. Now then, turn off the tap, that's it. And bring me the pail. Ain't your feet cold? Be careful of the wreaths there; lay them on the stool. That's right . . . Over there . . . (ST. ANTONY *brings her the pail*) Thank you. If you're half as honest as you are obliging. (*There is a sound of voices and of chairs being moved*) Listen! (*She goes to the glass door*) They're quarreling! No, they're just eating! Joseph's just helpin' the pastor. The master's coming out. I'll tell him you want to . . . Sh! Put down the pail! Sit down. (ST. ANTONY *obeys and is about to sit down on the stool on which the wreaths are lying*) Hey, what are you doing? You're sitting on the wreaths.

ST. ANTONY. Oh, I don't see very well!

VIRGINIA. Blockhead! They're a pretty sight now. What'll Mr. Gus say? Well, God be praised! They ain't so bad after all. Sit down over there, hold on to 'em and be quiet as a mouse. (*Kneeling in front of the Saint*) And now, sir, I would like to ask you one more thing.

ST. ANTONY. Speak; do not be afraid.

VIRGINIA. Could you give me your blessing, sir, now as we're alone? When the company comes in, I'll be sent out of the room; and I won't see you no more. I'm old and may need it.

ST. ANTONY (*rises and blesses her, his halo glowing*). I bless you, my daughter, for you are good; guileless of heart, open of mind; without fault, without fear; without reticence before the great secrets, and faithful in your small duties. Go in peace, my child, and tell your masters.

(*Exit* VIRGINIA. ST. ANTONY *sits down again on the stool. Presently the glass door opens and* GUSTAVUS *strides in followed by* VIRGINIA.)

GUSTAVUS (*his voice raised in anger*). What's the meaning of this? What do you want? Who are you?

ST. ANTONY (*rising discreetly*). Blessed Saint Antony.

GUSTAVUS. Blessed Saint——

ST. ANTONY. Of Padua.

GUSTAVUS. What kind of a hoax is this? I am not in the mood for laughing. I guess you have had too much to drink. Well, speak up: what are you here for? What do you want?

ST. ANTONY. To revive your aunt.

GUSTAVUS. Revive my—? (*To* VIRGINIA) He's drunk! Why did you let him in? (*To* ST. ANTONY) Listen to me, my man, we have no time for fooling; my aunt is to be buried today. You can come back tomorrow. Here! Here are a few farthings.

ST. ANTONY (*gently obstinate*). I wish to revive her today.

GUSTAVUS. All right, all right! after the ceremony. Come on now; here's the door.

ST. ANTONY. I shall not leave until I have revived her.

GUSTAVUS (*flaming out*). Here, you! I've had enough of this. You're getting tiresome; do you hear? My guests are waiting for me . . . (*He opens the street door*) Out with you now and quick.

ST. ANTONY. I shall not leave until I have revived . . .

GUSTAVUS. Oh, this is too . . . Well, well, we'll see whether you will or not. (*He opens the glass door and shouts*) Joseph!

JOSEPH (*appears on the step, a large steaming platter in his hand*). Yes, sir.

GUSTAVUS (*with a glance at the dish*). What's that?

JOSEPH. The fowl, sir.

GUSTAVUS. Give it to Virginia and kick this vagabond out on the street, do you hear? And promptly.

JOSEPH (*giving* VIRGINIA *the dish*). Certainly, sir. (*Going up to the Saint*) Come on, old codger, didn't you hear? You're in the wrong house! Come along with you! Get out! . . . You won't? Open the door, Virginia.

GUSTAVUS. I'll open it. (*He opens the street door.*)

JOSEPH. All right, that's enough; he ain't ridin' out . . . (*Rolling up his sleeves and spitting in his hands*) So, now, we'll see about you. (*He grasps* ST. ANTONY *firmly to swing him out, but the Saint stands rooted to the spot. Stupefied*) Well, what the . . .

GUSTAVUS. What's the matter?

JOSEPH. I don't know what's happened to him! There 'e stands like 'e was rooted and growing there. 'E won't budge.

GUSTAVUS. I'll help you. (*Both try to push* ST. ANTONY *out, but he remains immovable. Half-aside*) Well, on my soul! . . . He's dangerous. . . . Be careful . . . He's got the strength of a Hercules. We had better deal gently with him. Now listen to me, my friend, you understand, don't you, that on such a day, at the burial of my revered aunt . . .

ST. ANTONY. Whom I have come to revive from the dead . . .

GUSTAVUS. But you understand, surely, that this is scarcely the time . . . The fowl will be cold, my guests are waiting, and we are not in the mood for laughing. (ACHILLES *appears, napkin in hand, on the steps.*)

ACHILLES. What's the matter, Gus? What's wrong? We're waiting for the fowl.

GUSTAVUS. The fowl! It's this old fool who won't go out . . .

ACHILLES. Is he drunk?

GUSTAVUS. Of course.

ACHILLES. Put him out and be done with it. I don't see why our meal should be spoiled for a dirty tramp . . .

GUSTAVUS. He won't go.

ACHILLES. What's that? Won't go? We'll soon see about that.

GUSTAVUS. Try him yourself.

ACHILLES. I'm not going to take such a dirty beggar by the throat. It seems to me that's Joseph's business, or—or the coachman's . . .

GUSTAVUS. We've tried, we don't want to scuffle—in here—on such a day. (*Other guests appear at the door, most of them still with their mouths full and their napkins under their arms or around their necks.*)

A GUEST. What's it all about?

A SECOND. What are you doing, Gus?

A THIRD. What's the beggar want?

A FOURTH. Where has he sprung from?

GUSTAVUS. He won't go out. Another blunder of Virginia's. As soon as she catches sight of a beggar, she . . . she loses her head! She let this fool in; he insists on seeing Auntie and reviving her.

A GUEST. We must send for the police.

GUSTAVUS. For God's sake, no scene! I don't want the police in this house on a day like this.

ACHILLES. A moment, Gus.

GUSTAVUS. Well?

ACHILLES. Have you noticed that two or three tiles are cracked there on the left side, at the end of the corridor?

GUSTAVUS. Yes, I know. I'm going to have a mosaic floor laid in place of those tiles.

ACHILLES. It'll make it look more friendly.

GUSTAVUS. Yes—one more up to date. And in place of this door and these white curtains I thought of putting in painted window sashes, illustrating THE CHASE, INDUSTRY, and PROGRESS, with a garland of fruits and wild animals!

ACHILLES. Yes, that would be handsome.

GUSTAVUS. I'm thinking of having my office in there (*pointing to the room right*) and opposite the employees'.

ACHILLES. When are you moving in?

GUSTAVUS. A few days after the wake. It would scarcely be becoming to move in the very next day.

ACHILLES. Of course, but meanwhile, we must get rid of this—this unbidden guest.

GUSTAVUS. He acts as if he were quite at home!

ACHILLES (*to* ST. ANTONY, *sarcastically*). Won't you have a chair?

ST. ANTONY (*naïvely*). Thank you, I am not tired.

ACHILLES. Let me have a try, I'll get him out . . .
(*Approaching the* SAINT *with a friendly gesture.*)

Well, my friend, won't you tell us who you are?

ST. ANTONY. Blessed Saint Antony.

ACHILLES. Why, of course, you are! (*To the others*) He sticks to that, but he's not vicious. (*He notices the* PASTOR *among the* GUESTS *who have crowded around* SAINT ANTONY *with sceptical and derisive glances*) Ah, here's the pastor, he knows you, and wants to pay you his respects. Come on, pastor, saints are your business. I know more about farmers' machines and ploughshares. Here is a messenger from Heaven, pastor, the mighty Saint Antony himself, who would like to speak with you. (*Under his breath to the pastor*) We want you to get him quietly to the door, without letting him notice it; as soon as he is outside, good-bye and Godspeed to him!

THE PASTOR (*unctuously and paternally*). Mighty Saint Antony, your vassal in all humility bids you welcome to this world, which we praise God you have elected to honor with your presence. What does your Holiness desire?

ST. ANTONY. I wish to revive Miss Hortensia.

THE PASTOR. Poor lady, poor lady! However, such a miracle would assuredly present no difficulties to the greatest of our saints. The dear deceased had a particular cult for you. I will conduct you to her, if your Holiness will take the trouble to follow me . . . (*He goes to the street door and beckons to* ST. ANTONY) This way, please.

ST. ANTONY (*pointing to the door right*). No, that way.

THE PASTOR. Your Holiness will pardon me if I seem to contradict you; but on account of the press of mourners the corpse has been removed to the house opposite, which if I may mention it, also forms part of the property of dear deceased.

ST. ANTONY (*pointing to the door right*). In there, in there.

THE PASTOR (*more and more unctuous*). To convince yourself of the contrary, your Holiness has only to follow me a moment onto the street; from there you will see the candles and black hangings . . .

ST. ANTONY (*immovable, pointing to the door on the right*). There will I enter; there; there.

A GUEST. He's got a nerve!

GUSTAVUS. He's going a bit too far really . . .

A GUEST. Suppose we open the door and all of us rush him out . . .

GUSTAVUS. No! no! no scene! He might be nasty. He's not to be fooled with; he's got the strength of a bear. Keep your hands off. Joseph and I are strong men and we couldn't budge him.

ACHILLES. But who told him the corpse lay in there?

GUSTAVUS. Virginia, of course; she's babbled about as much as it was possible to babble.

VIRGINIA. Me, sir? No. sir! Not me, I was attending to my work. I answered Yes and No, nothing else —Didn't I, Saint Antony? (ST. ANTONY *does not reply*) Well,

Speak up when a body talks to you friendly.

ST. ANTONY. She told me nothing.

VIRGINIA. There now, you see. He's a blessed saint; he knew it all beforehand. I tell you, there's nothing he don't know.

ACHILLES (going up to the Saint ana clapping him amicably on the shoulder). Now, then, young fellow, come on; step along, come, come.

THE GUESTS. He's moving; no, he's not moving!

ACHILLES. I've an idea.

GUSTAVUS. Well?

ACHILLES. Where's the Doctor?

A GUEST. He's still at table; he's finishing his trout.

GUSTAVUS. Go and call him. (Some go off to get the doctor) You're right, he's a madman; it's the Doctor's business.

THE DOCTOR (appears with his mouth full, his napkin around his neck). What's up? Is he mad? Is he sick? Is he drunk? (Looking the SAINT over) A beggar! I can do nothing for him. Well, my friend, what's the matter with you?

ST. ANTONY. I wish to revive Miss Hortensia.

THE DOCTOR. I see you're not a medical man. Let me feel your pulse. (He feels his pulse) Do you feel any pain?

ST. ANTONY. No.

THE DOCTOR (feeling his head and brow). And here? Does it hurt when I press?

ST. ANTONY. No.

THE DOCTOR. Good, good. Do you ever suffer from vertigo?

ST. ANTONY. No.

THE DOCTOR. And in your younger days? No serious accidents? No . . . no youthful indiscretions? You understand what I mean? Or constipation? Eh? Well, and your tongue? Let me have a look at that. That's right. Now breathe deep. Deeper, deeper. That's right. What do you want here?

ST. ANTONY. To go in there.

THE DOCTOR. What for?

ST. ANTONY. To revive Miss Hortensia.

THE DOCTOR. She isn't there.

ST. ANTONY. She is there, I see her.

GUSTAVUS. He won't give it up.

ACHILLES. Couldn't you bleed him?

THE DOCTOR. What for?

ACHILLES. To put him to sleep. We could easily get him on the street then.

THE DOCTOR. No, no, that would be foolish. He's dangerous.

ACHILLES. That's the worst of it; he's equal to all of us put together. But, after all, we aren't called upon to put up with vagabonds, and drunkards and fools. Are we?

THE DOCTOR. Do you want my opinion?

GUSTAVUS. Please.

THE DOCTOR. We have to deal with a madman, who can easily become dangerous if we cross him. Furthermore, there is no disrespect intended to the dear deceased. I don't see why we should not gratify his simple desire and let him into the room for a moment.

GUSTAVUS. Never—as long as I live! What are we coming to if a stranger can force his way into a respectable family on the crazy pretext of reviving a dead woman who never did him any harm?

THE DOCTOR. As you please, it's for you to decide.

ACHILLES. The Doctor's right.

THE DOCTOR. There's nothing to fear. I hold myself personally responsible; and besides, we are all here and can go in with him.

GUSTAVUS. Well, as far as I am concerned, put an end to the matter. But don't let anybody talk about this ridiculous incident, will you?

ACHILLES. Auntie's jewels are on the chimney, Gus.

GUSTAVUS. I know. I'll keep an eye on them. (*To* THE SAINT) Well, then, come on, this way. We haven't finished lunch yet. So a little lively, please. (*All go into the room on the right, followed by* SAINT ANTONY, *whose halo suddenly flames out brilliantly.*)

SCENE TWO

A living room. In the rear on a huge canopy bedstead lies the corpse of the maiden lady, Hortensia. Two burning candles, some branches of box-wood, etc. Left, a door. Right, a glass door leading to the garden. All the characters of the first episode troop through the door (left) into the room, followed by SAINT ANTONY, *to whom* GUSTAVUS *shows the corpse.*

GUSTAVUS. Now, are you satisfied? Here lies the dear departed, quite dead, you see. And now I think we are entitled to be left alone. (*To* VIRGINIA) Lead the gentleman out by the garden door.

ST. ANTONY. One moment. (*He walks into the middle of the room and standing at the foot of the bed, turns toward the corpse and speaks in a strong, grave voice*) Arise!

GUSTAVUS. There, there, that's

enough. We can't stand by and have a stranger offend our most sacred feelings.

ST. ANTONY. Be quiet. (*He goes nearer the bed and raises his voice more commandingly*) Arise!

GUSTAVUS (*losing patience*). Now, that's enough. Here's the door.

ST. ANTONY (*in a deeper and yet more commanding voice*). Hortensia, return and arise from the dead!

(*To the consternation of all present the dead woman stirs slightly, half opens her eyes, spreads her folded hands, slowly sits up in bed, sets her cap straight on her head, and looks around her, vexed and reluctant; she then proceeds quietly to scratch off a spot of candle grease which she discovers on the arm of her night dress. For a moment an oppressive silence reigns, then* VIRGINIA *leaves the speechless group about her, hurries to the bed and throws herself into the arms of the resurrected woman.*)

VIRGINIA. Miss Hortensia! She's alive! Just look at her: she's scratching away a grease spot, she is looking for her glasses! Saint Antony! Saint Antony! A miracle! A miracle! Kneel down! Kneel down!

GUSTAVUS. Keep still, don't talk. This is not the time for . . .

ACHILLES. There is no doubt about it, she's alive.

A GUEST. It isn't possible. What has he done to her?

GUSTAVUS. You can't take it seriously. She'll relapse immediately.

ACHILLES. Just see how she stares at us.

GUSTAVUS. I don't believe it yet. What kind of a world do we live in? Where are the laws of nature? Doctor, what do you say to this?

THE DOCTOR (*embarrassed*). What do I say? Why, I say . . . I say . . . that it's none of my business—it's quite outside my field: quite absurd —and quite simple! She lives: ergo, she was never dead. That's no rea-son for throwing up your hands and crying, A Miracle!

GUSTAVUS. But didn't you say——

THE DOCTOR. What did I say? I beg you to recall that I asserted nothing, absolutely nothing; I beg you to recall that I never even certified her death, did I? I even had very grave doubts—though I did not see fit to impart them to you at the time— for fear of raising false hopes. Besides, it is not probable that she will survive this long.

ACHILLES. Meanwhile, though, we must accept the evidence of our senses, the blessed evidence of our senses!

VIRGINIA. There ain't no doubt! I told you he's a Saint, a big Saint . . . Just look, she's alive! And as fresh as a rose!

GUSTAVUS (*goes to the bed and embraces the resurrected woman*). Aunt, my dear aunt, is it really you?

ACHILLES (*also approaching the bed*). Do you know me, dear aunt? I am Achilles, your nephew.

AN OLD LADY. And me, auntie? I am your niece, Leontine.

A YOUNG GIRL. And me, godmother? I am your little Valentine to whom you left all your silver . . .

GUSTAVUS. She smiles! . . . She recognizes us all.

ACHILLES (*seeing the old lady open her mouth and move her lips*). Listen! She is trying to speak.

VIRGINIA. Heavenly Father! And she

has seen God Almighty! She'll tell us all about the marvels of Paradise! Kneel—kneel down!

ACHILLES. Listen! Listen!

HORTENSIA (*who has been eyeing* ST. ANTONY *with scorn and disgust, now speaks sharply*). What sort of a creature is that? Who has so far forgotten himself as to introduce into my apartment such a barefoot scamp? He'll ruin the carpets! Put him out at once! Virginia, haven't I told you you're not to let beggars . . .

ST. ANTONY (*raising his hand commandingly*). Silence.
(*The woman stops short and sits open-mouthed, unable to utter a sound.*)

GUSTAVUS. You must forgive her, she doesn't yet realize what she owes to you; but we—ah! we realize what we owe you! What you have accomplished today is something, I venture to say, which no one else in this room would—or rather could—accomplish! Whether it was an accident or—something higher—who can say? For my part, I will not presume to judge, but this much I will say: I am proud and happy to clasp your hand, sir.

ST. ANTONY. I wish to leave now, I have other work to do.

GUSTAVUS. Oh, don't be in such a hurry! We can't let you go empty-handed! I don't know what my aunt will want to give you—that's her business, but as far as I am concerned, I shall take the matter up with my brother-in-law, and whatever he may decide—accident or miracle—we'll pay—yes, sir, we'll

pay, and no words wasted either! Yes, sir: you shan't regret what you have done. Eh, Achilles?

ACHILLES. Why, certainly! He shan't regret what he has done.

GUSTAVUS. Well, we ain't very wealthy, of course; we've got children, and our . . . our expectations have all vanished now; but we'll prove our gratitude. The honor of the family demands it. We couldn't let it be said that a beggar, a stranger did us a—a peculiar service, and departed unrecompensed—eh? Of course, the reward will have to be in proportion to our means, which as I say are now sadly shrunken; but as far as in us lies, we will pay—pay for a good deed! To be sure, there are some services that cannot be bought—which indeed one should not attempt to pay for. But . . . Don't interrupt me . . . That's no reason for doing nothing at all. So now, tell us what you would like . . . hm . . .

ACHILLES. I propose we take up a little collection, not by way of settlement, but——

ST. ANTONY. I wish to leave. I have other work to do.

GUSTAVUS. Other work to do! It ain't polite. Now, listen to me, if you don't want to take anything—and I appreciate the delicacy of your feelings and bow to them—at least you will give us the pleasure, won't you, of accepting some small souvenir? A cigar-holder, say, or a stud-pin, or a meerschaum pipe. I can have your name, address, and date of birth engraved on it.

ST. ANTONY. I can accept nothing.

GUSTAVUS. You mean that?

ST. ANTONY. Yes.

ACHILLES (*taking out his cigar case*). Well, at least you'll do us the honor of smoking a cigar with us?

ST. ANTONY. Thank you. I don't smoke.

ACHILLES. Wait, I've an idea. Since the gentleman won't accept anything—and, like my brother, I appreciate and applaud his delicacy of feeling, as I am sure we all do—for life is a treasure that can't be bought —well, then, since he has shown himself so disinterested, perhaps he will do us the honor of lunching with us, of finishing the meal he has so auspiciously interrupted? What do you say?
(*Loud murmurs of assent.*)

GUSTAVUS. Yes, by all means! Come on, we are a sociable crowd: we haven't any pride or airs about us, you see . . .

ST. ANTONY. I am awaited elsewhere.

GUSTAVUS. Oh, come, you can't refuse us this! And who can be awaiting you anyway?

ST. ANTONY. Another corpse.

GUSTAVUS. Another corpse! Nothing but corpses . . . Well, I must say, I hope you don't prefer the dead to us.

ACHILLES. I know what it is . . . You would rather eat downstairs in the kitchen, wouldn't you? You'd feel more at home there.

GUSTAVUS. Then he can come upstairs for coffee.

ACHILLES. Yes, yes. Ha! Ha! That's more to his taste. Virginia, leave your mistress a moment; she doesn't need you now; take this gentleman downstairs and do him "the honors of your realm"! Ha! Ha! I guess Virginia and you won't go to sleep to-gether! (*He slaps the* SAINT *familiarly on the belly*) Ha! ha! You old hypocrite, I see through you! So run along . . . You old swindler, you damned old swindler!

VIRGINIA (*alarmed*). But, master!

GUSTAVUS. What's wrong?

VIRGINIA. I don't know; Miss Hortensia ain't free to speak no more.

GUSTAVUS. What?

VIRGINIA. No, sir, just take a look at her yourself, please, sir. She's got her mouth wide open, and moves her lips, and works her hands, but it's like her voice was gone.

GUSTAVUS. Dear Aunt, what's the matter? Is there something you want to say to us? (*She nods*) And you can't? Now, now, just make an effort, it's a little stiffness, that's all. It will soon pass. (*She makes a sign that she can no longer speak*) What's the matter with you? What do you want? (*To* ST. ANTONY) What's the meaning of this?

ST. ANTONY. She will speak no more.

GUSTAVUS. She will speak no more? But . . . but . . . she spoke just now. You heard her . . . She was rude to you.

ST. ANTONY. She will speak no more.

GUSTAVUS. Can't you give her back her voice?

ST. ANTONY. No.

GUSTAVUS. But when will her voice come back?

ST. ANTONY. Never again.

GUSTAVUS. She'll be dumb till the day of her death?

ST. ANTONY. Yes.

GUSTAVUS. Why?

ST. ANTONY. She has beheld secrets she may not reveal.

GUSTAVUS. Secrets? What secrets?

ST. ANTONY. In the world of the dead.

GUSTAVUS. In the world of the dead? This is going too far. She spoke, we heard her, we have witnesses. You've deprived her of speech with a purpose which I now begin to see through. You have betrayed our confidence.

ACHILLES. Yes, our confidence; you're absolutely irresponsible.

GUSTAVUS. Who asked you to come here anyway? It's a hard thing to say, but I'd rather see her dead than in this condition. This is too terrible, too painful for us who love her.

THE DOCTOR. Allow me a word. Be quiet, please. (Going up to the SAINT) Let me have a look at your eyes, my friend . . . Just what I thought . . . I knew what I had to expect . . . You see, she never was dead. There is nothing supernatural or mysterious about this. The fellow is simply gifted with a rather extraordinary nervous force. He came just at the right moment.

GUSTAVUS. But what are we going to do now?

THE DOCTOR. Send for the police. He's dangerous.

GUSTAVUS. That's what he deserves . . . (Shouting) Joseph!

JOSEPH. Yes, sir?

GUSTAVUS. Run to the station and fetch a couple of officers. Tell them to bring handcuffs.

JOSEPH. Yes, sir. (He runs out.)

ST. ANTONY. I ask your permission to withdraw.

GUSTAVUS. All right, you old rascal. Your time's up. You will be able to withdraw in a very few minutes, and in first rate company, too, just wait and see.

ACHILLES. And one more bit of advice . . . These gentlemen who are about to honor you with their company—talk to them of farming and stock—of stock and horseflesh! Let your trade be stock farming: that's the way to get along with them . . . Here they are.
(JOSEPH comes back accompanied by two officers and a police sergeant.)

SERGEANT (pointing to ST. ANTONY). Is that the offender?

GUSTAVUS. That's the man.

SERGEANT (laying his hand on ST. ANTONY). Your papers.

ST. ANTONY. What papers?

SERGEANT. You haven't none? I knew it. What's your name?

ST. ANTONY. Blessed Saint Antony.

SERGEANT. Saint Antony? What do you take me for? That's no Christian name. I want the other, your real one.

ST. ANTONY. I have no other.

SERGEANT. Where did you steal this garment?

ST. ANTONY. I didn't steal it. It's my own.

SERGEANT. Where were you born?

ST. ANTONY. In Padua.

SERGEANT. In Padua? Where's that? What province?

GUSTAVUS. It's in Italy, Sergeant.

SERGEANT. I know, I know, but I want him to tell me. So you're an Italian! Just what I thought. Where do you hail from?

ST. ANTONY. From Paradise.

SERGEANT. From Paradise? And what sort of a reformatory is that?

ST. ANTONY. It is the abode to which the souls of the departed in the bosom of their Maker turn . . .

SERGEANT. What has he done? . . . Stolen?

GUSTAVUS. I shouldn't like to say whether he has stolen or not. I haven't had time yet to see, and I don't believe in offhand accusations; but what he has done is, in my opinion, far worse.

SERGEANT. Of course . . . Of course!

GUSTAVUS. You know what an affliction we are laboring under, Sergeant. Apparently, he reckoned on the upset condition of the household and our grief to get a good haul. He had probably learned from an accomplice that the jewels and the silver of our dead aunt had been laid out on the chimney. Well, unluckily for him, our aunt was not dead. When she saw this suspicious-looking person in her room, she came to and began to scream for help; whereupon in revenge for his failure he deprives her of speech, and in spite of our pleading refuses to restore it to her,—naturally in the hope of being able to bring us to terms! I beg you to notice that I am not lodging a complaint, I am merely stating the facts of the case. Besides, you can ask the Doctor here.

THE DOCTOR. I will give the required information in the presence of the Police Lieutenant. If you wish I will draw up a report.

ACHILLES. He is either a malefactor or a madman, or both; in any case a dangerous individual who ought to be kept under lock and key.

SERGEANT. Of course. Rabutteau!

THE OFFICER. Yes, sir.

SERGEANT. The handcuffs.

GUSTAVUS. And now, gentlemen, after all this trouble, won't you do us the honor of drinking a glass of wine with us before you go?

SERGEANT. My word, we won't say No to that, eh, Rabutteau, particularly as our charge here don't look very sociable inclined.

GUSTAVUS. Joseph, a bottle of wine, and glasses. (*Exit* JOSEPH) We will drink to the recovery of my aunt.

SERGEANT. Not a bad idea—in such weather!

GUSTAVUS. Is it still raining?

SERGEANT. A regular flood, sir! I just stepped across the street, and look at this cloak!
(JOSEPH *returns with a tray and passes glasses to the assembled company.*)

SERGEANT (*raising his glass*). Ladies and gentlemen, your health!

GUSTAVUS. Your health, Sergeant. (*All touch glasses with the officers*) Won't you have another?

SERGEANT. I'm ready enough, I guess. (*Licking his lips*) It's a good wine, sir.

ST. ANTONY. I am thirsty. I would like a glass of water.

SERGEANT (*scornfully*). A glass of water! Ha, but to hark to the storm outside! You'll get plenty of water in a minute. Just wait, young man, till we get you out—you'll get your mouth full. Well, come on, we've delayed long enough.
(*The street bell rings.*)

GUSTAVUS. There's a ring. (JOSEPH *goes out to open the door*) How late is it? It's probably the after-dinner guests.

ACHILLES. Not yet . . . It's only three o'clock. (THE POLICE LIEUTENANT *strides in*) Here comes the Police Lieutenant, Mitou.

LIEUTENANT. Good day, ladies and gentlemen. I've heard all about it. (*Looking at* ST. ANTONY) Yes, I suspected as much, it is St. Antony himself . . . the great St. Antony of Padua.

GUSTAVUS. You know him then?

LIEUTENANT. I should say I do: We've turned him out of the hospital three times. You understand, he's a little (*he points to his forehead*) and each time he's turned out, he plays the same pranks, heals the sick, makes the halt whole, steals the doctors' work and all without a license! (*He goes up to the* SAINT *and looks him over carefully*) Yes, he's the man. Or at least, well, he's changed since his last escapade. But if it ain't he, it's his twin. I don't know, there's something about him don't seem to me quite right, but we'll see about that in court. Come on, I've got no time to waste. March, my man, march.

GUSTAVUS. Take him out this way through the garden, it won't attract so much attention.
(*The door to the garden is opened. Snow, wind, and rain drive into the room.*)

ACHILLES. Devilish weather!
(ST. ANTONY *is led to the door.*)

VIRGINIA (*hurrying forward*). But, master, the poor man . . . Look! He's barefooted!

GUSTAVUS. Well, what of it? Are we to get him a carriage or a holy shrine?

VIRGINIA. No, I'll lend him my sabots. Take them, Blessed Antony, I've got others.

ST. ANTONY (*putting on the sabots*). Thank you. (*His halo begins tc glow.*)

VIRGINIA. And aren't you wearing anything on your head? You'll catch cold.

ST. ANTONY. I have nothing.

VIRGINIA. Take my little handkerchief. I'll get you my umbrella. (*She hurries out.*)

ACHILLES. The old fool . . .

GUSTAVUS. That's all right, but meanwhile there's a devil of a draught coming in

VIRGINIA (*returns with a huge umbrella which she gives ST. ANTONY*). Here's my umbrella.

ST. ANTONY (*showing his hands*). They have bound my hands.

VIRGINIA. I'll go with you! (*She opens the umbrella and holds it over ST. ANTONY, who goes out between the two officers. The halo glows under the umbrella and the group disappears through the garden in the snow.*)

GUSTAVUS (*closing the door*). At last.

ACHILLES. What a rascal.

GUSTAVUS (*going to the bed*). Well, Aunt?

ACHILLES. What's the matter with her? She is failing.

THE DOCTOR (*hurrying up*). I don't know. I believe . . .

GUSTAVUS (*bending over the bed*). Aunt! Aunt! How are you?

THE DOCTOR. This time she is really dying. I told you so.

GUSTAVUS. Impossible.

ACHILLES. But, Doctor, is there nothing we can do?

THE DOCTOR. Nothing—unfortunately!
(*Silence. All gather around the bed.*)

GUSTAVUS (*the first to recover*). What a day!

ACHILLES. Listen! Did you ever hear such a storm?

GUSTAVUS. Well, now, you know, we were a bit hard on the poor beggar! When you come to think of it, he really didn't do us any harm . . .

The Monkey's Paw

A STORY IN THREE SCENES

BY W. W. JACOBS

DRAMATIZED BY LOUIS N. PARKER

CHARACTERS

Mr. White
Mrs. White
Herbert
Sergeant-Major Morris
Mr. Sampson

THE MONKEY'S PAW

SCENE—*The living-room of an old-fashioned cottage on the outskirts of Fulham. Set corner-wise in the left angle at the back a deep window; further front, three or four steps lead up to a door. Further forward a dresser, with plates, glasses, etc. At back an alcove with the street door fully visible. On the inside of the street door, a wire letter-box. On the right a cupboard, then a fireplace. In the center a round table. Against the wall, an old-fashioned piano. A comfortable armchair each side of the fireplace. Other chairs. On the mantelpiece a clock, old china figures, etc. An air of comfort pervades the room.*

SCENE ONE

At the rise of the curtain, MRS. WHITE, *a pleasant-looking old woman, is seated in the armchair below the fire, attending to a kettle which is steaming on the fire, and keeping a laughing eye on* MR. WHITE *and* HERBERT. *These two are seated at the right angle of the table nearest the fire with a chess-board between them.* MR. WHITE *is evidently losing. His hair is ruffled; his spectacles are high up on his forehead.* HERBERT, *a fine young fellow, is looking with satisfaction at the move he has just made.* MR. WHITE *makes several attempts to move, but thinks better of them. There is a shaded lamp on the table. The door is tightly shut. The curtains of the window are drawn; but every now and then the wind is heard whistling outside.*

MR. WHITE (*moving at last, and triumphant*). There, Herbert, my boy! Got you, I think.

HERBERT. Oh, you're a deep 'un, Dad, aren't you?

MRS. WHITE. Mean to say he's beaten you at last?

HERBERT. Lor, no! Why, he's overlooked——

MR. WHITE (*very excited*). I see it! Lemme have that back!

HERBERT. Not much. Rules of the game!

MR. WHITE (*disgusted*). I don't hold with them scientific rules. You turn what ought to be an innocent relaxation——

MRS. WHITE. Don't talk so much, Father. You put him off——

HERBERT (*laughing*). Not he!

MR. WHITE (*trying to distract his attention*). Hark at the wind.

191

HERBERT (*drily*). Ah! I'm listening. Check.

MR. WHITE (*still trying to distract him*). I should hardly think Sergeant-Major Morris'd come tonight.

HERBERT. Mate. (*Rises.*)

MR. WHITE (*with an outbreak of disgust and sweeping the chessmen off the board*). That's the worst of living so far out. Your friends can't come for a quiet chat, and you addle your brains over a confounded——

HERBERT. Now, Father! Morris'll turn up all right.

MR. WHITE (*still in a temper*). Lover's Lane, Fulham! Ho! Of all the beastly, slushy, out-o'-the-way places to live in——! Pathway's a bog, and the road's a torrent. (*To* MRS. WHITE, *who has risen, and is at his side*). What's the County Council thinking of, that's what I want to know? Because this is the only house in the road it doesn't matter if nobody can get near it, I s'pose.

MRS. WHITE. Never mind, dear. Perhaps you'll win tomorrow. (*She moves to back of table.*)

MR. WHITE. Perhaps I'll—perhaps I'll——! What d'you mean? (*Bursts out laughing*) There! You always know what's going on inside o' me, don't you, Mother?

MRS. WHITE. Ought to, after thirty years, John. (*She goes to dresser, and busies herself wiping tumblers on tray there. He rises, goes to fireplace and lights pipe.*)

HERBERT. And it's not such a bad place, Dad, after all. One of the few old-fashioned houses left near London. None o' your stucco villas. Home-like, I call it. And so do you, or you wouldn't ha bought it. (*Rolls a cigarette.*)

MR. WHITE (*growling*). Nice job I made o' that, too! With two hundred pounds owin' on it.

HERBERT (*on back of chair*). Why, I shall work that off in no time, Dad. Matter o' three years, with the rise promised me.

MR. WHITE. If you don't get married.

HERBERT. Not me. Not that sort.

MRS. WHITE. I wish you would, Herbert. A good, steady, lad——
(*She brings the tray with a bottle of whisky, glasses, a lemon, spoons, buns, and a knife to the table.*)

HERBERT. Lots o' time, Mother. Sufficient for the day—as the sayin' goes. Just now my dynamos don't leave me any time for love-making. Jealous they are, I tell you!

MR. WHITE (*chuckling*). I lay awake o' night often, and think: If Herbert took a nap, and let his what-d'you-call-ums—dynamos, run down, all Fulham would be in darkness. Lord! what a joke!

HERBERT. Joke! And me with the sack! Pretty idea of a joke you've got, I don't think.
(*Knock at outer door.*)

MRS. WHITE. Hark!
(*Knock repeated, louder.*)

MR. WHITE (*going toward door*). That's him. That's the Sergeant-Major. (*He unlocks door, back.*)

HERBERT (*removes chess-board*). Wonder what yarn he's got for us tonight. (*Places chess-board on piano.*)

MRS. WHITE (*goes up right, busies herself putting the other armchair nearer fire, etc.*). Don't let the door slam, John!
(MR. WHITE *opens the door a little, struggling with it. Wind.* SERGEANT-MAJOR MORRIS, *a veteran with a distinct military appearance—left arm gone—dressed as a commissionaire, is seen to enter.* MR. WHITE *helps him off with his coat, which he hangs up in the outer hall.*)

MR. WHITE (*at the door*). Slip in quick! It's as much as I can do to hold it against the wind.

SERGEANT. Awful! Awful! (*Busy taking off his cloak, etc.*) And a mile up the road—by the cemetery—it's worse. Enough to blow the hair off your head.

MR. WHITE. Give me your stick.

SERGEANT. If 'twasn't I knew what a welcome I'd get——

MR. WHITE (*preceding him into the room*). Sergeant-Major Morris!

MRS. WHITE. Tut! tut! So cold you must be! Come to the fire; do'ee, now.

SERGEANT. How are you, marm? (*To* HERBERT) How's yourself, laddie? Not on duty yet, eh? Day-week, eh?

HERBERT. No sir. Night week. But there's half an hour yet.

SERGEANT (*sitting in the armchair*

above the fire, toward which MRS. WHITE *is motioning him.* MR. WHITE *mixes grog for* MORRIS). Thank'ee kindly, marm. That's good—hah! That's a sight better than the trenches at Chitral. That's better than settin' in a puddle with the rain pourin' down in buckets, and the natives takin' pot-shots at you.

MRS. WHITE. Didn't you have no umbrellas? (*Corner below fire, kneels before it, stirs it, etc.*)

SERGEANT. Umbrell——? Ho! ho! That's good! Eh, White? That's good. Did ye hear what she said? Umbrellas!— *And* goloshes! *And* hot-water bottles!—Ho, yes! No offence, marm, but it's easy to see you was never a soldier.

HERBERT (*rather hurt*). Mother spoke out o' kindness, sir.

SERGEANT. And well I know it; and no offense intended. No, marm, 'ardship, 'ardship is the soldier's lot. Starvation, fever, and get yourself shot. That's a bit o' my own.

MRS. WHITE. You don't look to've taken much harm—except—— (*Indicates his empty sleeve. She takes kettle to table, then returns to fire.*)

SERGEANT (*showing a medal hidden under his coat*). And that I got this for. No, marm. Tough. Thomas Morris is tough. (MR. WHITE *is holding a glass of grog under the* SERGEANT'S *nose*) And sober. What's this now?

MR. WHITE. Put your nose in it; you'll see.

SERGEANT. Whisky? And hot? And sugar? And a slice o' lemon? No. I said I'd never—but seein' the sort o' night. Well! (*Waving the glass at them*) Here's another thousand a year!

MR. WHITE (*also with a glass*). Same to you, and many of 'em.

SERGEANT (*to* HERBERT, *who has no glass*). What? Not you?

HERBERT (*laughing and sitting across chair*). Oh! 'tisn't for want of being sociable. But my work don't go with it. Not if 'twas ever so little. I've got to keep a cool head, a steady eye, and a still hand. The fly-wheel might gobble me up.

MRS. WHITE. Don't, Herbert. (*Sits in armchair below fire.*)

HERBERT (*laughing*). No fear, Mother.

SERGEANT. Ah! You electricians!— Sort o' magicians, you are. Light! says you—and light it is. And, power! says you—and the trams go whizzin'. And, knowledge! says you —and words go 'ummin' to the ends o' the world. It fair beats me—and I've seen a bit in my time, too.

HERBERT (*nudges his father*). Your Indian magic? All a fake, Governor. The fakir's fake.

SERGEANT. Fake, you call it? I tell you, I've *seen* it.

HERBERT (*nudging his father with his foot*). Oh, come, now! Such as what? Come, now!

SERGEANT. I've seen a cove with no more clothes on than a babby, (*to* MRS. WHITE) if you know what I mean—take an empty basket—

empty, mind!—as empty as—as this here glass——

MR. WHITE. Hand it over, Morris. (*Hands it to* HERBERT, *who goes quickly behind table and fills it.*)

SERGEANT. Which was not my intentions, but used for illustration.

HERBERT (*while mixing*). Oh, I've seen the basket trick; and I've read how it was done. Why, I could do it myself, with a bit o' practice. Ladle out something stronger. (HERBERT *brings him the glass.*)

SERGEANT. Stronger?—What do you say to an old fakir chuckin' a rope up in the air—in the *air*, mind you! —and swarming up it, same as if it was 'ooked on—-and vanishing clean out o' sight?—I've seen *that*. (HERBERT *goes to table, plunges a knife into a bun and offers it to the* SERGEANT *with exaggerated politeness.*)

SERGEANT (*eyeing it with disgust*). Bun—? What for?

HERBERT. That yarn takes it. (MR. *and* MRS. WHITE *delighted.*)

SERGEANT. Mean to say you doubt my word?

MRS. WHITE. No, no! He's only taking you off.—You shouldn't, Herbert.

MR. WHITE. Herbert always was one for a bit o' fun!
(HERBERT *puts bun back on table, comes round in front, and moving the chair out of the way, sits cross-legged on the floor at his father's side.*)

SERGEANT. But it's true. Why, if I chose, I could tell you things—— But there! You don't get no more yarns out o' *me*.

MR. WHITE. Nonsense, old friend. (*Puts down his glass*) You're not going to get shirty about a bit o' fun. (*Moves his chair nearer* MOR-RIS's) What was that you started telling me the other day about a monkey's paw, or something? (*Nudges* HERBERT, *and winks at* MRS. WHITE.)

SERGEANT (*gravely*). Nothing. Leastways, nothing worth hearing.

MRS. WHITE (*with astonished curiosity*). Monkey's *paw*——?

MR. WHITE. Ah—you was tellin' me——

SERGEANT. Nothing. Don't go on about it. (*Puts his empty glass to his lips—then stares at it*) What? Empty again? There! When I begin thinkin' o' the paw, it makes me that absent-minded——

MR. WHITE (*rises and fills glass*). You said you always carried it on you.

SERGEANT. So I do, for fear o' what might happen. (*Sunk in thought*) Ay!—ay!

MR. WHITE (*handing him his glass refilled*). There. (*Sits again in same chair.*)

MRS. WHITE. What's it for?

SERGEANT. You wouldn't believe me, if I was to tell you.

HERBERT. *I* will, every word.

SERGEANT. Magic, then! Don't you laugh!

HERBERT. I'm not. Got it on you now?

SERGEANT. Of course.

HERBERT. Let's see it. (*Seeing the* SERGEANT *embarrassed with his glass,* MRS. WHITE *rises, takes it from him, places it on mantelpiece and remains standing.*)

SERGEANT. Oh, it's nothing to look at. (*Hunting in his pocket*) Just an ordinary—little paw—dried to a mummy. (*Produces it and holds it toward* MRS. WHITE) Here.

MRS. WHITE (*who has leant forward eagerly to see it, starts back with a little cry of disgust*). Oh!

HERBERT. Give us a look. (*MORRIS passes the paw to* MR. WHITE, *from whom* HERBERT *takes it*) Why, it's all dried up!

SERGEANT. I said so.
(*Wind.*)

MRS. WHITE (*with a slight shudder*). Hark at the wind! (*Sits again in her old place.*)

MR. WHITE (*taking the paw from* HERBERT). And what might there be special about it?

SERGEANT (*impressively*). That there paw has had a spell put upon it!

MR. WHITE No? (*In great alarm he thrusts the paw back into* MORRIS's *hand.*)

SERGEANT (*pensively, holding the paw in the palm of his hand*). Ah!

By an old fakir. He was a very holy man. He'd sat all doubled up in one spot, goin' on for fifteen year; thinkin' o' things. And he wanted to show that fate ruled people. That everything was cut and dried from the beginning, as you might say. That there warn't no gettin' away from it. And that, if you tried to, you caught it hot. (*Pauses solemnly*) So he put a spell on this bit of a paw. It might ha' been anything else, but he took the first thing that came handy. Ah! He put a spell on it, and made it so that three people (*looking at them and with deep meaning*) could each have three wishes.
(*All but* MRS. WHITE *laugh rather nervously.*)

MRS. WHITE. Ssh! Don't!

SERGEANT (*more gravely*). But——! But, mark you, though the wishes was granted, those three people would have cause to wish they *hadn't* been.

MR. WHITE. But how *could* the wishes be granted?

SERGEANT. He didn't say. It would all happen so natural, you might think it a coincidence if so disposed.

HERBERT. Why haven't you tried it, sir?

SERGEANT (*gravely, after a pause*). I have.

HERBERT (*eagerly*). You've had your three wishes?

SERGEANT (*gravely*). Yes.

MRS. WHITE. Were they granted?

SERGEANT (*staring at the fire*). They were.
(*A pause.*)

MR. WHITE. Has anybody else wished?

SERGEANT. Yes. The first owner had his three wish—— (*Lost in recollection*) Yes, oh, yes, he had his three wishes all right. I don't know what his first two were, (*very impressively*) but the third was for death. (*All shudder*) That's how I got the paw.
(*A pause.*)

HERBERT (*cheerfully*). Well! Seems to me you've only got to wish for things that *can't* have any bad luck about 'em—— (*Rises.*)

SERGEANT (*shaking his head*). Ah!

MR. WHITE (*tentatively*). Morris— if you've had your three wishes— it's no good to you, now—what do you keep it for?

SERGEANT (*still holding the paw; looking at it*). Fancy, I s'pose. I did have some idea of selling it, but I don't think I will. It's done mischief enough already. Besides, people won't buy. Some of 'em think it's a fairy tale. And some want to try it first, and pay after.
(*Nervous laugh from the others.*)

MRS. WHITE. If you could have another three wishes, would you?

SERGEANT (*slowly—weighing the paw in his hand and looking at it*) I don't know—I don't know—— (*Suddenly, with violence, flinging it in the fire*) No! I'm damned if I would!
(*Movement from all.*)

MR. WHITE (*rises and quickly snatches it out of the fire*). What are you doing? (WHITE *goes to the fireplace.*)

SERGEANT (*rising and following him and trying to prevent him*). Let it burn! Let the infernal thing burn!

MRS. WHITE (*rises*). Let it burn, Father!

MR. WHITE (*wiping it on his coatsleeve*). No. If you don't want it, give it to me.

SERGEANT (*violently*). I won't! I won't! My hands are clear of it. I threw it on the fire. If you keep it, don't blame me, whatever happens. Here! Pitch it back again.

MR. WHITE (*stubbornly*). I'm going to keep it. What do you say, Herbert?

HERBERT (*laughing*). I say, keep it if you want to. Stuff and nonsense, anyhow.

MR. WHITE (*looking at the paw thoughtfully*). Stuff and nonsense. Yes. I wonder—(*casually*) I wish —— (*He was going to say some ordinary thing, like "I wish I were certain."*)

SERGEANT (*misunderstanding him; violently*). Stop! Mind what you're doing. That's not the way.

MR. WHITE. What *is* the way?

MRS. WHITE (*moving away to back of table, and beginning to put the tumblers straight, and the chairs in their places*). Oh, don't have anything to do with it, John. (*Takes glasses on tray to dresser, busies*

herself there, rinsing them in a bowl of water on the dresser, and wiping them with a cloth.*)

SERGEANT. That's what I say, marm. But if I warn't to tell him, he might go wishing something he didn't mean to. You hold it in your right hand, and wish aloud. But I warn you! I warn you!

MRS. WHITE. Sounds like the Arabian Nights. Don't you think you might wish me four pair o' hands?

MR. WHITE (*laughing*). Right you are, Mother!— I wish——

SERGEANT (*pulling his arm down*). Stop it! If you must wish, wish for something sensible. Look here! I can't stand this. Gets on my nerves. Where's my coat? (*Goes into alcove.*)
(MR. WHITE *crosses to fireplace and carefully puts the paw on mantelpiece. He is absorbed in it to the end of the tableau.*)

HERBERT. I'm coming your way, to the works, in a minute. Won't you wait? (*Helps* MORRIS *with his coat.*)

SERGEANT (*putting on his coat*). No. I'm all shook up. I want fresh air. I don't want to be here when you wish. And wish you will as soon's my back's turned. I know. I know. But I've warned you, mind.

MR. WHITE (*helping him into his coat*). All right, Morris. Don't you fret about us. (*Gives him money*) Here.

SERGEANT (*refusing it*). No, I won't——

MR. WHITE (*forcing it into his hand*). Yes, you will. (*Opens door.*)

SERGEANT (*turning to the room*). Well, good night all. (*To* WHITE) Put it in the fire.

ALL. Good night.
(*Exit* SERGEANT. MR. WHITE *closes door, comes toward fireplace, absorbed in the paw.*)

HERBERT. If there's no more in this than there is in his other stories, we shan't make much out of it.

MRS. WHITE (*to* WHITE). Did you give him anything for it, Father?

MR. WHITE. A trifle. He didn't want it, but I made him take it.

MRS. WHITE. There, now! You shouldn't. Throwing your money about.

MR. WHITE (*looking at the paw which he has picked up again*). I wonder——

HERBERT. What?

MR. WHITE. I wonder, whether we hadn't better chuck it on the fire?

HERBERT (*laughing*). Likely! Why, we're all going to be rich and famous, and happy.

MRS. WHITE. Throw it on the fire, indeed, when you've given money for it! So like you, Father.

HERBERT. Wish to be an Emperor, Father, to begin with. Then you can't be henpecked!

MRS. WHITE (*going for him front of table with a duster*). You young——! (*Follows him to back of table.*)

HERBERT (*running away from her, hiding behind table*). Steady with that duster, Mother!

MR. WHITE. Be quiet, there! (HERBERT *catches* MRS. WHITE *in his arms and kisses her*) I wonder—— (*He has the paw in his hand*) I don't know what to wish for, and that's a fact. (*He looks about him with a happy smile*) I seem to've got all I want.

HERBERT (*with his hands on the old man's shoulders*). Old Dad! If you'd only cleared the debt on the house, you'd be quite happy, wouldn't you? (*Laughing*) Well—go ahead! —wish for the two hundred pounds: that'll just do it.

MR. WHITE (*half laughing*). Shall I?

HERBERT. Go on! Here!—I'll play slow music. (*Goes to piano.*)

MRS. WHITE. Don't 'ee, John. Don't have nothing to do with it!

HERBERT. Now, Dad! (*Plays.*)

MR. WHITE. I will! (*Holds up the paw, as if half ashamed*) I wish for two hundred pounds. (*Crash on the piano. At the same instant* MR. WHITE *utters a cry and lets the paw drop.*)

MRS. WHITE *and* HERBERT. What's the matter?

MR. WHITE (*gazing with horror at the paw*). It moved! As I wished, it twisted in my hand like a snake.

HERBERT (*goes down and picks the paw up*). Nonsense, Dad. Why, it's as stiff as a bone (*Lays it on the mantelpiece.*)

MRS. WHITE. Must have been your fancy, Father.

HERBERT (*laughing*). Well——? (*Looking round the room.*) I don't see the money; and I bet I never shall.

MR. WHITE (*relieved*). Thank God, there's no harm done! But it gave me a shock.

HERBERT. Half-past eleven. I must get along. I'm on at midnight. (*Fetches his coat, etc.*) We've had quite a merry evening.

MRS. WHITE. I'm off to bed. Don't be late for breakfast, Herbert.

HERBERT. I shall walk home as usual. Does me good. I shall be with you about nine. Don't wait, though.

MRS. WHITE. You know your father never waits.

HERBERT. Good night, Mother. (*Kisses her. She lights candle on dresser, goes up stairs and exit.*)

HERBERT (*coming to his father, who is sunk in thought*). Good night, Dad. You'll find the cash tied up in the middle of the bed.

MR. WHITE (*staring, seizes* HERBERT's *hand*). It moved, Herbert.

HERBERT. Ah! And a monkey hanging by his tail from the bed-post, watching you count the golden sovereigns.

MR. WHITE (*accompanying him to the door*). I wish you wouldn't joke, my boy.

HERBERT. All right, Dad. (*Opens door*) Lord! What weather! Good night. (*Exit.*)
(*The old man shakes his head, closes the door, locks it, puts the chain up, slips the lower bolt, has some difficulty with the upper bolt.*)

MR. WHITE. This bolt's stiff again! I must get Herbert to look to it in the morning. (*Comes into the room, puts out the lamp, crosses toward steps; but is irresistibly attracted toward fireplace. Sits down and stares into the fire. His expression changes: he sees something horrible.*)

MR. WHITE (*with an involuntary cry*). Mother! Mother!

MRS. WHITE (*appearing at the door at the top of the steps with candle*). What's the matter?

MR. WHITE (*mastering himself. Rises*). Nothing—I—haha!—I saw faces in the fire.

MRS. WHITE. Come along. (*She takes his arm and draws him toward the steps. He looks back frightened toward fireplace as they reach the first step.*)

TABLEAU CURTAIN

SCENE TWO

Bright sunshine. The table, which has been moved nearer the window, is laid for breakfast. MRS. WHITE *busy about the table.* MR. WHITE *standing in the window looking off. The inner door is open, showing the outer door.*

MR. WHITE. What a morning Herbert's got for walking home!

MRS. WHITE. What's o'clock? (*Looks at clock on mantelpiece*) Quarter to nine, I declare. He's off at eight. (*Crosses to fire.*)

MR. WHITE. Takes him half an hour to change and wash. He's just by the cemetery now.

MRS. WHITE. He'll be here in ten minutes.

MR. WHITE (*coming to the table*). What's for breakfast?

MRS. WHITE. Sausages. (*At the mantelpiece*) Why, if here isn't that dirty monkey's paw! (*Picks it up, looks at it with disgust, puts it back. Takes sausages in dish from before fire and places them on table*) Silly thing! The idea of us listening to such nonsense!

MR. WHITE (*goes up to window again*). Ay—the Sergeant-Major and his yarns! I suppose all old soldiers are alike——

MRS. WHITE. Come on, Father. Herbert hates us to wait. (*They both sit and begin breakfast.*)

MRS. WHITE. How could wishes be granted, nowadays?

MR. WHITE. Ah! Been thinking about it all night, have you?

MRS. WHITE. You kept me awake, with your tossing and tumbling——

MR. WHITE. Ay, I had a bad night.

MRS. WHITE. It was the storm, I expect. How it blew!

MR. WHITE. I didn't hear it. I was asleep and not asleep, if you know what I mean.

MRS. WHITE. And all that rubbish about its making you unhappy if your wish *was* granted! How could two hundred pounds hurt you, eh, Father?

MR. WHITE. Might drop on my head in a lump. Don't see any other way. And I'd try to bear that. Though, mind you, Morris said it would all happen so naturally that you might take it for a coincidence, if so disposed.

MRS. WHITE. Well—it hasn't happened. That's all I know. And it isn't going to. (*A letter is seen to drop in the letter-box*) And how you can sit there and talk about it—— (*Sharp postman's knock; she jumps to her feet*) What's that?

MR. WHITE. Postman, o' course.

MRS. WHITE (*seeing the letter from a distance; in an awed whisper*). He's brought a letter, John!

MR. WHITE (*laughing*). What did

vou think he'd bring? Ton o' coals?

MRS. WHITE. John—! John—! Suppose——?

MR. WHITE. Suppose what?

MRS. WHITE. Suppose it was two hundred pounds!

MR. WHITE (*suppressing his excitement*). Eh!— Here! Don't talk nonsense. Why don't you fetch it?

MRS. WHITE (*crosses and takes letter out of the box*). It's thick, John —(*feels it*)—and—and it's got something crisp inside it. (*Takes letter to* WHITE.)

MR. WHITE. Who—who's it for?

MRS. WHITE. You.

MR. WHITE. Hand it over, then. (*Feeling and examining it with ill-concealed excitement*) The idea! What a superstitious old woman you are! Where are my specs?

MRS. WHITE. Let me open it.

MR. WHITE. Don't you touch it. Where are my specs?

MRS. WHITE. Don't let sudden wealth sour your temper, John.

MR. WHITE. *Will* you find my specs?

MRS. WHITE (*taking them off mantelpiece*). Here, John, here. (*As he opens the letter*) Take care! Don't tear it!

MR. WHITE. Tear what?

MRS. WHITE. If it was banknotes, John!

MR. WHITE (*taking a thick, formal document out of the envelope and a crisp-looking slip*). You've gone dotty.—You've made me nervous. (*Reads*) "Sir,—Enclosed please find receipt for interest on the mortgage of £200 on your house, duly received." (*They look at each other.* MR. WHITE *sits down to finish his breakfast silently.* MRS. WHITE *goes to the window.*)

MRS. WHITE. That comes of listening to tipsy old soldiers.

MR. WHITE (*pettish*). What does?

MRS. WHITE. You thought there was banknotes in it.

MR. WHITE (*injured*). I didn't! I said all along——

MRS. WHITE. How Herbert will laugh, when I tell him!

MR. WHITE (*with gruff good-humor*). You're not going to tell him. You're going to keep your mouth shut. That's what you're going to do. Why, I should never hear the last of it.

MRS. WHITE. Serve you right. I shall tell him. You know you like his fun. See how he joked you last night when you said the paw moved. (*She is looking through the window.*)

MR. WHITE. So it did. It did move. That I'll swear to.

MRS. WHITE (*abstractedly; she is watching something outside*). You thought it did.

MR. WHITE. I say it did. There was no thinking about it. You saw how it upset me, didn't you? (*She doesn't answer*) *Didn't* you?—Why don't you listen? (*Turns round*) What is it?

MRS. WHITE. Nothing.

MR. WHITE (*turns back to his breakfast*). Do you see Herbert coming?

MRS. WHITE. No.

MR. WHITE. He's about due. What *is* it?

MRS. WHITE. Nothing. Only a man. Looks like a gentleman. Leastways, he's in black, and he's got a top-hat on.

MR. WHITE. What about him? (*He is not interested; goes on eating.*)

MRS. WHITE. He stood at the garden-gate as if he wanted to come in. But he couldn't seem to make up his mind.

MR. WHITE. Oh, go on! You're full o' fancies.

MRS. WHITE. He's going—no; he's coming back.

MR. WHITE. Don't let him see you peeping.

MRS. WHITE (*with increasing excitement*). He's looking at the house. He's got his hand on the latch. No. He turns away again. (*Eagerly*) John! He looks like a sort of a lawyer.

MR. WHITE. What of it?

MRS. WHITE. Oh, you'll only laugh again. But suppose—suppose he's coming about the two hundred——

MR. WHITE. You're not to mention it again! You're a foolish old woman. Come and eat your breakfast. (*Eagerly*) Where is he now?

MRS. WHITE. Gone down the road. He has turned back. He seems to've made up his mind. Here he comes! Oh, John, and me all untidy! (*Crosses to fire. There is a knock.*)

MR. WHITE (*to* MRS. WHITE *who is hastily smoothing her hair*). What's it matter? He's made a mistake. Come to the wrong house. (*Goes to fireplace.* MRS. WHITE *opens the door.* MR. SAMPSON, *dressed from head to foot in solemn black, with a top-hat, stands in the doorway.*)

SAMPSON (*outside*). Is this Mr. White's?

MRS. WHITE. Come in, sir. Please step in. (*She shows him into the room. He is awkward and nervous*) You must overlook our being so untidy; and the room all anyhow; and John in his garden-coat. (*To* MR. WHITE, *reproachfully*) Oh, John.

SAMPSON (*to* MR. WHITE). Morning. My name is Sampson.

MRS. WHITE (*offering a chair*). Won't you please be seated? (SAMPSON *stands quite still.*)

SAMPSON. Ah—thank you—no, I think not—I think not. (*Pause.*)

MR. WHITE (*awkwardly, trying to help him*). Fine weather for the time o' year.

SAMPSON. Ah — yes — yes —— (*Pause; he makes a renewed effort*) My name is Sampson—I've come——

MRS. WHITE. Perhaps you was wishful to see Herbert; he'll be home in a minute. (*Pointing*) Here's his breakfast waiting——

SAMPSON (*interrupting her hastily*). No, no! (*Pause*) I've come from the electrical works——

MRS. WHITE. Why, you might have come *with* him.
(MR. WHITE *sees something is wrong, tenderly puts his hand on her arm.*)

SAMPSON. No—no—I've come—alone.

MRS. WHITE (*with a little anxiety*). Is anything the matter?

SAMPSON. I was asked to call——

MRS. WHITE (*abruptly*). Herbert! Has anything happened? Is he hurt? Is he hurt?

MR. WHITE (*soothing her*). There, there, Mother. Don't you jump to conclusions. Let the gentleman speak. You've not brought bad news, I'm sure, sir.

SAMPSON. I'm—sorry——

MRS. WHITE. Is he hurt? (SAMPSON *bows*) Badly?

SAMPSON. Very badly. (*Turns away.*)

MRS. WHITE (*with a cry*). John—! (*She instinctively moves toward* WHITE.)

MR. WHITE. Is he in pain?

SAMPSON. He is not in pain.

MRS. WHITE. Oh, thank God! Thank God for that! Thank—— (*She looks in a startled fashion at* MR. WHITE —realizes what SAMPSON *means, catches his arm and tries to turn him toward her*) Do you mean——?
(SAMPSON *avoids her look; she gropes for her husband: he takes her two hands in his, and gently lets her sink into the armchair above the fireplace, then he stands on her right, between her and* SAMPSON.)

MR. WHITE (*hoarsely*). Go on, sir.

SAMPSON. He was telling his mates a story. Something that had happened here last night. He was laughing, and wasn't noticing and —and—(*hushed*) the machinery caught him——
(*A little cry from* MRS. WHITE, *her face shows her horror and agony.*)

MR. WHITE (*vague, holding* MRS. WHITE'S *hand*). The machinery caught him—yes—and him the only child—it's hard, sir—very hard——

SAMPSON (*subdued*). The Company wished me to convey their sincere sympathy with you in your great loss——

MR. WHITE (*staring blankly*). Our —great—loss——!

SAMPSON. I was to say further—(*as if apologizing*) I am only their servant—I am only obeying orders——

MR. WHITE. Our—great—loss——

SAMPSON (*laying an envelope on the table and edging toward the door*).

I was to say, the Company disclaim all responsibility, but, in consideration of your son's services, they wish to present you with a certain sum as compensation. (*Gets to door.*)

MR. WHITE. Our—great—loss—— (*Suddenly, with horror*) How—how much?

SAMPSON (*in the doorway*). Twc hundred pounds. (*Exit.*)

(MRS. WHITE *gives a cry. The old man takes no heed of her, smiles faintly, puts out his hands like a sightless man, and drops, a senseless heap, to the floor.* MRS. WHITE *stares at him blankly and her hands go out helplessly toward him.*)

TABLEAU CURTAIN

SCENE THREE

Night. On the table a candle is flickering at its last gasp. The room looks neglected. MR. WHITE *is dozing fitfully in the armchair.* MRS. WHITE *is in the window peering through the blind.* MR. WHITE *starts, wakes, looks around him.*

MR. WHITE (*fretfully*). Jenny—Jenny.

MRS. WHITE (*in the window*). Yes.

MR. WHITE. Where are you?

MRS. WHITE. At the window.

MR. WHITE. What are you doing?

MRS. WHITE. Looking up the road.

MR. WHITE (*falling back*). What's the use, Jenny? What's the use?

MRS. WHITE. That's where the cemetery is; that's where we've laid him.

MR. WHITE. Ay—ay—a week today —what o'clock is it?

MRS. WHITE. I don't know.

MR. WHITE. We don't take much account of time now, Jenny, do we?

MRS. WHITE. Why should we? He

don't come home. He'll never come home again. There's nothing to think about——

MR. WHITE. Or to talk about. (*Pause*) Come away from the window; you'll get cold.

MRS. WHITE. It's colder where *he* is.

MR. WHITE. Ay—gone for ever——

MRS. WHITE. And taken all our hopes with him——

MR. WHITE. And all our *wishes*——

MRS. WHITE. Ay, and all our—— (*With a sudden cry*) John! (*She comes quickly to him; he rises.*)

MR. WHITE. Jenny! For God's sake! What's the matter?

MRS. WHITE (*with dreadful eagerness*). The *paw!* The monkey's paw!

MR. WHITE (*bewildered*). Where? Where is it? What's wrong with it?

MRS. WHITE. I want it! You haven't done away with it?

MR. WHITE. I haven't seen it—since —why?

MRS. WHITE. I want it! Find it! Find it!

MR. WHITE (*groping on the mantelpiece*). Here! Here it is! What do you want of it? (*He leaves it there.*)

MRS. WHITE. Why didn't I think of it? Why didn't *you* think of it?

MR. WHITE. Think of what?

MRS. WHITE. The *other two* wishes!

MR. WHITE (*with horror*). What?

MRS. WHITE. We've only had one.

MR. WHITE (*tragically*). Wasn't that enough?

MRS. WHITE. No! We'll have one more. (WHITE *crosses.* MRS. WHITE *takes the paw and follows him*) Take it. Take it quickly. And wish——

MR. WHITE (*avoiding the paw*). Wish what?

MRS. WHITE. Oh, John! John! Wish our boy alive again!

MR. WHITE. Good God! Are you mad?

MRS. WHITE. Take it. Take it and wish. (*With a paroxysm of grief*) Oh, my boy! My boy!

MR. WHITE. Get to bed. Get to sleep. You don't know what you're saying.

MRS. WHITE. We had the first wish granted—why not the second?

MR. WHITE (*hushed*). He's been dead ten days, and—Jenny! Jenny! I only knew him by his clothing— if you wasn't allowed to see him then—how could you bear to see him *now*?

MRS. WHITE. I don't care. Bring him back.

MR. WHITE (*shrinking from the paw*). I daren't touch it!

MRS. WHITE (*thrusting it in his hand*). Here! Here! Wish!

MR. WHITE (*trembling*). Jenny!

MRS. WHITE (*fiercely*). Wish. (*She goes on frantically whispering "Wish."*)

MR. WHITE (*shuddering, but overcome by her insistence*). I—I— wish—my—son—alive again. (*He drops it with a cry. The candle goes out. Utter darkness. He sinks into a chair.* MRS. WHITE *hurries to the window and draws the blind back. She stands in the moonlight. Pause.*)

MRS. WHITE (*drearily*). Nothing.

MR. WHITE. Thank God! Thank God!

MRS. WHITE. Nothing at all. Along the whole length of the road not a living thing. (*Closes blind*) And nothing, nothing, nothing left in our lives, John.

MR. WHITE. Except each other, Jenny—and memories.

MRS. WHITE (coming back slowly to the fireplace). We're too old. We were only alive in him. We can't begin again. We can't feel anything now, John, but emptiness and darkness. (She sinks into armchair.)

MR. WHITE. 'Tisn't for long, Jenny. There's that to look forward to.

MRS. WHITE. Every minute's long, now.

MR. WHITE (rising). I can't bear the darkness!

MRS. WHITE. It's dreary—dreary.

MR. WHITE (goes to dresser). Where's the candle? (Finds it and brings it to table) And the matches? Where are the matches? We mustn't sit in the dark. 'Tisn't wholesome. (Lights match; the other candlestick is close to him) There. (Turning with the lighted match toward MRS. WHITE, who is rocking and moaning) Don't take on so, Mother.

MRS. WHITE. I'm a mother no longer.

MR. WHITE (lights candle). There now; there now. Go on up to bed. Go on, now—I'm a-coming.

MRS. WHITE. Whether I'm here or in bed, or wherever I am, I'm with my boy, I'm with——
(A low single knock at the street door.)

MRS. WHITE (starting). What's that!

MR. WHITE (mastering his horror). A rat. The house is full of 'em. (A louder single knock; she starts up. He catches her by the arm) Stop! What are you going to do?

MRS. WHITE (wildly). It's my boy! It's Herbert! I forgot it was a mile away! What are you holding me for? I must open the door!
(The knocking continues in single knocks at irregular intervals, constantly growing louder and more insistant.)

MR. WHITE (still holding her). For God's sake!

MRS. WHITE (struggling). Let me go!

MR. WHITE. Don't open the door!
(He drags her away.)

MRS. WHITE. Let me go!

MR. WHITE. Think what you might see!

MRS. WHITE (struggling fiercely). Do you think I fear the child I bore! Let me go! (She wrenches herself loose and rushes to the door which she tears open) I'm coming, Herbert! I'm coming!

MR. WHITE (cowering in the extreme corner, left front). Don't 'ee do it! Don't 'ee do it!
(MRS. WHITE is at work on the outer door, where the knocking still continues. She slips the chain, slips the lower bolt, unlocks the door.)

MR. WHITE (suddenly). The paw! Where's the monkey's paw? (He gets on his knees and feels along the floor for it.)

MRS. WHITE (tugging at the top bolt). John! The top bolt's stuck. I can't move it. Come and help. Quick!

MR. WHITE (wildly groping). The paw! There's a wish left.

(*The knocking is now loud, and in groups of increasing length between the speeches.*)

MRS. WHITE. D'ye hear him? John! Your child's knocking!

MR. WHITE. Where is it? Where did it fall?

MRS. WHITE (*tugging desperately at the bolt*). Help! Help! Will you keep your child from his home?

MR. WHITE. Where did it fall? I can't find it—I can't find——
(*The knocking is now tempestuous, and there are blows upon the door as of a body beating against it.*)

MRS. WHITE. Herbert! Herbert! My boy! Wait! Your mother's opening to you! Ah! It's moving! It's moving!

MR. WHITE. God forbid! (*Finds the paw*) Ah!

MRS. WHITE (*slipping the bolt*). Herbert!

MR. WHITE (*has raised himself to his knees; he holds the paw high*). I wish him dead. (*The knocking stops abruptly.*) I wish him dead and at peace!

MRS. WHITE (*flinging the door open simultaneously*). Herb——
(*A flood of moonlight. Emptiness. The old man sways in prayer on his knees. The old woman lies half swooning, wailing against the doorpost.*)

CURTAIN

The Little Man

A FARCICAL MORALITY IN THREE SCENES

BY JOHN GALSWORTHY

CHARACTERS

THE LITTLE MAN
THE AMERICAN
THE ENGLISHMAN
THE ENGLISHWOMAN
THE GERMAN
THE DUTCH BOY
THE MOTHER
THE BABY
THE WAITER
THE STATION OFFICIAL
THE POLICEMAN
THE PORTER

THE LITTLE MAN

SCENE ONE

Afternoon, on the departure platform of an Austrian railway station. At several little tables outside the buffet persons are taking refreshment, served by a pale young waiter. On a seat against the wall of the buffet a woman of lowly station is sitting beside two large bundles, on one of which she has placed her baby, swathed in a black shawl.

WAITER (*approaching a table whereat sit an English traveler and his wife*). Two coffee?

ENGLISHMAN (*paying*). Thanks. (*To his wife, in an Oxford voice*) Sugar?

ENGLISHWOMAN (*in a Cambridge voice*). One.

AMERICAN TRAVELER (*with field glasses and a pocket camera—from another table*). Waiter, I'd like to have you get my eggs. I've been sitting here quite a while.

WAITER. Yes, sare.

GERMAN TRAVELER. Kellner, bezahlen! (*His voice is, like his moustache, stiff and brushed up at the ends. His figure also is stiff and his hair a little gray; clearly once, if not now, a colonel.*)

WAITER. Komm' gleich!
(*The baby on the bundle wails. The mother takes it up to sooth it. A young, red-cheeked Dutchman at the fourth table stops eating and laughs.*)

AMERICAN. My eggs! Get a wiggle on you!

WAITER. Yes, sare. (*He rapidly recedes.*)
(*A LITTLE MAN in a soft hat is seen to the right of tables. He stands a moment looking after the hurrying waiter, then seats himself at the fifth table.*)

ENGLISHMAN (*looking at his watch*). Ten minutes more.

ENGLISHWOMAN. Bother!

AMERICAN (*addressing them*). 'Pears as if they'd a prejudice against eggs here, anyway.
(*The ENGLISH look at him, but do not speak.*)

GERMAN (*in creditable English*). In these places man can get nothing.
(*The WAITER comes flying back with a compote for the DUTCH YOUTH, who pays.*)

GERMAN. Kellner, bezahlen!

WAITER. Eine Krone sechzig.
(*The GERMAN pays.*)

AMERICAN (*rising, and taking out his watch—blandly*). See here. If I don't get my eggs before this watch ticks twenty, there'll be another waiter in heaven.

WAITER (*flying*). Komm' gleich!

AMERICAN (*seeking sympathy*). I'm gettin' kind of mad!
(*The* ENGLISHMAN *halves his newspaper and hands the advertisement half to his wife. The* BABY *wails. The* MOTHER *rocks it. The* DUTCH YOUTH *stops eating and laughs. The* GERMAN *lights a cigarette. The* LITTLE MAN *sits motionless, nursing his hat. The* WAITER *comes flying back with the eggs and places them before the* AMERICAN.)

AMERICAN (*putting away his watch*). Good! I don't like trouble. How much? (*He pays and eats. The* WAITER *stands a moment at the edge of the platform and passes his hand across his brow. The* LITTLE MAN *eyes him and speaks gently.*)

LITTLE MAN. Herr Ober! (*The* WAITER *turns*) Might I have a glass of beer?

WAITER. Yes, sare.

LITTLE MAN. Thank you very much. (*The* WAITER *goes.*)

AMERICAN (*pausing in the deglutition of his eggs—affably*). Pardon me, sir; I'd like to have you tell me why you called that little bit of a feller "Herr Ober." Reckon you would know what that means? Mr. Head Waiter.

LITTLE MAN. Yes, yes.

AMERICAN. I smile.

LITTLE MAN. Oughtn't I to call him that?

GERMAN (*abruptly*). Nein—Kellner.

AMERICAN. Why, yes! Just "waiter."
(*The* ENGLISHWOMAN *looks round her paper for a second. The* DUTCH YOUTH *stops eating and laughs. The* LITTLE MAN *gazes from face to face and nurses his hat.*)

LITTLE MAN. I didn't want to hurt his feelings.

GERMAN. Gott!

AMERICAN. In my country we're very democratic—but that's quite a proposition.

ENGLISHMAN (*handling coffee pot, to his wife*). More?

ENGLISHWOMAN. No, thanks.

GERMAN (*abruptly*). These fellows —if you treat them in this manner, at once they take liberties. You see, you will not get your beer. (*As he speaks the* WAITER *returns, bringing the* LITTLE MAN'S *beer, then retires.*)

AMERICAN. That 'pears to be one up to democracy. (*To the* LITTLE MAN) I judge you go in for brotherhood?

LITTLE MAN (*startled*). Oh, no!

AMERICAN. I take considerable stock in Leo Tolstoi myself. Grand man —grand-souled apparatus. But I guess you've got to pinch those waiters some to make 'em skip. (*To the* ENGLISH, *who have carelessly looked his way for a moment*) You'll appreciate that, the way he acted about my eggs. (*The* ENGLISH *make faint motions with their chins and avert their eyes. To the* WAITER, *who is standing at the door of the buffet*) Waiter! Flash of beer— jump, now!

WAITER. Komm' gleich!

GERMAN. Cigarren!

WAITER. Schön! (*He disappears.*)

AMERICAN (*affably—to the* LITTLE MAN). Now, if I don't get that flash of beer quicker'n you got yours, I shall admire.

GERMAN (*abruptly*). Tolstoi is nothing—nichts! No good! Ha?

AMERICAN (*relishing the approach of argument*). Well, that is a matter of temperament. Now, I'm all for equality. See that poor woman there —very humble woman—there she sits among us with her baby. Perhaps you'd like to locate her somewhere else?

GERMAN (*shrugging*). Tolstoi is sentimentalisch. Nietzsche is the true philosopher, the only one.

AMERICAN. Well, that's quite in the prospectus—very stimulating party —old Nietch—virgin mind. But give me Leo! (*He turns to the redcheeked* YOUTH) What do you opine, sir? I guess by your labels you'll be Dutch. Do they read Tolstoi in your country? (*The* DUTCH YOUTH *laughs.*)

AMERICAN. That is a very luminous answer.

GERMAN. Tolstoi is nothing. Man should himself express. He must push—he must be strong.

AMERICAN. That is so. In America we believe in virility; we like a man to expand. But we believe in brotherhood too. We draw the line at niggers; but we aspire. Social

barriers and distinctions we've not much use for.

ENGLISHMAN. Do you feel a draught?

ENGLISHWOMAN (*with a shiver of her shoulder toward the* AMERICAN). I do—rather.

GERMAN. Wait! You are a young people.

AMERICAN. That is so; there are no flies on us. (*To the* LITTLE MAN, *who has been gazing eagerly from face to face*) Say! I'd like to have you give us your sentiments in relation to the duty of man. (*The* LITTLE MAN *fidgets, and is about to open his mouth.*)

AMERICAN. For example—is it your opinion that we should kill off the weak and diseased, and all that can't jump around?

GERMAN (*nodding*). Ja, ja! That is coming.

LITTLE MAN (*looking from face to face*). They might be me. (*The* DUTCH YOUTH *laughs.*)

AMERICAN (*reproving him with a look*). That's true humility. 'Tisn't grammar. Now, here's a proposition that brings it nearer the bone: Would you step out of your way to help them when it was liable to bring you trouble?

GERMAN. Nein, nein! That is stupid.

LITTLE MAN (*eager but wistful*). I'm afraid not. Of course one wants to— There was St. Francis d'Assisi and St. Julien l'Hospitalier, and—

AMERICAN. Very lofty dispositions. Guess they died of them. (*He rises*) Shake hands, sir—my name is— (*He hands a card*) I am an ice-machine maker. (*He shakes the* LITTLE MAN'S *hand*) I like your sentiments—I feel kind of brotherly. (*Catching sight of the* WAITER *appearing in the doorway*) Waiter, where to h—ll is that flash of beer?

GERMAN. Cigarren!

WAITER. Komm' gleich! (*He vanishes.*)

ENGLISHMAN (*consulting watch*). Train's late.

ENGLISHWOMAN. Really! Nuisance! (*A station* POLICEMAN, *very square and uniformed, passes and repasses.*

AMERICAN (*resuming his seat—to the* GERMAN). Now, we don't have so much of that in America. Guess we feel more to trust in human nature.

GERMAN. Ah! ha! you will bresently find there is nothing in him but self.

LITTLE MAN (*wistfully*). Don't you believe in human nature?

AMERICAN. Very stimulating question. (*He looks round for opinions.*) (*The* DUTCH YOUTH *laughs.*)

ENGLISHMAN (*holding out his half of the paper to his wife*). Swap! (*His wife swaps.*)

GERMAN. In human nature I believe so far as I can see him—no more.

AMERICAN. Now that 'pears to me kind o' blasphemy. I believe in heroism. I opine there's not one of us

settin' around here that's not a hero —give him the occasion.

LITTLE MAN. Oh! Do you believe that?

AMERICAN. Well! I judge a hero is just a person that'll help another at the expense of himself. Take that poor woman there. Well, now, she's a heroine, I guess. She would die for her baby any old time.

GERMAN. Animals will die for their babies. That is nothing.

AMERICAN. I carry it further. I postulate we would all die for that baby if a locomotive was to trundle up right here and try to handle it. (*To the* GERMAN) I guess *you* don't know how good you are. (*As the* GERMAN *is twisting up the ends of his moustache—to the* ENGLISHWOMAN) I should like to have you express an opinion, ma'am.

ENGLISHWOMAN. I beg your pardon.

AMERICAN. The English are very humanitarian; they have a very high sense of duty. So have the Germans, so have the Americans. (*To the* DUTCH YOUTH) I judge even in your little country they have that. This is an epoch of equality and high-toned ideals. (*To the* LITTLE MAN) What is *your* nationality, sir?

LITTLE MAN. I'm afraid I'm nothing particular. My father was half-English and half-American, and my mother half-German and half-Dutch.

AMERICAN. My! That's a bit streaky, any old way. (*The* POLICEMAN *passes again*) Now, I don't believe we've much use any more for those

gentlemen in buttons. We've grown kind of mild—we don't think of self as we used to do.
(*The* WAITER *has appeared in the doorway.*)

GERMAN (*in a voice of thunder*). Cigarren! Donnerwetter!

AMERICAN (*shaking his fist at the vanishing* WAITER). That flash of beer!

WAITER. Komm' gleich!

AMERICAN. A little more, and he will join George Washington! I was about to remark when he intruded: In this year of grace 1913 the kingdom of Christ is quite a going concern. We are mighty near to universal brotherhood. The colonel here (*he indicates the* GERMAN) is a man of blood and iron, but give him an opportunity to be magnanimous, and he'll be right there. Oh, sir! yep!
(*The* GERMAN, *with a profound mixture of pleasure and cynicism, brushes up the ends of his moustache.*)

LITTLE MAN. I wonder. One wants to, but somehow—— (*He shakes his head.*)

AMERICAN. You seem kind of skeery about that. You've had experience, maybe. I'm an optimist—I think we're bound to make the devil hum in the near future. I opine we shall occasion a good deal of trouble to that old party. There's about to be a holocaust of selfish interests. The colonel there with old man Nietch —he won't know himself. There's going to be a very sacred opportunity.
(*As he speaks, the voice of a* RAIL-

WAY OFFICIAL *is heard in the distance calling out in German. It approaches, and the words become audible.*)

GERMAN (*startled*). Der Teufel! (*He gets up, and seizes the bag beside him.*)
(*The* STATION OFFICIAL *has appeared; he stands for a moment casting his commands at the seated group. The* DUTCH YOUTH *also rises, and takes his coat and hat. The* OFFICIAL *turns on his heel and retires, still issuing directions.*)

ENGLISHMAN. What does he say?

GERMAN. Our drain has come in, de oder platform; only one minute we haf.
(ALL *have risen in a fluster.*)

AMERICAN. Now, that's very provoking. I won't get that flash of beer.
(*There is a general scurry to gather coats and hats and wraps, during which the lowly* WOMAN *is seen making desperate attempts to deal with her baby and the two large bundles. Quite defeated, she suddenly puts all down, wrings her hands, and cries out: "Herr Jesu! Hilfe!" The flying procession turn their heads at that strange cry.*)

AMERICAN. What's that? Help? (*He continues to run.*)
(*The* LITTLE MAN *spins round, rushes back, picks up baby and bundle on which it was seated.*)

LITTLE MAN. Come along, good woman, come along!
(*The* WOMAN *picks up the other bundle and they run. The* WAITER, *appearing in the doorway with the bottle of beer, watches with his tired smile.*)

CURTAIN

SCENE TWO

A second-class compartment of a corridor carriage, in motion. In it are seated the ENGLISHMAN *and his* WIFE, *opposite each other at the corridor end, she with her face to the engine, he with his back. Both are somewhat protected from the rest of the travelers by newspapers. Next to her sits the* GERMAN, *and opposite him sits the* AMERICAN; *next the* AMERICAN *in one window corner is seated the* DUTCH YOUTH; *the other window corner is taken by the* GERMAN's *bag. The silence is only broken by the slight rushing noise of the train's progression and the crackling of the English newspapers.*

AMERICAN (*turning to the* DUTCH YOUTH). Guess I'd like that window raised; it's kind of chilly after that old run they gave us.
(*The* DUTCH YOUTH *laughs, and goes through the motions of raising the window. The* ENGLISH *regard the operation with uneasy irritation. The* GERMAN *opens his bag, which reposes on the corner seat next him, and takes out a book.*)

AMERICAN. The Germans are great readers. Very stimulating practice. I read most anything myself! (*The* GERMAN *holds up the book so that the title may be read*) "Don Quixote"—fine book. We Americans take considerable stock in old man Quixote. Bit of a wild-cat—but we don't laugh at him.

GERMAN. He is dead. Dead as a sheep. A good thing, too.

AMERICAN. In America we have still quite an amount of chivalry.

GERMAN. Chivalry is nothing—sentimentalisch. In modern days—no good. A man must push, he must pull.

AMERICAN. So you say. But I judge your form of chivalry is sacrifice to the state. We allow more freedom to the individual soul. Where there's something little and weak, we feel it kind of noble to give up to it. That way we feel elevated.
(*As he speaks there is seen in the corridor doorway the* LITTLE MAN, *with the* WOMAN's BABY *still on his arm and the bundle held in the other hand. He peers in anxiously. The* ENGLISH, *acutely conscious, try to dissociate themselves from his presence with their papers. The* DUTCH YOUTH *laughs.*)

GERMAN. Ach! So!

AMERICAN. Dear me!

LITTLE MAN. Is there room? I can't find a seat.

AMERICAN. Why, yes! There's a seat for one.

LITTLE MAN (*depositing bundle outside, and heaving* BABY). May I?

AMERICAN. Come right in!
(*The* GERMAN *sulkily moves his bag. The* LITTLE MAN *comes in and seats himself gingerly.*)

AMERICAN. Where's the mother?

LITTLE MAN (*ruefully*). Afraid she got left behind.
(*The* DUTCH YOUTH *laughs. The* ENGLISH *unconsciously emerge from their newspapers.*)

AMERICAN. My! That would appear to be quite a domestic incident.
(*The* ENGLISHMAN *suddenly utters a profound "Ha, Ha!" and disappears behind his paper. And that paper and the one opposite are seen to shake, and little squirls and squeaks emerge.*)

GERMAN. And you haf got her bundle, and her baby. Ha! (*He cackles dryly.*)

AMERICAN (*gravely*). I smile. I guess Providence has played it pretty low down on you. It's sure acted real mean.
(*The* BABY *wails, and the* LITTLE MAN *jigs it with a sort of gentle desperation, looking apologetically from face to face. His wistful glance renews the fire of merriment wherever it alights. The* AMERICAN *alone preserves a gravity which seems incapable of being broken.*)

AMERICAN. Maybe you'd better get off right smart and restore that baby. There's nothing can act madder than a mother.

LITTLE MAN. Poor thing, yes! What she must be suffering!
(*A gale of laughter shakes the carriage. The* ENGLISH *for a moment drop their papers, the better to indulge. The* LITTLE MAN *smiles a wintry smile.*)

AMERICAN (*in a lull*). How did it eventuate?

LITTLE MAN. We got there just as the train was going to start; and I jumped, thinking I could help her up. But it moved too quickly, and —and left her.
(*The gale of laughter blows up again.*)

AMERICAN. Guess I'd have thrown the baby out to her.

LITTLE MAN. I was afraid the poor little thing might break.
(*The* BABY *wails; the* LITTLE MAN *heaves it; the gale of laughter blows.*)

AMERICAN (*gravely*). It's highly entertaining—not for the baby. What kind of an old baby is it, anyway? (*He sniffs*) I judge it's a bit—niffy.

LITTLE MAN. Afraid I've hardly looked at it yet.

AMERICAN. Which end up is it?

LITTLE MAN. Oh! I think the right end. Yes, yes, it is.

AMERICAN. Well, that's something. Maybe you should hold it out of the window a bit. Very excitable things, babies!

ENGLISHWOMAN (*galvanized*). No, no!

ENGLISHMAN (*touching her knee*). My dear!

AMERICAN. You are right, ma'am. I opine there's a draught out there. This baby is precious. We've all of us got stock in this baby in a manner of speaking. This is a little bit of universal brotherhood. Is it a woman baby?

LITTLE MAN. I—I can only see the top of its head.

AMERICAN. You can't always tell from that. It looks kind of over-wrapped up. Maybe it had better be unbound.

GERMAN. Nein, nein, nein!

AMERICAN. I think you are very likely right, colonel. It might be a pity to unbind that baby. I guess the lady should be consulted in this matter.

ENGLISHWOMAN. Yes, yes, of course —I——

ENGLISHMAN (*touching her*). Let it be! Little beggar seems all right.

AMERICAN. That would seem only known to Providence at this moment. I judge it might be due to humanity to look at its face.

LITTLE MAN (*gladly*). It's sucking my finger. There, there—nice little thing—there!

AMERICAN. I would surmise in your leisure moments you have created babies, sir?

LITTLE MAN. Oh! no—indeed, no.

AMERICAN. Dear me!—That is a loss. (*Addressing himself to the carriage at large*) I think we may esteem ourselves fortunate to have this little stranger right here with us. Demonstrates what a hold the little and weak have upon us nowadays. The colonel here—a man of blood and iron—there he sits quite ca'm next door to it. (*He sniffs*) Now, this baby is ruther chastening —that is a sign of grace, in the colonel—that is true heroism.

LITTLE MAN (*faintly*). I—I can see its face a little now. (*All bend forward.*)

AMERICAN. What sort of a physiog-nomy has it, anyway?

LITTLE MAN (*still faintly*). I don't see anything but—but spots.

GERMAN. Oh! Ha! Pfui! (*The* DUTCH YOUTH *laughs.*)

AMERICAN. I am told that is not uncommon amongst babies. Perhaps we could have you inform us, ma'am.

ENGLISHWOMAN. Yes, of course— —only—what sort of——

LITTLE MAN. They seem all over its — (*At the slight recoil of everyone*) I feel sure it's—it's quite a good baby underneath.

AMERICAN. That will be ruther difficult to come at. I'm just a bit sensitive. I've very little use for affections of the epidermis.

GERMAN. Pfui! (*He has edged away as far as he can get, and is lighting a big cigar. The* DUTCH YOUTH *draws his legs back.*)

AMERICAN (*also taking out a cigar*). I guess it would be well to fumigate this carriage. Does it suffer, do you think?

LITTLE MAN (*peering*). Really, I don't—I'm not sure—I know so little about babies. I think it would have a nice expression—if—if it showed.

AMERICAN. Is it kind of boiled look-ing?

LITTLE MAN. Yes—yes, it is.

AMERICAN (*looking gravely round*). I judge this baby has the measles.

(*The* GERMAN *screws himself spasmodically against the arm of the* ENGLISHWOMAN'S *seat.*)

ENGLISHWOMAN. Poor little thing! Shall I——? (*She half rises.*)

ENGLISHMAN (*touching her*). No no— Dash it!

AMERICAN. I honor your emotion, ma'am. It does credit to us all. But I sympathize with your husband too. The measles *is* a very important pestilence in connection with a grown woman.

LITTLE MAN. It likes my finger awfully. Really, it's rather a sweet baby.

AMERICAN (*sniffing*). Well, that would appear to be quite a question. About them spots, now? Are they rosy?

LITTLE MAN. No-o; they're dark, almost black.

GERMAN. Gott! Typhus! (*He bounds up on to the arm of the* ENGLISHWOMAN'S *seat.*)

AMERICAN. Typhus! That's quite an indisposition!
(*The* DUTCH YOUTH *rises suddenly, and bolts out into the corridor. He is followed by the* GERMAN, *puffing clouds of smoke. The* ENGLISH *and* AMERICAN *sit a moment longer without speaking. The* ENGLISHWOMAN'S *face is turned with a curious expression—half pity, half fear —towards the* LITTLE MAN. *Then the* ENGLISHMAN *gets up.*)

ENGLISHMAN. Bit stuffy for you here, dear, isn't it? (*He puts his* arm *through hers, raises her, and' almost pushes her through the doorway. She goes, still looking back.*)

AMERICAN (*gravely*). There's nothing I admire more'n courage. Guess I'll go and smoke in the corridor.
(*As he goes out the* LITTLE MAN *looks very wistfully after him. Screwing up his mouth and nose, he holds the* BABY *away from him and wavers; then rising, he puts it on the seat opposite and goes through the motions of letting down the window. Having done so he looks at the* BABY, *who has begun to wail. Suddenly he raises his hands and clasps them, like a child praying. Since, however, the* BABY *does not stop wailing, he hovers over it in indecision; then, picking it up, sits down again to dandle it, with his face turned toward the open window. Finding that it still wails, he begins to sing to it in a cracked little voice. It is charmed at once. While he is singing, the* AMERICAN *appears in the corridor. Letting down the passage window, he stands there in the doorway with the draught blowing his hair and the smoke of his cigar all about him. The* LITTLE MAN *stops singing and shifts the shawl higher to protect the* BABY'S *head from the draught.*)

AMERICAN (*gravely*). This is the most sublime spectacle I have ever envisaged. There ought to be a record of this. (*The* LITTLE MAN *looks at him, wondering*) You are typical, sir, of the sentiments of modern Christianity. You illustrate the deepest feelings in the heart of every man. (*The* LITTLE MAN *rises with the* BABY *and a movement of approach*) Guess I'm wanted in the dining-car. (*He vanishes.*)
(*The* LITTLE MAN *sits down again,*

but back to the engine, away from the draught, and looks out of the window, patiently jogging the BABY *on his knee.*)

SCENE THREE

An arrival platform. The LITTLE MAN, *with the* BABY *and the bundle, is standing disconsolate, while travellers pass and luggage is being carried by. A* STATION OFFICIAL, *accompanied by a* POLICEMAN, *appears from a doorway, behind him.*

OFFICIAL (*consulting telegram in his hand*). Das ist der Herr. (*They advance to the* LITTLE MAN.)

OFFICIAL. Sie haben einen Buben gestohlen?

LITTLE MAN. I only speak English and American.

OFFICIAL. Dies ist nicht Ihr Bube? (*He touches the* BABY.)

LITTLE MAN (*shaking his head*). Take care—it's ill. (*The man does not understand*) Ill—the baby——

OFFICIAL (*shaking his head*). Verstehe nicht. Dis is nod your baby? No?

LITTLE MAN (*shaking his head violently*). No, it is not. No.

OFFICIAL (*tapping the telegram*). Gut! You are 'rested. (*He signs to the* POLICEMAN, *who takes the* LITTLE MAN'S *arm.*)

LITTLE MAN. Why? I don't want the poor baby.

OFFICIAL (*lifting the bundle*). Dies ist nicht Ihr Gepäck—pag?

LITTLE MAN. No.

OFFICIAL. Gut. You are 'rested.

LITTLE MAN. I only took it for the poor woman. I'm not a thief—I'm—I'm——

OFFICIAL (*shaking head*). Verstehe nicht.
(*The* LITTLE MAN *tries to tear his hair. The disturbed* BABY *wails.*)

LITTLE MAN (*dandling it as best he can*). There, there—poor, poor!

OFFICIAL. Halt still! You are 'rested. It is all right.

LITTLE MAN. Where is the mother?

OFFICIAL. She comm by next drain. Das telegram say: Halt einen Herrn mit schwarzem Buben and schwarzem Gepäck. 'Rest gentleman mit black baby und black—pag.
(*The* LITTLE MAN *turns up his eyes to heaven.*)

OFFICIAL. Komm mit us. (*They take the* LITTLE MAN *toward the door from which they have come. A voice stops them.*)

AMERICAN (*speaking from as far away as may be*). Just a moment! (*The* OFFICIAL *stops; the* LITTLE MAN *also stops and sits down on a bench against the wall. The* POLICEMAN *stands stolidly beside him. The* AMERICAN *approaches a step or two, beckoning; the* OFFICIAL *goes up to him.*)

AMERICAN. Guess you've got an angel from heaven there! What's the gentleman in buttons for?

OFFICIAL. Was ist das?

AMERICAN. Is there anybody here that can understand American?

OFFICIAL. Verstehe nicht.

AMERICAN. Well, just watch my gestures. I was saying (*he points to the* LITTLE MAN, *then makes gestures of flying*) you have an angel from heaven there. You have there a man in whom Gawd (*he points upward*) takes quite an amount of stock. You have no call to arrest him. (*He makes the gesture of arrest*) No, sir. Providence has acted pretty mean, loading off that baby on him. (*He makes the motion of dandling*) The little man has a heart of gold. (*He points to his heart, and takes out a gold coin.*)

OFFICIAL (*thinking he is about to be bribed*). Aber, das ist zu viel!

AMERICAN. Now, don't rattle me! (*Pointing to the* LITTLE MAN) Man (*pointing to his heart*) Herz (*pointing to the coin*) von Gold. This is a flower of the field—he don't want no gentleman in buttons to pluck him up. (*A little crowd is gathering, including the* TWO ENGLISH, *the* GERMAN, *and the* DUTCH YOUTH.)

OFFICIAL. Verstehe absolut nichts. (*He taps the telegram*) Ich muss mein duty do.

AMERICAN. But I'm telling you. This is a white man. This is probably the whitest man on Gawd's earth.

OFFICIAL. Das macht nichts—gut or no gut, I muss mein duty do. (*He turns to go toward the* LITTLE MAN.)

AMERICAN. Oh! Very well, arrest him; do your duty. This baby has typhus. (*At the word "typhus" the* OFFICIAL *stops.*)

AMERICAN (*making gestures*). First-class typhus, black typhus, schwarzen typhus. Now you have it. I'm kind o' sorry for you and the gentleman in buttons. Do your duty!

OFFICIAL. Typhus? Der Bub'—die baby hat typhus?

AMERICAN. I'm telling you.

OFFICIAL. Gott im Himmel!

AMERICAN (*spotting the* GERMAN *in the little throng*). Here's a gentleman will corroborate me.

OFFICIAL (*much disturbed, and signing to the* POLICEMAN *to stand clear*). Typhus! Aber das ist grässlich!

AMERICAN. I kind o' thought you'd feel like that.

OFFICIAL. Die Sanitätsmachine! Gleich! (*A* PORTER *goes to get it. From either side the broken half-moon of persons stand gazing at the* LITTLE

MAN *who sits unhappily dandling the* BABY *in the center.*)

OFFICIAL (*raising his hands*). Was zu thun?

AMERICAN. Guess you'd better isolate the baby.
(*A silence, during which the* LITTLE MAN *is heard faintly whistling and clucking to the* BABY.)

OFFICIAL (*referring once more to his telegram*). " 'Rest gentleman mit black baby." (*Shaking his head*) Wir must de gentleman hold. (*To the* GERMAN) Bitte, mein Herr, sagen Sie ihm, den Buben zu niedersetzen. (*He makes the gesture of deposit.*)

GERMAN (*to the* LITTLE MAN). He say: Put down the baby.
(*The* LITTLE MAN *shakes his head, and continues to dandle the* BABY.)

OFFICIAL. You must.
(*The* LITTLE MAN *glowers, in silence.*)

ENGLISHMAN (*in background—muttering*). Good man!

GERMAN. His spirit ever denies.

OFFICIAL (*again making his gesture*). Aber er muss! (*The* LITTLE MAN *makes a face at him*) Sag' Ihm: Instantly put down baby, and komm' mit us.
(*The* BABY *wails.*)

LITTLE MAN. Leave the poor ill baby here alone? Be—be—be d——d to you!

AMERICAN (*jumping on to a trunk —with enthusiasm*). Bully!
(*The* ENGLISH *clap their hands; the*

DUTCH YOUTH *laughs. The* OFFICIAL *is muttering, greatly incensed.*)

AMERICAN. What does that body snatcher say?

GERMAN. He say this man use the baby to save himself from arrest Very smart—he say.

AMERICAN. I judge you do him an injustice. (*Showing off the* LITTLE MAN *with a sweep of his arm*) This is a white man. He's got a black baby, and he won't leave it in the lurch. Guess we would all act noble, that way, give us the chance.
(*The* LITTLE MAN *rises, holding out the* BABY, *and advances a step or two. The half-moon at once gives, increasing its size; the* AMERICAN *climbs on to a higher trunk. The* LITTLE MAN *retires and again sits down.*)

AMERICAN (*addressing the* OFFICIAL). Guess you'd better go out of business and wait for the mother.

OFFICIAL (*stamping his foot*). Die Mutter sall 'rested be for taking out baby mit typhus. Ha! (*To the* LITTLE MAN) Put ze baby down! (*The* LITTLE MAN *smiles*) Do you 'ear?

AMERICAN (*addressing the* OFFICIAL). Now, see here. 'Pears to me you don't suspicion just how beautiful this is. Here we have a man giving his life for that old baby that's got no claim on him This is not a baby of his own making. No, sir, this is a very Christ-like proposition in the gentleman.

OFFICIAL. Put ze baby down, or ich will gommand someone it to do.

AMERICAN. That will be very interesting to watch.

OFFICIAL (*to* POLICEMAN). Dake it vrom him.
(*The* POLICEMAN *mutters, but does not.*)

AMERICAN (*to the* GERMAN). Guess I lost that.

GERMAN. He say he is not his officier.

AMERICAN. That just tickles me to death.

OFFICIAL (*looking round*). Vill nobody dake ze Bub'?

ENGLISHWOMAN (*moving a step—faintly*). Yes—I——

ENGLISHMAN (*grasping her arm*). By Jove! Will you!

OFFICIAL (*gathering himself for a great effort to take the* BABY, *and advancing two steps*). Zen I gommand you—— (*He stops and his voice dies away*) Zit dere!

AMERICAN. My! That's wonderful. What a man this is! What a sublime sense of duty!
(*The* DUTCH YOUTH *laughs. The* OFFICIAL *turns on him, but as he does so the* MOTHER *of the* BABY *is seen hurrying.*)

MOTHER. Ach! Ach! Mei' Bubi!
(*Her face is illumined; she is about to rush to the* LITTLE MAN.)

OFFICIAL (*to the* POLICEMAN). Nimm die Frau!
(*The* POLICEMAN *catches hold of the* WOMAN.)

OFFICIAL (*to the frightened* WOMAN). Warum haben Sie einen Buben mit Typhus mit ausgebracht?

AMERICAN (*eagerly, from his perch*). What was that? I don't want to miss any.

GERMAN. He say: Why did you a baby with typhus with you bring out?

AMERICAN. Well, that's quite a question. (*He takes out the field-glasses slung around him and adjusts them on the* BABY.)

MOTHER (*bewildered*). Mei' Bubi —Typhus—aber Typhus? (*She shakes her head violently*) Nein, nein, nein! Typhus!

OFFICIAL. Er hat Typhus.

MOTHER (*shaking her head*). Nein, nein, nein!

AMERICAN (*looking through his glasses*). Guess she's kind of right! I judge the typhus is where the baby's slobbered on the shawl, and it's come off on him.
(*The* DUTCH YOUTH *laughs.*)

OFFICIAL (*turning on him furiously*). Er hat Typhus.

AMERICAN. Now, that's where you slop over. Come right here.
(*The* OFFICIAL *mounts, and looks through the glasses.*)

AMERICAN (*to the* LITTLE MAN). Skin out the baby's leg. If we don't locate spots on that, it'll be good enough for me.
(*The* LITTLE MAN *fumbles out the* BABY's *little white foot.*)

MOTHER. Mei' Bubi! (*She tries to break away.*)

AMERICAN. White as a banana. (*To the* OFFICIAL—*affably*) Guess you've made kind of a fool of us with your old typhus.

OFFICIAL. Lass die Frau! (*The* POLICEMAN *lets her go, and she rushes to her* BABY.)

MOTHER. Mei' Bubi! (*The* BABY, *exchanging the warmth of the* LITTLE MAN *for the momentary chill of its* MOTHER, *wails.*)

OFFICIAL (*descending and beckoning to the* POLICEMAN). Sie wollen den Herrn accusiren? (*The* POLICEMAN *takes the* LITTLE MAN'S *arm.*)

AMERICAN. What's that? They goin' to pinch him after all? (*The* MOTHER, *still hugging her* BABY, *who has stopped crying, gazes at the* LITTLE MAN, *who sits dazedly looking up. Suddenly she drops on her knees, and with her free hand lifts his booted foot and kisses it.*)

AMERICAN (*waving his hat*). Ra! Ra! (*He descends swiftly, goes up to the* LITTLE MAN, *whose arm the* POLICEMAN *has dropped, and takes his hand*) Brother, I am proud to know you. This is one of the greatest moments I have ever experienced. (*Displaying the* LITTLE MAN *to the assembled company*) I think I sense the situation when I say that we all esteem it an honor to breathe the rather inferior atmosphere of this station here along with our little friend. I guess we shall all go home and treasure the memory of his face as the whitest thing in our museum of recollections. And perhaps this good woman will also go home and wash the face of our little brother here. I am inspired with a new faith in mankind. Ladies and gentlemen, I wish to present to you a sure-enough saint—only wants a halo, to be transfigured. (*To the* LITTLE MAN) Stand right up. (*The* LITTLE MAN *stands up bewildered. They come about him. The* OFFICIAL *bows to him, the* POLICEMAN *salutes him. The* DUTCH YOUTH *shakes his head and laughs. The* GERMAN *draws himself up very straight, and bows quickly twice. The* ENGLISHMAN *and his* WIFE *approach at least two steps, then, thinking better of it, turn to each other and recede. The* MOTHER *kisses his hand. The* PORTER *returning with the Sanitätsmachine, turns it on from behind, and its pinkish shower, goldened by a ray of sunlight, falls around the* LITTLE MAN'S *head, transfiguring it as he stands with eyes upraised to see whence the portent comes.*)

AMERICAN (*rushing forward and dropping on his knees*). Hold on just a minute! Guess I'll take a snapshot of the miracle. (*He adjusts his pocket camera*) This ought to look bully!

CURTAIN

Riders to the Sea

BY J. M. SYNGE

CHARACTERS

MAURYA, *an old woman*
BARTLEY, *her son*
CATHLEEN, *her daughter*
NORA, *a younger daughter*
MEN AND WOMEN

RIDERS TO THE SEA

SCENE—*An Island off the West of Ireland.*
Cottage kitchen, with nets, oil-skins, spinning wheel, some new boards
standing by the wall, etc. CATHLEEN, *a girl of about twenty, finishes knead*
ing cake, and puts it down in the pot-oven by the fire; then wipes her hands,
and begins to spin at the wheel. NORA, *a young girl, puts her head in at*
the door.

NORA (*in a low voice*). Where is she?

CATHLEEN. She's lying down, God help her, and may be sleeping, if she's able.

(NORA *comes in softly, and takes a bundle from under her shawl.*)

CATHLEEN (*spinning the wheel rapidly*). What is it you have?

NORA. The young priest is after bringing them. It's a shirt and a plain stocking were got off a drowned man in Donegal.

(CATHLEEN *stops her wheel with a sudden movement, and leans out to listen.*)

NORA. We're to find out if it's Michael's they are, some time herself will be down looking by the sea.

CATHLEEN. How would they be Michael's, Nora? How would he go the length of that way to the far north?

NORA. The young priest says he's known the like of it. "If it's Michael's they are," says he, "you can tell herself he's got a clean burial by the grace of God, and if they're not his, let no one say a word about them, for she'll be getting her death," says he, "with crying and lamenting."

(*The door which* NORA *half closed is blown open by a gust of wind.*)

CATHLEEN (*looking out anxiously*). Did you ask him would he stop Bartley going this day with the horses to the Galway fair?

NORA. "I won't stop him," says he, "but let you not be afraid. Herself does be saying prayers half through the night, and the Almighty God won't leave her destitute," says he, "with no son living."

CATHLEEN. Is the sea bad by the white rocks, Nora?

NORA. Middling bad, God help us. There's a great roaring in the west, and it's worse it'll be getting when the tide's turned to the wind. (*She goes over to the table with the bundle*) Shall I open it now?

CATHLEEN. Maybe she'd wake up on us, and come in before we'd done. (*Coming to the table*) It's a long time we'll be, and the two of us crying.

NORA (*goes to the inner door and listens*). She's moving about on the bed. She'll be coming in a minute.

CATHLEEN. Give me the ladder, and I'll put them up in the turf-loft, the way she won't know of them at all, and maybe when the tide turns she'll be going down to see would he be floating from the east. (*They put the ladder against the gable of the chimney;* CATHLEEN *goes up a few steps and hides the bundle in the turf-loft.* MAURYA *comes from the inner room.*)

MAURYA (*looking up at* CATHLEEN *and speaking querulously*). Isn't it turf enough you have for this day and evening?

CATHLEEN. There's a cake baking at the fire for a short space (*throwing down the turf*) and BARTLEY will want it when the tide turns if he goes to Connemara. (NORA *picks up the turf and puts it round the pot-oven.*)

MAURYA (*sitting down on a stool at the fire*). He won't go this day with the wind rising from the south and west. He won't go this day, for the young priest will stop him surely.

NORA. He'll not stop him, Mother, and I heard Eamon Simon and Stephen Pheety and Colum Shawn saying he would go.

MAURYA. Where is he itself?

NORA. He went down to see would there be another boat sailing in the week, and I'm thinking it won't be long till he's here now, for the tide's turning at the green head, and the hooker's tacking from the east.

CATHLEEN. I hear some one passing the big stones.

NORA (*looking out*). He's coming now, and he in a hurry.

BARTLEY (*comes in and looks round the room. Speaking sadly and quietly*). Where is the bit of new rope, Cathleen, was bought in Connemara?

CATHLEEN (*coming down*). Give it to him, Nora; it's on a nail by the white boards. I hung it up this morning, for the pig with the black feet was eating it.

NORA (*giving him a rope*). Is that it, Bartley?

MAURYA. You'd do right to leave that rope, Bartley, hanging by the boards. (BARTLEY *takes the rope*) It will be wanting in this place, I'm telling you, if Michael is washed up tomorrow morning, or the next morning, or any morning in the week, for it's a deep grave we'll make him by the grace of God.

BARTLEY (*beginning to work with the rope*). I've no halter the way I can ride down on the mare, and I must go now quickly. This is the one boat going for two weeks or beyond it, and the fair will be a good fair for horses I heard them saying below.

MAURYA It's a hard thing they'll be saying below if the body is washed up and there's no man in it to make the coffin, and I after giving a big price for the finest white boards you'd find in Connemara. (*She looks round at the boards.*)

BARTLEY. How would it be washed up, and we after looking each day for nine days, and a strong wind blowing a while back from the west and south?

MAURYA. If it wasn't found itself,

that wind is raising the sea, and there was a star up against the moon, and it rising in the night. If it was a hundred horses, or a thousand horses you had itself, what is the price of a thousand horses against a son where there is one son only?

BARTLEY (*working at the halter, to* CATHLEEN). Let you go down each day, and see the sheep aren't jumping in on the rye, and if the jobber comes you can sell the pig with the black feet if there is a good price going.

MAURYA. How would the like of her get a good price for a pig?

BARTLEY (*to* CATHLEEN). If the west wind holds with the last bit of the moon let you and Nora get up weed enough for another cock for the kelp. It's hard set we'll be from this day with no one in it but one man to work.

MAURYA. It's hard set we'll be surely the day you're drownd'd with the rest. What way will I live and the girls with me, and I an old woman looking for the grave? (*Bartley lays down the halter, takes off his old coat, and puts on a newer one of the same flannel.*)

BARTLEY (*to* NORA). Is she coming to the pier?

NORA (*looking out*). She's passing the green head and letting fall her sails.

BARTLEY (*getting his purse and tobacco*). I'll have half an hour to go down, and you'll see me coming again in two days, or in three days, or maybe in four days if the wind is bad.

MAURYA (*turning round to the fire and putting her shawl over her head*). Isn't it a hard and cruel man won't hear a word from an old woman, and she holding him from the sea?

CATHLEEN. It's the life of a young man to be going on the sea, and who would listen to an old woman with one thing and she saying it over?

BARTLEY (*taking the halter*). I must go now quickly. I'll ride down on the red mare, and the gray pony'll run behind me. . . . The blessing of God on you. (*He goes out.*)

MAURYA (*crying out as he is in the door*). He's gone now, God spare us, and we'll not see him again. He's gone now, and when the black night is falling I'll have no son left me in the world.

CATHLEEN. Why wouldn't you give him your blessing and he looking round in the door? Isn't it sorrow enough is on every one in this house without your sending him out with an unlucky word behind him, and a hard word in his ear? (*MAURYA takes up the tongs and begins raking the fire aimlessly without looking round.*)

NORA (*turning towards her*). You're taking away the turf from the cake.

CATHLEEN (*crying out*). The Son of God forgive us, Nora, we're after forgetting his bit of bread. (*She comes over to the fire.*)

NORA. And it's destroyed he'll be going till dark night, and he after eating nothing since the sun went up.

CATHLEEN (*turning the cake out of the oven*). It's destroyed he'll be, surely. There's no sense left on any person in a house where an old woman will be talking for ever. (MAURYA *sways herself on her stool.*)

CATHLEEN (*cutting off some of the bread and rolling it in a cloth; to Maurya*). Let you go down now to the spring well and give him this and he passing. You'll see him then and the dark world will be broken, and you can say "God speed you," the way he'll be easy in his mind.

MAURYA (*taking the bread*). Will I be in it as soon as himself?

CATHLEEN. If you go now quickly.

MAURYA (*standing up unsteadily*). It's hard set I am to walk.

CATHLEEN (*looking at her anxiously*). Give her the stick, NORA, or maybe she'll slip on the big stones.

NORA. What stick?

CATHLEEN. The stick Michael brought from Connemara.

MAURYA (*taking a stick* NORA *gives her*). In the big world the old people do be leaving things after them for their sons and children, but in this place it is the young men do be leaving things behind for them that do be old. (*She goes out slowly.* NORA *goes over to the ladder.*)

CATHLEEN. Wait, NORA, maybe she'd turn back quickly. She's that sorry, God help her, you wouldn't know the thing she'd do.

NORA. Is she gone round by the bush?

CATHLEEN (*looking out*). She's gone now. Throw it down quickly, for the Lord knows when she'll be out of it again.

NORA (*getting the bundle from the loft*). The young priest said he'd be passing tomorrow, and we might go down and speak to him below if it's Michael's they are surely.

CATHLEEN (*taking the bundle*). Did he say what way they were found?

NORA (*coming down*). "There were two men," says he, "and they rowing round with poteen before the cocks crowed, and the oar of one of them caught the body, and they passing the black cliffs of the north."

CATHLEEN (*trying to open the bundle*). Give me a knife, NORA, the string's perished with the salt water, and there's a black knot on it you wouldn't loosen in a week.

NORA (*giving her a knife*). I've heard tell it was a long way to Donegal.

CATHLEEN (*cutting the string*). It is surely. There was a man in here a while ago—the man sold us that knife—and he said if you set off walking from the rocks beyond, it would be seven days you'd be in Donegal.

NORA. And what time would a man take, and he floating? (CATHLEEN *opens the bundle and takes out a bit of a stocking. They look at them eagerly.*)

CATHLEEN (*in a low voice*). The Lord spare us, Nora! isn't it a queer hard thing to say if it's his they are surely?

NORA. I'll get his shirt off the hook the way we can put the one flannel on the other. (*She looks through some clothes hanging in the corner*) It's not with them, Cathleen, and where will it be?

CATHLEEN. I'm thinking Bartley put it on him in the morning, for his own shirt was heavy with the salt in it. (*Pointing to the corner*) There's a bit of a sleeve was of the same stuff. Give me that and it will do.
(NORA *brings it to her and they compare the flannel.*)

CATHLEEN. It's the same stuff, Nora; but if it is itself aren't there great rolls of it in the shops of Galway, and isn't it many another man may have a shirt of it as well as Michael himself?

NORA (*who has taken up the stocking and counted the stitches, crying out*). It's Michael, Cathleen, it's Michael; God spare his soul, and what will herself say when she hears this story, and Bartley on the sea?

CATHLEEN (*taking the stocking*). It's a plain stocking.

NORA. It's the second one of the third pair I knitted, and I put up three score stitches, and I dropped four of them.

CATHLEEN (*counts the stitches*). It's that number is in it. (*Crying out*) Ah, Nora, isn't it a bitter thing to think of him floating that way to the far north, and no one to keen him but the black hags that do be flying on the sea?

NORA (*swinging herself round, and throwing out her arms on the clothes*). And isn't it a pitiful thing

when there is nothing left of a man who was a great rower and fisher, but a bit of an old shirt and a plain stocking?

CATHLEEN (*after an instant*). Tell me is herself coming, Nora? I hear a little sound on the path.

NORA (*looking out*). She is, Cathleen. She's coming up to the door.

CATHLEEN. Put these things away before she'll come in. Maybe it's easier she'll be after giving her blessing to Bartley, and we won't let on we've heard anything the time he's on the sea.

NORA (*helping* CATHLEEN *to close the bundle*). We'll put them here in the corner. (*They put them into a hole in the chimney corner.* CATHLEEN *goes back to the spinning-wheel.*)

NORA. Will she see it was crying I was?

CATHLEEN. Keep your back to the door the way the light'll not be on you.
(NORA *sits down at the chimney corner, with her back to the door.* MAURYA *comes in very slowly, without looking at the girls, and goes over to her stool at the other side of the fire. The cloth with the bread is still in her hand. The girls look at each other, and* NORA *points to the bundle of bread.*)

CATHLEEN (*after spinning for a moment*). You didn't give him his bit of bread?
(MAURYA *begins to keen softly, without turning round.*)

CATHLEEN. Did you see him riding down?
(MAURYA *goes on keening.*)

CATHLEEN (*a little impatiently*).

God forgive ycu; isn't it a better thing to raise your voice and tell what you seen, than to be making lamentation for a thing that's done? Did you see Bartley, I'm saying to you.

MAURYA (*with a weak voice*). My heart's broken from this day.

CATHLEEN (*as before*). Did you see Bartley?

MAURYA. I seen the fearfulest thing.

CATHLEEN (*leaves her wheel and looks out*). God forgive you; he's riding the mare now over the green head, and the gray pony behind him.

MAURYA (*starts, so that her shawl falls back from her head and shows her white tossed hair. With a frightened voice*). The gray pony behind him.

CATHLEEN (*coming to the fire*). What is it ails you, at all?

MAURYA (*speaking very slowly*). I've seen the fearfulest thing any person has seen, since the day Bride Dara seen the dead man with the child in his arms.

CATHLEEN and NORA. Uah. (*They crouch down in front of the old woman at the fire.*)

NORA. Tell us what it is you seen.

MAURYA. I went down to the spring well, and I stood there saying a prayer to myself. Then Bartley came along, and he riding on the red mare with the gray pony behind him. (*She puts up her hands, as if to hide something from her eyes*) The Son of God spare us, Nora!

CATHLEEN. What is it you seen?

MAURYA. I seen Michael himself.

CATHLEEN (*speaking softly*). You did not, Mother; it wasn't Michael you seen, for his body is after being found in the far north, and he's got a clean burial by the grace of God.

MAURYA (*a little defiantly*). I'm after seeing him this day, and he riding and galloping. Bartley came first on the red mare; and I tried to say "God speed you," but something choked the words in my throat. He went by quickly; and "the blessing of God on you," says he, and I could say nothing. I looked up then, and I crying, at the gray pony, and there was Michael upon it—with fine clothes on him, and new shoes on his feet.

CATHLEEN (*begins to keen*). It's destroyed we are from this day. It's destroyed, surely.

NORA. Didn't the young priest say the Almighty God wouldn't leave her destitute with no son living?

MAURYA (*in a low voice, bui clearly*). It's little the like of him knows of the sea. . . . Bartley will be lost now, and let you call in Eamon and make me a good coffin out of the white boards, for I won't live after them. I've had a husband, and a husband's father, and six sons in this house—six fine men, though it was a hard birth I had with every one of them and they coming to the world—and some of them were found and some of them were not found, but they're gone now the lot of them. . . . There were Stephen, and Shawn, were lost in the great wind, and found after in the Bay of Gregory of the Golden Mouth, and carried up the two of them on the one plank, and in by that door. (*She pauses for a moment, the girls start as if they heard something through the door that is half open behind them.*)

NORA (*in a whisper*). Did you hear that, Cathleen? Did you hear a noise in the north-east?

CATHLEEN (*in a whisper*). There's some one after crying out by the seashore.

MAURYA (*continues without hearing anything*). There was Sheamus and his father, and his own father again, were lost in a dark night, and not a stick or sign was seen of them when the sun went up. There was Patch after was drowned out of a curagh that turned over. I was sitting here with Bartley, and he a baby, lying on my two knees, and I seen two women, and three women, and four women coming in, and they crossing themselves, and not saying a word. I looked out then, and there were men coming after them, and they holding a thing in the half of a red sail, and water dripping out of it— it was a dry day, Nora—and leaving a track to the door. (*She pauses again with her hand stretched out towards the door. It opens softly and old women begin to come in, crossing themselves on the threshold, and kneeling down in front of the stage with red petticoats over their heads.*)

MAURYA (*half in a dream, to* CATHLEEN). Is it Patch, or Michael, or what is it at all?

CATHLEEN. Michael is after being found in the far north, and when he is found there how could he be here in this place?

MAURYA. There does be a power of young men floating round in the sea, and what way would they know if it was Michael they had, or another man like him, for when a man is nine days in the sea, and the wind blowing, it's hard set his own mother would be to say what man was it.

CATHLEEN. It's Michael, God spare him, for they're after sending us a bit of his clothes from the far north. (*She reaches out and hands* MAURYA *the clothes that belonged to* MICHAEL. MAURYA *stands up slowly, and takes them in her hands.* NORA *looks out.*)

NORA. They're carrying a thing among them and there's water dripping out of it and leaving a track by the big stones.

CATHLEEN (*in a whisper to the women who have come in*). Is it Bartley it is?

ONE OF THE WOMEN. It is surely, God rest his soul.

(*Two younger women come in and pull out the table. Then men carry in the body of* BARTLEY, *laid on a plank, with a bit of a sail over it, and lay it on the table.*)

CATHLEEN (*to the women, as they are doing so*). What way was he drowned?

ONE OF THE WOMEN. The gray pony knocked him into the sea, and he was washed out where there is a great surf on the white rocks. (MAURYA *has gone over and knelt down at the head of the table. The women are keening softly and swaying themselves with a slow movement.* CATHLEEN *and* NORA *kneel at the other end of the table. The men kneel near the door.*)

MAURYA (*raising her head and speaking as if she did not see the people around her*). They're all gone now, and there isn't anything more the sea can do to me. . . . I'll have no call now to be up crying and praying when the wind breaks from the south, and you can hear the surf is in the east, and the surf is in the west, making a great stir with the two noises, and they hitting one on the other. I'll have no call now to be going down and getting Holy Water in the dark nights after Samhain, and I won't care what way the sea is when the other women will be keening. (*To* NORA) Give me the Holy Water, Nora, there's a small sup still on the dresser.

(NORA *gives it to her.*)

MAURYA (*drops* MICHAEL's *clothes across* BARTLEY's *feet, and sprinkles the Holy Water over him*). It isn't that I haven't prayed for you, Bartley, to the Almighty God. It isn't that I haven't said prayers in the dark night till you wouldn't know what I'ld be saying; but it's a great rest I'll have now, and it's time surely. It's a great rest I'll have now, and great sleeping in the long nights after Samhain, if it's only a bit of wet flour we do have to eat, and maybe a fish that would be stinking. (*She kneels down again, crossing herself, and saying prayers under her breath.*)

CATHLEEN (*to an old man*). Maybe yourself and Eamon would make a coffin when the sun rises. We have fine white boards herself bought, God help her, thinking Michael would be found, and I have a new cake you can eat while you'll be working.

THE OLD MAN (*looking at the boards*). Are there nails with them?

CATHLEEN. There are not, Colum; we didn't think of the nails.

ANOTHER MAN. It's a great wonder she wouldn't think of the nails, and all the coffins she's seen made already.

CATHLEEN. It's getting old she is, and broken.

(MAURYA *stands up again very slowly and spreads out the pieces of* MICHAEL's *clothes beside the body, sprinkling them with the last of the Holy Water.*)

NORA (*in a whisper to* CATHLEEN). She's quiet now and easy; but the day Michael was drowned you could hear her crying out from this to the spring well. It's fonder she was of Michael, and would any one have thought that?

CATHLEEN (*slowly and clearly*). An old woman will be soon tired with anything she will do, and isn't it nine days herself is after crying and keening, and making great sorrow in the house?

MAURYA (*puts the empty cup mouth downwards on the table, and lays her hands together on* BART-LEY's *feet*). They're all together this time, and the end is come. May the Almighty God have mercy on Bartley's soul, and on Michael's soul, and on the souls of Sheamus and Patch, and Stephen and Shawn (*bending her head*); and may He have mercy on my soul, Nora, and on the soul of every one is left living in the world. (*She pauses, and the keen rises a little more loudly from the women, then sinks away.*)

MAURYA (*continuing*). Michael has a clean burial in the far north, by the grace of the Almighty God. Bartley will have a fine coffin out of the white boards, and a deep grave surely. What more can we want than that? No man at all can be living for ever, and we must be satisfied. (*She kneels down again and the curtain falls slowly.*)

A Sunny Morning

A COMEDY OF MADRID IN ONE ACT

BY SERAFIN AND JOAQUIN ALVAREZ QUINTERO

TRANSLATED FROM THE SPANISH BY
LUCRETIA XAVIER FLOYD

CHARACTERS

DOÑA LAURA
PETRA, *her maid*
DON GONZALO
JUANITO, *his servant*

SCENE: A retired corner in a Park in Madrid
TIME: The present

A SUNNY MORNING

SCENE—*A sunny morning in a retired corner of a park in Madrid. Autumn. A bench at Right.*

DOÑA LAURA, *a handsome, white-haired old lady of about seventy, refined in appearance, her bright eyes and entire manner giving evidence that despite her age her mental faculties are unimpaired, enters leaning upon the arm of her maid,* PETRA. *In her free hand she carries a parasol, which serves also as a cane.*

DOÑA LAURA. I am so glad to be here. I feared my seat would be occupied. What a beautiful morning!

PETRA. The sun is hot.

DOÑA LAURA. Yes, you are only twenty. (*She sits down on the bench*) Oh, I feel more tired today than usual. (*Noticing* PETRA, *who seems impatient*) Go, if you wish to chat with your guard.

PETRA. He is not mine, señora; he belongs to the park.

DOÑA LAURA. He belongs more to you than he does to the park. Go find him, but remain within calling distance.

PETRA. I see him over there waiting for me.

DOÑA LAURA. Do not remain more than ten minutes.

PETRA. Very well, señora. (*Walks toward* R.)

DOÑA LAURA. Wait a moment.

PETRA. What does the señora wish?

DOÑA LAURA. Give me the bread crumbs.

PETRA. I don't know what is the matter with me.

DOÑA LAURA (*smiling*). I do. Your head is where your heart is—with the guard.

PETRA. Here, señora. (*She hands* DOÑA LAURA *a small bag. Exit* PETRA *by* R.)

DOÑA LAURA. Adiós. (*Glances toward trees at* R.) Here they come! They know just when to expect me. (*She rises, walks toward* R., *and throws three handfuls of bread crumbs*) These are for the spryest, these for the gluttons, and these for the little ones which are the most persistent. (*Laughs. She returns to her seat and watches, with a pleased expression, the pigeons feeding*) There, that big one is always first! I know him by his big head. Now one, now another, now two, now three—— That little fellow is the least timid. I believe he would eat from my hand. That one takes his piece and flies up to that branch alone. He is a philosopher. But where do they all come from? It seems as if the news had spread. Ha, ha! Don't quarrel. There is enough for all. I'll bring more tomorrow.

(*Enter* DON GONZALO *and* JUANITO *from* L.C. DON GONZALO *is an old gentleman of seventy, gouty and impatient. He leans upon* JUANITO's *arm and drags his feet somewhat as he walks.*)

DON GONZALO. Idling their time away! They should be saying mass.

JUANITO. You can sit here, señor. There is only a lady. (DOÑA LAURA *turns her head and listens.*)

DON GONZALO. I won't, Juanito. I want a bench to myself.

JUANITO. But there is none.

DON GONZALO. That one over there is mine.

JUANITO. There are three priests sitting there.

DON GONZALO. Rout them out. Have they gone?

JUANITO. No, indeed. They are talking.

DON GONZALO. Just as if they were glued to the seat. No hope of their leaving. Come this way, Juanito. (*They walked toward the birds, Right.*)

DOÑA LAURA (*indignantly*). Look out!

DON GONZALO. Are you speaking to me, señora?

DOÑA LAURA. Yes, to you.

DON GONZALO. What do you wish?

DOÑA LAURA. You have scared away the birds who were feeding on my crumbs.

DON GONZALO. What do I care about the birds?

DOÑA LAURA. But I do.

DON GONZALO. This is a public park.

DOÑA LAURA. Then why do you complain that the priests have taken your bench?

DON GONZALO. Señora, we have not met. I cannot imagine why you take the liberty of addressing me. Come, Juanito. (*Both go out* R.)

DOÑA LAURA. What an ill-natured old man! Why must people get so fussy and cross when they reach a certain age? (*Looking toward* R.) I am glad. He lost that bench, too. Serves him right for scaring the birds. He is furious. Yes, yes; find a seat if you can. Poor man! He is wiping the perspiration from his face. Here he comes. A carriage would not raise more dust than his feet. (*Enter* DON GONZALO *and* JUANITO *by* R. *and walk toward* L.)

DON GONZALO. Have the priests gone yet, Juanito?

JUANITO. No, indeed, señor. They are still there.

DON GONZALO. The authorities should place more benches here for these sunny mornings. Well, I suppose I must resign myself and sit on the bench with the old lady. (*Muttering to himself, he sits at the extreme end of* DOÑA LAURA's *bench and looks at her indignantly. Touches his hat as he greets her*) Good morning.

DOÑA LAURA. What, you here again?

DON GONZALO. I repeat that we have not met.

DOÑA LAURA. I was responding to your salute.

DON GONZALO. "Good morning" should be answered by "good morning," and that is all you should have said.

DOÑA LAURA. You should have asked permission to sit on this bench, which is mine.

DON GONZALO. The benches here are public property.

DOÑA LAURA. Why, you said the one the priests have was yours.

DON GONZALO. Very well, very well. I have nothing more to say. (*Between his teeth*) Senile old lady! She ought to be at home knitting and counting her beads.

DOÑA LAURA. Don't grumble any more. I'm not going to leave just to please you.

DON GONZALO (*brushing the dust from his shoes with his handkerchief*). If the ground were sprinkled a little it would be an improvement.

DOÑA LAURA. Do you use your handkerchief as a shoe brush?

DON GONZALO. Why not?

DOÑA LAURA. Do you use a shoe brush as a handkerchief?

DON GONZALO. What right have you to criticize my actions?

DOÑA LAURA. A neighbor's right.

DON GONZALO. Juanito, my book. I do not care to listen to nonsense.

DOÑA LAURA. You are very polite.

DON GONZALO. Pardon me, señora, but never interfere with what does not concern you.

DOÑA LAURA. I generally say what I think.

DON GONZALO. And more to the same effect. Give me the book, Juanito.

JUANITO. Here, señor. (*JUANITO takes a book from his pocket, hands it to DON GONZALO, then exits by R. DON GONZALO, casting indignant glances at DOÑA LAURA, puts on an enormous pair of glasses, takes from his pocket a reading-glass, adjusts both to suit him, and opens his book.*)

DOÑA LAURA. I thought you were taking out a telescope.

DON GONZALO. Was that you?

DOÑA LAURA. Your sight must be keen.

DON GONZALO. Keener than yours is.

DOÑA LAURA. Yes, evidently.

DON GONZALO. Ask the hares and partridges.

DOÑA LAURA. Ah! Do you hunt?

DON GONZALO. I did, and even now——

DOÑA LAURA. Oh, yes, of course!

DON GONZALO. Yes, señora. Every

Sunday I take my gun and dog, you understand, and go to one of my estates near Aravaca and kill time.

DOÑA LAURA. Yes, kill time. That is all you kill.

DON GONZALO. Do you think so? I could show you a wild boar's head in my study——

DOÑA LAURA. Yes, and I could show you a tiger's skin in my boudoir. What does that prove?

DON GONZALO. Very well, señora, please allow me to read. Enough conversation.

DOÑA LAURA. Well, you subside, then.

DON GONZALO. But first I shall take a pinch of snuff. (*Takes out snuff box*) Will you have some? (*Offers box to* DOÑA LAURA.)

DOÑA LAURA. If it is good.

DON GONZALO. It is of the finest. You will like it.

DOÑA LAURA (*taking pinch of snuff*). It clears my head.

DON GONZALO. And mine.

DOÑA LAURA. Do you sneeze?

DON GONZALO. Yes, señora, three times.

DOÑA LAURA. And so do I. What a coincidence! (*After taking the snuff, they await the sneezes, both anxiously, and sneeze alternately three times each.*)

DON GONZALO. There, I feel better.

DOÑA LAURA. So do I. (*Aside*) The snuff has made peace between us.

DON GONZALO. You will excuse me if I read aloud?

DOÑA LAURA. Read as loud as you please; you will not disturb me.

DON GONZALO (*reading*). "All love is sad, but sad as it is, it is the best thing that we know." That is from Campoamor.

DOÑA LAURA. Ah!

DON GONZALO (*reading*). "The daughters of the mothers I once loved kiss me now as they would a graven image." Those lines, I take it, are in a humorous vein.

DOÑA LAURA (*laughing*). I take them so, too.

DON GONZALO. There are some beautiful poems in this book. Here. "Twenty years pass. He returns."

DOÑA LAURA. You cannot imagine how it affects me to see you reading with all those glasses.

DON GONZALO. Can you read without any?

DOÑA LAURA. Certainly.

DON GONZALO. At your age? You're jesting.

DOÑA LAURA. Pass me the book, then. (*Takes book; reads aloud.*)
"*Twenty years pass. He returns.
And each, beholding the other,
exclaims—
Can it be that this is he?
Heavens, is it she?*"
(DOÑA LAURA *returns the book to* DON GONZALO.)

DON GONZALO. Indeed, I envy you your wonderful eyesight.

DOÑA LAURA (*aside*). I know every word by heart.

DON GONZALO. I am very fond of good verses, very fond. I even composed some in my youth.

DOÑA LAURA. Good ones?

DON GONZALO. Of all kinds. I was a great friend of Espronceda, Zorrilla, Bécquer, and others. I first met Zorrilla in America.

DOÑA LAURA. Why, have you been in America?

DON GONZALO. Several times. The first time I went I was only six years old.

DOÑA LAURA. You must have gone with Columbus in one of his caravels!

DON GONZALO (*laughing*). Not quite as bad as that. I am old, I admit, but I did not know Ferdinand and Isabella. (*They both laugh*) I was also a great friend of Campoamor. I met him in Valencia. I am a native of that city.

DOÑA LAURA. You are?

DON GONZALO. I was brought up there and there I spent my early youth. Have you ever visited that city?

DOÑA LAURA. Yes, señor. Not far from Valencia there was a villa that, if still there, should retain memories of me. I spent several seasons there. It was many, many years ago. It was near the sea, hidden away among lemon and orange trees. They called it—let me see, what did they call it —Maricela.

DON GONZALO (*startled*). Maricela?

DOÑA LAURA. Maricela. Is the name familiar to you?

DON GONZALO. Yes, very familiar. If my memory serves me right, for we forget as we grow old, there lived in that villa the most beautiful woman I have ever seen, and I assure you I have seen many. Let me see—what was her name? Laura— Laura—Laura Llorente.

DOÑA LAURA (*startled*). Laura Llorente?

DON GONZALO. Yes. (*They look at each other intently.*)

DOÑA LAURA (*recovering herself*). Nothing. You reminded me of my best friend.

DON GONZALO. How strange!

DOÑA LAURA. It is strange. She was called "The Silver Maiden."

DON GONZALO. Precisely, "The Silver Maiden." By that name she was known in that locality. I seem to see her as if she were before me now, at that window with the red roses. Do you remember that window?

DOÑA LAURA. Yes, I remember. It was the window of her room.

DON GONZALO. She spent many hours there. I mean in my day.

DOÑA LAURA (*sighing*). And in mine, too.

DON GONZALO. She was ideal. Fair as a lily, jet black hair and black eyes, with an uncommonly sweet expression. She seemed to cast a radiance wherever she was. Her figure was beautiful, perfect. "What forms of sovereign beauty God models in human clay!" She was a dream.

DOÑA LAURA (*aside*). If you but knew that dream was now by your side, you would realize what dreams come to. (*Aloud*) She was very unfortunate and had a sad love affair.

DON GONZALO. Very sad. (*They look at each other.*)

DOÑA LAURA. Did you hear of it?

DON GONZALO. Yes.

DOÑA LAURA. The ways of Providence are strange. (*Aside*) Gonzalo!

DON GONZALO. The gallant lover, in the same affair——

DOÑA LAURA. Ah, the duel?

DON GONZALO. Precisely, the duel. The gallant lover was—my cousin, of whom I was very fond.

DOÑA LAURA. Oh, yes, a cousin? My friend told me in one of her letters the story of that affair, which was truly romantic. He, your cousin, passed by on horseback every morning down the rose path under her window, and tossed up to her balcony a bouquet of flowers which she caught.

DON GONZALO. And later in the afternoon the gallant horseman would return by the same path. and catch the bouquet of flowers she would toss him. Am I right?

DOÑA LAURA. Yes. They wanted to marry her to a merchant whom she would not have.

DON GONZALO. And one night, when my cousin waited under her window to hear her sing, this other person presented himself unexpectedly.

DOÑA LAURA. And insulted your cousin.

DON GONZALO. There was a quarrel.

DOÑA LAURA. And later a duel.

DON GONZALO. Yes, at sunrise, on the beach, and the merchant was badly wounded. My cousin had to conceal himself for a few days and later to fly.

DOÑA LAURA. You seem to know the story well.

DON GONZALO. And so do you.

DOÑA LAURA. I have explained that a friend repeated it to me.

DON GONZALO. As my cousin did to me. (*Aside*) This is Laura!

DOÑA LAURA (*aside*). Why tell him? He does not suspect.

DON GONZALO (*aside*). She is entirely innocent.

DOÑA LAURA. And was it you, by any chance, who advised your cousin to forget Laura?

DON GONZALO. Why, my cousin never forgot her!

DOÑA LAURA. How do you account, then, for his conduct?

DON GONZALO. I will tell you. The young man took refuge in my house, fearful of the consequences of a duel with a person highly regarded in that locality. From my home he went to Seville, then came to Madrid. He wrote Laura many letters, some of them in verse. But undoubtedly they were intercepted by her parents, for she never answered at all. Gonzalo then, in despair, believing his love lost to him forever, joined the army, went to Africa, and there, in a trench, met a glorious death, grasping the flag of Spain and whispering the name of his beloved Laura——

DOÑA LAURA (*aside*). What an atrocious lie!

DON GONZALO (*aside*). I could not have killed myself more gloriously.

DOÑA LAURA. You must have been prostrated by the calamity.

DON GONZALO. Yes, indeed, señora. As if he were my brother. I presume, though, on the contrary, that Laura in a short time was chasing butterflies in her garden, indifferent to regret.

DOÑA LAURA. No, señor, no!

DON GONZALO. It is woman's way.

DOÑA LAURA. Even if it were woman's way, "The Silver Maiden" was not of that disposition. My friend awaited news for days, months, a year, and no letter came. One afternoon, just at sunset, as the first stars were appearing, she was seen to leave the house, and with quickening steps wend her way toward the beach, the beach where her beloved had risked his life. She wrote his name on the sand, then sat down upon a rock, her gaze fixed upon the horizon. The waves murmured their eternal threnody and slowly crept up to the rock where the maiden sat. The tide rose with a boom and swept her out to sea.

DON GONZALO. Good heavens!

DOÑA LAURA. The fishermen of that shore who often tell the story affirm that it was a long time before the waves washed away that name written on the sand. (*Aside*) You will not get ahead of me in decorating my own funeral.

DON GONZALO (*aside*). She lies worse than I do.

DOÑA LAURA. Poor Laura!

DON GONZALO. Poor Gonzalo!

DOÑA LAURA (*aside*). I will not tell him that I married two years later.

DON GONZALO (*aside*). In three months I ran off to Paris with a ballet dancer.

DOÑA LAURA. Fate is curious. Here are you and I, complete strangers, met by chance, discussing the romance of old friends of long ago! We have been conversing as if we were old friends.

DON GONZALO. Yes, it is curious, considering the ill-natured prelude to our conversation.

DOÑA LAURA. You scared away the birds.

DON GONZALO. I was unreasonable, perhaps.

DOÑA LAURA. Yes, that was evident. (*Sweetly*) Are you coming again tomorrow?

DON GONZALO. Most certainly, if it is a sunny morning. And not only will I not scare away the birds, but I will bring a few crumbs.

DOÑA LAURA. Thank you very much. Birds are grateful and repay attention. I wonder where my maid is? Petra! (*Signals for her maid.*)

DON GONZALO (*aside, looking at* LAURA, *whose back is turned*). No, no, I will not reveal myself. I am grotesque now. Better that she recall the gallant horseman who passed daily beneath her window tossing flowers.

DOÑA LAURA. Here she comes.

DON GONZALO. That Juanito! He plays havoc with the nursemaids. (*Looks* R. *and signals with his hand.*)

DOÑA LAURA (*aside, looking at* GONZALO, *whose back is turned*). No, I am too sadly changed. It is better he should remember me as the black-eyed girl tossing flowers as he passed among the roses in the garden. (JUANITO *enters by* R., PETRA *by* L. *She has a bunch of violets in her hand.*)

DOÑA LAURA. Well, Petra! At last!

DON GONZALO. Juanito, you are late.

PETRA (*to* DOÑA LAURA). The guard gave me these violets for you, señora.

DOÑA LAURA. How very nice! Thank him for me. They are fragrant. (*As she takes the violets from her maid a few loose ones fall to the ground.*)

DON GONZALO. My dear lady, this has been a great honor and a great pleasure.

DOÑA LAURA. It has also been a pleasure to me.

DON GONZALO. Good-bye until tomorrow.

DOÑA LAURA. Until tomorrow.

DON GONZALO. If it *is* sunny.

DOÑA LAURA. A sunny morning. Will you go to your bench?

DON GONZALO. No, I will come to this—if you do not object?

DOÑA LAURA. This bench is at your disposal.

DON GONZALO. And I will surely bring the crumbs.

DOÑA LAURA. Tomorrow, then?

DON GONZALO. Tomorrow! (LAURA *walks away toward* R., *supported by her* MAID. GONZALO, *before leaving with* JUANITO, *trembling and with a great effort, stoops to pick up the violets* LAURA *dropped. Just then* LAURA *turns her head and surprises him picking up the flowers.*)

JUANITO. What are you doing, señor?

DON GONZALO. Juanito, wait——

DOÑA LAURA (*aside*). Yes, it is he!

DON GONZALO (*aside*). It is she, and no mistake. (DOÑA LAURA *and* DON GONZALO *wave farewell.*)

DOÑA LAURA. "Can it be that this is he?"

DON GONZALO. "Heavens, is it she?" (*They smile once more, as if she were again at the window and he below in the rose garden, and then disappear upon the arms of their servants.*)

CURTAIN

A Night at an Inn

BY LORD DUNSANY

CHARACTERS

A. E. Scott-Fortescue
  (The Toff) *a dilapidated*
  gentleman ⎫
William Jones (Bill) ⎬ *Merchant Sailors*
Albert Thomas ⎭
Jacob Smith (Sniggers)
1st Priest of Klesh
2nd Priest of Klesh
3rd Priest of Klesh
Klesh

The Curtain rises on a room in an inn

A NIGHT AT AN INN

SNIGGERS *and* BILL *are talking.* THE TOFF *is reading a paper.* ALBERT *sits a little apart.*

SNIGGERS. What's the idea, I wonder?

BILL. I don't know.

SNIGGERS. And how much longer will he keep us here?

BILL. We've been here three days.

SNIGGERS. And 'aven't seen a soul.

BILL. And a pretty penny it cost us when he rented the pub.

SNIGGERS. 'Ow long did 'e rent the pub for?

BILL. You never know with him.

SNIGGERS. It's lonely enough.

BILL. 'Ow long did you rent the pub for, Toffy?
(THE TOFF *continues to read a sporting paper; he takes no notice of what is said.*)

SNIGGERS. 'E's *such* a toff.

BILL. Yet 'e's clever, no mistake.

SNIGGERS. Those clever ones are the beggars to make a muddle. Their plans are clever enough, but they don't work, and then they make a mess of things much worse than you or me.

BILL. Ah.

SNIGGERS. I don't like this place.

BILL. Why not?

SNIGGERS. I don't like the looks of it.

BILL. He's keeping us here because here those niggers can't find us. The three heathen priests what was looking for us so. But we want to go and sell our ruby soon.

ALBERT. There's no sense in it.

BILL. Why not, Albert?

ALBERT. Because I gave those black devils the slip in Hull.

BILL. You give 'em the slip, Albert?

ALBERT. The slip, all three of them. The fellows with the gold spots on their foreheads. I had the ruby then and I give them the slip in Hull.

BILL. How did you do it, Albert?

ALBERT. I had the ruby and they were following me. . . .

BILL. Who told them you had the ruby? You didn't show it?

ALBERT. No. . . . But they kind of know.

SNIGGERS. They kind of know, Albert?

ALBERT. Yes, they know if you've

got it. Well, they sort of mouched after me, and I tells a policeman, and he says, Oh, they were only three poor niggers and they wouldn't hurt me. Ugh! When I thought of what they did in Malta to poor old Jim.

BILL. Yes and to George in Bombay before we started.

SNIGGERS. Ugh!

BILL. Why didn't you give 'em in charge?

ALBERT. What about the ruby, Bill?

BILL. Ah!

ALBERT. Well, I did better than that. I walks up and down through Hull. I walks slow enough. And then I turns a corner and I runs. I never sees a corner but I turns it. But sometimes I let a corner pass just to fool them. I twists about like a hare. Then I sits down and waits. No priests.

SNIGGERS. What?

ALBERT. No heathen black devils with gold spots on their face. I give 'em the slip.

BILL. Well done, Albert.

SNIGGERS (*after a sigh of content*). Why didn't you tell us?

ALBERT. 'Cause 'e won't let you speak. 'E's got 'is plans and 'e thinks we're silly folk. Things must be done 'is way. And all the time I've give 'em the slip. Might 'ave 'ad one o' them crooked knives in him before now but for me who give 'em the slip in Hull.

BILL. Well done. Albert.

SNIGGERS. Do you hear that, Tolfy? Albert has give 'em the slip.

THE TOFF. Yes, I hear.

SNIGGERS. Well, what do you say to that?

THE TOFF. Oh . . . Well done, Albert.

ALBERT. And what a' you going to do?

THE TOFF. Going to wait.

ALBERT. Don't seem to know what 'e's waiting for.

SNIGGERS. It's a nasty place.

ALBERT. It's getting silly, Bill. Our money's gone and we want to sell the ruby. Let's get on to a town.

BILL. But 'e won't come.

ALBERT. Then we'll leave him.

SNIGGERS. We'll be all right if we keep away from Hull.

ALBERT. We'll go to London.

BILL. But 'e must 'ave 'is share.

SNIGGERS. All right. Only let's go. (*To* THE TOFF) We're going, do you hear? Give us the ruby.

THE TOFF. Certainly. (*He gives them a ruby from his waist-coat pocket, it is the size of a small hen's egg*) (*He goes on reading his paper.*)

ALBERT. Come on, Sniggers. (*Exeunt* ALBERT *and* SNIGGERS.)

BILL. Good-bye, old man. We'll give you your fair share, but there's nothing to do here, no girls, no halls, and we must sell the ruby.

THE TOFF. I'm not a fool, Bill.

BILL. No, no, of course not. Of course you ain't, and you've helped us a lot. Good-bye. You'll say good-bye.

THE TOFF. Oh, yes. Good-bye. (*Still reads paper. Exit* BILL.)
(THE TOFF *puts a revolver on the table beside him and goes on with his paper.*)

SNIGGERS (*out of breath*). We've come back, Toffy.

THE TOFF. So you have.

ALBERT. Toffy—How did they get here?

THE TOFF. They walked, of course.

ALBERT. But it's eighty miles.

SNIGGERS. Did you know they were here, Toffy?

THE TOFF. Expected them about now.

ALBERT. Eighty miles.

BILL. Toffy, old man—what are we to do?

THE TOFF. Ask Albert.

BILL. If they can do things like this there's no one can save us but you, Toffy—I always knew you were a clever one. We won't be fools any more. We'll obey you, Toffy.

THE TOFF. You're brave enough and strong enough. There isn't many that would steal a ruby eye out of an idol's head, and such an idol as that was to look at, and on such a night. You're brave enough, Bill. But you're all three of you fools. Jim would have none of my plans and where's Jim? And George. What did they do to him?

SNIGGERS. Don't Toffy!

THE TOFF. Well then your strength is no use to you. You want cleverness; or they'll have you the way that they had George and Jim.

ALL. Ugh!

THE TOFF. These black priests would follow you round the world in circles. Year after year, till they got their idol's eye. And if we died with it they'd follow our grandchildren. That fool thinks he can escape men like that by running round three streets in the town of Hull.

ALBERT. God's truth, *you* 'aven't escaped them, because they're 'ere.

THE TOFF. So I supposed.

ALBERT. You *supposed?*

THE TOFF. Yes, I believe there's no announcement in the society papers. But I took this country seat especially to receive them. There's plenty of room if you dig, it is pleasantly situated, and, what is most important, it is in a very quiet neighborhood. So I am at home to them this afternoon.

BILL. Well, you're a deep one.

THE TOFF. And remember you've only my wits between you and death, and don't put your futile plans against those of an educated gentleman.

ALBERT. If you're a gentleman why don't you go about among gentlemen instead of the likes of us?

THE TOFF. Because I was too clever for them as I am too clever for you.

ALBERT. Too clever for them?

THE TOFF. I never lost a game of cards in my life.

BILL. You never lost a game!

THE TOFF. Not when there was money on it.

BILL. Well, well.

THE TOFF. Have a game of poker?

ALL. No thanks.

THE TOFF. Then do as you're told.

BILL. All right, Toffy.

SNIGGERS. I saw something just then. Hadn't we better draw the curtains?

THE TOFF. No.

SNIGGERS. What?

THE TOFF. Don't draw the curtains.

SNIGGERS. Oh all right.

BILL. But Toffy they can see us. One doesn't let the enemy do that. I don't see why. . . .

THE TOFF. No, of course you don't.

BILL. Oh all right, Toffy.

(*All begin to pull out revolvers.*)

THE TOFF (*putting his own away*). No revolvers, please.

ALBERT. Why not?

THE TOFF. Because I don't want any noise at my party. We might get guests that hadn't been invited. *Knives* are a different matter.

(ALL *draw knives.* THE TOFF *signs to them not to draw them yet.* THE TOFF *has already taken back his ruby.*)

BILL. I think they're coming, Toffy.

THE TOFF. Not yet.

ALBERT. When will they come?

THE TOFF. When I am quite ready to receive them. Not before.

SNIGGERS. I should like to get this over.

THE TOFF. Should you? Then we'll have them now.

SNIGGERS. Now?

THE TOFF. Yes. Listen to me. You shall do as you see me do. You will all pretend to go out. I'll show you how. I've got the ruby. When they see me alone they will come for their idol's eye.

BILL. How can they tell like this which of us has it?

THE TOFF. I confess I don't know, but they seem to.

SNIGGERS. What will you do when they come in?

THE TOFF. I shall do nothing.

SNIGGERS. What?

THE TOFF. They will creep up behind me. Then my friends, Sniggers and Bill and Albert, who gave them the slip, will do what they can.

BILL. All right, Toffy. Trust us.

THE TOFF. If you're a little slow you will see enacted the cheerful spectacle that accompanied the demise of Jim.

SNIGGERS. Don't, Toffy. We'll be there all right.

THE TOFF. Very well. Now watch me. (*He goes past the windows to the inner door Right; he opens it inwards, and then under cover of the open door he slips down on his knee and closes it, remaining on the inside, appearing to have gone out. He signs to the others who understand. Then he appears to re-enter in the same manner.*)

THE TOFF. Now. I shall sit with my back to the door. You go out one by one so far as our friends can make out. Crouch very low, to be on the safe side. They mustn't see you through the window.*
(BILL *makes his sham exit.*)

THE TOFF. Remember, no revolvers. The police are, I believe, proverbially inquisitive.
(*The other two follow* BILL. *All three are now crouching inside the door Right.* THE TOFF *puts the ruby beside him on the table. He lights a cigarette.*)
(*The door in back opens so slowly that you can hardly say at what moment it began.* THE TOFF *picks up his paper.*)

(A NATIVE *of India wriggles along the floor ever so slowly, seeking cover from chairs. He moves Left where* THE TOFF *is. The three sailors are Right.* SNIGGERS *and* ALBERT *lean forward.* BILL'S *arm keeps them back. An arm-chair had better conceal them from the Indian. The black* PRIEST *nears* THE TOFF.)
(BILL *watches to see if any more are coming. Then he leaps forward alone (he has taken his boots off) and knifes the* PRIEST.)
(*The* PRIEST *tries to shout, but* BILL'S *left hand is over his mouth.*)
(THE TOFF *continues to read his sporting paper. He never looks round.*)

BILL (*sotto voce*). There's only one, Toffy. What shall we do?

THE TOFF (*without turning his head*). Only one?

BILL. Yes.

THE TOFF. Wait a moment. Let me think. (*Still apparently absorbed in his paper*) Ah, yes. You go back, Bill. We must attract another guest. Now are you ready?

BILL. Yes.

THE TOFF. All right. You shall now see my demise at my Yorkshire residence. You must receive guests for me. (*He leaps up in full view of the window, flings up both arms and falls on to the floor near the dead* PRIEST) Now be ready. (*His eyes close.*)
(*There is a long pause. Again the door opens, very, very slowly. Another* PRIEST *creeps in. He has three golden spots upon his forehead. He looks round, then he creeps up to his companion and turns him over*

and looks inside each of his clenched hands. Then he looks at the recumbent TOFF. *Then he creeps towards him.* BILL *slips after him and knifes him like the other with his left hand over his mouth.*)

BILL (*sotto voce*). We've only got two, Toffy.

THE TOFF. Still another.

BILL. What'll we do?

THE TOFF (*sitting up*). Hum.

BILL. This is the best way, much.

THE TOFF. Out of the question. Never play the same game twice.

BILL. Why not, Toffy?

THE TOFF. Doesn't work if you do.

BILL. Well?

THE TOFF. I have it, Albert. You will now walk into the room. I showed you how to do it.

ALBERT. Yes.

THE TOFF. Just run over here and have a fight at this window with these two men.

ALBERT. But they're——

THE TOFF. Yes, they're dead, my perspicuous Albert. But Bill and I are going to resuscitate them——. Come on.
(BILL *picks up a body under the arms.*)

THE TOFF. That's right, Bill. (*Does the same*) Come and help us, Sniggers—— (SNIGGERS *comes*) Keep low, keep low. Wave their arms about, Sniggers. Don't show yourself. Now, Albert, over you go. Our Albert is slain. Back you get, Bill. Back Sniggers. Still Albert. Mustn't move when he comes. Not a muscle.
(A FACE *appears at the window and stays for some time. Then the door opens and looking craftily round the third* PRIEST *enters. He looks at his companion's bodies and turns round. He suspects something. He takes up one of the knives and with a knife in each hand he puts his back to the wall. He looks to the left and right.*)

THE TOFF. Come on, Bill.
(*The* PRIEST *rushes to the door.* THE TOFF *knifes the last* PRIEST *from behind.*)

THE TOFF. A good day's work, my friends.

BILL. Well done, Toffy. Oh, you are a deep one.

ALBERT. A deep one if ever there was one.

SNIGGERS. There ain't any more, Bill, are there?

THE TOFF. No more in the world, my friend.

BILL. Aye, that's all there are. There were only three in the temple. Three priests and their beastly idol.

ALBERT. What is it worth, Toffy? Is it worth a thousand pounds?

THE TOFF. It's worth all they've got in the shop. Worth just whatever we like to ask for it.

ALBERT. Then we're millionaires now.

THE TOFF. Yes, and what is more important, we no longer have any heirs.

BILL. We'll have to sell it now.

ALBERT. That won't be easy. It's a pity it isn't small and we had half a dozen. Hadn't the idol any other on him?

BILL. No, he was green jade all over and only had this one eye. He had it in the middle of his forehead, and was a long sight uglier than anything else in the world.

SNIGGERS. I'm sure we ought all to be very grateful to Toffy.

BILL. And indeed we ought.

ALBERT. If it hadn't 'ave been for him——

BILL. Yes, if it hadn't a been for old Toffy.

SNIGGERS. He's a deep one.

THE TOFF. Well you see I just have a knack of foreseeing things.

SNIGGERS. I should think you did.

BILL. Why, I don't suppose anything happens that our Toff doesn't foresee. Does it, Toffy?

THE TOFF. Well, I don't think it does, Bill. I don't think it often does.

BILL. Life is no more than just a game of cards to our old Toff.

THE TOFF. Well, we've taken these fellows' trick.

SNIGGERS (going to the window).

It wouldn't do for anyone to see them.

THE TOFF. Oh nobody will come this way. We're all alone on a moor.

BILL. Where will we put them?

THE TOFF. Bury them in the cellar but there's no hurry.

BILL. And what then, Toffy?

THE TOFF. Why, then we'll go to London and upset the ruby business. We have really come through this job very nicely.

BILL. I think the first thing that we ought to do is to give a little supper to old Toffy. We'll bury these fellows tonight.

ALBERT. Yes, let's.

SNIGGERS. The very thing.

BILL. And we'll all drink his health.

ALBERT. Good old Toffy.

SNIGGERS. He ought to have been a general or a premier.
(They get bottles from cupboard, etc.)

THE TOFF. Well, we've earned our bit of a supper.
(They sit down.)

BILL (glass in hand). Here's to old Toffy who guessed everything.

ALBERT and SNIGGERS. Good old Toffy.

BILL. Toffy who saved our lives and made our fortunes.

ALBERT *and* SNIGGERS. Hear. Hear.

THE TOFF. And here's to Bill who saved me twice tonight.

BILL. Couldn't have done it but for your cleverness, Toffy.

SNIGGERS. Hear, hear. Hear, hear.

ALBERT. He foresees everything.

BILL. A speech, Toffy. A speech from our general.

ALL. Yes, a speech.

SNIGGERS. A speech.

THE TOFF. Well, get me some water. This whiskey's too much for my head, and I must keep it clear till our friends are safe in the cellar.

BILL. Water. Yes, of course. Get him some water, Sniggers.

SNIGGERS. We don't use water here. Where shall I get it?

BILL. Outside in the garden. (*Exit* SNIGGERS.)

ALBERT. Here's to fortune. (*They all drink.*)

BILL. Here's to Albert Thomas, Esquire. (*He drinks.*)

THE TOFF. Albert Thomas, Esquire. (*He drinks.*)

ALBERT. And William Jones, Esquire.

THE TOFF. William Jones, Esquire. (THE TOFF *and* ALBERT *drinks.*) (*Re-enter* SNIGGERS *terrified.*)

THE TOFF. Hullo, here's Jacob Smith, Esquire, J.P., alias Sniggers, back again.

SNIGGERS. Toffy, I've been a thinking about my share in that ruby. I don't want it, Toffy, I don't want it.

THE TOFF. Nonsense, Sniggers, nonsense.

SNIGGERS. You shall have it, Toffy, you shall have it yourself, only say Sniggers has no share in this 'ere ruby. Say it Toffy, say it.

BILL. Want to turn informer, Sniggers?

SNIGGERS. No, no. Only I don't want the ruby, Toffy. . . .

THE TOFF. No more nonsense, Sniggers, we're all in together in this, if one hangs we all hang; but they won't outwit me. Besides, it's not a hanging affair, they had their knives.

SNIGGERS. Toffy, Toffy, I always treated you fair, Toffy. I was always one to say, give Toffy a chance. Take back my share, Toffy.

THE TOFF. What's the matter? What are you driving at?

SNIGGERS. Take it back, Toffy.

THE TOFF. Answer me, what are you up to?

SNIGGERS. I don't want my share any more.

BILL. Have you seen the police? (ALBERT *pulls out his knife.*)

THE TOFF. No, no knives, Albert.

ALBERT. What then?

THE TOFF. The honest truth in open court, barring the ruby. We were attacked.

SNIGGERS. There's no police.

THE TOFF. Well, then, what's the matter?

BILL. Out with it.

SNIGGERS. I swear to God . . .

ALBERT. Well?

THE TOFF. Don't interrupt.

SNIGGERS. I swear I saw something what I didn't like.

THE TOFF. What you didn't like?

SNIGGERS (*in tears*). O Toffy, Toffy, take it back. Take my share. Say you take it.

THE TOFF. What has he seen?
(*Dead silence only broken by* SNIGGERS' *sobs. Then stony steps are heard.*)
(*Enter a hideous* IDOL. *It is blind and gropes its way. It gropes its way to the ruby and picks it up and screws it into a socket in the forehead.*)
(SNIGGERS *still weeps softly, the rest stare in horror. The* IDOL *steps out not groping. Its steps move off then stop.*)

THE TOFF. Oh, great heavens!

ALBERT (*in a childish, plaintive voice*). What is it, Toffy?

BILL. Albert, it is that obscene idol (*in a whisper*) come from India.

ALBERT. It is gone.

BILL. It has taken its eye.

SNIGGERS. We are saved.

OFF, A VOICE (*with outlandish accent*). Meestaire William Jones, Able Seaman.

(THE TOFF *has never spoken, never moved. He only gazes stupidly in horror.*)

BILL. Albert, Albert, what is this? (*He rises and walks out. One moan is heard.* SNIGGERS *goes to window. He falls back sickly.*)

ALBERT (*in a whisper*). What has happened?

SNIGGERS. I have seen it. I have seen it. Oh, I have seen it. (*He returns to table.*)

THE TOFF (*laying his hand very gently on* SNIGGERS' *arm, speaking softly and winningly*). What was it, Sniggers?

SNIGGERS. I have seen it.

ALBERT. What?

SNIGGERS. Oh . . .

VOICE. Meestaire Albert Thomas, Able Seaman.

ALBERT. Must I go, Toffy? Toffy, must I go?

SNIGGERS (*clutching him*). Don't move.

ALBERT (*going*). Toffy, Toffy. (*Exit.*)

VOICE. Meestaire Jacob Smith, Able Seaman.

SNIGGERS. I can't go, Toffy. I can't go. I can't do it. (*He goes.*)

VOICE. Meestaire Arnold Everett Scott-Fortescue, late Esquire, Able Seaman.

THE TOFF. I did not foresee it. (*Exit.*)

CURTAIN

The Dear Departed

A COMEDY IN ONE ACT

BY STANLEY HOUGHTON

CHARACTERS

MRS. SLATER ⎱ *sisters*
MRS. JORDAN ⎰

HENRY SLATER ⎱ *their husbands*
BEN JORDAN ⎰

VICTORIA SLATER, *a girl of ten*
ABEL MERRYWEATHER

The action takes place in a provincial town on a Saturday afternoon.

THE DEAR DEPARTED

The scene is the sitting-room of a small house in a lower middle-class district of a provincial town. On the spectator's left is the window, with the blinds down. A sofa is in front of it. On his right is a fireplace with an armchair by it. In the middle of the wall facing the spectator is the door into the passage. To the left of the door a cheap, shabby chest of drawers, to the right a sideboard. In the middle of the room is the table, with chairs round it. Ornaments and a cheap American clock are on the mantelpiece, in the hearth a kettle. By the sideboard a pair of gaudy new carpet slippers. The table is partly laid for tea, and the necessaries for the meal are on the side-board, as also are copies of an evening paper and of Tit-Bits *and* Pearson's Weekly. *Turning to the left through the door takes you to the front door; to the right, upstairs. In the passage a hat-stand is visible.*

When the curtain rises MRS. SLATER *is seen laying the table. She is a vigorous, plump, red-faced vulgar woman, prepared to do any amount of straight talking to get her own way. She is in black, but not in complete mourning. She listens a moment and then goes to the window, opens it and calls into the street.*

MRS. SLATER (*sharply*). Victoria, Victoria! D'ye hear? Come in, will you?
(MRS. SLATER *closes window and puts the blind straight and then returns to her work at the table.* VICTORIA, *a precocious girl of ten, dressed in colors, enters.*)

MRS. S. I'm amazed at you, Victoria; I really am. How you can be gallivanting about in the street with your grandfather lying dead and cold upstairs, I don't know. Be off now, and change your dress before your Aunt Elizabeth and your Uncle Ben come. It would never do for them to find you in colors.

VICTORIA. What are they coming for? They haven't been here for ages.

MRS. S. They're coming to talk over poor grandpa's affairs. Your father sent them a telegram as soon as we found he was dead. (*A noise is heard*) Good gracious, that's never them. (MRS. SLATER *hurries to the door and opens it*) No, thank goodness: it's only your father.
(HENRY SLATER, *a stooping, heavy man with a drooping moustache, enters. He is wearing a black tail coat, gray trousers, a black tie and a bowler hat. He carries a little paper parcel.*)

HENRY. Not come yet, eh?

MRS. S. You can see they haven't, can't you? Now, Victoria, be off upstairs and that quick. Put your white frock on with a black sash.
(VICTORIA *goes out.*)

MRS. S. (*to* HENRY). I'm not satisfied, but it's the best we can do till our new black's ready, and Ben and Elizabeth will never have thought about mourning yet, so we'll outshine them there. (HENRY *sits in the armchair by the fire*) Get your boots off, Henry; Elizabeth's that prying she notices the least speck of dirt.

HENRY. I'm wondering if they'll come at all. When you and Elizabeth quarrelled she said she'd never set foot in your house again.

MRS. S. She'll come fast enough after her share of what grandfather's left. You know how hard she can be when she likes. Where she gets it from I can't tell.
(MRS. SLATER *unwraps the parcel* HENRY *has brought. It contains sliced tongue, which she puts on a dish on the table.*)

HENRY. I suppose it's in the family.

MRS. S. What do you mean by that, Henry Slater?

HENRY. I was referring to your father, not to you. Where are my slippers?

MRS. S. In the kitchen; but you want a new pair, those old ones are nearly worn out. (*Nearly breaking down*) You don't seem to realize what it's costing me to bear up like I am doing. My heart's fit to break when I see the little trifles that belonged to grandfather lying around, and think he'll never use them again. (*Briskly*) Here! you'd better wear these slippers of grandfather's now. It's lucky he'd just got a new pair.

HENRY. They'll be very small for me, my dear.

MRS. S. They'll stretch, won't they? I'm not going to have them wasted.

(*She has finished laying the table.*) Henry, I've been thinking about that bureau of grandfather's that's in his bedroom. You know I always wanted to have it after he died.

HENRY. You must arrange with Elizabeth when you're dividing things up.

MRS. S. Elizabeth's that sharp she'll see I'm after it, and she'll drive a hard bargain over it. Eh, what it is to have a low, money-grubbing spirit!

HENRY. Perhaps she's got her eye on the bureau as well.

MRS. S. She's never been here since grandfather bought it. If it was only down here instead of in his room, she'd never guess it wasn't our own.

HENRY (*startled*). Amelia! (*He rises.*)

MRS. S. Henry, why shouldn't we bring that bureau down here now? We could do it before they come.

HENRY (*stupefied*). I wouldn't care to.

MRS. S. Don't look so daft. Why not?

HENRY. It doesn't seem delicate, somehow.

MRS. S. We could put that shabby old chest of drawers upstairs where the bureau is now. Elizabeth could have that and welcome. I've always wanted to get rid of it. (*She points to the drawers.*)

HENRY. Suppose they come when we're doing it.

MRS. S. I'll fasten the front door. Get your coat off, Henry; we'll change it.

(MRS. SLATER *goes out to fasten the front door.* HENRY *takes his coat off.* MRS. SLATER *reappears.*)

MRS. S. I'll run up and move the chairs out of the way.

(VICTORIA *appears, dressed according to her mother's instructions.*)

VIC. Will you fasten my frock up the back, Mother?

MRS. S. I'm busy; get your father to do it.

(MRS. SLATER *hurries upstairs, and* HENRY *fastens the frock.*)

VIC. What have you got your coat off for, Father?

HENRY. Mother and me is going to bring grandfather's bureau down here.

VIC. (*after a moment's thought*). Are we pinching it before Aunt Elizabeth comes?

HENRY (*shocked*). No, my child. Grandpa gave it your mother before he died.

VIC. This morning?

HENRY. Yes.

VIC. Ah! He was drunk this morning.

HENRY. Hush; you mustn't ever say he was drunk, now.

(HENRY *has fastened the frock, and* MRS. SLATER *appears carrying a handsome clock under her arm.*)

MRS. S. I thought I'd fetch this down as well. (*She puts it on the mantelpiece*) Our clock's worth nothing and this always appealed to me.

VIC. That's grandpa's clock.

MRS. S. Chut! Be quiet! It's ours now. Come, Henry, lift your end. Victoria, don't breathe a word to your aunt about the clock and the bureau. (*They carry the chest of drawers through the doorway.*)

VIC. (*to herself*). I thought we'd pinched them.

(*After a short pause there is a sharp knock at the front door.*)

MRS. S. (*from upstairs*). Victoria, if that's your aunt and uncle you're not to open the door.

(VICTORIA *peeps through the window.*)

VIC. Mother, it's them!

MRS. S. You're not to open the door till I come down. (*Knocking repeated*) Let them knock away. (*There is a heavy bumping noise.*) Mind the wall, Henry.

(HENRY *and* MRS. SLATER, *very hot and flushed, stagger in with a pretty old-fashioned bureau containing a locked desk. They put it where the chest of drawers was, and straighten the ornaments, etc. The knocking is repeated.*)

MRS. S. That was a near thing. Open the door, Victoria. Now, Henry, get your coat on. (*She helps him.*)

HENRY. Did we knock much plaster off the wall?

MRS. S. Never mind the plaster. Do I look all right? (*Straightening her hair at the glass*) Just watch

Elizabeth's face when she sees we're all in half mourning. (*Throwing him* Tit-Bits) Take this and sit down. Try and look as if we'd been waiting for them.

(HENRY *sits in the armchair and* MRS. SLATER *left of table. They read ostentatiously.* VICTORIA *ushers in* BEN *and* MRS. JORDAN. *The latter is a stout, complacent woman with an impassive face and an irritating air of being always right. She is wearing a complete and deadly outfit of new mourning crowned by a great black hat with plumes.* BEN *is also in complete new mourning, with black gloves and a band round his hat. He is rather a jolly little man, accustomed to be humorous, but at present trying to adapt himself to the regrettable occasion. He has a bright, chirpy little voice.* MRS. JORDAN *sails into the room and solemnly goes straight to* MRS. SLATER *and kisses her. The men shake hands.* MRS. JORDAN *kisses* HENRY. BEN *kisses* MRS. SLATER. *Not a word is spoken.* MRS. SLATER *furtively inspects the new mourning.*)

MRS. JORDAN. Well, Amelia, and so he's "gone" at last.

MRS. S. Yes, he's gone. He was seventy-two a fortnight last Sunday. (*She sniffs back a tear,* MRS. JORDAN *sits on the left of the table.* MRS. SLATER *on the right.* HENRY *in the armchair.* BEN *on the sofa with* VICTORIA *near him.*)

BEN (*chirpily*). Now, Amelia, you mustn't give way. We've all got to die some time or other. It might have been worse.

MRS. S. I don't see how.

BEN. It might have been one of us.

HENRY. It's taken you a long time to get here, Elizabeth.

MRS. J. Oh, I couldn't do it. I really couldn't do it.

MRS. S. (*suspiciously*). Couldn't do what?

MRS. J. I couldn't start without getting the mourning. (*Glancing at her sister.*)

MRS. S. We've ordered ours, you may be sure. (*Acidly*) I never could fancy buying ready-made things.

MRS. J. No? For myself it's such a relief to get into the black. And now perhaps you'll tell us all about it. What did the doctor say?

MRS. S. Oh, he's not been near yet.

MRS. J. Not been near?

BEN (*in the same breath*). Didn't you send for him at once?

MRS. S. Of course I did. Do you take me for a fool? I sent Henry at once for Dr. Pringle, but he was out.

BEN. You should have gone for another. Eh, Eliza?

MRS. J. Oh, yes. It's a fatal mistake.

MRS. S. Pringle attended him when he was alive and Pringle shall attend him when he's dead. That's professional etiquette.

BEN. Well, you know your own business best, but——

MRS. J. Yes—it's a fatal mistake.

MRS. S. Don't talk so silly, Elizabeth. What good could a doctor have done?

MRS. J. Look at the many cases of persons being restored to life hours after they were thought to be "gone."

HENRY. That's when they've been drowned. Your father wasn't drowned, Elizabeth.

BEN (*humorously*). There wasn't much fear of that. If there was one thing he couldn't bear it was water. (*He laughs, but no one else does.*)

MRS. J. (*pained*). Ben!
(BEN *is crushed at once.*)

MRS. S. (*piqued*). I'm sure he washed regular enough.

MRS. J. If he did take a drop too much at times, we'll not dwell on that, now.

MRS. S. Father had been "merry" this morning. He went out soon after breakfast to pay his insurance.

BEN. My word, it's a good thing he did.

MRS. J. He always was thoughtful in that way. He was too honorable to have "gone" without paying his premium.

MRS. S. Well, he must have gone round to the *Ring-o'-Bells* afterwards, for he came in as merry as a sandboy. I says, "We're only waiting Henry to start dinner." "Dinner," he says, "I don't want no dinner, I'm going to bed!"

BEN (*shaking his head*). Ah! Dear, dear.

HENRY. And when I came in I found him undressed sure enough and snug in bed. (*He rises and stands on the hearthrug.*)

MRS. J. (*definitely*). Yes, he'd had a "warning." I'm sure of that. Did he know you?

HENRY. Yes. He spoke to me.

MRS. J. Did he say he'd had a "warning"?

HENRY. No. He said, "Henry, would you mind taking my boots off; I forgot before I got into bed."

MRS. J. He must have been wandering.

HENRY. No, he'd got 'em on all right.

MRS. S. And when we'd finished dinner I thought I'd take up a bit of something on a tray. He was lying there for all the world as if he was asleep, so I put the tray down on the bureau—(*correcting herself*) on the chest of drawers—and went to waken him. (*A pause*) He was quite cold.

HENRY. Then I heard Amelia calling for me, and I ran upstairs.

MRS. S. Of course we could do nothing.

MRS. J. He was "gone"?

HENRY. There wasn't any doubt.

MRS. J. I always knew he'd go sudden in the end.
(*A pause, they wipe their eyes and sniff back tears.*)

MRS. S. (*rising briskly at length; in a*

businesslike tone). Well, will you go up and look at him now, or shall we have tea?

MRS. J. What do you say, Ben?

BEN. I'm not particular.

MRS. J. (*surveying the table*). Well then, if the kettle's nearly ready we may as well have tea first.

(MRS. SLATER *puts the kettle on the fire and gets tea ready.*)

HENRY. One thing we may as well decide now: the announcement in the papers.

MRS. J. I was thinking of that. What would you put?

MRS. S. At the residence of his daughter, 235, Upper Cornbank Street, etc.

HENRY. You wouldn't care for a bit of poetry?

MRS. J. I like "Never Forgotten." It's refined.

HENRY. Yes, but it's rather soon for that.

BEN. You couldn't very well have forgot him the day after.

MRS. S. I always fancy "A loving husband, a kind father, and a faithful friend."

BEN (*doubtfully*). Do you think that's right?

HENRY. I don't think it matters whether it's right or not.

MRS. J. No, it's more for the look of the thing.

HENRY. I saw a verse in *The Evening News* yesterday. Proper poetry, it was. It rhymed. (*He gets the paper and reads*)
"Despised and forgotten by some
    you may be
But the spot that contains you is
    sacred to we."

MRS. J. That'll never do. You don't say "Sacred to we."

HENRY. It's in the paper.

MRS. S. You wouldn't say it if you were speaking properly, but it's different in poetry.

HENRY. Poetic license, you know.

MRS. J. No, that'll never do. We want a verse that says how much we loved him and refers to all his good qualities and says what a heavy loss we've had.

MRS. S. You want a whole poem. That'll cost a good lot.

MRS. J. Well, we'll think about it after tea, and then we'll look through his bits of things and make a list of them. There's all the furniture in his room.

HENRY. There's no jewellery or valuables of that sort.

MRS. J. Except his gold watch. He promised that to our Jimmy.

MRS. S. Promised your Jimmy! I never heard of that.

MRS. J. Oh, but he did, Amelia, when he was living with us. He was very fond of Jimmy.

MRS. S. Well. (*Amazed*) I don't know!

BEN. Anyhow, there's his insurance money. Have you got the receipt for the premium he paid this morning?

MRS. S. I've not seen it.
(VICTORIA *jumps up from the sofa and comes behind the table.*)

VIC. Mother, I don't think grandpa went to pay his insurance this morning.

MRS. S. He went out.

VIC. Yes, but he didn't go into the town. He met old Mr. Tattersall down the street, and they went off past St. Philips's Church.

MRS. S. To the *Ring-o'-Bells*, I'll be bound.

BEN. The *Ring-o'-Bells?*

MRS. S. That public-house that John Shorrock's widow keeps. He is always hanging about there. Oh, if he hasn't paid it——

BEN. Do you think he hasn't paid it? Was it overdue?

MRS. S. I should think it was overdue.

MRS. J. Something tells me he's not paid it. I've a "warning," I know it; he's not paid it.

BEN. The drunken old beggar.

MRS. J. He's done it on purpose, just to annoy us.

MRS. S. After all I've done for him, having to put up with him in the house these three years. It's nothing short of swindling.

MRS. J. I had to put up with him for five years.

MRS. S. And you were trying to turn him over to us all the time.

HENRY. But we don't know for certain that he's not paid the premium.

MRS. J. I do. It's come over me all at once that he hasn't.

MRS. S. Victoria, run upstairs and fetch that bunch of keys that's on your grandpa's dressing table.

VIC (*timidly*). In grandpa's room?

MRS. S. Yes.

VIC. I—I don't like to.

MRS. S. Don't talk so silly. There's no one can hurt you. (VICTORIA *goes out reluctantly*) We'll see if he's locked the receipt up in the bureau.

BEN. In where? In this thing? (*He rises and examines it.*)

MRS. J. (*also rising*). Where did you pick that up, Amelia? It's new since last I was here.
(*They examine it closely.*)

MRS. S. Oh—Henry picked it up one day.

MRS. J. I like it. It's artistic. Did you buy it at an auction?

HENRY. Eh? Where did I buy it, Amelia?

MRS. J. Yes, at an auction.

BEN (*disparagingly*). Oh, second-hand.

MRS. J. Don't show your ignorance, Ben. All artistic things are second-hand. Look at those old masters. (VICTORIA *returns, very scared. She closes the door after her.*)

VIC. Mother! Mother!

MRS. S. What is it, child?

VIC. Grandpa's getting up.

BEN. What?

MRS. S. What do you say?

VIC. Grandpa's getting up.

MRS. J. The child's crazy.

MRS. S. Don't talk so silly. Don't you know your grandpa's dead?

VIC. No, no; he's getting up. I saw him. (*They are transfixed with amazement;* BEN *and* MRS. JORDAN *left of table;* VICTORIA *clings to* MRS. SLATER, *right of table;* HENRY *near fireplace.*)

MRS. J. You'd better go up and see for yourself, Amelia.

MRS. S. Here—come with me, Henry. (HENRY *draws back terrified.*)

BEN (*suddenly*). Hist! Listen. (*They look at the door. A slight chuckling is heard outside. The door opens, revealing an old man clad in a faded but gay dressing-gown. He is in his stockinged feet. Although over seventy he is vigorous and well colored; his bright, malicious eyes twinkle under his heavy, reddish-gray eyebrows. He is obviously either grandfather* ABEL MERRY-WEATHER *or else his ghost.*)

ABEL. What's the matter with little Vicky? (*He sees* BEN *and* MRS. JORDAN.) Hello! What brings you here? How's yourself, Ben? (ABEL *thrusts his hand at* BEN, *who skips back smartly and retreats with* MRS. JORDAN *to a safe distance below the sofa.*)

MRS. S. (*approaching* ABEL *gingerly*). Grandfather, is that you? (*She pokes him with her hand to see if he is solid.*)

ABEL. Of course it's me. Don't do that, 'Melia. What the devil do you mean by this tomfoolery?

MRS. S. (*to the others*). He's not dead.

BEN. Doesn't seem like it.

ABEL (*irritated by the whispering*). You've kept away long enough, Lizzie; and now you've come you don't seem over-pleased to see me.

MRS. J. You took us by surprise, Father. Are you keeping quite well?

ABEL (*trying to catch the words*). Eh? What?

MRS. J. Are you quite well?

ABEL. Ay, I'm right enough but for a bit of a headache. I wouldn't mind betting that I'm not the first in this house to be carried to the cemetery. I always think Henry there looks none too healthy.

MRS. J. Well, I never! (ABEL *crosses to the armchair and* HENRY *gets out of his way to the front of the table.*)

ABEL. 'Melia, what the dickens did I do with my new slippers?

MRS. S. (*confused*). Aren't they by the hearth, Grandfather?

ABEL. I don't see them. (*Observing* HENRY *trying to remove the slippers*) Why, you've got 'em on, Henry.

MRS. S. (*promptly*). I told him to put them on to stretch them, they were that new and hard. Now, Henry. (MRS. SLATER *snatches the slippers from* HENRY *and gives them to* ABEL, *who puts them on and sits in armchair.*)

MRS. J. (*to* BEN). Well, I don't call that delicate, stepping into a dead man's shoes in such haste.
(HENRY *goes up to the window and pulls up the blind.* VICTORIA *runs across to* ABEL *and sits on the floor at his feet.*)

VIC. Oh, Grandpa, I'm so glad you're not dead.

MRS. S. (*in a vindictive whisper*). Hold your tongue, Victoria.

ABEL. Eh? What's that? Who's gone dead?

MRS. S. (*loudly*). Victoria says she's sorry about your head.

ABEL. Ah, thank you, Vicky, but I'm feeling better.

MRS. S. (*to* MRS. J.). He's so fond of Victoria.

MRS. J. (*to* MRS. S.). Yes; he's fond of our Jimmy, too.

MRS. S. You'd better ask him if he promised your Jimmy his gold watch.

MRS. J. (*disconcerted*). I couldn't just now. I don't feel equal to it.

ABEL. Why, Ben, you're in mourning! And Lizzie too. And 'Melia, and Henry and little Vicky! Who's gone dead? It's some one in the family. (*He chuckles.*)

MRS. S. No one you know, Father. A relation of Ben's.

ABEL. And what relation of Ben's?

MRS. S. His brother.

BEN (*to* MRS. S.). Dang it, I never had one.

ABEL. Dear, dear. And what was his name, Ben?

BEN (*at a loss*). Er—er. (*He crosses to front of table.*)

MRS. S. (*prompting*). Frederick.

MRS. J. (*prompting*). Albert.

BEN. Er—Fred—Alb—Isaac.

ABEL. Isaac? And where did your brother Isaac die?

BEN. In—er—in Australia.

ABEL. Dear, dear. He'd be older than you, eh?

BEN. Yes, five year.

ABEL. Ay, ay. Are you going to the funeral?

BEN. Oh, yes.

MRS. S. *and* MRS. J. No, no.

BEN. No, of course not. (*He retires to the left.*)

ABEL (*rising*). Well, I suppose you've only been waiting for me to begin tea. I'm feeling hungry.

MRS. S. (*taking up the kettle*). I'll make tea.

ABEL. Come along, now; sit you down and let's be jolly.
(ABEL *sits at the head of the table, facing spectator.* BEN *and* MRS. JORDAN *on the left.* VICTORIA *brings a chair and sits by* ABEL. MRS. SLATER *and* HENRY *sit on the right. Both the women are next to* ABEL.)

MRS. S. Henry, give Grandpa some tongue.

ABEL. Thank you. I'll make a start. (*He helps himself to bread and butter.*)
(HENRY *serves the tongue and* MRS. SLATER *pours out tea. Only* ABEL *eats with any heartiness.*)

BEN. Glad to see you've got an appetite, Mr. Merryweather, although you've not been so well.

ABEL. Nothing serious. I've been lying down for a bit.

MRS. S. Been to sleep, Grandfather?

ABEL. No, I've not been to sleep.

MRS. S. *and* HENRY. Oh!

ABEL (*eating and drinking*). I can't exactly call everything to mind, but I remember I was a bit dazed, like. I couldn't move an inch, hand or foot.

BEN. And could you see and hear Mr. Merryweather?

ABEL. Yes, but I don't remember seeing anything particular. Mustard, Ben.
(BEN *passes the mustard.*)

MRS. S. Of course not, Grandfather. It was all your fancy. You must have been asleep.

ABEL (*snappishly*). I tell you I wasn't asleep, 'Melia. Damn it, I ought to know.

MRS. J. Didn't you see Henry or Amelia come into the room?

ABEL (*scratching his head*). Now let me think——

MRS. S. I wouldn't press him, Elizabeth. Don't press him.

HENRY. No. I wouldn't worry him.

ABEL (*suddenly recollecting*). Ay, begad! 'Melia and Henry, what the devil did you mean by shifting my bureau out of my bedroom? (HENRY *and* MRS. SLATER *are speechless*) D'you hear me? Henry! 'Melia!

MRS. J. What bureau was that, Father?

ABEL. Why, my bureau, the one I bought——

MRS. J. (*pointing to the bureau*). Was it that one, Father?

ABEL. Ah, that's it. What's it doing here? Eh? (*A pause. The clock on the mantelpiece strikes six. Every one looks at it*) Drat me if that isn't my clock, too. What the devil's been going on in this house? (*A slight pause.*)

BEN. Well, I'll be hanged.

MRS. J. (*rising*). I'll tell you what's been going on in this house, Father. Nothing short of robbery.

MRS. S. Be quiet, Elizabeth.

MRS. J. I'll not be quiet. Oh, I call it double-faced.

HENRY. Now, now, Elizabeth.

MRS. J. And you, too. Are you such a poor creature that you must do every dirty thing she tells you?

MRS. S. (*rising*). Remember where you are, Elizabeth.

HENRY (*rising*). Come, come. No quarrelling.

BEN (*rising*). My wife's every right to speak her own mind.

MRS. S. Then she can speak it outside, not here.

ABEL (*thumping the table*). Damn it all, will some one tell me what's been going on?

MRS. J. Yes, I will. I'll not see you robbed.

ABEL. Who's been robbing me?

MRS. J. Amelia and Henry. They've stolen your clock and bureau. (*Working herself up*) They sneaked into your room like a thief in the night and stole them after you were dead.

HENRY *and* MRS. S. Hush! Quiet, Elizabeth!

MRS. J. I'll not be stopped. After you were dead, I say.

ABEL. After who was dead?

MRS. J. You.

ABEL. But I'm not dead.

MRS. J. No, but they thought you were. (*A pause.* ABEL *gazes round at them.*)

ABEL. Oho! So that's why you're all in black today. You thought I was dead. (*He chuckles*) That was a big mistake. (*He sits and resumes his tea.*)

MRS. S. (*sobbing*). Grandfather.

ABEL. It didn't take you long to start dividing my things between you.

MRS. J. No, Father; you mustn't think that. Amelia was simply getting hold of them on her own account.

ABEL. You always were a keen one, Amelia. I suppose you thought the will wasn't fair.

HENRY. Did you make a will?

ABEL. Yes, it was locked up in the bureau.

MRS. J. And what was in it, Father?

ABEL. That doesn't matter now. I'm thinking of destroying it and making another.

MRS. S. (*sobbing*). Grandfather, you'll not be hard on me.

ABEL. I'll trouble you for another cup of tea, 'Melia; two lumps and plenty of milk.

MRS. S. With pleasure, Grandfather. (*She pours out the tea.*)

ABEL. I don't want to be hard on any one. I'll tell you what I'm going to do. Since your mother died, I've lived part of the time with you, 'Melia, and part with you, Lizzie. Well, I shall make a new will, leaving all my bits of things to whoever I'm living with when I die. How does that strike you?

HENRY. It's a bit of a lottery, like.

MRS. J. And who do you intend to live with from now?

ABEL (*drinking his tea*). I'm just coming to that.

MRS. J. You know, Father, it's quite time you came to live with us again. We'd make you very comfortable.

MRS. S. No, he's not been with us as long as he was with you.

MRS. J. I may be wrong, but I don't think Father will fancy living on with you after what's happened to-day.

ABEL. So you'd like to have me again, Lizzie?

MRS. J. You know we're ready for you to make your home with us for as long as you please.

ABEL. What do you say to that, 'Melia?

MRS. S. All I can say is that Elizabeth's changed her mind in the last two years. (*Rising*) Grandfather, do you know what the quarrel between us was about?

MRS. J. Amelia, don't be a fool; sit down.

MRS. S. No, if I'm not to have him, you shan't either. We quarrelled because Elizabeth said she wouldn't take you off our hands at any price. She said she'd had enough of you to last a life-time, and we'd got to keep you.

ABEL. It seems to me that neither of you has any cause to feel proud about the way you've treated me.

MRS. S. If I've done anything wrong, I'm sure I'm sorry for it.

MRS. J. And I can't say more than that, too.

ABEL. It's a bit late to say it, now. You neither of you cared to put up with me.

MRS. S. *and* MRS. J. No, no, Grandfather.

ABEL. Ay, you both say that because of what I've told you about leaving my money. Well, since you don't want me I'll go to some one that does.

BEN. Come, Mr. Merryweather, you've got to live with one of your daughters.

ABEL. I'll tell you what I've got to do. On Monday next I've got to do three things. I've got to go to the lawyer's and alter my will; and I've got to go to the insurance office and pay my premium; and I've got to go to St. Philips's Church and get married.

BEN *and* HENRY. What!

MRS. J. Get married!

MRS. S. He's out of his senses. (*General consternation.*)

ABEL. I say I'm going to get married.

MRS. S. Who to?

ABEL. To Mrs. John Shorrocks who keeps the *Ring-o'-Bells*. We've had it fixed up a good while now, but I was keeping it for a pleasant surprise. (*He rises*) I felt I was a bit of a burden to you, so I found some one who'd think it a pleasure to look after me. We shall be very glad to see you at the ceremony. (*He gets to the door*) Till Monday then. Twelve o'clock at St. Philips's Church. (*Opening the door*) It's a good thing you brought that bureau downstairs, 'Melia. It'll be handier to carry across to the *Ring-o'-Bells* on Monday. (*He goes out.*)

CURTAIN

The Drums of Oude

A DRAMA IN ONE ACT

BY AUSTIN STRONG

Dedicated to my wife—Mary Strong.
A. S.

CHARACTERS

Captain Hector McGregor
Lieutenant Alan Hartley
Sergeant McDougal
Stewart, *the sentry*
Two Hindustani Servants
Mrs. Jack Clayton, *Hartley's sister*
A Private

Scene: *An interior of a palace in Northern India, occupied by British troops.*
Time: *Spring of 1857.*

THE DRUMS OF OUDE

*Music before curtain rises to be of that mysterious, nervous Indian quality,
in a minor key, with the barbaric drum-beat measure throughout.*

*All lights out. Theater in total darkness. Drumming is heard from beyond
the stage, mingled with faint cries. This drumming must be great in volume, yet low in key. It stops short.*

*Repeats itself and again stops short. The curtain has gone up in the dark-
ness. The audience first becomes aware of the moonlit Indian City, in the
distance, over the top of an intervening forest.*

*Then they see the outline of the archway and the stage itself, which is a
store-room in an old Indian Palace, now occupied by the British. There is
no furniture in the room except a piano, R., and a business desk, R., rear.
A large Indian carpet is upon the floor. The only decorations are two
crossed swords on either side of the arch.*

Sentry STEWART, *in Highland uniform, passes beyond the arch, in the
moonlight, from R. to L. Pause. He returns. Pause. Then again from R. to
L. The drumming swells in the distance and seems to come from the Indian
City. As the* SENTRY *appears on his return beat, the drumming ceases. He
halts center of archway and turns a puzzled face toward the audience and
listens intently. Dead silence.*

*He is seen to breathe a sigh of relief, straighten himself and continue his
stolid march. Silence.*

Then with a crash door L. bursts open and MCGREGOR *slides in. He shuts
the door softly and swiftly and listens intently with his ear to the panels.
He gives a glance at the open arch, then takes three steps center, stoops,
takes hold of the corner of carpet and flings it back. Rises, goes back to door
L. and listens at panels again. Then returns center and opens a trap-door
which was beneath the carpet. The trap-door is three feet square and eight
inches thick.*

*He looks carefully in and then closing it returns the carpet to its place,
stands on it, and listens intently, his eyes to the audience. He then draws
from his left-hand coat pocket a large leather cigar case. Chooses a cigar
and returns case. He then slowly backs to wall R. When he reaches it he
strikes a match upon it with a downward sweep of his hand. He lights cigar
and carefully putting out the match, he assumes a graceful, easy position,
his back against the wall, his hands rammed deep in his coat pockets and
his right foot crossed over his left, his eyes always on the corner of the
carpet.*

STEWART, *the sentry, is seen to pass at rear. He halts again and listens as
if he heard something. He turns his face toward the audience to listen better, and with a start becomes aware of* MCGREGOR's *presence. He brings his
musket sharply to the shoulder, comes down the stage and halts three paces
from* MCGREGOR, *his face toward the audience. He makes the stiff soldier's
salute, right hand across the body.*

MCGREGOR *continues smoking and regarding the carpet. (Pause.)*

MCGREGOR (*cigar between his teeth*). Well, Stewart?

STEWART. Please, sir! Beg pardon, sir, but did you 'ear anything, sir?

MCGREGOR. Eh?

STEWART. Listen, sir!
(MCGREGOR *removes the cigar from his mouth and listens. Dead silence.*)

MCGREGOR. What do you mean?

STEWART (*intensely*). Listen, sir! (*The drumming heard. It stops abruptly*) There, sir!

MCGREGOR. Well?

STEWART. Beg pardon, sir—but me and the men don't fancy it, sir.

MCGREGOR. That will do, Stewart.

STEWART. Yes, sir! (*Salutes stiffly—faces about—marches out and resumes sentry duty, and is seen at stated intervals passing and repassing beyond the arch.*

Door L. *softly opens and two* HINDUSTANI SERVANTS *enter, one bearing* c *standard lamp with a red shade. The lamp is lighted. The other bears a small table which he places at* L. *center. The standard lamp is placed near the business desk.* SERGEANT MCDOUGAL *enters* L. *with* PRIVATE, *both in Highland uniform and carrying telegraphic apparatus. They cross the stage and exeunt door* R. *After a moment ticking is heard from that room. The two* SERVANTS *have by this time returned with the two wicker chairs, which they place* R. *and* L. *and then exeunt.* SERGEANT MCDOUGAL *and* PRIVATE *return through door* R. *The* PRIVATE *crosses stage and exits door* L. SERGEANT MCDOUGAL *comes down center.*
Enter FIRST *and* SECOND HINDUSTANI SERVANTS *through door* L. *They go over to* MCGREGOR *and salaam deeply before him.*)

MCGREGOR. I want you to serve supper up here for two. (*They do not move. A pause*) Did you hear what I said? I said—serve supper—supper—up here for two. (*They salaam and exeunt softly.*)

MCDOUGAL. The telegraph is in working order, sir! (*He faces about and goes toward door* L. *Just as he is about to exit——*)

MCGREGOR. Sergeant.

MCDOUGAL (*stopping abruptly*). Y-y-yes, sir!

MCGREGOR. How many men on guard duty?

MCDOUGAL (*in a surprised tone*). Seven, sir! (*Pause.*)

MCGREGOR. Wake the others up!

MCDOUGAL (*his tone more surprised*). B-b-beg p-pardon, sir!

MCGREGOR. Double the sentries. Put Neill and ten men on the ground floor with orders to let no one enter except women and civilians. Take the rest yourself and string them along the walls. North and West sides as much as possible, towards the dome.

MCDOUGAL. Yes, sir! (*Is about to exit*) Pardon, sir—but—but do you know when the regiment will be back?

MCGREGOR. Can't say, McDougal.

MCDOUGAL. Thank you, sir. (*Is about to exit.*)

MCGREGOR. Sergeant!

MCDOUGAL. Yes, sir!

MCGREGOR. Lieutenant Hartley will take command. Kindly wake him up with my compliments and ask him up here.

MCDOUGAL. Yes, sir. (*Exits.*) (*Drumming is heard again.* SENTRY *is seen to pass from* R. *to* L., *then* L. *to* R. MCGREGOR *still regards the corner of the carpet, the cigar between his teeth. Door* L. *opens and* LIEUTENANT HARTLEY *enters; a tall fair-haired English lad, garrulous and pink-cheeked. He is buttoning his tunic and wears the expression of one who has been aroused from a deep sleep. He looks vaguely about for* MCGREGOR, *but does not see him.*)

MCGREGOR. Ah, Hartley.

HARTLEY (*in a thick, sleepy voice*). Oh, there you are—didn't see where you were at first. Why in thunder— (*yawns*)—d-d-did y-y-you w-wake me u-up at this hour? Must be near one or two or something—your man bounced me out of bed as if the house was afire. (*Goes over to table and mixes brandy and soda*) And why have you moved up to this outlandish store-room? (*Drinks glass, his voice becoming more awake*) Shifted all your things, too! (*He pauses, and then becoming wide awake he suddenly asks*) I say, McGregor, what's up?

MCGREGOR. Listen!
(*The drumming a shade louder.*)

HARTLEY. Oh, that's the Mohurrum business they're having. Guess the beggars will keep it up all night. They tell me it is a religious festival they hold here once a year. (HARTLEY *takes a few strides nearer* MC-GREGOR) I say, you don't think there is anything nasty about it, do you?

MCGREGOR. India is a queer place, Hartley.

HARTLEY. By Jove—come to think of it—I—did you hear that queer rumor this morning?

MCGREGOR. Rumors. You're all alike, you youngsters. I was the same myself once—well, out with it!

HARTLEY. Something about a small cake——!

MCGREGOR (*sharply*). What?—— Quick——where was it seen?

HARTLEY (*blithely*). The chaps I was talking to said that it was a sure sign that these devils meant mischief. They called it the fiery cross of India and they said that this little cake passes from hand to hand— from village to village—and the message which means mutiny and disaster flies faster than our telegraph!

MCGREGOR. Oh, yes—I know all that—— But where was it seen?

HARTLEY. This morning on the steps of the Mission! (*A pause while* HARTLEY *watches face of* MCGREGOR *who goes on smoking.* HARTLEY, *in an eager voice*) I say——by Jove ——you don't think there's a chance for a row, do you?

MCGREGOR. Hartley.

HARTLEY. Yes, old chap?

MCGREGOR. You are standing over forty tons of gunpowder!

HARTLEY (*standing back and looking down at the carpet*). What?

MCGREGOR. Beneath you is the magazine!

HARTLEY. The magazine! (*Stooping and lifting edge of carpet*) I didn't know it was here! Thought it was by the Colonel's quarters.

MCGREGOR. Hartley, these Sepoys want that powder.

HARTLEY. Eh?

MCGREGOR. I'm afraid they will be disappointed.

HARTLEY. I say, McGregor—do you really think——

MCGREGOR. The regiment is away— we don't know when it will be back. The town is full of strangers. . . . (*Pause*) Hartley, there are women in this town—white women—English women.

HARTLEY. Rather. And, by Jove, there's my sister, Mrs. Clayton, the widow—I hadn't thought of her!

MCGREGOR. Well, you see—I had, Hartley!

HARTLEY (*surprised*). Why, what do you mean . . . ?

MCGREGOR. Only that I bribed her woman—her faithful ayah—to bring her here tonight under some pretext or other. I expect her any minute now.

HARTLEY. I say, that was clever of you! (*Pause.* MCGREGOR *goes over center for the first time and looks through archway.* HARTLEY, *in* c *queer voice*) You have known my sister, Mrs. Clayton, a long time out here, haven't you?

MCGREGOR. I remember her before she left England—when you were still at Sandhurst.

HARTLEY. She used often to write me of you.

MCGREGOR (*turning*). She did?

HARTLEY. You have been a better friend to her than ever Clayton, her husband, was.

MCGREGOR. The man's dead, Hartley.

HARTLEY. Oh yes, I know—but it was all the mater's fault she ever married him. (*Pause.* HARTLEY *goes over to* MCGREGOR *in a shy, boyish manner*) I say, McGregor—give us a chance if there's a row?

MCGREGOR (*smiling*). I woke you up for that purpose. You'll take command of the walls in a few minutes. I don't trust anyone here except myself. That is why I had my things shifted. (*Takes out watch*) The Colonel ought to be near Bandagaar by this time. You stay here a moment—I'll telegraph along the line. (*Goes toward the door at* R.)

HARTLEY. McGregor!

MCGREGOR. Eh?

HARTLEY. You're a brick to give a fellow such a chance—thanks!

MCGREGOR (*laughing*). Don't be too sanguine, Hartley—it's a bad habit. Perhaps, after all, this is nothing. (*Exits into next room, at* R., *and after a moment is heard telegraphing.*)

(HARTLEY *takes another look at the magazine, then goes to the center of the archway and listens a moment to the drumming, which, by fine degrees has grown louder. The* SENTRY *passes at rear, but doesn't see* HARTLEY. HARTLEY *goes over* R. *to business desk and idly looks over it. Picks up a newspaper, looks at it a moment, and then drops it. He sees writing materials upon the desk. He seats himself, spreads paper, leans forward and dips pen in ink.*)

HARTLEY (*as he writes*). "Dear mater . . . This is the slowest station in Northern India . . . there is nothing to do . . . no society . . . nothing! Sis is practically the only Englishwoman of any account, except the Major's wife and Mrs. Indermaur. By the way, Captain McGregor, my senior, you remember him . . . the chap Sis used to write us about. . . . Well, he's a thoroughbred and dead nuts on Sis . . . has been all his life, it seems. I think McGregor is the only man Sis ever cared a straw about, but she won't have a word said against Clayton's memory." . . . (HARTLEY *leans back in his chair, lifting his pen and searching the ceiling for ideas. Then leans forward and continues writing in silence.*)

(*Door* L. *softly opens and* FIRST *and* SECOND SERVANTS *glide noiselessly in, walking as Orientals do, straight from the hips. They move about quietly setting the table. The drumming ceases suddenly. The* SERVANTS *raise their heads slowly and look deep into each other's eyes, across the table. They both come forward center without changing their relative positions or shifting their gaze from each other's eyes. They stand center a moment listening. Then a small white cake, the size of a griddle cake, flies through the archway and falls between the* SERVANTS. *The* FIRST SERVANT *drops on one knee and covers the cake with his right hand, and watches his companion.* SECOND SERVANT *takes four deliberate steps backwards, which brings him immediately behind* HARTLEY, *who is deep in his letter.* SECOND SERVANT *slowly draws from his bosom a pistol which he levels at* HARTLEY'S *neck, about two feet distant.* HARTLEY *blots letter with a satisfied air, throws down pen, leans far back in his chair, which brings the muzzle of the pistol within two inches of his neck. He passes his hand through his hair and reads. Reading in a satisfied air*) . . . "and I always wear my flannels as you asked me to, and take my two grains of quinine regularly. I forgot to say in my last letter that Spiffy Watkins may have my cricket bat. I shan't need it again, but don't let anyone touch my fishing rod on any account! (*Leans forward to underline—"any"*) You needn't be anxious about me, mother dear—there is no danger in India. It's positively dull, it's so safe. Love to everybody—shall write the girls next mail. Your affectionate son, Alan Hartley. P.S.—I repeat— don't let anyone touch my fishing rod."

(*The ticking of the telegraph is heard to stop suddenly.* SECOND SERVANT *hides pistol in his bosom,* FIRST SERVANT *rises and hides cake in his sash. Both assume position at door* L., *one immediately behind the*

other—watching HARTLEY *intently.*
HARTLEY *rises, folds letter, slips it
into envelope, and is about to lick
it when he becomes aware of the
two Indians staring at him. He is
taken aback. They drop their eyes
—salaam, and exeunt together.*)

HARTLEY (*taking five paces after
them and stopping with a startled
expression*). By Gad, I didn't know
those men were in the room. I wish
these servant fellows would laugh
or make a noise, or anything—instead of bowing and gliding about.
(*With a slight shudder*) Makes a
fellow feel deuced uncanny!

MCGREGOR (*entering with papers
which he throws on business desk,
then comes center, sits*). Can't get
the Colonel yet. They haven't
reached the station—or they have
passed it.

HARTLEY (*still looking after the
servants*). I say, McGregor, do you
trust those two servants of yours?

MCGREGOR (*laughing and coming
forward*). Implicitly. . . . Come,
my dear boy, take a seat and have
some supper. (*Motions* HARTLEY *to
a seat opposite to him at the table*)
I would trust those two men with
my life.

HARTLEY. Well, I suppose you
know. For myself, I don't like them.
Fact is, I never liked the looks of
any of these vermin—they're so
damned slippery.

MCGREGOR. Hartley, may I give you
a piece of advice?

HARTLEY (*taking a large piece of
toast. His mouth full*). Go ahead.

MCGREGOR. You are new to India—
you have only joined the regiment
three weeks, and you have an imagination. . . . My boy, quell it—
stifle it—for if you let it grow in this
hotbed of rumors and strange
noises, it will devour you! I have
seen brave men made cowards by
it. . . . Sherry?

HARTLEY. Thanks. (MCGREGOR
pours it out) Perhaps you're right,
but talking of rumors—do tell me
more about this chuppattie cake!

MCGREGOR. Fact is, no one knows
much about them. A chuppattie
cake is the commonest thing in India. Why, it's the food of the people
—it's their bread.

HARTLEY. These chaps told me it
was a signal of mutiny—they told
me of a sentence that went with it
—do you know it?

MCGREGOR. "Sub lal hogga hi."
(*Pronounced "Sub lal hoyarggi."*)

HARTLEY. And what does that mean,
pray?

MCGREGOR (*slowly*). Everything is
to become red!

HARTLEY (*watching* MCGREGOR,
who goes on calmly eating). Do—
do you believe in it?

MCGREGOR. Depends, Hartley,
where I saw one.

HARTLEY. What do you mean?

MCGREGOR. If I saw a chuppattie in
an out-of-the-way place—

HARTLEY (*eagerly*). Yes?

MCGREGOR (*smiling*). India's a queer place, Hartley. (*Pause*) I remember when I was with a Sepoy regiment once, the Colonel had us out on a surprise inspection one night, and we found that a corporal had two chuppatties under his pillow. . . . (*Pause*) We had a narrow escape that night. (*They both rise suddenly to their feet.*)

HARTLEY. Did you hear that?

MCGREGOR (*listening*). Yes.

HARTLEY. Sounded like . . . sounded like a whistle!

MCGREGOR. Sit down! (*They both sit down. Enter the* TWO HINDUSTANI SERVANTS *with more dishes for dinner.*)

MCGREGOR (*to* FIRST SERVANT). Abdul, that lamp is smoking—turn it down.
(FIRST SERVANT *crosses the stage to* R. *to standing lamp, which he lowers. He listens all the while intently, with his eyes fixed upon his companion, who is immediately behind* HARTLEY. *As he reaches center of stage on his return, unnoticed by himself or any of the others, the chuppattie falls from his sash to the floor near* MCGREGOR. *Exeunt* SERVANTS *softly.*)

HARTLEY (*using a siphon*). I don't like those two men!

MCGREGOR. Oh, you will get over that, Hartley.
(*Door* L. *bursts open and* SERGEANT MCDOUGAL *enters, breathless—he salutes and stands.*)

MCGREGOR (*going on eating*). Well, McDougal?

MCDOUGAL (*breathlessly*). Please. sir—Mrs. Cameron, Miss Williams and five other ladies, Mr. Palmer and Judge Lawson with some civilian gentlemen, have come into the walls, sir! They seek protection, sir! They're afraid of a rising, sir!

MCGREGOR. Ah! Is—is Mrs. Clayton with them?

MCDOUGAL. N-n-no, sir! P-p-please, s-sir—what'll I do with them, sir?

MCGREGOR (*thoughtfully*). Well, I can't very well leave this room. . . .

HARTLEY (*rising abruptly*). I'll go!

MCGREGOR. Sit down—I want you here, Hartley! McDougal, put the ladies in the Mess Room and see that they are properly cared for. Give the gentlemen muskets and put them on the North Side as much as possible. Lieut. Hartley will take command in a few minutes. McDougal!

MCDOUGAL. Yes, sir! (*About to exit.*)

MCGREGOR. And McDougal—

MCDOUGAL. Yes, sir!

MCGREGOR. If Mrs. Clayton comes, show her up here.

MCDOUGAL. Yes, sir. (*Salutes and exits.*)
(*They go on eating in silence.* HARTLEY *tries to hide his excitement and watches* MCGREGOR *excitedly. At last, with a great show of unconcern he drains his cup of coffee, uses a napkin, throws it down, and speaks in an obviously careless manner.*)

HARTLEY. My sister. . . . You think she will get here safely?

MCGREGOR. I have known this servant of hers for years. Your sister will
be here—don't you worry. (*Rises—
another pause.* HARTLEY *tries again
to hide his excitement.*)

HARTLEY (*obviously making conversation*). I say, McGregor—I am
interested about these chuppattie
cakes—tell me what does one look
like?

MCGREGOR (*going over to business
desk. He gets cigar box from a
drawer and returns across stage. He
pauses in the center and looks out
into the moonlight*). Hartley, I don't
see that sentry! (*He remains silent
a moment, looking out, then comes
over to the table and throws the
cigar box among the dishes*) Have
a cheroot? (*Business of* HARTLEY
choosing one. MCGREGOR *puts a
match into the candle and facing
audience holds it in the air, his eyes
to the ceiling*) What's a chuppattie
look like? Why, let me see if I can
describe it to you. (*Lights cigar
thoughtfully—then looks upon the
floor, match still burning in his right
hand. Sees cake at his feet. Shakes
out the lighted match slowly. Puts
it carefully in the saucer. Takes a
draw at his cigar, all the while examining the cake intently*) Well, it
looks like a griddle cake . . . it's
thick — and — er — white. (*Leans
down and picks up with his right
hand and weighs it*) Weighs about
an ounce—looks deuced indigesti-
ble! (HARTLEY *at this word is in the
act of lighting his cigar under the
candle shade.* MCGREGOR *carelessly
throws cake on table and it falls
with a clatter among the dishes*)
Something like that, Hartley.

HARTLEY (*sternly, back*). My God
—how did that get here?

MCGREGOR (*looking over the heads
of the audience*). I told you India
was a queer place, Hartley.
(HARTLEY *puts his cigar on his plate
and watches* MCGREGOR'S *face excitedly.*)

MCGREGOR (*slowly*). The first thing
to be done, Hartley, is to see if that
sentry is there.

HARTLEY (*quickly*). I'll go and see!
(*Turns and runs towards arch.*)

MCGREGOR. Stop! (HARTLEY *stops
abruptly*) Are you armed?

HARTLEY (*with a rising inflection*).
No! (*Looks about.*)

MCGREGOR. You will find one in the
left-hand drawer of my desk.
(HARTLEY *goes to desk, opens
drawer, takes out pistol, comes back
center holding the pistol in front of
him. Is seen to collect himself,
square his shoulders and march out
into the moonlight with military
step. Halts without, his back to the
audience*) What do you see?

HARTLEY. All the men seem to be at
their posts. I see Mr. Palmer and
Judge Lawson—they have given
them muskets.

MCGREGOR. And Stewart—the sentry?
(HARTLEY *disappears* R. *of archway,
then returns at a run. He arrives
breathless at* MCGREGOR'S *side.*)

HARTLEY (*in a whisper*). They've
cut his throat!

MCGREGOR. Hartley! Hartley!
(*Draws his cigar sharply from his
mouth. Pause*) Hartley, would you
mind going into that room and telegraphing?

HARTLEY (*flying to the door R., breathless with excitement*). What will I say?

MCGREGOR. Get Bandagaar. . . . If they don't answer get Sir John at Hadraa . . . then the Bulbud Residency. . . . Repeat the one word "massacre" till someone answers you! (*Exit* HARTLEY, *banging the door. Then the sound of the machine repeating the same message over and over again. Drumming begins again.* MCGREGOR *stands a moment longer looking over the heads of the audience, then goes quickly to the business desk and begins pulling out with feverish hurry papers and documents which he tears to pieces. His cigar between his teeth. Door L. opens with a bang and the* TWO HINDUSTANI SERVANTS *burst into the room, wildly searching for the lost chuppattie cake.* FIRST SERVANT *is seen feeling in his sash.* MCGREGOR *turns sharply around*) What the devil—(SERVANTS *immediately salaam and make a pretense of going towards the table*) Oh yes, we have finished—you may clear away the things. (*He turns his back to them and goes on tearing up the papers. As soon as his back is turned,* FIRST SERVANT *signals through door at L. and out troop all the other* SERVANTS. *They tiptoe down stage, all with their eyes on* MCGREGOR's *back. They pass through arch and one by one leap lightly over the parapet and out of sight. When all have gone—*MCGREGOR *speaks through his teeth, still tearing up his papers, his back to the empty stage*) Look here, you men—I didn't like the way you burst into the room just now! (*Pause, he goes on tearing up papers*) What did you mean by it? (*Pause*) I said, what did you mean

by it? (*He turns sharply*) Look here, when I ask a question I expect an answer. . . . (*The words die on his lips as he sees the empty stage. Stands silent a moment, looking at the untouched supper table. Then takes three deliberate steps backwards, which brings him to R. of arch. He raises his hand and unhooks one of the Indian swords that decorates the wall, and throws it lightly on the desk within easy reach. He then leans comfortably on the side of the archway, looking out into the moonlight, smoking his cigar. A sound of running feet approaching.* MCGREGOR's *hand is seen to move towards the sword on the desk. He continues smoking and looking out.*)

A WOMAN'S VOICE. Captain McGregor! Captain McGregor! (MCGREGOR *removes the cigar from his mouth and gives a quick look at the magazine door. Then, breathless and half crying with excitement,* MRS. CLAYTON *enters wildly and leans fainting against wall L. of archway. She covers her eyes with her arm.*)

MRS. CLAYTON (*wildly*). Captain McGregor . . . your men . . . your men showed me up here . . . the town is rising! Save me! Save me!

MCGREGOR (*in a polite voice, carefully putting cigar out in a small ashtray beside him on the desk*). Why, how do you do, Mrs. Clayton?

MRS. CLAYTON. No—no—no—the Sepoys—they're rising—where is my brother?—I escaped just in time! . . .

MCGREGOR (*wheeling an easy chair towards her*). I know, but won't you sit down? . . . Your brother is here . . . in the next room.

MRS. CLAYTON. Can't you hear them? . . . they're coming . . . we'll all be massacred!

MCGREGOR. Come, Mrs. Clayton. . . . (*Forces her gently into a chair*) Sit down. Your nerves are all awry. Calm yourself!

MRS. CLAYTON. Calm myself! . . . Listen! (*They listen a moment to the drumming.*)

MCGREGOR (*going over to the table, taking a decanter with which he fills a small glass*). Why, you know what that is, Mrs. Clayton; it's the Mohurrum business—religious affair—pious riot—quite harmless. Won't you try some of my sherry? (*Offers glass.*)

MRS. CLAYTON (*waving glass aside*). Captain McGregor, the natives are pouring into the town by thousands! They are collecting at the bazaar! There is danger! I feel it here! (*Puts hand on heart.*)

MCGREGOR. Do you think, Mrs. Clayton, that if there was much danger I would be here enjoying a cigar alone?

MRS. CLAYTON. I—I—I—suppose —after all—I—I—I—I have let my nerves get the better of me . . . but, oh, Captain McGregor—just as I was going to bed I began to hear that horrid, queer noise they are making! (*Listens a moment*) I called Rebottie—you know her— my faithful ayah. Well, she told me that all the servants had fled!

MCGREGOR (*laughing*). You can no more keep a native from a Mohurrum than a small boy from a circus. My servants have left me, too!

MRS. CLAYTON. But this kind of thing never happened to me before! We flew to the stables to saddle our own horses, but they were all gone —they had taken them too. . . . So we ran here on foot—choosing the back street. I could see the town was full of strangers—they are pouring from all quarters! When we came to your gates they sent me up here!

MCGREGOR. They did right—but after all this, you must calm yourself. (*Gives her the glass again, which she reluctantly drinks. While she is in the act, he turns his head slowly and looks through the archway.*)

MRS. CLAYTON (*weakly*). I'm afraid I've made an awful fool of myself. You'll have to forgive me, Captain McGregor. You know, really, I am not often frightened, but India has always been a land of horror to me. Full of sounds and strange noises— terrible—terrible silences . . . and always those eyes looking at you! One can't help thinking of what these Sepoys will do when they are once let loose! Remember that Oude massacre. . . . Massacre! Massacre! . . . I can't get that word out of my brain.

MCGREGOR (*still listening and not looking up*). Come—rest a bit. You're worn out!

MRS. CLAYTON (*suddenly, after a pause*). But I can't stay here—it's late! If you really think, Captain McGregor, that there is no cause for alarm, will you forgive a silly woman and let her return home?

MCGREGOR (*slowly*). Won't you stay a bit? . . . Your brother is here.

MRS. CLAYTON. I'd like to . . . (*laughing*)—but it's growing very late!

MCGREGOR. Then I'll call Stewart and have him take you home. (*Goes toward arch, thinking deeply. Then stopping*) By the way, won't you in the meantime play me something on my new piano? I had it shifted up here with my other things —I want you to try it for me. (*Reluctant, yet to humor him, she pulls off her gloves and goes towards the piano. She pauses to put her gloves upon the table, and sees the chuppattie cake lying among the dishes. She turns quickly with a face full of horror to* MCGREGOR, *who is leaning against the archway and looking out.*)

MRS. CLAYTON (*in an awed and intense voice*). How did this get here?

MCGREGOR. Eh? . . . Oh . . . the chuppattie. . . . Why, you know, I rather like them. Always have them for supper. . . . I'm quite an Indian in my tastes.

MRS. CLAYTON (*with a short laugh of relief*). You must think I'm an awful coward—but you know the rumor of these cakes, and that awful sentence, "All is to become red!" (*Stands still, looking down at it with a frightened face.*)

MCGREGOR. Come—you have been badly frightened, and I don't blame you. Do try my piano and forget for a moment this country which you detest so heartily!

(MRS. CLAYTON *goes over to the piano, seats herself and commences playing* "THE WATER LILY" *softly and with deep feeling. The drumming goes on.* HARTLEY *is heard repeating the one word incessantly on the telegraph.* MCGREGOR *keeps his position at the side of the archway, looking out.* MRS. CLAYTON *plays for some time in silence.*)

MRS. CLAYTON (*stopping abruptly, and in a queer voice*). Did you call that man to take me home, Captain McGregor?

MCGREGOR. Yes.

MRS. CLAYTON. I didn't hear you.

MCGREGOR (*coming down stage and leaning over the edge of the piano*). He will be here in a moment. (*She goes on playing again, looking up at him. His voice changes to one of emotion*) That was the melody you played at the Maharajah's ball.

MRS. CLAYTON. You remember that?

MCGREGOR. Remember! . . . My life is made up of memories. (*Pause*) I remember the day when a fresh, young English girl arrived on the decks of a great East Indiaman— and how we cheered her pretty face! I remember a military wedding at Calcutta and Mrs. Jack Clayton, the toast of the regiment. And then I remember when I first saw you in mourning. . . . I remember many things! (*Sighs. Here a long pause.* MCGREGOR *turns his face slowly and looks through archway.*)

MRS. CLAYTON (*her voice low and full*). You have been a loyal friend! (*She plays.*)

MCGREGOR (*turning to her with a smile*). How wonderfully you play! (*A pause*) What a strange and beautiful thing awakened memory is! One can live again those hours one has thought forever lost. Do you—can you—remember and live over those wonderful days—in the old bungalow by the river—the queer lights and tall shadows—when in the gaiety of your heart you called me Major Dobbin?

MRS. CLAYTON. Because you were so awkward and were always upsetting my tea cups and things—oh, yes—I remember.

MCGREGOR. I thought you called me Major Dobbin because I was so faithful.

MRS. CLAYTON. Perhaps I did. (*She plays on a moment, and then stops and sits looking out into the moonlight in silence,* MCGREGOR *watching her intently the while*) What a dear fellow you were, Major Dobbin! Ah, a woman never forgets a man's friendship in a time like that—and it seems I can never get the chance —(*turning to him*) to thank you enough!

MCGREGOR. Thank me! . . . Why, I stood by you, as you call it, because I couldn't help myself—because you're the only woman worthy of the name . . . because you took your trouble like a thoroughbred . . . because . . . because you are beautiful . . . because you're straight and tall and your hair is brown . . . because you're true, and clean-hearted . . . because, old friend, I have loved you all my life!

MRS. CLAYTON (*her voice broken*). Major Dobbin!

MCGREGOR (*coming to her side and kneeling on one knee*). Aye—Major Dobbin—as ever was!

MRS. CLAYTON (*putting her hand on his shoulder and looking down into his eyes*). You know 'way down deep in your heart that you were the first and only one—and now, old friend, tried and trusted—after all these years of silence and pain— here is your reward. (*With a low laugh*) A poor thing, Major, but myself—my honor—my life—my— my—(*tenderly drawing his head with both hands to her bosom and putting her lips to his hair*) . . . my Major Dobbin!
(MCGREGOR *raises his head and their lips meet.* MCGREGOR *then stands straight and breathes deep.*)

MCGREGOR. It was worth it—it was worth the waiting for!
(*The sound of a chair being violently overturned in room at* R.)

MRS. CLAYTON. What is that?
(*Door bursts open and* HARTLEY *bursts in.*)

HARTLEY (*shouting*). McGregor! McGregor!

MCGREGOR (*going quickly up to him and speaking in a calm, rapid voice*). Ah, Hartley . . . (*Turning*) here is Mrs. Clayton, your sister . . . she sought our protection, thinking that perhaps this Mohurrum was a Sepoy rising, but I have assured her that there is no cause for alarm.

HARTLEY (*breathlessly*). It's all right, Sis . . . you needn't be alarmed . . . —I—I—I—if there had been any danger we would have heard of it.

MRS. CLAYTON. You must forgive us poor women our cowardice, Alan— it is only when we realize our helplessness that we are frightened. Sometimes I wish that I were a man—a soldier—a Highlander like yourselves—instead of a woman who has to wait and listen . . . and listen . . . and listen!

HARTLEY (*blatantly*). It is not all beer and skittles being a man, I can assure you, Sis . . . Why, do you know—just now . . . !

MCGREGOR (*sharply*). Hartley!

HARTLEY. Eh?

MCGREGOR. Would you kindly take a message for me?

HARTLEY. Pardon me, Sis. (*She inclines her head and goes on playing, her eyes to the keys.* HARTLEY *goes over to* MCGREGOR *and both watch her as they speak.*)

MCGREGOR (*in an undertone*). Well, what is it?

HARTLEY (*in an excited whisper*). They have cut the wires!

MCGREGOR. Ah—I thought as much!

HARTLEY. Sir John says, don't let them get the powder!

MCGREGOR. He needn't worry.

MRS. CLAYTON (*stopping her playing and looking up*). Is your man ready, Captain McGregor? (*Politely*) It is growing very late!

MCGREGOR. I am sending your brother to hurry him up. (MRS. CLAYTON *goes on playing.*)

HARTLEY (*to* MCGREGOR). Well?

MCGREGOR. You'll take command now at once, as they will be on us in a moment. Hold them off as long as possible. I'll stay here and watch that powder. (*Points to the corner of the carpet*) I daren't trust anyone in this room except myself. If they once get over the walls. . . .

HARTLEY. We're lost!

MCGREGOR. If they once do, Hartley. . . .

HARTLEY. Yes?

MCGREGOR. Have the bugler sound the charge so that I can hear it. Make him play it loudly, mind you!

HARTLEY. And then—?

MCGREGOR. I shall blow up the magazine!

HARTLEY. By Jove—

MCGREGOR. Quick—say a word to your sister, and go! (HARTLEY *backs down stage, watching* MCGREGOR, *who is looking out into the moonlight—he feels the air behind him for his sister.*)

HARTLEY (*as he reaches her. She continues to play*). I say, Sis, I'm going for the man. I won't be back myself—he'll see you safe home. I want to say good—good night!

MRS. CLAYTON (*continuing her music*). Good night, old fellow!

HARTLEY. Sis?

MRS. CLAYTON (*stopping and looking around*). Yes, Alan?

HARTLEY. Pardon my asking, but— has McGregor said anything to you?

MRS. CLAYTON (*looking up and smiling*). Yes.

HARTLEY (*with enthusiasm*). I'm glad! (*Bending and kissing her tenderly*) Good night, old girl!

MRS. CLAYTON. Good night, my brother!

HARTLEY (*goes up to* MCGREGOR *and gives him his hand in silence*). I congratulate you. . . . By Jove, you are a brick. . . . (*Lower*) Good-bye!
(MCGREGOR *gives him his hand in silence and* HARTLEY *exits, drawing his pistol.* MCGREGOR *remains a moment looking after him, and then comes down stage and leans on the piano and watches* MRS. CLAYTON *as she continues to play softly. A Sepoy's head and shoulders rise up stealthily from behind the balustrade—beyond the arch. First an arm appearing, then a turban, and then a white-trousered leg is thrown over the balustrade.* MCGREGOR *turns quickly and sees the Sepoy who instantly drops out of sight.* MRS. CLAYTON *has seen nothing and continues playing dreamily.* MCGREGOR *goes at once to the desk and quickly opens a drawer and takes out a black coil of fuse. He comes down center. He throws back the corner of the carpet, opens the magazine door, gives a quick look through the archway, and lowers one end of the fuse deep into the magazine.*)

MRS. CLAYTON (*not looking up*). Ah! I'm so happy. . . . Tell me, dear, you like my brother?

MCGREGOR (*backing and uncoiling fuse*). Rather! (MCGREGOR *leaves end of fuse near center.*)

MRS. CLAYTON. I suppose India will spoil him like all the rest—but it's like a breath of old England to see his boyish honest face!

MCGREGOR. Rather. . . . (*He says this as he is in the act of taking one of the silver candlesticks, removes the shade, and places it with the lighted candle near the end of the fuse.*)

MRS. CLAYTON. I remember when I first saw India—how terrified I was —the bronze and blackened faces. . . . (*She happens to look around. She stops playing and rises slowly.* MCGREGOR *is standing over the lighted candle with his hands rammed in his coat pockets. He is looking out into the moonlight. She looks from him to the open magazine, and back to him again.*)

MRS. CLAYTON. What are you doing?

MCGREGOR (*turning his face towards the audience*). You will pardon me—I have lied to you. I am afraid, after all, there is danger. (*A pause—*MRS. CLAYTON *remains perfectly still*) I thought perhaps I'd spare you unnecessary alarm, but I'm afraid I can't—you see, the regiment is not on time. I know you for a thoroughbred—you've the blood of soldiers in your veins. So I can tell you plainly how we stand?

MRS. CLAYTON (*after drawing a quick breath*). Tell me!

MCGREGOR. That door you see open is the powder magazine. . . . You know what it means if these Sepoys capture it—*You* know what it means if I let them capture you. *You* know what it means when they get an Englishwoman in their power! My Highlanders will hold them off as long as possible, and if they fail . . . you see my duty?

MRS. CLAYTON (*after a pause, while she struggles with herself*). Yes!

MCGREGOR. I thought it would seem a hard thing to do, but with you beside me—why, girl, I am going to blow up that magazine. . . . Will you stand by me?

MRS. CLAYTON. With my last breath! (*The sound of musket shooting without, rapid and terrifying.*)

MCGREGOR. Ah, they've begun already! (*They stand listening*) Tell me if you hear the bugle call! (*The noise without becomes deafening. Savage yells, hoots and firing. The sky through the archway turns scarlet as if the city were afire. Suddenly the standing lamp at R. is shot to pieces by a stray bullet.* MRS. CLAYTON *screams, but still stands beside piano*) What's that? (*They listen. A sudden lull in the battle and a tiny call is heard gallantly playing in the distance.* MCGREGOR *slowly leans down and takes the lighted candlestick in his hand and looks up at* MRS. CLAYTON. *She goes*

to him. *He then slowly and carefully touches the fuse with the lighted candle. It burns with great display towards the magazine. Together they watch the fuse as it hisses and splutters towards the yawning pit. The noise without becomes deafening. The red light flares more brilliantly—when suddenly the noise stops. Dead silence.*)

MRS. CLAYTON (*dashes for* MC-GREGOR's *side*). Stop it! Stop it! (*She flies to the fuse and stamps it out.*) Can't you hear it? . . . Listen!
(*Pause. They both listen. Then far away in the distance is heard fife, drum and bagpipes playing, "The Campbells Are Coming, Ye Ho, Ye Ho." It swells louder at each approaching step.* HARTLEY *enters wildly, his coat torn off his back; he carries his smoking revolver, which he waves madly.*)

HARTLEY (*hoarsely, and with excitement*). McGregor—McGregor—it's all right! The Highlanders are here! We're saved—saved! (*Exits reeling and shouting.*)
(MCGREGOR *puts the candle out by striking the flame with his open palm and catches* MRS. CLAYTON *just as she faints, falling backwards into his arms. Curtain falls on this tableau now lit with red fire smoke and resounding with rousing British cheers, drums and bagpipes.*)

CURTAIN

Helena's Husband

AN HISTORICAL COMEDY

BY PHILIP MOELLER

CHARACTERS

HELENA, *the Queen*
TSUMU, *a black woman, slave to Helena*
MENELAUS, *the King*
ANALYTIKOS, *the King's librarian*
PARIS, *a shepherd*

HELENA'S HUSBAND

SCENE *is that archæological mystery, a Greek interior. A door on the right leads to the King's library, one on the left to the apartment of the Queen. Back right is the main entrance leading to the palace. Next this, running the full length of the wall, is a window with a platform, built out over the main court. Beyond is a view of hills bright with lemon groves, and in the far distance shimmers the sea. On the wall near the Queen's room hangs an old shield rusty with disuse. A bust of Zeus stands on a pedestal against the right wall. There are low coffers about the room from which hang the ends of vivid colored robes. The scene is bathed in intense sunlight.* TSUMU *is massaging the Queen.*

HELENA. There's no doubt about it. Menelaus has been too long out of battle.

TSUMU. Analytikos says there is much doubt about all things.

HELENA. Never mind what he says. I envy you your complexion.

TSUMU (*falling prostrate before* HELENA). Whom the Queen envies should beware.

HELENA (*annoyed*). Get up, Tsumu. You make me nervous tumbling about like that.

TSUMU (*still on floor*). Why does the great Queen envy Tsumu?

HELENA. Get up, you silly. (*She kicks her*) I envy you because you can run about and never worry about getting sunburnt.

TSUMU (*on her knees*). The radiant beauty of the Queen is unspoilable.

HELENA. That's just what's worrying me, Tsumu. When beauty is so perfect the slightest jar may mean a jolt. (*She goes over and looks at her reflection in the shield*) I can't see myself as well as I would like to. The King's shield is tarnished.

TSUMU (*handing her a hand mirror*). The Gods will keep Sparta free from strife.

HELENA. I'll have you beaten if you assume that prophetic tone with me. There's one thing I can't stand, and that's a know-all. (*Flinging the hand mirror to the floor.*)

TSUMU (*in alarm*). Gods grant you haven't bent it.

HELENA. These little mirrors are useless. His shield is the only thing in which I can see myself full-length. If he only went to war, he'd have to have it cleaned.

TSUMU (*putting the mirror on a table near the Queen*). The King is a lover of peace.

HELENA. The King is a lover of comfort. Have you noticed that he spends more time than he used to in the library?

TSUMU. He is busy with questions of State.

HELENA. You know perfectly well that when anything's the matter with the Government it's always straightened out at the other end of the palace. Finish my shoulder. (*She examines her arm*) I doubt if there is a finer skin than this in Sparta.

(TSUMU *begins to massage the Queen's shoulder.*)

HELENA (*taking up a mirror*). That touch of deep carmine right here in the center of my lips was quite an idea.

TSUMU (*busily pounding the Queen*). An inspiration of the Gods!

HELENA. The Gods have nothing to do with it. I copied it from a low woman I saw at the circus. I can't understand how these bad women have such good ideas. (HELENA *twists about.*)

TSUMU. If Your Majesty doesn't sit still, I may pinch you.

HELENA (*boxing her ears*). None of your tricks, you ebony fiend!

TSUMU (*crouching*). Descendant of paradise, forgive me.

HELENA. If you bruise my perfect flesh, the King will kill you. My beauty is his religion. He can sit for hours, as if at prayer, just examining the arch of my foot. Tsumu, you may kiss my foot.

TSUMU (*prostrate*). May the Gods make me worthy of your kindness!

HELENA. That's enough, Tsumu, are you married?

TSUMU (*getting up*). I've been so busy having babies I never had time to get married.

HELENA. It's a great disillusionment.

TSUMU (*aghast*). What!

HELENA. I'm not complaining. Moo Moo is the best of husbands, but sometimes being adored too much is trying. (*She sighs deeply*) I think I'll wear my heliotrope this afternoon.

(*A trumpet sounds below in the courtyard.* TSUMU *goes to the window.*)

TSUMU. They are changing the guards at the gates of the palace. It's almost time for your bath. (*She begins scraping the massage ointment back into the box.*)

HELENA. You're as careful with that ointment as Moo Moo is with me.

TSUMU. Precious things need precious guarding.

HELENA. It's very short-sighted on Moo Moo's part to send everybody to the galleys who dares lift a head when I pass by—and all these nice-looking soldiers! Why—the only men I ever see besides Moo Moo are Analytikos and a lot of useless eunuchs.

TSUMU. Oh, those eunuchs!

HELENA (*as she sits dreaming*). I wish, I wish— (*She stops short.*)

TSUMU. You have but to speak your desire to the King.

HELENA (*shocked*). Tsumu! How can you think of such a thing? I'm not a bad woman.

TSUMU. He would die for you.

HELENA (*relieved*). Ah! Do you think so, Tsumu?

TSUMU. All Sparta knows that His Majesty is a lover of peace, and yet he would rush into battle to save you.

HELENA. I should love to have men fighting for me.

TSUMU (*in high alarm*). May Zeus turn a deaf ear to your voice.

HELENA. Don't be impertinent, Tsumu. I've got to have some sort of amusement.

TSUMU. You've only to wait till next week, and you can see another of the priestesses sacrificed to Diana.

HELENA. That doesn't interest me any longer. The girls are positively beginning to like it. No! My mind is set on war.

TSUMU (*terrified*). I have five fathers of my children to lose.

HELENA. War, or—or—

TSUMU (*hopefully*). Have I been so long your slave that I no longer know your wish?

HELENA (*very simply*). Well, I should like to have a lover.

TSUMU (*springs up and rushes over in horror to draw the curtains across the door of the library. All of a tremble*). Gods grant they didn't hear you.

HELENA. Don't be alarmed, Tsumu. Analytikos is over eighty. (*She*

bursts into a loud peal of laughter and MENELAUS *rushes into the room.*)

MENELAUS (*in high irritation*). I wish you wouldn't make so much noise in here. A King might at least expect quiet in his own palace.

HELENA. Tsumu, see if my bath is ready. (TSUMU *exits*) You used not speak like that to me, Moo Moo.

MENELAUS (*in a temper*). How many times must I tell you that my name is Menelaus and that it isn't "Moo Moo"?

HELENA (*sweetly*). I'll never do it again, Moo Moo. (*She giggles.*)

MENELAUS. Your laugh gets on my nerves. It's louder than it used to be.

HELENA. If you wish it, I'll never, never laugh again.

MENELAUS. You've promised that too often.

HELENA (*sadly*). Things are not as they used to be.

MENELAUS. Are you going to start that again?

HELENA (*with a tinge of melancholy*). I suppose you'd like me to be still and sad.

MENELAUS (*bitterly*). Is it too much to hope that you might be still and happy?

HELENA (*speaking very quickly and tragically*). Don't treat me cruelly, Moo Moo. You don't understand me. No man ever really understands a woman. There are terrible depths to my nature. I had a long talk with Dr. Æsculapius only last week, and he told me I'm too introspective. It's the curse of us emotional women. I'm really quite worried, but much you care, much you care. (*A note of tears comes into her voice*) I'm sure you don't love me any more, Moo Moo. No! No! Don't answer me! If you did you couldn't speak to me the way you do. I've never wronged you in deed or in thought. No, never—never. I've given up my hopes and aspirations, because I knew you wanted me around you. And now, NOW— (*She can contain the tears no longer*) Because I have neglected my beauty and because I am old and ugly, you regret that Ulysses or Agamemnon didn't marry me when you all wanted me, and I know you curse the day you ever saw me. (*She is breathless.*)

MENELAUS (*fuming*). Well! Have you done?

HELENA. No. I could say a great deal more, but I'm not a talkative woman.
(ANALYTIKOS *comes in from the library.*)

ANALYTIKOS. Your Majesty, are we to read no longer today?

HELENA. I have something to say to the King.
(ANALYTIKOS *goes toward the library.* MENELAUS *anxiously stops him.*)

MENELAUS. No. Stay here. You are a wise man and well understand the wisdom of the Queen.

ANALYTIKOS (*bowing to* HELENA). Helena is wise as she is beautiful.

MENELAUS. She is attempting to prove to me in a thousand words that she's a silent woman.

ANALYTIKOS. Women are seldom silent. (HELENA *resents this*) Their beauty is forever speaking for them.

HELENA. The years have, indeed, taught you wisdom.
(TSUMU *enters.*)

TSUMU. The almond water awaits Your Majesty.

HELENA. I hope you haven't forgotten the chiropodist.

TSUMU. He has been commanded but he's always late. He's so busy.

HELENA (*in a purring tone to* MENELAUS). Moo Moo.
(MENELAUS, *bored, turns away.*)

HELENA (*to* TSUMU). I think after all I'll wear my Sicily blue. (*She and* TSUMU *go into the Queen's apartment.*)

ANALYTIKOS. Shall we go back to the library?

MENELAUS. My mind is unhinged again—that woman with her endless protestations.

ANALYTIKOS. I am sorry the poets no longer divert you.

MENELAUS. A little poetry is always too much.

ANALYTIKOS. Tomorrow we will try the historians.

MENELAUS. No! Not the historians. I want the truth for a change.

ANALYTIKOS. The truth!

MENELAUS. Where in books can I find escape from the grim reality of being hitched for life to such a wife? Bah!

ANALYTIKOS. Philosophy teaches—

MENELAUS. Why have the Gods made woman necessary to man, and made them fools?

ANALYTIKOS. For seventy years I have been resolving the problem of woman and even at my age—

MENELAUS. Give it up, old man. The answer is—don't.

ANALYTIKOS. Such endless variety, and yet—

MENELAUS (with the conviction of finality). There are only two sorts of women! Those who are failures and those who realize it.

ANALYTIKOS. Is not Penelope, the model wife of your cousin Ulysses, an exception?

MENELAUS. Duty is the refuge of the unbeautiful. She is as commonplace as she is ugly. (And then with deep bitterness) Why didn't he marry Helen when we all wanted her? He was too wise for that. He is the only man I've ever known who seems able to direct destiny.

ANALYTIKOS. You should not blame the Gods for a lack of will.

MENELAUS (shouting). Will! Heaven knows I do not lack the will to rid myself of this painted puppet, but where is the instrument ready to my hand?

(At this moment a Shepherd of Apollonian beauty leaps across the rail of the balcony and bounds into the room. MENELAUS and ANALYTIKOS start back in amazement.)

ANALYTIKOS. Who are you?

PARIS. An adventurer.

ANALYTIKOS. Then you have reached the end of your story. In a moment you will die.

PARIS. I have no faith in prophets.

ANALYTIKOS. The soldiers of the King will give you faith. Don't you know that it means death for any man to enter the apartments of the Queen?

PARIS (looking from one to the other). Oh! So you're a couple of eunuchs.
(Though nearly eighty this is too much for ANALYTIKOS to bear. He rushes to call the guard, but MENELAUS stops him.)

PARIS (to ANALYTIKOS). Thanks.

ANALYTIKOS. You thank me for telling you your doom?

PARIS. No—for convincing me that I'm where I want to be. It's taken me a long while, but I knew I'd get here. (And then very intimately to MENELAUS) Where's the Queen?

MENELAUS. Where do you come from?

PARIS. From the hills. I had come down into the market-place to sell my sheep. I had my hood filled with apples. They were golden-red like a thousand sunsets.

MENELAUS (*annoyed*). You might skip those bucolic details.

PARIS. At the fair I met three ancient gypsies.

MENELAUS. What have they to do with you coming here?

PARIS. You don't seem very patient. Can't I tell my story in my own way? They asked me for the apple I was eating and I asked them what they'd give for it.

MENELAUS. I'm not interested in market quotations.

PARIS. You take everything so literally. I'm sure you're easily bored.

MENELAUS (*with meaning*). I am.

PARIS (*going on cheerfully*). The first was to give me all the money she could beg, and the second was to tell me all the truth she could learn by listening, and the third promised me a pretty girl. So I chose— (*He hesitates.*)

ANALYTIKOS. You cannot escape by spinning out your tale.

PARIS. Death is the end of one story and the beginning of another.

MENELAUS. Well! Well! Come to the point. Which did you choose?

PARIS (*smiling*). Well, you see I'd been in the hills for a long while, so I picked the girl.

ANALYTIKOS. It would have been better for you if you had chosen wisdom.

PARIS. I knew you'd say that.

ANALYTIKOS. I have spoken truly. In a moment you will die.

PARIS. It is because the old have forgotten life that they preach wisdom.

MENELAUS. So you chose the girl? Well, go on.

PARIS. This made the other cronies angry, and when I tossed her the apple one of the others yelped at me: "You may as well seek the Queen of Sparta: she is the fairest of women." And as I turned away I heard their laughter, but the words had set my heart aflame and though it cost me my life, I'll follow the adventure.

ANALYTIKOS (*scandalized*). Haven't we heard enough of this?

MENELAUS (*deeply*). No! I want to hear how the story ends. It may amuse the King. (*He makes a sign to* ANALYTIKOS.)

PARIS. And on the ship at night I looked long at the stars and dreamed of possessing Helen.
(ANALYTIKOS *makes an involuntary movement toward the balcony, but* MENELAUS *stops him.*)

PARIS. Desire has been my guiding Mercury; the Fates are with me, and here I am.

ANALYTIKOS. The wrath of the King will show you no mercy.

PARIS (*nonchalantly*). I'm not afraid of the King. He's fat, and—a fool.

ANALYTIKOS. Shall I call the guards? (MENELAUS *stops him.*)

MENELAUS (*very significantly*). So you would give your life for a glimpse of the Queen?

PARIS (*swiftly*). Yes! My immortal soul, and if the fables tell the truth, the sight will be worth the forfeit.

MENELAUS (*suddenly jumping up*). It shall be as you wish!

PARIS (*buoyantly*). Venus has smiled on me.

MENELAUS. In there beyond the library you will find a room with a bath. Wait there till I call you.

PARIS. Is this some trick to catch me?

MENELAUS. A Spartan cannot lie.

PARIS. What will happen to you if the King hears of this?

MENELAUS. I will answer for the King. Go.
(PARIS *exits into the library.*)

ANALYTIKOS (*rubbing his hands*) Shall I order the boiling oil?

MENELAUS (*surprised*). Oil?

ANALYTIKOS. Now that he is being cleaned for the sacrifice.

MENELAUS. His torture will be greater than being boiled alive.

ANALYTIKOS (*eagerly*). You'll have him hurled from the wall of the palace to a forest of waiting spears below?

MENELAUS. None is so blind as he who sees too much.

ANALYTIKOS. Your Majesty is subtle in his cruelty.

MENELAUS. Haven't the years taught you the cheapness of revenge?

ANALYTIKOS (*mystified*). You do not intend to alter destiny.

MENELAUS. Never before has destiny been so clear to me.

ANALYTIKOS. Then the boy must die.

MENELAUS (*with slow determination*). No! He has been sent by the Gods to save me!

ANALYTIKOS. Your Majesty! (*He is trembling with apprehension.*)

MENELAUS (*with unbudgeable conviction*). Helena must elope with him!

ANALYTIKOS (*falling into a seat*). Ye Gods!

MENELAUS (*quietly*). I couldn't divorce the Queen. That would set a bad example.

ANALYTIKOS. Yes, very.

MENELAUS. I couldn't desert her. That would be beneath my honor.

ANALYTIKOS (*deeply*). Was there no other way?

MENELAUS (*pompously*). The King can do no wrong, and besides I hate the smell of blood. Are you a prophet as well as a scholar? Will she go?

ANALYTIKOS. Tonight I will read the stars.

MENELAUS (*meaningfully*). By tonight I'll not need you to tell me.
(ANALYTIKOS *sits deep in thought*) Well?

ANALYTIKOS. Ethics cite no precedent.

MENELAUS. Do you mean to say I'm not justified?

ANALYTIKOS (*cogitating*). Who can establish the punctilious ratio between necessity and desire?

MENELAUS (*beginning to fume*). This is no time for language. Just put yourself in my place.

ANALYTIKOS. Being you, how can I judge as I?

MENELAUS (*losing control*). May you choke on your dialectics! Zeus himself could have stood it no longer.

ANALYTIKOS. Have you given her soul a chance to grow?

MENELAUS. Her soul, indeed! It's shut in her rouge pot. (*He has been strutting about. Suddenly he sits down crushing a roll of papyrus. He takes it up and in utter disgust reads*) "The perfect hip, its development and permanence." Bah! (*He flings it to the floor*) I've done what I had to do, and Gods grant the bait may be sweet enough to catch the Queen.

ANALYTIKOS. If you had diverted yourself with a war or two you might have forgotten your troubles at home.

MENELAUS (*frightened*). I detest dissension of any kind—my dream was perpetual peace in comfortable domesticity with a womanly woman to warm my sandals.

ANALYTIKOS. Is not the Queen—?

MENELAUS. No! No! The whole world is but her mirror. And I'm expected to face that woman every morning at breakfast for the rest of my life, and by Venus that's more than even a King can bear!

ANALYTIKOS. Even a King cannot alter destiny. I warn you, whom the Gods have joined together—

MENELAUS (*in an outburst*). Is for man to break asunder!

ANALYTIKOS (*deeply shocked*). You talk like an atheist.

MENELAUS. I never allow religion to interfere with life. Go call the victim and see that he be left alone with the Queen.
(MENELAUS *exits and* ANALYTIKOS *goes over to the door of the library and summons* PARIS, *who enters clad in a gorgeous robe.*)

PARIS. I found this in there. It looks rather well, doesn't it? Ah! So you're alone. I suppose that stupid friend of yours has gone to tell the King. When do I see the Queen?

ANALYTIKOS. At once. (*He goes to the door of the Queen's apartment and claps his hand.* TSUMU *enters and at the sight of her* PARIS *recoils the full length of the room.*)

PARIS. I thought the Queen was a blonde!

ANALYTIKOS. Tell Her Majesty a stranger awaits her here. (TSUMU *exits, her eyes wide on* PARIS) You should thank the Gods for this moment.

PARIS (*his eyes on the door*). You do it for me. I can never remember all their names.

(HELENA *enters clad in her Sicily blue, crowned with a garland of golden flowers. She and* PARIS *stand riveted, looking at each other. Their attitude might be described as fantastic.* ANALYTIKOS *watches them for a moment and then with hands and head lifted to heaven he goes into the library.*)

PARIS (*quivering with emotion*). I have the most strange sensation of having seen you before. Something I can't explain—

HELENA (*quite practically*). Please don't bother about all sorts of fine distinctions. Under the influence of Analytikos and my husband, life has become a mess of indecision. I'm a simple, direct woman and I expect you to say just what you think.

PARIS. Do you? Very well, then— (*He comes a step nearer to her*) Fate is impelling me toward you.

HELENA. Yes. That's much better. So you're a fatalist. It's very Greek. I don't see what our dramatists would do without it.

PARIS. In my country there are no dramatists. We are too busy with reality.

HELENA. Your people must be uncivilized barbarians.

PARIS. My people are a genuine people. There is but one thing we worship.

HELENA. Don't tell me it's money.

PARIS. It's—

HELENA. Analytikos says if there weren't any money, there wouldn't be any of those ridiculous socialists.

PARIS. It isn't money. It's sincerity.

HELENA. I, too, believe in sincerity. It's the loveliest thing in the world.

PARIS. And the most dangerous.

HELENA. The truth is never dangerous.

PARIS. Except when told.

HELENA (*making room on the couch for him to sit next to her*). You mustn't say wicked things to me.

PARIS. Can your theories survive a test?

HELENA (*beautifully*). Truth is eternal and survives all tests.

PARIS. No. Perhaps, after all, your soul is not ready for the supremest heights.

HELENA. Do you mean to say I'm not religious? Religion teaches the meaning of love.

PARIS. Has it taught you to love your husband?

HELENA (*starting up and immediately sitting down again*). How dare you speak to me like that?

PARIS. You see. I was right. (*He goes toward the balcony.*)

HELENA (*stopping him*). Whatever made you think so?

PARIS. I've heard people talk of the King. You could never love a man like that.

HELENA (*beautifully*). A woman's first duty is to love her husband.

PARIS. There is a higher right than duty.

HELENA (*with conviction*). Right is right.

PARIS (*with admiration*). The world has libeled you.

HELENA. Me! The Queen?

PARIS. You are as wise as you are beautiful.

HELENA (*smiling coyly*). Why, you hardly know me.

PARIS. I know you! I, better than all men.

HELENA. You?

PARIS (*rapturously*). Human law has given you to Menelaus, but divine law makes you mine.

HELENA (*in amazement*). What!

PARIS. I alone appreciate your beauty. I alone can reach your soul.

HELENA. Ah!

PARIS. You hate your husband!

HELENA (*drawing back*). Why do you look at me like that?

PARIS. To see if there's one woman in the world who dares tell the truth.

HELENA. My husband doesn't understand me.

PARIS (*with conviction*). I knew you detested him.

HELENA. He never listens to my aspirations.

PARIS. Egoist.

HELENA (*assuming an irresistible pose*). I'm tired of being only lovely. He doesn't realize the meaning of spiritual intercourse, of soul communion.

PARIS. Fool!

HELENA. You dare call Moo Moo a fool?

PARIS. Has he not been too blind to see that your soul outshines your beauty? (*Then, very dramatically*) You're stifling!

HELENA (*clearing her throat*). I— I—

PARIS. He has made you sit upon your wings. (HELENA, *jumping up, shifts her position*) You are groping in the darkness.

HELENA. Don't be silly. It's very light in here.

PARIS (*undisturbed*). You are stumbling, and I have come to lead you. (*He steps toward her.*)

HELENA. Stop right there! (PARIS *stops*) No man but the King can come within ten feet of me. It's a court tradition.

PARIS. Necessity knows no tradition. (*He falls on his knees before her*) I shall come close to you, though the flame of your beauty consume me.

HELENA. You'd better be careful what you say to me. Remember I'm the Queen.

PARIS. No man weighs his words who has but a moment to live.

HELENA. You said that exactly like an actor. (*He leans very close to her*) What are you doing now?

PARIS. I am looking into you. You are the clear glass in which I read the secret of the universe.

HELENA. The secret of the universe. Ah! Perhaps you could understand me.

PARIS. First you must understand yourself.

HELENA (*instinctively taking up a mirror*). How?

PARIS. You must break with all this prose. (*With an unconscious gesture he sweeps a tray of toilet articles from the table.* HELENA *emits a little shriek.*)

HELENA. The ointment!

PARIS (*rushing to the window and pointing to the distance*). And climb to infinite poesy!

HELENA (*catching his enthusiasm, says very blandly*). There is nothing in the world like poetry.

PARIS (*lyrically*). Have you ever heard the poignant breathing of the stars?

HELENA. No. I don't believe in astrology.

PARIS. Have you ever smelt the powdery mists of the sun?

HELENA. I should sneeze myself to death.

PARIS. Have you ever listened to the sapphire soul of the sea?

HELENA. Has the sea a soul? But please don't stop talking. You do it so beautifully.

PARIS. Deeds are sweeter than words. Shall we go hand in hand to meet eternity?

HELENA (*not comprehending him*). That's very pretty. Say it again.

PARIS (*passionately*). There's but a moment of life left me. I shall stifle it in ecstasy. Helena, Helena, I adore you!

HELENA (*jumping up in high surprise*). You're not making love to me, you naughty boy?

PARIS. Helena.

HELENA. You've spoken to me so little, and already you dare to do that.

PARIS (*impetuously*). I am a lover of life. I skip the inessentials.

HELENA. Remember who I am.

PARIS. I have not forgotten, Daughter of Heaven. (*Suddenly he leaps to his feet*) Listen!

HELENA. Shhh! That's the King and Analytikos in the library.

PARIS. No! No! Don't you hear the flutter of wings?

HELENA. Wings?

PARIS (*ecstatically*). Venus, mother of Love!

HELENA (*alarmed*). What is it?

PARIS. She has sent her messenger. I hear the patter of little feet.

HELENA. Those little feet are the soldiers below in the courtyard.
(*A trumpet sounds.*)

PARIS (*the truth of the situation breaking through his emotion*). In a moment I shall be killed.

HELENA. Killed?

PARIS. Save me and save yourself!

HELENA. Myself?

PARIS. I shall rescue you and lead you on to life.

HELENA. No one has ever spoken to me like that before.

PARIS. This is the first time your ears have heard the truth.

HELENA. Was it of you I've been dreaming?

PARIS. Your dream was but your unrealized desire.

HELENA. Menelaus has never made me feel like this. (*And then with a sudden shriek*) Oh! I'm a wicked woman!

PARIS. No! No!

HELENA. For years I've been living with a man I didn't love.

PARIS. Yes! Yes!

HELENA. I'm lost!

PARIS (*at a loss*). No! Yes! Yes! No!

HELENA. It was a profanation of the most holy.

PARIS. The holiest awaits you, Helena! Our love will lighten the Plutonian realms.

HELENA. Menelaus never spoke to me like that.

PARIS. 'Tis but the first whisper of my adoration.

HELENA. I can't face him every morning at breakfast for the rest of my life. That's even more than a Queen can bear.

PARIS. I am waiting to release you.

HELENA. I've stood it for seven years.

PARIS. I've been coming to you since the beginning of time.

HELENA. There is something urging me to go with you, something I do not understand.

PARIS. Quick! There is but a moment left us. (*He takes her rapturously in his arms. There is a passionate embrace in the midst of which* TSUMU *enters.*)

TSUMU. The chiropodist has come.

HELENA. Bring me my outer garment and my purse.
(TSUMU *exits, her eyes wide on* PARIS.)

PARIS. Helena! Helena!
(HELENA *looks about her and takes up the papyrus that* MENELAUS *has flung to the floor.*)

HELENA. A last word to the King. (*She looks at the papyrus*) No, this won't do; I shall have to take this with me.

PARIS What is it?

HELENA Maskanda's discourse on the hip.
(*A trumpet sounds below in the courtyard.*)

PARIS (*excitedly*). Leave it—or your hip may cost me my head. We haven't a minute to spare. Hurry! Hurry!
(HELENA *takes up an eyebrow pencil and writes on the back of the papyrus. She looks for a place to put it and seeing the shield she smears it with some of the ointment and sticks the papyrus to it.*)

PARIS (*watching her in ecstasy*). You are the fairest of all fair women and your name will blaze as a symbol throughout eternity.
(TSUMU *enters with the purse and the Queen's outer robe.*)

HELENA (*tossing the purse to* PARIS). Here, we may need this.

PARIS (*throwing it back to* TSUMU). This for your silence, daughter of darkness. A prince has no need of purses.

TSUMU (*looking at him*). A prince!

HELENA (*gloriously*). My prince of poetry. My deliverer!

PARIS (*divinely*). My queen of love!
(*They go out,* TSUMU *looking after them in speechless amazement. Suddenly she sees the papyrus on the shield, runs over and reads it and then rushes to the door of the library.*)

TSUMU (*calling*). Analytikos. (*She hides the purse in her bosom.* ANALYTIKOS *enters, scroll in hand.*)

ANALYTIKOS. Has the Queen summoned me?

TSUMU (*mysteriously*). A terrible thing has happened.

ANALYTIKOS. What's the matter?

TSUMU. Where's the King?

ANALYTIKOS. In the library.

TSUMU. I have news more precious than the gold of Midas.

ANALYTIKOS (*giving her a purse*). Well! What is it?

TSUMU (*speaking very dramatically and watching the effect of her words*). The Queen has deserted Menelaus.

ANALYTIKOS (*receiving the shock philosophically*). Swift are the ways of Nature. The Gods have smiled upon him.

TSUMU. The Gods have forsaken the King to smile upon a prince.

ANALYTIKOS. What?

TSUMU. He was a prince.

ANALYTIKOS (*apprehensively*). Why do you say that?

TSUMU (*clutching her bosom*). I have a good reason to know. (*There is a sound of voices below in the courtyard.* MENELAUS *rushes in expectantly.* TSUMU *falls prostrate before him*) Oh, King, in thy bottomless agony blame not a blameless Negress. The Queen has fled!

MENELAUS (*in his delight forgetting himself and flinging her a purse*). Is it true?

TSUMU. Woe! Woe is me!

MENELAUS (*storming*). Out of my sight, you eyeless Argus!

ANALYTIKOS (to TSUMU). Quick, send a messenger. Find out who he was.
(TSUMU *sticks the third purse in her bosom and runs out.*)

MENELAUS (*with radiant happiness, kneeling before the bust of Zeus*). Ye Gods, I thank ye. Peace and a happy life at last.
(*The shouts in the courtyard grow louder.*)

ANALYTIKOS. The news has spread through the palace.

MENELAUS (*in trepidation, springing up*). No one would dare stop the progress of the Queen.

TSUMU (*rushes in and prostrates herself before the King*). Woe is me! They have gone by the road to the harbor.

MENELAUS (*anxiously*). Yes! Yes!

TSUMU. By the King's orders no man has dared gaze upon Her Majesty. They all fell prostrate before her.

MENELAUS. Good! Good! (*Attempting to cover his delight*) Go! Go! You garrulous dog.
(TSUMU *gets up and points to shield.* ANALYTIKOS *and the King look toward it.* ANALYTIKOS *tears off the papyrus and brings it to* MENELAUS. TSUMU, *watching them, exits.*)

MENELAUS (*reading*). "I am not a bad woman. I did what I had to do." How Greek to blame fate for what one wants to do.
(TSUMU *again comes tumbling in.*)

TSUMU (*again prostrate before the King*). A rumor flies through the city. He—he—

ANALYTIKOS (*anxiously*). Well? Well?

TSUMU. He—he—

MENELAUS (*furiously to* ANALYTIKOS). Rid me of this croaking raven.

TSUMU. Evil has fallen on Sparta. He—

ANALYTIKOS. Yes—yes—

MENELAUS (*in a rage*). Out of my sight, perfidious Nubian.
(*Sounds of confusion in the courtyard. Suddenly she springs to her feet and yells at the top of her voice.*)

TSUMU. He was Paris, Prince of Troy!
(*They all start back.* ANALYTIKOS *stumbles into a seat.* MENELAUS *turns pale.* TSUMU *leers like a black Nemesis.*)

ANALYTIKOS (*very ominously*). Who can read the secret of the Fates?

MENELAUS (*frightened*). What do you mean?

ANALYTIKOS. He is the son of Priam, King of Troy.

TSUMU (*adding fuel*). And of Hecuba, Queen of the Trojans. (*She rushes out to spread the news.*)

ANALYTIKOS. That makes the matter international.

MENELAUS (*quickly*). But we have treaties with Troy.

ANALYTIKOS. Circumstances alter treaties. They will mean nothing.

MENELAUS. Nothing?

ANALYTIKOS. No more than a scrap of papyrus. Sparta will fight to regain her Queen.

MENELAUS. But I don't want her back.

ANALYTIKOS. Can you tell that to Sparta? Remember, the King can do no wrong. Last night I dreamed of war.

MENELAUS. No! No! Don't say that. After the scandal I can't be expected to fight to get her back.

ANALYTIKOS. Sparta will see with the eyes of chivalry.

MENELAUS (fuming). But I don't believe in war.

ANALYTIKOS (still obdurate). Have you forgotten the oath pledged of old, with Ulysses and Agamemnon? They have sworn, if ever the time came, to fight and defend the Queen.

MENELAUS (bitterly). I didn't think of the triple alliance.

ANALYTIKOS. Can Sparta ask less of her King?

MENELAUS. Let's hear the other side. We can perhaps arbitrate. Peace at any price.

ANALYTIKOS. Some bargains are too cheap.

MENELAUS (hopelessly). But I am a pacifist.

ANALYTIKOS. You are Menelaus of Sparta, and Sparta's a nation of soldiers.

MENELAUS (desperately). I am too proud to fight!

ANALYTIKOS. Here, put on your shield. (A great clamor comes up from the courtyard. ANALYTIKOS steps out on the balcony and is greeted with shouts of "The King! The King!" Addressing the crowd) People of Sparta, this calamity has been forced upon us. (MENELAUS winces) We are a peaceful people. But thanks to our unparalleled efficiency, the military system of Sparta is the most powerful in all Greece and we can mobilize in half an hour. (Loud acclaims from the people. MENELAUS, the papyrus still in hand, crawls over and attempts to stop ANALYTIKOS.)

ANALYTIKOS (not noticing him). In the midst of connubial and communal peace the thunderbolt has fallen on the King. (MENELAUS tugs at ANALYTIKOS' robe) Broken in spirit as he is, he is already pawing the ground like a battle steed. Never will we lay down our arms! We and Jupiter! (Cheers) Never until the Queen is restored to Menelaus. Never, even if it takes ten years. (MENELAUS squirms. A loud cheer) Even now the King is buckling on his shield. (More cheers. ANALYTIKOS steps farther forward and then with bursting eloquence) One hate we have and one alone! (Yells from below.)

Hate by water and hate by land,
Hate of the head and hate of the
    hand,
Hate of Paris and hate of Troy
That has broken the Queen for a
    moment's toy.

(*The yells grow fiercer.*)
Zeus' thunder will shatter the Trojan throne.
We have one hate and one alone!
(MENELAUS *sits on the floor dejectedly looking at the papyrus. A thunder of voices from the people.*)

We have one hate and one alone.
    Troy! Troy!

(*Helmets and swords are thrown into the air. The cheers grow tumultuous, trumpets are blown, and the Curtain falls.*)

Suppressed Desires

A COMEDY IN TWO EPISODES

BY SUSAN GLASPELL

IN COLLABORATION WITH
GEORGE CRAM COOK

CHARACTERS

Henrietta Brewster
Stephen Brewster
Mabel

Scene—*A Studio Apartment*

SUPPRESSED DESIRES

SCENE I—*A studio apartment in an upper story, Washington Square South. Through an immense north window in the back wall appear tree tops and the upper part of the Washington Arch. Beyond it you look up Fifth Avenue. Near the window is a big table, loaded at one end with serious-looking books and austere scientific periodicals. At the other end are architect's drawings, blue prints, dividing compasses, square, ruler, etc. At the left is a door leading to the rest of the apartment; at the right the outer door. A breakfast table is set for three, but only two are seated at it—*HENRIETTA *and* STEPHEN BREWSTER. *As the curtains withdraw* STEVE *pushes back his coffee cup and sits dejected.*

HENRIETTA. It isn't the coffee, Steve dear. There's nothing the matter with the coffee. There's something the matter with *you.*

STEVE *(doggedly)*. There may be something the matter with my stomach.

HENRIETTA *(scornfully)*. Your stomach! The trouble is not with your stomach but in your subconscious mind.

STEVE. Subconscious piffle! *(Takes morning paper and tries to read.)*

HENRIETTA. Steve, you never used to be so disagreeable. You certainly have got some sort of a complex. You're all inhibited. You're no longer open to new ideas. You won't listen to a word about psychoanalysis.

STEVE. A word! I've listened to volumes!

HENRIETTA. You've ceased to be creative in architecture—your work isn't going well. You're not sleeping well—.

STEVE. How can I sleep, Henrietta, when you're always waking me up to find out what I'm dreaming?

HENRIETTA. But dreams are so important, Steve. If you'd tell yours to Dr. Russell he'd find out exactly what's wrong with you.

STEVE. There's nothing wrong with me.

HENRIETTA. You don't even talk as well as you used to.

STEVE. Talk? I can't say a thing without you looking at me in that dark fashion you have when you're on the trail of a complex.

HENRIETTA. This very irritability indicates that you're suffering from some suppressed desire.

STEVE. I'm suffering from a suppressed desire for a little peace.

HENRIETTA. Dr. Russell is doing simply wonderful things with nervous cases. Won't you go to him, Steve?

STEVE *(slamming down his newspaper)*. No, Henrietta, I won't!

HENRIETTA. But Stephen—!

STEVE. 'Ist! I hear Mabel coming. Let's not be at each other's throats the first day of her visit. (*He takes out cigarettes.* MABEL *comes in from door left, the side opposite* STEVE, *so that he is facing her. She is wearing a rather fussy negligee in contrast to* HENRIETTA, *who wears "radical" clothes.* MABEL *is what is called plump.*)

MABEL. Good morning.

HENRIETTA. Oh, here you are, little sister.

STEVE. Good morning, Mabel. (MABEL *nods to him and turns, her face lighting up, to* HENRIETTA.)

HENRIETTA (*giving* MABEL *a hug as she leans against her*). It's so good to have you here. I was going to let you sleep, thinking you'd be tired after the long trip. Sit down. There'll be fresh toast in a minute and (*rising*) will you have—

MABEL. Oh, I ought to have told you, Henrietta. Don't get anything for me. I'm not eating breakfast.

HENRIETTA (*at first in mere surprise*). Not eating breakfast? (*She sits down, then leans toward* MABEL *who is seated now, and scrutinizes her.*)

STEVE (*half to himself*). The psychoanalytical look!

HENRIETTA. Mabel, why are you not eating breakfast?

MABEL (*a little startled*). Why, no particular reason. I just don't care much for breakfast, and they say it

keeps down— (*A hand on her hip —the gesture of one who is "reducing"*) that is, it's a good thing to go without it.

HENRIETTA. Don't you sleep well? Did you sleep well last night?

MABEL. Oh, yes, I slept all right. Yes, I slept fine last night, only (*laughing*) I did have the funniest dream!

STEVE. S-h! S-t!

HENRIETTA (*moving closer*). And what did you dream, Mabel?

STEVE. Look-a-here, Mabel, I feel it's my duty to put you on. Don't tell Henrietta your dreams. If you do she'll find out that you have an underground desire to kill your father and marry your mother—

HENRIETTA. Don't be absurd, Stephen Brewster. (*Sweetly to* MABEL) What was your dream, dear?

MABEL (*laughing*). Well, I dreamed I was a hen.

HENRIETTA. A hen?

MABEL. Yes; and I was pushing along through a crowd as fast as I could, but being a hen I couldn't walk very fast—it was like having a tight skirt, you know; and there was some sort of creature in a blue cap —you know how mixed up dreams are—and it kept shouting after me, "Step, Hen! Step, Hen!" until I got all excited and just couldn't move at all.

HENRIETTA (*resting chin in palm and peering*). You say you became much excited?

MABEL (*laughing*). Oh, yes; I was in a terrible state.

HENRIETTA (*leaning back, murmurs*). This is significant.

STEVE. She dreams she's a hen. She is told to step lively. She becomes violently agitated. What can it mean?

HENRIETTA (*turning impatiently from him*). Mabel, do you know anything about psychoanalysis?

MABEL (*feebly*). Oh—not much. No—I— (*Brightening*) It's something about the war, isn't it?

STEVE. Not that kind of war.

MABEL (*abashed*). I thought it might be the name of a new explosive.

STEVE. It *is.*

MABEL (*apologetically to* HENRIETTA, *who is frowning*). You see, Henrietta, I—we do not live in touch with intellectual things, as you do. Bob being a dentist—somehow our friends—

STEVE (*softly*). Oh, to be a dentist! (*Goes to window and stands looking out.*)

HENRIETTA. Don't you see anything more of that editorial writer—what was his name?

MABEL. Lyman Eggleston?

HENRIETTA. Yes, Eggleston. He was in touch with things. Don't you see him?

MABEL. Yes, I see him once in a while. Bob doesn't like him very well.

HENRIETTA. Your husband does not like Lyman Eggleston? (*Mysteriously*) Mabel, are you perfectly happy with your husband?

STEVE (*sharply*). Oh, come now, Henrietta—that's going a little strong!

HENRIETTA. Are you perfectly happy with him, Mabel?
(STEVE *goes to work-table.*)

MABEL. Why—yes—I guess so. Why—of course I am!

HENRIETTA. Are you happy? Or do you only think you are? Or do you only think you *ought* to be?

MABEL. Why, Henrietta, I don't know what you mean!

STEVE (*seizes stack of books and magazines and dumps them on the breakfast table*). This is what she means, Mabel. Psychoanalysis. My work-table groans with it. Books by Freud, the new Messiah; books by Jung, the new St. Paul; the Psychoanalytical Review—back numbers two-fifty per.

MABEL. But what's it all about?

STEVE. All about your sub-un-non-conscious mind and desires you know not of. They may be doing you a great deal of harm. You may go crazy with them. Oh, yes! People are doing it right and left. Your dreaming you're a hen— (*Shakes his head darkly.*)

HENRIETTA. Any fool can ridicule anything.

MABEL (*hastily, to avert a quarrel*). But what do you say it is, Henrietta?

STEVE (*looking at his watch*). Oh, if Henrietta's going to start that! (*During* HENRIETTA'S *next speech settles himself at work-table and sharpens a lead pencil.*)

HENRIETTA. It's like this, Mabel. You want something. You think you can't have it. You think it's wrong. So you try to think you don't want it. Your mind protects you—avoids pain—by refusing to think the forbidden thing. But it's there just the same. It stays there shut up in your unconscious mind, and it festers.

STEVE. Sort of an ingrowing mental toenail.

HENRIETTA. Precisely. The forbidden impulse is there full of energy which has simply got to do something. It breaks into your consciousness in disguise, masks itself in dreams, makes all sorts of trouble. In extreme cases it drives you insane.

MABEL (*with a gesture of horror*). Oh!

HENRIETTA (*reassuring*). But psychoanalysis has found out how to save us from that. It brings into consciousness the suppressed desire that was making all the trouble. Psychoanalysis is simply the latest scientific method of preventing and curing insanity.

STEVE (*from his table*). It is also the latest scientific method of separating families.

HENRIETTA (*mildly*). Families that ought to be separated.

STEVE. The Dwights, for instance. You must have met them, Mabel, when you were here before. Helen was living, apparently, in peace and happiness with good old Joe. Well —she went to this psychoanalyzer —she was "psyched," and biff!— bang!—home she comes with an unsuppressed desire to leave her husband. (*He starts work, drawing lines on a drawing board with a T-square.*)

MABEL. How terrible! Yes, I remember Helen Dwight. But—but did she have such a desire?

STEVE. First she'd known of it.

MABEL. And she *left* him?

HENRIETTA (*coolly*). Yes, she did.

MABEL. Wasn't he good to her?

HENRIETTA. Why, yes, good enough.

MABEL. Wasn't he kind to her?

HENRIETTA. Oh, yes—kind to her.

MABEL. And she left her good, kind husband—!

HENRIETTA. Oh, Mabel! "Left her good, kind husband!" How naïve— forgive me, dear, but how bourgeois you are! She came to know herself. And she had the courage!

MABEL. I may be very naïve and— bourgeois—but I don't see the good of a new science that breaks up homes. (STEVE *applauds.*)

STEVE. in enlightening Mabel, we mustn't neglect to mention the case of Art Holden's private secretary, Mary Snow, who has just been informed of her suppressed desire for her employer.

MABEL. Why, I think it is terrible, Henrietta! It would be better if we didn't know such things about ourselves.

HENRIETTA. No, Mabel, that is the old way.

MABEL. But—but her employer? Is he married?

STEVE (*grunts*). Wife and four children.

MABEL. Well, then, what good does it do the girl to be told she has a desire for him? There's nothing can be done about it.

HENRIETTA. Old institutions will have to be reshaped so that something can be done in such cases. It happens, Mabel, that this suppressed desire was on the point of landing Mary Snow in the insane asylum. Are you so tight-minded that you'd rather have her in the insane asylum than break the conventions?

MABEL. But—but have people always had these awful suppressed desires?

HENRIETTA. Always.

STEVE. But they've just been discovered.

HENRIETTA. The harm they do has just been discovered. And free, sane people must face the fact that they have to be dealt with.

MABEL (*stoutly*). I don't believe they have them in Chicago.

HENRIETTA (*business of giving* MABEL *up*). People "have them" wherever the living Libido—the center of the soul's energy—is in conflict with petrified moral codes. That means everywhere in civilization. Psychoanalysis—

STEVE. Good God! I've got the roof in the cellar!

HENRIETTA. The roof in the cellar!

STEVE (*holding plan at arm's length*). That's what psychoanalysis does!

HENRIETTA. That's what psychoanalysis could *un*-do. Is it any wonder I'm concerned about Steve? He dreamed the other night that the walls of his room melted away and he found himself alone in a forest. Don't you see how significant it is for an architect to have *walls* slip away from him? It symbolizes his loss of grip in his work. There's some suppressed desire—

STEVE (*hurling his ruined plan viciously to the floor*). Suppressed hell!

HENRIETTA. You speak more truly than you know. It is through suppressions that hells are formed in us.

MABEL (*looking at* STEVE, *who is tearing his hair*). Don't you think it would be a good thing, Henrietta, if we went somewhere else? (*They rise and begin to pick up the dishes.* MABEL *drops a plate which breaks.* HENRIETTA *draws up short and looks at her—the psychoanalytic look*) I'm sorry, Henrietta. One of the Spode plates, too. (*Surprised and resentful as* HENRIETTA *continues to peer at her*) Don't take it so to heart, Henrietta.

HENRIETTA. I can't help taking it to heart.

MABEL. I'll get you another. (*Pause. More sharply as* HENRIETTA *does not answer*) I said I'll get you another plate, Henrietta.

HENRIETTA. It's not the plate.

MABEL. For heaven's sake, what is it then?

HENRIETTA. It's the significant little false movement that made you drop it.

MABEL. Well, I suppose everyone makes a false movement once in a while.

HENRIETTA. Yes, Mabel, but these false movements all mean something.

MABEL (*about to cry*). I don't think that's very nice! It was just because I happened to think of that Mabel Snow you were talking about—

HENRIETTA. *Mabel* Snow!

MABEL. Snow—Snow—well, what was her name, then?

HENRIETTA. Her name is Mary. You substituted *your own* name for hers.

MABEL. Well, *Mary* Snow, then; *Mary* Snow. I never heard her name but once. I don't see anything to make such a fuss about.

HENRIETTA (*gently*). Mabel dear—mistakes like that in names—

MABEL (*desperately*). They don't mean something, too, do they?

HENRIETTA (*gently*). I am sorry, dear, but they do.

MABEL. But I'm always doing that!

HENRIETTA (*after a start of horror*). My poor little sister, tell me about it.

MABEL. About what?

HENRIETTA. About your not being happy. About your longing for another sort of life.

MABEL. But I *don't*.

HENRIETTA. Ah, I understand these things, dear. You feel Bob is limiting you to a life in which you do not feel free—

MABEL. Henrietta! When did I ever say such a thing?

HENRIETTA. You said you are not in touch with things intellectual. You showed your feeling that it is Bob's profession—that has engendered a resentment which has colored your whole life with him.

MABEL. Why—Henrietta!

HENRIETTA. Don't be afraid of me. little sister. There's nothing can shock me or turn me from you. I am not like that. I wanted you to come for this visit because I had a feeling that you needed more from life than you were getting. No one of these things I have seen would excite my suspicion. It's the combination. You don't eat breakfast (*enumerating on her fingers*); you make false moves; you substitute your own name for the name of another *whose love is misdirected.* You're nervous; you *look* queer; in your eyes there's a frightened look that is most unlike you. And this dream. A *hen.* Come with me this afternoon to Dr. Russell! Your whole life may be at stake, Mabel.

MABEL (*gasping*). Henrietta, I— you—you always were the smartest in the family, and all that, but—this is terrible! I don't think we *ought* to think such things. (*Brightening*) Why, I'll tell you why I dreamed I was a hen. It was because last night, telling about that time in Chicago, you said I was as mad as a wet hen.

HENRIETTA (*superior*). Did you dream you were a *wet* hen?

MABEL (*forced to admit it*). No.

HENRIETTA. No. You dreamed you were a *dry* hen. And why, being a hen, were you urged to step?

MABEL. Maybe it's because when I am getting on a street car it always irritates me to have them call "Step lively."

HENRIETTA. No, Mabel, that is only a child's view of it—if you will forgive me. You see merely the elements used in the dream. You do not see into the dream; you do not see its meaning. This dream of the hen—

STEVE. Hen—hen—wet hen—dry hen—mad hen! (*Jumps up in a rage*) Let me out of this!

HENRIETTA (*hastily picking up dishes, speaks soothingly*). Just a minute, dear, and we'll have things so you can work in quiet. Mabel and I are going to sit in my room. (*She goes out left, carrying dishes.*)

STEVE (*seizing hat and coat from an alcove near the outside door*). I'm going to be psychoanalyzed. I'm going now! I'm going straight to that infallible doctor of hers—that priest of this new religion. If he's got honesty enough to tell Henrietta there's nothing the matter with my unconscious mind, perhaps I can be let alone about it, and then I *will* be all right. (*From the door in a low voice*) Don't tell Henrietta I'm going. It might take weeks, and I couldn't stand all the talk. (*He hurries out.*)

HENRIETTA (*returning*). Where's Steve? Gone? (*With a hopeless gesture*) You see how impatient he is —how unlike himself! I tell you, Mabel, I'm nearly distracted about Steve.

MABEL. I think he's a little distracted, too.

HENRIETTA. Well, if he's gone— you might as well stay here. I have a committee meeting at the bookshop, and will have to leave you to yourself for an hour or two. (*As she puts her hat on, taking it from the alcove where* STEVE *found his, her eye, lighting up almost carnivorously, falls on an enormous volume on the floor beside the worktable. The book has been half hidden by the wastebasket. She picks it up and carries it around the table toward* MABEL) Here, dear, is one of the simplest statements of psychoanalysis. You just read this and then we can talk more intelligently. (MABEL *takes volume and staggers back under its weight to chair rear center,* HENRIETTA *goes to outer door, stops and asks abruptly*) How old is Lyman Eggleston?

MABEL (*promptly*). He isn't forty yet. Why, what made you ask that, Henrietta? (*As she turns her head to look at* HENRIETTA *her hands move toward the upper corners of the book balanced on her knees.*)

HENRIETTA. Oh, nothing. Au revoir.

(*She goes out.* MABEL *stares at the ceiling. The book slides to the floor. She starts; looks at the book, then at the broken plate on the table*) The plate! The book! (*She lifts her eyes, leans forward, elbow on knee, chin on knuckles and plaintively queries*) Am I unhappy?

CURTAIN

SCENE II—*Two weeks later. The stage is as in Scene I, except that the breakfast table has been removed. During the first few minutes the dusk of a winter afternoon deepens. Out of the darkness spring rows of double street-lights almost meeting in the distance.* HENRIETTA *is at the psycho-analytical end of* STEVE's *work-table, surrounded by open books and periodicals, writing.* STEVE *enters briskly.*

STEVE. What are you doing, my dear?

HENRIETTA. My paper for the Liberal Club.

STEVE. Your paper on—?

HENRIETTA. On a subject which does not have your sympathy.

STEVE. Oh, I'm not sure I'm wholly out of sympathy with psychoanalysis, Henrietta. You worked it so hard. I couldn't even take a bath without its meaning something.

HENRIETTA (*loftily*). I talked it because I knew you needed it.

STEVE. You haven't said much about it these last two weeks. Uh—your faith in it hasn't weakened any?

HENRIETTA. Weakened? It's grown stronger with each new thing I've come to know. And Mabel. She is with Dr. Russell now. Dr. Russell is

wonderful! From what Mabel tells me I believe his analysis is going to prove that I was right. Today I discovered a remarkable confirmation of my theory in the hen-dream.

STEVE. What is your theory?

HENRIETTA. Well, you know about Lyman Eggleston. I've wondered about him. I've never seen him, but I know he's less bourgeois than Mabel's other friends—more intellectual—and (*significantly*) she doesn't see much of him because Bob doesn't like him.

STEVE. But what's the confirmation?

HENRIETTA. Today I noticed the first syllable of his name.

STEVE. Ly?

HENRIETTA. No—egg.

STEVE. Egg?

HENRIETTA (*patiently*). Mabel dreamed she was a *hen*. (STEVE *laughs*) You wouldn't laugh if you knew how important names are in interpreting dreams. Freud is full of just such cases in which a whole hidden complex is revealed by a single significant syllable—like this egg.

STEVE. Doesn't the traditional relation of hen and egg suggest rather a maternal feeling?

HENRIETTA. There is something maternal in Mabel's love, of course, but that's only one element.

STEVE. Well, suppose Mabel hasn't a suppressed desire to be this gentleman's mother, but his beloved. What's to be done about it? What about Bob? Don't you think it's going to be a little rough on him?

HENRIETTA. That can't be helped. Bob, like everyone else, must face the facts of life. If Dr. Russell should arrive independently at this same interpretation I shall not hesitate to advise Mabel to leave her present husband.

STEVE. Um—hum! (*The lights go up on Fifth Avenue.* STEVE *goes to the window and looks out*) How long is it we've lived here, Henrietta?

HENRIETTA. Why, this is the third year, Steve.

STEVE. I—we—one would miss this view if one went away, wouldn't one?

HENRIETTA. How strangely you speak! Oh, Stephen, I *wish* you'd go to Dr. Russell. Don't think my fears have abated because I've been able to restrain myself. I had to on account of Mabel. But now, dear —won't you go?

STEVE. I— (*He breaks off, turns on the light, then comes and sits beside* HENRIETTA) How long have we been married, Henrietta?

HENRIETTA. Stephen, I don't understand you! You *must* go to Dr. Russell.

STEVE. I have gone.

HENRIETTA. You—what?

STEVE (*jauntily*). Yes, Henrietta, I've been psyched.

HENRIETTA. You went to Dr. Russell?

STEVE. The same.

HENRIETTA. And what did he say?

STEVE. He said—I—I was a little surprised by what he said, Henrietta.

HENRIETTA (*breathlessly*). Of course—one can so seldom anticipate. But tell me—your dream, Stephen? It means—?

STEVE. It means—I was considerably surprised by what it means.

HENRIETTA. *Don't* be so exasperating!

STEVE. It means—you really want to know, Henrietta?

HENRIETTA. Stephen, you'll drive me mad!

STEVE. He said—of course he may be wrong in what he said.

HENRIETTA. He *isn't* wrong. *Tell me!*

STEVE. He said my dream of the walls receding and leaving me alone in a forest indicates a suppressed desire—

HENRIETTA. Yes—yes!

STEVE. To be freed from—

HENRIETTA. Yes—freed from—?

STEVE. Marriage.

HENRIETTA (*crumples. Stares*). Marriage!

STEVE. He—he may be mistaken, you know.

HENRIETTA. *May* be mistaken?

STEVE. I—well, of course, I hadn't taken any stock in it myself. It was only your great confidence—

HENRIETTA. Stephen, are you telling me that Dr. Russell—Dr. A. E. Russell—told you this? (STEVE *nods*) Told you you have a suppressed desire to separate from *me?*

STEVE. That's what he said.

HENRIETTA. Did he know who you were?

STEVE. Yes.

HENRIETTA. That you were married to me?

STEVE. Yes, he knew that.

HENRIETTA. And he told you to leave me?

STEVE. It seems he must be wrong, Henrietta.

HENRIETTA (*rising*). And I've sent him more patients—! (*Catches herself and resumes coldly*) What reason did he give for this analysis?

STEVE. He says the confining walls are a symbol of my feeling about marriage and that their fading away is a wish-fulfillment.

HENRIETTA (*gulping*). Well, is it? Do you want our marriage to end?

STEVE. It was a great surprise to me that I did. You see I hadn't known what was in my unconscious mind.

HENRIETTA (*flaming*). What did you tell Dr. Russell about me to make him think you weren't happy?

STEVE. I never told him a thing, Henrietta. He got it all from his confounded clever inferences. I—I tried to refute them, but he said that was only part of my self-protective lying.

HENRIETTA. And that's why you were so—happy—when you came in just now!

STEVE. Why, Henrietta, how can you say such a thing? I was *sad*. Didn't I speak sadly of—of the view? Didn't I ask how long we had been married?

HENRIETTA (*rising*). Stephen Brewster, have you no sense of the seriousness of this? Dr. Russell doesn't know what our marriage has been. You do. You should have laughed him down! Confined—in life with me? Did you tell him that I *believe* in freedom?

STEVE. I very emphatically told him that his results were a great surprise to me.

HENRIETTA. But you accepted them.

STEVE. Oh, not at all. I merely couldn't refute his arguments. I'm not a psychologist. I came home to talk it over with you. You being a disciple of psychoanalysis—

HENRIETTA. If you are going, I wish you would go tonight!

STEVE. Oh, my dear! I—surely I couldn't do that! Think of my feelings. And my laundry hasn't come home.

HENRIETTA. I ask you to go tonight. Some women would falter at this, Steve, but I am not such a woman. I leave you free. I do not repudiate psychoanalysis; I say again that it has done great things. It has also made mistakes, of course. But since you accept this analysis— (*She sits down and pretends to begin work*) I have to finish this paper. I wish you would leave me.

STEVE (*scratches his head, goes to the inner door*). I'm sorry, Henrietta, about my unconscious mind. (*Alone,* HENRIETTA's *face betrays her outraged state of mind—disconcerted, resentful, trying to pull herself together. She attains an air of bravely bearing an outrageous thing.—The outer door opens and* MABEL *enters in great excitement.*)

MABEL (*breathless*). Henrietta, I'm so glad you're here. And alone?

(*Looks toward the inner door*) Are you alone, Henrietta?

HENRIETTA (*with reproving dignity*). Very much so.

MABEL (*rushing to her*). Henrietta, he's found it!

HENRIETTA (*aloof*). Who has found what?

MABEL. Who has found what? Dr. Russell has found my suppressed desire!

HENRIETTA. That is interesting.

MABEL. He finished with me today —he got hold of my complex—in the most amazing way! But, oh, Henrietta—it is so terrible!

HENRIETTA. Do calm yourself, Mabel. Surely there's no occasion for all this agitation.

MABEL. But there is! And when you think of the lives that are affected —the readjustments that must be made in order to bring the suppressed hell out of me and save me from the insane asylum—!

HENRIETTA. The insane asylum!

MABEL. You said that's where these complexes brought people!

HENRIETTA. What did the doctor tell you, Mabel?

MABEL. Oh, I don't know how I can tell you—it is so awful—so unbelievable.

HENRIETTA. I rather have my hand in at hearing the unbelievable.

MABEL. Henrietta, who would ever have thought it? How can it be true? But the doctor is perfectly certain that I have a suppressed desire for — (*Looks at* HENRIETTA, *is unable to continue.*)

HENRIETTA. Oh, go on, Mabel. I'm not unprepared for what you have to say.

MABEL. Not unprepared? You mean you have suspected it?

HENRIETTA. From the first. It's been my theory all along.

MABEL. But, Henrietta, I didn't know myself that I had this secret desire for Stephen.

HENRIETTA (*jumps up*). Stephen!

MABEL. My brother-in-law! My own sister's husband!

HENRIETTA. *You* have a suppressed desire for *Stephen!*

MABEL. Oh, Henrietta, aren't these unconscious selves terrible? They seem so unlike *us!*

HENRIETTA. What insane thing are you driving at?

MABEL (*blubbering*). Henrietta, don't you use that word to me. I don't *want* to go to the insane asylum.

HENRIETTA. What did Dr. Russell say?

MABEL. Well, you see—oh, it's the strangest thing! But you know the voice in my dream that called "Step, Hen!" Dr. Russell found out today that when I was a little girl I

had a story-book in words of one syllable and I read the name Stephen wrong. I used to read it S-t-e-p, step, h-e-n, hen. (*Dramatically*) Step Hen is Stephen. (*Enter* STEPHEN, *his head bent over a time-table*) Stephen is Step Hen!

STEVE. I? Step Hen?

MABEL (*triumphantly*). S-t-e-p, step, H-e-n, hen, Stephen!

HENRIETTA (*exploding*). Well, what if Stephen is Step Hen? (*Scornfully*) Step Hen! Step Hen! For that ridiculous coincidence—

MABEL. Coincidence! But it's childish to look at the mere elements of a dream. You have to look *into* it— you have to see what it *means!*

HENRIETTA. On account of that trivial, meaningless play on syllables— on that flimsy basis—you are ready — (*Wails*) O-h!

STEVE. What on earth's the matter? What has happened? Suppose I *am* Step Hen? What about it? What does it mean?

MABEL (*crying*). It means—that I —have a suppressed desire for *you!*

STEVE. For me! The deuce you have! (*Feebly*) What—er—makes you think so?

MABEL. Dr. Russell has worked it out scientifically.

HENRIETTA. Yes. Through the amazing discovery that Step Hen equals Stephen!

MABEL (*tearfully*). Oh, that isn't all —that isn't near all. Henrietta won't give me a chance to tell it. She'd rather I'd go to the insane asylum than be unconventional.

HENRIETTA. We'll all go there if you can't control yourself. We are still waiting for some rational report.

MABEL (drying her eyes). Oh, there's such a lot about names. (With some pride) I don't see how I ever did it. It all works in together. I dreamed I was a hen because that's the first syllable of Henrietta's name, and when I dreamed I was a hen, I was putting myself in Henrietta's place.

HENRIETTA. With Stephen?

MABEL. With Stephen.

HENRIETTA (outraged). Oh! (Turns in rage upon STEPHEN, who is fanning himself with the time-table) What are you doing with that time-table?

STEVE. Why—I thought—you were so keen to have me go tonight—I thought I'd just take a run up to Canada, and join Billy—a little shooting—but—

MABEL. But there's more about the names.

HENRIETTA. Mabel, have you thought of Bob—dear old Bob—your good, kind husband?

MABEL. Oh, Henrietta, "my good, kind husband!"

HENRIETTA. Think of him, Mabel, out there alone in Chicago, working his head off, fixing people's teeth--for you!

MABEL. Yes, but think of the living Libido—in conflict with petrified moral codes! And think of the perfectly wonderful way the names all prove it. Dr. Russell said he's never seen anything more convincing. Just look at Stephen's last name—Brewster. I dream I'm a hen, and the name Brewster—you have to say its first letter by itself—and then the hen, that's me, she says to him: "Stephen, Be Rooster!" (HENRIETTA and STEPHEN collapse into the nearest chairs.)

MABEL. I think it's perfectly wonderful! Why, if it wasn't for psychoanalysis you'd never find out how wonderful your own mind is!

STEVE (begins to chuckle). Be Rooster! Stephen, Be Rooster!

HENRIETTA. You think it's funny, do you?

STEVE. Well, what's to be done about it? Does Mabel have to go away with me?

HENRIETTA. Do you want Mabel to go away with you?

STEVE. Well, but Mabel herself— her complex, her suppressed desire—!

HENRIETTA (going to her). Mabel, are you going to insist on going away with Stephen?

MABEL. I'd rather go with Stephen than go to the insane asylum!

HENRIETTA. For heaven's sake, Mabel, drop that insane asylum! If you did have a suppressed desire for Stephen hidden away in you—God knows it isn't hidden now. Dr. Russell has brought it into your consciousness—with a vengeance. That's all that's necessary to break up a complex. Psychoanalysis doesn't say you have to *gratify* every suppressed desire.

STEVE (*softly*). Unless it's for Lyman Eggleston.

HENRIETTA (*turning on him*). Well, if it comes to that, Stephen Brewster, I'd like to know why that interpretation of mine isn't as good as this one? Step, Hen!

STEVE. But Be Rooster! (*He pauses, chuckling to himself*) Step-Hen B-rooster. And *H*enrietta. Pshaw, my dear, Doc Russell's got you beat a mile! (*He turns away and chuckles*) Be rooster!

MABEL. What has Lyman Eggleston got to do with it?

STEVE. According to Henrietta, you, the hen, have a suppressed desire for *Egg*leston, the egg.

MABEL. Henrietta, I think that's indecent of you! He is bald as an egg and little and fat—the idea of you thinking such a thing of me!

HENRIETTA. Well, Bob isn't little and bald and fat! Why don't you stick to your own husband? (*To* STEPHEN) What if Dr. Russell's interpretation has got mine "beat a mile"? (*Resentful look at him*) It would only mean that Mabel doesn't want Eggleston and does want you. Does that mean she has to have you?

MABEL. But you said Mabel Snow—

HENRIETTA. *Mary* Snow! You're not as much like her as you think—substituting your name for hers! The cases are entirely different. Oh, I wouldn't have *believed* this of you, Mabel. (*Beginning to cry*) I brought you here for a pleasant visit—thought you needed brightening *up* —wanted to be *nice* to you—and now you—my husband—you insist — (*In fumbling her way to her chair she brushes to the floor some sheets from the psychoanalytical table.*)

STEVE (*with solicitude*). Careful, dear. Your paper on psychoanalysis! (*Gathers up sheets and offers them to her.*)

HENRIETTA. I don't want my paper on psychoanalysis! I'm sick of psychoanalysis!

STEVE (*eagerly*). Do you mean that, Henrietta?

HENRIETTA. Why shouldn't I mean it? Look at all I've done for psychoanalysis—and— (*Raising a tear-stained face*) what has psychoanalysis done for me?

STEVE. Do you mean, Henrietta, that you're going to stop *talking* psychoanalysis?

HENRIETTA. Why shouldn't I stop talking it? Haven't I seen what it does to people? Mabel has gone crazy about psychoanalysis! (*At the word "crazy" with a moan* MABEL *sinks to chair and buries her face in her hands.*)

STEVE (*solemnly*). Do you swear never to wake me up in the night to find out what I'm dreaming?

HENRIETTA *Dream* what you please —I don't care what you're dreaming.

STEVE. Will you clear off my worktable so the Journal of Morbid Psychology doesn't stare me in the face when I'm trying to plan a house?

HENRIETTA (*pushing a stack of periodicals off the table*). I'll *burn* the Journal of Morbid Psychology!

STEVE. My dear Henrietta, if you're going to separate from psychoanaly-sis, there's no reason why I should separate from *you*.

(*They embrace ardently.* MABEL *lifts her head and looks at them woefully.*)

MABEL (*jumping up and going toward them*). But what about me? What am I to do with my suppressed desire?

STEVE (*with one arm still around* HENRIETTA, *gives* MABEL *a brotherly hug*). Mabel, you just keep right on suppressing it!

CURTAIN

The Game of Chess

A PLAY IN ONE ACT

BY
KENNETH SAWYER GOODMAN

CHARACTERS

THE GAME OF CHESS

The Scene is a wainscoted room in the house of ALEXIS. *High windows at the back left; at the right back is a double door giving into an ante-room; against the right wall is a couch; in the left wall near the back is a small door; nearer the audience, on the same wall a chimney breast with a carved mantel; under the window, at the back, another couch and several chairs give the room a luxurious air.* ALEXIS *and* CONSTANTINE *are playing chess at a small table in front of an open fire. There is a large table in the center of the stage with fruit, a flagon of wine and glasses.*

ALEXIS. You seem to have lost your cunning, Constantine.

CONSTANTINE. Wait!

ALEXIS. Perhaps the pawn?

CONSTANTINE. No. (*He moves*) So!

ALEXIS. Ah, ha! That, eh? Well, well! The cunning is returning, is it? (*He strikes a little bell beside him and again scans the board.*)

CONSTANTINE. Is the hour up, Your Excellency?

ALEXIS. No, no! We still have ten minutes to play.

CONSTANTINE. Your Excellency tires of the game, perhaps?

ALEXIS. No, I never tire of the game. When I do that, I shall tire of life itself. Chess is as much a gauge of a man's mental development as love or war or politics or any other game. When I play bad chess, I shall have ceased to be a competent governor. We patricians do not justify our lives by the toil of our hands. We should tune the machinery inside our skulls to its highest effectiveness. We must keep it

tuned and timed and oiled. Ah, yes, it is that way we serve. When the machine balks or stops we are nothing.

CONSTANTINE. But Your Excellency was thinking of other things.

ALEXIS. Was I so? Well, well! We shall see, we shall see! I was thinking of other things, eh? (*He makes a move swiftly*) There, match me that if you can.

CONSTANTINE. Ah! The one move that could have saved your king!

ALEXIS. There you have it! I doze, I dream, my mind wanders, and then it comes in a flash. The one move on the board! It is by such flashes I know myself.

CONSTANTINE. Your Excellency has inspiration.

ALEXIS. Perhaps! But behind inspiration, always, the technique of the game.
(*A footman enters.*)

FOOTMAN. Your Excellency rang?

ALEXIS. Is the man, Shamrayeff, waiting?

347

FOOTMAN. A man, Boris Ivanovitch Shamrayeff, with a letter from Your Excellency, is waiting in the secretary's room.

ALEXIS. You may bring him here in three minutes.

FOOTMAN. Pardon, Excellency, but the secretary wishes to know if the orders received from Mr. Constantine are correct?

ALEXIS. What orders?

FOOTMAN. That the man, Boris Ivanovitch Shamrayeff, is not to be searched.

ALEXIS. There is no occasion to search the man.
(FOOTMAN bows and withdraws.)

ALEXIS (to CONSTANTINE). Your move, my dear Constantine. We have exactly two minutes to finish the game and one minute for questions. (He lays his watch beside the chessboard.)

CONSTANTINE (moves). So!

ALEXIS. Ah! One moment! There! What now? (He moves.)

CONSTANTINE. This. (He moves.)

ALEXIS. And this! (He moves.)

CONSTANTINE. Ah ha! I could check-mate Your Excellency in five more moves.

ALEXIS. The two minutes are up. Tell me, you are quite certain that your agents made no mistake in the matter of this man, Shamrayeff?

CONSTANTINE. Quite certain, Your Excellency. I begged you to have him put under arrest yesterday. There is absolutely no question. The man's entire history is in your hands.

ALEXIS. And, in spite of all this, I have granted him a personal interview. I have given explicit orders that he is not to be searched. In short, I must be a fool, eh?

CONSTANTINE. I cannot question. Your Excellency's judgment.

ALEXIS. Ah, you can't question my judgment, eh? But you think! I saw something behind your eyes just now when you said you would check-mate me in five moves. You were thinking, "Alexis Alexandrovitch, for all his fine talk, is not what he used to be. Something has slipped away from him." Do you think I've become a coward?

CONSTANTINE. Your Excellency!

ALEXIS. I sometimes think so, myself; that some time there will be no flash, that I shall be check-mated once and for all. That's why I keep you here, hour after hour, playing chess with me; that's why I am tempted to try another kind of game with this man, Shamrayeff.

CONSTANTINE. Then you have a definite reason for seeing this man?

ALEXIS. None that you would understand.

CONSTANTINE. But, in that case, might I point out to Your Excellency—Surely it would be safer—

ALEXIS. Don't speak to me as if you were speaking to a child. I know what you think: "Alexis Alexandrovitch is not what he was. Things are slipping past him, he needs watching." Well, the time is up. You have your orders.

CONSTANTINE. Shall I take away the chessmen?

ALEXIS. No, leave them as they are. We'll finish the game when I ring for you. (CONSTANTINE *rises and hesitates*) Well, well, well! You're going to say something. You think the game won't be finished. We'll see. We'll see about that!

CONSTANTINE. I beg Your Excellency—
(FOOTMAN *enters, followed by* SHAMRAYEFF.)

FOOTMAN. Boris Ivanovitch Shamrayeff.
(SHAMRAYEFF *wears the clothes of a respectable artisan. He is, apparently, somewhat younger than* ALEXIS, *strongly built and has a rather fine but stolid face. He stands with his cap in his hand.*)

ALEXIS. So, so! You are Boris Ivanovitch Shamrayeff, are you? Well, well!

BORIS. Yes, I am Boris Ivanovitch Shamrayeff!

ALEXIS. You found it hard to get at me, did you? Hard to get an interview with Alexis Alexandrovitch?

BORIS. Not so hard as I had expected, Your Excellency.

ALEXIS (*to* CONSTANTINE *and* FOOTMAN). Well, what are you waiting for? This man has something important to say to me. He's bashful. He can't speak out before so many people.

CONSTANTINE. Your Excellency, I will wait in the passage.

ALEXIS. Nonsense, nonsense! Go into the garden and think about your game of chess! Go!
(CONSTANTINE *and* FOOTMAN *go out.*)

ALEXIS (*to* BORIS). Sit down in that chair. I want to look at you. (BORIS *looks around uneasily*) Ah! There is no one watching us. This room is in a corner of the house—nothing but windows behind you, no balcony, no hangings. Open the door you came in by—there is no one in the passage. Turn the key, if you like. (BORIS *steps quickly to the main doors, throws them open, looks into the passage, shuts them again, turns the key in the lock and slips it into his pocket*) You see we won't be disturbed. Now, sit down and tell me what you want. (BORIS *sits down but says nothing*) Tongue-tied, eh? You don't know how to begin? Embarrassed, eh?

BORIS. No, I was only wondering.

ALEXIS. Ha, ha! Wondering, eh?

BORIS. I was wondering why Your Excellency chose to give me this opportunity?

ALEXIS This opportunity?

BORIS (*looking up*). This opportunity to kill Your Excellency.

ALEXIS. So, so! To kill me? That's it, is it? Well, well! I thought as much, but of course, I couldn't be sure. Well, well! Go on, go on!

BORIS (*simply*). God has delivered you into my hands.

ALEXIS. Pah! Leave God out of it! Don't give me any such cant nonsense. I doubt if God takes any interest in either of us. I have delivered myself into your hands. That's the simple fact of the matter. I could have trapped you so easily, too, but I didn't even have you searched. You may as well take the pistol out of your pocket.

BORIS. Your Excellency seems amused.

ALEXIS. No, no, not amused! I'm only curious to see you handle the thing—morbid curiosity, if you like. Take it out, man, take it out!

BORIS. This is a solemn moment for us both, Your Excellency.

ALEXIS. Solemn, eh? Well, well! Solemn! Oh, I suppose it is solemn for you, Boris Ivanovitch. To me it is simply curious grotesque. Well, well!

BORIS (*takes out pistol*). Keep your hand a little further from that bell, if you please.

ALEXIS. I shan't ring. You would hardly wait for them to answer the bell, would you? No, no! I'm not such a fool as to think you'd do that? Well, well! I lift my hand and you shoot.

BORIS. Yes.

ALEXIS. Exactly. Well, I won't lift my hand.

BORIS. Nothing on earth can save you, Alexis Alexandrovitch.

ALEXIS. Nor you, my friend, for that matter! You hardly expect to leave the house, shall we say, unmolested?

BORIS. I do not expect to leave it alive, Excellency.

ALEXIS. No, that would be asking too much. I was here to let you in. I won't be able to let you out again. You will have lost a useful friend, Boris Ivanovitch.

BORIS. Your Excellency!

ALEXIS. It is in your hands to end the interview. Come, come, you must hate me a great deal, my friend, to give your own life for the sake of taking mine.

BORIS. I do not hate you.

ALEXIS. So? How odd! I thought that everyone of your sort hated me. You might at least flatter me to the extent of showing some emotion. Come, come, flatter me to that extent.

BORIS. I do not care to flatter you.

ALEXIS. Ah, well, well! I shall have to do without it then.

BORIS. My own feelings have nothing to do with it. I am an instrument of God.

ALEXIS. God again! What has God to do with it? Do you happen to play a good game of chess?

BORIS (*nervously*). Why do you ask me such a thing?

ALEXIS. Because you interrupted a game here. Constantine threatened me with check-mate in five more moves. Check-mate in five moves! No, no! Not so easy as that.

BORIS. I have had enough of your jestings, Excellency.

ALEXIS. You won't play then? Well, well! I had promised myself to finish the game. We shall see! We shall see!

BORIS. Surely Your Excellency has something you wish to say—

ALEXIS. I have told you once, when you tire of the interview it is in your hands to end it. What are you waiting for? You become tedious!

BORIS. Have you no desire to pray, Excellency?

ALEXIS. Pray? Pray? Who would listen to me? No, I'd rather chat.

BORIS. As Your Excellency likes.

ALEXIS. Yes, yes, we'll chat until you gather courage to do what you came for.

BORIS. It takes no courage to kill a thing like you.

ALEXIS. It takes a certain kind of courage to kill—rats.

BORIS. I have been chosen, Excellency.

ALEXIS. So, so! The lot fell on you, did it? The honor! The distinction! You look at it in that way, don't you? Like the rest of your kind, you have political ideas, eh?

BORIS. I have no political ideas.

ALEXIS. No political ideas? Well, well! No personal hatred? Pray explain yourself, man.

BORIS. I am a peasant. My father and my father's father were peasants. You are a noble. Your line runs back to Tartar princes. It is a matter of centuries of pain and slavery against centuries of oppression and violence. I take no account of today, only of yesterday and tomorrow. Your acts have been cruel and harsh, doubtless. I hardly know. I throw them out of the scale. I throw out my own sufferings. They are not enough in themselves to tip the balance. You and I are nothing. It is caste against caste. I gave myself to the revolutionary party, yes! I am their agent as you say, but I know little of their ideas for Russia. I care less. I only know that the band to which I belong represents the struggle which I feel in my own breast. I am their willing tool. I do their will because the right of vengeance comes down to me in the blood.

ALEXIS. Yes, yes! A fanatic!

BORIS. It is my order against yours.

ALEXIS. Ah, your order against mine, eh? Centuries of pain against centuries of oppression. Well, well! You set aside today, do you? You throw your own little pains and penalties out of the scale on one side, and my little tyrannies and floggings and acts of villainy out on the other? You see yourself only as the avenger of a caste against a caste. The right of vengeance and the need of it comes down to you in the blood, does it? You're exalted by the breath of dead peasants, are you? It's because of that and only because of it that you take pride in the work you have set your hand to. Huh! Grotesque! You strike the air with a rod of smoke. You've stumbled upon the essence of the inane.

You're about to commit a fantastic mockery of Justice.

BORIS. I have held my hand too long!

ALEXIS. Wait! There is still something to be said; something for you to think of in the moment between the time you take my life and the time you take your own. You are about to kill the man you might have been yourself. You are about to —I, and not you, am Boris Ivanovitch.

BORIS. What rubbish are you talking now?

ALEXIS. You are Alexis Alexandrovitch!

BORIS. Why! You are mad!

ALEXIS. Wait! When you were a child, you had a foster-brother. You ran with him in the fields. You slept by his side at night. You fought with him over rough toys and bits of food. When you were seven years old, a man on horseback came and took him away. You never knew his true parentage and your father flogged you when you cried for him. Can you remember that?

BORIS. Aye, I can remember that well.

ALEXIS. Your father deserted your mother the following year. A little later she died. She told you nothing of the other child. You went to Kieff, to the house of your uncle, and became apprenticed to a boot-maker.

BORIS. Leave off! You can't mystify me by telling me the story of my own life. It proves nothing. Your

agents have ways of knowing such things: what I was, what I am, everything.

ALEXIS. Yes! Leave all that! As you say, it proves nothing. Yet we are foster-brothers, you and I.

BORIS. A sign!

ALEXIS. Our good mother was endowed with a grim sense of humor. She sent her own boy to be reared as the son of princes, and the little aristocrat, left with her for safety at the time of the Makaroff meeting, she sent to—well, you know to what sort of a life she sent him.

BORIS. Give me a sign!

ALEXIS. I have no sign to give you.

BORIS. Ah, ah! What else? What else have you to tell me?

ALEXIS. I, and not you, am the son of peasants. Do you see now why I call your errand grotesque?

BORIS. Lies! Lies! Lies! What do you expect to gain by telling me such lies?

ALEXIS. Nothing.

BORIS. Do you expect me to believe you? Do you expect me to embrace you and clap my hat on my head and toss this pistol out the window and tell you to do what you like with me?

ALEXIS. I expect nothing. I know that I am one dead man talking to another.

BORIS. I can't fathom you. I know there must be some trick up your sleeve, but I can't fathom you.

ALEXIS. There is no trick. You asked me why I chose to give you this opportunity to kill me. I'm telling you, that's all.

BORIS. Lies! Utterly useless lies!

ALEXIS. No! Utterly useless truth! Do you think I wish to believe myself Boris Ivanovitch Shamrayeff, born a peasant? I, who have sat in high places and given my life to preserving an order of men to which I do not belong, which my blood ought to cry out against. Do you think I would have believed it if the belief had not been forced upon me? I have ways of knowing truth from falsehood, my friend. You are striking at a man who is dead before you touch him. What I have found out in the past week, others already know. I have come to the end, I tell you. I have been a fantastic dupe. I cannot go on. I would have killed myself today, but I have a horror of taking my own life. You have come in time to save me from that.

BORIS. Was that your only reason for seeing me?

ALEXIS. I admit I was curious to see another man who had been as great a dupe as myself.

BORIS. Lies! Lies! What else? Have you anything more to say?

ALEXIS. I only ask you to finish your work. Unless you have a scruple against killing your— In which case, go! The door is still open to you.

BORIS (sneering). Very pretty! Very touching! Go back, eh? And tell my comrades that I let Alexis the Red slip through my fingers because he told me a child's story of changeling foster-brothers? No, no! (He cocks his pistol.)

ALEXIS. Kill me, then!
(BORIS raises the pistol.)

BORIS. I—

ALEXIS. Pull the trigger, man!

BORIS. I can't. There's a chance that what you have said may be true after all. (He lays down the pistol) And yet, I can't live if it's false. And, by God, I can't live if it's true!

ALEXIS. In either case, we must both die.

BORIS. Aye, you speak the truth there, but I dare not kill you. I tell you, I dare not! There must be some way out! Some other way!

ALEXIS. Are you brave enough to take poison? Yes! Good! Do you see this ring? I press a spring, so. There is a fine powder under the stone, so! I drop a few grains into one of these glasses. We draw lots. One of us drinks the wine and the other still has your pistol to use! It is very simple after all.

BORIS (rises). Yah! Now, by God, I see the trick! Lies! Lies! Every word of it was lies! I can see through you now. You're devilishly cunning with your sleight-of-hand, but I draw no lots for poison with the like of you.

ALEXIS. Have it your own way. See, there's more than enough for both. Take the glass in your own hands, divide it yourself, pour the wine yourself, and then, to satisfy you, I'll drink first.

BORIS. You carry the bluff to the bitter end, do you? Well, we'll see. (*He mixes the powder and pours the wine and hands one glass to* ALEXIS.)

ALEXIS. To your easy death, brother. (*He lifts the glass and drinks.*)

BORIS. Ah! So you're a brave man after all! (*He lifts the glass and pauses*) What if I were to leave you now, eh?

ALEXIS. My men have orders to seize you the moment you leave the room.

BORIS. In that case! (*He lifts the glass*) To your final redemption, brother!

ALEXIS. Sit down! (BORIS *sits down.*)

BORIS. Have we long to wait?

ALEXIS. Perhaps five minutes. It's a Chinese concoction. They call it the draught of final oblivion. I believe it to be painless. I'm told that one becomes numb. Do you find yourself becoming drowsy?

BORIS. No. My senses seem to be becoming more alert. Your voice sounds very sharp and clear.

ALEXIS. Lift your hand.

BORIS. It seems very heavy. Are you afraid of death, Excellency?

ALEXIS (*eyeing him sharply*). No, I am not afraid of death, brother, not in the least.

BORIS. Nor I!

ALEXIS. Good! Now, move your feet.

BORIS. I don't seem to be able to. That's strange. I can't feel anything.

ALEXIS. Nor I! Can you get out of your chair?

BORIS (*slowly*). I—I can hardly move my hand. I might move by a supreme effort but I haven't the will. I—I feel no pain, only a ringing in my head.

ALEXIS. So? Well, well! Can you still hear perfectly?

BORIS. Yes—yes, I can still hear.

ALEXIS. H'm, h'm.

BORIS. Tell me, on your hope of redemption, was what you said to me just now the truth?

ALEXIS. On my hope of redemption, eh?

BORIS. If it was, I ask you to forgive me.

ALEXIS. I have nothing to forgive.

BORIS. Thanks!

ALEXIS. On my hope of redemption, Boris Shamrayeff, everything I told you was lies! Lies! Lies! (BORIS *struggles painfully to his feet and lurches toward the table, where he has laid the pistol.* ALEXIS *springs to the table, seizes the pistol and tosses it out of the window.* BORIS *supports himself against the edge of table, half sitting, half leaning against it, his mouth open, his eyes staring. He sways dizzily.* ALEXIS *stands before him.*)

ALEXIS. Well, you can still speak, can't you?

BORIS. You fiend! You dog! You liar! Ha, ha, ha! At least you can't escape! No need for me to strike you!

ALEXIS. Ha, ha!

BORIS. Well! Sneer at me if you like. You are feeling the agony too, Alexis Alexandrovitch. You can't deny it.

ALEXIS. I am not dying, Boris Shamrayeff.

BORIS. But, I know! I saw! I saw you drink! You're dying, Excellency!

ALEXIS. Yes, we drank together, didn't we? Well, well! And your eye wasn't off me an instant, was it? And you didn't lift your cup till I'd drained the last drop of mine, did you? Well, well, well!

BORIS. I saw you drink what I drank.

ALEXIS. Yes, I did drink it, Boris Ivanovitch, didn't I? But what is sending you down to fry in Hell with the stupid ghosts of your bestial ancestors is only embarrassing me with the slightest of headaches. (*He chuckles.*)

BORIS. It—it is not possible!

ALEXIS. Eh? An oriental trick. A man in constant fear of poison may accustom himself, little by little, to a dose that would blast the life of an ordinary man. A fantastic precaution these days, only interesting to an antiquarian like myself. Well, well, you can hear me, can't you? I tell you I could have taken the entire mess; half of it seems to have been enough for you. (BORIS *makes an effort to get at* ALEXIS *but almost sinks to the floor*) No use, Boris Shamrayeff! I advise you to hold fast to the table.

BORIS. Why? Why have you done this thing to me?

ALEXIS. Body of St. Michael! I am of one order, you of another. You are a terrorist, a Red; the blood of my brother, shot down in the streets of Kronstadt, the lives of my friends, the preservation of the sacred empire—are these nothing? Nothing—beside your dirty petitions of right! Pah! God has delivered YOU into MY hands. I, and not you, am the instrument of God today! Boris Ivanovitch, can you still hear me? Eh?

BORIS. Yes!

ALEXIS. So! So! One thing more! Why did I risk my own life to get yours? You would like to know that, wouldn't you? Why did I let you in here at all? You'd ask that if you could. Ha, ha! Well, it was because men were thinking that Alexis Alexandrovitch wasn't what he used to be; because I was beginning to think so myself. Because I had begun to doubt my own wits. I had to let myself be brought to bay. I had to look into the muzzle of your pistol. I had to pit my life against yours in a struggle where I had no other weapon, no other help, than this. (*He taps his forehead*) I think it unlikely that Constantine will check-mate me in five moves today!

BORIS. Fiend! Fiend! Fiend! (*He crumples up and falls to the floor.*)

ALEXIS. So, it's over, is it? Well, well, well! (*He takes a cover from the couch and throws it over* BORIS *and stands over him.*)

ALEXIS (*as if exorcising a ghost*). To the night without stars! To the mist that never lifts! To the bottom of nothingness! Peace be with you! (*He turns and taps the bell and then seats himself at the chessboard. The* FOOTMAN *enters.*)

FOOTMAN. Your Excellency rang?

ALEXIS. Go into the garden and find Mr. Constantine. Tell him I am ready to finish our game of chess.

(*The* FOOTMAN *bows and with draws.*)

ALEXIS (*studying the moves on the chessboard*). So! So! The bishop— the queen! No! Yes, yes! I have it! I have it! Body of St. Michael, not in five moves, not in five moves tonight! Ah! Ha, ha! So! So! Well, well, well! (*He rubs his hands softly and looks up just as* CONSTANTINE *enters.*)

CURTAIN

Lithuania

A DRAMA IN ONE ACT

BY RUPERT BROOKE

CHARACTERS

A STRANGER
THE MOTHER
THE DAUGHTER
THE FATHER
A YOUNG MAN
A VODKA-SHOPKEEPER
THE VODKA-SHOPKEEPER'S SON

LITHUANIA

The inside of a hut in Lithuania. Table in center. To the left of the table a ladder up to the upper story. Behind, in the back wall, a long low window. Doors in the right end of the back wall, and the near end of the left wall. Projecting from the right wall, a large stone stove. Beyond it, a dresser with a basin, etc. It is early night in autumn. Outside the window is a space of moonlight; pine trees are vaguely visible beyond.

At the left end of the table, facing sideways, is sitting the STRANGER, *finishing a meal. The* DAUGHTER *is sitting on a stool before the stove, back to the audience, occasionally glancing at the* STRANGER. *The* MOTHER *is moving to and fro with plates, food, etc., between the table, the stove, and the dresser. There is a lamp on the table.*

The STRANGER *is in young middle-age, expensively, rather flashily dressed, medium height, rather weakly built, with black, greased hair, mustaches, and a small pointed beard. Excitable manner. The* MOTHER *is fifty or more, medium height, strongly built, but worn and rather bent, thin face, quiet, and occasionally voluble. The* DAUGHTER *is just past her youth, a little shorter than the* MOTHER, *but squarer, heavy-faced and immobile.*

STRANGER (*pushing chair back, and finishing vodka*). That's good. That's good. I think I'll be turning in now. I'm dog-tired after that tramp through the woods. By Jove, I was lucky to find this house!

MOTHER. If you'd bide a small bit. My man'll be in from the fields, any minute now.

STRANGER (*getting up*). And aren't you two women afraid, being alone in a lonely house like this, these evenings . . . ?

MOTHER. What's there for fear? Who'd want anything here, to rob us? And is it likely any one'ld want me? And Anna—Anna'ld give them more than they came for. She's stronger than most men.

STRANGER (*rather uneasily, bowing slightly*). Your daughter's a very well-built girl.

MOTHER. She's strong. She has to work in the fields, with her Dad.

STRANGER. Ah, I suppose it's hard enough to keep things going, with only one man in the family,—or (*quickly*) have you some sons, no doubt?

MOTHER. No. There was one. He ran off when he was thirteen.

STRANGER (*with a nervous, polite little laugh*). It's a pity. Women want someone to protect them, I always think. Now wouldn't you, as a mother, welcome him if ever he came back again to help you in your old age?

MOTHER (*undecidedly*). Well, I don't know——

DAUGHTER. He was drowned. (*Short pause.*)

STRANGER. Oh! I beg your pardon —But your husband, does he leave you alone— (*A man's shout, from some distance.*)

MOTHER. That's him. I'll go and meet him. If you'd bide a minute— I'd rather you saw him before you go to bed. (*Exit.*) (STRANGER *strolls, rather swaggeringly, to the stove.*)

STRANGER (*apparently with slight suppressed excitement*). I suppose a fine young girl like you must sometimes be sick of a life of working, working, in this gloomy place,— beautiful as it is.

DAUGHTER (*looks at him steadily*). Um——

STRANGER. I'll warrant there's not much fun round here; not many young men, no dancing and so on; ah, you ought to be in a big town!

DAUGHTER (*half to herself*). I have my fun—

STRANGER. It's wonderful in a big city! The glare and the roar of the streets. Your blood swims with it. It's a shame you should never know it. Don't you see that you'll only grow hard and worn here; stiffer and duller every day; working, working, working; then you'll be like your mother; and at last you'll shrivel and be ugly; and then you'll die. Now, what'd you say (*laughing a little, rather hysterically*) if some good fairy suddenly came (*looking at her*) and promised to take you to a big city and show you everything, and buy you dresses and jewels, and give you the best of everything, like a lady? (*Pause.*)

DAUGHTER (*gets up suddenly and crosses to him, limping slightly*). I'm lame. A dog bit me. Would you like to see? (*Pulls up her skirt and down her stocking and shows place under knee*) Are ladies' legs like that? See that cut? (*Holding out her hand*) That's a big nail did that. What'ld they say in cities to that hand? Feel! (*She grips him, with her right hand, just above the left knee; and looks up, smiling slightly. He gives a little exclamation and draws back, rather embarrassed*) Have you ever felt a lady's hand like that? (*A small pause. She lets go, and goes, swinging, across to the ladder and slowly up it, and, turning to the right, exit.*) (*He sits down, his hand on his leg. Enter* FATHER *and* MOTHER. *The* FATHER *is of middle height, not very broad, aged about fifty, clean-shaven, of a rather excitable manner, dark-brown hair beginning to go gray.*)

MOTHER. This is my husband.

STRANGER (*going toward him, looking hard at him; a little nervously*). Are you the master of the house? How do you do? Your wife was kind enough to promise me a bed here. I got lost in the forest, and benighted. I was very lucky to find a house.

FATHER. How were you in the wood: dressed like that, sir?

STRANGER (*slight agitation*). I'd lost my way. I was trying to walk to Mohilev. It was so fine—I'm very fond of walking—I thought I'd like to walk. I'm going round the small towns of this part on—business. Government business.

FATHER. Mohilev? You're a lot out of your way. You must be tired as a horse. And with that bag. You might have been robbed.

STRANGER (*opening the bag*). Oh, there's nothing much but papers in the bag. But (*excitedly*) I've a lot of money about me. (*Fumbling, and pulling some notes from under his waistcoat*) See. There's a lot of money! It'ld buy this house twice over, and all in it. I dare bet you've never seen as much money as that on this table in your life before (*Pulls out some more, laughing hysterically. Finishes the glass of vodka.*)

FATHER (*looking up at him*). No, Baron.
(*A pause.* MOTHER *goes to the stove.*)

MOTHER. It's not safe, walking in these woods with all that upon you.

STRANGER. I didn't meet a soul the whole day, or see a house. This was the first I came to. I came on it straight out of the forest—from the west there. I was glad to see the light!
(*Short pause.* DAUGHTER *comes back quietly, across back of room and sits down; meanwhile* STRANGER *continues.*)

STRANGER. It must be frightfully lonely here. I should think it would get on one's nerves. To hear the wind in the branches, and watch the night coming on, month after month. I declare, I began to feel quite queer today walking all day alone among the trees. A merry company for me!
(*Short pause.*)

FATHER. There's a fistful of houses down below in the valley; three minutes down. You didn't get to them, Baron; they lie east. There's people there.

MOTHER (*setting table again*). He goes down to them.

FATHER. And there's work enough to be done about the fields.

STRANGER. But in winter you must find time heavy on your hands?

FATHER. Ah—winter's coming.

STRANGER. I expect you'll all be glad when you've saved up a bit and go away and live by some town.

FATHER. That—that'll be when the rams milk—when God wakes from his snoring and remembers his poor.

MOTHER (*reproving mechanically*). Oh, Ivan!

FATHER. There's no living off this land.
(*Pause.*)

STRANGER. Well, I'm dog-tired after that tramp through the woods. I think I'll be turning in. It must be late?

FATHER. It should be after eight.

STRANGER (*laughing*). Why, I declare, you've no clock! (*Pause. Laughing loud*) Why, you'll not know what time to go to bed! I must leave you mine for the night. I really must. (*Taking his out of his waistcoat*) Look! It's good gold, all of it! I'll hang it up there. I'll bet you've never seen a gold watch hanging up on your wall, eh?

(DAUGHTER *looks at* MOTHER *behind his back,* MOTHER *at* DAUGHTER. FATHER *looks at each of the three, drumming on the table. Pause.*)

MOTHER (*taking up the lamp*). Shall I show you the bed, Baron?

STRANGER. Yes. I really must turn in. (*Turns to the watch*) There, what do you say to that! (*Goes up to* DAUGHTER) Good night, my little Anna. (*Puts hand on her shoulder, and presses it*) Good night! (*She stands stiffly up, dropping a slight curtsey.* STRANGER *turns to* FATHER) Good night! Good night! I'm afraid I've robbed you of the best part of your meal. I must apologize! But I'll pay for it. You shan't regret your hospitality. (*Goes up toward him as if to shake his hand or embrace him: hesitates and passes on after* MOTHER, *up the ladder.*)

FATHER (*after him*). It's poor food, but you're welcome to it.

MOTHER (*up the ladder*). It's a poor room for you—we sleep to the right here. You'll not be troubled if you hear us moving—— (*Exeunt, talking.*)
(*Light from stove.* DAUGHTER *standing at stove.* FATHER *sits down to eat, at end of table, facing audience.*)

FATHER (*eating*). You're always talking about men. There's one for you. Why don't you go to him? He was looking at you. And he's drunk a lot.

DAUGHTER (*bringing soup and pouring it in*). He's an undersized, white-handed, dirty little man.

FATHER. You're afraid. You're always afraid.

DAUGHTER. He's not a man. He's a little, weak, chattering, half a man: like you.

(FATHER *turns round savagely and catches her with wrench by the upper arm. A spoon is knocked from her hand.*)

DAUGHTER (*twisting her arm free and hitting his hand down; without raising her voice*). If you hit me, I'll kill you. (*Goes to seat and sits down with her back to the audience.*)

MOTHER (*enters with lamp, places it on table, and puts it out*). Have you brought anything?

FATHER. No. There's a curse on these woods. There's not a hare nor a bird in them. They're as quiet as the dead.

MOTHER (*sits down on the farther side of the stove, three-quarters face to the audience*). We can't get through the winter. We've nothing.

FATHER. I'm hungry. There's never food enough in this bloody house. There's no living off this land.

MOTHER. I gave him all there was. I knew he was a rich man. We'll get enough from him for eight days, maybe.

FATHER. And then?

MOTHER. We've always got through.

FATHER (*getting up excitedly*). I'm sick of it, I say. I'll go off to the towns. There's money there. Why should I stay here and work for you two as well as myself? I'll go off alone. (*Catches sight of watch*)

Look at that! Why should he have that and we be starving? It would keep us a year. How did he get it? Who is he? Why did he talk like that?

MOTHER. He had drunk. He is a rich man.

FATHER. He's mad, I say. Who ever heard tell of a man walking through these woods because he liked it, if he wasn't mad? And in that coat, and with a bag?

DAUGHTER. No one saw him come.

MOTHER. If he's mad, we might get a reward for keeping him. His parents would be very rich.

FATHER. He's not mad. But he's queer. Something was driving him mad. Why should he have come here? All that money—the way he talked—— Do you think it's his? (MOTHER *and* DAUGHTER *look at each other, scarcely moving their heads, at intervals through the conversation.*)

MOTHER. If it's not nis——

FATHER. He looked like a thief. He's a thief's manner. He stole it, I say. He's escaping, hiding. That's why he came here.

DAUGHTER. No one knows he's here.

MOTHER. If he's a thief, we might get a reward for giving him up, or something.

FATHER (*snatching down watch*). This gold thing, and all that money, what right has he to it? There may be people starving because he stole it? He looked like a thief.

DAUGHTER. He was a little weak, undersized man——
(*Pause.*)

FATHER (*leaning against the end of the table*). I'm working, and keeping you two, and doing my best, and I'm starving. And he's a thief and alone, and he has all that money. If there were a God, would He let that be?

MOTHER. Ivan!
(*Pause.*)

FATHER (*as if unwillingly, and still louder*). We've as good right to it as him. What's money to a hunted man, alone?

MOTHER. Hush! You'll wake him!

FATHER (*much lower*). Why do I care if he hears?
(*Pause.*)

DAUGHTER. He'll sleep deep, being tired.
(*Pause. The light from the stove is lower.*)

FATHER. Why do you look at me?
(*Pause.*)

MOTHER (*her hands fumbling, drawing silently closer to the stove*). We'll never get through the winter.
(*Pause.*)

FATHER (*shrilly*). Why do you look at me? What are you both thinking? I don't know what you're thinking.
(*Pause.*)

MOTHER. You're shaking, Ivan. You're making the table rattle—
(*Pause.*)

FATHER. Why are you looking at me? I can't see your eyes. (*Longer pause.*)

FATHER (*nearly crying*). I killed a man in fight, once—in fight. My God, I—not—— (*Small pause. They all rise silently*) I must think. Say something. Tomorrow—

DAUGHTER. Now.

FATHER. Tomorrow.

MOTHER. Now.

FATHER. He's our guest—

MOTHER. He's a thief. (*Small pause.* DAUGHTER *begins to light lamp.*)

MOTHER (*very low and quick*). He's asleep—— Only once! He can't struggle. We'll hold him. No one'll ever know. We *must* have the money.—You're a coward! (FATHER *meanwhile pulls knife out of sheath, takes lamp mechanically from* DAUGHTER *and makes a few steps toward the ladder. The women follow.*)

FATHER. I can do it. (*Takes a few steps; looks back*) You're filthy. Stay here. You're not to touch him. I'll do it. (*Goes up ladder quickly and quietly.*) (*The* DAUGHTER *stands by bottom of ladder, leaning against it.* MOTHER *goes back toward stove. Long pause. Slight sounds.* DAUGHTER *puts one foot slowly on bottom rung of ladder. Suddenly* FATHER *appears and comes down. Puts lamp on table. Leans against table, shivering.* MOTHER *comes forward. Pause.* FATHER *nods.*)

DAUGHTER. The knife's clean.

MOTHER. Did you? —

FATHER. I—— (*Crumblingly*) No! I feel dead-sick. I couldn't. I didn't go in. I've been working all day. I'm sick. (*Coughs and retches slightly.*)

MOTHER. You *must*.

FATHER. I can't—like this. Vodka. I want drink in me.

MOTHER. He drank it. You *must*. (FATHER *goes unsteadily to back of stage. Puts on his coat.*)

FATHER (*fumbling in his pocket*). I'm going down to the shop to get drink. I've got a few *kopeks*. I'll get so I can do it. I'll drink till I'd stick Almighty God. (*Straightens himself, speaks more controledly*) When I come back you'll see: I'll be ready to knife anybody. I tell you I'm tired now, and sick. You can't kill a man when your throat's full of stink, and you're going to be sick. I've been working all day. (*Fumbling at the door*) I'll be back in no time. I swear I'll kill him. I'll drink murder into me. My God! (*Exit.*) (*His figure is seen passing the window, going across to the left, running, rather slowly.* MOTHER *and* DAUGHTER *watch him cross; then listen a moment. No sound from above.* MOTHER *puts out the lamp. They sit down by the stove in their usual places,* DAUGHTER *with her back to the audience. The* DAUGHTER *opens the mouth of the stove, puts log of wood in, and leaves the mouth open. A certain amount of light comes out.*)

DAUGHTER. He's a coward.

MOTHER. He's all right.

DAUGHTER. He's a coward.

MOTHER. He's not that. He thinks so much. *You* can't understand. He'll be all right when he's got drink in him. It'll stop him thinking.

DAUGHTER. If I'd started off to kill a man, I wouldn't need to stop to drink.

MOTHER. You'd—— I was afraid we wouldn't get him to it.

DAUGHTER. He'll get drunk.

MOTHER. He's not got enough money to get drunk on.—Besides, he knows what he's gone for.

DAUGHTER. He's gone to get away. (*Short pause*) It's hard, waiting.

MOTHER. He'll do it when he comes back. (*Gets up and goes to foot of ladder, and wanders back again. Standing*) I know him. (*Takes down watch and examines it*) Do you think he's a thief?

DAUGHTER. I don't know. We'll be rich. We'll get away from here.

MOTHER (*hangs up watch*). It's the same anywhere. But we won't starve, then.

DAUGHTER. It's hell, waiting. (*Pause*) One must do things straight, and not think. It'll be harder.

MOTHER (*going irresolutely toward the window*). It's bright, outside. (*Suddenly*) No one can have seen in, can they? When *he* was at supper? (*Turns.*)

DAUGHTER. No. They couldn't see from the road.

MOTHER (*comes back and sits down*). Anyhow, who could come by here at night?

DAUGHTER. They come here, sometimes.

MOTHER. "Sometimes!" They come a lot to see you, don't they?—Young men. Twice a year! When I was a girl—

DAUGHTER. You're always jealous of me—
(*The voices get a little shrill, naggingly, not angrily.*)

MOTHER. Jealous! When I was a girl, I'd a dozen after me.
(*STRANGER appears silently, at top of ladder, in shirt and trousers, barefoot, and comes quickly down, holding a burning match in his left hand, looking rather dazedly excited.*)

DAUGHTER. It's a dirty thing to be old and jealous.

MOTHER. You've always hated me. I'm your mother, it's wrong to hate your mother—you're not natural.

DAUGHTER. It's you hate me. You're my mother, right enough. I've seen love turn—

MOTHER. You don't know what it is to be a mother. You never will, very like.
(*The STRANGER reaches the bottom of the ladder; it creaks. The DAUGHTER, at the second creak, looks round and stares agape, startled. The MOTHER sees her face, breaks off, looks round, and jumps up exclaiming. Short pause.*)

MOTHER. What do you want?

STRANGER. Oh! Isn't your husband here?

MOTHER. He's gone out.—Has anything disturbed you, Baron?

STRANGER. No—you—see—no—I wanted to speak to him. I thought —I wanted to do it tonight.—It doesn't matter.—When will he be back?

MOTHER. I—I don't know—

DAUGHTER. Not for hours, maybe. He comes back very late.

STRANGER (*advancing a step or two*). Oh, tomorrow'll do.

MOTHER (*going quickly to the window*). It's very cold. (*Folds rather old wooden shutters across and bars them with a great rusty iron bar. The* STRANGER *is staring with a vague uneasiness*) We'll lock up and go to bed. My man comes in later. Did you want anything, Baron?

STRANGER. No, I only thought, if he was here; I'd something I wanted to get clear before I could sleep. It's nothing. (*Drifts back to ladder.*)

MOTHER. We didn't disturb you, Baron?—Our talking?

STRANGER. Oh, no, I assure you! I —I went to sleep for a bit, and woke up suddenly. I felt, somehow, I shouldn't go to sleep again until I'd got clear——

MOTHER. You'll sleep sound enough, Baron. You'll not hear anything.

STRANGER (*more abruptly*). Yes. I'm sorry to have startled you.—A fancy— — Tomorrow'll do—I'll sleep like a log. (*Starts climbing up ladder.*)

MOTHER (*still in front of window*). Yes. You must be tired.
(DAUGHTER *stands up. Exit* STRANGER. MOTHER *comes forward.* MOTHER *and* DAUGHTER *converse in whispers.*)

MOTHER. What did he mean? Why did he come down?

DAUGHTER. I don't know.

MOTHER. Had he heard?

DAUGHTER. I don't think so. Perhaps he woke up frightened.

MOTHER. Or he's mad.

DAUGHTER. He was queer all the time.

MOTHER. Could he have been drunk —on that little? Men do queer, restless things when they're drunk—

DAUGHTER. Will he come again?

MOTHER. It makes it worse—that he's like that—that— (*Knocks at door. The women clutch at each other, and stand looking around. Knocks again.* MOTHER *whispers*) We must open. (DAUGHTER *nods.* MOTHER *goes over to door.* DAUGHTER *moves quickly to fireplace and takes watch down and thrusts it in her bosom.* MOTHER *opens door slightly: looks out: opens it wider, saying*) Ah, step in Paul! (*She admits a* YOUNG MAN, *carrying a hare. The* YOUNG MAN *stamps his feet, and takes off his coat. He is rather tall, neutral colored, solid-faced, aged 25, clean-shaven.*)

MOTHER. You're calling very late—

YOUNG MAN. It's not half-past eight. I only stepped in for a minute.

MOTHER. I was just tidying up. We go to bed early. (*Keeps looking round toward the ladder.*)

YOUNG MAN. I just stepped in to bring you this. (*Throwing hare on table.*)

MOTHER. It's very good of you. (*Taking it up and looking at it.*)

YOUNG MAN. I'd like to get warm a minute. (DAUGHTER *and* YOUNG MAN *come toward stove.*)

MOTHER (*takes lantern and goes toward ladder*). I'll be putting straight, upstairs. (*Goes up ladder. To* DAUGHTER) You'll be coming soon. (*Exit, right.*) (DAUGHTER *takes up hare, and handles it.*)

YOUNG MAN. It's close in here. (*Pause*) It's dirty and cold outside. Is your father here?

DAUGHTER. He's gone down, to drink.

YOUNG MAN. It's good of your mother to leave us.

DAUGHTER. She's putting straight, upstairs.

YOUNG MAN (*grinning*). She's not moving about. There's no noise.

DAUGHTER. Never mind her! (*Pause.*)

YOUNG MAN. I didn't know you went to bed so early.

DAUGHTER. You've not often been.

YOUNG MAN. Maybe I'd not have come, if I'd known— You're not very hospitable in this house.

DAUGHTER. It was good of you to bring this.

YOUNG MAN. I snared her today.

DAUGHTER. I wish—— I think Mother wants to shut the house up.

YOUNG MAN. Don't you want to see me?

DAUGHTER. It's not that. I'm very tired. You'd better go, Paul.

YOUNG MAN. You weren't in your fields today. I went to look.

DAUGHTER. I've done a lot. (*Comes up nearer to him*) Go. Paul, I want to see you. Come—any day. (*In sudden anger*) Go, will you?

YOUNG MAN (*putting a hand on each of her shoulders*). Why do you never say things? I've never understood you.

DAUGHTER (*hitting his arm down and shaking herself free*). Go! I'll see you again.

YOUNG MAN (*catching her quietly by the wrist as she hits his arm down*). I'll stay a bit, maybe.

DAUGHTER (*pulls herself free*). Go!

YOUNG MAN. What if I don't.

DAUGHTER (*seizing him by the upper arm in a passion and making him reel*). Go, will you?

YOUNG MAN (*pulls her in to him; they struggle*). You're not so strong! (*After a second's struggle he kisses her on the mouth. Their mouths part, and she kisses him again. She is pressed back and strikes the edge of the table, which rattles. Released, she leans back against it. He grins.*)

DAUGHTER (*half whispering*). You'll have something over!

YOUNG MAN. You're not so strong!

DAUGHTER. Go, for God's sake.

YOUNG MAN. I'll come again.

DAUGHTER. Yes; tomorrow.

YOUNG MAN (*picking up his coat*). I'll come earlier, one day. Come out into the lane and meet me.

DAUGHTER. Yes.

YOUNG MAN (*putting on his coat*). We'll have things to say.

DAUGHTER. I've got to go to bed now.

YOUNG MAN. Give me a kiss! (*She stands impassive. He kisses her*) Good night.
(*Exit* YOUNG MAN. *She shuts the door after him, quietly.*)

MOTHER (*comes quickly down*). He's gone.
{DAUGHTER *nods.*}

MOTHER (*jerking her head toward the ladder*). If *he* had come down when Paul was here!——

DAUGHTER. Someone else may come in.

MOTHER. A lot of young men smell you out, don't they?

DAUGHTER. You fool!—— We *must* have the money. I want to get away from here.

MOTHER. Do you think anyone'd look at you in a town? They like them fine made there.

DAUGHTER. He *must* come soon. He must do it. (*Sits down.*)
(*Pause.*)

DAUGHTER. He's been away an hour.

MOTHER. Five minutes, more like.
(*Pause.*)

MOTHER (*starting suddenly up*). What was that?

DAUGHTER. What?

MOTHER. A step.

DAUGHTER. Where?

MOTHER. Outside. It's Ivan.

DAUGHTER. I heard nothing.

MOTHER. Perhaps it's somebody else.
(*Pause. Silence.*)

DAUGHTER. It wasn't anything.

MOTHER. If he daren't, again, this time——

DAUGHTER. He's a coward.

MOTHER. He's tired. Perhaps he'll be drunk.
(*Pause.*)

MOTHER (*shifting*). I can't bear waiting. It's as if somebody's watching us.
(*Pause.*)
(DAUGHTER *rises and limps over to a box on ledge beyond the stove: rummages there.*)

MOTHER (*huskily*) What are you doing?

DAUGHTER. These knives are old and weak.

MOTHER. You—— Sit down. He'll come.

DAUGHTER (*stooping over box of firewood*). I'll go mad, waiting. (*Rises with an axe in her hand*) This isn't very sharp. But it's heavy.

MOTHER. What do you mean?

DAUGHTER (*lighting lamp on the table*). Hush. We can do it.

MOTHER (*getting up*). You mustn't. Do you think?—

DAUGHTER. He's a weak little man. Take off your skirt and throw it over him up to the neck and hold it down so as he can't get his hands out. Hold fast.
(MOTHER *slips off her outer skirt.* DAUGHTER *takes up the lantern.*)

MOTHER (*going to the ladder*). Come on quickly, for Christ's sake. Oh, thank God.

DAUGHTER. We'll put the lantern on the shelf.
(*They go quietly up the ladder—* DAUGHTER *first, and disappear left. Pause. Slight muffled noises. A shout. A crashing thud. A groan broken by a thud. A succession of rather regular heavy thuds. While these are still going on there is the sound of quick steps above, and the* MOTHER *comes, half falling down the ladder, sobbing quietly. The thuds cease.*)

MOTHER (*collapsing onto a stool at the table*). O Christ! Stop! Stop! O Christ!
(*The* DAUGHTER *comes slowly downstairs, the light in one hand, holding the axe stiffly down with the other; drawing long difficult audible breaths. The* MOTHER *ceases sobbing.*)

MOTHER. Why did you go on hitting?

DAUGHTER (*putting lamp on table*). I couldn't help it.

MOTHER. You went on and on. I thought you were mad. He cried out on his mother, at first.

DAUGHTER (*standing*). He didn't.

MOTHER. He cried on his mother. She'll never know. You went on and on hitting. You were horrible. Why did you?

DAUGHTER. I couldn't stop. (*Goes round and stands by the stove.*)

MOTHER. Why did you go on and on hitting? I thought you were mad. I hated you.

DAUGHTER. I couldn't help it.
(*Pause.*)

MOTHER. Why are you still holding that thing?
(DAUGHTER *goes up beyond stove and throws axe into woodbasket. Returns and sits in her seat, back to audience.*)

MOTHER. I'll never use that skirt again.

DAUGHTER. You'll never need to.
(*Pause.* MOTHER *begins slowly clearing remains of supper away.* DAUGHTER *puts her head in her hands and begins sobbing.*)

MOTHER. Well; he won't move now. We'll make Ivan bury him out in the woods tonight; or tomorrow. We'll get away from here before the thick of winter. (*Faint noise from outside, some distance away*) We'll have plenty— What's that? It's Ivan coming back. (*Noise louder and increasing*) Get ready, lass. It's done. There's someone with him. I hear talking. Perhaps it's somebody else. Get up—look yourself. We must be ready.

DAUGHTER (*jumping up*). It's done. We can tell him it's done. I'm glad. We can get away. We'll be rich. I'll wear silk.

MOTHER (*breaking in*). It's Ivan. I hear his name. Who's he bringing with him? Is he mad?

DAUGHTER. He's drunk.
(*Rattling at door.*)

MOTHER. He's arrested. (*Goes to door and opens it.*)
(VODKA-SHOPKEEPER *and his* SON *enter, the* FATHER *between them.*

VODKA-SHOPKEEPER a tall, blond, *jolly man of about forty, hairy face and inclined to be stout. His* SON *eighteen, slight, rather darker, and self-conscious.* VODKA-SHOPKEEPER *holds a boot in his right hand. His* SON *holds a vodka bottle. They are supporting the* FATHER, *who is drunk, dazed-looking and dragging. He has only one boot on. The* VODKA-SHOPKEEPER *and his* SON *are also slightly drunk;* VODKA-SHOPKEEPER *excited.* SON *sly and flushed.* MOTHER *and* DAUGHTER *both standing.*)

VODKA-SHOPKEEPER. Evening, missus! We've brought your man home. (*Laughing.*)

MOTHER. Ivan——?

VODKA-SHOPKEEPER. He wanted to come alone. He said he had something to do. (*Laughs*) He said he had to go quietly. He *would* take his boot off. (*Holds boot up*) We couldn't stop him. He couldn't get the other off. Said he had to go "quietly." You should have seen him going quietly—laugh—my God!
(FATHER, *asleep, collapses at the foot of the ladder.*)

VODKA-SHOPKEEPER. Here—hold up. He's gone dazed from the open air. Give him a drop to wake him up.
(SON *pours from bottle into glass left on table, shakes* FATHER *and makes him drink it.*)

VODKA-SHOPKEEPER'S SON. He came into the shop shivering and white. My God! "Drink," he says. I gave him a glass. He drank two before he spoke. "I've got something to do," he said. (*Giggling.*)

VODKA-SHOPKEEPER. When I came in he was drunk—blind. He can't have eaten all day, getting like that on three glasses. He was talking big about his luck. We all had a glass to his luck. "As much as you like, now," I said.

FATHER (*suddenly*). Hush! (*Tries to begin to climb ladder—falls against it.*)

MOTHER (*screaming*). Ivan!

VODKA-SHOPKEEPER (*delightedly*). That's it. Oh, he's all right. He won't hurt himself. You should 'a seen him, hopping along in the mud like a lame hare. "I've got to go quietly," he said. Laugh! We were nearly sick. "I've luck," he said. "God's good to me." "Here's to God," I said. "*I* know your luck. No more starving now!" We all drank. (*Pours out, and drinks from glass.*)
(MOTHER *and* DAUGHTER *stare suddenly at him.* FATHER *rises to his feet and stands wavering—holds up one hand.*)

FATHER. Quietly! Quietly! (*Nods his head.*)
(MOTHER *runs to him and holds him by the arm, still staring at the* VODKA-SHOPKEEPER.)

VODKA-SHOPKEEPER'S SON (*giggling*). He kept saying it. "Quietly," he said, Didn't he, Dad? "I've something to do—*quietly*," he said. "Not a sound," he said. He took his boot off and hopped through the mud like—like—a lame hare!

MOTHER (*to* VODKA-SHOPKEEPER). You know—

VODKA-SHOPKEEPER (*grinning*). Rather.

MOTHER (*calmly*). Of course, you share—the luck.

VODKA-SHOPKEEPER (*cheerfully*). I get what comes to me. I told him so. We all get a little. It's a great day. He's up there, I suppose. (*Nodding to the upper story.*)
(MOTHER *nods.*)

VODKA-SHOPKEEPER. Tired, eh? (*Laughs.*)

MOTHER (*after a short pause, leaving go of* IVAN). You see—— (*Begins again*) He told you?

VODKA-SHOPKEEPER (*expanding*). Rather! First in the village he came to. (FATHER *drinks again*) I'd never have known him. He knew me—after twenty years! We had a glass. He told me of his joke. "I'll be the first to congratulate them in the morning," I said, " 'tisn't often one gets a son back! Ivan'll be glad of a son!"
(*Pause*—IVAN *waves his glass, puts on an air of mystery, says "Somethin' to be done," sits down on the ladder and gets into a doze. His glass crashes to the ground.*)

MOTHER (*vacantly*). Son—— Son —— (*Leaning on table.*)
(DAUGHTER *stands stiff.*)

VODKA-SHOPKEEPER (*roaring with laughter*). It's turned all their heads! He said to me, "I've such a game on. I'll knock and say I'm a rich man who's lost his way in the woods, and I want a night's lodging, and I'll show 'em my money, and I'll watch 'em and see 'em all again, and then in the morning I'll say: "Behold, your son which was lost and is found!" Excited—wasn't he just. "You'll never keep the secret all

night," I said. And he hasn't; I knew he wouldn't. "I'll be the first to congratulate them in the morning," I said. And I'm doing it tonight!
(*Drinks from bottle.*)
(*Pause.* MOTHER *looking down at the table.*)

DAUGHTER. You knew him?

VODKA-SHOPKEEPER (*blearily*). Bless you, yes! When he talked of old times. What are you all looking like that for? Didn't he come on here?

DAUGHTER. He did.
(*Pause.* VODKA-SHOPKEEPER *stares resentfully.*)

VODKA-SHOPKEEPER. You're not very cheerful.
(MOTHER *goes suddenly to her chair, saying:*)

MOTHER. He cried out "Mother!"
(*Sits down.*)

VODKA-SHOPKEEPER (*genially*). I'll be bound he did!

FATHER (*waking up, suddenly*). Something to be done.
(MOTHER *suddenly screams.*)

DAUGHTER. Stop it, Mother!

VODKA-SHOPKEEPER. What is it? What have you done?
(VODKA-SHOPKEEPER *and his* SON *step a little backward toward door.* MOTHER *continues crying and sobbing loudly.*)

VODKA-SHOPKEEPER (*to* DAUGHTER).

Why are you looking like that? Didn't he tell you who he was?

DAUGHTER. No.

VODKA-SHOPKEEPER. What have you done? Where is he? (*Raises his head suddenly and shouts*) Ivan! Young Ivan! Ivan!

FATHER (*fumbling with his other boot*). Not a sound!
(*Pause.*)

MOTHER. He cried out "Mother!" You went on and on hitting. (*Screams.*)

VODKA-SHOPKEEPER. What have you done? You've— (*Backs toward the door, staring—the* SON *behind him.*)

VODKA-SHOPKEEPER'S SON. She's got something on her hands, Father! (MOTHER *still screaming.*)

DAUGHTER. Stop it, Mother!
(FATHER *starts clambering up ladder, stumbling.* SON *slips out of door.*)

VODKA-SHOPKEEPER. You've— (*Hurries out, slamming door.*)
(MOTHER *screaming.*)

DAUGHTER. Stop it, Mother!

FATHER (*vaguely, with immense air of mystery and determination*). Very softly, now. Quietly, quietly! Quietly— (*Falls onto ladder.*)

DAUGHTER. They'll put me in prison!

CURTAIN

The Valiant

A PLAY IN ONE ACT

BY HOLWORTHY HALL AND
ROBERT MIDDLEMASS

CHARACTERS

WARDEN HOLT, *about 60*
FATHER DALY, *the prison chaplain*
JAMES DYKE, *the Prisoner*
JOSEPHINE PARIS. *the Girl, about 18*
DAN, *a Jailer*
AN ATTENDANT

SCENE—*The Warden's office in the State's Prison at Wethersfield. Connecticut.*
   TIME—*About half-past eleven on a rainy night.*

THE VALIANT

The curtain rises upon the WARDEN'S *office in the State's Prison at Wethers-field, Connecticut. It is a large, cold, unfriendly apartment, with bare floors and staring, whitewashed walls; it is furnished only with the* WARDEN'S *flat-topped desk, and swivel-chair, with a few straight-backed chairs, one beside the desk and others against the walls, with a water-cooler and an eight-day clock. On the* WARDEN'S *desk are a telephone instrument, a row of electric push-buttons, and a bundle of forty or fifty letters. At the back of the room are two large windows, crossed with heavy bars; at the left there is a door to an anteroom, and at the right there are two doors, of which the more distant leads to the office of the deputy warden, and the nearer is seldom used.*

WARDEN HOLT, *dressed in a dark-brown sack suit, with a negligee shirt and black string-tie, carelessly knotted in a bow, is seated at his desk, re-flectively smoking a long, thin cigar. He is verging toward sixty, and his responsibilities have printed themselves in italics upon his countenance. His brown hair and bushy eyebrows are heavily shot with gray; there is a deep parenthesis of wrinkles at the corners of his mouth and innumerable fine lines about his eyes. His bearing indicates that he is accustomed to rank as a despot, and yet his expression is far from that of an unreasoning tyrant. He is no sentimentalist, but he believes that in each of us there is a constant oscillation of good and evil; and that all evil should be justly punished in this world, and that all good should be generously rewarded—in the next.*

Behind the WARDEN, *the prison chaplain stands at one of the barred win-dows, gazing steadily out into the night.* FATHER DALY *is a slender, white-haired priest of somewhat more than middle age; he is dressed in slightly shabby clericals. His face is calm, intellectual and inspiring; but just at this moment, it gives evidence of a peculiar depression.*

The WARDEN *blows a cloud of smoke to the ceiling, inspects the cigar critically, drums on the desk, and finally peers over his shoulder at the chaplain. He clears his throat and speaks brusquely.*

THE WARDEN. Has it started to rain?

FATHER DALY (*answers without turning*). Yes, it has.

THE WARDEN (*glaring at his cigar and impatiently tossing it aside*). It would rain tonight. (*His tone is vaguely resentful, as though the weather had added a needless frac-tion to his impatience.*)

FATHER DALY (*glances at a big sil-ver watch*). It's past eleven o'clock.

(*He draws a deep breath and comes slowly to the center of the room*) We haven't much longer to wait.

THE WARDEN. No, thank God! (*He gets up, and goes to the water-cooler; with the glass halfway to his lips he pauses*) Was he quiet when you left him?

FATHER DALY (*a trifle abstractedly*). Yes, yes, he was perfectly calm and I believe he'll stay so to the very end.

THE WARDEN (*finishes his drink, comes back to his desk, and lights a fresh cigar*). You've got to hand it to him, Father; I never saw such nerve in all my life. It isn't bluff, and it isn't a trance, either, like some of 'em have—it's plain nerve. You've certainly got to hand it to him. (*He shakes his head in frank admiration.*)

FATHER DALY (*sorrowfully*). That's the pity of it—that a man with all his courage hasn't a better use for it. Even now, it's very difficult for me to reconcile his character, as I see it, with what we know he's done.

THE WARDEN (*continues to shake his head*). He's got my goat, all right.

FATHER DALY (*with a slight grimace*). Yes, and he's got mine, too.

THE WARDEN. When he sent for you tonight, I hoped he was going to talk.

FATHER DALY. He did talk, very freely.

THE WARDEN. What about?

FATHER DALY (*smiles faintly, and sits beside the desk*). Most everything.

THE WARDEN (*looks up quickly*). Himself?

FATHER DALY. No. That seems to be the only subject he isn't interested in.

THE WARDEN (*sits up to his desk, and leans upon it with both elbows*). He still won't give you any hint about who he really is?

FATHER DALY. Not the slightest. He doesn't intend to, either. He intends to die as a man of mystery to us. Sometimes I wonder if he isn't just as much of a mystery to himself.

THE WARDEN. Oh, he's trying to shield somebody, that's all. James Dyke isn't his right name—we know that; and we know all the rest of his story is a fake, too. Well, where s his motive? I'll tell you where it is. It's to keep his family and his friends, wherever they are, from knowing what's happened to him. Lots of 'em have the same idea but I never knew one to carry it as far as this, before. You've certainly got to hand it to him. All we know is that we've got a man under sentence; and we don't know who he is, or where he comes from, or anything else about him, any more than we did four months ago.

FATHER DALY. It takes moral courage for a man to shut himself away from his family and his friends like that. They would have comforted him.

THE WARDEN. Not necessarily. What time is it?

FATHER DALY. Half-past eleven.

THE WARDEN (*rises and walks over to peer out of one of the barred windows*). I guess I'm getting too old for this sort of thing. A necktie party didn't use to bother me so much; but every time one comes along nowadays, I've got the blue devils beforehand and afterward. And this one is just about the limit.

FATHER DALY. It certainly isn't a pleasant duty even with the worst of them.

THE WARDEN (*wheels back abruptly*). But what gets *me* is why I should hate this one more than any of the others. The boy is guilty as hell.

FATHER DALY. Yes, he killed a man. "Wilfully, feloniously, and with malice aforethought."

THE WARDEN. And he pleaded guilty. So he deserves just what he's going to get.

FATHER DALY. That is the law. But has it ever occurred to you, Warden, that every now and then when a criminal behaves in a rather gentlemanly fashion to us, we instinctively think of him as just a little less of a criminal?

THE WARDEN. Yes, it has. But, all the same, this front of his makes me as nervous as the devil. He pleaded guilty all right, but he doesn't *act* guilty. I feel just as if tonight I was going to do something every bit as criminal as he did. I can't help it. And when I get to feeling like that, why, I guess it's pretty nearly time I sent in my resignation.

FATHER DALY (*reflectively*). His whole attitude has been very remarkable. Why, only a few minutes ago I found myself comparing it with the fortitude that the Christian martyrs carried to their death, and yet—

THE WARDEN. He's no martyr.

FATHER DALY. I know it. And he's anything in the world but a Christian. That was just what I was going to say.

THE WARDEN. Has he got any religious streak in him at all?

FATHER DALY. I'm afraid he hasn't. He listens to me very attentively, but— (*He shrugs his shoulders*) It's only because I offer him companionship. Anybody else would do quite as well—and any other topic would suit him better.

THE WARDEN. Well, if he wants to face God as a heathen, *we* can't force him to change his mind.

FATHER DALY (*with gentle reproach*). No, but we can never give up trying to save his immortal soul. And his soul tonight seems as dark and foreboding to me as a haunted house would seem to the small boys down in Wethersfield. But I haven't given up hope.

THE WARDEN. No—you wouldn't.

FATHER DALY. Are you going to talk with him again yourself?

THE WARDEN (*opens a drawer of his desk, and brings out a large envelope*). I'll have to. I've still got some Liberty Bonds that belong to him. (*He gazes at the envelope, and smiles grimly*) That was a funny thing—when the newspaper syndicate offered him twenty-five hundred for his autobiography, he jumped at it so quick I was sure he wanted the money for something or other. (*He slaps the envelope on the desk*) But now the bonds are here, waiting for him, he won't say what to do with 'em. Know why? (FATHER DALY *shakes his head*) Why, of course you do! Because the story he wrote was pure bunk from start to finish and the only reason he jumped at the chance of writing it was so's he could pull the wool over everybody's head a little farther. He don't want the bonds, but

I've got to do *something* with 'em.
(*He pushes a button on the desk*)
And besides, I want to make one
more try at finding out who he is.

FATHER DALY. Shall I go with you
to see him or do you want to see
him alone?

THE WARDEN (*sits deliberating with
one hand at his forehead, and the
other hand tapping the desk*). Father, you gave me a thought—I believe I'm going to do something
tonight that's never been done before in this prison—that is to say—
not in all the twenty-eight years
that *I've* been warden.

FATHER DALY. What's that?

THE WARDEN (*who has evidently
come to an important decision, raps
the desk more forcibly with his
knuckles*). Instead of our going to
see him, I'll have that boy brought
into this office and let him sit here
with you and me until the time
comes for us all to walk through
that door to the execution room.

FATHER DALY (*startled*). What on
earth is your idea in doing a thing
like that?

THE WARDEN. Because maybe if he
sits here awhile with just you and
me, and we go at him right, he'll
loosen up and tell us about himself.
It'll be different from being in his
cell; it'll be sort of free and easy, and
maybe he'll weaken. And then, besides, if we take him to the scaffold
through this passage-way, maybe I
can keep the others quiet. If they
don't know when the job's being
done, they may behave 'emselves.
I don't want any such yelling and
screeching tonight as we had with

that Greek. (*A* JAILER *in blue uniform enters from the deputy's room
and stands waiting*) Dan, I want
you to get Dyke and bring him to
me here. (*The* JAILER *stares
blankly at him and the* WARDEN'S
*voice takes on an added note of
authority*) Get Dyke and bring him
in here to me.

THE JAILER. Yes, sir. (*He starts to
obey the order but halts in the doorway and turns as the* WARDEN
speaks again. It is apparent that the
WARDEN *is a strict disciplinarian of
the prison staff.*)

THE WARDEN. Oh, Dan!

THE JAILER. Yes, sir?

THE WARDEN. How nearly ready are
they?

THE JAILER. They'll be all set in ten
or fifteen minutes, sir. Twenty minutes at the outside.

THE WARDEN (*very sharp and mag-
isterial*). Now, I don't want any
hitch or delay in this thing tonight.
If there is, somebody's going to get
in awful Dutch with me. Pass that
along.

THE JAILER. There won't be none,
sir.

THE WARDEN. When everything's
ready—not a second before—you
let me know.

THE JAILER. Yes, sir.

THE WARDEN. I'll be right here with
Dyke and Father Daly.

THE JAILER (*eyes widening*). Here?

THE WARDEN (*peremptorily*). Yes, here!

THE JAILER (*crushes down his astonishment*). Yes, sir.

THE WARDEN. When everything and everybody is ready, you come from the execution room through the passage— (*He gestures toward the nearer door on the right*) Open that door quietly and stand there.

THE JAILER. Yes, sir.

THE WARDEN. You don't have to say anything, and I don't *want* you to say anything. Just stand there. That all clear?

THE JAILER. Yes, sir.

THE WARDEN. That'll be the signal for us to start—understand?

THE JAILER. Yes, sir.

THE WARDEN (*draws a deep breath*). All right. Now bring Dyke to me.

THE JAILER. Yes, sir. (*He goes out dazedly.*)

FATHER DALY. What about the witnesses and the reporters?

THE WARDEN. They're having their sandwiches and coffee now—the deputy'll have 'em seated in another ten or fifteen minutes. Let 'em wait. (*His voice becomes savage*) I'd like to poison the lot of 'em. Reporters! Witnesses! (*The telephone bell rings*) Hello—yes—yes— what's that?—Yes, yes, right here —who wants him? (*To* FATHER DALY) Father, it's the Governor! (*His expression is tense.*)

FATHER DALY (*his voice also gives evidence of incredulity and hope*). What! (*He walks swiftly over to the desk*) Is it about Dyke?

THE WARDEN. Ssh. (*He turns to the telephone*) Yes, this is Warden Holt speaking. Hello—oh, hello, Gov·ernor Fuller, how are you? Oh, I'm between grass and hay, thanks. Well, this isn't my idea of a picnic exactly—yes—yes— Oh, I should say in about half an hour or so— everything's just about ready. (*His expression gradually relaxes, and* FATHER DALY, *with a little sigh and shake of the head, turns away*) Oh, no, there won't be any slip-up—yes, we made the regular tests, one this afternoon and another at nine o'clock tonight— Oh, no, Governor, nothing can go wrong— Well, according to the law I've got to get it done as soon as possible after midnight, but you're the Governor of the state— How long?— Certainly, Governor, I can hold it off as long as you want me to— What say?— A *girl!*—You're going to send her to me?—you *have* sent her!—she ought to be here by this time?— All right, Governor, I'll ring you up when it's over. Good-bye. (*He hangs up the receiver, mops his forehead with his handkerchief, and turns to* FATHER DALY *in great excitement*) Did you get *that?* Some girl thinks Dyke's her long-lost brother, and she's persuaded the old man to let her come out here tonight—he wants me to hold up the job until she's had a chance to see him. She's due here any minute, he says—in his own car—escorted by his own private secretary! Can you beat it?

FATHER DALY (*downcast*). Poor girl!

THE WARDEN (*blots his forehead vigorously*). For a minute there I thought it was going to be a reprieve at the very least. Whew!

FATHER DALY. So did I.

(*The door from the deputy's room is opened, and* DYKE *comes in, followed immediately by the* JAILER. DYKE *halts just inside the door and waits passively to be told what to do next. He has a lean, pale face, with a high forehead, good eyes, and a strong chin; his mouth is ruled in a firm straight line. His wavy hair is prematurely gray. His figure has the elasticity of youth, but he might pass among strangers either as a man of forty, or as a man of twenty-five, depending upon the mobility of his features at a given moment. He is dressed in a dark shirt open at the throat, dark trousers without belt or suspenders, and soft slippers. The* JAILER *receives a nod from the* WARDEN, *and goes out promptly, closing the door behind him.*)

THE WARDEN (*swings half-way around in his swivel-chair*). Sit down, Dyke. (*He points to the chair at the right of his desk.*)

DYKE. Thanks. (*He goes directly to the chair and sits down.*)

THE WARDEN (*leans back, and surveys him thoughtfully.* FATHER DALY *remains in the background*). Dyke, you've been here under my charge for nearly four months and I want to tell you that from first to last you've behaved yourself like a gentleman.

DYKE (*his manner is vaguely cynical without being in the least impertinent*). Why should I make you any trouble?

THE WARDEN. Well, you *haven't* made me any trouble, and I've tried to show what I think about it. I've made you every bit as comfortable as the law would let me.

DYKE. You've been very kind to me. (*He glances over his shoulder at the chaplain*) And you, too, Father.

THE WARDEN. I've had you brought in here to stay from now on. (DYKE *looks inquiringly at him*) No, you won't have to go back to your cell again. You're to stay right here with Father Daly and me.

DYKE (*carelessly*). All right.

THE WARDEN (*piqued by this cool reception of the distinguished favor*). You don't seem to understand that I'm doing something a long way out of the ordinary for you.

DYKE. Oh, yes, I do, but maybe *you* don't understand why it doesn't give me much of a thrill.

FATHER DALY (*comes forward*). My son, the Warden is only trying to do you one more kindness.

DYKE. I know he is, Father, but the Warden isn't taking very much of a gamble. From now on, one place is about the same as another.

THE WARDEN. What do you mean?

DYKE (*his voice is very faintly sarcastic*). Why, I mean that I'm just as much a condemned prisoner here as when I was in my cell. That door (*he points to it*) leads right *back* to my cell. Outside those windows are armed guards every few feet. You yourself can't get through the iron door in that anteroom (*he indicates the door to the left*) until somebody on the outside unlocks it; and I know as well as you do where *that* door (*he points to the nearer door on the right*) leads to.

THE WARDEN (*stiffly*). Would you rather wait in your cell?

DYKE. Oh, no, this is a little pleasanter. Except—

THE WARDEN. Except what?

DYKE. In my cell, I could smoke.

THE WARDEN (*shrugs his shoulders*). What do you want—cigar or cigarette?

DYKE. A cigarette, if it's all the same. (*The* WARDEN *opens a drawer of his desk, takes out a box of cigarettes, removes one and hands it to* DYKE. *The* WARDEN *striking a match, lights* DYKE's *cigarette, and then carefully puts out the match.*)

DYKE (*smiles faintly*). Thanks. You're a good host.

THE WARDEN. Dyke, before it's too late I wish you'd think over what Father Daly and I've said to you so many times.

DYKE. I've thought of nothing else.

THE WARDEN. Then—as man to man—and this is your last chance —who are you?

DYKE (*inspects his cigarette*). Who am I? James Dyke—a murderer.

THE WARDEN. That isn't your real name and we know it.

DYKE. You're not going to execute a name—you're going to execute a man. What difference does it make whether you call me Dyke or something else?

THE WARDEN. You had another name once. What was it?

DYKE. If I had, I've forgotten it.

FATHER DALY. Your mind is made up, my son?

DYKE. Yes, Father, it is.

THE WARDEN. Dyke.

DYKE. Yes, sir?

THE WARDEN. Do you see this pile of letters? (*He places his hand over it.*)

DYKE. Yes, sir.

THE WARDEN (*fingers them*). Every one of these letters is about the same thing and all put together we've got maybe four thousand of 'em. These here are just a few samples.

DYKE. What about them?

THE WARDEN. We've had letters from every State in the Union and every province in Canada. We've had fifteen or twenty from England, four or five from France, two from Australia and one from Russia.

DYKE. Well?

THE WARDEN (*inclines toward him*). Do you know what every one of those letters says—what four thousand different people are writing to me about?

DYKE. No, sir.

THE WARDEN (*speaks slowly and impressively*). Who *are* you—and are you the missing son—or brother —or husband—or sweetheart?

DYKE (*flicks his cigarette ashes to the floor*). Have you answered them?

THE WARDEN. No, I couldn't. I want you to.

DYKE. How's that?

THE WARDEN. I want you to tell me who you are. (DYKE *shakes his head*) Can't you see you *ought* to do it?

DYKE. No, sir, I can't exactly see that. Suppose you explain it to me.

THE WARDEN (*suddenly*). You're trying to shield somebody, aren't you?

DYKE. Yes—no, I'm not!

THE WARDEN (*glances at* FATHER DALY *and nods with elation*). Who is it? Your family?

DYKE. I said I'm not.

THE WARDEN. But first, you said you were.

DYKE. That was a slip of the tongue.

THE WARDEN (*has grown persuasive*). Dyke, just listen to me a minute. Don't be narrow, look at this thing in a big, broad way. Suppose you should tell me your real name, and I publish it, it'll bring an awful lot of sorrow, let's say, to *one* family, *one* home, and that's your own. That's probably what you're thinking about. Am I right? You

want to spare your family and I don't blame you. On the surface, it sure would look like a mighty white thing for you to do. But look at it *this* way: suppose you came out with the truth, flat-footed, why, you might put all that sorrow into *one* home—your own—but at the same time you'd be putting an immense amount of relief in four thousand— others. Don't you get that? Don't you figure you owe something to all these other people?

DYKE. Not a thing.

FATHER DALY (*has been fidgeting*). My boy, the Warden is absolutely right. You do owe something to the other people—you owe them peace of mind—and for the sake of all those thousands of poor, distressed women, who imagine God knows what, I beg of you to tell us who you are.

DYKE. Father, I simply can't do it.

FATHER DALY. Think carefully, my boy, think very carefully. We're not asking out of idle curiosity.

DYKE. I know that, but please don't let's talk about it any more. (*To the* WARDEN) You can answer those letters whenever you want to, and you can say I'm not the man they're looking for. That'll be the truth, too. Because I haven't any mother—or father—or sister—or wife—or sweetheart. That's fair enough, isn't it?

FATHER DALY (*sighs wearily*). As you will, my son.

THE WARDEN. Dyke, there's one more thing.

DYKE. Yes?

THE WARDEN. Here are the Liberty Bonds (*he takes up the large envelope from his desk*) that belong to you. Twenty-five hundred dollars in real money.

DYKE (*removes the bonds and examines them*). Good-looking, aren't they?

THE WARDEN (*casually*). What do you want me to do with them?

DYKE. Well, I can't very well take them with me, so, under the circumstances, I'd like to put them where they'll do the most good.

THE WARDEN (*more casually yet*). Who do you want me to send 'em to?

DYKE (*laughs quietly*). Now, Warden Holt, you didn't think you were going to catch me that way, did you?

THE WARDEN (*scowls*). Who'll I send 'em to? I can't keep 'em here, and I can't destroy 'em. What do you want to do with 'em?

DYKE (*ponders diligently and tosses the envelopes to the desk*). I don't know. I'll think of something to do with them. I'll tell you in just a minute. Is there anything else?

THE WARDEN. Not unless you want to make some sort of statement.

DYKE. No, I guess I've said everything. I killed a man and I'm not sorry for it—that is, I'm not sorry I killed that particular person. I—

FATHER DALY (*raises his hand*). Repentance—

DYKE (*raises his own hand in turn*). I've heard that repentance, Father, is the sick bed of the soul—and mine is very well and flourishing. The man deserved to be killed; he wasn't fit to live. It was my duty to kill him, and I did it. I'd never struck a man in anger in all my life, but when I knew what that fellow had done, I knew I had to kill him, and I did it deliberately and intentionally—and carefully. I knew what I was doing, and I haven't any excuse—that is, I haven't any excuse that satisfies the law. Now, I learned pretty early in life that whatever you do in this world you have to pay for in one way or another. If you kill a man, the price you have to pay is this (*he makes a gesture which sweeps the entire room*) and that (*he points to the nearer door on the right*) and I'm going to pay it. That's all there is to that. And an hour from now, while my body is lying in there, if a couple of angel policemen grab my soul and haul it up before God—

FATHER DALY (*profoundly shocked*). My boy, my boy, please—

DYKE. I beg your pardon, Father. I don't mean to trample on anything that's sacred to you, but what I do mean to say is this: If I've got to be judged by God Almighty for the crime of murder, I'm not afraid, because the other fellow will certainly be there, too, won't he? And when God hears the whole story and both sides of it, which *you* never heard and never will—and they never heard it in the court room, either—why, then, if he's any kind of a God at all, I'm willing to take my chances with the other fellow. That's how concerned I am about the hereafter. And, if it'll make you feel any better, Father, why I *do* rather think there's going to be a hereafter. I read a book once that said a milligram of musk will give out perfume for seven thousand years, and a milligram of radium will give out light for *seventy* thousand. Why shouldn't a soul—mine, for instance—live more than twenty-seven? But if there *isn't* any hereafter—if we just die and are dead and that's all—why, I'm still not sorry and I'm not afraid, because I'm quits with the other fellow—the law is quits with me, and it's all balanced on the books. And that's all there is to that.

(*An* ATTENDANT *enters from the anteroom.*)

THE WARDEN. Well? What is it?

THE ATTENDANT. Visitor to see you, sir. With note from Governor Fuller. (*He presents it.*)

THE WARDEN (*barely glances at the envelope*). Oh! A young woman?

THE ATTENDANT. Yes, sir.

THE WARDEN. Is Mrs. Case there?

THE ATTENDANT. Yes, sir.

THE WARDEN. Have the girl searched, and then take her into the anteroom and wait till I call you.

THE ATTENDANT. Yes, sir. (*He goes out.*)

THE WARDEN. Dyke, a young woman has just come to see you— do you want to see her?

DYKE. I don't think so. What does she want?

THE WARDEN. She thinks maybe she's your sister, and she's come a thousand miles to find out.

DYKE. She's wrong. I haven't any sister.

THE WARDEN (*hesitates*). Will I tell her that, or do you want to tell it to her yourself?

DYKE. Oh, you tell her.

THE WARDEN. All right. (*He starts to rise but resumes his seat as* DYKE *speaks.*)

DYKE. Just a second—she's come a thousand miles to see me, did you say?

THE WARDEN. Yes, and she's got special permission from the Governor to talk to you—that is, with my O. K.

DYKE. A year ago, nobody'd have crossed the street to look at me, and now they come a thousand miles!

FATHER DALY. This is one of your debts to humanity, my boy. It wouldn't take you two minutes to see her, and, if you don't, after she's made that long journey in hope and dread and suffering—

DYKE. Where can I talk with her—here?

THE WARDEN. Yes.

DYKE. Alone? (*The* WARDEN *is doubtful*) Why, you don't need to be afraid. I haven't the faintest idea who the girl is, but if she happens to be some poor misguided sentimental fool, with a gun or a pocket full of cyanide of potassium, she's wasting her time. I wouldn't cheat the sovereign state of Connecticut for anything in the world—not even to please a young lady.

THE WARDEN. Dyke, there's something about you that gets everybody.

DYKE. How about the jury?

THE WARDEN. You've got a sort of way with you—

DYKE. How about that spread-eagle district attorney?

THE WARDEN. I'm going to let you talk with that girl in here—alone.

DYKE. Thanks.

THE WARDEN. It's a sort of thing that's never been done before, but if I put you on your honor—

DYKE (cynically). My honor! Thank you, so much.

FATHER DALY. Warden, are you sure it's wise?

DYKE. Father, I'm disappointed in you. Do you imagine I'd do anything that could reflect on Warden Holt—or you—or the young lady— or me?

THE WARDEN. Father, will you take Dyke into the deputy's room? I want to speak to the young lady first.

FATHER DALY. Certainly. Come, my boy. (FATHER DALY and DYKE start toward the Deputy's room.)

THE WARDEN. I'll call you in just a couple of minutes.

DYKE. We promise not to run away (They go out together.)

THE WARDEN (calls). Wilson! (The ATTENDANT enters from the left.)

THE ATTENDANT. Yes, sir.

THE WARDEN. Is the girl there?

THE ATTENDANT. Yes, sir.

THE WARDEN. Frisked?

THE ATTENDANT. Yes, sir.

THE WARDEN. Everything all right?

THE ATTENDANT. Yes, sir.

THE WARDEN (throws away his cigar). Bring her in.

THE ATTENDANT. Yes, sir. (He speaks through the door at the left) Step this way, Miss. This here's the Warden.

(A young girl appears on the threshold, and casts about in mingled curiosity and apprehension. She is fresh and wholesome, and rather pretty; but her manner betrays a certain spiritual aloofness from the ultra-modern world—a certain delicate reticence of the flesh—which immediately separates her from the metropolitan class. Indeed, she is dressed far too simply for a metropolitan girl of her age; she wears a blue tailored suit with deep white cuffs and a starched white sailor-collar, and a small blue hat which fits snugly over her fluffy hair. Her costume is not quite conservative enough to be literally old-fashioned, but it hints at the taste and repression of an old-fashioned home.

She is neither timid nor aggressive; she is self-unconscious. She looks at the WARDEN *squarely, but not in boldness, and yet not in feminine appeal; she has rather the fearlessness of a girl who has lost none of her illusions about men in general. Her expression is essentially serious; it conveys, however, the idea that her seriousness is due to her present mission, and that ordinarily she takes an active joy in the mere pleasure of existence.*)

THE WARDEN (*he had expected a very different type of visitor, so that he is somewhat taken aback*). All right, Wilson.

THE ATTENDANT. Yes, sir. (*He goes out.*)

THE WARDEN (*with grave deference, half rises*). Will you sit down?

THE GIRL. Why—thank you very much. (*She sits in the chair beside the desk and regards him trustfully.*)

THE WARDEN (*he is palpably affected by her youth and innocence, and he is not quite sure how best to proceed, but eventually he makes an awkward beginning*). You've had an interview with the Governor, I understand?

THE GIRL. Yes, sir. I was with him almost an hour.

THE WARDEN. And you want to see Dyke, do you?

THE GIRL. Yes, sir. I *hope* I'm not— too late.

THE WARDEN. No, you're not too late. (*He is appraising her carefully*) But I want to ask you a few

questions beforehand. (*Her reaction of uncertainty induces him to soften his tone*) There isn't anything to get upset about. I just want to make it easier for you, not harder. Where do you live?

THE GIRL. In Ohio.

THE WARDEN (*very kindly*). What place?

THE GIRL. In Pennington, sir. It's a little town not far from Columbus.

THE WARDEN. And you live out there with your father and mother?

THE GIRL. No, sir—just my mother and I. My father died when I was a little baby.

THE WARDEN. Why didn't your mother come here herself, instead of sending you?

THE GIRL. She couldn't. She's sick.

THE WARDEN. I see. Have you any brothers or sisters?

THE GIRL (*slightly more at ease*). Just one brother, sir—this one. He and I were the only children. We were very fond of each other.

THE WARDEN. He was considerably older than you?

THE GIRL. Oh, yes. He's ten years older.

THE WARDEN. Why did he leave home?

THE GIRL. I don't really know, sir, except he just wanted to be in the city. Pennington's pretty small.

THE WARDEN. How long is it since you've seen him?

THE GIRL. It's eight years.

THE WARDEN (*his voice is almost paternal*). As long as that? Hm! And how old are you now?

THE GIRL. I'm almost eighteen.

THE WARDEN (*repeats slowly*). Almost eighteen. Hm! And are you sure after all this time you'd recognize your brother if you saw him?

THE GIRL. Well— (*She looks down, as if embarrassed to make the admission*) Of course I think so, but maybe I couldn't. You see, I was only a little girl when he went away —he wasn't a bad boy, sir, I don't think he could ever be really bad— but if this *is* my brother, why he's been in a great deal of trouble and you know that trouble makes people look different.

THE WARDEN. Yes, it does. But what makes you think this man Dyke may be your brother—and why didn't you think of it sooner? The case has been in the papers for the last six months.

THE GIRL. Why, it wasn't until last Tuesday that Mother saw a piece in the *Journal*—that's the Columbus paper—that he'd written all about himself, and there was one little part of it that sounded so like Joe—like the funny way he used to say things —and then there was a picture that looked the least little *bit* like him— well, Mother just wanted me to come East and find out for sure.

THE WARDEN. It's too bad she couldn't come herself. She'd prob-ably know him whether he'd changed or not.

THE GIRL. Yes, sir. But I'll do the best I can.

THE WARDEN. When was the last time you heard from him, and where was he, and what was he doing?

THE GIRL. Why, it's about five or six years since we had a letter from Joe. He was in Seattle, Washington.

THE WARDEN. What doing?

THE GIRL. I don't remember. At home, though, he worked in the stationery store. He liked books.

THE WARDEN (*suspiciously*). Why do you suppose he didn't write home?

THE GIRL. I—couldn't say. He was just—thoughtless.

THE WARDEN. Wasn't in trouble of any kind?

THE GIRL. Oh, *no!* Never. That is —unless he's—here now.

THE WARDEN (*deliberates*). How are you going to tell him?

THE GIRL. I don't know what you mean.

THE WARDEN. Why, you say maybe you wouldn't know him even if you saw him—and I'll guarantee this man Dyke won't help you out very much. How do you think you're going to tell? Suppose he don't want to be recognized by you or anybody else? Suppose he's so ashamed of himself he—

THE GIRL. I'd thought of that. I'm just going to talk to him—ask him questions—about things he and I used to do together—I'll watch his face, and if he's my brother, I'm sure I can tell.

THE WARDEN (*with tolerant doubt*). What did you and your brother ever used to do that would help you out now?

THE GIRL. He used to play games with me when I was a little girl, and tell me stories—that's what I'm counting on mostly—the stories.

THE WARDEN. I'm afraid—

THE GIRL. Especially Shakespeare stories.

THE WARDEN. Shakespeare!

THE GIRL. Why, yes. He used to get the plots of the plays—all the Shakespeare plays—out of a book by a man named Lamb, and then he'd tell me the stories in his own words. It was wonderful!

THE WARDEN. I'm certainly afraid he—

THE GIRL. But best of all he'd learn some of the speeches from the plays themselves. He liked to do it—he was sure he was going to be an actor or something—he was in all the high school plays, always. And then he'd teach some of the speeches to me, and we'd say them to each other. And one thing—every night he'd sit side of my bed, and when I got sleepy there were two speeches we'd always say to each other, like good night—two speeches out of *Romeo and Juliet,* and then I'd go to sleep. I can see it all. (*The* WAR-

DEN *shakes his head*) Why do you do that?

THE WARDEN. This boy isn't your brother.

THE GIRL. Do you think he isn't?

THE WARDEN. I *know* he isn't.

THE GIRL. How do you?

THE WARDEN. This boy never heard of Shakespeare—much less learned him. (*He presses a button on his desk*) Oh, I'll let you see him for yourself, only you might as well be prepared. (*The* ATTENDANT *enters from the anteroom*) Tell Dyke and Father Daly to come in here— they're in the deputy's room.

THE ATTENDANT. Yes, sir. (*He crosses behind the* WARDEN, *and goes off to the right.*)

THE WARDEN. If he turns out to be your brother—which he won't—you can have, say, an hour with him. If he don't, you'll oblige me by cutting it as short as you can.

THE GIRL. You see, I've got to tell Mother something perfectly definite. She's worried so long about him, and—and *now* the suspense is perfectly terrible for her.

THE WARDEN. I can understand that. You're a plucky girl.

THE GIRL. Of course, it would be awful for us if this *is* Joe, but even that would be better for Mother than just to stay awake nights, and wonder and wonder, and never *know* what became of him. (*The* ATTENDANT *opens the door of the Deputy's room, and when* DYKE and FATHER DALY *have come in, he crosses again behind the* WARDEN, *and is going out at the left when the* WARDEN *signs to him and he stops.*)

THE WARDEN (*gets to his feet*). Dyke, this is the young lady that's come all the way from Pennington, Ohio, to see you.

DYKE (*who has been talking in an undertone to* FATHER DALY, *raises his head quickly*). Yes, sir?

THE WARDEN. I've decided you can talk with her here—alone.
(THE GIRL *has risen, breathless, and stands fixed;* DYKE *inspects her coldly from head to foot.*)

DYKE. Thank you. It won't take long.

THE WARDEN (*has been scanning the girl's expression; now, as he sees that she has neither recognized* DYKE *nor failed to recognize him, he makes a little grimace in confirmation of his own judgment*). Father Daly and I'll stay in the deputy's office. We'll leave the door open. Wilson, you stand in the anteroom with the door open.

DYKE (*bitterly*). My honor!

THE WARDEN. What say?

DYKE. I didn't say anything.

THE WARDEN (*to the* GIRL). Will you please remember what I told you about the time?

THE GIRL. Oh, yes, sir.

THE WARDEN. Come, Father.
(*They go off into the Deputy's room, and the* ATTENDANT, *at a nod from the* WARDEN, *goes off at the left.*)
(DYKE *and the* GIRL *are now facing each other;* DYKE *is well poised and insouciant and gives the impression of complete indifference to the moment. The* GIRL, *on the other hand, is deeply agitated and her agitation is gradually increased by* DYKE's *own attitude.*)

THE GIRL (*after several efforts to speak*). Mother sent me to see you.

DYKE (*politely callous*). Yes?

THE GIRL (*compelled to drop her eyes*). You see, we haven't seen or heard of my brother Joe for ever so long, and mother thought—after what we read in the papers—

DYKE. That I might be your brother Joe?

THE GIRL (*obviously relieved*). Yes, that's it.

DYKE. Well, you can easily see that I'm not your brother, can't you?

THE GIRL (*stares at him again*). I'm not sure. You look a little like him, just as the picture in the paper did, but then again, it's so long— (*she shakes her head dubiously*) and I'd thought of Joe so differently—

DYKE (*his manner is somewhat indulgent, as though to a child*). As a matter of fact, I couldn't be *your* brother, or anybody else's brother, because I never had a sister. So *that* rather settles it.

THE GIRL. Honestly?

DYKE. Honestly.

THE GIRL. (*unconvinced, becomes more appealing*). What's your real name?

DYKE. Dyke—James Dyke.

THE GIRL. That's sure enough your name?

DYKE. Sure enough. You don't think I'd tell a lie at this stage of the game, do you?

THE GIRL (*musing*). No, I don't believe you would. Where do you come from—I mean where were you born?

DYKE. In Canada, but I've lived all over.

THE GIRL. Didn't you ever live in Ohio?

DYKE. No. Never.

THE GIRL. What kind of work did you do—what was your business?

DYKE. Oh, I'm sort of Jack-of-all-trades. I've been everything a man could be—except a success.

THE GIRL. Do you like books?

DYKE. Books?

THE GIRL. Yes—books to read.

DYKE. I don't read when there's anything better to do. I've read a lot here.

THE GIRL. Did you ever sell books—for a living, I mean?

DYKE. Oh, no.

THE GIRL (*growing confused*). I hope you don't mind my asking so many questions. But I—

DYKE. No—go ahead, if it'll relieve your mind any.

THE GIRL. You went to school somewhere, of course—high school?

DYKE. No, I never got that far.

THE GIRL. Did you ever want to be an actor? Or *were* you ever?

DYKE. No, just a convict.

THE GIRL (*helplessly*). Do you know any poetry?

DYKE. Not to speak of.

THE GIRL (*delays a moment, and then, watching him very earnestly, she recites just above her breath*).

*Thou knowst the mask of night is
   on my face
Else would a maiden blush be-
   paint my cheek
For that which—*

(*Realizing that* DYKE's *expression is one of utter vacuity she falters, and breaks off the quotation, but she continues to watch him unwaveringly*) Don't you know what that is?

DYKE. No, but to tell the truth, it sounds sort of silly to *me*. Doesn't it to you?

THE GIRL (*her intonation has become slightly forlorn, but she gathers courage, and puts him to one more test*).

*Good night, good night, parting
   is such sweet sorrow
That I shall say good night till it
   be morrow.*

DYKE (*his mouth twitches in amusement*). Eh?

THE GIRL. What comes next?

DYKE. Good Lord, I don't know.

THE GIRL (*gazes intently, almost imploringly, at him as though she is making a struggle to read his mind. Then she relaxes and holds out her hand*). Good-bye. You—you're not Joe, are you? I—had to come and find out, though. I hope I've not made you too unhappy.

DYKE (*ignores her hand*). You're not going now?

THE GIRL (*spiritless*). Yes. I promised the—is he the Warden? that man in there?—I said I'd go right away if you weren't my brother. And you aren't, so—

DYKE. You're going back to your mother?

THE GIRL. Yes.

DYKE. I'm surprised that she sent a girl like you on a sorry errand like this, instead of—

THE GIRL. She's very sick.

DYKE. Oh, that's too bad.

THE GIRL (*twisting her handkerchief*). No, she's not well at all. And most of it's from worrying about Joe.

DYKE. Still, when you tell her that her son isn't a murderer—at least, that he isn't *this* one—that'll comfort her a good deal, won't it?

THE GIRL (*reluctantly*). Yes, I think maybe it will, only—

DYKE. Only what?

THE GIRL. I don't think Mother'll ever be *really* well again until she finds out for certain where Joe is and what's become of him.

DYKE (*shakes his head compassionately*). Mothers ought not to be treated like that. I wish I'd treated *mine* better. By the way, you didn't tell me what your name is.

THE GIRL. Josephine Paris.

DYKE (*is suddenly attentive*). Paris? That's an unusual name. I've heard it somewhere, too.

THE GIRL. Just like the name of the city—in France.

DYKE (*knitting his brows*). And your brother's name was Joseph?

THE GIRL. Yes—they used to call us Joe and Josie—that's funny, isn't it?

DYKE (*thoughtfully*). No, I don't think it's so very funny. I rather like it. (*He passes his hand over his forehead as if trying to coerce his memory.*)

THE GIRL. What's the matter?

DYKE (*frowning*). I was thinking of something—now, what on earth was that boy's name! Wait a minute, don't tell me—wait a minute—I've got it! (*He punctuates his triumph with one fist in the palm of the other hand*) Joseph Anthony Paris!

THE GIRL (*amazed*). Why, that's his name! That's Joe! How did you ever—

DYKE (*his manner is very forcible and convincing*). Wait! Now listen carefully to what I say, and don't interrupt me, because we've only got a minute, and I want you to get this all straight, so you can tell your mother. When the war came along I enlisted and I was overseas for four years—with the Canadians. Early one morning we'd staged a big trench raid, and there was an officer who'd been wounded coming back, and was lying out there in a shell-hole under fire. The Jerries were getting ready for a raid of their own, so they were putting down a box barrage with light guns and howitzers and a few heavies. This officer was lying right in the middle of it. Well, all of a sudden a young fellow dashed out of a trench not far from where I was, and went for that officer. He had to go through a curtain of shells and, more than that, they opened on him with rifles and machine guns. The chances were just about a million to one against him, and he must have known it, but he went out just the same. He got the officer in his arms and started back, but he'd only gone a few yards when a five point nine landed right on top of the two of them. Afterward, we got what was left—the identification tag was still there—and that was the name— Joseph Anthony Paris!

THE GIRL (*carries both hands to her breast*). Oh!

DYKE. If that was your brother's name, then you can tell your mother that he died like a brave man and a soldier, three years ago, in France.

THE GIRL. Joe—my brother Joe—is dead?

DYKE. On the field of battle. It was one of the wonderful, heroic things that went almost unnoticed, as so

many of them did. If an officer had seen it, there'd have been a decoration for your mother to keep and remember him by.

THE GIRL. And you were there— and saw it?

DYKE. I was there and saw it. It was three years ago. That's why you and your mother haven't heard from him. And if you don't believe what I've said, why, you just write up to Ottawa and get the official record. Of course (*he shrugs his shoulders contemptuously*) those records are in terribly poor shape, but at least they can tell you what battalion he fought with, when he went overseas. Only you mustn't be surprised no matter whether they say he was killed in action, or died of wounds, or is missing, or even went through the whole war with his outfit, and was honorably discharged. They really don't know what happened to half the men. But I've told you the truth. And it certainly ought to make your mother happy when she knows that her boy died as a soldier, and not as a criminal.

THE GIRL (*is transfigured*). Yes, yes, it will!

DYKE. And does it make you happy, too?

THE GIRL (*nods repeatedly*). Yes. So happy—after what we were both afraid of—I can't even cry—yet. (*She brushes her eyes with her handkerchief*) I can hardly wait to take it to her.

DYKE (*struck by a sudden inspiration*). I want to give you something else to take to her. (*He picks up from the desk the envelope contain ing the Liberty Bonds ana seals it)* I want you to give this to your mother from me. Tell her it's from a man who was at Vimy Ridge and saw your brother die, so it's a sort of memorial for him. *(He touches her arm as she absently begins to tear open the envelope)* No, don't you open it—let her do it.

THE GIRL. What is it? Can't I know?

DYKE. Never mind now, but give it to her. It's all I've got in the world and it's too late now for me to do anything else with it. And have your mother buy a little gold star to wear for her son—and you get one, too, and wear it—here— *(He touches his heart)* Will you?

THE GIRL. Yes—I will. And yet somehow I'll almost feel that I'm wearing it for you, too.

DYKE *(shakes his head soberly)*. Oh, no! You mustn't ever do that. I'm not fit to be mentioned in the same breath with a boy like your brother, and now I'm afraid it *is* time for you to go. I'm sorry, but—you'd better. I'm glad you came before it was too late, though.

THE GIRL *(gives him her hand)*. Good-bye, and thank you. You've done more for me—and Mother— than I could possibly tell you. And— and I'm so sorry for you—so *truly sorry*—I wish I could only do something to make you a tiny bit happier, too. Is there anything I could do?

DYKE *(stares at her and by degrees he becomes wistful)*. Why—yes, there is. Only I— *(He leaves the sentence uncompleted.)*

THE GIRL. What is it?

DYKE *(looks away)*. I can't tell you. I never should have let myself think of it.

THE GIRL. Please tell me. I want you to. For—for Joe's sake, tell me what I can do.

DYKE *(his voice is low and desolate)*. Well—in all the months I've been in this hideous place, you're the first girl I've seen. I didn't ever expect to see one again. I'd forgot ten how much like angels women look. I've been terribly lonesome to· night, especially, and if you really do want to do something for me— for your brother's sake—you see, you're going to leave me in just a minute and—and I haven't any sister of my own, or anybody else, to say good-bye to me—so, if you could—*really* say good-bye— *(She gazes at him for a moment, understands, flushes, and then slowly moves into his outstretched arms. He holds her close to him, touches his lips to her forehead twice, and releases her.)*

DYKE *(thickly)*. Good-bye, my dear.

THE GIRL. Good night. *(She endeavors to smile, but her voice catches in her throat)* Good-bye.

DYKE *(impulsively)*. What is it?

THE GIRL *(shakes her head)*. N-nothing.

DYKE. Nothing?

THE GIRL *(clutches her handkerchief tight in her palm)*. I was thinking—I was thinking what I used to say to my brother—for good night. *(She very nearly breaks down)* If I only could have—have said it to him just once more—for good-bye.

DYKE. What was it?

THE GIRL. I—I told it to you once, and you said it was silly.

DYKE (*softly*). Say it again.

THE GIRL (*she cannot quite control her voice*).

Good night, good night, parting is such sweet sorrow
That I shall say good night till it be morrow.

(*She goes uncertainly toward the anteroom, hesitates, almost turns back, and then with a choking sob she hurries through the door and closes it behind her. For several seconds DYKE stands rigidly intent upon that door; until at length, without changing his attitude or his expression, he speaks very tenderly and reminiscently.*)

Sleep dwell upon thine eyes, peace in thy breast;
Would I were sleep and peace, so sweet to rest.

(*The WARDEN and FATHER DALY come in quietly from the Deputy's room; and as they behold DYKE, how rapt and unconscious of them he is, they look at each other, questioningly. The WARDEN glances at the clock and makes as though to interrupt DYKE'S solitary reflections but FATHER DALY quietly restrains him. The CHAPLAIN sits down in one of the chairs at the back wall; the WARDEN crosses on tip-toe and sits at his desk; he is excessively nervous and he continually refers to the clock. DYKE turns, as though unwillingly, from the door; there are depths in his eyes, and his thoughts are evidently far away. He sits in the chair*

to the right of the WARDEN's desk and leans outward, his right hand on his knee. He puts his left hand to his throat as though to protect it from a sudden pain. He gazes straight ahead into the unknown and speaks in reverie.*)

Of all the wonders that I yet have heard,
It seems to me most strange that men should fear;
Seeing that death, a necessary end,
Will come when it will come.

(*He stops and muses for a time, while the WARDEN glances perplexedly at FATHER DALY to discover if the PRIEST can interpret what DYKE is saying. FATHER DALY shakes his head. Abruptly DYKE'S face is illumined by a new and welcome recollection; and again he speaks, while the WARDEN tries in vain to comprehend him.*)

Cowards die many times before their death;
The valiant never taste of death but once.

(*He stops again and shudders a trifle; his head droops and he repeats, barely above a whisper.*)

The valiant never taste of death but once.

(*The nearer door on the right is opened noiselessly and the JAILER, in obedience to his instructions, steps just inside the room and stands there mute. FATHER DALY and the WARDEN glance at the JAILER, and with significance at each other, and both rise, tardily. The WARDEN's hand, as it rests on his desk is seen to tremble. There is a moment of dead silence; presently* DYKE *lifts his head and catches sight of the motionless* ATTENDANT *at the open door. With a quick intake of his breath, he starts half out of his seat and stares, fascinated; he sinks back slowly, and turns his head to gaze first at* FATHER DALY *and then at the* WARDEN. *The* WARDEN *averts his eyes, but* FATHER DALY's *expression is of supreme pity and encouragement. Involuntarily,* DYKE's *hand again goes creeping upward toward his throat, but he arrests it. He grasps the arms of his chair and braces himself; he rises then, and stands very erect, in almost the position of a soldier at attention.*)

THE WARDEN (*swallows hard*). Dyke!

FATHER DALY (*brushes past the* WARDEN, *his right hand lifted as though in benediction*). My son!

DYKE (*regards them fixedly; his voice is low and steady*). All right, let's go. (*He faces about, and with his head held proud and high, and his shoulders squared to the world, he moves slowly toward the open door.* FATHER DALY, *with the light of his calling in his eyes, steps in line just ahead of* DYKE. *The* WARDEN,

his mouth set hard, falls in behind. When they have all gone forward a pace or two, FATHER DALY *begins to speak, and* DYKE *to reply.* FATHER DALY's *voice is strong and sweet; and* DYKE *speaks just after him, not mechanically, but in brave and unfaltering response.*)

FATHER DALY. "I will lift up mine eyes unto the hills—"

DYKE. "The valiant never taste of death but once."

FATHER DALY. "From whence cometh my help."

DYKE. "The valiant never taste of death but once."

FATHER DALY (*has almost reached the door; his voice rises a semi-tone, and gains in emotion*). "My help cometh from the Lord which made Heaven and earth."

DYKE. "The valiant never taste of death—but once."
(*When the* WARDEN, *whose hands are tightly clenched, has passed the threshold, the* JAILER *follows and closes the door behind him. There is a very brief pause and then*)

CURTAIN

In the Zone

BY EUGENE O'NEILL

CHARACTERS

SMITTY
DAVIS
SWANSON
SCOTTY
IVAN   *Seamen on the British Tramp*
PAUL   *Steamer* Glencairn
JACK
DRISCOLL
COCKY

IN THE ZONE

SCENE—*The seamen's forecastle. On the right above the bunks three or four portholes covered with black cloth can be seen. On the floor near the doorway is a pail with a tin dipper. A lantern in the middle of the floor, turned down very low, throws a dim light around the place. Five men, SCOTTY, IVAN, SWANSON, SMITTY and PAUL, are in their bunks apparently asleep. It is about ten minutes of twelve on a night in the fall of the year 1915.*

SMITTY turns slowly in his bunk and, leaning out over the side, looks from one to another of the men as if to assure himself that they are asleep. Then he climbs carefully out of his bunk and stands in the middle of the forecastle fully dressed, but in his stocking feet, glancing around him suspiciously. Reassured, he leans down and cautiously pulls out a suit-case from under the bunks in front of him.

Just at this moment DAVIS appears in the doorway, carrying a large steaming coffee-pot in his hand. He stops short when he sees SMITTY. A puzzled expression comes over his face, followed by one of suspicion, and he retreats farther back in the alleyway, where he can watch SMITTY without being seen.

All the latter's movements indicate a fear of discovery. He takes out a small bunch of keys and unlocks the suit-case, making a slight noise as he does so. SCOTTY wakes up and peers at him over the side of the bunk. SMITTY opens the suit-case and takes out a small black tin box, carefully places this under his mattress, shoves the suit-case back under the bunk, climbs into his bunk again, closes his eyes and begins to snore loudly.

DAVIS enters the forecastle, places the coffee-pot beside the lantern, and goes from one to the other of the sleepers and shakes them vigorously, saying to each in a low voice: Near eight bells, Scotty. Arise and shine, Swanson. Eight bells, Ivan. *SMITTY yawns loudly with a great pretense of having been dead asleep. All of the rest of the men tumble out of their bunks, stretching and gaping, and commence to pull on their shoes. They go one by one to the cupboard near the open door, take out their cups and spoons, and sit down together on the benches. The coffee-pot is passed around. They munch their biscuits and sip their coffee in dull silence.*

DAVIS (*suddenly jumping to his feet—nervously*). Where's that air comin' from?
(*All are startled and look at him wonderingly.*)

SWANSON (*a squat, surly-faced Swede—grumpily*). What air? I don't feel nothing.

DAVIS (*excitedly*). I kin feel it—a draft. (*He stands on the bench and looks around—suddenly exploding*) Damn fool square-head! (*He leans over the upper bunk in which PAUL is sleeping and slams the porthole shut*) I got a good notion to report him. Serve him bloody well right! What's the use o' blindin' the ports when that thick-head goes an' leaves 'em open?

SWANSON (*yawning—too sleepy to be aroused by anything—carelessly*). Dey don't see what little light go out yust one port.

SCOTTY (*protestingly*). Dinna be a loon, Swanson! D'ye no ken the dangerr o' showin' a licht wi' a pack o' submarrines lyin' aboot?

IVAN (*shaking his shaggy ox-like head in an emphatic affirmative*). Dot's right, Scotty. I don' li-ke blow up, no, by devil!

SMITTY (*his manner slightly contemptuous*). I don't think there's much danger of meeting any of their submarines, not until we get into the war zone, at any rate.

DAVIS (*he and* SCOTTY *look at* SMITTY *suspiciously—harshly*). You don't, eh? (*He lowers his voice and speaks slowly*) Well, we're in the war zone right this minit if you wants to know.
(*The effect of this speech is instantaneous. All sit bolt upright on their benches and stare at* DAVIS.)

SMITTY. How do you know, Davis?

DAVIS (*angrily*). 'Cos Drisc heard the First send the Third below to wake the skipper when we fetched the zone—bout five bells, it was. Now whata y' got to say?

SMITTY (*conciliatingly*). Oh, I wasn't doubting your word, Davis; but you know they're not pasting up bulletins to let the crew know when the zone is reached—especially on ammunition ships like this.

IVAN (*decidedly*). I don't li-ike dees voyage. Next time I ship on windjammer Boston to River Plate, load with wood only so it float, by golly!

SWANSON (*fretfully*). I hope British navy blow 'em to hell, those submarines, py damn!

SCOTTY (*looking at* SMITTY, *who is staring at the doorway in a dream, his chin on his hands. Meaningly*). It is no the submarrines only we've to fear, I'm thinkin'.

DAVIS (*assenting eagerly*). That's no lie, Scotty.

SWANSON. You mean the mines?

SCOTTY. I wasna thinkin' o' mines eitherr.

DAVIS. There's many a good ship blown up and at the bottom of the sea, what never hit no mine or torpedo.

SCOTTY. Did ye neverr read of the German spies and the dirrty work they're doin' all the war? (*He and* DAVIS *both glance at* SMITTY, *who is deep in thought and is not listening to the conversation.*)

DAVIS. An' the clever way they fool you!

SWANSON. Sure; I read it in paper many time.

DAVIS. Well— (*He is about to speak but hesitates and finishes lamely.*) you got to watch out, that's all I says.

IVAN (*drinking the last of his coffee and slamming his fist on the bench explosively*). I tell you dis rotten coffee give me belly-ache, yes!
(*They all look at him in amused disgust.*)

SCOTTY (*sardonically*). Dinna fret about it, Ivan. If we blow up ye'll no be mindin' the pain in your middle.

(JACK *enters. He is a young American with a tough, good-natured face. He wears dungarees and a heavy jersey.*)

JACK. Eight bells, fellers.

IVAN (*stupidly*). I don' hear bell ring.

JACK. No, and yuh won't hear any ring, yuh boob— (*Lowering his voice unconsciously*) Now we're in the war zone.

SWANSON (*anxiously*). Is the boats all ready?

JACK. Sure; we can lower 'em in a second.

DAVIS. A lot o' good the boats'll do, with us loaded deep with all kinds o' dynamite and stuff the like o' that! If a torpedo hits this hooker we'll all be in hell b'fore you could wink your eye.

JACK. They ain't goin' to hit us, see? That's my dope. Whose wheel is it?

IVAN (*sullenly*). My wheel. (*He lumbers out.*)

JACK. And whose lookout?

SWANSON. Mine, I tink. (*He follows* IVAN.)

JACK (*scornfully*). A hell of a lot of use keepin' a lookout! We couldn't run away or fight if we wanted to. (*To* SCOTTY *and* SMITTY) Better look up the bo'sun or the Fourth, you two, and let 'em see you're awake. (SCOTTY *goes to the doorway and turns to wait for*

SMITTY, *who is still in the same position, head on hands, seemingly unconscious of everything.* JACK *slaps him roughly on the shoulder and he comes to with a start*) Aft and report, Duke! What's the matter with yuh—in a dope dream? (SMITTY *goes out after* SCOTTY *without answering.* JACK *looks after him with a frown*) He's a queer guy. I can't figger him out.

DAVIS. Nor no one else. (*Lowering his voice—meaningly*) An' he's liable to turn out queerer than any of us think if we ain't careful.

JACK (*suspiciously*). What d'yuh mean? (*They are interrupted by the entrance of* DRISCOLL *and* COCKY.)

COCKY (*protestingly*). Blimey if I don't fink I'll put in this 'ere watch ahtside on deck. (*He and* DRISCOLL *go over and get their cups*) I down't want to be caught in this 'ole if they 'its us. (*He pours out coffee.*)

DRISCOLL (*pouring his*). Divil a bit ut wud matther where ye arre. Ye'd be blown to smithereens b'fore ye cud say your name. (*He sits down, over-turning as he does so the untouched cup of coffee which* SMITTY *had forgotten and left on the bench. They all jump nervously as the tin cup hits the floor with a bang.* DRISCOLL *flies into an unreasoning rage*) Who's the dirty scut left this cup where a man 'ud sit on ut?

DAVIS. It's Smitty's.

DRISCOLL (*kicking the cup across the forecastle*). Does he think he's too much av a bloody gentleman to put his own away loike the rist av us? If he does I'm the bye'll beat that noshun out av his head.

COCKY. Be the airs 'e puts on you'd think 'e was the Prince of Wales. Wot's 'e doin' on a ship, I arsks yer? 'E ain't now good as a sailor, is 'e? —dawdlin' abaht on deck like a chicken wiv 'is 'ead cut orf!

JACK (*good-naturedly*). Aw, the Duke's all right. S'posin' he did forget his cup—what's the dif! (*He picks up the cup and puts it away —with a grin*) This war zone stuff's got yer goat, Drisc—and yours too, Cocky—and I ain't cheerin' much fur it myself, neither.

COCKY (*with a sigh*). Blimey, it ain't no bleedin' joke, yer first trip, to know as ther's a ship full of shells li'ble to go orf in under your bloomin' feet, as you might say, if we gets 'it be a torpedo or mine. (*With sudden savagery*) Calls theyselves 'uman bein's, too! Blarsted 'Uns!

DRISCOLL (*gloomily*). 'Tis me last trip in the bloody zone, God help me. The divil take their twenty-foive percent bonus—and be drowned like a rat in a trap in the bargain, maybe.

DAVIS. Wouldn't be so bad if she wasn't carryin' ammunition. Them's the kind the subs is layin' for.

DRISCOLL (*irritably*). Fur the love av hivin, don't be talkin' about ut. I'm sick wid thinkin' and jumpin' at iviry bit av a noise. (*There is a pause during which they all stare gloomily at the floor.*)

JACK. Hey, Davis, what was you sayin' about Smitty when they come in?

DAVIS (*with a great air of mystery*). I'll tell you in a minit. I want to wait an' see if he's comin' back. (*Impressively*) You won't be callin' him all right when you hears what I seen with my own eyes. (*He adds with an air of satisfaction*) An' you won't be feelin' no safer, neither. (*They all look at him with puzzled glances full of a vague apprehension.*)

DRISCOLL. God blarst ut! (*He fills his pipe and lights it. The others, with an air of remembering something they had forgotten, do the same.* SCOTTY *enters.*)

SCOTTY (*in awed tones*). Mon, but it's clear outside the nicht! Like day.

DAVIS (*in low tones*). Where's Smitty, Scotty?

SCOTTY. Out on the hatch starin' at the moon like a mon half-daft.

DAVIS. Kin you see him from the doorway?

SCOTTY (*goes to doorway and carefully peeks out*). Aye; he's still there.

DAVIS. Keep your eyes on him for a moment. I've got something I wants to tell the boys and I don't want him walkin' in the middle of it. Give a shout if he starts this way.

SCOTTY (*with suppressed excitement*). Aye, I'll watch him. And I've somethin' myself to tell aboot his Lordship.

DRISCOLL (*impatiently*). Out wid ut! You're talkin' more than a pair av auld women wud be standin' in the road, and gittin' no further along

DAVIS. Listen! You 'member when I went to git the coffee, Jack?

JACK. Sure, I do.

DAVIS. Well, I brings it down here same as usual and got as far as the door there when I sees him.

JACK. Smitty?

DAVIS. Yes, Smitty! He was standin' in the middle of the fo'c's'tle there (*pointing*) lookin' around sneakin'-like at Ivan and Swanson and the rest 's if he wants to make certain they're asleep. (*He pauses significantly, looking from one to the other of his listeners.* SCOTTY *is nervously dividing his attention between* SMITTY *on the hatch outside and* DAVIS' *story, fairly bursting to break in with his own revelations.*)

JACK (*impatiently*). What of it?

DAVIS. Listen! He was standin' right there— (*Pointing again*) In his stockin' feet—no shoes on, mind, so he wouldn't make no noise!

JACK (*spitting disgustedly*). Aw!

DAVIS (*not heeding the interruption*). I seen right away somethin' on the queer was up so I slides back into the alleyway where I kin see him but he can't see me. After he makes sure they're all asleep he goes in under the bunks there—bein' careful not to raise a noise, mind!— an' takes out his bag there. (*By this time every one,* JACK *included, is listening breathlessly to his story*) Then he fishes in his pocket an' takes out a bunch o' keys an' kneels down beside the bag an' opens it.

SCOTTY (*unable to keep silent longer*). Mon, didn't I see him do that same thing wi' these two eyes. 'Twas just that moment I woke and spied him.

DAVIS (*surprised, and a bit nettled to have to share his story with any one*). Oh, you seen him, too, eh? (*To the others*) Then Scotty kin tell you if I'm lyin' or not.

DRISCOLL. An' what did he do whin he'd the bag opened?

DAVIS. He bends down and reaches out his hand sort o' scared-like, like it was somethin' dang'rous he was after, an' feels round in under his duds—hidden in under his duds an' wrapped up in 'em, it was—an' he brings out a black iron box!

COCKY (*looking around him with a frightened glance*). Gawd blimey! (*The others likewise betray their uneasiness, shuffling their feet nervously.*)

DAVIS. Ain't that right, Scotty?

SCOTTY. Right as rain, I'm tellin' ye'!

DAVIS (*to the others with an air of satisfaction*). There you are! (*Lowering his voice*) An' then what d'you suppose he did? Sneaks to his bunk an' slips the black box in under his mattress—in under his mattress, mind!—

JACK. And it's there now?

DAVIS. Course it is!
(JACK *starts toward* SMITTY'S *bunk.* DRISCOLL *grabs him by the arm.*)

DRISCOLL. Don't be touchin' ut, Jack!

JACK. Yuh needn't worry. I ain't goin' to touch it. (*He pulls up* SMITTY'S *mattress and looks down. The others stare at him, holding their breaths. He turns to them, trying hard to assume a careless tone*) It's there, aw right.

COCKY (*miserably upset*). I'm goin-ter 'op it aht on deck. (*He gets up but* DRISCOLL *pulls him down again.* COCKY *protests*) It fair guvs me the trembles sittin' still in 'ere.

DRISCOLL (*scornfully*). Are ye frightened, ye toad? 'Tis a hell av a thing fur grown men to be shiverin' loike childer at a bit av a black box. (*Scratching his head in uneasy perplexity*) Still, ut's damn queer, the looks av ut.

DAVIS (*sarcastically*). A bit of a black box, eh? How big d'you think them— (*he hesitates*) things has to be—big as this fo'c's'tle?

JACK (*in a voice meant to be reassuring*). Aw, hell! I'll bet it ain't nothin' but some coin he's saved he's got locked up in there.

DAVIS (scornfully). That's likely, ain't it? Then why does he act so s'picious? He's been on ship near two year, ain't he? He knows damn well there ain't no thiefs in this fo'c's'tle, don't he? An' you know 's well 's I do he didn't have no money when he came on board an' he ain't saved none since. Don't you? (JACK *doesn't answer*) Listen! D'you know what he done after he put that thing in under his mattress?—an' Scotty'll tell you if I ain't speakin' truth. He looks round to see if any one's woke up——

SCOTTY. I clapped my eyes shut when he turned round.

DAVIS. An' then he crawls into his bunk an' shuts his eyes, an' starts in snorin', pretendin' he was asleep, mind!

SCOTTY. Aye, I could hear him.

DAVIS. An' when I goes to call him I don't even shake him. I just says, "Eight bells, Smitty," in a'most a whisper-like, an' up he gets yawnin' an' stretchin' fit to kill hisself 's if he's been dead asleep.

COCKY. Gawd blimey!

DRISCOLL (*shaking his head*). Ut looks bad, divil a doubt av ut.

DAVIS (*excitedly*). An' now I come to think of it, there's the porthole. How'd it come to git open, tell me that? I know'd well Paul never opened it. Ain't he grumblin' about bein' cold all the time?

SCOTTY. The mon that opened it meant no good to this ship, whoever he was.

JACK (*sourly*). What porthole? What're yuh talkin' about?

DAVIS (*pointing over* PAUL'S *bunk*). There. It was open when I come in. I felt the cold air on my neck an' shut it. It would'a been clear's a lighthouse to any sub that was watchin'—an' we s'posed to have all the ports blinded! Who'd do a dirty trick like that? It wasn't none of us, nor Scotty here, nor Swanson, nor Ivan. Who would it be, then?

COCKY (*angrily*). Must'a been 'is bloody Lordship.

DAVIS. For all's we know he might'a been signallin' with it. They does it like that by winkin' a light. Ain't you read how they gets caught doin' it in London an' on the coast?

COCKY (*firmly convinced now*). An' wots 'e doin' aht alone on the 'atch —keepin' 'isself clear of us like 'e was afraid?

DRISCOLL. Kape your eye on him, Scotty.

SCOTTY. There's no a move oot o' him.

JACK (*in irritated perplexity*). But, hell, ain't he an Englishman? What'd he wanta——

DAVIS. English? How d'we know he's English? Cos he talks it? That ain't no proof. Ain't you read in the papers how all them German spies they been catchin' in England has been livin' there for ten, often as not twenty years, an' talks English as good's any one? An' look here, ain't you noticed he don't talk natural? He talks it too damn good, that's what I mean. He don't talk exactly like a toff, does he, Cocky?

COCKY. Not like any toff as I ever met up wiv.

DAVIS. No; an' he don't talk it like us, that's certain. An' he don't look English. An' what d'we know about him when you come to look at it? Nothin'! He ain't ever said where he comes from or why. All we knows is he ships on here in London 'bout a year b'fore the war starts, as an A. B. —stole his papers most lik'ly— when he don't know how to box the compass, hardly. Ain't that queer in itself? An' was he ever open with us like a good shipmate? No; he's always had that sly air about him 's if he was hidin' somethin'.

DRISCOLL (*slapping his thigh—angrily*). Divil take me if I don't think ye have the truth av ut, Davis.

COCKY (*scornfully*). Lettin' on be 'is silly airs, and all, 'e's the son of a blarsted earl or somethink!

DAVIS. An' the name he calls hisself —Smith! I'd risk a quid of my next pay day that his real name is Schmidt, if the truth was known.

JACK (*evidently fighting against his own conviction*). Aw, say, you guys give me a pain! What'd they want puttin' a spy on this old tub for?

DAVIS (*shaking his head sagely*). They're deep ones, an' there's a lot o' things a sailor'll see in the ports he puts in ought to be useful to 'em. An' if he kin signal to 'em an' they blow us up it's one ship less, ain't it? (*Lowering his voice and indicating* SMITTY's *bunk*) Or if he blows us up hisself.

SCOTTY (*in alarmed tones*). Hush, mon! Here he comes! (SCOTTY *hurries over to a bench and sits down. A thick silence settles over the forecastle. The men look from one to another with uneasy glances.* SMITTY *enters and sits down beside his bunk. He is seemingly unaware of the dark glances of suspicion directed at him from all sides. He slides his hand back stealthily over his mattress and his fingers move, evidently feeling to make sure the box is still there. The others follow this movement carefully with quick looks out of the corners of their eyes. Their attitudes grow tense as if they were about to spring at him. Satisfied the box is safe,* SMITTY *draws his hand away slowly and utters a sigh of relief.*)

SMITTY (*in a casual tone which to them sounds sinister*). It's a good light night for the subs if there's any about. (*For a moment he sits staring in front of him. Finally he seems to sense the hostile atmosphere of the forecastle and looks from one to the other of the men in surprise. All of them avoid his eyes. He sighs with a puzzled expression and gets up and walks out of the doorway. There is silence for a moment after his departure and then a storm of excited talk breaks loose.*)

DAVIS. Did you see him feelin' if it was there?

COCKY. 'E ain't arf a sly one wiv 'is talk of submarines, Gawd blind 'im!

SCOTTY. Did ye see the sneakin' looks he gave us?

DRISCOLL. If ivir I saw black shame on a man's face 'twas on his whin he sat there!

JACK (*thoroughly convinced at last*). He looked bad to me. He's a crook, aw right.

DAVIS (*excitedly*). What'll we do? We gotter do somethin' quick or—— (*He is interrupted by the sound of something hitting against the port side of the forecastle with a dull, heavy thud. The men start to their feet in wild-eyed terror and turn as if they were going to rush for the deck. They stand that way for a strained moment, scarcely breathing and listening intently.*)

JACK (*with a sickly smile*). Hell! It's on'y a piece of driftwood or a floatin' log. (*He sits down again.*)

DAVIS (*sarcastically*). Or a mine that

didn't go off—that time—or a piece o' wreckage from some ship they've sent to Davy Jones.

COCKY (*mopping his brow with a trembling hand*). Blimey! (*He sinks back weakly on a bench.*)

DRISCOLL (*furiously*). God blarst ut! No man at all cud be puttin' up wid the loike av this—an' I'm not wan to be fearin' anything or any man in the worrld'll stand up to me face to face; but this divil's trickery in the darrk—— (*He starts for SMITTY's bunk*) I'll throw ut out wan av the portholes an' be done wid ut. (*He reaches toward the mattress.*)

SCOTTY (*grabbing his arm—wildly*). Arre ye daft, mon?

DAVIS. Don't monkey with it, Drisc. I knows what to do. Bring the bucket o' water here, Jack, will you? (*JACK gets it and brings it over to DAVIS*) An' you, Scotty, see if he's back on the hatch.

SCOTTY (*cautiously peering out*). Aye, he's sittin' there the noo.

DAVIS. Sing out if he makes a move. Lift up the mattress, Drisc—careful now! (*DRISCOLL does so with infinite caution*) Take it out, Jack—careful—don't shake it now, for Christ's sake! Here—put it in the water—easy! There, that's fixed it! (*They all sit down with great sighs of relief*) The water'll git in and spoil it.

DRISCOLL (*slapping DAVIS on the back*). Good wurrk for ye, Davis, ye scut! (*He spits on his hands aggressively*) An' now what's to be done wid that black-hearted thraitor?

COCKY (*belligerently*). Guv 'im a shove in the marf and 'eave 'im over the side!

DAVIS. An' serve him right!

JACK. Aw, say, give him a chance. Yuh can't prove nothin' till yuh find out what's in there.

DRISCOLL (*heatedly*). Is ut more proof ye'd be needin' afther what we've seen an' heard? Then listen to me—an' ut's Driscoll talkin'—if there's divilmint in that box an' we see plain 'twas his plan to murrdher his own shipmates that have served him fair—— (*He raises his fist*) I'll choke his rotten hearrt out wid me own hands, an' over the side wid him, and one man missin' in the mornin'.

DAVIS. An' no one the wiser. He's the balmy kind what commits suicide.

COCKY. They 'angs spies ashore.

JACK (*resentfully*). If he's done what yuh think I'll croak him myself. Is that good enough for yuh?

DRISCOLL (*looking down at the box*). How'll we be openin' this, I wonder?

SCOTTY (*from the doorway—warningly*). He's standin' up.

DAVIS. We'll take his keys away from him when he comes in. Quick, Drisc! You an' Jack get beside the door and grab him. (*They get on either side of the door.* DAVIS *snatches a small coil of rope from one of the upper bunks*) This'll do for me an' Scotty to tie him.

SCOTTY. He's turrnin' this way—he's comin'! (*He moves away from door.*)

DAVIS. Stand by to lend a hand, Cocky.

COCKY. Righto. (*As* SMITTY *enters the forecastle he is seized roughly from both sides and his arms pinned behind him. At first he struggles fiercely, but seeing the uselessness of this, he finally stands calmly and allows* DAVIS *and* SCOTTY *to tie up his arms.*)

SMITTY (*when they have finished—with cold contempt*). If this is your idea of a joke I'll have to confess it's a bit too thick for me to enjoy.

COCKY (*angrily*). Shut yer marf, 'ear!

DRISCOLL (*roughly*). Ye'll find ut's no joke, me bucko, b'fore we're done wid you. (*To* SCOTTY) Kape your eye peeled, Scotty, and sing out if any one's comin'. (SCOTTY *resumes his post at the door.*)

SMITTY (*with the same icy contempt*). If you'd be good enough to explain——

DRISCOLL (*furiously*). Explain, is ut? 'Tis you'll do the explainin'—an' damn quick, or we'll know the reason why. (*To* JACK *and* DAVIS) Bring him here, now. (*They push* SMITTY *over to the bucket*) Look here, ye murrdherin' swab. D'you see ut? (SMITTY *looks down with an expression of amazement which rapidly changes to one of anguish.*)

DAVIS (*with a sneer*). Look at him! S'prised, ain't you? If you wants to try your dirty spyin' tricks on us you've gotter git up earlier in the mornin'.

COCKY. Thorght yer weren't 'arf a fox, didn't yer?

SMITTY (*trying to restrain his growing rage*). What—what do you mean? That's only—How dare— What are you doing with my private belongings?

COCKY (*sarcastically*). Ho yus! Private b'longings!

DRISCOLL (*shouting*). What is ut, ye swine? Will you tell us to our faces? What's in ut?

SMITTY (*biting his lips—holding himself in check with a great effort*). Nothing but—— That's my business. You'll please attend to your own.

DRISCOLL. Oho, ut is, is ut? (*Shaking his fist in* SMITTY's *face*) Talk aisy now if ye know what's best for you. Your business, indade! Then we'll be makin' ut ours, I'm thinkin'. (*To* JACK *and* DAVIS) Take his keys away from him an' we'll see if there's one'll open ut, maybe. (*They start in searching* SMITTY, *who tries to resist and kicks out at the bucket.* DRISCOLL *leaps forward and helps them push him away*) Try to kick ut over, wud ye? Did ye see him then? Tryin' to murrdher us all, the scut! Take that pail out av his way, Cocky. (SMITTY *struggles with all of his strength and keeps them busy for a few seconds. As* COCKY *grabs the pail* SMITTY *makes a final effort and, lunging forward, kicks again* at the bucket but only succeeds in hitting COCKY *on the shin.* COCKY *immediately sets down the pail with a bang and, clutching his knee in both hands, starts hopping around the forecastle, groaning and swearing.*)

COCKY. Ooow! Gawd strike me pink! Kicked me, 'e did! Bloody, bleedin', rotten Dutch 'og! (*Approaching* SMITTY, *who has given up the fight and is pushed back against the wall near the doorway with* JACK *and* DAVIS *holding him on either side— wrathfully, at the top of his lungs*) Kick me, will yer? I'll show yer what for, yer bleedin' sneak! (*He draws back his fist.* DRISCOLL *pushes him to one side.*)

DRISCOLL. Shut your mouth! D'you want to wake the whole ship? (COCKY *grumbles and retires to a bench, nursing his sore shin.*)

JACK (*taking a small bunch of keys from* SMITTY's *pocket*). Here yuh are, Drisc.

DRISCOLL (*taking them*). We'll soon be knowin'. (*He takes the pail and sits down, placing it on the floor between his feet.* SMITTY *again tries to break loose but he is too tired and is easily held back against the wall.*)

SMITTY (*breathing heavily and very pale*). Cowards!

JACK (*with a growl*). Nix on the rough talk, see! That don't git yuh nothin'.

DRISCOLL (*looking at the lock on the box in the water and then scrutinizing the keys in his hand*). This'll be ut, I'm thinkin'. (*He selects one and gingerly reaches his hand in the water.*)

SMITTY (*his face grown livid—chokingly*). Don't you open that box, Driscoll. If you do, so help me God, I'll kill you if I have to hang for it.

DRISCOLL (*pausing—his hand in the water*). Whin I open this box I'll not be the wan to be kilt, me sonny bye! I'm no dirty spy.

SMITTY (*his voice trembling with rage. His eyes are fixed on DRIS-COLL's hand*). Spy? What are you talking about? I only put that box there so I could get it quick in case we were torpedoed. Are you all mad? Do you think I'm—— (*Chokingly*) You stupid curs! You cowardly dolts!
(DAVIS *claps his hand over* SMITTY's *mouth.*)

DAVIS. That'll be enough from you! (DRISCOLL *takes the dripping box from the water and starts to fit in the key.* SMITTY *springs forward furiously, almost escaping from their grasp, and drags them after him half-way across the forecastle.*)

DRISCOLL. Hold him, ye divils! (*He puts the box back in the water and jumps to their aid.* COCKY *hovers on the outskirts of the battle, mindful of the kick he received.*)

SMITTY (*raging*). Cowards! Damn you! Rotten curs! (*He is thrown to the floor and held there*) Cowards! Cowards!

DRISCOLL. I'll shut your dirty mouth for you. (*He goes to his bunk and pulls out a big wad of waste and comes back to* SMITTY.)

SMITTY. Cowards! Cowards!

DRISCOLL (*with no gentle hand slaps the waste over* SMITTY's *mouth*). That'll teach you to be misnamin' a man, ye sneak. Have ye a handkerchief, Jack? (JACK *hands him one and he ties it tightly around* SMITTY's *head over the waste*) That'll fix your gab. Stand him up, now, and tie his feet, too, so he'll not be movin'. (*They do so and leave him with his back against the wall near* SCOTTY. *Then they all sit down beside* DRISCOLL, *who again lifts the box out of the water and sets it carefully on his knees. He picks out the key, then hesitates, looking from one to the other uncertainly*) We'd best be takin' this to the skipper, d'you think, maybe?

JACK (*irritably*). To hell with the Old Man. This is our game and we c'n play it without no help.

COCKY. Now bleedin' horficers, I says!

DAVIS. They'd only be takin' all the credit and makin' heroes of theyselves.

DRISCOLL (*boldly*). Here goes, thin! (*He slowly turns the key in the lock. The others instinctively turn away. He carefully pushes the cover back on its hinges and looks at what he sees inside with an expression of puzzled astonishment. The others crowd up close. Even* SCOTTY *leaves his post to take a look*) What is ut, Davis?

DAVIS (*mystified*). Looks funny, don't it? Somethin' square tied up in a rubber bag. Maybe it's dynamite—or somethin'—you can't never tell.

JACK. Aw, it ain't got no works so it ain't no bomb, I'll bet.

DAVIS (*dubiously*). They makes them all kinds, they do.

JACK. Open it up, Drisc.

DAVIS. Careful now!

(DRISCOLL *takes a black rubber bag resembling a large tobacco pouch from the box and unties the string which is wound tightly around the top. He opens it and takes out a small packet of letters also tied up with string. He turns these over in his hands and looks at the others questioningly.*)

JACK (*with a broad grin*). On'y letters! (*Slapping* DAVIS *on the back*) Yuh're a hell of a Sherlock Holmes, ain't yuh? Letters from his best girl too, I'll bet. Let's turn the Duke loose, what d'yuh say? (*He starts to get up.*)

DAVIS (*fixing him with a withering look*). Don't be so damn smart, Jack. Letters, you says, 's if there never was no harm in 'em. How d'you s'pose spies gets their orders and sends back what they finds out if it ain't by letters and such things? There's many a letter is worser'n any bomb.

COCKY. Righto! They ain't as inner-cent as they looks, I'll take me oath, when you read 'em. (*Pointing at* SMITTY) Not 'is Lordship's letters; not be no means!

JACK (*sitting down again*). Well, read 'em and find out.

(DRISCOLL *commences untying the packet. There is a muffled groan of rage and protest from* SMITTY.)

DAVIS (*triumphantly*). There! Listen to him! Look at him tryin' to git loose! Ain't that proof enough? He knows well we're findin' him out. Listen to me! Love letters, you says, Jack, 's if they couldn't harm nothin'. Listen! I was reading in some magazine in New York on'y two weeks back how some German spy in Paris was writin' love letters to some woman spy in Switzerland who sent 'em on to Berlin Germany. To read 'em you wouldn't s'pect nothin'—just mush and all. (*Impressively*) But they had a way o' doin' it—a damn sneakin' way. They had a piece o' plain paper with pieces cut out of it an' when they puts it on top o' the letter they sees on'y the words what tells them what they wants to know. An' the Frenchies gets beat in a fight all on account o' that letter.

COCKY (*awed*). Gawd blimey! They ain't 'arf smart bleeders!

DAVIS (*seeing his audience is again all with him*). An' even if these letters of his do sound all right they may have what they calls a code. You can't never tell. (*To* DRISCOLL, *who has finished untying the packet*) Read one of 'em, Drisc. My eyes is weak.

DRISCOLL (*takes the first one out of its envelope and bends down to the lantern with it. He turns up the wick to give him a better light*). I'm no hand to be readin' but I'll try ut. (*Again there is a muffled groan from* SMITTY *as he strains at his bonds.*)

DAVIS (*gloatingly*). Listen to him! He knows. Go ahead, Drisc.

DRISCOLL (*his brow furrowed with concentration*). Ut begins: Dearest Man—— (*His eyes travel down the page*) An' thin there's a lot av

blarney tellin' him how much she misses him now she's gone away to singin' school—an' how she hopes he'll settle down to rale worrk an' not be skylarkin' around now that she's away loike he used to before she met up wid him—and ut ends: "I love you betther than anythin' in the worrld. You know that, don't you, dear? But b'fore I can agree to live out my life wid you, you must prove to me that the black shadow —I won't menshun uts hateful name but you know what I mean—which might wreck both our lives, does not exist for you. You can do that, can't you, dear? Don't you see you must for my sake?" (*He pauses for a moment—then adds gruffly*) Uts signed: "Edith."
(*At the sound of the name* SMITTY, *who has stood tensely with his eyes shut as if he were undergoing torture during the reading, makes a muffled sound like a sob and half turns his face to the wall.*)

JACK (*sympathetically*). Hell! What's the use of readin' that stuff even if——

DAVIS (*interrupting him sharply*). Wait! Where's that letter from, Drisc?

DRISCOLL. There's no address on the top av ut.

DAVIS (*meaningly*). What'd I tell you? Look at the postmark, Drisc, —on the envelope.

DRISCOLL. The name that's written is Sidney Davidson, wan hundred an'——

DAVIS. Never mind that. O' course it's a false name. Look at the postmark.

DRISCOLL. There's a furrin stamp on ut by the looks av ut. The mark's blurred so it's hard to read. (*He spells it out laboriously*) B-e-r—the nixt is an l, I think—i—an' an n.

DAVIS (*excitedly*). Berlin! What did I tell you? I knew them letters was from Germany.

COCKY (*shaking his fist in* SMITTY's *direction*). Rotten 'ound!
(*The others look at* SMITTY *as if this last fact had utterly condemned him in their eyes.*)

DAVIS. Give me the letter, Drisc. Maybe I kin make somethin' out of it. (DRISCOLL *hands the letter to him*) You go through the others, Drisc, and sing out if you sees anythin' queer. (*He bends over the first letter as if he were determined to figure out its secret meaning.* JACK, COCKY *and* SCOTTY *look over his shoulder with eager curiosity.* DRISCOLL *takes out some of the other letters, running his eyes quickly down the pages. He looks curiously over at* SMITTY *from time to time, and sighs frequently with a puzzled frown.*)

DAVIS (*disappointedly*). I gotter give it up. It's too deep for me, but we'll turn 'em over to the perlice when we docks at Liverpool to look through. This one I got was written a year before the war started, anyway. Find anythin' in yours, Drisc?

DRISCOLL. They're all the same as the first—lovin' blarney, an' how her singin' is doin' and the great things the Dutch teacher rays about her voice, an' how glad she is that her Sidney bye is worrkin' harrd an' makin' a man av himself for her sake.

(SMITTY *turns his face completely to the wall.*)

DAVIS (*disgustedly*). If we on'y had the code!

DRISCOLL (*taking up the bottom letter*). Hullo! Here's wan addressed to this ship—s. s. Glencairn, ut says —whin we was in Cape Town sivin months ago—— (*Looking at the postmark*) Ut's from London.

DAVIS (*eagerly*). Read it!
(*There is another choking groan from* SMITTY.)

DRISCOLL (*reads slowly—his voice becomes lower and lower as he goes on*). Ut begins wid simply the name Sidney Davidson—no dearest or sweetheart to this wan. "Ut is only from your chance meetin' with Harry—whin you were drunk— that I happen to know where to reach you. So you have run away to sea loike the coward you are be- cause you knew I had found out the truth—the truth you have covered over with your mean little lies all the time I was away in Berlin and blindly trusted you. Very well, you have chosen. You have shown that your drunkenness means more to you than any love or faith av mine. I am sorry—for I loved you, Sid- ney Davidson—but this is the end. I lave you—the mem'ries; an' if ut is any satisfaction to you I lave you the real-i-zation that you have wrecked my loife as you have wrecked your own. My one re- mainin' hope is that nivir in God's worrld will I ivir see your face again. Good-by. Edith." (*As he finishes there is a deep silence, broken only by* SMITTY'S *muffled*

sobbing. *The men cannot look at each other.* DRISCOLL *holds the rub- ber bag limply in his hand and some small white object falls out of it and drops noiselessly on the floor. Me- chanically* DRISCOLL *leans over and picks it up, and looks at it wonder- ingly.*)

DAVIS (*in a dull voice*). What's that?

DRISCOLL (*slowly*). A bit av a dried-up flower—a rose, maybe. (*He drops it into the bag and gath- ers up the letters and puts them back. He replaces the bag in the box, and locks it and puts it back under* SMITTY'S *mattress. The others follow him with their eyes. He steps softly over to* SMITTY *and cuts the ropes about his arms and ankles with his sheath knife, and unties the handkerchief over the gag.* SMITTY *does not turn around but covers his face with his hands and leans his head against the wall. His shoulders continue to heave spas- modically but he makes no further sound.*)

DRISCOLL (*stalks back to the others —there is a moment of silence, in which each man is in agony with the hopelessness of finding a word he can say—then* DRISCOLL *ex- plodes*) God stiffen us, are we never goin' to turn in fur a wink av sleep?
(*They all start as if awakening from a bad dream and gratefully crawl into their bunks, shoes and all, turning their faces to the wall, and pulling their blankets up over their shoulders.* SCOTTY *tiptoes past* SMITTY *out into the darkness . . .* DRISCOLL *turns down the light and crawls into his bunk as*)

THE CURTAIN FALLS

If Men Played Cards as Women Do

A COMEDY IN ONE ACT

BY GEORGE S. KAUFMAN

CHARACTERS

JOHN
BOB
MARC
GEORGE

IF MEN PLAYED CARDS
AS WOMEN DO

SCENE—*The scene is* JOHN's *home.*

NOTE—*It is suggested that, prior to the rise of the curtain, a* PAGE *appear from each side of the stage, bearing a card on which is printed the title of the sketch. They cross, and exit on opposite sides.*

The scene is JOHN's *home—the living room. There are two doors, one leading to an outside hall, the other to the other rooms of the house. A card table has been set up in the middle of the room, with four chairs around it, and above it is another table on which are piled the necessary adjuncts for a poker game—a fancy cover for the table, cards, chips, a humidor. For the rest, you have only to imagine an average and good-looking room.*

RISE—*As the curtain rises,* JOHN *enters from another room, then turns and calls back through the open door, as though he had forgotten something.*

IMPERTINENCE FROM THE AUTHOR—*It is perhaps unnecessary to remark that the sketch derives its entire value from the fact that it is played in forthright and manly fashion. In other words, the actors must not imitate the voices of women.*

JOHN. And don't forget, I want things served very nicely. Use the best china and the filigree doilies. (*He starts to close the door—remembers another instruction*) And at eleven o'clock just put the cigars and drinks right on the table and we'll stop playing. (*He closes the door and advances into the room. He looks the place over; rubs a suspecting finger along the table top in a quest for dust. He moves one chair a fraction of an inch and seems to think that that makes a difference in the appearance of the room. Then there comes a knock on the outer door.* JOHN *darts to the mirror and takes a quick look at himself; adjusts his tie*) Come in! (BOB *enters*) Hello, Bob!

BOB. Hello, John! I thought I'd run over early to see if I could help you with the lunch.

JOHN. Thanks—everything is ready. I baked a cake. Oh, say! That's a new hat, isn't it?

BOB. Why, no—don't you remember? It's the one I got at Knox's in the Spring. Then when they began wearing the bands higher, I said to myself, why should I buy a new hat when I can have a man in and get him to put on another band for me, just as easily as not? Do you like it?

JOHN. Very attractive. I wonder how it would look on me? (*Takes it; starts to try it on, then smooths his hair before he finally puts it on. He looks at himself in the mirror; turns*) What do you think?

BOB. Lovely! Makes your face look thinner. (*Looks at the card table*) Who's playing tonight?

JOHN. George and Marc.

423

BOB. Really? (*He takes his seat*) Tell me—don't you think George is looking older these days? How are he and Ethel getting along? Any better?

JOHN. Not as good.

BOB. Funny what she saw in him. (*There is a knock on the door.*)

JOHN. Come in! (GEORGE *enters.*)

GEORGE (*greatly surprised, as though they were the last people he had expected to see*). Hello, boys!

JOHN. Hello, George! Well, well, well!

BOB (*rises*). Hello, George! Never saw you look so young!

GEORGE (*in great excitement*). Say, I just met Ed Jennings down the street and what do you think? He says Jim Perkins told him that Will Harper's wife may leave him!

BOB. You don't say so! (*Sits again.*)

GEORGE. What do you think of that? (*His excitement dies a little; he looks around*) The room looks lovely, John. You've changed things around, haven't you? Awfully nice. But if you don't mind just a little suggestion—I'm not sure that I like that table up there where you've got it. (*Another critical look*) And if you had these chairs re-uphol-stered in blue——

JOHN. Well, what do you think of a plain chintz?

GEORGE. That would be nice. Oh, say! I've got a T. L. for you, Bob.

BOB. Oh, good! What is it?

GEORGE. Well, you owe me one first.

BOB. Oh, tell me mine! Don't be mean!

GEORGE. Well, all right. Frank Williams said you looked lovely in your dinner coat.

BOB. That *is* nice.

JOHN. How's the baby, George?

GEORGE. Awfully cranky lately. He's teething. I left him with the nurse tonight—first chance I've had to get out. (*Takes a seat at the table*) Who else is coming?

JOHN. Just Marc.

GEORGE (*with meaning*). Oh, is he? I want to speak to you boys about Marc. Don't you think he's been seeing a lot of that Fleming woman lately?

BOB. He certainly has. He was at the Biltmore, having tea with her yesterday—I know because a cousin of Tom Hennessey's saw him.

JOHN. Which cousin is that?

BOB. I don't know whether you know him—Ralph Wilson. He married that Akron girl—they have two children.

GEORGE. *You* remember—one of them is backward.

JOHN. Oh, yes! I heard that. (*Another knock on the door.*) Come in! (MARC *enters.*)

MARC. Hello, everybody!

GEORGE, JOHN *and* BOB. Hello, Marc!

MARC. I'm sorry to be the last, but we have a new maid, and you know what that means.

JOHN. That's all right. Say, I like the cut of that vest, Marc. Look, boys! Don't you like that vest?

MARC. It is nice, isn't it?

GEORGE. Oh, lovely! Turn around and let's see the back.
(GEORGE *and* JOHN *both get up and examine his clothes, pull down his trousers, etc.*)

MARC. I had it made right in the house—I have a little tailor that comes in. Four dollars a day.

GEORGE. Excuse me—there's a little spot—— (*He moistens a finger and rubs* MARC's *lapel.*)

JOHN. Well, shall we play a little poker?

MARC (*sitting*). Yes, sure. Oh, John, may I trouble you for a glass of water?

JOHN. Why, of course, Marc. (GEORGE *and* BOB *sit again.*)

MARC. I'll get it myself if you'll tell me where—

JOHN. Oh, no—that's all right. (*He goes out. A pause. The men look at each other, meaningly. Their heads come together.*)

MARC. John doesn't look well, does he?

BOB. No. Did you notice those lines? He can't hide them much longer.

MARC. He was very good-looking as a boy.

GEORGE. Isn't this room the most terrible thing you ever saw?
(MARC *goes to the table up stage; picks up a cigar and shows it to the others. They are scornful.*)

MARC. Huh! Ten cents. (*Pause*) I really wanted to get that water myself. I'd like to see his kitchen. (JOHN *re-enters with the water*) Oh, thanks, John. (MARC *drinks.*)

JOHN. Is it cold enough, Marc?

MARC (*indicating that it isn't*). Oh, yes. Of course, I generally put ice in, myself. (*Sits.*)

GEORGE. Say, we had the loveliest new dessert tonight!

BOB. Oh! What was it? It's awfully hard to find a new dessert.

MARC (*with emphasis*). Is it?

GEORGE. Well, it was a sort of prune whip. You make it out of just nothing at all. And then, if company comes when you don't expect them——

BOB. I want the recipe.

MARC. How many eggs?
(JOHN *up at the rear table. Turns on this speech.*)

JOHN. Does it take much butter?

GEORGE. Oh, no—very little. I'll bring you the recipe Tuesday afternoon.
(MARC *feels a rough place on his chin. Rubs it, then takes a good-sized mirror out of his pocket and*

stands it on the table. Examines his chin. Then takes out a safety razor and starts to shave. After that he takes out two military brushes and combs his hair. The others pay no attention to this. JOHN *is at the rear table, with his back to the audience;* BOB *is seated, fooling with the cards;* GEORGE *is seated, calmly smoking. After* MARC *has put everything away,* BOB *breaks the silence.*)

BOB. Are we ready?

JOHN. No! Wait just a minute. (*He brings down the fancy table cover, which he spreads on the table*) There we are!

MARC (*feeling it*). That's nice, John. Where'd you get it?

JOHN. Why, I bought a yard of this plain sateen down at Macy's——

GEORGE. Really? How much was it?

JOHN. A dollar sixty-three. It was reduced. Then I had this edging in the house.

BOB. Awfully nice!

MARC. Oh, say! Walter Sharp just got back from Paris——

GEORGE. He did?

MARC. Yes. And *he* says they're wearing trousers longer over there.

GEORGE. Really?
(*There is quite a fuss about it.*)

JOHN (*brings chips and takes his seat*). What'll we play for?

BOB. Oh, what's the difference? One cent limit?

GEORGE. Does it matter who deals? (*Takes the cards from* BOB.)

MARC. Say, did you hear about Eddie Parker?

JOHN. No.

MARC. Well, it seems he saw these advertisements about how to get thin, and he thought he'd try them. You know Eddie's taken on a lot of weight since his marriage.

GEORGE. Twenty pounds—absolutely.

MARC. Well, they sent him some powders and he began taking them, and what do you think?

GEORGE. Well? (MARC *whispers to him*) You don't say so?

JOHN *and* BOB (*excited*). What was it? What was it?
(GEORGE *whispers to* JOHN, *who whispers to* BOB; *great excitement.*)

MARC. Who has the cards?

GEORGE. Here they are. (*Starts to deal—poker hands.*)

MARC. I don't want to play late. I've been shopping all day.

GEORGE. And I have an appointment at the barber's tomorrow. I'm going to try a new way of getting my hair cut.
(*The deal is completed.*)

BOB (*picking up a few cards*). Which is higher—aces or kings?

GEORGE. Now, who bets first?

JOHN. Are these funny little things clubs?

MARC. What are the chips worth?

JOHN. Let's have them all worth the same thing.

BOB. A penny apiece. . . .

GEORGE. Say, Lord & Taylor are having a wonderful sale of nightgowns!

MARC. What do you pay your maid?

BOB. Sixty-five, but she isn't worth it.
(*The three start talking at once about maids, and* JOHN *has a hard time being heard.*)

JOHN (*excited*). Boys! Boys! Listen to this! Boys!

ALL. Well?

JOHN (*excited*). I *knew* there was something I wanted to tell you!

ALL (*they must not speak together*). What is it?

JOHN. Well, now in the first place you must promise not to breathe a word of it to anybody, because I got it in absolute confidence and I promised I wouldn't tell.

GEORGE. What is it?

MARC. Well?

BOB. Well?

JOHN. It's about Sid Heflin! Now, you won't tell anybody? At least, don't let on you got it from me!

ALL. No!

JOHN. Well, I'm told—and I got this pretty straight, mind you—I'm told that he's going to—ah——— (*He puts the message across with his eyes.*)

MARC. I don't believe it!

BOB. What do you mean?

GEORGE. When?

JOHN. In April!

MARC. April!
(*They count on their fingers, up to four.*)

GEORGE. What do you mean?

JOHN. Exactly! They were married late in January!
(*They all throw down their hands and begin talking at once.*)

CURTAIN

Another Way Out

A COMEDY

BY LAWRENCE LANGNER

CHARACTERS

Margaret Marshall
Mrs. Abbey
Pomeroy Pendleton
Baroness de Meauville
Charles P. K. Fenton

Time: *The Present.*

ANOTHER WAY OUT

Scene—*The studio in* PENDLETON's *apartment. A large room, with sky-light in center wall, doors right and left, table set for breakfast; a vase with red flowers decorates the table. Center back stage, in front of sky-light, modeling stand upon which is placed a rough statuette, covered by cloth. To one side of this is a large screen. The furnishings are many hued, the cushions a flare of color, and the pictures fantastically futuristic.*

At Rise: MRS. ABBEY, *a benevolent-looking, middle-aged woman, in neat clothes and apron, is arranging some dishes on the table.* MARGARET, *a very modern young woman, is exercising vigorously. She is decidedly good-looking. Her eyes are direct, her complexion fresh, and her movements free. Her brown hair is "bobbed," and she wears a picturesque Grecian robe.*

MRS. ABBEY. Breakfast is ready, ma'am.

(MARGARET *sits at table and helps herself. Exit* MRS. ABBEY, *left.*)

MARGARET (*calling*). Pommy dear. Breakfast is on the table.

PENDLETON (*from without*). I'll be there in a moment.

(MARGARET *glances through paper;* PENDLETON *enters, door right. He is tall and thin, and of æsthetic appearance. His long blond hair is brushed loosely over his forehead and he is dressed in a heliotrope-colored dressing gown. He lights a cigarette.*)

MARGARET. I thought you were going to stop smoking before breakfast.

PENDLETON. My dear, I can't possibly stand the taste of tooth paste in my mouth all day. (PENDLETON *sits at table. Enters* MRS. ABBEY *with tray.* PENDLETON *helps himself, then drops his knife and fork with a clang.* MRS. ABBEY *and* MARGARET *are startled.*)

MRS. ABBEY. Anything the matter, sir?

PENDLETON. Dear, dear! My breakfast is quite spoiled again.

MRS. ABBEY (*concerned*). Spoiled, sir?

PENDLETON (*pointing to red flowers on breakfast table*). Look at those flowers, Mrs. Abbey. Not only are they quite out of harmony with the color scheme in this room, but they're positively red, and you know I have a perfect horror of red.

MRS. ABBEY. But you like them that color sometimes, sir. What am I to do when you're so temperamental about 'em?

MARGARET. Temperamental. I should say bad-tempered.

MRS. ABBEY (*soothingly*). Oh no, ma'am. It isn't bad temper. I understand Mr. Pendleton. It's just another bad night he's had, that's what it is.

PENDLETON (*sarcastically polite*). Mrs. Abbey, you appear to have an intimate knowledge of how I pass the nights. It's becoming quite embarrassing.

MRS. ABBEY. You mustn't mind an old woman like me, sir.

(*The sound of a piano hopelessly out of tune, in the apartment upstairs, is heard, the player banging out Mendelssohn's Wedding March with unusual insistence.*)

PENDLETON. There! That confounded piano again!

MARGARET. And they always play the Wedding March. There must be an old maid living there.

MRS. ABBEY. They're doing that for a reason.

MARGARET. What reason?

MRS. ABBEY. Their cook told me yesterday that her missus thinks if she keeps on a-playing of the Wedding March, p'raps it'll give you an' Mr. Pendleton the idea of getting married. She don't believe in couples livin' together, like you an' Mr. Pendleton.

MARGARET. No?

MRS. ABBEY. And I just said you an' Mr. Pendleton had been living together so long, it was my opinion you might just as well be married an' done with it.

MARGARET (*angrily*). Your opinion is quite uncalled for, Mrs. Abbey.

PENDLETON. Why shouldn't Mrs. Abbey give us her opinion? It may be valuable. Look at her experiences in matrimony.

MRS. ABBEY. In matrimony, and out of it, too.

MARGARET (*sitting*). But Mrs. Abbey has no right to discuss our affairs with other people's maids.

MRS. ABBEY. I'll be glad to quit if I don't suit the mistress.

MARGARET (*angrily*). There! Mistress again! How often have I asked you not to refer to me as the mistress?

MRS. ABBEY. No offense, ma'am.

PENDLETON. You'd better see if there's any mail, Mrs. Abbey, and take those flowers away with you.

MRS. ABBEY. Very well, sir. (*Exit.*)

MARGARET. What an old-fashioned point of view Mrs. Abbey has. (PENDLETON *takes up paper and commences to read.*)

MARGARET. Pommy, why do you stoop so?

PENDLETON. Am I stooping?

MARGARET. I'm tired of telling you. You ought to take more exercise. (PENDLETON *continues to read.*)

MARGARET. One reason why the Greeks were the greatest of artists was because they cultivated the body as carefully as the mind.

PENDLETON. Oh! Hang the Greeks! (*Enter* MRS. ABBEY *right, with letters.*)

MRS. ABBEY. There are your letters, sir. (*Coldly*) And these are yours, ma'am. (*Exit* MRS. ABBEY *left.*)

MARGARET (*who has opened her letters meanwhile*). How delightful! Tom Del Valli has asked us to a party at his studio next Friday.

PENDLETON (*opening his letters*). Both of us?

MARGARET (*giving him letter*). Yes, and Helen Marsden wants us for Saturday.

PENDLETON. Both of us?

MARGARET (*picking up another letter*). Yes, and here's one from Bobby Watson for Sunday.

PENDLETON. Both of us?

MARGARET. Yes.

PENDLETON. Really, Margaret, this is becoming exasperating. (*Holds up letters*) Here are four more, I suppose for both of us. People keep on inviting us out together time after time as though we were the most conventional married couple on God's earth.

MARGARET. Do you object to going out with me?

PENDLETON (*doubtfully*). No, it isn't that. But we're having too much of a good thing. And I've come to the conclusion that it's your fault.

MARGARET (*indignantly*). Oh! it's my fault? Of course you'd blame me. Why?

PENDLETON. Because you have such an absurd habit of boasting to people of your devotion for me, when we're out.

MARGARET. You surely don't expect me to quarrel with you in public?

PENDLETON. It isn't necessary to go to that extent. But then everybody believes that we're utterly, almost stupidly in love with one another, what can you expect?

MARGARET. You said once you never wanted me to suppress anything.

PENDLETON. That was before we began to live together.

MARGARET. What could I have done?

PENDLETON (*stands up*). Anything just so we could have a little more freedom instead of being tied to one another the way we are. Never a moment when we're not together, never a day when I'm not interviewed by special article writers from almost every paper and magazine in the country, as the only successful exponent of the theory that love can be so perfect that the marriage contract degrades it. I put it to you, Margaret, if this is a free union it is simply intolerable!

MARGARET. But aren't we living together so as to have more freedom? Think of what it might be if we were married. Didn't you once write that "When marriage comes in at the door, freedom flies out at the window"?

PENDLETON. Are we any better off, with everybody treating us as though we were living together to prove a principle?

MARGARET. Well, aren't we, incidentally? You said so yourself. We can be a beautiful example to other people, and show them how to lead the pure natural lives of the later Greeks?

PENDLETON. Damn the later Greeks! Why do you always throw those confounded later Greeks in my face? We've got to look at it from our standpoint. This situation must come to an end.

MARGARET. What can we do?

PENDLETON. It rests with you.

MARGARET. With me?

PENDLETON. You can compromise yourself with somebody publicly. That'll put an end to everything.

MARGARET. How will that end it?

PENDLETON. It'll break down the morally sanctified atmosphere in which we're living. Then perhaps, people will regard us as immoral and treat us like decent human beings again.

MARGARET. But I don't want to compromise myself.

PENDLETON. If you believe in your own ideas, you must.

MARGARET. But why should I have to do it?

PENDLETON. It will be so easy for you.

MARGARET. Why can't we both be compromised? That would be better still.

PENDLETON. I should find it a bore. You, unless my memory fails me, would enjoy it.

MARGARET. You needn't be cynical. Even if you don't enjoy it, you can work it into a novel.

PENDLETON. It's less exertion to imagine an affair of that sort, and the result would probably be more sale-able. Besides I have no interest whatsoever in women, at least, in the women we know.

MARGARET. For that matter, I don't know any eligible men.

PENDLETON. What about Bob Lockwood?

MARGARET. But he's your best friend!

PENDLETON. Exactly—no man ever really trusts his best friend. He'll probably compromise you without compunction.

MARGARET. I'm afraid he'd be too dangerous—he tells you all his secrets. Whom will you choose?

PENDLETON. It's a matter of complete indifference to me.

MARGARET. I've heard a lot of queer stories about Jean Roberts. How would she do?

PENDLETON (firmly). Margaret, I don't mind being party to a flirtation —but I draw the line at being the victim of a seduction.

MARGARET. Why not leave it to chance? Let it be the next interesting woman you meet.

PENDLETON. That might be amusing. But there must be an age limit. And how about you?

MARGARET (takes cloth off statuette and discloses figure of Apollo in rough modeling clay). Me! Why not the new model who is coming today to pose for my Apollo?

PENDLETON. Well, if he's anything

like that, you ought to be able to create a sensation. Then, perhaps, we shall have some real freedom.

MARGARET. Pommy, do you still love me as much as you did?

PENDLETON. How you sentimentalize! Do you think I'd be willing to enter into a flirtation with a strange woman, if I didn't want to keep on living with you?

MARGARET. And we won't have to break up our little home, will we?

PENDLETON. No, anything to save the home. (*Catches himself*) My God! If any of my readers should hear me say that! To think that I, Pomeroy Pendleton, should be trying to save my own home. And yet, how characteristically paradoxical!

MARGARET (*interrupting*). You are going to philosophize! Give me a kiss. (*She goes to him, sits on his lap, and places her arm on his shoulder; he takes out cigarette; she lights it for him.*)

PENDLETON (*brought back to reality*). I have some work to do—I must go.

MARGARET. A kiss!

PENDLETON (*kisses her carelessly*). There let me go.

MARGARET. I want a real kiss.

PENDLETON. Don't be silly, dear, I can't play this morning. I've simply got to finish my last chapter. (*A bell rings.* MRS. ABBEY *enters and goes to door.*)

MRS. ABBEY. There's a lady to see Mr. Pendleton.

MARGARET. Tell her to come in!

PENDLETON. But, Margaret!

MARGARET. Remember! (*Significantly*) The first woman you meet! (*Exit* MARGARET. MRS. ABBEY *enters with* BARONESS DE MEAUVILLE. *Exit* MRS. ABBEY.)

BARONESS DE MEAUVILLE (*speaking with a pronounced English accent*). Good morning, Mr. Pendleton, I'm the Baroness de Meauville!

PENDLETON (*recalling her name*). Baroness de Meauville? Ah, the costumiere?

BARONESS. Not a costumiere, Mr. Pendleton, I am an artist, an artist in modern attire. A woman is to me what a canvas is to a painter.

PENDLETON. Excuse me for receiving you in my dressing gown. I was at work.

BARONESS. I like to see men in dressing gowns—yours is charming.

PENDLETON (*flattered and pleased*). Do you like it? I designed it myself.

BARONESS (*looking seductively into his eyes*). How few really creative artists there are in America.

PENDLETON (*modestly*). You flatter me.

BARONESS. Not at all. You must know that I'm a great admirer of yours, Mr. Pendleton. I've read every one of your books. I feel I know you as an old friend.

PENDLETON. That's very nice of you!

(*The* BARONESS *reclines on couch; takes jeweled cigarette case from reticule and offers* PENDLETON *a cigarette.*)

BARONESS. Will you smoke?

PENDLETON. Thanks. (PENDLETON *lights her cigarette, then his own. He draws his chair up to the couch. An atmosphere of mutual interest is established.*)

BARONESS. Mr. Pendleton, I have a mission in life. It is to make the American woman the best-dressed woman in the world. I came here today because I want you to help me.

PENDLETON. But I have no ambitions in that direction.

BARONESS. Why should you have ambitions? Only the bourgeoisie have ambitions. We artists have inspirations. I want to breathe into you the spirit of my great undertaking. Already I have opened my place in the smartest part of the Avenue. Already I have drawn my assistants from all parts of the world. Nothing is lacking to complete my plans but you.

PENDLETON. Me? Why me?

BARONESS (*endearingly*). Are you not considered one of the foremost men of letters in America?

PENDLETON (*modestly*). Didn't you say you had read all my books?

BARONESS. Are you not the only writer who has successfully portrayed the emotional side of American life?

PENDLETON (*decidedly*). Yes.

BARONESS. Exactly. That is why I have chosen you to write my advertisements.

PENDLETON (*aghast*). But, Baroness!

BARONESS. You're not going to say that. It's so ordinary.

PENDLETON. But, but, you want me to write advertisements!

BARONESS. Please don't disappoint me.

PENDLETON. Yes, I suppose that's so. But one has a sense of pride.

BARONESS. Art comes before Pride. Consider my feelings, an aristocrat, coming here to America and engaging in commerce, and advertising, and other dreadful things, and all for the sake of Art!

PENDLETON. But you make money out of it!

BARONESS. Only incidentally. Just as you, in writing my advertisements, would make, say ten thousand or so, as a sort of accident. But don't let us talk of money. It's perfectly revolting, isn't it? Art is Life, and I believe in Life for Art's sake. That's why I'm a success.

PENDLETON. Indeed? How interesting. Please go on.

BARONESS. When a woman comes to me for a gown, I don't measure body, why should I? I measure her mind. I find her color harmony. In a moment I can tell whether she ought to wear scarlet, mauve, taupe, magenta, or any other color, so as to fall into her proper rhythm. Every one has a rhythm, you know. (PEN-DLETON *sits on sofa*) But I don't have to explain all this to you, Mr. Pendleton. You understand it intuitively. This heliotrope you are wearing shows me at once that you are in rhythm.

PENDLETON (*thinks of* MARGARET). I'm not so sure that I am. What you say interests me. May I ask you a question?

BARONESS. Yes, but I may not answer it.

PENDLETON. Why do you wear heliotrope and the same shade as mine?

BARONESS (*with mock mystery*). You mustn't ask me that.

PENDLETON. I'm all curiosity.

BARONESS. Curiosity is dangerous.

PENDLETON. Supposing I try to find out?

BARONESS. That may be even more dangerous.

PENDLETON. I'm fond of that kind of danger.

BARONESS. Take care! I'm very fragile.

PENDLETON. Isn't heliotrope in rhythm with the faint reflection of passion?

BARONESS. How brutal of you to have said it!

PENDLETON (*coming closer to her*). I, too, am in rhythm with heliotrope.

BARONESS (*with joy*). How glad I am. Thank God you've no desire to kiss my lips.

PENDLETON. Only your finger-tips. (*They exchange kisses on finger-tips.*)

PENDLETON. Your fingers are like soft, pale, waxen tapers!

BARONESS. Your kisses are the breathings that light them into quivering flame!

PENDLETON. Exquisite—exquisite!

BARONESS (*withdrawing her hands*). *That* was a moment!

PENDLETON. We must have many such.

BARONESS. Many? That's too near too much.

PENDLETON (*feverishly*). We shall, dear lady.

BARONESS. How I adore your writings! They have made me realize the beauty of an ideal union, the love of one man for one woman at a time. Let us have such a union, you and me.

PENDLETON (*taken back*). But I live in such a union already.

BARONESS (*rising in amazement*). And only a moment ago you kissed me!

PENDLETON. Well—what of it?

BARONESS. Don't you see what we've done? You are living in one of those wonderful unions you describe in your books—and I've let you kiss me. I've committed a sacrilege.

PENDLETON. You're mistaken. It isn't a sacrilege. It's an opportunity.

BARONESS (*dramatically*). How can you say that—you whose words have inspired my deepest intimacies. No, I must go. (*Makes for the door*) I—must—go.

PENDLETON. You don't understand. I exaggerated everything so in my confounded books.

BARONESS. Please ask her to forgive me. Please tell her I thought you were married, otherwise, never, never, would I have permitted you to kiss me.

PENDLETON. What made you think I was married?

BARONESS. One often believes what one hopes.

PENDLETON. You take it too seriously. Let me explain.

BARONESS. What is there to explain? Our experience has been complete. Why spoil it by anti-climax?

PENDLETON. Am I never to see you again?

BARONESS. Who knows? If your present union should end, and some day your soul needs—some one? (*Exit door center, her manner full of promise.*)

PENDLETON (*with feeling*). Goodbye—long, pale fingers.
(*Enter* MARGARET, *door right.*)

MARGARET. Did you get a good start with the scandal?

PENDLETON. Not exactly. I may as well admit it was a failure through no fault of mine, of course. And now, I simply must finish that last chapter. (*He exits.* MARGARET *rings.* MRS. ABBEY *enters.*)

MARGARET. You may clear, Mrs. Abbey.

MRS. ABBEY. Very well, ma'am. (*She attends to clearing the table.*)

MARGARET. Mrs. Abbey, have you worked for many people living together, like Mr. Pendleton and myself?

MRS. ABBEY. Lor', Ma'am, yes. I've worked in nearly every house on the south side of Washington Square.

MARGARET. Mr. Pendleton says I'm as domestic as any wife could be. Were the others like me?

MRS. ABBEY. Most of them, ma'am, but some was regular hussies; not only a-livin' with their fellers—but havin' a good time, too. That's what I call real immoral.
(*Bell rings.* MRS. ABBEY *opens door center and passes out. Conversation with* FENTON *without is heard.* MRS. ABBEY *comes back.*)

MRS. ABBEY. A young man wants to see you, ma'am.

MARGARET. That's the new model. I'll get my working apron. (*Exit* MARGARET, *door right.* MRS. ABBEY *calls through door center.*)

MRS. ABBEY. You c'n come in. (*Enter door left,* CHARLES P. K. FENTON, *dictionary salesman. He is a strikingly handsome young man, offensively smartly dressed in a black and white check suit, gaudy tie, and white socks. His hair is brushed back from his forehead like a glossy sheath. He carries a black bag. His manner is distinctly "male."*)

MRS. ABBEY (*points to screen*). You can undress behind there.

FENTON. Undress? Say, what's this? A Turkish bath?

MRS. ABBEY. Did you expect to have a private room all to yourself?

FENTON (*looking around*). What am I to undress for?

MRS. ABBEY. The Missus will be here in a minute.

FENTON. Good night! I'm goin'. (*Makes for door.*)

MRS. ABBEY. What's the matter? Ain't you the Missus' new model?

FENTON. A model! Ha! Ha! You've sure got the wrong number this time. I'm in the dictionary line, ma'am.

MRS. ABBEY. Well, of all the impudence! You a book agent, and a-walkin' in here.

FENTON. Well, you asked me in, didn't you? Can't I see the Missus, jest for a minute?

MRS. ABBEY (*good-naturedly*). Very well. Here she is. (*Confidentially*) And I advise you to remove that Spearmint from your mouth, if you want to sell any dictionaries in this house.

FENTON (*placing hand to mouth*). Where shall I put it?

MRS. ABBEY. You'd better swallow it!
(*FENTON tries to do so, chokes, turns red, and places his hand to mouth.*)

MARGARET (*to FENTON*). I'm so glad to see you.
(*FENTON is most embarrassed. MRS. ABBEY, in surprise, attempts to explain situation.*)

MRS. ABBEY. But, ma'am—

MARGARET. You may go, Mrs. Abbey.

MRS. ABBEY. But, but, ma'am—

MARGARET (*severely*). You may go, Mrs. Abbey. (*Exit MRS. ABBEY in a huff*) I'm so glad they sent you up to see me. Won't you sit down?
(*FENTON finds it a difficult matter to handle the situation. He adopts his usual formula for an "opening," but his speech is mechanical and without conviction. MARGARET adds to the embarrassment by stepping around him and examining him with professional interest.*)

FENTON. Madam, I represent the Globe Advertising Publishing Sales Co., the largest publishers of dictionaries in the world.

MARGARET (*continuing to appraise him*). Then you're not the new model?

FENTON. No, ma'am.

MARGARET. What a pity! Never mind, go on.

FENTON. As I was saying, ma'am, I represent the Advertising Globe Publishing—I mean the Globe Publishing Sales Publishing Co., the largest publishers of dictionaries in the world. For some time past we have felt there was a demand for a new Encyclopaedic Dictionary, madam, one that would not only fill up a good deal of space in the bookshelf, making an attractive addition to the home, but also containing the most complete collection of words in the English language.

MARGARET (*who has taken a pencil and is measuring* FENTON *while he speaks;* FENTON's *discomfort is obvious. He attempts to rearrange his tie and coat, thinking she is examining him*). Please go on talking, it's so interesting.

FENTON. Statistics show that the Woman of Average Education in America, Madam, has command of but fifteen hundred words. This new dictionary, Madam (*produces book from bag*), will give you command of over eight hundred and fifty thousand.

MARGARET (*archly*). So you are a dealer in words—how perfectly romantic.

FENTON (*warming*). Most of these words, madam, are not used more than a dozen times a year. They are our Heritage from the Past. And all these words, to say nothing of the fact that the dictionary fills five inches in a book-shelf, making an attractive addition to the library, being handsomely bound in half-cloth—all these are yours, ma'am, for the price of one dollar. (*He places dictionary in her hand. She examines it.*) If you have a son, madam, the possession of this dictionary will give him an opportunity of acquiring that knowledge of our language which made Abraham Lincoln the Father of our Country. Madam, opportunity knocks at the door only once and *this* is *your* opportunity at one dollar.

MARGARET (*meaningly*). Yes, this is my opportunity! I'll buy the dictionary, and now (*sweetly*) won't you tell me your name?

FENTON (*pocketing dollar*). My name is Charles P. K. Fenton.

MARGARET. Mr. Fenton, would you mind doing me a favor?

FENTON (*looking dubiously toward the screen*). Why, I guess not, ma'am.

MARGARET. I want you to take off your coat.

FENTON (*puzzled*). You're not trying to kid me, ma'am?

MARGARET. I just want to see your development. Do you mind?

FENTON (*removes coat*). Why, no, ma'am, if that's all you want.

MARGARET. Now, bring your arm up, tighten the muscles. (*FENTON does as she bids;* MARGARET *thumps his arm approvingly*) Splendid! You must take lots of exercise, Mr. Fenton.

FENTON. Not me, ma'am. I never had no time for exercise; I got that workin' in a freight yard.

MARGARET. I suppose you think me rather peculiar, Mr. Fenton.

FENTON. You said it, Miss.

MARGARET. You see I'm a sculptress. (*Points to statuette*) This is my work.

FENTON. You made that? Gee! that's great. (*Examines statuette*) Just

like them statues at the Metropolitan.

MARGARET That figure is Apollo,
Mr. Fenton.

FENTON. Oh, Apollo.

MARGARET. I was to engage a professional model for it, but I could
never hope to get a professional as
fine a type as you. Will you pose for
it?

FENTON (aghast). Me? That feller
there without any clothes. (Dubiously) Well, I don't know. It's
kind of chilly here.

MARGARET. If I draped you, it
would spoil some of your lines.
(Seeing his hesitation) But I will if
you like.

FENTON (relieved). Ah, now you're
talking.

MARGARET. So, you'll really come?

FENTON. How about this evening?

MARGARET. Splendid! Sit down.
(FENTON does so) Mr. Fenton,
you've quite aroused my curiosity. I
know so few business men. Is your
work interesting?

FENTON. Well, I can't say it was,
until I started selling around this
neighborhood.

MARGARET. Is it difficult?

FENTON. Not if you've got personality, Miss. That's the thing, personality. If a feller hasn't got personality, he can't sell goods, that's
sure.

MARGARET. What do you mean by
personality, Mr. Fenton.

FENTON. Well, it's what sells the
goods. I don't know how else to explain it exactly. I'll look it up in the
dictionary. (Takes dictionary and
turns pages) Here it is, ma'am. Per
—per—why, it isn't in here. I guess
they don't put in words that everybody knows. We all know what personality means. It's what sells the
goods.

MARGARET. I adore a strong, virile,
masculine personality.

FENTON. I don't quite get you, madam.

MARGARET. The men I know have
so much of the feminine in them.

FENTON. Oh, "Cissies"!

MARGARET (flirtingly). They lack
the magnetic forcefulness which I
like so much in you.

FENTON. I believe you are kidding
me. Does that mean you like me?

MARGARET. That's rather an embarrassing question.

FENTON. You must or you wouldn't
let me speak to you this way.

MARGARET (archly). Never mind
whether I like you. Tell me whether
you like me?

FENTON (feeling more at home).
Gee! I didn't get on to you at first.
Sure I like you.

MARGARET. Then we're going to be
good friends.

FENTON. You just bet we are. Say, got a date for tomorrow evening?

MARGARET. No.

FENTON. How about the movies? There's a fine feature film at the Strand. Theda Bara in "The Lonesome Vampire," five reels. They say it's got "Gloria's Romance" beat a mile.

MARGARET. I don't know that I'd care to go there.

FENTON. How about a run down to Coney?

MARGARET. Coney! I've always wanted to do wild pagan things.

FENTON. Say, you'll tell me your name, won't you?

MARGARET. Margaret Marshall.

FENTON. Do you mind if I call you Margie?

MARGARET. If you do, I must call you—

FENTON. Charley. Gee, I like the name of Margie. Some class to that.

MARGARET. I'm glad you like it.

FENTON (*moving nearer*). And some class to you!

MARGARET (*coyly*). So you really like me?

FENTON. You bet. Say, before I go, you've got to give me a kiss, Margie.

MARGARET. Well, I don't know. Aren't you rather "rushing" me?

FENTON. Say, you are a kidder. (*He draws her up from her chair, and kisses her warmly on the lips.*)

MARGARET (*ecstatically*). You have the true Greek spirit! (*They kiss again*) If only Pommy would kiss me that way!

FENTON. Pommy? Who's Pommy?

MARGARET. Pommy is the man I live with.

FENTON. Your husband!

MARGARET. No, we just live together. You see, we don't believe in marriage.

FENTON (*pushing her away in horror*). I thought there was something queer about all this. Does he live here?

MARGARET. Yes. (*Points to door*) He's in there now.

FENTON (*excitedly*). Good night! I'm goin'. (*Looks for hat.*)

MARGARET (*speaking with real anguish*). You're surely not going just on that account.

FENTON (*taking hat and bag*). Isn't that enough?

MARGARET (*emotionally*). Please don't go. Listen, I can't suppress my feeling for you; I never do with anybody. I liked you the moment I saw you, I want you as a friend, a good friend. You can't go now, just when everything's about to begin.

FENTON (*severely*). Fair's fair, Miss. If he's keeping you, you can't be taking up with me at the same time. That puts the finish on it.

MARGARET. But he doesn't keep me. I keep myself.

FENTON. Wait a minute. You support yourself, and live with him of your own free will. Then you've got no excuse for being immoral; 'tisn't like you had to make your living at it. (*At door*) Good-bye.

MARGARET. But I can explain everything.

FENTON. It's no use, Miss. Even though I am a salesman, I've got a sense of honor. I sized you up as a married woman when I came in just now, or I never would have made love to you at all.

MARGARET. Oh—wait! Supposing I should want to buy some more dictionaries.

FENTON (*returning*). You've got my card, Miss. The 'phone number is on it. Bryant 4253. (*Sees* MARGARET *hang her head*) Don't feel hurt, Miss. You'll get over these queer ideas some day, and when you do, well, you've got my number. So long, kid. (*Exit* FENTON.)

MARGARET (*taking his card from table and placing it to her lips soulfully*). My Apollo, Bryant 4253! (PENDLETON *enters.*)

PENDLETON. Did you get a good start with your scandal? (MARGARET *hangs her head*) It's no use; I'm convinced we're in a hopeless muddle.

MARGARET. I heartily agree with you.

PENDLETON. You've changed your mind very suddenly.

MARGARET. I have my reasons.

PENDLETON. The fact is, Margaret, that so long as we live together we're public figures, with everybody else as our jury.

MARGARET. But lots of people read your books and respect us.

PENDLETON. The people that respect us are worse than the people that don't.

MARGARET. If they wouldn't always be bothering about our morals!

PENDLETON. If we continue living together, we shall simply be giving up our freedom to prove we are free.

MARGARET (*faltering*). I suppose we ought to separate.

PENDLETON. I believe we should.

MARGARET. We'll have to give up the studio.

PENDLETON (*regretfully*). Yes.

MARGARET. It's taken a long time to make the place homelike.

PENDLETON. We've been very comfortable here.

MARGARET. I shall miss you at meals.

PENDLETON. I shall have to start eating at clubs and restaurants again; no more good home cooking.

MARGARET. We're kind of used to one another, aren't we?

PENDLETON. It isn't an easy matter to break, after five years.

MARGARET. And there are mighty few studios with as good a light as this; I don't want to separate if you don't.

PENDLETON. But, Margaret. (*Piano starts playing wedding march*) There, that confounded piano again. (*Seized with an idea*) Margaret, there's another way out!

MARGARET (*with same idea*). You mean, we ought to marry!

PENDLETON. Yes, marry, and do it at once. That'll end everything.

MARGARET. Let's do it right away and get it over with; I simply must finish my Apollo.

PENDLETON. I'm going to buy you a new gown to get married in, a wedding present from Baroness de Meauville's.

MARGARET. I don't know that I want a De Meauville gown.

PENDLETON. Please let me. I want to give you something to symbolize our new life together.

MARGARET. Very well. And in return, I'll buy you a dictionary, so that I won't have to keep on correcting your spelling.

(*Exit* PENDLETON. MARGARET *goes to 'phone, and consults* FENTON'S *card.*)

MARGARET. Bryant 4253? Can I speak to Mr. Fenton? (*Enter* MRS. ABBEY) Mrs. Abbey. What do you think? We're going to get married!

MRS. ABBEY. Well, bless my soul! That's right. You can take it from me, ma'am, you'll find that respectability pays.

MARGARET (*at 'phone*). Bryant 4253? (*Sweetly*) Is that Mr. Fenton? (*Pause*) Hello, Charley!

CURTAIN

The Clod

A ONE-ACT PLAY

BY LEWIS BEACH

Suggested by *The Least of These*—a
short-story by DONAL HAMILTON HAINES

CHARACTERS

THADDEUS TRASK
MARY TRASK
A NORTHERN PRIVATE
A SOUTHERN SERGEANT
A SOUTHERN PRIVATE

THE CLOD

SCENE—*The kitchen of a farmhouse on the borderline between the Northern and Southern states. It is ten o'clock in the evening, September, 1863.*
The back wall is broken at stage left by the projection at right angles of a partially enclosed staircase; the four steps leading to the landing cut into the room. Underneath the enclosed part of the stairway, a cubby-hole; in front of it a small table which partially hides the door. To the left of the table a kitchen chair. A door, leading to the yard, is the center of the unbroken wall, back. To the right of the door, a cupboard; to the left, a small cooking-stove. Two windows in the right wall. Between them a bench on which a pail and a tin dipper stand. Above the bench a towel hanging on a nail, and above the towel a double-barrelled shotgun suspended on two pegs. Well downstage left, a closed door leading to a second room. In the center of the kitchen a large table; straight-backed chairs to the right and left of it. A lighted candle on this table. ("Right" and "left" are the actors' "right" and "left.")
The moon shines into the room through the windows, but at no time is the kitchen brightly lighted. The characters appear as silhouettes except when they stand near the candle or the lantern, and then the lights throw huge shadows on the roughly plastered walls. When the door, back, is opened one sees a bit of the farmyard, desolate even in the moonlight.
As the curtain rises, THADDEUS TRASK, *a man of sixty-odd years, short and thick-set, slow in speech and action, yet in perfect health, sits at the left of the center table. He is pressing tobacco into his corncob pipe. He lights it with the candle. After a moment,* MARY TRASK, *a tired, emaciated woman, whose years equal her husband's, enters from the yard carrying a heavy pail of water and a lighted lantern. She puts the pail on the bench and hangs the lantern above it; then crosses to the stove.*

MARY. Ain't got wood 'nough fer breakfast, Thad.

THADDEUS. I'm too tired t' go out now. Wait 'til mornin'. (*Pause.* MARY *lays the fire in the stove*) Did I tell yuh that old man Reed saw three Southern troopers pass his house this mornin'?

MARY (*takes coffee-pot from stove, crosses to bench, fills pot with water*). I wish them soldiers would git out o' the neighborhood. Whenever I see 'em passin', I have t' steady myself 'gainst somethin' or I'd fall. I couldn't hardly breathe yesterday when them Southerners came after fodder. I'd died if they'd spoke t' me.

THADDEUS. Yuh needn't be afraid o' Northern soldiers.

MARY (*carries coffee-pot to stove*). I hate 'em all—Union or Southern. I can't make head or tail t' what all this fightin's 'bout. An' I don't care who wins, so long as they git through, an' them soldiers stop stealin' our corn an' potatoes.

THADDEUS. Yuh can't hardly blame 'em if they're hungry, ken yuh?

MARY. It ain't right that they should steal from us poor folk. (*Lifts a huge gunny sack of potatoes from the table, and begins setting the table for breakfast, getting knives, forks, spoons, plates, cups and saucers—two of each—from the cupboard*) We have hard 'nough times t' make things meet now. I ain't set down onct today 'cept fer meals. An' when I think o' the work I got t' do t'morrow, I ought t' been in bed hours ago.

THADDEUS. I'd help if I could, but it ain't my fault if the Lord seed fit t' lay me up so I'm always ailin'. (*Rises lazily*) Yuh better try an' take things easy t'morrow.

MARY. It's well enough t' say, but them apples is got t' be picked an' the rest o' the potatoes sorted. If I could sleep at night it'd be all right, but with them soldiers 'bout, I can't.

THADDEUS (*crosses right, fondly handles his gun*). Golly wish I'd see a flock o' birds.

MARY (*nervously*) I'd rather go without than hear yuh fire. I wish yuh didn't keep it loaded.

THADDEUS. Yuh know I ain't got time t' stop an' load when I see the birds. They don't wait fer yuh. (*Hangs gun on wall, drops into his chair; dejectedly*) Them pigs has got t' be butchered.

MARY. Wait 'til I git a chance t' go t' sister's. I can't stand it t' hear 'em squeal.

THADDEUS (*pulling off his boots—*

grunting meanwhile*). Best go soon then, 'cause they's fat as they'll ever be, an' there ain't no use in wastin' feed on 'em. (*Pause; rises*) Ain't yuh 'most ready fer bed?

MARY. Go on up. (THADDEUS *takes the candle in one hand, his boots in the other, and climbs the stairs.* MARY *speaks when he reaches the landing*) An' Thad, try not t' snore t'night.

THADDEUS. Poke me if I do. (*Disappears.*)

(MARY *fills the kettle with water and puts it on the stove; closes the door, back; takes the lantern from the wall and tries twice before she succeeds in blowing it out. Puts the lantern on the table before the cubby-hole. Slowly drags herself up the stairs, pausing a moment on the top step for breath before she disappears. There is a silence. Then the door, back, is opened a trifle and a man's hand is seen. Cautiously the door is opened wide and a young Northern private stands silhouetted on the threshold. He wears a dirty uniform, and a bloody bandage is tied about his head. He is wounded, sick, and exhausted. He stands at the door a moment, listening intently; then hastily moves to the center table looking for food. He bumps against a chair and mutters an oath. Finding nothing on the table, he hurries to the cupboard. Suddenly the galloping of horses is heard in the distance. The NORTHERNER starts, then rushes to the window nearer the audience. For a moment the sound ceases, then it begins again, growing gradually louder and louder. The NORTHERNER hurries into the room at the left. Horses and voices are heard in the yard, and almost immediately heavy, thundering knocks sound on the door, back. The men at the door grow impatient and push the door open. A large, powerfully built* SOUTHERN SERGEANT, *and a smaller, younger trooper of the same army enter.* THADDEUS *appears on the stairs, carrying a candle.*)

SERGEANT (*to* THADDEUS; *not unkindly*). Sorry, my friend, but you were so darn slow 'bout openin' the door that we had to walk in. Has there been a Northern soldier round here today?

THADDEUS (*timidly*). I ain't seed one. (*Comes down the stairs.*)

SERGEANT. Have you been here all day?

THADDEUS. I ain't stirred from the place.

SERGEANT. Call the rest of your family down.

THADDEUS. My wife's all there is. (*Goes to foot of stairs, and calls loudly and excitedly*) Mary! Mary! Come down. Right off!

SERGEANT. You better not lie to me or it'll go tough with you.

THADDEUS. I swear I ain't seed no one. (MARY *comes downstairs slowly. She is all atremble*) Say, Mary, you was here——

SERGEANT. Keep still, man. I'll do the talkin' (*To* MARY) You were here at the house all day? (MARY *is very frightened and embarrassed, but after a moment manages to nod her head slowly*) You didn't take a trip down to the store? (MARY *shakes her head slowly*) Haven't you got a tongue?

MARY (*with difficulty*). Y-e-s.

SERGEANT. Then use it. The Northern soldier who came here a while ago was pretty badly wounded, wasn't he?

MARY. I—I—no one's been here.

SERGEANT. Come, come, woman, don't lie. (MARY *shows a slight sign of anger*) He had a bad cut in his forehead, and you felt sorry for him, and gave him a bite to eat.

MARY (*haltingly*). No one's been near the house t'day.

SERGEANT (*trying a different tone*). We're not going to hurt him, woman. He's a friend of ours. We want to find him, and put him in a hospital, don't we, Dick? (*Turning to his companion.*)

DICK. He's sick and needs to go to bed for a while.

MARY. He ain't here.

SERGEANT. What do you want to lie for?

MARY (*quickly*). I ain't lyin'. I ain't seed no soldier. (*She stands rooted to the spot where she stopped when she came downstairs. Her eyes are still fixed on the* SERGEANT.)

SERGEANT. I reckon you know what'll happen if you are hidin' the spy.

THADDEUS. There ain't no one here. We both been here all day, an' there couldn't no one come without our knowin' it. What would they want round here anyway?

SERGEANT. We'll search the place, Dick.

MARY (quickly). Yuh ain't got no—

SERGEANT (sharply). What's that, woman?

MARY. There ain't no one here, an' yer keepin' us from our sleep.

SERGEANT. Your sleep? This is an affair of life and death. Get us a lantern. (THADDEUS moves to the small table and lights the lantern with the candle which he holds in his hand. He gives the lantern to the SERGEANT. The SERGEANT notices the door to the cubby-hole) Ha! Tryin' to hide the door, are you, by puttin' a table in front of it? You can't fool me. (To THADDEUS) Pull the table away and let's see what's behind the door.

THADDEUS. It's a cubby-hole an' ain't been opened in years.

SERGEANT (sternly and emphatically). I said to open the door. (THADDEUS sets the candle on the larger table, moves the smaller table to the right, and opens the door to the cubby-hole. MARY is angry. The SERGEANT takes a long-barreled revolver from his belt and peers into the cubby-hole. Returning his revolver to his belt) We're goin' to tear this place to pieces 'til we find him. You might just as well hand him over now.

MARY. There ain't no one here.

SERGEANT. All right. Now we'll see. Dick, you stand guard at the door. (DICK goes to the door, back, and stands gazing out into the night,—his back to the audience. To THAD-DEUS) Come along, man. I'll have to look at the upstairs. (To MARY) You sit down in that chair. (Points to chair at right of center table, and feels for a sufficiently strong threat) Don't you stir or I'll—I'll set fire to your house. (To THADDEUS) Go on ahead.

(THADDEUS and the SERGEANT go upstairs. MARY sinks lifelessly into the chair. She is the picture of fear. She sits facing left. Suddenly she leans forward. She opens her eyes wide, and draws her breath sharply. She opens her mouth as though she would scream, but makes no sound. The NORTHERNER has opened the door. He enters slowly and cautiously, his gun pointed at MARY. DICK cannot see him because of the jog in the wall. MARY only stares in bewilderment at the NORTHERNER, as he, with eyes fixed appealingly on her, opens the door to the cubby-hole and crawls inside.)

DICK. Woman!

MARY (almost with a cry, thinking that DICK has seen the NORTHERNER). Yes.

DICK. Have you got an apple handy? I'm starved.

(MARY rises and moves to the cupboard. The SERGEANT and THADDEUS come downstairs. The SERGEANT, seeing that MARY is not where he left her, looks about rapidly and discovers her at the cupboard.)

SERGEANT. Here, what did I tell you I'd do if you moved from that chair?

MARY (terrified). Oh, I didn't—I only—he wanted——

DICK. It's all right, Sergeant. I asked her to get me an apple.

SERGEANT. Take this lantern and search the barn. (DICK *takes the lantern from the* SERGEANT *and goes out, back. To* THADDEUS) Come in here with me. (*The* SERGEANT *picks up the candle. He and* THADDEUS *move toward the door, left. As though in a stupor,* MARY *starts to follow*) Sit down! (MARY *drops into the chair at the right of the table. The* SERGEANT *and* THADDEUS *go into the room, left. They can be heard moving furniture about.* MARY *sees a pin on the floor. She stoops, picks it up, and fastens it in her belt. The* SERGEANT *and* THADDEUS *return*) If I find him now after all the trouble you've given me, you know what'll happen. There's likely to be two dead men and a woman, instead of only the Yankee.

DICK (*bounding into the room*). Sergeant!

SERGEANT. What is it? (DICK *hurries to the* SERGEANT *and says something to him in a low voice. The* SERGEANT *smiles*) Now, my good people, how did that horse get here?

THADDEUS. What horse?

DICK. There's a horse in the barn with a saddle on his back. I swear he's been ridden lately.

THADDEUS (*amazed*). There is?

SERGEANT. You know it. (*To* MARY) Come, woman, who drove that horse here?

MARY (*silent for a moment, her eyes on the floor*). I don't know. I didn't hear nothin'.

THADDEUS (*moving toward the door*). Let me go an' see.

SERGEANT (*pushing* THADDEUS *back*). No, you don't. You two have done enough to justify the harshest measures. Show us the man's hiding place.

THADDEUS. If there's anybody here, he's come in the night without our knowin' it. I tell yuh I didn't see anybody, an' she didn't, an'——

SERGEANT (*has been watching* MARY). Where is he? (*His tone makes* THADDEUS *jump. There is a pause, during which* MARY *seems trying to compose herself. Then slowly she lifts her eyes and looks at the* SERGEANT.)

MARY. There ain't nobody in the house 'cept us two.

SERGEANT (*to* DICK). Did you search all the out-buildings?

DICK. Yes. There's not a trace of him except the horse.

SERGEANT (*wiping the perspiration from his face; speaks with apparent deliberation at first, but becomes very emphatic*). He didn't have much of a start of us, and I think he was wounded. A farmer down the road said he heard hoof-beats. The man the other side of you heard nothin', *and the horse is in your barn.* (*Slowly draws his revolver and points it at* THADDEUS) There are ways of making people confess.

THADDEUS (*covering his face with his hands*). For God's sake, don't. I know that horse looks bad, but, as I live, I ain't heard a sound, or seen anybody. I'd give the man up in a minute if he was here.

SERGEANT (*lowering his gun*). Yes.

I guess you would. You wouldn't want me to hand you and your wife over to our army to be shot down like dogs. (MARY *shivers.* SERGEANT *swings round sharply and points the gun at* MARY) Your wife knows where he's hid.

MARY (*breaking out in irritating, rasping voice*). I'm sure I wish I did. I'd tell yuh quick an' git yuh out o' here. 'Tain't no fun fer me t' have yuh prowlin' all over my house, trackin' it up with yer dirty boots. Yuh ain't got no right t' torment me like this. Lord knows how I'll git my day's work done, if I can't have my sleep out.

SERGEANT (*has been gazing at her in astonishment; lowers his gun*). Good God! Nothing but her own petty existence. (*In different voice to* MARY) I'll have to ask you to get us some breakfast. We're famished. (*With relief but showing some an ger,* MARY *turns to the stove. She lights the fire and puts more coffee in the pot*) Come, Dick, we better give our horses some water. They're all tired out. (*In lower voice*) The man isn't here. If he were he couldn't get away while we're in the yard. (*To* THADDEUS) Get us a pail to give the horses some water in. (*Sees the pails on the bench. Picks one of them up and moves toward the door.*)

MARY. That ain't the horses' pail.

SERGEANT (*to* THADDEUS). Come along. You can help.

MARY (*louder*). That's the drinkin' water pail.

SERGEANT. That's all right. (*The* SERGEANT, THADDEUS, *and*

DICK—*carrying the lantern—go out back.* MARY *needs more wood for the fire, so she follows in a moment. When she has disappeared, the* NORTHERNER *drags himself from the cubby-hole.* MARY *returns with an armful of wood.*)

MARY (*sees the* NORTHERNER. *Shows no sympathy for him in this speech nor during the entire scene*). Yuh git back! Them soldiers'll see yuh.

NORTHERNER. Some water. Quick. (*Falls into chair at left of table*) It was so hot in there.

MARY (*gives him water in the dipper*). Don't yuh faint here! If them soldiers git yuh, they'll kill me an' Thad. Hustle an' git back in that cubby-hole. (*Turns quickly to the stove.*)
(*The* NORTHERNER *drinks the water, puts the dipper on the table. Then, summoning all his strength, rises and crosses to* MARY. *He touches her on the sleeve.* MARY *is so startled that she jumps and utters a faint cry.*)

NORTHERNER. Be still or they'll hear you. How are you going to get me out of here?

MARY. Yuh git out! Why did yuh come here, a-bringin' me all this extra work, an' maybe death?

NORTHERNER. I couldn't go any farther. My horse and I were ready to drop. Won't you help me?

MARY. No, I won't. I don't know who yuh are or nothin' 'bout yuh, 'cept that them men want t' ketch yuh. (*In a changed tone of curi-*

osity) Did yuh steal somethin' from
'em?

NORTHERNER. Don't you understand? Those men belong to the
Confederacy, and I'm a Northerner.
They've been chasing me all day.
*(Pulling a bit of crumpled paper
from his breast)* They want this paper. If they get it before tomorrow
morning it will mean the greatest
disaster that's ever come to the
Union army.

MARY *(with frank curiosity)*. Was it
yuh rode by yesterday?

NORTHERNER. Don't you see what
you can do? Get me out of here and
away from those men, and you'll
have done more than any soldier
could do for the country—for *your*
country.

MARY. I ain't got no country. Me an'
Thad's only got this farm. Thad's
ailin', an' I do most the work, an'—

NORTHERNER. The lives of thirty
thousand men hang by a thread. I
must save them. And you must help
me!

MARY. I don't know nothin' 'bout
yuh, an' I don't know what yer
talkin' 'bout.

NORTHERNER. Only help me get
away.

MARY *(angrily)*. No one ever helped
me or Thad. I lift no finger in this
business. Why yuh come here in the
first place is beyond me—sneakin'
in our house, spoilin' our well-
earned sleep. If them soldiers ketch
yuh, they'll kill me an' Thad. Maybe you didn't know that.

NORTHERNER. What's your life and
your husband's compared to thirty
thousand? I haven't any money or
I'd give it to you.

MARY. I don't want yer money.

NORTHERNER. What do you want?

MARY. I want yuh t' git out. I don't
care what happens t' yuh. Only git
out o' here.

NORTHERNER. I can't with the Southerners in the yard. They'd shoot me
like a dog. Besides, I've got to have
my horse.

MARY *(with naïve curiosity)*. What
kind o' lookin' horse is it?

NORTHERNER *(dropping into the
chair at left of center table in disgust and despair)*. Oh, God! If I'd
only turned in at the other farm. I
might have found people with red
blood. *(Pulls out his gun and hopelessly opens the empty chamber.)*

MARY *(alarmed)*. What yuh goin'
t' do with that gun?

NORTHERNER. Don't be afraid.

MARY. I'd call 'em if I wasn't——

NORTHERNER *(leaping to the wall,
left, and bracing himself against
it)*. Go call them in. Save your poor
skin and your husband's if you can.
Call them in. You can't save yourself. *(Laughs hysterically)* You
can't save your miserable skin.
'Cause if they get me, and don't
shoot you, *I will.*

MARY *(leaning against the left side
of the table for support; in agony)*.
Oh!

NORTHERNER. You see? You've got to help me whether you want to or not.

MARY (*feeling absolutely caught*). I ain't done nothin'. I don't see why yuh an' them others come here a-threatenin' t' shoot me. I don't want nothin'. I don't want t' do nothin'. I jest want yuh all t' git out o' here an' leave me an' Thad t' go t' sleep. Oh, I don't know what t' do. Yuh got me in a corner where I can't move. (*Passes her hand back along the table. Touches the dipper accidentally, and it falls to the floor. Screams at the sound.*)

NORTHERNER (*leaping toward her*). Now you've done it. They'll be here in a minute. You can't give me up. They'll shoot me if you do. *They'll shoot.* (*Hurries up the stairs and disappears.*)
(MARY *stands beside the table, trembling terribly. The* SERGEANT DICK, *and* THADDEUS *come running in.*)

SERGEANT. What did you yell for? (MARY *does not answer. He seizes her by the arm*) Answer!

MARY. I knocked the dipper off the table. It scared me.

SERGEANT (*dropping wearily into chair at left of center table*). Well, don't drop our breakfast. Put it on the table. We're ready.

MARY (*stands looking at the* SERGEANT). It ain't finished.

SERGEANT (*worn out by his day's work and* MARY's *stupidity, from now on absolutely brutish*). You've had time to cook a dozen meals.

What did you do all the time we were in the yard?

MARY. I didn't do nothin'.

SERGEANT. You good-for-nothin'—— Get a move on and give us something fit to eat. Don't try to get rid of any left-overs on us. If you do, you'll suffer for it. (MARY *stands looking at him*) Don't you know anything, you brainless farm-drudge? *Hurry*, I said.
(MARY *picks up the dipper and turns to the stove.* THADDEUS *sits in the chair at left of smaller table.*)

DICK. What a night! My stomach's as hollow as these people's heads. (*Takes towel which hangs above the bench, and wipes the barrel of his gun with it.*)

MARY. That's one of my best towels.

DICK. Can't help it.

SERGEANT. 'Tend to the breakfast. That's enough for you to do at one time. (DICK *puts his gun on the smaller table, and sits at the right of the larger. Then the* SERGEANT *speaks, quietly*) I don't see how he gave us the slip.

DICK. He knew we were after him, drove his horse in here, and went on afoot. Clever scheme, I must admit.

THADDEUS (*endeavoring to get them into conversation*). Have yuh rid far t'night, Misters?

DICK (*shortly*). Far enough.

THADDEUS. Twenty miles or so?

DICK. Perhaps.

THADDEUS. How long yuh been chasin' the critter?

SERGEANT. Oh, shut up! Don't you see we don't want to talk to you? Take hold and hurry, woman. My patience's at an end.
(MARY *puts a loaf of bread, some fried eggs, and a coffee-pot on the table.*)

MARY. There! I hope yer satisfied.
(DICK *and the* SERGEANT *pull up their chairs and begin to eat.*)

SERGEANT. Is this all we get? Come, it won't do you any good to be stingy.

MARY. It's all I got.

SERGEANT. It isn't a mouthful for a chickadee! Give us some butter.

MARY. There ain't none.

SERGEANT. No butter on a farm? God, the way you lie.

MARY. I——

SERGEANT. Shut up!

DICK. Have you got any cider?

SERGEANT. Don't ask. She and the man probably drank themselves stupid on it. (*Throws fork on floor*) I never struck such a place in my life. Get me another fork. How do you expect me to eat with that bent thing? (MARY *stoops with difficulty and picks up the fork. Gets another from the cupboard and gives it to the* SERGEANT) Now give me some salt. Don't you know that folks eat it on eggs? (MARY *crosses to the cup-*board; *mistakes the pepper for the salt and puts it on the table.* SERGEANT *sprinkles pepper on his food*) I said salt, woman. (*Spelling*) S-a-l-t. Salt! Salt! (MARY *gets the salt and gives it to the* SERGEANT. *Almost ready to drop, she drags herself to the window nearer the back and leans against it, watching the* SOUTHERNERS *like a hunted animal.* THADDEUS *is nodding in the corner. The* SERGEANT *and* DICK *go on devouring the food. The former pours the coffee, puts his cup to his lips, takes one swallow; then, jumping to his feet and upsetting his chair as he does so, he hurls his cup to the floor. Bellowing and pointing to the fluid trickling on the floor*) Have you tried to poison us, you God damn hag?
(MARY *screams and the faces of the men turn white. It is the cry of an animal goaded beyond endurance.*)

MARY (*screeching*). Break my cup? Call my coffee poison? Call me a hag, will yuh? I'll learn yuh! I'm a woman, but yer drivin' me crazy. (*She has snatched the gun from the wall and pointed it at the* SERGEANT. *Fires.*)
(*The* SERGEANT *falls to the floor.* MARY *keeps on screeching.* DICK *rushes for his gun.*)

THADDEUS. Mary! Mary!

MARY (*aiming at* DICK *and firing*). I ain't a hag. I'm a woman, but yer killin' me.
(DICK *falls just as he reaches his gun.* THADDEUS *is in the corner with his hands over his ears. The* NORTHERNER *stands on the stairs.* MARY *continues to pull the trigger of the empty gun. The* NORTHERNER *is motionless for a moment; then he goes to* THADDEUS *and shakes him.*)

NORTHERNER. Go get my horse. Quick! (THADDEUS *hurries out. The* NORTHERNER *turns to* MARY *and speaks with great fervor. She gazes at him but does not understand a word he says*) I'm ashamed of what I said. The whole country will hear of this, and you. (*He takes her hand and presses it to his lips; then turns and hurries out of the house.*)

(MARY *still holds the gun in her hand. She pushes a strand of gray hair back from her face, and begins to pick up the fragments of the broken cup.*)

MARY (*in dead, flat tone*). I'll have t' drink out the tin cup now. (*The hoof-beats of the* NORTHERN-ER's *horse are heard.*)

CURTAIN

Aria Da Capo

A PLAY

BY EDNA ST. VINCENT MILLAY

CHARACTERS

PIERROT
COLUMBINE
COTHURNUS, *masque of tragedy*
THYRSIS, *shepherd*
CORYDON, *shepherd*

ARIA DA CAPO

SCENE—*A Stage. The curtain rises on a stage set for a Harlequinade, a merry black and white interior. Directly behind the footlights, and running parallel with them, is a long table, covered with a gay black and white cloth, on which is spread a banquet. At the opposite ends of this table, seated on delicate thin-legged chairs with high backs, are* PIERROT *and* COLUMBINE, *dressed according to the tradition, excepting that* PIERROT *is in lilac, and* COLUMBINE *in pink. They are dining.*

COLUMBINE
          Pierrot, a macaroon!
I cannot *live*
Without a macaroon!

PIERROT
          My only love,
You are *so* intense . . . It is Tuesday, Columbine?——
I'll kiss you if it's Tuesday.

COLUMBINE
          It is Wednesday,
If you must know. . . . Is this my artichoke,
Or yours?

PIERROT
          Ah, Columbine,—as if it mattered!
Wednesday. . . . Will it be Tuesday, then, tomorrow,
By any chance?

COLUMBINE
          Tomorrow will be—
Pierrot,
That isn't funny!

PIERROT
          I thought it rather nice.
Well, let us drink some wine and lose our heads
And love each other.

COLUMBINE
          Pierrot, don't you love
Me now?

PIERROT
          La, what a woman!—
How should I know?
Pour me some wine: I'll tell you presently.

COLUMBINE
Pierrot, do you know, I think you drink too much.

PIERROT
Yes, I dare say I do. . . . Or else too little.
It's hard to tell. You see, I am always wanting
A little more than what I have—or else
A little less. There's something wrong. My dear,
How many fingers have you?

COLUMBINE
          La, indeed,
How should I know?—It always takes me one hand
To count the other with. It's too confusing.
Why?

465

PIERROT
Why?—I am a student,
Columbine;
And search into all matters.

COLUMBINE
La, indeed?—
Count them yourself, then!

PIERROT
No. Or, rather, nay.
'Tis of no consequence. . . . I am
  become
A painter, suddenly,—and you im-
  press me—
Ah, yes!—six orange bull's-eyes,
  four green pin-wheels,
And one magenta jelly-roll—the
  title
As follows: *Woman Taking in
Cheese from Fire-Escape.*

COLUMBINE
Well, I like that! So that is all
  I've meant
To you!

PIERROT
Hush! All at once I
am become
A pianist. I will image you in sound.
On a new scale . . . without tonal-
  ity . . .
Vivace senza tempo senza tutto. . . .
Title: *Uptown Express at Six O'-
Clock.*
Pour me a drink.

COLUMBINE
Pierrot, you work too hard.
You need a rest. Come on out into
  the garden,
And sing me something sad.

PIERROT
Don't stand so near me!
I am become a socialist. I love
Humanity; but I hate people. Col-
umbine,

Put on your mittens, child; your
hands are cold.

COLUMBINE
My hands are *not* cold

PIERROT
Oh, I am sure they are.
And you must have a shawl to wrap
  about you,
And sit by the fire.

COLUMBINE
Why, I'll do no such thing!
I'm hot as a spoon in a tea-cup!

PIERROT
Columbine,
I'm a philanthropist. I know I am,
Because I feel so restless. Do not
  scream,
Or it will be the worse for you!

COLUMBINE
Pierrot,
My vinaigrette: I cannot *live* with-
out
My vinaigrette!

PIERROT
My only love, you are
So fundamental! . . . How would
  you like to be
An actress, Columbine?—I am be-
come
Your manager.

COLUMBINE
Why, Pierrot, *I* can't act.

PIERROT
Can't act! Can't act! La, listen to the
  woman!
What's that to do with the price of
  furs?—You're blonde,
Are you not?—You have no education, have you?—
Can't act! You under-rate yourself,
  my dear!

COLUMBINE

Yes, I suppose I do.

PIERROT

As for the rest,
I'll teach you how to cry, and how
to die,
And other little tricks; and the house
will love you.
You'll be a star by five o'clock . . .
That is,
If you will let me pay for your apart-
ment.

COLUMBINE

Let you?—well, that's a good one!
Ha! Ha! Ha!
But why?

PIERROT

But why?—well, as to that,
my dear,
I cannot say. It's just a matter of
form.

COLUMBINE

Pierrot, I'm getting
tired of caviar
And peacocks' livers. Isn't there
something else
That people eat?—some humble
vegetable,
That grows in the ground?

PIERROT

Well, there are mushrooms.

COLUMBINE

Mushrooms!
That's so! I had forgotten . . .
mushrooms . . . mushrooms. . . .
I cannot live with. . . . How do you
like this gown?

PIERROT

Not much. I'm tired of gowns that
have the waist-line
About the waist, and the hem
around the bottom—

And women with their breasts in
front of them!—
Zut and ehé! Where does one go
from here!

COLUMBINE

Here's a persimmon, love. You always liked them.

PIERROT

I am become a critic; there
is nothing I can enjoy. . . . However, set it aside;
I'll eat it between meals.

COLUMBINE

Pierrot, do you know,
Sometimes I think you're making
fun of me.

PIERROT

My love, by yon black moon, you
wrong us both.

COLUMBINE

There isn't a sign of a moon,
Pierrot.

PIERROT

Of course not.
There never was. "Moon's" just a
word to swear by,
"Mutton!"—now there's a thing you
can lay the hands on,
And set the tooth in! Listen, Colum-
bine:
I always lied about the moon and
you.
Food is my only lust.

COLUMBINE

Well, eat it, then,
For heaven's sake, and stop your
silly noise!
I haven't heard the clock tick for an
hour.

PIERROT

It's ticking all the same. If you were
a fly,

You would be dead by now. And if I
were a parrot,
I could be talking for a thousand
years!
(*Enters* COTHURNUS.)

PIERROT

Hello, what's this, for God's sake?
—What's the matter?
Say, whadda you mean?—get off
the stage, my friend,
And pinch yourself,—you're walk-
ing in your sleep!

COTHURNUS
I never sleep.

PIERROT
Well, anyhow, clear out.
You don't belong on here. Wait for
your own scene!
Whadda you think this is—a dress-
rehearsal?

COTHURNUS
Sir, I am tired of waiting. I
will wait
No longer.

PIERROT
Well, but what are you
going to do?
The scene is set for me!

COTHURNUS
True, sir; yet I
Can play the scene.

PIERROT
Your scene is down for
later!

COTHURNUS
That, too, is true, sir; but I
play it now.

PIERROT
Oh, very well!—Anyway,
I am tired
Of black and white. At least, I think
I am.

(*Exit* COLUMBINE.)
Yes, I am sure I am. I know what
I'll do!—
I'll go and strum the moon, that's
what I'll do. . . .
Unless, perhaps, . . . you never can
tell . . . I may be,
You know, tired of the moon. Well,
anyway,
I'll go find Columbine. . . . And
when I find her,
I will address her thus: "*Ehé* Pier-
rette!"—
There's something in that.
(*Exit* PIERROT.)

COTHURNUS
You, Thyrsis! Corydon!
Where are you?

THYRSIS
Sir, we are in our dressing-
room!

COTHURNUS
Come out and do the scene.

CORYDON
You are mocking us!—
The scene is down for later.

COTHURNUS
That is true;
But we will play it now. I am the
scene.
(*Seats himself on high place in
back of stage. Enter* CORY-
DON *and* THYRSIS.)

CORYDON
Sir, we were counting on this
little hour.
We said, "Here is an hour,—in
which to think
A mighty thought, and sing a tri-
fling song,
And look at nothing."—And, behold! the hour.

Even as we spoke, was over, and the
act begun,
'Under our feet!

THYRSIS

Sir, we are not in the
fancy
To play the play. We had thought to
play it later.

CORYDON

Besides, this is the setting
for a farce.
Our scene requires a wall; we cannot build
A wall of tissue-paper!

THYRSIS

We cannot act
A tragedy with comic properties!

COTHURNUS

Try it and see. I think you'll find you
can.
One wall is like another. And re-
garding
The matter of your insufficient wood,
The important thing is that you
speak the lines,
And make the gestures. Wherefore
I shall remain
Throughout, and hold the prompt-
book. Are you ready?

CORYDON-THYRSIS

(Sorrowfully.)
Sir, we are always ready.

COTHURNUS

Play the play!

(CORYDON and THYRSIS move
the table and chairs to one
side out of the way, and seat
themselves in a half-reclin-
ing position on the floor, left
of the center of the stage,
propped up by crêpe paper

pillows and bolsters, in place
of rocks.)

THYRSIS

How gently in the silence,
Corydon,
Our sheep go up the bank. They
crop a grass
That's yellow where the sun is out,
and black
Where the clouds drag their shad-
ows.
Have you noticed
How steadily, yet with what a slant-
ing eye,
They graze?

CORYDON

As if they thought of other
things.
What say you, Thyrsis, do they only
question
Where next to pull?—Or do their
far minds draw them
Thus vaguely north of west and
south of east?

THYRSIS

One cannot say. . . . The black
lamb wears its burdocks
As if they were a garland—have
you noticed?—
Purple and white—and drinks the
bitten grass
As if it were a wine.

CORYDON

I've noticed that.
What say you, Thyrsis, shall we
make a song
About a lamb that thought himself a
shepherd?

THYRSIS

Why, yes!—that is, why—no. (I
have forgotten
My line.)

COTHURNUS
(*Prompting.*)
"I know a game worth two of that."

THYRSIS
Oh, yes. . . . I know a game worth
two of that:
Let's gather rocks, and build a wall
between us;
And say that over there belongs to
me,
And over here to you!

CORYDON
Why—very well.
And say you may not come upon my
side
Unless I say you may!

THYRSIS
Nor you on mine!
And if you should, 'twould be the
worse for you!
(*They weave a wall of colored
crêpe paper ribbons from the
center front to the center
back of the stage, fastening
the ends to* COLUMBINE'S
chair in front and to PIER-
ROT'S *chair in the back.*)

CORYDON
Now there's a wall a man may see
across,
But not attempt to scale.

THYRSIS
An excellent wall.

CORYDON
Come, let us separate,
and sit alone
A little while, and lay a plot where-
by
We may outdo each other.
(*They seat themselves on op-
posite sides of the wall.*)

PIERROT
(*Off stage.*)
Ehé, Pierrette!

COLUMBINE
(*Off stage.*)
My name is Columbine! Leave me
alone!

THYRSIS
(*Coming up to the wall.*)
Corydon, after all, and in spite of
the fact
I started it myself, I do not like this
So very much. What is the sense of
saying
I do not want you on my side the
wall?
It is a silly game. I'd much prefer
Making the little song you spoke of
making,
About the lamb, you know, that
thought himself
A shepherd!—what do you say?
(*Pause.*)

CORYDON
(*At wall.*)
I have forgotten
The line.

COTHURNUS
(*Prompting.*)
"How do I know this isn't a trick."

CORYDON
Oh, yes. . . . How do I know this
isn't a trick
To get upon my land?

THYRSIS
Oh, Corydon,
You *know* it's not a trick. I do not
like
The game, that's all. Come over
here, or let me
Come over there.

CORYDON

It is a clever trick
To get upon my land.
(*Seats himself as before.*)

THYRSIS

Oh, very well!
(*Seats himself as before.*)
(*To himself.*)
I think I never knew a sillier game.

CORYDON

(*Coming to wall.*)
Oh, Thyrsis, just a minute!—all the water
Is on your side the wall, and the sheep are thirsty.
I hadn't thought of that.

THYRSIS
Oh, hadn't you?

CORYDON
Why, what do you mean?

THYRSIS
What do I mean?—I mean
That I can play a game as well as you can.
And if the pool is on my side, it's on
My side, that's all.

CORYDON
You mean you'd let the sheep
Go thirsty?

THYRSIS
Well, they're not my sheep.
My sheep
Have water enough.

CORYDON
Your sheep! You are mad, to call them.
Yours—mine—they are all one flock! Thyrsis, you can't mean
To keep the water from them, just because

They happened to be grazing over here
Instead of over there, when we set the wall up?

THYRSIS

Oh, can't I?—wait and see!—and if you try
To lead them over here, you'll wish you hadn't!

CORYDON
I wonder how it happens all the water
Is on your side. . . . I'll say you had an eye out
For lots of little things, my innocent friend,
When I said, "Let us make a song," and you said,
"I know a game worth two of that!"

COLUMBINE
(*Off stage.*)
D'you know, I think you must be getting old,
Or fat, or something—stupid, anyway!—
Can't you put on some other kind of collar?

THYRSIS
You know as well as I do, Corydon,
I never thought of anything of the kind.
Don't you?

CORYDON
I *do* not.

THYRSIS
Don't you?

CORYDON
Oh, I suppose so.
Thyrsis, let's drop this—what do you say?—it's only

A game, you know . . . we seem to be forgetting
It's only a game . . . a pretty serious game
It's getting to be, when one of us is willing
To let the sheep go thirsty, for the sake of it.

THYRSIS

I know it, Corydon.
(*They reach out their arms to each other across the wall.*)

COTHURNUS

(*Prompting.*)
"But how do I know?"

THYRSIS

Oh, yes. . . . But how do I know this isn't a trick
To water your sheep, and get the laugh on me?

CORYDON

You can't know, that's the difficult thing about it,
Of course—you can't be sure. You have to take
My word for it. And I know just how you feel.
But one of us has to take a risk, or else,
Why don't you see?—the game goes on forever—
It's terrible, when you stop to think of it. . . .
Oh, Thyrsis, now for the first time I feel
This wall is actually a wall, a thing
Come up between us, shutting me away
From you. . . . I do not know you any more!

THYRSIS

No, don't say that! Oh, Corydon, I'm willing

To drop it all, if you will! Come on over
And water your sheep! It is an ugly game.
I hate it from the first. . . . How did it start?

CORYDON

I do not know . . . I do not know . . . I think
I am afraid of you!—you are a stranger!
I never set eyes on you before! "Come over
And water my sheep," indeed!—They'll be more thirsty
Than they are now, before I bring them over
Into your land, and have you mixing them up
With yours, and calling them yours, and trying to keep them!
(*Enter* COLUMBINE.)

COLUMBINE

(*To* COTHURNUS.)
Glummy, I want my hat.

THYRSIS

Take it, and go.

COLUMBINE

Take it and go, indeed! Is it my hat,
Or isn't it? Is this my scene, or not?
Take it and go! Really, you know, you two
Are awfully funny!
(*Exit* COLUMBINE.)

THYRSIS

Corydon, my friend,
I'm going to leave you now, and whittle me
A pipe, or sing a song, or go to sleep.
When you have come to your senses, let me know.
(*Goes back to where he has*

*been sitting, lies down and
sleeps.*)
(CORYDON, *in going back to
where he has been sitting,
stumbles over bowl of colored confetti and colored
paper ribbons.*)

CORYDON

Why, what is this?—Red stones—
and purple stones—
And stones stuck full of gold!—The
ground is full
Of gold and colored stones! . . .
I'm glad the wall
Was up before I found them!—
Otherwise,
I should have had to share them. As
it is,
They all belong to me. . . . Un-
less—
(*He goes to wall and digs up
and down the length of it, to
see if there are jewels on the
other side.*)
None here—
None here—none here— They all
belong to me!
(*Sits.*)

THYRSIS

(*Awakening.*)
How curious! I thought the little
black lamb
Came up and licked my hair! I saw
the wool
About its neck as plain as anything!
It must have been a dream. The lit-
tle black lamb
Is on the other side of the wall, I'm
sure.
(*Goes to wall and looks over.
CORYDON is seated on the
ground, tossing the confetti
up into the air and catching
it.*)
Hello, what's that you've got there,
Corydon?

CORYDON

Jewels.

THYRSIS

Jewels?—And where did you ever
get them?

CORYDON

Oh, over here.

THYRSIS

You mean to say you found
them,
By digging around in the ground for
them?

CORYDON

(*Unpleasantly.*)
No, Thyrsis.
By digging down for water for my
sheep.

THYRSIS

Corydon, come to the wall a minute,
will you?
I want to talk to you.

CORYDON

I haven't time.
I'm making me a necklace of red
stones.

THYRSIS

I'll give you all the water that you
want,
For one of those red stones—if it's
a good one.

CORYDON

Water?—what for?—what do I
want of water?

THYRSIS

Why, for your sheep.

CORYDON

My sheep?—I'm not a
shepherd!

THYRSIS

Your sheep are dying
of thirst.

CORYDON

Man, haven't I told you
I can't be bothered with a few un-
tidy
Brown sheep all full of burdocks?—
I'm a merchant,
That's what I am!—And I set my
mind to it,
I dare say I could be an emperor!
(*To himself.*)
Wouldn't I be a fool to spend my
time
Watching a flock of sheep go up a
hill,
When I have these to play with—
when I have these
To think about?—I can't make up
my mind
Whether to buy a city, and have a
thousand
Beautiful girls to bathe me, and be
happy
Until I die, or build a bridge, and
name it
The Bridge of Corydon—and be re-
membered
After I'm dead.

THYRSIS

Corydon, come to the wall,
Won't you?—I want to tell you
something.

CORYDON

Hush!
Be off! Be off! Go finish your nap,
I tell you!

THYRSIS

Corydon, listen: If you don't want
your sheep,
Give them to me.

CORYDON

Be off. Go finish your nap.
A red one—and a blue one—and a
red one—

And a purple one—give you my
sheep, did you say?—
Come, come! What do you take me
for, a fool?
I've a lot of thinking to do—and
while I'm thinking,
The sheep might just as well be over
here
As over there. . . . A blue one—
and a red one—

THYRSIS

But they will die!

CORYDON

And a green one—and a couple
Of white ones, for a change.

THYRSIS

Maybe I have
Some jewels on my side.

CORYDON

And another green one—
Maybe, but I don't think so. You
see, this rock
Isn't so very wide. It stops before
It gets to the wall. It seems to go
quite deep,
However.

THYRSIS

(*With hatred.*)
I see.

COLUMBINE

(*Off stage.*)
Look, Pierrot, there's the moon!

PIERROT

(*Off stage.*)
Nonsense!

THYRSIS

I see.

COLUMBINE

(*Off stage.*)
Sing me an old song, Pierrot—
Something I can remember.

PIERROT

(*Off stage.*)
                    Columbine,
Your mind is made of crumbs—like
    an escallop
Of oysters—first a layer of crumbs,
    and then
An oystery taste, and then a layer of
    crumbs.

THYRSIS

I find no jewels . . . but I wonder
    what
The root of this black weed would
    do to a man
If he should taste it . . . I have
    seen a sheep die,
With half the stalk still drooling
    from its mouth.
'Twould be a speedy remedy, I
    should think,
For a festered pride and a feverish
    ambition.
It has a curious root. I think I'll hack
    it
In little pieces. . . . First I'll get
    me a drink;
And then I'll hack that root in little
    pieces
As small as dust, and see what the
    color is
Inside.
        (*Goes to bowl on floor.*)
            The pool is very clear. I see
A shepherd standing on the brink,
    with a red cloak
About him, and a black weed in his
    hand. . . .
'Tis I.
        (*Kneels and drinks.*)

CORYDON

(*Coming to wall.*)
Hello, what are you doing, Thyrsis?

THYRSIS

Digging for gold.

CORYDON

            I'll give you all the gold
You want, if you'll give me a bowl
    of water.
If you don't want too much, that is
    to say.

THYRSIS

Ho, so you've changed your mind?
    —It's different,
Isn't it, when you want a drink your-
    self?

CORYDON

Of course it is.

THYRSIS

            Well, let me see . . . a bowl
Of water—come back in an hour,
    Corydon. I'm busy now.

CORYDON

Oh, Thyrsis, give me a bowl
Of water!—and I'll fill the bowl
    with jewels,
And bring it back!

THYRSIS

            Be off, I'm busy now.
        (*He catches sight of the weed,
        picks it up and looks at it,
        unseen by* CORYDON.)
Wait!—Pick me out the finest stones
    you have . . .
I'll bring you a drink of water pres-
    ently.

CORYDON

(*Goes back and sits down, with
    the jewels before him.*)
A bowl of jewels is a lot of jewels.

THYRSIS

(*Chopping up the weed.*)
I wonder if it has a bitter taste?

CORYDON

There's sure to be a stone or two
    among them

I have grown fond of, pouring them
     from one hand
Into the other.

THYRSIS

               I hope it doesn't taste
Too bitter, just at first.

CORYDON

               A bowl of jewels
Is far too many jewels to give away,
And not get back again.

THYRSIS

               I don't believe
He'll notice. He's thirsty. He'll gulp
     it down
And never notice.

CORYDON

     There ought to be some way
To get them back again. . . . I could
     give him a necklace,
And snatch it back, after I'd drunk
     the water,
I suppose . . . why, as for that, of
     course, a *necklace*. . . .
     (*He puts two or three of the
     colored tapes together and
     tries their strength by pull-
     ing them, after which he
     puts them around his neck
     and pulls them, gently, nod-
     ding to himself. He gets up
     and goes to the wall, with
     the colored tapes in his
     hands.*
     THYRSIS *in the meantime has
     poured the powdered root—
     black confetti—into the pot
     which contains the flower
     and filled it up with wine
     from the punch-bowl on the
     floor. He comes to the wall
     at the same time, holding the
     bowl of poison.*)

THYRSIS

Come and get your bowl of water,
     Corydon.

CORYDON

Ah, very good!—and for such a gift
     as that
I'll give you more than a bowl of
     unset stones.
I'll give you three long necklaces,
     my friend.
Come closer. Here they are.
     (*Puts the ribbons about* THYR-
     SIS' *neck.*)

THYRSIS

     (*Putting bowl to* CORYDON's
     mouth.)
I'll hold the bowl
Until you've drunk it all.

CORYDON

               Then hold it steady.
For every drop you spill I'll have a
     stone back
Out of this chain.

THYRSIS

     I shall not spill a drop.
     (CORYDON *drinks, meanwhile
     beginning to strangle* THYR-
     SIS.*)

THYRSIS

Don't pull the string so tight.

CORYDON

               You're spilling the
     water.

THYRSIS

You've had enough—you've had
     enough—stop pulling
The string so tight!

CORYDON

     Why, that's not tight at all. . . .
How's this?

THYRSIS

(*Drops bowl.*)
You're strangling me! Oh, Corydon!
It's only a game!—and you are
strangling me!

CORYDON

It's only a game, is it?—Yet I be-
lieve
You've poisoned me in earnest!
(*Writhes and pulls the strings
tighter, winding them about
THYRSIS' neck.*)

THYRSIS

Corydon!
(*Dies.*)

CORYDON

You've poisoned me in earnest. . . .
I feel so cold. . . .
So cold . . . this is a very silly game.
Why do we play it?—let's not play
this game
A minute more . . . let's make a little song
About a lamb. . . . I'm coming over
the wall,
No matter what you say—I want to
be near you. . . .
(*Groping his way, with arms
wide before him, he strides
through the frail papers of
the wall without knowing it,
and continues seeking for
the wall straight across the
stage.*)
Where is the wall?
(*Gropes his way back, and
stands very near THYRSIS
without knowing it; he
speaks slowly.*)
There isn't any wall,
I think.
(*Takes a step forward, his foot
touches THYRSIS' body, and
he falls down beside him.*)
Thyrsis, where is your cloak?
—just give me

A little bit of your cloak! . . .
(*Draws corner of THYRSIS'
cloak over his shoulders, falls
across THYRSIS' body, and
dies.*)
(COTHURNUS *closes the prompt-
book with a bang, arises
matter-of-factly, comes down
stage, and places the table
over the two bodies, drawing down the cover so that
they are hidden from any
actors on the stage, but visible to the audience, pushing
in their feet and hands with
his boot. He then turns his
back to the audience, and
claps his hands twice.*)

COTHURNUS

Strike the scene!
(*Exit* COTHURNUS. *Enter* PIER-
ROT *and* COLUMBINE.)

PIERROT

Don't puff so, Columbine!

COLUMBINE

Lord, what a mess
This set is in! If there's one thing I
hate
Above everything else—even more
than getting my feet wet—
It's clutter!—He might at least have
left the scene
The way he found it. . . . don't you
say so, Pierrot?
(*She picks up punch bowl.
They arrange chairs as be-
fore at ends of table.*)

PIERROT

Well, I don't know. I think it rather
diverting
The way it is.
(*Yawns, picks up confetti
bowl.*)
Shall we begin?

COLUMBINE

(*Screams.*)
                    My God!
What's that there under the table?

PIERROT

                    It is the bodies
Of the two shepherds from the other
play.

COLUMBINE

(*Slowly.*)
How curious to strangle him like
    that,
With colored paper ribbons!

PIERROT

                    Yes, and yet
I dare say he is just as dead.
    (*Pause. Calls* COTHURNUS.)
Come drag these bodies out of here!
    We can't
Sit down and eat with two dead
    bodies lying
Under the table! . . . The audience
    wouldn't stand for it!

COTHURNUS

(*Off stage.*)
What makes you think so?—Pull
    down the tablecloth
On the other play, and hide them
    from the house,
And play the farce. The audience
    will forget.

PIERROT

That's so. Give me a hand there,
Columbine.

(PIERROT *and* COLUMBINE *pull
down the table cover in such
a way that the two bodies
are hidden from the house,
then merrily set their bowls
back on the table, draw up
their chairs, and begin the
play exactly as before, speaking even more rapidly and
artificially.*)

COLUMBINE

Pierrot, a macaroon—I cannot *live*
Without a macaroon!

PIERROT

                    My only love,
You are *so* intense! . . . Is it Tues-
    day, Columbine?—
I'll kiss you if it's Tuesday.
    (*Curtains begin to close
    slowly.*)

COLUMBINE

                    It is Wednesday,
If you must know. . . . Is this my
    artichoke,
Or yours?

PIERROT

                    Ah, Columbine, as if it
    mattered!
Wednesday. . . . Will it be Tues-
    day, then tomorrow,
By any chance?

CURTAIN

Overtones

A ONE-ACT PLAY

BY ALICE GERSTENBERG

CHARACTERS

HARRIET, *a cultured woman*
HETTY, *her primitive self*
MARGARET, *a cultured woman*
MAGGIE, *her primitive self*

OVERTONES

TIME—*The present.*

SCENE—HARRIET'S *fashionable living-room. The door at the back leads to the hall. In the center a tea table with a high-backed chair at each side.*

HARRIET'S *gown is a light, "jealous" green. Her counterpart,* HETTY, *wears a gown of the same design but in a darker shade.* MARGARET *wears a gown of lavender chiffon while her counterpart,* MAGGIE, *wears a gown of the same design in purple, a purple scarf veiling her face. Chiffon is used to give a sheer effect, suggesting a possibility of primitive and cultured selves merging into one woman. The primitive and cultured selves never come into actual physical contact but try to sustain the impression of mental conflict.* HARRIET *never sees* HETTY, *never talks to her but rather thinks aloud looking into space.* HETTY, *however, looks at* HARRIET, *talks intently and shadows her continually. The same is true of* MARGARET *and* MAGGIE. *The voices of the cultured women are affected and lingering, the voices of the primitive impulsive and more or less staccato.*

When the curtain rises HARRIET *is seated right of tea table, busying herself with the tea things.*

HETTY. Harriet. (*There is no answer*) Harriet, my other self. (*There is no answer*) My trained self.

HARRIET (*Listens intently*). Yes?

(*From behind* HARRIET'S *chair* HETTY *rises slowly.*)

HETTY. I want to talk to you.

HARRIET. Well?

HETTY (*looking at* HARRIET *admiringly*). Oh, Harriet, you are beautiful today.

HARRIET. Am I presentable, Hetty?

HETTY. Suits me.

HARRIET. I've tried to make the best of the good points.

HETTY. My passions are deeper than yours. I can't keep on the mask as you do. I'm crude and real, you are my appearance in the world.

HARRIET. I am what you wish the world to believe you are.

HETTY. You are the part of me that has been trained.

HARRIET. I am your educated self.

HETTY. I am the rushing river; you are the ice over the current.

HARRIET. I am your subtle overtones.

HETTY. But together we are one woman, the wife of Charles Goodrich.

HARRIET. There I disagree with you, Hetty, I alone am his wife.

HETTY (*indignantly*). Harriet, how can you say such a thing!

HARRIET. Certainly. I am the one who flatters him. I have to be the one who talks to him. If I gave you a chance you would tell him at once that you dislike him.

HETTY (*moving away*). I don't love him, that's certain.

HARRIET. You leave all the fibbing to me. He doesn't suspect that my calm, suave manner hides your hatred. Considering the amount of scheming it causes me it can safely be said that he is my husband.

HETTY. Oh, if you love him—

HARRIET. I? I haven't any feelings. It isn't my business to love anybody.

HETTY. Then why need you object to calling him my husband?

HARRIET. I resent your appropriation of a man who is managed only through the cleverness of my artifice.

HETTY. You may be clever enough to deceive him, Harriet, but I am still the one who suffers. I can't forget he is my husband. I can't forget that I might have married John Caldwell.

HARRIET. How foolish of you to remember John, just because we met his wife by chance.

HETTY. That's what I want to talk to you about. She may be here at any moment. I want to advise you about what to say to her this afternoon.

HARRIET. By all means tell me now and don't interrupt while she is here. You have a most annoying habit of talking to me when people are present. Sometimes it is all I can do to keep my poise and appear *not* to be listening to you.

HETTY. Impress her.

HARRIET. Hetty, dear, is it not my custom to impress people?

HETTY. I hate her.

HARRIET. I can't let her see that.

HETTY. I hate her because she married John.

HARRIET. Only after you had refused him.

HETTY (*turning to* HARRIET). Was it my fault that I refused him?

HARRIET. That's right, blame me.

HETTY. It was your fault. You told me he was too poor and never would be able to do anything in painting. Look at him now, known in Europe, just returned from eight years in Paris, famous.

HARRIET. It was too poor a gamble at the time. It was much safer to accept Charles's money and position.

HETTY. And then John married Margaret within the year.

HARRIET. Out of spite.

HETTY. Freckled, gauky-looking thing she was, too.

HARRIET (*a little sadly*). Europe improved her. She was stunning the other morning.

HETTY. Make her jealous today.

HARRIET. Shall I be haughty or cordial or caustic or—

HETTY. Above all else you must let her know that we are rich.

HARRIET. Oh, yes, I do that quite easily now.

HETTY. You must put it on a bit.

HARRIET. Never fear.

HETTY. Tell her I love my husband.

HARRIET. My husband—

HETTY. Are you going to quarrel with me?

HARRIET (*moves away*). No, I have no desire to quarrel with you. It is quite too uncomfortable. I couldn't get away from you if I tried.

HETTY (*stamping her foot and following* HARRIET). You were a stupid fool to make me refuse John, I'll never forgive you—never—

HARRIET (*stopping and holding up her hand*). Don't get me all excited. I'll be in no condition to meet her properly this afternoon.

HETTY (*passionately*). I could choke you for robbing me of John.

HARRIET (*retreating*). Don't muss me!

HETTY. You don't know how you have made me suffer.

HARRIET (*beginning to feel the strength of* HETTY's *emotion surge through her and trying to conquer it*). It is not my business to have heartaches.

HETTY. You're bloodless. Nothing but sham—sham—while I—

HARRIET (*emotionally*). Be quiet! I can't let her see that I have been fighting with my inner self.

HETTY. And now after all my suffering you say it has cost you more than it has cost me to be married to Charles. But it's the pain here in my heart—I've paid the price—I've paid—Charles is not your husband!

HARRIET (*trying to conquer emotion*). He is.

HETTY (*follows* HARRIET). He isn't.

HARRIET (*weakly*). He is.

HETTY (*towering over* HARRIET). He isn't! I'll kill you!

HARRIET (*overpowered, sinks into a chair*). Don't—don't you're stronger than I—you're—

HETTY. Say he's mine.

HARRIET. He's ours.

HETTY (*the telephone rings*). There she is now. (HETTY *hurries to* 'phone *but* HARRIET *regains her supremacy*.)

HARRIET (*authoritatively*). Wait! I can't let the telephone girl down there hear my real self. It isn't proper. (*At* 'phone) Show Mrs. Caldwell up.

HETTY. I'm so excited, my heart's in my mouth.

HARRIET (*at the mirror*). A nice state you've put my nerves into.

HETTY. Don't let her see you're nervous.

HARRIET. Quick, put the veil on, or she'll see *you* shining through me. (HARRIET *takes a scarf of chiffon that has been lying over the back of a chair and drapes it on* HETTY, *covering her face. The chiffon is the same color of their gowns but paler in shade so that it pales* HETTY's *darker gown to match* HARRIET's *lighter one. As* HETTY *moves in the following scene the chiffon falls away revealing now and then the gown of deeper dye underneath.*)

HETTY. Tell her Charles is rich and fascinating—boast of our friends, make her feel she needs us.

HARRIET. I'll make her ask John to paint us.

HETTY. That's just my thought—if John paints our portrait—

HARRIET. We can wear an exquisite gown—

HETTY. And make him fall in love again and—

HARRIET (*schemingly*). Yes. (MARGARET *parts the portières back center and extends her hand.* MARGARET *is followed by her counterpart* MAGGIE) Oh, Margaret, I'm so glad to see you!

HETTY (*to* MAGGIE). That's a lie.

MARGARET (*in superficial voice throughout*). It's enchanting to see you, Harriet.

MAGGIE (*in emotional voice throughout*). I'd bite you, if I dared.

HARRIET (*to* MARGARET). Wasn't our meeting a stroke of luck?

MARGARET (*coming down left of table*). I've thought of you so often, Harriet; and to come back and find you living in New York.

HARRIET (*coming down right of table*). Mr. Goodrich has many interests here.

MAGGIE (*to* MARGARET). Flatter her.

MARGARET. I know, Mr. Goodrich is so successful.

HETTY (*to* HARRIET). Tell her we're rich.

HARRIET (*to* MARGARET). Won't you sit down?

MARGARET (*takes a chair*). What a beautiful cabinet!

HARRIET. Do you like it? I'm afraid Charles paid an extravagant price.

MAGGIE (*to* HETTY). I don't believe it.

MARGARET (*sitting down. To* HARRIET). I am sure he must have.

HARRIET (*sitting down*). How well you are looking, Margaret.

HETTY. Yes, you are not. There are circles under your eyes.

MAGGIE (*to* HETTY). I haven't eaten since breakfast and I'm hungry.

MARGARET (*to* HARRIET). How well you are looking, too.

MAGGIE (*to* HETTY). You have hard

lines about your lips, are you happy?

HETTY (*to* HARRIET). Don't let her know that I'm unhappy.

HARRIET (*to* MARGARET). Why shouldn't I look well? My life is full, happy, complete—

MAGGIE. I wonder.

HETTY (*in* HARRIET'S *ear*). Tell her we have an automobile.

MARGARET (*to* HARRIET). My life is complete, too.

MAGGIE. My heart is torn with sorrow; my husband cannot make a living. He will kill himself if he does not get an order for a painting.

MARGARET (*laughs*). You must come and see us in our studio. John has been doing some excellent portraits. He cannot begin to fill his orders.

HETTY (*to* HARRIET). Tell her we have an automobile.

HARRIET (*to* MARGARET). Do you take lemon in your tea?

MAGGIE. Take cream. It's more filling.

MARGARET (*looking nonchalantly at tea things*). No, cream, if you please. How cozy!

MAGGIE (*glaring at tea things*) Only cakes! I could eat them all!

HARRIET (*to* MARGARET). How many lumps?

MAGGIE (*to* MARGARET). Sugar is nourishing.

MARGARET (*to* HARRIET). Three, please. I used to drink very sweet coffee in Turkey and ever since I've—

HETTY. I don't believe you were ever in Turkey.

MAGGIE. I wasn't, but it is none of your business.

HARRIET (*pouring tea*). Have you been in Turkey? Do tell me about it.

MAGGIE (*to* MARGARET). Change the subject.

MARGARET (*to* HARRIET). You must go there. You have so much taste in dress you would enjoy seeing their costumes.

MAGGIE. Isn't she going to pass the cake?

MARGARET (*to* HARRIET). John painted several portraits there.

HETTY (*to* HARRIET). Why don't you stop her bragging and tell her we have an automobile?

HARRIET (*offers cake across the table to* MARGARET). Cake?

MAGGIE (*stands back of* MARGARET, *shadowing her as* HETTY *shadows* HARRIET. MAGGIE *reaches claws out for the cake and groans with joy*). At last! (*But her claws do not touch the cake.*)

MARGARET (*with a graceful, nonchalant hand places cake upon her plate and bites at it slowly and delicately*). Thank you.

HETTY (*to* HARRIET). Automobile!

MAGGIE (*to* MARGARET). Follow up the costumes with the suggestion that she would make a good model for John. It isn't too early to begin getting what you came for.

MARGARET (*ignoring* MAGGIE). What delicious cake.

HETTY (*excitedly to* HARRIET). There's your chance for the auto.

HARRIET (*nonchalantly to* MARGARET). Yes, it is good cake, isn't it? There are always a great many people buying it at Harper's. I sat in my automobile fifteen minutes this morning waiting for my chauffeur to get it.

MAGGIE (*to* MARGARET). Make her order a portrait.

MARGARET (*to* HARRIET). If you stopped at Harper's you must have noticed the new gowns at Henderson's. Aren't the shop windows alluring these days?

HARRIET. Even my chauffeur notices them.

MAGGIE. I know you have an automobile, I heard you the first time.

MARGARET. I notice gowns now with an artist's eye as John does. The one you have on, my dear, is very paintable.

HETTY. Don't let her see you're anxious to be painted.

HARRIET (*nonchalantly*). Oh, it's just a little model.

MAGGIE (*to* MARGARET). Don't seem anxious to get the order.

MARGARET (*nonchalantly*). Perhaps it isn't the gown itself but the way you wear it that pleases the eye. Some people can wear anything with grace.

HETTY. Yes, I'm very graceful.

HARRIET (*to* MARGARET). You flatter me, my dear.

MARGARET. On the contrary, Harriet, I have an intense admiration for you. I remember how beautiful you were—as a girl. In fact, I was quite jealous when John was paying you so much attention.

HETTY. She is gloating because I lost him.

HARRIET. Those were childhood days in a country town.

MAGGIE (*to* MARGARET). She's trying to make you feel that John was only a country boy.

MARGARET. Most great men have come from the country. There is a fair chance that John will be added to the list.

HETTY. I know it and I am bitterly jealous of you.

HARRIET. Undoubtedly he owes much of his success to you, Margaret, your experience in economy and your ability to endure hardship. Those first few years in Paris must have been a struggle.

MAGGIE. She is sneering at your poverty.

MARGARET. Yes, we did find life difficult at first, not the luxurious start a girl has who marries wealth.

HETTY (*to* HARRIET). Deny that you married Charles for his money. (HARRIET *deems it wise to ignore* HETTY's *advice*.)

MARGARET. But John and I are so congenial in our tastes, that we were impervious to hardship or unhappiness.

HETTY (*in anguish*). Do you love each other? Is it really true?

HARRIET (*sweetly*). Did you have all the romance of starving for his art?

MAGGIE (*to* MARGARET). She's taunting you. Get even with her.

MARGARET. Not for long. Prince Rier soon discovered John's genius, and introduced him royally to wealthy Parisians who gave him many orders.

HETTY (*to* MAGGIE). Are you telling the truth or are you lying?

HARRIET. If he had so many opportunities there, you must have had great inducements to come back to the States.

MAGGIE (*to* HETTY). We did, but not the kind you think.

MARGARET. John became the rage among Americans traveling in France, too, and they simply insisted upon his coming here.

HARRIET. Whom is he going to paint here?

MAGGIE (*frightened*). What names dare I make up?

MARGARET (*calmly*). Just at present Miss Dorothy Ainsworth of Oregon is posing. You may not know the name, but she is the daughter of a wealthy miner who found gold in Alaska.

HARRIET. I dare say there are many Western people we have never heard of.

MARGARET. You must have found social life in New York very interesting, Harriet, after the simplicity of our home town.

HETTY (*to* MAGGIE). There's no need to remind us that our beginnings were the same.

HARRIET. Of course Charles's family made everything delightful for me. They are so well connected.

MAGGIE (*to* MARGARET). Flatter her.

MARGARET. I heard it mentioned yesterday that you had made yourself very popular. Some one said you were very clever!

HARRIET (*pleased*). Who told you that?

MAGGIE. Nobody!

MARGARET (*pleasantly*). Oh, confidences should be suspected—respected, I mean. They said, too, that you are gaining some reputation as a critic of art.

HARRIET. I make no pretenses.

MARGARET. Are you and Mr. Goodrich interested in the same things, too?

HETTY. No!

HARRIET. Yes, indeed, Charles and I are inseparable.

MAGGIE. I wonder.

HARRIET. Do have another cake.

MAGGIE (*in relief*). Oh, yes. (*Again her claws extend but do not touch the cake.*)

MARGARET (*takes cake delicately*). I really shouldn't—after my big luncheon. John took me to the Ritz and we are invited to the Bedford's for dinner—they have such a magnificent house near the drive—I really shouldn't, but the cakes are so good.

MAGGIE. Starving!

HARRIET (*to* MARGARET). More tea?

MAGGIE. Yes!

MARGARET. No, thank you. How wonderfully life has arranged itself for you. Wealth, position, a happy marriage, every opportunity to enjoy all pleasures; beauty, art—how happy you must be.

HETTY (*in anguish*). Don't call me happy. I've never been happy since I gave up John. All these years without him—a future without him—no —no—I shall win him back—away from you—away from you—

HARRIET (*does not see* MAGGIE *pointing to cream and* MARGARET *stealing some*). I sometimes think it is unfair for anyone to be as happy

as I am. Charles and I are just as much in love now as when we married. To me he is just the dearest man in the world.

MAGGIE (*passionately*). My John is. I love him so much I could die for him. I'm going through hunger and want to make him great and he loves me. He worships me!

MARGARET (*leisurely to* HARRIET). I should like to meet Mr. Goodrich. Bring him to our studio. John has some sketches to show. Not many, because all the portraits have been purchased by the subjects. He gets as much as four thousand dollars now.

HETTY (*to* HARRIET). Don't pay that much.

HARRIET (*to* MARGARET). As much as that?

MARGARET. It is not really too much when one considers that John is in the foremost ranks of artists today. A picture painted by him now will double and treble in value.

MAGGIE. It's a lie. He is growing weak with despair.

HARRIET. Does he paint all day long?

MAGGIE. No, he draws advertisements for our bread.

MARGARET (*to* HARRIET). When you and your husband come to see us, telephone first—

MAGGIE. Yes, so he can get the advertisements out of the way.

MARGARET. Otherwise you might

arrive while he has a sitter, and John refuses to let me disturb him then.

HETTY. Make her ask for an order.

HARRIET (*to* MARGARET). Le Grange offered to paint me for a thousand.

MARGARET. Louis Le Grange's reputation isn't worth more than that.

HARRIET. Well, I've heard his work well mentioned.

MAGGIE. Yes, he is doing splendid work.

MARGARET. Oh, dear me, no. He is only praised by the masses. He is accepted not at all by artists themselves.

HETTY (*anxiously*). Must I really pay the full price?

HARRIET. Le Grange thought I would make a good subject.

MAGGIE (*to* MARGARET). Let her fish for it.

MARGARET. Of course you would. Why don't you let Le Grange paint you, if you *trust* him?

HETTY. She doesn't seem anxious to have John do it.

HARRIET. But if Le Grange isn't accepted by artists, it would be a waste of time to pose for him, wouldn't it?

MARGARET. Yes, I think it would.

MAGGIE (*passionately to* HETTY *across back of table*). Give us the order. John is so despondent he can't endure much longer. Help us! Help me! Save us!

HETTY (*to* HARRIET). Don't seem too eager.

HARRIET. And yet if he charges only a thousand one might consider it.

MARGARET. If you really wish to be painted, why don't you give a little more and have a portrait really worth while? John might be induced to do you for a little below his usual price considering that you used to be such good friends.

HETTY (*in glee*). Hurrah!

HARRIET (*quietly to* MARGARET). That's very nice of you to suggest— of course I don't know—

MAGGIE (*in fear*). For God's sake, say yes.

MARGARET (*quietly to* HARRIET). Of course, I don't know whether John would. He is very peculiar in these matters. He sets his value on his work and thinks it beneath him to discuss price.

HETTY (*to* MAGGIE). You needn't try to make us feel small.

MARGARET. Still, I might quite delicately mention to him that inasmuch as you have many influential friends you would be very glad to—to—

MAGGIE (*to* HETTY). Finish what I don't want to say.

HETTY (*to* HARRIET). Help her out.

HARRIET. Oh, yes, introductions will follow the exhibition of my portrait No doubt I—

HETTY (*to* HARRIET). Be patroniz ing.

HARRIET. No doubt I shall be able to introduce your husband to his advantage.

MAGGIE (*relieved*). Saved.

MARGARET. If I find John in a propitious mood I shall take pleasure, for your sake, in telling him about your beauty. Just as you are sitting now would be a lovely pose.

MAGGIE (*to* MARGARET). We can go now.

HETTY (*to* HARRIET). Don't let her think she is doing us a favor.

HARRIET. It will give me pleasure to add my name to your husband's list of patronesses.

MAGGIE (*excitedly to* MARGARET). Run home and tell John the good news.

MARGARET (*leisurely to* HARRIET). I little guessed when I came for a pleasant chat about old times that it would develop into business arrangements. I had no idea, Harriet, that you had any intention of being painted. By Le Grange, too. Well, I came just in time to rescue you.

MAGGIE (*to* MARGARET). Run home and tell John. Hurry, hurry!

HETTY (*to* HARRIET). You managed the order very neatly. She doesn't suspect that you wanted it.

HARRIET. Now if I am not satisfied with my portrait I shall blame you, Margaret, dear. I am relying upon your opinion of John's talent.

MAGGIE (*to* MARGARET). She doesn't suspect what you came for. Run home and tell John!

HARRIET. You always had a brilliant mind, Margaret.

MARGARET. Ah, it is you who flatter, now.

MAGGIE (*to* MARGARET). You don't have to stay so long. Hurry home!

HARRIET. Ah, one does not flatter when one tells the truth.

MARGARET (*smiles*). I must be going or you will have me completely under your spell.

HETTY (*looks at clock*). Yes, do go. I have to dress for dinner.

HARRIET (*to* MARGARET). Oh, don't hurry.

MAGGIE (*to* HETTIE). I hate you!

MARGARET (*to* HARRIET). No, really I must, but I hope we shall see each other often at the studio. I find you so stimulating.

HETTY (*to* MAGGIE). I hate you!

HARRIET (*to* MARGARET). It is indeed gratifying to find a kindred spirit.

MAGGIE (*to* HETTY). I came for your gold.

MARGARET (*to* HARRIET). How delightful it is to know you again.

HETTY (*to* MAGGIE). I am going to make you and your husband suffer.

HARRIET. My kind regards to John.

MAGGIE (*to* HETTY). He has forgotten all about you.

MARGARET (*rises*). He will be so happy to receive them.

HETTY (*to* MAGGIE). I can hardly wait to talk to him again.

HARRIET. I shall wait, then, until you send me word?

MARGARET (*offering her hand*). I'll speak to John about it as soon as I can and tell you when to come.
(HARRIET *takes* MARGARET'*s hand affectionately.* HETTY *and* MAGGIE *rush at each other, throw back their veils, and fling their speeches fiercely at each other.*)

HETTY. I love him—I love him—

MAGGIE. He's starving—I'm starving—

HETTY. I'm going to take him away from you—

MAGGIE. I want your money—and your influence.

HETTY *and* MAGGIE. I'm going to rob you—rob you.
(*There is a cymbal crash, the lights go out and come up again slowly, leaving only* MARGARET *and* HARRIET *visible.*)

MARGARET (*quietly to* HARRIET). I've had such a delightful afternoon.

HARRIET (*offering her hand*). It has been a joy to see you.

MARGARET (*sweetly to* HARRIET). Good-bye.

HARRIET (*sweetly to* MARGARET *as she kisses her*). Good-bye, my dear.

CURTAIN

Fumed Oak

AN UNPLEASANT COMEDY IN TWO SCENES

BY NOEL COWARD

From Tonight at 8:30

CHARACTERS

HENRY GOW
DORIS, *his wife*
ELSIE, *his daughter*
MRS. ROCKETT, *his mother-in-law*

SCENE I. Morning.
SCENE II. Evening.

The action of the play passes in the sitting-room of the Gows' house in South London.

The time is the present day.

FUMED OAK

SCENE ONE

The Gows' sitting-room is indistinguishable from several thousand other suburban sitting-rooms. The dominant note is refinement. There are French windows at the back opening on to a narrow lane of garden. These are veiled discreetly by lace curtains set off by pieces of rather faded blue casement cloth. There is a tiled fireplace on the L.; an upright piano between it and the window; a fumed-oak sideboard on the R. and, below it, a door leading to the hall, the stairs and the front door. There is a fumed-oak dining-room set consisting of a table and six chairs; a sofa; an armchair in front of the fire; and a plentiful sprinkling over the entire room of ornaments and framed photographs.

When the curtain rises it is about eight-thirty on a spring morning. Rain is trickling down the windows and breakfast is laid on the table.

MRS. ROCKETT is seated in the armchair by the fire; on a small table next to her is a workbasket. She is a fattish, gray-looking woman dressed in a blouse and skirt and a pepper-and-salt jumper of artificial silk. Her pince-nez snap in and out of a little clip on her bosom and her feet are bad, which necessitates the wearing of large quilted slippers in the house. DORIS, aged about thirty-five, is seated R. of the table reading a newspaper propped up against the cruet. She is thin and anæmic, and whatever traces of past prettiness she might have are obscured by the pursed-up, rather sour gentility of her expression. She wears a nondescript coat-frock, a slave bangle and a necklace of amber glass beads. ELSIE, her daughter, aged about fourteen, is sitting opposite to her, cutting her toast into strips in order to dip them into her boiled egg. She is a straight-haired ordinary-looking girl dressed in a navy blue school dress with a glacé red leather waist-belt.

There is complete silence broken only by the occasional rattle of a spoon in a cup or a sniffle from ELSIE, who has a slight head cold.

HENRY GOW comes into the room. He is tall and spare, neatly dressed in a blue serge suit. He wears rimless glasses and his hair is going gray at the sides and thin on the top. He sits down at the table, up stage, without a word. DORIS automatically rises and goes out, returning in a moment with a plate of haddock, which she places in front of him and resumes her place. HENRY pours himself out some tea. DORIS, without looking at him, being reimmersed in the paper, passes him the milk and sugar. HENRY stretches for toast across the table.

The silence continues until ELSIE breaks it.

ELSIE. Mum?

DORIS. What?

ELSIE. When can I put my hair up?

DORIS (*snappily*). When you're old enough.

ELSIE. Gladys Pierce is the same age as me and she's got hers up.

499

DORIS. Never you mind about Gladys Pierce, get on with your breakfast.

ELSIE. I don't see why I can't have it cut. That would be better than nothing. (*This remark is ignored*) Maisie Blake had hers cut last week and it looks lovely.

DORIS. Never you mind about Maisie Blake neither. She's common.

ELSIE. Miss Pritchard doesn't think so. Miss Pritchard likes Maisie Blake a lot, she said it looked ever so nice.

DORIS (*irritably*). What?

ELSIE. Her hair.

DORIS. Get on with your breakfast. You'll be late.

ELSIE (*petulantly*). Oh, Mum——

DORIS. And stop sniffling. Sniffle, sniffle, sniffle! Haven't you got a handkerchief?

ELSIE. Yes, but it's a clean one.

DORIS. Never mind, use it.

MRS. ROCKETT. The child can't help having a cold.

DORIS. She can blow her nose, can't she, even if she has got a cold?

ELSIE (*conversationally*). Dodie Watson's got a terrible cold, she's had it for weeks. It went to her chest and then it went back to her head again.

MRS. ROCKETT. That's the worst of schools, you're always catching something.

ELSIE. Miss Pritchard's awful mean to Dodie Watson, she said she'd had enough of it.

DORIS. Enough of what?

ELSIE. Her cold.
(*There is silence again, which is presently shattered by the wailing of a baby in the house next door.*)

MRS. ROCKETT. There's that child again. It kept me awake all night

DORIS. I'm very sorry, I'm sure. (*She picks up the newspaper.*)

MRS. ROCKETT (*fiddling in her work-basket*). I wasn't blaming you.

DORIS. The night before last it was the hot-water pipes.

MRS. ROCKETT. You ought to have them seen to.

DORIS. You know as well as I do you can't stop them making that noise every now and then.

MRS. ROCKETT (*threading a needle*). I'm sure I don't know why you don't get a plumber in.

DORIS (*grandly*). Because I do not consider it necessary.

MRS. ROCKETT. You would if you slept in my room—gurgle gurgle gurgle all night long—it's all very fine for you, you're at the end of the passage.

DORIS (*with meaning*). You don't have to sleep there.

MRS. ROCKETT. What do you mean by that?

DORIS. You know perfectly well what I mean.

MRS. ROCKETT (*with spirit*). Listen to me, Doris Gow. I've got a perfect right to complain if I want to, and well you know it. It isn't as if I was staying here for nothing.

DORIS. I really don't know what's the matter with you lately, Mother, you do nothing but grumble.

MRS. ROCKETT. Me, grumble! I like that, I'm sure. That's rich, that is.

DORIS. Well, you do. It gives me a headache.

MRS. ROCKETT. You ought to do something about those headaches of yours. They seem to pop on and off at the least thing.

DORIS. And I wish you wouldn't keep passing remarks about not staying here for nothing.

MRS. ROCKETT. Well, it's true, I don't.

DORIS. Anyone would think we was taking advantage of you, to hear you talk.

MRS. ROCKETT. Well, they wouldn't be far wrong.

DORIS. Mother, how can you! You're not paying a penny more than you can afford.

MRS. ROCKETT. I never said I was. It isn't the money, it's the lack of consideration.
(ELSIE *puts her exercise book away in her satchel.*)

DORIS. Pity you don't go and live with Nora for a change.

MRS. ROCKETT. Nora hasn't got a spare room.

DORIS. Phyllis has, a lovely one, looking out over the railway. I'm sure her hot-water pipes wouldn't keep you awake, there isn't enough hot water in them.

MRS. ROCKETT. Of course, if I'm not wanted here, I can always go to a boarding-house or a private hotel.

DORIS. Catch you!

MRS. ROCKETT. I'm not the sort to outstay my welcome anywhere . . .

DORIS. Oh, for heaven's sake don't start that again . . . (*She bangs the paper down on the table.*)

MRS. ROCKETT (*addressing the air*). It seems as though some of us had got out of bed the wrong side this morning.

ELSIE. Mum, can I have some more toast?

DORIS. No.

ELSIE. I could make it myself over the kitchen fire.

DORIS. No, I tell you. Can't you understand plain English? You've had quite enough and you'll be late for school.

MRS. ROCKETT. Never mind, Elsie, here's twopence. (*Taking it out of her purse*) You can buy yourself a sponge-cake at Barrets.

ELSIE (*rising and taking the twopence*). Thanks, Grandma.

DORIS. You'll do no such thing, Elsie.

I'm not going to have a child of mine stuffing herself with cake in the middle of the High Street.

MRS. ROCKETT (*sweetly*). Eat it in the shop, dear.

DORIS. Go on, you'll be late.

ELSIE. Oh, Mum, it's only ten to.

DORIS. Do as I tell you.

ELSIE. Oh, all right. (*She crosses in front of the table and goes sullenly out of the room and can be heard scampering noisily up the stairs.*)

MRS. ROCKETT (*irritatingly*). Poor little soul.

DORIS. I'll trouble you not to spoil Elsie, Mother.

MRS. ROCKETT. Spoil her! I like that. Better than half-starving her.

DORIS (*hotly*). Are you insinuating . . .

MRS. ROCKETT. I'm not insinuating anything. Elsie's getting a big girl, she only had one bit of toast for her breakfast and she used that for her egg. I saw her.

DORIS (*rising and putting away the paper in the sideboard drawer*). It's none of your business, and in future I'd be much obliged if you'd keep your twopences to yourself (*She returns to her seat at the table.*)
(HENRY *rises and fetches the paper out.*)

MRS. ROCKETT (*hurt*). Very well, of course if I'm to be abused every time I try to bring a little happiness into the child's life . . .

DORIS. Anyone would think I ill-treated her the way you talk.

MRS. ROCKETT. You certainly nag her enough.

DORIS. I don't do any such thing— and I wish you'd leave me to bring up my own child in my own way.

MRS. ROCKETT. That cold's been hanging over her for weeks and a fat lot you care——

DORIS (*rising and getting tray from beside the sideboard*). I've dosed her for it, haven't I? The whole house stinks of Vapex. What more can I do?

MRS. ROCKETT. She ought to have had Doctor Bristow last Saturday when it was so bad. He'd have cleared it up in no time.

DORIS (*putting tray on her chair and beginning to clear things onto it*). You and your Doctor Bristow.

MRS. ROCKETT. Nice thing if it turned to bronchitis. (DORIS *throws scraps into the fire*) Mrs. Henderson's Muriel got bronchitis, all through neglecting a cold; the poor child couldn't breathe, they had to have two kettles going night and day——

DORIS. I suppose your precious Doctor Bristow told you that.

MRS. ROCKETT. Yes, he did, and what's more, he saved the girl's life, you ask Mrs. Henderson.

DORIS. Catch me ask Mrs. Henderson anything, stuck up thing. . . .

MRS. ROCKETT. Mrs. Henderson's a very nice ladylike woman, just because she's quiet and a bit reserved you say she's stuck up . . .

DORIS. Who does she think she is, anyway, Lady Mountbatten? (*She takes the cruet to the sideboard.*)

MRS. ROCKETT. Really, Doris, you make me tired sometimes, you do really.

DORIS. If you're so fond of Mrs. Henderson it's a pity you don't see more of her. I notice you don't go there often.

MRS. ROCKETT (*with dignity*). I go when I am invited.

DORIS (*triumphantly*). Exactly.

MRS. ROCKETT. She's not the kind of woman that likes people popping in and out all the time. We can't all be Amy Fawcetts.

DORIS. What's the matter with Amy Fawcett? (*She takes the teapot to the sideboard.*)

MRS. ROCKETT. Well, she's common for one thing, she dyes her hair for another, and she's a bit too free and easy all round for my taste.

DORIS. She doesn't put on airs, anyway.

MRS. ROCKETT. I should think not, after the sort of life she's led.

DORIS (*takes bread to sideboard*). How do you know what sort of a life she's led?

MRS. ROCKETT. Everybody knows, you only have to look at her; I'm a woman of the world, I am, you can't pull the wool over my eyes——

(ELSIE *comes into the room wearing a mackintosh and a tam-o'-shanter.*)

ELSIE. Mum, we want a new roll of toilet paper.

DORIS. How many times have I told you ladies don't talk about such things!

ELSIE (*as she stamps over to the piano and begins to search untidily through a pile of music on it*). It's right down to the bit of cardboard.

DORIS (*scraping the bottom of her cup on the saucer*). Don't untidy everything like that. What are you looking for?

ELSIE. "The Pixies' Parade," I had it last night.

DORIS. If it's the one with the blue cover it's at the bottom.

ELSIE. It isn't—oh dear, Miss Pritchard will be mad at me if I can't find it.

MRS. ROCKETT (*rising*). Perhaps you put it in your satchel, dear. Here, let me look—— (*She opens* ELSIE'S *satchel which is hanging over the back of a chair and fumbles in it*) Is this it?

ELSIE. Oh yes, thanks, Grandma.

DORIS. Go along now, for heaven's sake, you'll be late.

(MRS. ROCKETT *helps* ELSIE *on with her satchel.*)

ELSIE. Oh, all right, Mum. Goodbye, Grandma, good-bye, Dad.

HENRY. Good-bye.

MRS. ROCKETT. Good-bye, dear, give Grandma a kiss.
(ELSIE *does so.*)

DORIS (*pushing* ELSIE *out of the door*). Don't dawdle on the way home.

ELSIE. Oh, all right, Mum. (*She goes out. The slam of the front door shakes the house.*)

DORIS (*irritably*). There now.

MRS. ROCKETT (*with studied politeness*). If you are going down to the shops this morning, would it be troubling you too much to get me a reel of white cotton? (*She sits in the armchair.*)

DORIS (*tidying the piano*). I thought you were coming with me.

MRS. ROCKETT. I really don't feel up to it.

DORIS. I'll put it on my list. (*She takes a piece of paper out of the sideboard drawer and scribbles on it.*)

MRS. ROCKETT. If it's out of your way, please don't trouble. It'll do another time.

DORIS. Henry, it's past nine.

HENRY (*without looking up*). I know.

DORIS. You'll be late.

HENRY. Never mind.

DORIS. That's a nice way to talk, I must say.

MRS. ROCKETT. I'm sure if my Rob-

ert had ever lazed about like that in the mornings, I'd have thought the world had come to an end.

DORIS. Henry'll do it once too often, mark my words. (*She crosses behind* HENRY.)

MRS. ROCKETT (*biting off her thread*). Well, that corner's finished. (*She puts away her embroidery and starts to knit.*)

DORIS (*to* HENRY). You'll have to move now, I've got to clear. (*Taking first his saucer, then his cup, from his hand.*)
(HENRY *rises absently.*)

MRS. ROCKETT. Where's Ethel?

DORIS. Doing the bedroom. (HENRY *quietly goes out of the room*) (*Throwing more scraps on the* fire) Look at that wicked waste.

MRS. ROCKETT. What's the matter with him?

DORIS. Don't ask me, I'm sure I couldn't tell you.

MRS. ROCKETT. He came in very late last night, I heard him go into the bathroom. (*There is a pause*) That cistern makes a terrible noise.

DORIS (*emptying crumbs from cloth into fire and folding it*). Does it indeed!

MRS. ROCKETT. Yes, it does.

DORIS (*slamming the teapot onto the tray*). Very sorry, I'm sure.

MRS. ROCKETT. Where's he been?

DORIS. How do I know?

MRS. ROCKETT. Didn't you ask him?

DORIS. I wouldn't demean myself.

MRS. ROCKETT. Been drinking?

DORIS. No.

MRS. ROCKETT. Sounded very like it to me, all that banging about.

DORIS. You know Henry never touches a drop.

MRS. ROCKETT. I know he says he doesn't.

DORIS. Oh, do shut up, Mother, we're not all like Father. (*She puts the cloth in the sideboard drawer, then scrapes grease with her nail from the green cloth on the table.*)

MRS. ROCKETT. You watch your tongue, Doris Gow, don't let me hear you saying anything against the memory of your poor father.

DORIS. I wasn't.

MRS. ROCKETT (*belligerently*). Oh yes, you were, you were insinuating again.

DORIS (*hoisting up the tray*). Father drank and you know it, everybody knew it. (*She moves* L.)

MRS. ROCKETT. You're a wicked woman.

DORIS. It's true.

MRS. ROCKETT. Your father was a gentleman, which is more than your husband will ever be, with all his night-classes and his book reading —night-classes, indeed!

DORIS (*poking the fire*). Who's insinuating now?

MRS. ROCKETT (*angrily*). I am, and I'm not afraid to say so.

DORIS. What of it?

MRS. ROCKETT (*with heavy sarcasm*). I suppose he was at a night-class last night?

DORIS (*loudly*). Mind your own business.
(HENRY *comes in, wearing his mackintosh and a bowler hat.*)

HENRY. What's up?

DORIS. Where were you last night?

HENRY. Why?

DORIS. Mother wants to know and so do I.

HENRY. I was kept late at the shop and I had a bit of dinner in town.

DORIS. Who with?

HENRY. Charlie Henderson. (*He picks up the paper off the table and goes out. The baby next door bursts into fresh wails.*)

MRS. ROCKETT. There goes that child again. It's my belief it's hungry.

DORIS. Wonder you don't go and give it twopence to buy sponge-cake. (*She pulls the door open with her foot and goes out with the tray as the lights fade on the scene.*)

SCENE TWO

It is about seven-thirty in the evening. ELSIE *is sitting at the piano practising with the loud pedal firmly down all the time.* MRS. ROCKETT *is sitting
in her chair by the fire, but she is dressed in her street things and wearing
a black hat with a veil.* DORIS, *also in street clothes, is trying on paper pat-
terns.*

*There is a cloth across the upstage end of the table on which is set a loaf,
a plate of cold ham, a saucer with two tomatoes in it, a bottle of A1 sauce
and a teapot, tea-cup, sugar basin and milk jug.*

HENRY *comes in, taking off his mackintosh. He gives one look round the
room and goes out into the hall again to hang up his things.* ELSIE *stops
playing and comes over to* DORIS.

ELSIE. Mum, can we go now?

DORIS. In a minute.

ELSIE. We'll miss the Mickey.

DORIS. Put on your hat and don't
worry.

ELSIE (*grabbing her hat from the
sideboard*). Oh, all right.
(HENRY *re-enters.*)

DORIS. Your supper's all ready, the
kettle's on the gas stove when you
want it. (*Folding up paper pat-
terns*) We've had ours.

HENRY. Oh!

DORIS. And you needn't look injured,
either.

HENRY. Very well. (*He crosses in
front of the table.*)

DORIS. If you managed to get home a
bit earlier it'd save a lot of trouble
all round.

HENRY (*amiably*). Sorry, dear. (*He
warms his hands at the fire.*)

DORIS. It's all very fine to be sorry,
you've been getting later and later
these last few weeks, they can't
keep you overtime every night.

HENRY. All right, dear, I'll tell them.

DORIS. Here, Elsie, put these away
in the cupboard. Mind your fingers
with the scissors. (*She hands her a
pile of material and pieces of paper.*
ELSIE *obediently takes them and
puts them in the lefthand cupboard
of the sideboard.*)

HENRY (*sitting at the table*). Cold
ham, what a surprise!

DORIS (*looking at him sharply*).
What's the matter with it? (*She puts
on her coat.*)

HENRY. I don't know, yet.

DORIS. It's perfectly fresh, if that's
what you mean.
(ELSIE *crosses to* L.C.)

HENRY. Why are you all so dressed
up?

ELSIE. We're going to the pictures.
(*She picks up her bag and gloves.*)

HENRY. Oh, I see.

DORIS (*putting on her gloves*). You can put everything on the tray when you've finished and leave it in the kitchen for Ethel.

HENRY. Good old Ethel.

DORIS (*surprised*). What?

HENRY. I said good old Ethel.

DORIS. Well, it sounded very silly, I'm sure.

MRS. ROCKETT (*scrutinizing him*). What's the matter with you?

HENRY. Nothing, why?

MRS. ROCKETT. You look funny.

HENRY. I feel funny.

MRS. ROCKETT. Have you been drinking?

HENRY. Yes.

DORIS. Henry!

MRS. ROCKETT. I knew it!

HENRY. I had a whisky and soda in town and another one at the Plough.

DORIS (*astounded*). What for?

HENRY. Because I felt like it.

DORIS. You ought to be ashamed of yourself.

HENRY. I'm going to have another one too, a bit later on.

DORIS. You'll do no such thing.

HENRY. That hat looks awful.

DORIS (*furiously*). Don't you speak to me like that.

HENRY. Why not?

DORIS (*slightly non-plussed*). Because I won't have it—that's why not.

HENRY. It's a common little hat and it looks awful.

DORIS (*with an admirable effort at control*). Now listen to me, Henry Gow, the next time I catch you drinking and coming home here and insulting me, I'll . . .

HENRY (*interrupting her gently*). What will you do, Dorrie?

DORIS (*hotly*). I'll give you a piece of my mind, that's what I'll do.

HENRY (*rising*). It'll have to be a very little piece. You can't afford much! (*He laughs delightedly at his own joke.*)

DORIS. I'd be very much obliged if you'd kindly tell me what this means?

HENRY. I'm celebrating.

DORIS. Celebrating! What do you mean, celebrating?

HENRY (*up* L.C.). Tonight's our anniversary.

DORIS (R.C.). Don't talk so soft, our anniversary's not until November.

HENRY. I don't mean that one. Tonight's the anniversary of the first time I had an affair with you and you got in the family way.

DORIS (*shrieking*). Henry! (*She moves down stage.*)

HENRY (*delighted with his carefully calculated effect*). Hurray!

DORIS (*beside herself*). How dare you say such a dreadful thing, in front of the child, too.

HENRY (*in romantic tones*). Three years and a bit after that wonderful night our child was born! (*Lapsing into his normal voice*) Considering all the time you took forming yourself, Else, I'm surprised you're not a nicer little girl than you are.

DORIS. Go upstairs, Elsie.

HENRY. Stay here, Elsie.
(ELSIE *dithers.*)

DORIS. Do as I tell you.

ELSIE (L.C.). But, Mum . . .

DORIS. Mother, take her, for God's sake! There's going to be a row.
(MRS. ROCKETT *rises.*)

HENRY (*firmly*). Leave her alone and sit down. Leave her alone and sit down.
(MRS. ROCKETT *hesitates.* ELSIE *sits on the piano stool.*)

MRS. ROCKETT (*subsiding into the chair*). Well, I never, I . . .

HENRY (*happily*). See? It works like a charm.

DORIS. A fine exhibition you're making of yourself, I must say.

HENRY. Not bad, is it? As a matter of fact, I'm rather pleased with it myself.

DORIS. Go to bed!

HENRY. Stop ordering me about, see. (*Crossing* C.) What right have you got to nag at me and boss me? No right at all. I'm the one that pays the rent and works for you and keeps you. What do you give me in return, I'd like to know? Nothing. (*He bangs the table*) I sit through breakfast while you and Mother wrangle. You're too busy being snappy and bad-tempered even to say good-morning. I come home tired after working all day and ten to one there isn't even a hot dinner for me; here, see this ham? That's what I think of the ham. (*He throws it at her feet*) And the tomatoes and the A1 bloody sauce! (*He throws them too.*)

DORIS (*screaming*). Henry! All over the carpet. (*Getting plate and knife.*)

HENRY (*throwing the butter-dish face downwards on the floor*). And that's what I think of the carpet. (*He moves* L.)

DORIS (*scraping up the butter onto the plate*). That I should live to see this! That I should live to see the man I married make such a beast of himself!

HENRY. Stop working yourself up into a state, you'll need all your control when you've heard what I'm going to say to you.

DORIS (*making a move to him*). Look here . . .

HENRY. Sit down. And you. And you. (MRS. ROCKETT *and* ELSIE *sit again*) I'm afraid you'll have to miss the pictures for once.

DORIS. Elsie, you come with me.

MRS. ROCKETT. Yes, go on, Ducks. (DORIS *makes a movement towards the door, but* HENRY *is too quick for her. He locks the door and slips the key into his pocket.*)

HENRY. I've been waiting for this moment for fifteen years, and believe me it's not going to be spoilt for me by you running away.

DORIS (*on the verge of tears*). Let me out of this room.

HENRY. You'll stay where you are until I've had my say.

DORIS. Let me out of this room. Don't you lay your hands on me. (*Bursting into tears and sinking down at the table*) Oh! Oh! Oh! ... (*She falls into the chair* R. *of the table as he pushes her.*)

ELSIE (*starting to cry too*). Mum— Oh, Mum . . .

HENRY. Here you, shut up, go and get the port out of the sideboard and give some to your mother . . . Go on, do as I tell you. (ELSIE, *terrified and hypnotized into submission, goes to the sideboard cupboard and brings out a bottle of invalid port and some glasses, snivelling as she does so.* DORIS *continues to sob*) That's right. (*He crosses up* C.)

MRS. ROCKETT (*quietly*). You drunken brute, you!

HENRY (*cheerfully*). Worse than that, Mother, far worse. Just you wait and see.
(ELSIE *sits on the chair* L. *of the table.*)

MRS. ROCKETT (*ignoring him*). Take some port, Dorrie, it'll do you good.

DORIS. I couldn't touch any—it'd choke me . . .

HENRY (*pouring some out*). Come on—here . . .

DORIS. Keep away from me.

HENRY. Drink it and stop snivelling.

DORIS. I'll never forgive you for this, never, never, never, as long as I live. (*She gulps down some port.*)

HENRY (*noting her gesture*). That's better.

MRS. ROCKETT. Pay no attention, Dorrie, he's drunk.

HENRY. I'm not drunk. I've only had two whiskies and sodas, just to give me enough guts to take the first plunge. You'd never believe how scared I was, thinking it over in cold blood. I'm not scared any more though, it's much easier than I thought it was going to be. My only regret is that I didn't come to the boil a long time ago, and tell you to your face, Dorrie, what I think of you, what I've been thinking of you for years, and this horrid little kid, and that old bitch of a mother of yours.

MRS. ROCKETT (*shrilly*). Henry Gow!

HENRY. You heard me, old bitch was what I said and old bitch was what I meant.

MRS. ROCKETT. Let me out of this room. (*Rising and crossing to the*

window) I'm not going to stay here and be insulted—I'm not . . .
(*They all rise.*)

HENRY. You're going to stay here just as long as I want you to.

MRS. ROCKETT. Oh, am I? We'll see about that. . . . (*With astonishing quickness she darts over to the window and manages to drag one open. HENRY grabs her by the arm.*)

HENRY. No, you don't.

MRS. ROCKETT. Let go of me.

DORIS. Oh, Mother, don't let the neighbors know all your business.

HENRY. Not on your life!

MRS. ROCKETT (*suddenly screaming powerfully*). Help! Help! Police! Help! Mrs. Harrison—help! . . . (*HENRY drags her away from the window, turns her round and gives her a light slap on the face; she staggers against the piano. Meanwhile he shuts the window again, locks it and pockets the key.*)

DORIS (*looking at him in horror— runs to below the table*). Oh, God! Oh, my God!

ELSIE (*bursting into tears again*). Oh, Mum, Mum, he hit Grandma! Oh, Mum . . . (*She runs to DORIS, who puts her arm round her protectively.*)

MRS. ROCKETT (*gasping*). Oh—my heart! I think I'm going to faint— Oh—my heart— Oh— Oh— Oh, dear— (*MRS. ROCKETT slides onto the floor, perceptibly breaking her fall by clinging on to the piano stool.*)

DORIS. Mother!

HENRY. Stay where you are. (*HENRY goes to the sideboard and pours out a glass of water. DORIS, disobeying him, runs over to her mother. ELSIE wails*) Stand out of the way, Doris, we don't all want to get wet. (*He approaches with the glass of water. MRS. ROCKETT sits up weakly.*)

MRS. ROCKETT (*in a far-away voice*). Where am I?

HENRY. Number Seventeen Cranworth Road, Clapham.

MRS. ROCKETT. Oh—oh, dear!

HENRY. Look here, Mother, I don't want there to be any misunderstanding about this. I liked slapping you just now, see? It was lovely, and if you don't behave yourself and keep quiet I shall slap you again. Go and sit in your chair and remember if you feel faint the water's all ready for you. (*He helps her up and escorts her to her chair by the fire. She collapses into it and looks at him balefully*) Now then. Sit down, Dorrie, you look silly standing about.

DORIS (*with a great effort at control —sits in HENRY's chair*). Henry——

HENRY (*slowly, but very firmly*). Sit down! And keep her quiet or I'll fetch her one too.

DORIS (*with dignity*). Come here, Elsie. (*ELSIE sits on the chair R. of the table*) (*Banging her back*) Shut up, will you!

HENRY. That's right. (*He walks round the room slowly and in si-*

lence, looking at them with an expression of the greatest satisfaction on his face. Finally he goes over to the fireplace; MRS. ROCKETT *jumps slightly as he approaches her, but he smiles at her reassuringly. Meanwhile* DORIS, *recovering from her fear, is beginning to simmer with rage; she remains still, however, watching*) (*Sitting on the piano stool*) Now then. I'm going to start, quite quietly, explaining a few things to you.

DORIS. Enjoying yourself, aren't you?
(MRS. ROCKETT *wipes her neck with her handkerchief.*)

HENRY. You've said it.

DORIS (*gaining courage*). You'll grin on the other side of your face before I've done with you.

HENRY (*politely*). Very likely, Dorrie, very likely indeed!

DORIS. And don't you Dorrie me either! Coming home here drunk, hitting poor Mother and frightening Elsie out of her wits.

HENRY. Out of her what?—— Do her good, do 'em both good, a little excitement in the home. God knows, it's dull enough as a rule.

DORIS. (*with biting sarcasm*). Very clever, oh, very clever, I'm sure.

HENRY. Sixteen years ago tonight, Dorrie, you and me had a little rough and tumble in your Aunt Daisy's house in Stansfield Road, do you remember?

DORIS. Henry—— (*Pointing to* ELSIE. *)*

HENRY. (*ignoring her*). We had the house to ourselves, it being a Sunday, your aunt had popped over to the Golden Calf with Mr. Simmonds, the lodger, which, as the writers say, was her wont——

MRS. ROCKETT (*rising*). This is disgusting, I won't listen to another word.

HENRY. (*rising—rounding on her*). You will! Shut up!
(MRS. ROCKETT *sits.*)

DORIS. Pay no attention, Mother, he's gone mad.

HENRY. Let me see now, where was I? Oh yes, Stansfield Road. You'd been after me for a long while, Dorrie. I didn't know it then, but I realized it soon after. You had to have a husband, what with Nora married and Phyllis engaged, both of them younger than you, you had to have a husband, and quick, so you fixed on me. You were pretty enough and I fell for it hook, line and sinker; then, a couple of months later you told me you'd clicked, you cried a hell of a lot, I remember, said the disgrace would kill your mother if she ever found out. I didn't know then that it'd take a sight more than that to kill that leathery old mare——

MRS. ROCKETT (*bursting into tears*). I won't stand it, I won't! I won't!

HENRY (*rising above her sobs*). I expect you were in on the whole business, in a refined way of course, you knew what was going on all right, you knew that Dorrie was no more in the family way than I was, but we got married; you both saw to that, and I chucked up all the plans I had for getting on, perhaps being a steward in a ship and seeing a bit of the world. Oh yes, all that had to go and we settled down in rooms and I went into Ferguson's Hosiery.

DORIS. I've given you the best years of my life and don't you forget it.

HENRY. You've never given me the best of anything, not even yourself. You didn't even have Elsie willingly.

DORIS (*wildly*). It's not true—stop up your ears, Elsie, don't listen to him, he's wicked—he's wicked—— (ELSIE *makes to do it.*)

HENRY (*grimly*). It's true all right, and you know it as well as I do.

DORIS (*shrilly*). It was only right that you married me. It was only fair! You took advantage of me, didn't you? You took away my innocence. It was only right that you paid for it.

HENRY. Come off it, Dorrie, don't talk so silly. I was the innocent one, not you. I found out you'd cheated me a long long time ago, and when I found out, realized it for certain, I started cheating you. (*He leans on the chair* L. *of the table*) Prepare yourself, Dorrie, my girl, you're going to be really upset this time. I've been saving! Every week for over ten years I've been earning a little bit more than you thought I was. I've managed, by hook and by crook, to put by five hundred and seventy-two pounds—d'you hear me?—five hundred and seventy-two pounds!

MRS. ROCKETT (*jumping to her feet*). Henry! You never have—it's not true——

DORIS (*also jumping up*). You couldn't have—you'd have given it away—I should have found out——

HENRY. I thought that'd rouse you, but don't get excited. (MRS. ROCK-ETT *sits again*) I haven't got it on me, it's in the bank. And it's not for you, it's for me—all but fifty pounds of it, that much is for you, just fifty pounds, the last you'll ever get from me——

DORIS. Henry! You couldn't be so cruel! You couldn't be so mean!

HENRY. I've done what I think's fair and what I think's fair is a damn sight more than you deserve. To start with I've transferred the freehold of this house into your name so you'll always have a roof over your head—you can take in lodgers at a pinch, though God help the poor bleeders if you do!

DORIS. Five hundred and seventy-two pounds! You've got all that and you're going to leave me to starve! (*She takes off her coat and puts it on the chair down* R.)

HENRY. Cut out the drama, Dorrie, and have a look at your mother's savings bank book—I bet you'll find she's got enough to keep you in comfort till the day you die. She soaked her old man plenty, I'm sure—before he took to soaking himself!

MRS. ROCKETT. It's a lie! (*She rises.*)

HENRY. Now listen to me! Mother Machree—you've 'ad one sock in the jaw this evening and you're not just asking for another, you're sitting up and begging for it. (DORIS *pulls the curtains back.*)

MRS. ROCKETT. I'll have you up for assault. I'll have the police on you, my fine fellow!

HENRY. They'll have to be pretty nippy—my boat sails first thing in the morning.

DORIS (*horrified*). Boat! (*At the window.*)

(MRS. ROCKETT *sits.*)

HENRY (*moving up* C.). I'm going away. I've got my ticket here in my pocket, and my passport. My passport photo's a fair scream, I wish I could show it to you, but I don't want you to see the nice new name I've got.

DORIS (*crossing to him*). Henry, you can't do it, I can have you stopped by law. It's desertion.

HENRY. That's right, Dorrie, you've said it. Desertion's just what it is.

DORIS (*breathlessly*). Where are you going, you've got to tell me. Where are you going?

HENRY. Wouldn't you like to know? Maybe Africa, maybe China, maybe Australia. There are lots of places in the world you know nothing about, Dorrie. You've often laughed at me for reading books, but I've found out a hell of a lot from books. (DORIS *sits on* HENRY's *chair*) There are islands in the South Seas, for instance, with coco palms and turtles and sunshine all the year round—you can live there for practically nothing, then there's Australia or New Zealand; with a little bit of capital I might start in a small way sheep farming. Think of it; miles and miles of open country stretching as far as the eye can see

—good food and fresh air—that might be very nice, that might suit me beautifully. Then there's South America. There are coffee plantations there, and sugar plantations, and banana plantations. If I go to South America I'll send you a whole crate. 'Ave a banana, Dorrie! 'Ave a banana!

DORIS. Henry, listen to me, you can't do this dreadful thing, you can't! If you don't love me any more, think of Elsie.

HENRY (*still in his dream*). Then there's the sea, not the sea we know at Worthing with the tide going in and out regular and the band playing on the pier. The real sea's what I mean. The sea that Joseph Conrad wrote about, and Rudyard Kipling and lots of other people, too, a sea with whacking great waves and water spouts and typhoons and flying-fish and phosphorus making the foam look as if it was lit up. (DORIS *turns up stage on her chair*) Those people knew a thing or two, I can tell you. They knew what life could be like if you give it a chance. They knew there was a bit more to it than refinement and fumed oak and getting old and miserable with nothing to show for it. I'm a middle-aged man, but my health's not too bad, taken all round. There's still time for me to see a little bit of real life before I conk out. I'm still fit enough to do a job of work—real work, mind you—not bowing and scraping and wearing myself out showing fussy old cows the way to the lace and the china ware and the bargain basement. (*He crosses to the fireplace.*)

DORIS (*hysterically*). God will punish you, you just see if He doesn't, you just see——

HENRY. God's been punishing me for fifteen years, it's high time He laid off me now. He's been punishing me good and proud for being damn fool enough to let you get your claws into me in the first place——

DORIS (*changing her tactics*). Henry, have pity, for God's sake have pity.

HENRY. And don't start weeping and wailing either, because it won't wash. I know you, Dorrie, I know you through and through. You're frightened now, scared out of your wits, but give you half a chance and you'd be worse than ever you were. You're a bad lot, Dorrie, not what the world would call a bad lot but what I call a bad lot. Mean and cold and respectable.

DORIS (*rising and going to him*). Listen to me, Henry, you've got to listen—you must. You can't leave us to starve, you can't throw us on to the streets—if I've been a bad wife to you, I'm sorry—I'll try to be better, really I will, I swear to God I will—— You can't do this. If you won't forgive me, think of Elsie, think of poor little Elsie——

HENRY. Poor little Elsie, my eye! I think Elsie's awful, I always have ever since she was little. She's never done anything but whine and snivel and try to get something for nothing ——

ELSIE (*wailing*). Oh, Mum, did you hear what he said? Oh, Dad, oh dear——

MRS. ROCKETT (*crossing and comforting her*). There, there, dear, don't listen to him—— (*She sits in the chair L. of the table.*)

HENRY. Elsie can go to work in a year or so; in the meantime, Dorrie, you can go to work yourself, you're quite a young woman still and strong as an ox.—Here's your fifty pounds—— (*He takes an envelope out of his pocket and throws it on to the table. Then he goes towards the door.* DORIS *rushes after him and hangs on to his arm.*)

DORIS. Henry, Henry, you shan't go, you shan't——
(ELSIE *rises.*)

HENRY (*struggling with her*). Leave hold of me. (*He goes to the door.*)

DORIS (*following him*). Mother, Mother—help—help me, don't let him go——

MRS. ROCKETT. Run, Doris, run!
(HENRY *frees himself from her and, taking her by the shoulders, forces her back into a chair, then he unlocks the door and opens it.*)
(ELSIE *sits in the C. chair.*)

HENRY. I'm taking my last look at you, Dorrie. I shall never see you again as long as I live—— It's a dream come true.
(DORIS *buries her head in her arms and starts to sob loudly.* MRS. ROCKETT *sits transfixed, staring at him murderously.*)
(*Quietly.*) Three generations. Grandmother, Mother and Kid. Made of the same bones and sinews and muscles and glands, millions of you, millions just like you. You're past it now, Mother, you're past the thick of the fray, you're nothing but a music-hall joke, a mother-in-law with a bit of money put by. Dorrie, the next few years will show whether you've got guts or not.

Maybe what I'm doing to you will save your immortal soul in the long run. That'd be a bit of all right, wouldn't it? I doubt it, though, your immortal soul's too measly. You're a natural bully and a cheat and I'm sick of the sight of you; I should also like to take this opportunity of saying that I hate that bloody awful slave bangle and I always have. As for you, Elsie, you've got a chance, it's a slim one, I grant you, but still it's a chance. If you learn to work and be independent and, when the time comes, give what you have to give freely and without demanding lifelong payment for it, there's just a bit of hope that you'll turn into a decent human being. At all events, if you'll take one parting piece of advice from your cruel, ungrateful father, you'll spend the first money you ever earn on having your adenoids out. Good-bye, one and all. Nice to have known you!

(*The wails of* DORIS *and* ELSIE *rise in volume as he goes jauntily out, slamming the door behind him.*)

CURTAIN

Waiting for Lefty

BY CLIFFORD ODETS

CHARACTERS

FATT
JOE
EDNA
MILLER
FAYETTE
IRV
FLORRIE
SID
CLAYTON
AGATE KELLER
HENCHMAN
SECRETARY
ACTOR
REILLY
DR. BARNES
DR. BENJAMIN
A MAN

WAITING FOR LEFTY

As the curtain goes up we see a bare stage. On it are sitting six or seven men in a semi-circle. Lolling against the proscenium down left is a young man chewing a toothpick: a gunman. A fat man of porcine appearance is talk-ing directly to the audience. In other words he is the head of a union and the men ranged behind him are a committee of workers. They are now seated in interesting different attitudes and present a wide diversity of type, as we shall soon see. The fat man is hot and heavy under the collar, near the end of a long talk, but not too hot: he is well fed and confident. His name is HARRY FATT.

FATT. You're so wrong I ain't laugh-ing. Any guy with eyes to read knows it. Look at the textile strike—out like lions and in like lambs. Take the San Francisco tie-up—starvation and broken heads. The steel boys wanted to walk out too, but they changed their minds. It's the trend of the times, that's what it is. All we workers got a good man behind us now. He's top man of the country—looking out for our inter-ests—the man in the White House is the one I'm referrin' to. That's why the times ain't ripe for a strike. He's working day and night—

VOICE FROM THE AUDIENCE. For who?
(*The* GUNMAN *stirs himself.*)

FATT. For you! The records prove it. If this was the Hoover régime, would I say don't go out, boys? Not on your tintype! But things is differ-ent now. You read the papers as well as me. You know it. And that's why I'm against the strike. Because we gotta stand behind the man who's standin' behind us! The whole coun-try——

ANOTHER VOICE. Is on the blink!
(*The* GUNMAN *looks grave.*)

FATT. Stand up and show yourself, you damn red! Be a man, let's see what you look like! (*Waits in vain*) Yellow from the word go! Red and yellow makes a dirty color, boys. I got my eyes on four or five of them in the union here. What the hell'll they do for you? Pull you out and run away when trouble starts. Give those birds a chance and they'll have your sisters and wives in the whore houses, like they done in Russia. They'll tear Christ off his bleeding cross. They'll wreck your homes and throw your babies in the river. You think that's bunk? Read the papers! Now listen. we can't stay here all night. I gave you the facts in the case. You boys got hot suppers to go to and——

ANOTHER VOICE. Says you!

GUNMAN. Sit down, Punk!

ANOTHER VOICE. Where's Lefty? (*Now this question is taken up by the others in unison.* FATT *pounds with gavel.*)

FATT. That's what I wanna know. Where's your pal, Lefty? You elected him chairman—where the hell did he disappear?

521

VOICES. We want Lefty! Lefty! Lefty!

FATT (*pounding*). What the hell is this—a circus? You got the committee here. This bunch of cowboys you elected. (*Pointing to man on extreme right end.*)

MAN. Benjamin.

FATT. Yeah, Doc Benjamin. (*Pointing to other men in circle in seated order*) Benjamin, Miller, Stein, Mitchell, Phillips, Keller. It ain't my fault Lefty took a run-out powder. If you guys——

A GOOD VOICE. What's the committee say?

OTHERS. The committee! Let's hear from the committee!
(FATT *tries to quiet the crowd, but one of the seated men suddenly comes to the front. The* GUNMAN *moves over to center stage, but* FATT *says*):

FATT. Sure, let him talk. Let's hear what the red boys gotta say!
(*Various shouts are coming from the audience.* FATT *insolently goes back to his seat in the middle of the circle. He sits on his raised platform and relights his cigar. The* GUNMAN *goes back to his post.* JOE, *the new speaker, raises his hand for quiet. Gets it quickly. He is sore.*)

JOE. You boys know me. I ain't a red boy one bit! Here I'm carryin' a shrapnel that big I picked up in the war. And maybe I don't know it when it rains! Don't tell me red! You know what we are? The black and blue boys! We been kicked around so long we're black and blue from head to toes. But I guess anyone who says straight out he don't like it, he's a red boy to the leaders of the union. What's this crap about goin' home to hot suppers? I'm asking to your faces how many's got hot suppers to go home to? Anyone who's sure of his next meal, raise your hand! A certain gent sitting behind me can raise them both. But not in front here! And that's why we're talking strike—to get a living wage!

VOICE. Where's Lefty?

JOE. I honest to God don't know, but he didn't take no run-out powder. That Wop's got more guts than a slaughter house. Maybe a traffic jam got him, but he'll be here. But don't let this red stuff scare you. Unless fighting for a living scares you. We gotta make up our minds. My wife made up my mind last week, if you want the truth. It's plain as the nose on Sol Feinberg's face we need a strike. There's us comin' home every night—eight, ten hours on the cab. "God," the wife says, "eighty cents ain't money—don't buy beans almost. You're workin' for the company," she says to me, "Joe, you ain't workin' for me or the family no more!" She says to me, "If you don't start. . . ."

I. JOE AND EDNA

The lights fade out and a white spot picks out the playing space within the space of seated men. The seated men are very dimly visible in the outer dark, but more prominent is FATT *smoking his cigar and often blowing the smoke in the lighted circle.*

A tired but attractive woman of thirty comes into the room, drying her hands on an apron. She stands there sullenly as JOE *comes in from the other side, home from work. For a moment they stand and look at each other in silence.*

JOE. Where's all the furniture, honey?

EDNA. They took it away. No installments paid.

JOE. When?

EDNA. Three o'clock.

JOE. They can't do that.

EDNA. Can't? They did it.

JOE. Why, the palookas, we paid three-quarters.

EDNA. The man said read the contract.

JOE. We must have signed a phony. . . .

EDNA. It's a regular contract and you signed it.

JOE. Don't be so sour, Edna. . . . (*Tries to embrace her.*)

EDNA. Do it in the movies, Joe—they pay Clark Gable big money for it.

JOE. This is a helluva house to come home to. Take my word!

EDNA. Take MY word! Whose fault is it?

JOE. Must you start that stuff again?

EDNA. Maybe you'd like to talk about books?

JOE. I'd like to slap you in the mouth!

EDNA. No, you won't.

JOE (*sheepish*). Jeez, Edna, you get me sore some time. . . .

EDNA. But just look at me—I'm laughing all over!

JOE. Don't insult me. Can I help it if times are bad? What the hell do you want me to do, jump off a bridge or something?

EDNA. Don't yell. I just put the kids to bed so they won't know they missed a meal. If I don't have Emmy's shoes soled tomorrow, she can't go to school. In the meantime let her sleep.

JOE. Honey, I rode the wheels off the chariot today. I cruised around five hours without a call. It's conditions.

EDNA Tell it to the A & P!

JOE. I booked two-twenty on the clock. A lady with a dog was lit . . . she gave me a quarter tip by mistake. If you'd only listen to me—we're rolling in wealth.

EDNA. Yeah? How much?

JOE. I had "coffee and—" in a beanery. (*Hands her silver coins*) A buck four.

EDNA. The second month's rent is due tomorrow.

JOE. Don't look at me that way, Edna.

EDNA. I'm looking through you, not at you. . . . Everything was gonna be so ducky! A cottage by the waterfall, roses in Picardy. You're a four-star-bust! If you think I'm standing for it much longer, you're crazy as a bedbug.

JOE. I'd get another job if I could. There's no work—you know it.

EDNA. I only know we're at the bottom of the ocean.

JOE. What can I do?

EDNA. Who's the man in the family, you or me?

JOE. That's no answer. Get down to brass tacks. Christ, gimme a break, too! A coffee cake and java all day. I'm hungry, too, Babe. I'd work my fingers to the bone if—

EDNA. I'll open a can of salmon.

JOE. Not now. Tell me what to do!

EDNA. I'm not God!

JOE. Jeez, I wish I was a kid again and didn't have to think about the next minute.

EDNA. But you're not a kid and you do have to think about the next minute. You got two blondie kids sleeping in the next room. They need food and clothes. I'm not mentioning anything else—But we're stalled like a flivver in the snow. For five years I laid awake at night listening to my heart pound. For God's sake, do something, Joe, get wise. Maybe get your buddies together, maybe go on strike for better money. Poppa did it during the war and they won out. I'm turning into a sour old nag.

JOE (*defending himself*). Strikes don't work!

EDNA. Who told you?

JOE. Besides that means not a nickel a week while we're out. Then when it's over they don't take you back.

EDNA. Suppose they don't! What's to lose?

JOE. Well, we're averaging six-seven dollars a week now.

EDNA. That just pays for the rent.

JOE. That is something, Edna.

EDNA. It isn't. They'll push you down to three and four a week before you know it. Then you'll say, "That's somethin'," too!

JOE. There's too many cabs on the street, that's the whole damn trouble.

EDNA. Let the company worry about that, you big fool! If their cabs didn't make a profit, they'd take them off the streets. Or maybe you think they're in business just to pay Joe Mitchell's rent!

JOE. You don't know a-b-c, Edna.

EDNA. I know this—your boss is making suckers outa you boys every minute. Yes, and suckers out of all the wives and the poor innocent kids who'll grow up with crooked spines and sick bones. Sure, I see it in the papers, how good orange juice is for kids. But dammit our kids get colds one on top of the other. They look like little ghosts. Betty never saw a grapefruit. I took her to the store last week and she pointed to a stack of grapefruits. "What's that!" she said. My God, Joe—the world is supposed to be for all of us.

JOE. You'll wake them up.

EDNA. I don't care, as long as I can maybe wake you up.

JOE. Don't insult me. One man can't make a strike.

EDNA. Who says one? You got hundreds in your rotten union!

JOE. The Union ain't rotten.

EDNA. No? Then what are they doing? Collecting dues and patting your back?

JOE. They're making plans.

EDNA. What kind?

JOE. They don't tell us.

EDNA. It's too damn bad about you.

They don't tell little Joey what's happening in his bitsie witsie union. What do you think it is—a ping pong game?

JOE. You know they're racketeers. The guys at the top would shoot you for a nickel.

EDNA. Why do you stand for that stuff?

JOE. Don't you wanna see me alive?

EDNA (after a deep pause). No . . . I don't think I do, Joe. Not if you can lift a finger to do something about it, and don't. No, I don't care.

JOE. Honey, you don't understand what—

EDNA. And any other hackie that won't fight . . . let them all be ground to hamburger!

JOE. It's one thing to—

EDNA. Take your hand away! Only they don't grind me to little pieces! I got different plans. (Starts to take off her apron.)

JOE. Where are you going?

EDNA. None of your business.

JOE. What's up your sleeve?

EDNA. My arm'd be up my sleeve, darling, if I had a sleeve to wear. (Puts neatly folded apron on back of chair.)

JOE. Tell me!

EDNA. Tell you what?

JOE. Where are you going?

EDNA. Don't you remember my old boy friend?

JOE. Who?

EDNA. Bud Haas. He still has my picture in his watch. He earns a living.

JOE. What the hell are you talking about.

EDNA. I heard worse than I'm talking about.

JOE. Have you seen Bud since we got married?

EDNA. Maybe.

JOE. If I thought . . . (*He stands looking at her.*)

EDNA. See much? Listen, boy friend, if you think I won't do this it just means you can't see straight.

JOE. Stop talking bull!

EDNA. This isn't five years ago, Joe.

JOE. You mean you'd leave me and the kids?

EDNA. I'd leave *you* like a shot!

JOE. No. . . .

EDNA. Yes!
(JOE *turns away, sitting on a chair with his back to her. Outside the lighted circle of the playing stage we hear the other seated members of the strike committee.* "She will . . . she will . . . it happens that way," *etc. This group should be used throughout for various com-ments, political, emotional and as general chorus. Whispering. . . . The fat boss now blows a heavy cloud of smoke into the scene.*)

JOE (*finally*). Well, I guess I ain't got a leg to stand on.

EDNA. No?

JOE (*suddenly mad*). No, you lousy tart, no! Get the hell out of here. Go pick up that bull-thrower on the corner and stop at some cushy hotel downtown. He's probably been coming here every morning and laying you while I hacked my guts out!

EDNA. You're crawling like a worm!

JOE. You'll be crawling in a minute.

EDNA. You don't scare me that much! (*Indicates a half inch on her finger.*)

JOE. This is what I slaved for!

EDNA. Tell it to your boss!

JOE. He don't give a damn for you or me!

EDNA. That's what I say.

JOE. Don't change the subject!

EDNA. This is the subject, the EX-ACT SUBJECT! Your boss makes this subject. I never saw him in my life, but he's putting ideas in my head a mile a minute. He's giving your kids that fancy disease called the rickets. He's making a jelly-fish outa you and putting wrinkles in my face. This is the subject every inch of the way! He's throwing me into

Bud Haas' lap. When in hell will you get wise——

JOE. I'm not so dumb as you think! But you are talking like a Red.

EDNA. I don't know what that means. But when a man knocks you down you get up and kiss his fist! You gutless piece of boloney.

JOE. One man can't——

EDNA (*with great joy*). I don't say one man! I say a hundred, a thousand, a whole million, I say. But start in your own union. Get those hack boys together! Sweep out those racketeers like a pile of dirt! Stand up like men and fight for the crying kids and wives. Goddammit! I'm tired of slavery and sleepless nights.

JOE (*with her*). Sure, sure! . . .

EDNA. Yes. Get brass toes on your shoes and know where to kick!

JOE (*suddenly jumping up and kissing his wife full on the mouth*). Listen, Edna. I'm goin' down to 174th Street to look up Lefty Costello. Lefty was saying the other day. . . . (*He suddenly stops*) How about this Haas guy?

EDNA. Get out of here!

JOE. I'll be back! (*Runs out.*)
(*For a moment* EDNA *stands triumphant. There is a blackout and when the regular lights come up,* JOE MITCHELL *is concluding what he has been saying.*)

JOE. You guys know this stuff better than me. We gotta walk out! (*Abruptly he turns and goes back to his seat and blackout.*)

BLACKOUT

II. LAB ASSISTANT EPISODE

Discovered: MILLER, *a lab assistant, looking around; and* FAYETTE, *an industrialist.*

FAY. Like it?

MILLER. Very much. I've never seen an office like this outside the movies.

FAY. Yes, I often wonder if interior decorators and bathroom fixture people don't get all their ideas from Hollywood. Our country's extraordinary that way. Soap, cosmetics, electric refrigerators—just let Mrs. Consumer know they're used by the Crawfords and Garbos—more volume of sale than one plant can handle!

MILL. I'm afraid it isn't that easy, Mr. Fayette.

FAY. No, you're right—gross exaggeration on my part. Competition is cut-throat today. Markets up flush against a stone wall. The astronomers had better hurry- -open Mars to trade expansion.

MILL. Or it will be just too bad!

FAY. Cigar?

MILL. Thank you, don't smoke.

FAY. Drink?

MILL. Ditto, Mr. Fayette.

FAY. I like sobriety in my workers . . . the trained ones, I mean. The Pollacks and niggers, they're better drunk—keeps them out of mischief. Wondering why I had you come over?

MILL. If you don't mind my saying --very much.

FAY (patting him on the knee). I like your work.

MILL. Thanks.

FAY. No reason why a talented young man like yourself shouldn't string along with us—a growing concern. Loyalty is well repaid in our organization. Did you see Siegfried this morning?

MILL. He hasn't been in the laboratory all day.

FAY. I told him yesterday to raise you twenty dollars a month. Starts this week.

MILL. You don't know how happy my wife'll be.

FAY. Oh, I can appreciate it. (He laughs.)

MILL. Was that all, Mr. Fayette?

FAY. Yes, except that we're switching you to laboratory A tomorrow. Siegfried knows about it. That's why I had you in. The new work is very important. Siegfried recommended you very highly as a man to trust. You'll work directly under Dr. Brenner. Make you happy?

MILL. Very. He's an important chemist!

FAY (leaning over seriously). We think so, Miller. We think so to the extent of asking you to stay within the building throughout the time you work with him.

MILL. You mean sleep and eat in?

FAY. Yes. . . .

MILL. It can be arranged.

FAY. Fine. You'll go far, Miller.

MILL. May I ask the nature of the new work?

FAY (looking around first). Poison gas. . . .

MILL. Poison!

FAY. Orders from above. I don't have to tell you from where. New type poison gas for modern warfare.

MILL. I see.

FAY. You didn't know a new war was that close, did you?

MILL. I guess I didn't.

FAY. I don't have to stress the importance of absolute secrecy.

MILL. I understand!

FAY. The world is an armed camp today. One match sets the whole world blazing in forty-eight hours. Uncle Sam won't be caught napping!

MILL (addressing his pencil). They

say 12 million men were killed in that last one and 20 million more wounded or missing.

FAY. That's not our worry. If big business went sentimental over human life there wouldn't be big business of any sort!

MILL. My brother and two cousins went in the last one.

FAY. They died in a good cause.

MILL. My mother says "no!"

FAY. She won't worry about you this time. You're too valuable behind the front.

MILL. That's right.

FAY. All right, Miller. See Siegfried for further orders.

MILL. You should have seen my brother—he could ride a bike without hands. . . .

FAY. You'd better move some clothes and shaving tools in tomorrow. Remember what I said—you're with a growing organization.

MILL. He could run the hundred yards in 9:8 flat. . . .

FAY. Who?

MILL. My brother. He's in the Meuse-Argonne Cemetery! Momma went there in 1926. . . .

FAY. Yes, those things stick. How's your handwriting, Miller, fairly legible?

MILL. Fairly so.

FAY. Once a week I'd like a little report from you.

MILL. What sort of report?

FAY. Just a few hundred words once a week on Dr. Brenner's progress.

MILL. Don't you think it might be better coming from the Doctor?

FAY. I didn't ask you that.

MILL. Sorry.

FAY. I want to know what progress he's making, the reports to be purely confidential—between you and me.

MILL. You mean I'm to watch him?

FAY. Yes!

MILL. I guess I can't do that. . . .

FAY. Thirty a month raise . . .

MILL. You said twenty. . . .

FAY. Thirty!

MILL. Guess I'm not built hat way.

FAY. Forty. . . .

MILL. Spying's not in my line, Mr Fayette!

FAY. You use ugly words, Mr. Miller!

MILL. For ugly activity? Yes!

FAY. Think about it, Miller. Your chances are excellent. . . .

MILL. No.

FAY. You're doing something for

your country. Assuring the United States that when those goddam Japs start a ruckus we'll have offensive weapons to back us up! Don't you read your newspapers, Miller?

MILL. Nothing but Andy Gump.

FAY. If you were on the inside you'd know I'm talking cold sober truth! Now, I'm not asking you to make up your mind on the spot. Think about it over your lunch period.

MILL. No. . . .

FAY. Made up your mind already?

MILL. Afraid so.

FAY. You understand the consequences?

MILL. I lose my raise——

(*Simulta-neously*) {
MILL. And my job!
FAY. And your job!
MILL. You misunder-stand——
}

MILL. Rather dig ditches first!

FAY. That's a big job for foreigners.

MILL. But sneaking—and making poison gas—that's for Americans?

FAY. It's up to you.

MILL. My mind's made up.

FAY. No hard feelings?

MILL. Sure hard feelings! I'm not the civilized type, Mr. Fayette. Nothing suave or sophisticated about me. Plenty of hard feelings! Enough to want to bust you and all your kind square in the mouth! (*Does exactly that.*)

BLACKOUT

III. THE YOUNG HACK AND HIS GIRL

Opens with girl and brother. FLORENCE *waiting for* SID *to take her to a dance.*

FLOR. I gotta right to have something out of life. I don't smoke, I don't drink. So if Sid wants to take me to a dance, I'll go. Maybe if you was in love you wouldn't talk so hard.

IRV. I'm saying it for your good.

FLOR. Don't be so good to me.

IRV. Mom's sick in bed and you'll be worryin' her to the grave. She don't

want that boy hanging around the house and she don't want you meeting him in Crotona Park.

FLOR. I'll meet him anytime I like!

IRV. If you do, yours truly'll take care of it in his own way. With just one hand, too!

FLOR. Why are you all so set against him?

IRV. Mom told you ten times—it ain't him It's that he ain't got nothing. Sure, we know he's serious, that he's stuck on you. But that don't cut no ice.

FLOR. Taxi drivers used to make good money.

IRV. Today they're makin' five and six dollars a week. Maybe you wanta raise a family on that. Then you'll be back here living with us again and I'll be supporting two families in one. Well . . . over my dead body.

FLOR. Irv, I don't care—I love him!

IRV. You're a little kid with half-baked ideas!

FLOR. I stand there behind the counter the whole day. I think about him—

IRV. If you thought more about Mom it would be better.

FLOR. Don't I take care of her every night when I come home? Don't I cook supper and iron your shirts and . . . you give me a pain in the neck, too. Don't try to shut me up! I bring a few dollars in the house, too. Don't you see I want something else out of life? Sure, I want romance, love, babies. I want everything in life I can get.

IRV. You take care of Mom and watch your step!

FLOR. And if I don't?

IRV. Yours truly'll watch it for you!

FLOR. You can talk that way to a girl. . . .

IRV. I'll talk that way to your boy friend, too, and it won't be with words! Florrie, if you had a pair of eyes you'd see it's for your own good we're talking. This ain't no time to get married. Maybe later—

FLOR. "Maybe Later" never comes for me, though. Why don't we send Mom to a hospital? She can die in peace there instead of looking at the clock on the mantelpiece all day.

IRV. That needs money. Which we don't have!

FLOR. Money, money, money!

IRV. Don't change the subject.

FLOR. This is the subject!

IRV. You gonna stop seeing him? (*She turns away*) Jesus, kiddie, I remember when you were a baby with curls down your back. Now I gotta stand here yellin' at you like this.

FLOR. I'll talk to him, Irv.

IRV. When?

FLOR. I asked him to come here tonight. We'll talk it over.

IRV. Don't get soft with him. Nowadays is no time to be soft. You gotta be hard as a rock or go under.

FLOR. I found that out. There's the bell. Take the egg off the stove *I* boiled for Mom. Leave us alone, Irv.
(SID *comes in—the two men look at each other for a second.* IRV *exits*)

SID (*enters*). Hello, Florrie.

FLOR. Hello, Honey. You're looking tired.

SID. Naw, I just need a shave.

FLOR. Well, draw your chair up to the fire and I'll ring for brandy and soda . . . like in the movies.

SID. If this was the movies I'd bring a big bunch of roses.

FLOR. How big?

SID. Fifty or sixty dozen—the kind with long, long stems—big as that. . . .

FLOR. You dope. . . .

SID. Your Paris gown is beautiful.

FLOR (acting grandly). Yes, Percy, velvet panels are coming back again. Madame La Farge told me today that Queen Marie herself designed it.

SID. Gee . . . !

FLOR. Every princess in the Balkans is wearing one like this. (Poses grandly.)

SID. Hold it. (Does a nose camera—thumbing nose and imitating grinding of camera with other hand. Suddenly she falls out of the posture and swiftly goes to him, to embrace him, to kiss him with love. Finally.)

SID. You look tired, Florrie.

FLOR. Naw, I just need a shave. (She laughs tremorously.)

SID. You worried about your mother?

FLOR No.

SID. What's on your mind?

FLOR. The French and Indian War.

SID. What's on your mind?

FLOR. I got us on my mind, Sid. Night and day, Sid!

SID. I smacked a beer truck today. Did I get hell! I was driving along thinking of us, too. You don't have to say it—I know what's on your mind. I'm rat poison around here.

FLOR. Not to me. . . .

SID. I know to who . . . and I know why. I don't blame them. We're engaged now for three years. . . .

FLOR. That's a long time. . . .

SID. My brother Sam joined the navy this morning—get a break that way. They'll send him down to Cuba with the hootchy-kootchy girls. He don't know from nothing, that dumb basket ball player!

FLOR. Don't you do that.

SID. Don't you worry, I'm not the kind who runs away. But I'm so tired of being a dog, Baby, I could choke. I don't even have to ask what's going on in your mind. I know from the word go, 'cause I'm thinking the same things, too.

FLOR. It's yes or no—nothing in between.

SID. The answer is no—a big electric sign looking down on Broadway!

FLOR. We wanted to have kids. . . .

SID. But that sort of life ain't for the dogs which is us. Christ, Baby! I get like thunder in my chest when we're together. If we went off together I could maybe look the world straight in the face, spit in its eye like a man should do. Goddamit, it's trying to be a man on the earth. Two in life together.

FLOR. But something wants us to be lonely like that—crawling alone in the dark. Or they want us trapped.

SID. Sure, the big shot money men want us like that.

FLOR. Highly insulting us——

SID. Keeping us in the dark about what is wrong with us in the money sense. They got the power an mean to be damn sure they keep it. They know if they give in just an inch, all the dogs like us will be down on them together—an ocean knocking them to hell and back and each singing cuckoo with stars coming from their nose and ears. I'm not raving, Florrie——

FLOR. I know you're not, I know.

SID. I don't have the words to tell you what I feel. I never finished school. . . .

FLOR. I know. . . .

SID. But it's relative, like the professors say. We worked like hell to send him to college—my kid brother Sam, I mean—and look what he done—joined the navy! The damn fool don't see the cards is stacked for all of us. The money man dealing himself a hot royal flush. Then giving you and me a phony hand like a pair of tens or something. Then keep on losing the pots 'cause

the cards is stacked against you. Then he says, what's the matter you can't win—no stuff on the ball, he says to you. And kids like my brother believe it 'cause they don't know better. For all their education, they don't know from nothing.

But wait a minute! Don't he come around and say to you—this millionaire with a jazz band—listen Sam or Sid or what's-your-name, you're no good, but here's a chance. The whole world'll know who you are. Yes sir, he says, get up on that ship and fight those bastards who's making the world a lousy place to live in. The Japs, the Turks, the Greeks. Take this gun—kill the slobs like a real hero, he says, a real American. Be a hero!

And the guy you're poking at? A real louse, just like you, 'cause they don't let him catch more than a pair of tens, too. On that foreign soil he's a guy like me and Sam, a guy who wants his baby like you and hot sun on his face! They'll teach Sam to point the guns the wrong way, that dumb basket ball player!

FLOR. I got a lump in my throat, Honey.

SID. You and me—we never even had a room to sit in somewhere.

FLOR. The park was nice . . .

SID. In Winter? The hallways . . . I'm glad we never got together. This way we don't know what we missed.

FLOR (in a burst). Sid, I'll go with you—we'll get a room somewhere.

SID. Naw . . . they're right. If we can't climb higher than this together —we better stay apart.

FLOR. I swear to God I wouldn't care.

SID. You would, you would—in a year, two years, you'd curse the day. I seen it happen.

FLOR. Oh, Sid. . . .

SID. Sure, I know. We got the blues, Babe—the 1935 blues. I'm talkin' this way 'cause I love you. If I didn't, I wouldn't care. . . .

FLOR. We'll work together, we'll—

SID. How about the backwash? Your family needs your nine bucks. My family——

FLOR. I don't care for them!

SID. You're making it up, Florrie. Little Florrie Canary in a cage.

FLOR. Don't make fun of me.

SID. I'm not, Baby.

FLOR. Yes, you're laughing at me.

SID. I'm not.
(*They stand looking at each other, unable to speak. Finally, he turns to*

a small portable phonograph and plays a cheap, sad, dance tune. He makes a motion with his hand; she comes to him. They begin to dance slowly. They hold each other tightly, almost as though they would merge into each other. The music stops, but the scratching record continues to the end of the scene. They stop dancing. He finally unlooses her clutch and seats her on the couch, where she sits, tense and expectant.)

SID. Hello, Babe.

FLOR. Hello. (*For a brief time they stand as though in a dream.*)

SID (*finally*). Good-by, Babe. (*He waits for an answer, but she is silent. They look at each other.*)

SID. Did you ever see my Pat Rooney imitation? (*He whistles Rosy O'Grady and soft shoes to it. Stops. He asks:*)

SID. Don't you like it?

FLOR (*finally*). No. (*Buries her face in her hands.*)
(*Suddenly he falls on his knees and buries his face in her lap.*)

BLACKOUT

IV. LABOR SPY EPISODE

FATT. You don't know how we work for you. Shooting off your mouth won't help. Hell, don't you guys ever look at the records like me? Look in your own industry. See what happened when the hacks walked out in Philly three months ago! Where's Philly? A thousand miles away? An hour's ride on the train.

VOICE. Two hours! !

FATT. Two hours . . . what the hell's the difference. Let's hear from someone who's got the practical experience to back him up. Fellers, there's a man here who's seen the whole parade in Philly, walked out with his pals, got knocked down like the rest—and blacklisted after they went back. That's why he's here. He's got a mighty interestin' word to say. (*Announces:*) TOM CLAYTON! (*As* CLAYTON *starts up from the audience,* FATT *gives him a hand which is sparsely followed in the audience.* CLAYTON *comes forward*) Fellers, this is a man with practical strike experience—Tom Clayton from little ole Philly.

CLAYTON (*a thin, modest individual*). Fellers, I don't mind your booing. If I thought it would help us hacks get better living conditions, I'd let you walk all over me, cut me up to little pieces. I'm one of you myself. But what I wanna say is that Harry Fatt's right. I only been working here in the big town five weeks, but I know conditions just like the rest of you. You know how it is—don't take long to feel the sore spots, no matter where you park.

CLEAR VOICE (*from audience*). Sit down!

CLAYTON. But Fatt's right. Our officers is right. The time ain't ripe. Like a fruit don't fall off the tree until it's ripe.

CLEAR VOICE. Sit down, you fruit!

FATT (*on his feet*). Take care of him, boys.

VOICE (*in audience, struggling*). No one takes care of me.
(*Struggle in house and finally the owner of the voice runs up on stage, says to speaker:*)

SAME VOICE. Where the hell did you pick up that name! Clayton! This rat's name is Clancy, from the old Clancys, way back! Fruit! I almost wet myself listening to that one!

FATT (*gunman with him*). This ain't a barn! What the hell do you think you're doing here!

SAME VOICE. Exposing a rat!

FATT. You can't get away with this. Throw him the hell outa here.

VOICE (*preparing to stand his ground*). Try it yourself. . . . When this bozo throws that slop around. You know who he is? That's a company spy.

FATT. Who the hell are you to make —

VOICE. I paid dues in this union for four years, that's who's me! I gotta right and this pussy-footed rat ain't coming in here with ideals like that. You know his record. Lemme say it out——

FATT. You'll prove all this or I'll bust you in every hack outfit in town!

VOICE. I gotta right. I gotta right. Looka *him,* he don't say boo!

CLAYTON. You're a liar and I never seen you before in my life!

VOICE. Boys, he spent two years in the coal fields breaking up any organization he touched. Fifty guys he put in jail. He's ranged up and down the east coast—shipping, textiles, steel—he's been in everything you can name. Right now——

CLAYTON. That's a lie!

VOICE. Right now he's working for that Bergman outfit on Columbus Circle who furnishes rats for any outfit in the country before, during, and after strikes.
(*The man who is the hero of the next episode goes down to his side with other committee men.*)

CLAYTON. He's trying to break up the meeting, fellers!

VOICE. We won't search you for credentials. . . .

CLAYTON. I got nothing to hide. Your own secretary knows I'm straight.

VOICE. Sure, Boys, you know who this sonovabitch is?

CLAYTON. I never seen you before in my life! !

VOICE. Boys, I slept with him in the same bed sixteen years. HE'S MY OWN LOUSY BROTHER! !

FATT (*after pause*). Is this true? (*No answer from* CLAYTON.)

VOICE *to* CLAYTON. Scram, before I break your neck!
(CLAYTON *scrams down center aisle.*)

VOICE (*says watching him*). Remember his map—he can't change that—Clancy! (*Standing in his place says:*) Too bad you didn't know about this, Fatt! (*After a pause*) The Clancy family tree is bearing nuts!
(*Standing isolated clear on the stage is the hero of the next episode.*)

BLACKOUT

V. THE YOUNG ACTOR

A New York theatrical producer's office. Present are a stenographer and a young actor. She is busy typing; he, waiting with card in hand.

STEN. He's taking a hot bath . . . says you should wait.

PHILIPS (*the actor*). A bath did you say? Where?

STEN. See that door? Right through there—leads to his apartment.

PHIL. Through there?

STEN. Mister, he's laying there in a hot perfumed bath. Don't say I said it.

PHIL. You don't say!

STEN. An oriental den he's got. Can you just see this big Irishman burning Chinese punk in the bedroom? And a big old rose canopy over his casting couch. . . .

PHIL. What's that—casting couch?

STEN. What's that? You from the sticks?

PHIL. I beg your pardon?

STEN (*rolls up her sleeves, makes elaborate deaf and dumb signs*).

No from side walkies of New Yorkie . . . savvy?

PHIL. Oh, you're right. Two years of dramatic stock out of town. One in Chicago.

STEN. Don't tell him, Baby Face. He wouldn't know a good actor if he fell over him in the dark. Say you had two years with the Group, two with the Guild.

PHIL. I'd like to get with the Guild. They say——

STEN. He won't know the difference. Don't say I said it!

PHIL. I really did play with Watson Findlay in "Early Birds."

STEN. (withering him). Don't tell him!

PHIL. He's a big producer, Mr. Grady. I wish I had his money. Don't you?

STEN. Say, I got a clean heart, Mister. I love my fellow man! (About to exit with typed letters) Stick around—Mr. Philips. You might be the type. If you were a woman——

PHIL. Please. Just a minute . . . please . . . I need the job.

STEN. Look at him!

PHIL. I mean . . . I don't know what buttons to push, and you do. What my father used to say—we had a gas station in Cleveland before the crash—"Know what buttons to push," Dad used to say, "and you'll go far."

STEN. You can't push me, Mister! I don't ring right these last few years!

PHIL. We don't know where the next meal's coming from. We——

STEN. Maybe . . . I'll lend you a dollar?

PHIL. Thanks very much: it won't help.

STEN. One of the old families of Virginia? Proud?

PHIL. Oh, not that. You see, I have a wife. We'll have our first baby next month . . . so . . . a dollar isn't much help.

STEN. Roped in?

PHIL. I love my wife!

STEN. Okay, you love her! Excuse me! You married her. Can't support her. No . . . not blaming you. But you're fools, all you actors. Old and young! Watch you parade in and out all day. You still got apples in your cheeks and pins for buttons. But in six months you'll be like them —putting on an act: Phony strutting "pishers"—that's French for dead codfish! It's not their fault. Here you get like that or go under. What kind of job is this for an adult man!

PHIL. When you have to make a living——

STEN. I know, but——

PHIL. Nothing else to do. If I could get something else——

STEN. You'd take it!

PHIL. Anything!

STEN. Telling me! With two brothers in my hair! (MR. GRADY now en-

ters; played by FATT) Mr. Brown sent this young man over.

GRADY. Call the hospital: see how Boris is. (*She assents and exits.*)

PHIL. Good morning, Mr. Grady. . . .

GRADY. The morning is lousy!

PHIL. Mr. Brown sent me. (*Hands over card.*)

GRADY. I heard that once already.

PHIL. Excuse me. . . .

GRADY. What experience?

PHIL. Oh, yes. . . .

GRADY. Where?

PHIL. Two years in stock, sir. A year with the Goodman Theatre in Chicago. . . .

GRADY. That all?

PHIL (*abashed*). Why, no . . . with the Theatre Guild . . . I was there. . .

GRADY. Never saw you in a Guild show!

PHIL. On the road, I mean . . . understudying Mr. Lunt . . .

GRADY. What part? (PHILIPS *can not answer*) You're a lousy liar, son.

PHIL. I did. . . .

GRADY. You don't look like what I want. Can't understand that Brown. Need a big man to play a soldier. Not a lousy soldier left on Broad-

way! All in pictures, and we get the nances! (*Turns to work on desk.*)

PHIL (*immediately playing the soldier*). I was in the ROTC in college . . . Reserve Officers' Training Corps. We trained twice a week. . . .

GRADY. Won't help.

PHIL. With real rifles. (*Waits*) Mr. Grady, I weigh a hundred and fifty-five!

GRADY. How many years back? Been eating regular since you left college?

PHIL (*very earnestly*). Mr. Grady, I could act this soldier part. I could build it up and act it. Make it up——

GRADY. Think I run a lousy acting school around here?

PHIL. Honest to God I would! I need the job—that's why I could do it! I'm strong. I know my business! You'll get an A-1 performance. Because I need this job! My wife's having a baby in a few weeks. We need the money. Give me a chance!

GRADY. What do I care if you can act it! I'm sorry about your baby. Use your head, son. Tank Town stock is different. Here we got investments to be protected. When I sink fifteen thousand in a show I don't take chances on some youngster. We cast to type!

PHIL. I'm an artist! I can——

GRADY. That's your headache. Nobody interested in artists here. Get a big bunch for a nickel on any corner. Two flops in a row on this lousy street nobody loves you—only God, and He don't count. We protect investments: we cast to *type*. Your face and height we want, not your soul, son. And Jesus Christ himself couldn't play a soldier in this show . . . with all his talent. (*Crosses himself in quick repentance for this remark.*)

PHIL. Anything . . . a bit, a walk-on?

GRADY. Sorry: small cast. (*Looking at papers on his desk*) You try Russia, son. I hear it's hot stuff over there.

PHIL. Stage manager? Assistant?

GRADY. All filled, sonny. (*Stands up; crumples several papers from the desk*) Better luck next time.

PHIL. Thanks. . . .

GRADY. Drop in from time to time. (*Crosses and about to exit*) You never know when something— (*The* STENOGRAPHER *enters with papers to put on desk*) What did the hospital say?

STEN. He's much better, Mr. Grady.

GRADY. Resting easy?

STEN. Dr. Martel said Boris is doing even better than he expected.

GRADY. A damn lousy operation!

STEN. Yes. . . .

GRADY (*belching*). Tell the nigger boy to send up a bromo seltzer.

STEN. Yes, Mr. Grady. (*He exits*) Boris wanted lady friends.

PHIL. What?

STEN. So they operated . . . poor dog!

PHIL. A dog?

STEN. His Russian wolf hound! They do the same to you, but you don't know it! (*Suddenly*) Want advice? In the next office, don't let them see you down in the mouth. They don't like it—makes them shiver.

PHIL. You treat me like a human being. Thanks. . . .

STEN. You're human!

PHIL. I used to think so.

STEN. He wants a bromo for his hangover. (*Goes to door*) Want that dollar?

PHIL. It won't help much.

STEN. One dollar buys ten loaves of bread, Mister. Or one dollar buys nine loaves of bread and one copy of The Communist Manifesto. Learn while you eat. Read while you run. . . .

PHIL. Manifesto? What's that? (*Takes dollar*) What is that, what you said. . . . Manifesto?

STEN. Stop off on your way out— I'll give you a copy. From Genesis to Revelation, Comrade Philips!

"And I saw a new earth and a new heaven; for the first earth and the first heaven were passed away; and there was no more sea."

PHIL. I don't understand that. . . .

STEN. I'm saying the meek shall not inherit the earth!

PHIL. No?

STEN. The MILITANT! Come out in the light, Comrade.

BLACKOUT

VI. INTERNE EPISODE

DR. BARNES, *an elderly distinguished man, is speaking on the telephone. He wears a white coat.*

DR. BARNES. No, I gave you my opinion twice. You outvoted me. You did this to Dr. Benjamin yourself. That is why you can tell him yourself. (*Hangs up phone, angrily. As he is about to pour himself a drink from a bottle on the table, a knock is heard.*)

BARNES. Who is it?

BENJAMIN (*without*). Can I see you a minute, please?

BARNES (*hiding the bottle*). Come in, Dr. Benjamin, come in.

BENJ. It's important—excuse me—they've got Leeds up there in my place—He's operating on Mrs. Lewis—the hysterectomy—it's my job. I washed up, prepared . . . they told me at the last minute. I don't mind being replaced, Doctor, but Leeds is a damn fool! He shouldn't be permitted—

BARNES (*dryly*). Leeds is the nephew of Senator Leeds.

BENJ. He's incompetent as hell.

BARNES (*obviously changing subject, picks up lab. jar*). They're doing splendid work in brain surgery these days. This is a very fine specimen. . . .

BENJ. I'm sorry, I thought you might be interested.

BARNES (*still examining jar*). Well, I am, young man, I am! Only remember it's a charity case!

BENJ. Of course. They wouldn't allow it for a second, otherwise.

BARNES. Her life is in danger?

BENJ. Of course! You know how serious the case is!

BARNES. Turn your gimlet eyes elsewhere, Doctor. Jigging around like a cricket on a hot grill won't help. Doctors don't run these hospitals. He's the Senator's nephew and there he stays.

BENJ. It's too bad.

BARNES. I'm not calling you down either. (*Plopping down jar suddenly*) Goddammit, do you think it's my fault?

BENJ. (*about to leave*). I know . . . I'm sorry.

BARNES. Just a minute. Sit down.

BENJ. Sorry, I can't sit.

BARNES. Stand then!

BENJ. (*sits*). Understand, Dr. Barnes, I don't mind being replaced at the last minute this way, but . . . well, this flagrant bit of class distinction—because she's poor—

BARNES. Be careful of words like that—"class distinction." Don't belong here. Lots of energy, you brilliant young men, but idiots. Discretion! Ever hear that word?

BENJ. Too radical?

BARNES. Precisely. And some day like in Germany, it might cost you your head.

BENJ. Not to mention my job.

BARNES. So they told you?

BENJ. Told me what?

BARNES. They're closing Ward C next month. I don't have to tell you the hospital isn't self supporting. Until last year that board of trustees met deficits. . . . You can guess the rest. At a board meeting Tuesday, our fine feathered friends discovered they couldn't meet the last quarter's deficit—a neat little sum well over $100,000. If the hospital is to continue at all, its damn—

BENJ. Necessary to close another charity ward!

BARNES. So they say. . . . (*A wait.*)

BENJ. But that's not all?

BARNES (*ashamed*). Have to cut down on staff too. . . .

BENJ. That's too bad. Does it touch me?

BARNES. Afraid it does.

BENJ. But after all I'm top man here. I don't mean I'm better than others, but I've worked harder.

BARNES. And shown more promise. . . .

BENJ. I always supposed they'd cut from the bottom first.

BARNES. Usually.

BENJ. But in this case?

BARNES. Complications.

BENJ. For instance?
(BARNES *hesitant.*)

BARNES. I like you, Benjamin. It's one ripping shame.

BENJ. I'm no sensitive plant—what's the answer?

BARNES. An old disease, malignant, tumescent. We need an anti-toxin for it.

BENJ. I see.

BARNES. What?

BENJ. I met that disease before— at Harvard first.

BARNES. You have seniority here, Benjamin.

BENJ. But I'm a Jew!
(BARNES *nods his head in agreement.* BENJ. *stands there a moment and blows his nose.*)

BARNES (*blows his nose*). Microbes!

BENJ. Pressure from above?

BARNES. Don't think Kennedy and I didn't fight for you!

BENJ. Such discrimination, with all those wealthy brother Jews on the board?

BARNES. I've remarked before— doesn't seem to be much difference between wealthy Jews and rich Gentiles. Cut from the same piece!

BENJ. For myself I don't feel sorry. My parents gave up an awful lot to get me this far. They ran a little dry goods shop in the Bronx until their pitiful savings went in the crash last year. Poppa's peddling neckties. . . . Saul Ezra Benjamin—a man who's read Spinoza all his life.

BARNES. Doctors don't run medicine in this country. The men who know their jobs don't run anything here, except the motormen on trolley cars. I've seen medicine change—plenty —anesthesia, sterilization—but not because of rich men—in *spite* of them! In a rich man's country your true self's buried deep. Microbes! Less. . . . Vermin! See this ankle, this delicate sensitive hand? Four hundred years to breed that. Out of a revolutionary background! Spirit of '76! Ancestors froze at Valley Forge! What's it all mean! Slops! The honest workers were sold out then, in '76. The Constitution's for rich men then and now. Slops! (*The phone rings.*)

BARNES (*angrily*). Dr. Barnes. (*Listens a moment, looks at* BENJAMIN) I see. (*Hangs up, turns slowly to the younger Doctor*) They lost your patient.

BENJ. (*stands solid with the shock of this news but finally hurls his operation gloves to the floor*).

BARNES. That's right . . . that's right. Young, hot, go and do it! I'm very ancient, fossil, but life's ahead of you, Dr. Benjamin, and when you fire the first shot say, "This one's for old Doc Barnes!" Too much dignity —bullets. Don't shoot vermin! Step on them! If I didn't have an invalid daughter— (BARNES *goes back to his seat, blows his nose in silence*) I have said my piece, Benjamin.

BENJ. Lots of things I wasn't certain of. Many things these radicals say . . . you don't believe theories until they happen to you.

BARNES. You lost a lot today, but you won a great point.

BENJ. Yes, to know I'm right? To really begin believing in something? Not to say, "What a world!" but to say, "Change the world!" I wanted to go to Russia. Last week I was thinking about it—the wonderful opportunity to do good work in their socialized medicine—

BARNES. Beautiful, beautiful!

BENJ. To be able to work—

BARNES. Why don't you go? I might be able—

BENJ. Nothing's nearer what I'd like to do!

BARNES. Do it!

BENJ. No! Our work's here—America! I'm scared. . . . What future's ahead, I don't know. Get some job to keep alive—maybe drive a cab—and study and work and learn my place—

BARNES. And step down hard!

BENJ. Fight! Maybe get killed, but goddam! We'll go ahead! (BENJAMIN *stands with clenched fist raised high.*)

BLACKOUT

AGATE. LADIES AND GENTLEMEN, and don't let anyone tell you we ain't got some ladies in this sea of upturned faces! Only they're wearin' pants. Well, maybe I don't know a thing; maybe I fell outa the cradle when I was a kid and ain't been right since—you can't tell!

VOICE. Sit down, cockeye!

AGATE. Who's paying you for those remarks, Buddy?—Moscow Gold? Maybe I got a *glass eye,* but it come from working in a factory at the age of eleven. They hooked it out because they didn't have a shield on the works. But I wear it like a medal 'cause it tells the world where I belong—deep down in the working class! We had delegates in the union there—all kinds of secretaries and treasurers . . . walkin' delegates, but not with blisters on their feet! Oh no! On their fat little ass from sitting on cushions and raking in mazuma. (SECRETARY *and* GUNMAN *remonstrate in words and actions here*) Sit down, boys. I'm just sayin' that about unions in general. I know it ain't true here! Why no, our officers is all aces. Why, I seen our own secretary Fatt walk outa his way not to step on a cockroach. No, boys, don't think—

FATT (*breaking in*). You're out of order!

AGATE (*to audience*). Am I outa order?

ALL. No, no. Speak. Go on, etc.

AGATE. Yes, our officers is all aces. But I'm a member here—and no experience in Philly either! Today I couldn't wear my union button. The damnedest thing happened. When I take the old coat off the wall, I see she's smoking. I'm a sonovagun if the old union button isn't on fire! Yep, the old celluloid was makin' the most god-awful stink: the landlady come up and give me hell! You know what happened?—that old union button just blushed itself to death! Ashamed! Can you beat it?

FATT. Sit down, Keller! Nobody's interested!

AGATE. Yes, they are!

GUNMAN. Sit down like he tells you!

AGATE (*continuing to audience*). And when I finish— (*His speech is broken by* FATT *and* GUNMAN *who physically handle him. He breaks away and gets to other side of stage. The two are about to make for him when some of the committee men come forward and get in between the struggling parties.* AGATE'S *shirt has been torn.*)

AGATE (*to audience*). What's the answer, boys? The answer is, if we're reds because we wanna strike, then we take over their salute too! Know how they do it? (*Makes Communist salute*) What is it? An uppercut! The good old uppercut to the chin! Hell, some of us boys ain't even got a shirt to our backs. What's the boss class tryin' to do—make a nudist colony outa us?

(*The audience laughs and suddenly* AGATE *comes to the middle of the stage so that the other cabmen back him up in a strong clump.*)

AGATE. Don't laugh! Nothing's funny! This is your life and mine! It's skull and bones every incha the road! Christ, we're dyin' by inches! For what? For the debutant-ees to have their sweet comin' out parties in the Ritz! Poppa's got a daughter she's gotta get her picture in the papers. Christ, they make 'em with our blood. Joe said it. Slow death or fight. It's war! (*Throughout this whole speech* AGATE *is backed up by the other six workers, so that from their activity it is plain that the whole group of them are saying these things. Several of them may take alternate lines out of this long last speech*) You Edna, God love your mouth! Sid and Florrie, the other boys, old Doc Barnes—fight with us for right! It's war! Working class, unite and fight! Tear down the slaughter house of our old lives! Let freedom really ring. These slick slobs stand here telling us about bogeymen. That's a new one for the kids—the reds is bogeymen! But the man who got me food in 1932, he called me Comrade! The one who picked me up where I bled—he called me Comrade too! What

are we waiting for. . . . Don't wait for Lefty! He might never come. Every minute—
(*This is broken into by a man who has dashed up the center aisle from the back of the house. He runs up on stage, says*)

MAN. Boys, they just found Lefty!

OTHERS. What? What? What?

SOME. Shhh. . . . Shhh. . . .

MAN. They found Lefty. . . .

AGATE. Where?

MAN. Behind the car barns with a bullet in his head!

AGATE (*crying*). Hear it, boys, hear it? Hell, listen to me! Coast to coast! HELLO AMERICA! HELLO! WE'RE STORMBIRDS OF THE WORKING-CLASS. WORKERS OF THE WORLD. . . . OUR BONES AND BLOOD! And when we die they'll know what we did to make a new world! Christ, cut us up to little pieces. We'll die for what is right! Put fruit trees where our ashes are! (*To audience*) Well, what's the answer?

ALL. STRIKE!

AGATE. LOUDER!

ALL. STRIKE!

AGATE *and* OTHERS (*on Stage*) AGAIN!

ALL. STRIKE, STRIKE, STRIKE!!!

CURTAIN

NOTES FOR PRODUCTION

The background of the episodes, a strike meeting, is not an excuse. Each of the committeemen shows in his episode the crucial moment of his life which brought him to this very platform. The dramatic structure on which the play has been built is simple but highly effective. The form used is the old black-face minstrel form of chorus, end men, specialty men and inter-locutor.

In Fatt's scenes before the "Spy Exposé," mention should again be made of Lefty's tardiness. Sitting next to Fatt in the center of the circle is a little henchman who sits with his back to the audience. On the other side of Fatt is Lefty's empty chair. This is so indicated by Fatt when he himself asks: "Yeah, where's your chairman?"

Fatt, of course, represents the capitalist system throughout the play. The audience should constantly be kept aware of him, the ugly menace which hangs over the lives of all the people who act out their own dramas. Perhaps he puffs smoke into the spotted playing space; perhaps during the action of a playlet he might insolently walk in and around the unseeing players. It is possible that some highly gratifying results can be achieved by the imaginative use of this character.

The strike committee on the platform during the acting out of the play-let should be used as chorus. Emotional, political, musical, they have in them possibilities of various comments on the scenes. This has been indicated once in the script in the place where Joe's wife is about to leave him. In the climaxes of each scene, slogans might very effectively be used—a voice coming out of the dark. Such a voice might announce at the appropriate moments in the "Young Interne's" scene that the USSR is the only country in the world where Anti-Semitism is a crime against the State.

Do not hesitate to use music wherever possible. It is very valuable in emotionally stirring an audience.

Hello Out There

A ONE-ACT PLAY

BY WILLIAM SAROYAN

For George Bernard Shaw

HELLO OUT THERE

There is a fellow in a small-town prison cell, tapping slowly on the floor with a spoon. After tapping half a minute, as if he were trying to telegraph words, he gets up and begins walking around the cell. At last he stops, stands at the center of the cell, and doesn't move for a long time. He feels his head, as if it were wounded. Then he looks around. Then he calls out dramatically, kidding the world.

YOUNG MAN. Hello—out there! (*Pause*) Hello—out there! Hello—out there! (*Long pause*) Nobody out there. (*Still more dramatically, but more comically, too*) Hello—out there! Hello—out there!

(*A GIRL'S VOICE is heard, very sweet and soft.*)
THE VOICE. Hello.

YOUNG MAN. Hello—out there

THE VOICE. Hello.

YOUNG MAN. Is that you, Katey?

THE VOICE. No—this here is Emily.

YOUNG MAN. Who? (*Swiftly*) Hello out there.

THE VOICE. Emily.

YOUNG MAN. Emily who? I don't know anybody named Emily. Are you that girl I met at Sam's in Salinas about three years ago?

THE VOICE. No—I'm the girl who cooks here. I'm the cook. I've never been in Salinas. I don't even know where it is.

YOUNG MAN. Hello out there. You say you cook here?

THE VOICE. Yes.

YOUNG MAN. Well, why don't you study up and learn to cook? How come I don't get no jello or anything good?

THE VOICE. I just cook what they tell me to. (*Pause*) You lonesome?

YOUNG MAN. Lonesome as a coyote. Hear me hollering? Hello out there!

THE VOICE. Who you hollering to?

YOUNG MAN. Well—nobody, I guess. I been trying to think of somebody to write a letter to, but I can't think of anybody.

THE VOICE. What about Katey?

YOUNG MAN. I don't know anybody named Katey.

THE VOICE. Then why did you say, Is that you, Katey?

YOUNG MAN. Katey's a good name. I always did like a name like Katey. I never *knew* anybody named Katey, though.

THE VOICE. *I* did.

YOUNG MAN. Yeah? What was she like? Tall girl, or little one?

THE VOICE. Kind of medium.

YOUNG MAN. Hello out there. What sort of a looking girl are *you*?

THE VOICE. Oh, I don't know.

YOUNG MAN. Didn't anybody ever tell you? Didn't anybody ever talk to you that way?

THE VOICE. What way?

YOUNG MAN. You know. Didn't they?

THE VOICE. No, they didn't.

YOUNG MAN. Ah, the fools—they should have. I can tell from your voice you're O.K.

THE VOICE. Maybe I am and maybe I ain't.

YOUNG MAN. I never missed yet.

THE VOICE. Yeah, I know. That's why you're in jail.

YOUNG MAN. The whole thing was a mistake.

THE VOICE. They claim it was rape.

YOUNG MAN. No—it wasn't.

THE VOICE. That's what they claim it was.

YOUNG MAN. They're a lot of fools.

THE VOICE. Well, you sure are in trouble. Are you scared?

YOUNG MAN. Scared to death. (*Suddenly*) Hello out there!

THE VOICE. What do you keep saying that for all the time?

YOUNG MAN. I'm lonesome. I'm as lonesome as a coyote. (*A long one*) Hello—out there!

(THE GIRL *appears, over to one side. She is a plain girl in plain clothes.*)
THE GIRL. I'm kind of lonesome, too.

YOUNG MAN (*turning and looking at her*). Hey— No fooling? Are you?

THE GIRL. Yeah— I'm almost as lonesome as a coyote myself.

YOUNG MAN. Who *you* lonesome for?

THE GIRL. I don't know.

YOUNG MAN. It's the same with me. The minute they put you in a place like this you remember all the girls you ever knew, and all the girls you didn't get to know, and it sure gets lonesome.

THE GIRL. I bet it does.

YOUNG MAN. Ah, it's awful. (*Pause*) You're a pretty kid, you know that?

THE GIRL. You're just talking.

YOUNG MAN. No, I'm not just talking—you *are* pretty. Any fool could see that. You're just about the prettiest kid in the whole world.

THE GIRL. I'm not—and you know it.

YOUNG MAN. No—you are. I never saw anyone prettier in all my born days, in all my travels. I knew Texas would bring me luck.

THE GIRL. Luck? You're in jail, aren't you? You've got a whole gang of people all worked up, haven't you?

YOUNG MAN. Ah, that's nothing. I'll get out of this.

THE GIRL. Maybe.

YOUNG MAN. No, I'll be all right— *now.*

THE GIRL. What do you mean— now?

YOUNG MAN. I mean after seeing you. I got something now. You know for a while there I didn't care one way or another. Tired. (*Pause*) Tired of trying for the best all the time and never getting it. (*Suddenly*) Hello out there!

THE GIRL. Who you calling now?

YOUNG MAN. You.

THE GIRL. Why, I'm right here.

YOUNG MAN. I know. (*Calling*) Hello out there!

THE GIRL. Hello.

YOUNG MAN. Ah, you're sweet. (*Pause*) I'm going to marry *you.* I'm going away with *you.* I'm going to take you to San Francisco or some place like that. I *am,* now. I'm going to win myself some real money, too. I'm going to study 'em real careful and pick myself some winners, and we're going to have a lot of money.

THE GIRL. Yeah?

YOUNG MAN. Yeah. Tell me your name and all that stuff.

THE GIRL. Emily.

YOUNG MAN. I know that. What's the rest of it? Where were you born? Come on, tell me the whole thing.

THE GIRL. Emily Smith.

YOUNG MAN. Honest to God?

THE GIRL. Honest. That's my name —Emily Smith.

YOUNG MAN. Ah, you're the sweetest girl in the whole world.

THE GIRL. Why?

YOUNG MAN. I don't know why, but you are, that's all. Where were you born?

THE GIRL. Matador, Texas.

YOUNG MAN. Where's that?

THE GIRL. Right here.

YOUNG MAN. Is this Matador, Texas?

THE GIRL. Yeah, it's Matador. They brought you here from Wheeling.

YOUNG MAN. Is that where I was— Wheeling?

THE GIRL. Didn't you even know what town you were in?

YOUNG MAN. All towns are alike. You don't go up and ask somebody what town you're in. It doesn't make any difference. How far away is Wheeling?

THE GIRL. Sixteen or seventeen miles. Didn't you know they moved you?

YOUNG MAN. How could I know, when I was out—cold? Somebody hit me over the head with a lead pipe or something. What'd they hit me for?

THE GIRL. Rape—that's what they *said*.

YOUNG MAN. Ah, that's a lie. (*Amazed, almost to himself*) She wanted me to give her money.

THE GIRL. Money?

YOUNG MAN. Yeah, if I'd have known she was a woman like that—well, by God, I'd have gone on down the street and stretched out in a park somewhere and gone to sleep.

THE GIRL. Is that what she wanted —money?

YOUNG MAN. Yeah. A fellow like me hopping freights all over the country, trying to break his bad luck, going from one poor little town to another, trying to get in on something good somewhere, and she asks for money. I thought she was lonesome. She *said* she was.

THE GIRL. Maybe she was.

YOUNG MAN. She was *something*.

THE GIRL. I guess I'd never see you, if it didn't happen, though.

YOUNG MAN. Oh, I don't know— maybe I'd just mosey along this way and see you in this town somewhere. I'd recognize you, too.

THE GIRL. Recognize me?

YOUNG MAN. Sure, I'd recognize you the minute I laid eyes on you.

THE GIRL. Well, who would I be?

YOUNG MAN. Mine, that's who.

THE GIRL. Honest?

YOUNG MAN. Honest to God.

THE GIRL. You just say that because you're in jail.

YOUNG MAN. No, I mean it. You just pack up and wait for me. We'll high-roll the hell out of here to Frisco.

THE GIRL. You're just lonesome.

YOUNG MAN. I been lonesome all my life—there's no cure for that—but you and me—we can have a lot of fun hanging around together. You'll bring me luck. I know it.

THE GIRL. What are you looking for luck for all the time?

YOUNG MAN. I'm a gambler. I don't work. I've *got* to have luck, or I'm a bum. I haven't had any decent luck in years. Two whole years now —one place to another. Bad luck all the time. That's why I got in trouble back there in Wheeling, too. That was no accident. That was my bad luck following me around. So here I am, with my head half busted. I guess it was her old man that did it.

THE GIRL. You mean her father?

YOUNG MAN. No, her husband. If I had an old lady like that, I'd throw her out.

THE GIRL. Do you think you'll have better luck, if I go with you?

YOUNG MAN. It's a cinch. I'm a good handicapper. All I need is somebody good like you with me. It's no good always walking around in the streets for anything that might be there at the time. You got to have somebody staying with you all the time— through winters when it's cold, and springtime when it's pretty, and summertime when it's nice and hot and you can go swimming—through *all* the times—rain and snow and all the different kinds of weather a man's got to go through before he dies. You got to have somebody who's right. Somebody who knows you, from away back. You got to have somebody who even knows you're wrong but likes you just the same. I know I'm wrong, but I just don't want anything the hard way, working like a dog, or the *easy* way, working like a dog—working's the hard way and the easy way both. All I got to do is beat the price, always—and then I don't feel lousy and don't hate anybody. If you go along with me, I'll be the finest guy anybody ever saw. I won't be wrong any more. You know when you get enough of that money, you *can't* be wrong any more—you're right because the money says so. I'll have a lot of money and you'll be just about the prettiest, most wonderful kid in the whole world. I'll be proud walking around Frisco with you on my arm and people turning around to look at us.

THE GIRL. Do you think they will?

YOUNG MAN. Sure they will. When I get back in some decent clothes, and you're on my arm—well, Katey, they'll turn around and look, and they'll see something, too.

THE GIRL. Katey?

YOUNG MAN. Yeah—that's your name from now on. You're the first girl I ever called Katey. I've been saving it for you. O.K.?

THE GIRL. O.K.

YOUNG MAN. How long have I been here?

THE GIRL. Since last night. You didn't wake up until late this morning, though.

YOUNG MAN. What time is it now? About nine?

THE GIRL. About ten.

YOUNG MAN. Have you got the key to this lousy cell?

THE GIRL. No. They don't let me fool with any keys.

YOUNG MAN. Well, can you get it?

THE GIRL. No.

YOUNG MAN. Can you *try?*

THE GIRL. They wouldn't let me get near any keys. I cook for this jail, when they've got somebody in it. I clean up and things like that.

YOUNG MAN. Well, I want to get out of here. Don't you know the guy that runs this joint?

THE GIRL. I know him, but he wouldn't let you out. They were talking of taking you to another jail in another town.

YOUNG MAN. Yeah? Why?

THE GIRL. Because they're afraid.

YOUNG MAN. What are they afraid of?

THE GIRL. They're afraid these people from Wheeling will come over in the middle of the night and break in.

YOUNG MAN. Yeah? What do they want to do that for?

THE GIRL. Don't *you* know what they want to do it for?

YOUNG MAN. Yeah, I know all right.

THE GIRL. Are you scared?

YOUNG MAN. Sure I'm scared. Nothing scares a man more than ignorance. You can argue with people who ain't fools, but you can't argue with fools—they just go to work and do what they're set on doing. Get me out of here.

THE GIRL. How?

YOUNG MAN. Well, go get the guy with the key, and let me talk to him.

THE GIRL. He's gone home. Everybody's gone home.

YOUNG MAN. You mean I'm in this little jail all alone?

THE GIRL. Well—yeah—except me.

YOUNG MAN. Well, what's the big idea—doesn't anybody stay here all the time?

THE GIRL. No, they go home every night. I clean up and then I go, too. I hung around tonight.

YOUNG MAN. What made you do that?

THE GIRL. I wanted to talk to you.

YOUNG MAN. Honest? What did you want to talk about?

THE GIRL. Oh, I don't know. I took care of you last night. You were talk-ing in your sleep. You liked me, too. I didn't think you'd like me when you woke up, though.

YOUNG MAN. Yeah? Why not?

THE GIRL. I don't know.

YOUNG MAN. Yeah? Well, you're wonderful, see?

THE GIRL. Nobody ever talked to me that way. All the fellows in town— (*Pause.*)

YOUNG MAN. What about 'em? (*Pause*) Well, what about 'em? Come on—tell me.

THE GIRL. They laugh at me.

YOUNG MAN. Laugh at *you*? They're fools. What do they know about anything? You go get your things and come back here. I'll take you with me to Frisco. How old are you?

THE GIRL. Oh, I'm of age.

YOUNG MAN. How old are you?— Don't lie to me! Sixteen?

THE GIRL. I'm seventeen.

YOUNG MAN. Well, bring your father and mother. We'll get married before we go.

THE GIRL. They wouldn't let me go.

YOUNG MAN. Why not?

THE GIRL. I don't know, but they wouldn't. I know they wouldn't.

YOUNG MAN. You go tell your father not to be a fool, see? What is he, a farmer?

THE GIRL. No—nothing. He gets a little relief from the government because he's supposed to be hurt or something—his side hurts, he says. I don't know what it is.

YOUNG MAN. Ah, he's a liar. Well, I'm taking you with me, see?

THE GIRL. He takes the money I earn, too.

YOUNG MAN. He's got no right to do that.

THE GIRL. I know it, but he d ɔes it.

YOUNG MAN (*almost to himself*). This world stinks. You shouldn't have been born in this town, anyway, and you shouldn't have had a man like that for a father, either.

THE GIRL. Sometimes I feel sorry for him.

YOUNG MAN. Never mind feeling sorry for him. (*Pointing a finger*) I'm going to talk to your father some day. I've got a few things to tell that guy.

THE GIRL. I know you have.

YOUNG MAN (*suddenly*). Hello—out there! See if you can get that fellow with the keys to come down and let me out.

THE GIRL. Oh, I couldn't.

YOUNG MAN. Why not?

THE GIRL. I'm nobody here—they give me fifty cents every day I work.

YOUNG MAN. How much?

THE GIRL. Fifty cents.

YOUNG MAN (*to the world*). You see? They ought to pay money to *look* at you. To breathe the *air* you breathe. I don't know. Sometimes I figure it never is going to make sense. Hello—out there! I'm scared. You try to get me out of here. I'm scared them fools are going to come here from Wheeling and go crazy, thinking they're heroes. Get me out of here, Katey.

THE GIRL. I don't know what to do. Maybe I could break the door down.

YOUNG MAN. No, you couldn't do that. Is there a hammer out there or anything?

THE GIRL. Only a broom. Maybe they've locked the broom up, too.

YOUNG MAN. Go see if you can find anything.

THE GIRL. All right. (*She goes.*)

YOUNG MAN. Hello—out there! Hello—out there! (*Pause*) Hello—out there! Hello—out there! (*Pause*) Putting me in jail. (*With contempt*) Rape! Rape? *They* rape everything good that was ever born. His side hurts. They laugh at her. Fifty cents a day. Little punk people. Hurting the only good thing that ever came their way. (*Suddenly*) Hello—out there!

THE GIRL (*returning*). There isn't a thing out there. They've locked everything up for the night.

YOUNG MAN. Any cigarettes?

THE GIRL. Everything's locked up—all the drawers of the desk, all the closet doors—everything.

YOUNG MAN. I ought to have a cigarette.

THE GIRL. I could get you a package maybe, somewhere. I guess the drug store's open. It's about a mile.

YOUNG MAN. A mile? I don't want to be alone that long.

THE GIRL. I could run all the way, and all the way back.

YOUNG MAN. You're the sweetest girl that ever lived.

THE GIRL. What kind do you want?

YOUNG MAN. Oh, any kind—Chesterfields or Camels or Lucky Strikes —any kind at all.

THE GIRL. I'll go get a package. (*She turns to go.*)

YOUNG MAN. What about the money?

THE GIRL. I've got some money. I've got a quarter I been saving. I'll run all the way. (*She is about to go.*)

YOUNG MAN. Come here.

THE GIRL (*going to him*). What?

YOUNG MAN. Give me your hand. (*He takes her hand and looks at it, smiling. He lifts it and kisses it*) I'm scared to death.

THE GIRL. I am, too.

YOUNG MAN. I'm not lying—I don't care what happens to me, but I'm scared nobody will ever come out here to this God-forsaken broken-down town and find you. I'm scared you'll get used to it and not mind. I'm scared you'll never get to Frisco

and have 'em all turning around to look at you. Listen—go get me a gun, because if they come, I'll kill 'em! They don't understand. Get me a gun!

THE GIRL. I could get my father's gun. I know where he hides it.

YOUNG MAN. Go get it. Never mind the cigarettes. Run all the way. (*Pause, smiling but seriously*) Hello, Katey.

THE GIRL. Hello. What's *your* name?

YOUNG MAN. Photo-Finish is what they *call* me. My races are always photo-finish races. You don't know what that means, but it means they're very close. So close the only way they can tell which horse wins is to look at a photograph after the race is over. Well, every race I bet turns out to be a photo-finish race, and my horse never wins. It's my bad luck, all the time. That's why they call me Photo-Finish. Say it before you go.

THE GIRL. Photo-Finish.

YOUNG MAN. Come here. (THE GIRL *moves close and he kisses her*) Now, hurry. Run all the way.

THE GIRL. I'll run. (THE GIRL *turns and runs. The* YOUNG MAN *stands at the center of the cell a long time.* THE GIRL *comes running back in. Almost crying*) I'm afraid. I'm afraid I won't see you again. If I come back and you're not here, I—

YOUNG MAN. Hello—out there!

THE GIRL. It's so lonely in this town. Nothing here but the lonesome wind all the time, lifting the dirt and blowing out to the prairie. I'll stay here. I won't *let* them take you away,

YOUNG MAN. Listen, Katey. Do what I tell you. Go get that gun and come back. Maybe they won't come tonight. Maybe they won't come at all. I'll hide the gun and when they let me out you can take it back and put it where you found it. And then we'll go away. But if they come, I'll kill 'em! Now, hurry—

THE GIRL. All right. (*Pause*) I want to tell you something.

YOUNG MAN. O.K.

THE GIRL (*very softly*). If you're not here when I come back, well, I'll have the gun and I'll know what to do with it.

YOUNG MAN. You know how to handle a gun?

THE GIRL. I know how.

YOUNG MAN. Don't be a fool. (*Takes off his shoe, brings out some currency*) Don't be a fool, see? Here's some money. Eighty dollars. Take it and go to Frisco. Look around and find somebody. Find somebody alive and halfway human, see? Promise me—if I'm not here when you come back, just throw the gun away and get the hell to Frisco. Look around and find somebody.

THE GIRL. I don't *want* to find anybody.

YOUNG MAN (*swiftly, desperately*). Listen, if I'm not here when you come back, how do you know I haven't gotten away? Now, do what

I tell you. I'll meet you in Frisco. I've got a couple of dollars in my other shoe. I'll see you in San Francisco.

THE GIRL (*with wonder*). San Francisco?

YOUNG MAN. That's right—San Francisco. That's where you and me belong.

THE GIRL. I've always wanted to go to *some* place like San Francisco—but how could I go alone?

YOUNG MAN. Well, you're not alone any more, see?

THE GIRL. Tell me a little what it's like.

YOUNG MAN (*very swiftly, almost impatiently at first, but gradually slower and with remembrance, smiling, and* THE GIRL *moving closer to him as he speaks*). Well, it's on the Pacific to begin with—ocean water all around. Cool fog and sea-gulls. Ships from all over the world. It's got seven hills. The little streets go up and down, around and all over. Every night the fog-horns bawl. But they won't be bawling for you and me.

THE GIRL. What else?

YOUNG MAN. That's about all, I guess.

THE GIRL. Are people different in San Francisco?

YOUNG MAN. People are the same everywhere. They're different only when they love somebody. That's the only thing that makes 'em different. More people in Frisco love somebody, that's all.

THE GIRL. Nobody anywhere loves anybody as much as I love you.

YOUNG MAN (*shouting, as if to the world*). You see? Hearing you say that, a man could die and still be ahead of the game. Now, hurry. And don't forget, if I'm not here when you come back, get the hell to San Francisco where you'll have a chance. Do you hear me?

(THE GIRL *stands a moment looking at him, then backs away, turns and runs. The* YOUNG MAN *stares after her, troubled and smiling. Then he turns away from the image of her and walks about like a lion in a cage. After a while he sits down suddenly and buries his head in his hands. From a distance the sound of several automobiles approaching is heard. He listens a moment, then ignores the implications of the sound, whatever they may be. Several automobile doors are slammed. He ignores this also. A wooden door is opened with a key and closed, and footsteps are heard in a hall. Walking easily, almost casually and yet arrogantly, a* MAN *comes in. The* YOUNG MAN *jumps up suddenly and shouts at the* MAN, *almost scaring him*) What the hell kind of a jail-keeper are you, anyway? Why don't you attend to your business? You get paid for it, don't you? Now, get me out of here.

THE MAN. But I'm not the jail-keeper.

YOUNG MAN. Yeah? Well, who are you, then?

THE MAN. I'm the husband.

YOUNG MAN. What husband you talking about?

THE MAN. You know what husband.

YOUNG MAN. Hey! (*Pause, looking at* THE MAN) Are you the guy that hit me over the head last night?

THE MAN. I am.

YOUNG MAN (*with righteous indignation*). What do you mean going around hitting people over the head?

THE MAN. Oh, I don't know. What do you *mean* going around—the way you do?

YOUNG MAN (*rubbing his head*). You hurt my head. You got no right to hit anybody over the head.

THE MAN (*suddenly angry, shouting*). Answer my question! What do you mean?

YOUNG MAN. Listen, you—don't be hollering at me just because I'm locked up.

THE MAN (*with contempt, slowly*). You're a dog!

YOUNG MAN. Yeah, Well, let me tell you something. You *think* you're the husband. You're the husband of nothing. (*Slowly*) What's more, your wife—if you want to call her that—is a tramp. Why don't you throw her out in the street where she belongs?

THE MAN (*draws a pistol*). Shut up!

YOUNG MAN. Yeah? Go ahead, shoot —(*Softly*) and spoil the fun.

What'll your pals think? They'll be disappointed, won't they. What's the fun hanging a man who's already dead? (THE MAN *puts the gun away*) That's right, because now you can have some fun yourself, telling me what you're going to do. That's what you came here for, isn't it? Well, you don't need to tell me. I *know* what you're going to do. I've read the papers and I know. They have fun. A mob of 'em fall on one man and beat him, don't they? They tear off his clothes and kick him, don't they? And women and little children stand around watching, don't they? Well, before you go on *this* picnic, I'm going to tell you a few things. Not that that's going to send you home with your pals—the other heroes. No. You've been outraged. A stranger has come to town and violated your women. Your pure, innocent, virtuous women. You fellows have got to set this thing right. You're men, not mice. You're home-makers, and you beat your children. (*Suddenly*) Listen, you—I didn't know she was your wife. I didn't know she was anybody's wife.

THE MAN. You're a liar!

YOUNG MAN. Sometimes—when it'll do somebody some good—but not this time. Do you want to hear about it? (THE MAN *doesn't answer*) All right, I'll tell you. I met her at a lunch counter. She came in and sat next to me. There was plenty of room, but she sat next to me. Somebody had put a nickel in the phonograph and a fellow was singing *New San Antonio Rose*. Well, she got to talking about the song. I thought she was talking to the waiter, but *he* didn't answer her, so after a while *I* answered her. That's

how I met her. I didn't think anything of it. We left the place together and started walking. The first thing I knew she said, This is where I live.

THE MAN. You're a dirty liar!

YOUNG MAN. Do you want to hear it? Or not? (THE MAN *does not answer*) O.K. She asked me to come in. Maybe she had something in mind, maybe she didn't. Didn't make any difference to me, one way or the other. If she was lonely, all right. If not, all right.

THE MAN. You're telling a lot of dirty lies!

YOUNG MAN. I'm telling the truth. Maybe your wife's out there with your pals. Well, call her in. I got nothing against her, or you—or any of you. Call her in, and ask her a few questions. Are you in love with her? (THE MAN *doesn't answer*) Well, that's too bad.

THE MAN. What do you mean, too bad?

YOUNG MAN. I mean this may not be the first time something like this has happened.

THE MAN (*swiftly*). Shut up!

YOUNG MAN. Oh, you know it. You've always known it. You're afraid of your pals, that's all. She asked me for money. That's all she wanted. I wouldn't be here now if I had given her the money.

THE MAN (*slowly*). How much did she ask for?

YOUNG MAN. I didn't ask her how much. I told her I'd made a mistake. She said she would make trouble if I didn't give her money. Well, I don't like bargaining, and I don't like being threatened, either. I told her to get the hell away from me. The next thing I knew she'd run out of the house and was hollering. (*Pause*) Now, why don't you go out there and tell em they took me to another jail—go home and pack up and leave her. You're a pretty good guy, you're just afraid of your pals. (THE MAN *draws his gun again. He is very frightened. He moves a step toward the* YOUNG MAN, *then fires three times. The* YOUNG MAN *falls to his knees.* THE MAN *turns and runs, horrified*) Hello—out there! (*He is bent forward.* THE GIRL *comes running in, and halts suddenly, looking at him.*)

THE GIRL. There were some people in the street, men and women and kids—so I came in through the back, through a window. I couldn't find the gun. I looked all over but I couldn't find it. What's the matter?

YOUNG MAN. Nothing—nothing. Everything's all right. Listen. Listen, kid. Get the hell out of here. Go out the same way you came in and run—run like hell—run all night. Get to another town and get on a train. Do you hear me?

THE GIRL. What's happened?

YOUNG MAN. Get away—just get away from here. Take any train that's going—you can get to Frisco later.

THE GIRL (*almost sobbing*). I don't want to go any place without you.

YOUNG MAN. I can't go. Something's happened. (*He looks at her*) But I'll be with you always—God damn it. Always! (*He falls forward.* THE GIRL *stands near him, then begins to sob softly, walking away. She stands over to one side, stops sobbing, and stares out. The excitement of the mob outside increases.* THE MAN, *with two of his pals, comes running in.* THE GIRL *watches, unseen.*)

THE MAN. Here's the son of a bitch!

ANOTHER MAN. O.K. Open the cell, Harry.
(*The* THIRD MAN *goes to the cell door, unlocks it, and swings it open.*)
(*A* WOMAN *comes running in.*)

THE WOMAN. Where is he? I want to see him. Is he dead? (*Looking down at him, as the* MEN *pick him up*) There he is. (*Pause*) Yeah, that's him. (*Her husband looks at her with contempt, then at the dead man.*)

THE MAN (*trying to laugh*). All right—let's get it over with.

THIRD MAN. Right you are, George. Give me a hand, Harry.
(*They lift the body.*)

THE GIRL (*suddenly, fiercely*). Put him down!

THE MAN. What's this?

SECOND MAN. What are you doing here? Why aren't you out in the street?

THE GIRL. Put him down and go away. (*She runs toward the* MEN THE WOMAN *grabs her.*)

THE WOMAN. Here—where do you think *you're* going?

THE GIRL. Let me go. You've no right to take him away.

THE WOMAN. Well, listen to her, will you? (*She slaps* THE GIRL *and pushes her to the floor*) Listen to the little slut, will you?

(*They all go, carrying the* YOUNG MAN'S *body.* THE GIRL *gets up slowly, no longer sobbing. She looks around at everything, then looks straight out, and whispers.*)

THE GIRL. Hello—out—there! Hello —out there!

Bury the Dead

BY IRWIN SHAW

*". . . what is this world that
you cling to it?"*

TO MY MOTHER

CHARACTERS

PRIVATE DRISCOLL
PRIVATE MORGAN
PRIVATE LEVY
PRIVATE WEBSTER
PRIVATE SCHELLING
PRIVATE DEAN
JOAN BURKE
BESS SCHELLING
MARTHA WEBSTER
JULIA BLAKE
KATHERINE DRISCOLL
ELIZABETH DEAN

GENERALS ONE, TWO AND THREE
A CAPTAIN, A SERGEANT, AND FOUR INFANTRYMEN, *employed as a burial detail.*
A PRIEST, A RABBI, A DOCTOR
A REPORTER AND AN EDITOR
TWO WHORES

TIME—*The second year of the war that is to begin tomorrow night.*

SCENE—*The stage is in two planes —in the foreground, the bare stage, in the rear, not too far back, going the entire length of the stage, a platform about seven feet above the level of the stage proper. No properties are used to adorn the stage save for some sandbags, whole and split, lying along the edge of the raised platform and some loose dirt also on the platform. The entire platform is painted dull black. It is lighted by a strong spotlight thrown along it at hip-height from the right wing. It is the only light on the stage. The platform is to represent a torn-over battlefield, now quiet, some miles behind the present lines, where a burial detail, standing in a shallow trench dug in the platform, so that the audience sees them only from the hip up, are digging a common grave to accommodate six bodies, piled on the right of the platform, wrapped in canvas. A* SERGEANT *stands on the right, on the edge of the grave, smoking. . . . The* SOLDIER *nearest him, in the shallow trench, stops his digging. . . .*

BURY THE DEAD

FIRST SOLDIER. Say, Sergeant, they stink. . . . (*Waving his shovel at the corpses*) Let's bury them in a hurry. . . .

SERGEANT. What the hell do you think you'd smell like, after you'd been lyin' out for two days—a goddamn lily of the valley? They'll be buried soon enough. Keep digging.

SECOND SOLDIER (*scratching himself*). Dig and scratch! Dig and scratch! What a war! When you're not diggin' trenches you're diggin' graves. . . .

THIRD SOLDIER. Who's got a cigarette? I'll take opium if nobody's got a cigarette.

SECOND SOLDIER. When you're not diggin' graves you're scratchin' at fleas. By God, there're more fleas in this army than . . .

FIRST SOLDIER. That's what the war's made for—the fleas. Somebody's got to feed 'em. . . .

FOURTH SOLDIER. I used to take a shower every day. Can you imagine?

SERGEANT. All right, Mr. Lifebuoy, we'll put your picture in the *Saturday Evening Post*—in color!

SECOND SOLDIER. When you're not scratchin' at fleas, you're bein' killed. That's a helluva life for a grown man.

THIRD SOLDIER. Who's got a cigarette? I'll trade my rifle—if I can find it—for a cigarette. For Christ's sake, don't they make cigarettes no more? (*Leaning, melancholy, on his shovel*) This country's goin' to the dogs for real now. . . .

SERGEANT. Lift dirt, soldier. Come on! This ain't no vacation.

THIRD SOLDIER (*disregarding him*). I heard of guys packin' weeds and cowflop into cigarettes in this man's army. They say it has a tang. (*Reflectively*) Got to try it some day. . . .

SERGEANT. Hurry up! (*Blowing on his hands*) I'm freezin' here. I don't want to hang around all night. I can't feel my feet no more. . . .

FOURTH SOLDIER. I ain't felt my feet for two weeks. I ain't had my shoes off in two weeks. (*Leaning on his shovel*) I wonder if the toes're still connected. I wear a 8A shoe. Aristocratic foot, the salesman always said. Funny—going around not even knowin' whether you still got toes or not. . . . It's not hygienic really. . . .

SERGEANT. All right, friend, we'll make sure the next war you're in is run hygienic.

FOURTH SOLDIER. In the Spanish-American War more men died of fever than . . .

FIRST SOLDIER (*beating viciously at*

567

something in the grave). Get him! Get him! Kill the bastard!

FOURTH SOLDIER (*savagely*). He's coming this way! We got him cornered!

FIRST SOLDIER. Bash his brains out!

SECOND SOLDIER. You got him with that one! (*All the soldiers in the grave beat at it, yelling demoniacally, triumphantly.*)

SERGEANT (*remonstrating*). Come on now, you're wasting time. . . .

FIRST SOLDIER (*swinging savagely*). There. That fixed him. The goddamn . . .

FOURTH SOLDIER (*sadly*). You'd think the rats'd at least wait until the stiffs were underground.

FIRST SOLDIER. Did you ever see such a fat rat in your whole life? I bet he ate like a horse—this one.

SERGEANT. All right, all right. You're not fightin' the war against rats. Get back to your business.

FIRST SOLDIER. I get a lot more pleasure killin' rats than killin' them. (*Gesture toward the front lines.*)

SERGEANT. Rats got to live, too. They don't know no better.

FIRST SOLDIER (*suddenly scooping up rat on his shovel and presenting it to* SERGEANT). Here you are, Sergeant. A little token of our regard from Company A.

SERGEANT. Stop the smart stuff! I don't like it.

FIRST SOLDIER (*still with rat upheld on shovel*). Ah, Sergeant, I'm disappointed. This rat's a fine pedigreed animal—fed only on the choicest young men the United State's turned out in the last twenty years.

SERGEANT. Come on, wise guy. (FIRST SOLDIER *goes right on.*)

FIRST SOLDIER. Notice the heavy, powerful shoulders to this rat, notice the well-covered flanks, notice the round belly—bank clerks, mechanics, society-leaders, farmers— good feeding— (*Suddenly he throws the rat away*) Ah—I'm gettin' awful tired of this. I didn't enlist in this bloody war to be no bloody grave-digger!

SERGEANT. Tell that to the President. Keep diggin'.

SECOND SOLDIER. Say, this is deep enough. What're we supposed to do —dig right down to hell and deliver them over first-hand?

SERGEANT. A man's entitled to six feet a' dirt over his face. We gotta show respect to the dead. Keep diggin'. . . .

FOURTH SOLDIER. I hope they don't put me too far under when my turn comes. I want to be able to come up and get a smell of air every once in so often.

SERGEANT. Stow the gab, you guys! Keep diggin'. . . .

FIRST SOLDIER. They stink! Bury them!

SERGEANT. All right, Fanny. From now on we'll perfume 'em before we ask you to put them away. Will that please you?

FIRST SOLDIER. I don't like the way they smell, that's all. I don't have to like the way they smell, do I? That ain't in the regulations, is it? A man's got a right to use his nose, ain't he, even though he's in this god-damn army. . . .

SERGEANT. Talk respectful when you talk about the army, you!

FIRST SOLDIER. Oh, the lovely army . . . (*He heaves up clod of dirt.*)

SECOND SOLDIER. Oh, the dear army . . . (*He heaves up clod of dirt.*)

THIRD SOLDIER. Oh, the sweet army . . . (*He heaves up clod of dirt.*)

FIRST SOLDIER. Oh, the scummy, stinking, god-damn army . . . (*He heaves up three shovelfuls in rapid succession.*)

SERGEANT. That's a fine way to talk in the presence of death. . . .

FIRST SOLDIER. We'd talk in blank verse for you, Sergeant, only we ran out of it our third day in the front line. What do you expect, Sergeant, we're just common soldiers . . .

SECOND SOLDIER. Come on. Let's put 'em away. I'm getting blisters big enough to use for balloons here. What's the difference? They'll just be turned up anyway, the next time the artillery wakes up. . . .

SERGEANT. All right! All right! If you're in such a hurry—put 'em in. . . . (*The* SOLDIERS *nearest the right-hand edge of the grave jump out and start carrying the bodies*

over, one at each corner of the canvas. The other* SOLDIERS, *still in the trench, take the bodies from them and carry them over to the other side of the trench, where they lay them down, out of sight of the audience.*)

SERGEANT. Put 'em in neat, there. . . .

FIRST SOLDIER. File 'em away alphabetically, boys. We may want to refer to them, later. The General might want to look up some past cases.

FOURTH SOLDIER. This one's just a kid. I knew him a little. Nice kid. He used to write dirty poems. Funny as hell. He don't even look dead. . . .

FIRST SOLDIER. Bury him! He stinks!

SERGEANT. If you think *you* smell so sweet, yourself, Baby, you oughta wake up. You ain't exactly a perfume-ad, soldier. (*Laughter.*)

THIRD SOLDIER. Chalk one up for the Sergeant.

FIRST SOLDIER. You ain't a combination of roses and wistaria, either, Sergeant, but I can stand you, especially when you don't talk. At least you're alive. There's something about the smell of dead ones that gives me the willies. . . . Come on, let's pile the dirt in on them. . . . (*The* SOLDIERS *scramble out of the grave.*)

SERGEANT. Hold it.

THIRD SOLDIER. What's the matter now? Do we have to do a dance around them?

SERGEANT. We have to wait for chaplains. . . . They gotta say some prayers over them.

FIRST SOLDIER. Oh, for Christ's sake, ain't I ever going to get any sleep tonight?

SERGEANT. Don't begrudge a man his prayers, soldier. You'd want 'em, wouldn't you?

FIRST SOLDIER. God, no. I want to sleep peaceful when I go. . . . Well, where are they? Why don't they come? Do we have to stand here all night waiting for those guys to come and talk to God about these fellers?

THIRD SOLDIER. Who's got a cigarette? (*Plaintively.*)

SERGEANT. Attention! Here they are! (*A Roman-Catholic* PRIEST *and a* RABBI *come in.*)

PRIEST. Is everything ready?

SERGEANT. Yes, Father . . .

FIRST SOLDIER. Make it snappy! I'm awful tired.

PRIEST. God must be served slowly, my son. . . .

FIRST SOLDIER. He's gettin' plenty of service these days—and not so slow, either. He can stand a little rushin'. . . .

SERGEANT. Shut up, soldier.

RABBI. Do you want to hold your services first, Father?

SERGEANT. There ain't no Jewish boys in there. (*Gesture to grave*)

Reverend, I don't think we'll need you.

RABBI. I understand one of them is named Levy.

SERGEANT. Yes. But he's no Jew.

RABBI. With that name we won't take any chances. Father, will you be first?

PRIEST. Perhaps we had better wait. There is an Episcopal bishop in this sector. He expressed the desire to conduct a burial service here. He's doing that in all the sectors he is visiting. I think we had better wait for him. Episcopal bishops are rather sensitive about order. . . .

RABBI. He's not coming. He's having his supper.

FIRST SOLDIER. What does God do while the bishop has his supper?

SERGEANT. If you don't keep quiet, I'll bring you up on charges.

FIRST SOLDIER. I want to get it over with! Bury them! They stink!

PRIEST. Young man, that is not the way to talk about one of God's creatures. . . .

FIRST SOLDIER. If *that's* (*gesture to grave*) one of God's creatures, all I can say is, He's slippin' . . .

PRIEST. Ah, my son, you seem so bitter. . . .

FIRST SOLDIER. For God's sake, stop talking and get this over with. I want to throw dirt over them! I can't stand the smell of them! Sergeant, get 'em to do it fast. They ain't got no right to keep us up all night. We got work to do tomorrow. . . . Let 'em say their prayers together! God'll be able to understand. . . .

PRIEST. Yes. There is really no need to prolong it. We must think of the living as well as the dead. As he says, Reverend, God will be able to understand. . . .
(*He stands at the head of the grave, chants the Latin prayer for the dead. The* RABBI *goes around to the other end and recites the Hebrew prayer. In the middle of it, a groan is heard, low, but clear. The chants keep on. Another groan is heard.*)

FIRST SOLDIER (*while the Hebrew and Latin go on*). I heard a groan. (*The* RABBI *and* PRIEST *continue*) I heard a groan!

SERGEANT. Shut up, soldier!
(*The Latin and Hebrew go on.*)

FIRST SOLDIER (*gets down on one knee by side of grave and listens. Another groan*). Stop it! I heard a groan . . .

SERGEANT. What about it? Can you have war without groans? Keep quiet!
(*The prayers go on undisturbed. Another groan. The* FIRST SOLDIER *jumps into the grave.*)

FIRST SOLDIER. It's from here! Hold it! (*Screaming*) Hold it! Stop those god-damned parrots! (*Throws a clod of dirt at end of trench*) Hold it! Somebody down here groaned. . . .
(*A head appears slowly above the trench rim at the left end, a man stands up, slowly facing the rear. All the men sigh—the service goes on.*)

SERGEANT. Oh, my God . . .

FIRST SOLDIER. He's alive. . . .

SERGEANT. Why the hell don't they get these things straight? Pull him out!

FIRST SOLDIER. Stop them! (*As the services go on*) Get them out of here! Live men don't need them. . . .

SERGEANT. Please, Father, this has nothing to do with you. . . . There's been some mistake. . . .

PRIEST. I see. All right, Sergeant. (*He and* RABBI *join, hand in hand, and leave. Nobody notices them. All the men are hypnotically watching the man in the trench, arisen from the dead. The* CORPSE *passes his hand over his eyes. The men sigh— horrible, dry sighs. . . . Another groan is heard from the left side of the trench.*)

FIRST SOLDIER (*in trench*). There! (*Pointing*) It came from there! I heard it! (*A head, then shoulders appear over the rim of trench at left side. The* SECOND CORPSE *stands up, passes his hands over eyes in same gesture which drew sighs from the men before. There is absolute silence as the men watch the arisen corpses. Then, silently, a corpse rises in the middle of the trench, next to the* FIRST SOLDIER. *The* FIRST SOLDIER *screams, scrambles out of the trench in rear, and stands, bent over, watching the trench, middle-rear. There is no sound save the very light rumble of the guns. One by one the* CORPSES *arise and stand silently in their places, facing the rear, their backs to the audience. The* SOLDIERS *don't move, scarcely breathe, as, one by one, the* CORPSES *appear. They stand there, a frozen tableau. Suddenly, the* SERGEANT *talks.*)

SERGEANT. What do you want?

FIRST CORPSE. Don't bury us.

THIRD SOLDIER. Let's get the hell out of here!

SERGEANT (*drawing pistol*). Stay where you are! I'll shoot the first man that moves.

FIRST CORPSE. Don't bury us. We don't want to be buried.

SERGEANT. Christ! (*To men*) Carry on! (*The men stand still*) Christ! (*The* SERGEANT *rushes off, calling*) Captain! Captain! Where the hell is the Captain? (*His voice fades, terror-stricken. The* SOLDIERS *watch the* CORPSES, *then slowly, all together, start to back off.*)

SIXTH CORPSE. Don't go away.

SECOND CORPSE. Stay with us.

THIRD CORPSE. We want to hear the sound of men talking.

SIXTH CORPSE. Don't be afraid of us.

FIRST CORPSE. We're not really different from you. We're dead.

SECOND CORPSE. That's all . . .?

FOURTH CORPSE. All—all . . .

FIRST SOLDIER. That's all . . .?

THIRD CORPSE. Are you afraid of six dead men? You, who've lived with the dead, the so-many dead, and eaten your bread by their side when there was no time to bury them and you were hungry?

SECOND CORPSE. Are we different from you? An ounce or so of lead in our hearts, and none in yours. A small difference between us.

THIRD CORPSE. Tomorrow or the next day, the lead will be yours, too. Talk as our equals.

FOURTH SOLDIER. It's the kid—the one who wrote the dirty poems.

FIRST CORPSE. Say something to us. Forget the grave, as we would forget it. . . .

THIRD SOLDIER. Do you—do you want a cigarette?
(SERGEANT *re-enters with* CAPTAIN.)

SERGEANT. I'm not drunk! I'm not crazy, either! They just—got up, all together—and looked at us. . . . Look—look for yourself, Captain! (*The* CAPTAIN *stands off to one side, looking. The men stand at attention.*)

SERGEANT. See?

CAPTAIN. I see. (*He laughs sadly*) I was expecting it to happen—some day. So many men each day. It's too bad it had to happen in my company. Gentlemen! At ease! (*The men stand at ease. The* CAPTAIN *leaves. The guns roar suddenly. Fadeout.*)
(*The spotlight is turned on to the lower stage, right, below the platform on which the action, until now, has taken place. Discovered in its glare are three* GENERALS, *around a table. The* CAPTAIN *is standing before them, talking.*)

CAPTAIN. I'm only telling the Generals what I saw.

FIRST GENERAL. You're not making this up, Captain?

CAPTAIN. No, General.

SECOND GENERAL. Have you any proof, Captain?

CAPTAIN. The four men in the burial detail and the Sergeant, Sir.

THIRD GENERAL. In time of war, Captain, men see strange things.

CAPTAIN. Yes, General.

SECOND GENERAL. You've been drinking, Captain.

CAPTAIN. Yes, General.

SECOND GENERAL. When a man has been drinking, he is not responsible for what he sees.

CAPTAIN. Yes, General. I am not responsible for what I saw. I am glad of that. I would not like to carry that burden, along with all the others. . . .

FIRST GENERAL. Come, come, Captain, confess now. You were drinking and you walked out into the cold air over a field just lately won and what with the liquor and the air and the flush of victory . . .

CAPTAIN. I told the General what I saw.

SECOND GENERAL. Yes, we heard. We forgive you for it. We don't think any the worse of you for taking a nip. It's only natural. We understand. So take another drink with us now and forget your ghosts. . . .

CAPTAIN. They weren't ghosts. They were men—killed two days, standing in their graves and looking at me.

FIRST GENERAL. Captain, you're becoming trying. . . .

CAPTAIN. I'm sorry, Sir. It was a trying sight. I saw them and what are the Generals going to do about it?

SECOND GENERAL. Forget it! A man is taken for dead and put in a grave. He wakes from his coma and stands up. It happens every day—you've got to expect such things in a war. Take him out and send him to a hospital!

CAPTAIN. Hospitals aren't for dead men. What are the Generals going to do about them?

THIRD GENERAL. Don't stand there croaking, "What are the Generals going to do about them?" Have 'em examined by a doctor. If they're alive send them to a hospital. If they're dead, bury them! It's very simple.

CAPTAIN. But . . .

THIRD GENERAL. No buts, Sir!

CAPTAIN. Yes, Sir.

THIRD GENERAL. Take a doctor down with you, Sir, and a stenographer. Have the doctor dictate official reports. Have them witnessed. And let's hear no more of it.

CAPTAIN. Yes, Sir. Very good, Sir. (Wheels to go out.)

SECOND GENERAL. Oh, and Captain . . .

CAPTAIN (*stopping*). Yes, Sir.

SECOND GENERAL. Stay away from the bottle.

CAPTAIN. Yes, Sir. Is that all, Sir?

SECOND GENERAL. That's all.

CAPTAIN. Yes, Sir.
(*The light fades from the* GENERALS. *It follows the* CAPTAIN *as he walks across stage. The* CAPTAIN *stops, takes out a bottle. Takes two long swigs. Blackout.*)
(*The guns rumble, growing louder. They have been almost mute during* GENERALS' *scene. The light is thrown on the burial scene again, where the* DOCTOR *is seen examining the* CORPSES *in their graves. The* DOCTOR *is armed with a stethoscope and is followed by a soldier* STENOGRAPHER, *two of the* SOLDIERS, *impressed as witnesses, and the* CAPTAIN. *The* DOCTOR *is talking, as he passes from the first man.*)

DOCTOR. Number one. Evisceration of the lower intestine. Dead forty-eight hours.

STENOGRAPHER (*repeating*). Number one. Evisceration of the lower intestine. Dead forty-eight hours. (*To witnesses*) Sign here. (*They sign.*)

DOCTOR (*on the next man*). Number two. Bullet penetrated the left ventricle. Dead forty-eight hours.

STENOGRAPHER. Number two. Bullet penetrated the left ventricle. Dead forty-eight hours. (*To witnesses*) Sign here. (*They sign.*)

DOCTOR (*on the next* CORPSE). Number three. Bullets penetrated both lungs. Severe hemorrhages. Dead forty-eight hours.

STENOGRAPHER (*chanting*). Number three. Bullets penetrated both lungs. Severe hemorrhages. Dead forty-eight hours. Sign here. (*The witnesses sign.*)

DOCTOR (*on next* CORPSE). Number four. Fracture of the skull and avulsion of the cerebellum. Dead forty-eight hours.

STENOGRAPHER. Number four. Fracture of the skull and avulsion of the cerebellum. Dead forty-eight hours. Sign here. (*The witnesses sign.*)

DOCTOR (*moving on to next* CORPSE). Number five. Destruction of the genito-urinary system by shell-splinters. Death from hemorrhages. Dead forty-eight hours. Ummn. (*Looks curiously at* CORPSE's *face*) Hum . . . (*Moves on.*)

STENOGRAPHER. Number five. Destruction of the genito-urinary system by shell-splinters. Death from hemorrhages. Dead forty-eight hours. Sign here. (*The witnesses sign.*)

DOCTOR (*on the next* CORPSE). Number six. Destruction of right side of head from supra-orbital ridges through jaw-bone. Hum. You'd be a pretty sight for your mother, you would. Dead forty-eight hours . . .

STENOGRAPHER. Number six. Destruction of right side of head from supra-orbital ridges through jaw-bone. You'd be a pretty sight for your mother, you would. Dead forty-eight hours. Sign here.

DOCTOR. What are you doing there?

STENOGRAPHER. That's what you said, Sir. . . .

DOCTOR. I know. Leave out— "You'd be a pretty sight for your mother, you would . . ." The Generals wouldn't be interested in that.

STENOGRAPHER. Yes, Sir. Sign here. (*The witnesses sign.*)

DOCTOR. Six, is that all?

CAPTAIN. Yes, Doctor. They're all dead?
(*The* FOURTH CORPSE *offers the* THIRD SOLDIER *a cigarette. The* THIRD SOLDIER *hesitates a second before taking it, then accepts it with a half grin.*)

THIRD SOLDIER. Thanks, Buddy. I— I'm awful sorry—I—Thanks . . . (*He saves cigarette.*)

DOCTOR (*eyes on* FOURTH CORPSE *and* THIRD SOLDIER). All dead.

CAPTAIN. A drink, Doctor?

DOCTOR. Yes, thank you. (*He takes the proffered bottle. Drinks long from it. Holds it, puts stethoscope in pocket with other hand. Stands looking at the* CORPSES, *lined up, facing the rear, nods, then takes another long drink. Silently hands bottle to* CAPTAIN, *who looks around him from one* CORPSE *to another, then takes a long drink. Blackout.*)
(*Spotlight on the* GENERALS, *facing the* CAPTAIN *and the* DOCTOR. *The* FIRST GENERAL *has the* DOCTOR's *reports in his hands.*)

FIRST GENERAL. Doctor!

DOCTOR. Yes, Sir.

FIRST GENERAL. In your reports here you say each of these six men is dead.

DOCTOR. Yes, Sir.

FIRST GENERAL. Then I don't see what all the fuss is about, Captain. They're dead—bury them. . . .

CAPTAIN. I am afraid, Sir, that that can't be done. . . . They are standing in their graves. They refuse to be buried.

THIRD GENERAL. Do we have to go into that again? We have the doctor's report. They're dead. Aren't they, Doctor?

DOCTOR. Yes, Sir.

THIRD GENERAL. Then they aren't standing in their graves, refusing to be buried, are they?

DOCTOR. Yes, Sir.

SECOND GENERAL. Doctor, would you know a dead man if you saw one?

DOCTOR. The symptoms are easily recognized.

FIRST GENERAL. You've been drinking, too. . . .

DOCTOR. Yes, Sir.

FIRST GENERAL. The whole damned army is drunk! I want a regulation announced tomorrow morning in all regiments. No more liquor is to be allowed within twenty miles of the front line upon pain of death. Got it?

SECOND GENERAL. Yes, General. But then how'll we get the men to fight?

FIRST GENERAL. Damn the fighting! We can't have stories like this springing up. It's bad for the morale! Did you hear me, Doctor, it's bad for the morale and you ought to be ashamed of yourself!

DOCTOR. Yes, Sir.

THIRD GENERAL. This has gone far enough. If it goes any farther, the men will get wind of it. We have witnessed certificates from a registered surgeon that these men are dead. Bury them! Waste no more time on it. Did you hear me, Captain?

CAPTAIN. Yes, Sir. I'm afraid, Sir, that I must refuse to bury these men.

THIRD GENERAL. That's insubordination, Sir. . . .

CAPTAIN. I'm sorry, Sir. It is not within the line of my military duties to bury men against their will. If the General will only think for a moment he will see that this is impossible. . . .

FIRST GENERAL. The Captain's right. It might get back to Congress. God only knows what *they'd* make of it!

THIRD GENERAL. What are we going to do then?

FIRST GENERAL. Captain, what do you suggest?

CAPTAIN. Stop the war.

CHORUS OF GENERALS. Captain!

FIRST GENERAL (*with great dignity*). Captain, we beg of you to remember the gravity of the situation. It admits of no levity. Is that the best suggestion you can make, Captain?

CAPTAIN. Yes. But I have another— If the Generals would come down to the grave themselves and attempt to influence these—ah—corpses—to lie down, perhaps that would prove effective. We're seven miles behind the line now and we could screen the roads to protect your arrival. . . .

FIRST GENERAL (*coughing*). Umm —uh—usually, of course, that would be—uh . . . We'll see. In the meantime it must be kept quiet! Remember that! Not a word! Nobody must know! God only knows what would happen if people began to suspect we couldn't even get our dead to lie down and be buried! This is the god-damndest war! They never said anything about this sort of thing at West Point. Remember, not a word, nobody must know, quiet as the grave, *mum! ssssh!* (*All the* GENERALS *repeat the ssssh after him.*)
(*The light fades—but the hiss of the* GENERALS *hushing each other is still heard as the light falls on another part of the stage proper, where two soldiers are on post in the front lines, behind a barricade of sandbags. The sound of guns is very strong. There are flashes of gunfire.*)

BEVINS (*a soldier past forty, fat, with a pot-belly and graying hair showing under his helmet*). Did you hear about those guys that won't let themselves be buried, Charley?

CHARLEY. I heard. You never know what's gonna happen next in this lousy war.

BEVINS. What do you think about it, Charley?

CHARLEY. What're they gettin' out of it, that's what I'd like to know. They're just makin' things harder. I heard all about 'em. They stink! Bury 'em. That's what I say.

BEVINS. I don't know, Charley. I kinda can see what they're aimin' at. Christ, I wouldn't like to be put six foot under now, I wouldn't. What the hell for?

CHARLEY. What's the difference?

BEVINS. There's a difference, all right. It's kinda good, bein' alive. It's kinda nice, bein' on top of the earth and seein' things and hearin' things and smellin' things. . . .

CHARLEY. Yeah, smellin' stiffs that ain't had time to be buried. That sure is sweet.

BEVINS. Yeah, but it's better than havin' the dirt packed onto your face. I guess those guys felt sorta gypped when they started throwin' the dirt in on 'em and they just couldn't stand it, dead or no dead.

CHARLEY. They're dead, ain't they? Nobody's puttin' them under while they're alive.

BEVINS. It amounts to the same thing, Charley. They should be alive now. What are they—a parcel of kids? Kids shouldn't be dead, Charley. That's what they musta figured when the dirt started fallin' in on 'em. What the hell are they doin' dead? Did they get anything out of it? Did anybody ask them? Did they want to be standin' there when the lead poured in? They're just kids, or guys with wives and young kids of their own. They wanted to be home readin' a book or teachin' their kid c-a-t spells cat or takin' a woman out into the country in a open car with the wind blowin'. . . . That's the way it musta come to them, when the dirt smacked on their faces, dead or no dead. . . .

CHARLEY. Bury them. That's what I say. . . .
(*There is the chatter of a machine gun off in the night.* BEVINS *is hit. He staggers.*)

BEVINS (*clutching his throat*). Charley—Charley . . . (*His fingers bring down the top sandbag as he falls. The machine gun chatters again and* CHARLEY *is hit. He staggers.*)

CHARLEY. Oh, my God . . . (*The machine gun chatters again. He falls over* BEVINS. *There is quiet for a moment. Then the eternal artillery again. Blackout.*)
(*A baby spotlight, white, picks out the* FIRST GENERAL, *standing over the prone forms of the two soldiers. He has his fingers to his lips.*)

FIRST GENERAL (*in a hoarse whisper*). Sssh! Keep it quiet! Nobody must know! Not a word! Sssh! (*Blackout.*)
(*A spotlight picks out another part of the stage—a newspaper office.* EDITOR *at his desk,* REPORTER *before him, hat on head.*)

REPORTER. That's the story! It's as straight as a rifle-barrel, so help me God.

EDITOR (*looking down at manuscript in hand*). This is a freak, all right. I never came across anything like it in all the years I've been putting out a newspaper.

REPORTER. There never was anything like it before. It's somethin' new. Somethin's happening. Somebody's waking up. . . .

EDITOR. It didn't happen.

REPORTER. So help me God, I got it straight. Those guys just stood up in the grave and said, "The hell with it, you can't bury us!" God's honest truth.

EDITOR (*picks up telephone*). Get me Macready at the War Department. . . . It's an awfully funny story. . . .

REPORTER. What about it? It's the story of the year—the story of the century—the biggest story of all time—men gettin' up with bullets in their hearts and refusin' to be buried. . . .

EDITOR. Who do they think they are—Jesus Christ?

REPORTER. What's the difference? That's the story! You can't miss it! You goin' to put it in? Lissen—are you goin' to put it in?

EDITOR. Hold it! (*Into telephone*) Macready!

REPORTER. What's he got to do with it?

EDITOR. I'll find out. What are *you* so hot about? . . . Hello! Macready? Hansen from the New York . . . Yeah. . . . Listen, Macready,

I got this story about six guys who refuse to be . . . Yeah. . . .

REPORTER. What does he say?

EDITOR. Okay, Macready. Yeah, if that's the way the Government feels about it. . . . Yeah. . . .

REPORTER. Well?

EDITOR (*putting down telephone*). No.

REPORTER. Holy god-damn, you got to. People got a right to know.

EDITOR. In time of war, people have a right to know nothing. If we put it in, it'd be censored anyway.

REPORTER. Ah, this is a lousy business. . . .

EDITOR. Write another human interest story about the boys at the front. That'll keep you busy. You know . . . that one about how the boys in the front-line sing "I Can't Give You Anything but Love," before they go over the top. . . .

REPORTER. But I wrote that last week.

EDITOR. It made a great hit. Write it again.

REPORTER. But these guys in the grave, Boss. Lloyds are giving three to one they won't go down. That's a story!

EDITOR. Save it. You can write a book of memoirs twenty years from now. Make that "I Can't Give You Anything but Love" story a thousand words, and make it snappy. The casualty lists run into two pages today and we got to balance them with something. . . . (*Blackout.*)

(*Rumble of guns. The spotlight illuminates the grave on the platform, where the* CORPSES *are still standing, hip-deep, facing the rear. The burial squad is there, and the* CAPTAIN, *and the* GENERALS.)

CAPTAIN. There they are. What are the Generals going to do about them?

FIRST GENERAL (*pettishly*). I see them. Stop saying "What are the Generals going to do about them?"

SECOND GENERAL. Who do they think they are?

THIRD GENERAL. It's against all regulations.

FIRST GENERAL. Quiet, please, quiet. Let's not have any scenes. . . . This must be handled with authority—but tactfully. I'll talk to them! (*He goes over to brink of grave*) Men! Listen to me! This is a strange situation in which we find ourselves. I have no doubt but that it is giving you as much embarrassment as it is us. . . .

SECOND GENERAL (*confidentially to* THIRD GENERAL). The wrong note. He's good on artillery, but when it comes to using his head, he's lost. . . . He's been that way ever since I knew him.

FIRST GENERAL. We're all anxious to get this thing over with just as quickly and quietly as possible. I know that you men are with me on this. There's no reason why we can't get together and settle this in jig time. I grant, my friends, that it's unfortunate that you're dead. I'm sure that you'll all listen to reason. Listen, too, to the voice of duty, the voice that sent you here to die bravely for your country. Gentlemen, your country demands of you that you lie down and allow yourselves to be buried. Must our flag fly at half-mast and droop in the wind while you so far forget your duty to the lovely land that bore and nurtured you? I love America, gentlemen, its hills and valleys. If you loved America as I do, you would not . . . (*He breaks down, overcome*) I find it difficult to go on. (*He pauses*) I have studied this matter and come to the conclusion that the best thing for all concerned would be for you men to lie down peaceably in your graves and allow yourselves to be buried. (*He waits. The* CORPSES *do not move.*)

THIRD GENERAL. It didn't work. He's not firm enough. You've got to be firm right from the beginning or you're lost.

FIRST GENERAL. Men, perhaps you don't understand. (*To* CORPSES) I advise you to allow yourselves to be buried. (*They stand, motionless*) You're dead, men, don't you realize that? You can't be dead and stand there like that. Here . . . here . . . I'll prove it to you! (*He gets out* DOCTOR'S *reports*) Look! A doctor's reports. Witnessed! Witnessed by Privates McGurk and Butler. (*He reads the names*) This ought to show you! (*He waves the reports. He stands on the brink of the grave, middle-rear, glaring at the* CORPSES. *He shouts at them*) You're dead, officially, all of you! I won't mince words! You heard! We're a civilized race, we bury our dead. Lie down! (*The* CORPSES *stand*) Private Driscoll! Private Schelling! Private

Morgan! Private Levy! Private Webster! Private Dean! Lie down! As Commander-in-Chief of the Army as appointed by the President of the United States in accordance with the Constitution of the United States, and as your superior officer, I command you to lie down and allow yourselves to be buried. (*They stand, silent and motionless*) Tell me—What is it going to get you, staying above the earth? (*Not a sound from the* CORPSES) I asked you a question, men. Answer me! What is it going to get you? If I were dead I wouldn't hesitate to be buried. Answer me . . . what do you want? What is it going to get you you . . . (*As they remain silent*) Tell me! Answer me! Why don't you talk? Explain it to me, make me understand . . .

SECOND GENERAL (*in whisper to* THIRD GENERAL, *as* FIRST GENERAL *glares hopelessly at the* CORPSES). He's licked. It was a mistake—moving him off the artillery.

THIRD GENERAL. They ought to let me handle them. I'd show 'em. You've got to use force.

FIRST GENERAL (*bursting out—after walking along entire row of* CORPSES *and back*). Lie down! (*The* CORPSES *stand, immobile. The* GENERAL *rushes out, moaning*) Oh, God, oh, my God . . . (*Blackout.*) (*Spotlight, red, picks out two* WHORES, *dressed in the uniform of their trade, on a street corner.*)

FIRST WHORE. I'd lay 'em, all right. They oughta call me in. I'd lay 'em. There wouldn't be any doubt in anybody's mind after I got through with 'em. Why don't they call me in instead of those Generals? What do

Generals know about such things? (*Both* WHORES *go off into fits of wild laughter*) Call the War Department, Mabel, tell 'em we'll come to their rescue at the prevailing rates. (*Laugh wildly again*) We're willing to do our part, like the papers say—share the burden! Oh, my Gawd, I ain't laughed so much . . . (*Laugh again. A* MAN *crosses their path. Still laughing, but professional*) Say, Johnny, Johnny, what'cha doin' tonight? How'd ya like . . . ? (*The* MAN *passes on. The women laugh*) Share the burden—Oh, my Gawd . . . (*They laugh and laugh and laugh, clinging to each other. . . . Blackout. But the laughter goes on.*) (*The spotlight illuminates the grave—*SOLDIERS *of burial detail are sitting around a covered fire.* SECOND SOLDIER *is singing "Swing Low, Sweet Chariot."*)

THIRD SOLDIER. This is a funny war. It's rollin' downhill. Everybody's waitin'. Personally, I think it's those guys there that . . . (*He gestures to grave.*)

SERGEANT. Nobody asked you. You're not supposed to talk about it.

FIRST SOLDIER. Regulation 2035a . . .

SERGEANT. Well, I just told ya. (SECOND SOLDIER *starts to sing again.* SERGEANT *breaks in on him*) Say, lissen, think about those guys there. How do you think they feel with you howlin' like this? They got more important things to think about.

SECOND SOLDIER. I won't distract 'em. I got an easy-flowin' voice.

SERGEANT. They don't like it. I can tell.

FIRST SOLDIER. Well, *I* like to hear him sing. And I'll bet they do, too. I'm gonna ask 'em . . . (*He jumps up.*)

SERGEANT. Now lissen! (FIRST SOLDIER *slowly approaches the grave. He is embarrassed, a little frightened.*)

FIRST SOLDIER. Say, men, I . . . (CAPTAIN *comes on.* FIRST SOLDIER *stands at attention.*)

CAPTAIN. Sergeant . . .

SERGEANT. Yes, Sir!

CAPTAIN. You know that none of the men is to talk to *them.* . . .

SERGEANT. Yes, Sir. Only, Sir . . .

CAPTAIN. All right. (*To* FIRST SOLDIER) Get back there, please.

FIRST SOLDIER. Yes, Sir! (*He salutes and goes back.*)

SERGEANT (*under his breath to* FIRST SOLDIER). I warned ya.

FIRST SOLDIER. Shut up! I wanna lissen to what's goin' on there! (CAPTAIN *has meanwhile seated himself on the edge of the grave and has brought out a pair of eyeglasses with which he plays as he talks.*)

CAPTAIN. Gentlemen, I have been asked by the Generals to talk to you. My work is not this . . . (*He indicates his uniform*) I am a philosopher, a scientist, my uniform is a pair of eye-glasses, my ususal weapons test-tubes and books. At a time

like this perhaps we need philosophy, need science. First I must say that your General has ordered you to lie down.

FIRST CORPSE. We used to have a General.

THIRD CORPSE. No more.

FOURTH CORPSE. They sold us.

CAPTAIN. What do you mean—sold you!

FIFTH CORPSE. Sold us for twenty-five yards of bloody mud.

SIXTH CORPSE. A life for four yards of bloody mud.

CAPTAIN. We had to take that hill. General's orders. You're soldiers. You understand.

FIRST CORPSE. We understand now. The real estate operations of Generals are always carried on at boom prices.

SIXTH CORPSE. A life for four yards of bloody mud. Gold is cheaper, and rare jewels, pearls and rubies. . . .

THIRD CORPSE. I fell in the first yard. . . .

SECOND CORPSE. I caught on the wire and hung there while the machine gun stitched me through the middle to it. . . .

FOURTH CORPSE. I was there at the end and thought I had life in my hands for another day, but a shell came and my life dripped into the mud.

SIXTH CORPSE. Ask the General how he'd like to be dead at twenty. (*Calling, as though to the* GENERALS) Twenty, General, twenty . . .

CAPTAIN. Other men are dead.

FIRST CORPSE. Too many.

CAPTAIN. Men must die for their country's sake—if not you, then others. This has always been. Men died for Pharaoh and Cæsar and Rome two thousand years ago and more, and went into the earth with their wounds. Why not you . . . ?

FIRST CORPSE. Men, even the men who die for Pharaoh and Cæsar and Rome, must, in the end, before all hope is gone, discover that a man can die happy and be contentedly buried only when he dies for himself or for a cause that is his own and not Pharaoh's or Cæsar's or Rome's. . . .

CAPTAIN. Still—what is this world, that you cling to it? A speck of dust, a flaw in the skies, a thumb-print on the margin of a page printed in an incomprehensible language. . . .

SECOND CORPSE. It is our home.

THIRD CORPSE. We have been dispossessed by force, but we are reclaiming our home. It is time that mankind claimed its home—this earth—its home. . . .

CAPTAIN. We have no home. We are strangers in the universe and cling, desperate and grimy, to the crust of our world, and if there is a God and this His earth, we must be a terrible sight in His eyes.

FOURTH CORPSE. We are not disturbed by the notion of our appearance in the eyes of God. . . .

CAPTAIN. The earth is an unpleasant place and when you are rid of it you are well rid of it. Man cheats man here and the only sure things are death and despair. Of what use, then, to remain on it once you have the permission to leave?

FIFTH CORPSE. It is the one thing we know.

SIXTH CORPSE. We did not ask permission to leave. Nobody asked us whether we wanted it or not. The Generals pushed us out and closed the door on us. Who are the Generals that they are to close doors on us?

CAPTAIN. The earth, I assure you, is a mean place, insignificantly miserable. . . .

FIRST CORPSE. We must find out for ourselves. That is our right.

CAPTAIN. Man has no rights. . . .

FIRST CORPSE. Man can make rights for himself. It requires only determination and the good-will of ordinary men. We have made ourselves the right to walk this earth, seeing it and judging it for ourselves.

CAPTAIN. There is peace in the grave. . . .

THIRD CORPSE. Peace and the worms and the roots of grass. There is a deeper peace than that which comes with feeding the roots of the grass.

CAPTAIN (*looks slowly at them, in turn*). Yes, gentlemen . . . (*Turns away and walks off.* FIRST SOLDIER *moves slowly up to the grave.)*

FIRST SOLDIER (*to the* CORPSES). I . . . I'm glad you . . . you didn't . . . I'm glad. Say, is there anything we can do for you?

SERGEANT. Lissen, soldier!

FIRST SOLDIER (*passionately, harshly*). Shut up, Sergeant! (*Then very softly and warmly to* FIRST CORPSE) Is there anything we can do for you, Friend?

FIRST CORPSE. Yeah. You can sing . . . (*There is a pause in which the* FIRST SOLDIER *turns around and looks at the* SECOND SOLDIER, *then back to the* FIRST CORPSE. *Then the silence is broken by the* SECOND SOLDIER's *voice, raised in song. It goes on for a few moments, then fades as the light dims.)*
(*Colored spotlights pick out three* BUSINESS MEN *on different parts of the stage.)*

FIRST BUSINESS MAN. Ssh! Keep it quiet!

THIRD BUSINESS MAN. Sink 'em with lead. . . .

SECOND BUSINESS MAN. Bury them! Bury them six feet under!

FIRST BUSINESS MAN. What are we going to do?

SECOND BUSINESS MAN. We must keep up the morale.

THIRD BUSINESS MAN. Lead! Lead! A lot of lead!

SECOND BUSINESS MAN. What do we pay our Generals for?

CHORUS OF BUSINESS MEN. Ssssh! (*Blackout.*)
(*Spotlight on the congregation of a church, kneeling, with a* PRIEST *praying over them.)*

PRIEST. O Jesus, our God and our Christ, Who has redeemed us with Thy blood on the Cross at Calvary, give us Thy blessing on this holy day, and cause it that our soldiers allow themselves to be buried in peace, and bring victory to our arms, enlisted in Thy Cause and the cause of all righteousness on the field of battle . . . Amen . . . (*Blackout.*)

FIRST GENERAL (*in purple baby spotlight*). Please, God, keep it quiet . . .
(*Spotlight on newspaper office.*)

REPORTER. Well? What are you going to do?

EDITOR. Do I have to do anything?

REPORTER. God damn right you do. . . . They're still standing up. They're going to stand up from now till Doomsday. They're not going to be able to bury soldiers any more. It's in the stars. . . . You got to say something about it. . . .

EDITOR. All right. Put this in. "It is alleged that certain members of an infantry regiment refuse to allow themselves to be buried. . . ."

REPORTER. Well?

EDITOR. That's all.

REPORTER (*incredulous*). That's all?

EDITOR. Yes, Christ, isn't that enough? (*Blackout.*)

(Spotlight on a radio-loudspeaker. A VOICE, *mellow and beautiful, comes out of it.)*

THE VOICE. It has been reported that certain American soldiers, killed on the field of battle, have refused to allow themselves to be buried. Whether this is true or not, the Coast-to-Coast Broadcasting System feels that this must give the American public an idea of the indomitable spirit of the American doughboy in this war. We cannot rest until this war is won—not even our brave dead boys . . . (*Blackout.*)

(*Guns. Spotlight on* FIRST GENERAL *and* CAPTAIN.)

FIRST GENERAL. Have you any suggestions . . . ?

CAPTAIN. I think so. Get their women. . . .

FIRST GENERAL. What good'll their women do?

CAPTAIN. Women are always conservative. It's a conservative notion —this one of lying down and allowing yourself to be buried when you're dead. The women'll fight the General's battle for them—in the best possible way—through their emotions. . . . It's the General's best bet. . . .

FIRST GENERAL. Women—Of course! You've got it there, Captain! Get out their women! Get them in a hurry! We'll have these boys underground in a jiffy. Women! By God, I never thought of it. . . . Send out the call. . . . Women! (*Fadeout.*) (*A baby spotlight on the loudspeaker. The* VOICE *again, just as mellow, just as persuasive.*)

VOICE. We have been asked by the War Department to broadcast an appeal to the women of Privates Driscoll, Schelling, Morgan, Webster, Levy, and Dean, reported dead. The War Department requests that the women of these men present themselves at the War Department Office immediately. It is within their power to do a great service to their country. . . . (*Blackout.*)
(*The spotlight illuminates the* FIRST GENERAL, *where he stands, addressing six women.*)

FIRST GENERAL. Go to your men .. talk to them . . . make them see the error of their ways, ladies. You women represent what is dearest in our civilization—the sacred foundations of the home. We are fighting this war to protect the foundations of the homes of America! Those foundations will crumble utterly if these men of yours come back from the dead. I shudder to think of the consequences of such an act. Our entire system will be mortally struck. Our banks will close, our buildings collapse . . . our army will desert the field and leave our fair land open to be overrun by the enemy. Ladies, you are all Gold Star mothers and wives and sweethearts. You want to win this war. I know it. I know the high fire of patriotism that burns in women's breasts. That is why I have called upon you. Ladies, let me make this clear to you. If you do not get your men to lie down and allow themselves to be buried, I fear that our cause is lost. The burden of the war is upon your shoulders now. Wars are not fought with guns and powder alone, ladies. Here is your chance to do your part, a glorious part. . . . You are fighting for your homes, your children, your sisters' lives, your country's honor. You are fighting for religion, for love, for all decent human life. Wars can be fought and won only when the dead are buried and forgotten. How can we forget the dead who refuse to be buried? And we *must* forget them! There is no room in this world for dead men. They will lead only to the bitterest unhappiness—for you, for them, for everybody. Go, ladies, do your duty. Your country waits upon you. . . . (*Blackout.*)

(*Spotlight immediately illuminates the place where* PRIVATE SCHELLING, CORPSE TWO, *is talking to his wife.* MRS. SCHELLING *is a spare, taciturn woman, a farmer's wife, who might be twenty or forty or anything in between.*)

BESS SCHELLING. Did it hurt much, John?

SCHELLING. How's the kid, Bess?

BESS. He's fine. He talks now. He weighs twenty-eight pounds. He'll be a big boy. Did it hurt much, John?

SCHELLING. How is the farm? Is it going all right, Bess?

BESS. It's going. The rye was heavy this year. Did it hurt much, John?

SCHELLING. Who did the reapin' for you, Bess?

BESS. Schmidt took care of it—and his boys. Schmidt's too old for the war and his boys are too young. Took 'em nearly two weeks. The wheat's not bad this year. Schmidt's oldest boy expects to be called in a month or two. He practises behind the barn with that old shotgun Schmidt uses for duck.

SCHELLING. The Schmidts were always fools. When the kid grows up, Bess, you make sure you pump some sense into his head. What color's his hair?

BESS. Blond. Like you. . . . What are you going to do, John?

SCHELLING. I would like to see the kid—and the farm—and . . .

BESS. They say you're dead, John. . . .

SCHELLING. I'm dead, all right.

BESS. Then how is it . . . ?

SCHELLING. I don't know. Maybe there's too many of us under the ground now. Maybe the earth can't stand it no more. You got to change crops sometime. What are you doing here, Bess?

BESS. They asked me to get you to let yourself be buried.

SCHELLING. What do you think?

BESS. You're dead, John. . . .

SCHELLING. Well . . . ?

BESS. What's the good . . . ?

SCHELLING. I don't know. Only there's something in me, dead or no dead, that won't let me be buried.

BESS. You were a queer man, John. I never did understand what you were about. But what's the good . . . ?

SCHELLING. Bess, I never talked so that I could get you to understand what I wanted while I—while I—

before . . . Maybe now . . . There's a couple of things, Bess, that I ain't had enough of. Easy things, the things you see when you look outa your window at night, after supper, or when you wake up in the mornin'. Things you smell when you step outside the door when summer's on and the sun starts to turn the grass brown. Things you hear when you're busy with the horses or pitchin' the hay and you don't really notice them and yet they come back to you. Things like the fuzz of green over a field in spring where you planted wheat and it's started to come out overnight. Things like lookin' at rows of corn scrapin' in the breeze, tall and green, with the silk flying off the ears in the wind. Things like seeing the sweat come out all over on your horse's fat flank and seein' it shine like silk in front of you, smelling horsey and strong. Things like seein' the loam turn back all fat and deep brown on both sides as the plough turns it over so that it gets to be awful hard walkin' behind it. Things like taking a cold drink of water outa the well after you've boiled in the sun all afternoon, and feelin' the water go down and down into you coolin' you off all through from the inside out. . . . Things like seein' a blond kid, all busy and serious, playin' with a dog on the shady side of a house. . . . There ain't nothin' like that down here, Bess. . . .

BESS. Everything has its place, John. Dead men have theirs.

SCHELLING. My place is on the earth, Bess. My business is with the top of the earth, not the under-side. It was a trap that yanked me down. I'm not smart, Bess, and I'm easy trapped—but I can tell now . . .

I got some stories to tell farmers before I'm through—I'm going to tell 'em. . . .

BESS. We could bury you home, John, near the creek—it's cool there and quiet and there's always a breeze in the trees. . . .

SCHELLING. Later, Bess, when I've had my fill of lookin' and smellin' and talkin'. . . . A man should be able to walk into his grave, not be dragged into it. . . .

BESS. How'll I feel—and the kid— with you walkin' around—like— like that . . . ?

SCHELLING. I won't bother you. . . . I won't come near you. . . .

BESS. Even so. Just knowin' . .

SCHELLING. I can't help it. This is somethin' bigger'n you—bigger'n me. It's somethin' I ain't had nothin' to do with startin'. . . . It's somethin' that just grew up outa the earth—like—like a weed—a flower. Cut it down now and it'll jump up in a dozen new places. You can't stop it. The earth's ready for it. . . .

BESS. You were a good husband, John. For the kid—and me—won't you?

SCHELLING (*quietly*). Go home, Bess. *Go home!* (*Blackout.*)
(*The spotlight picks out* CORPSE NUMBER FIVE, PRIVATE LEVY, *where he stands in the grave, with his back to the audience. His woman, a pert, attractive young lady, is sitting next to him, above him, facing him, talking to him.*)

JOAN. You loved me best, didn't you, Henry—of all of them—all those women—you loved me the best, didn't you?

LEVY (FIFTH CORPSE). What's the difference, now?

JOAN. I want to know it.

LEVY. It's not important.

JOAN. It's important to me. I knew about the others, about Doris and that shifty-eyed Janet. . . . Henry, you're not a live man, are you, Henry?

LEVY. No, I'm all shot away inside.

JOAN. Must wars always be fought in the mud like this? I never expected it to look like this. It . . . it looks like a dump heap.

LEVY. You've gotten your shoes muddy. They're pretty shoes, Joan.

JOAN. Do you think so, Henry? They're lizard. I like them too. It's so hard to get a good pair of shoes nowadays.

LEVY. Do you still dance, Joan?

JOAN. Oh, I'm really much better than I used to be. There are so many dances back home nowadays. Dances for orphan relief and convalescent hospitals and Victory Loans. I'm busy seven nights a week. I sold more Victory Loans than any other girl in the League. I got a helmet . . . one of *their* helmets . . . one with a bullet-hole in it, for selling eleven thousand dollars' worth.

LEVY. Out here we get them for nothing, by the million—bullet-holes and all.

JOAN. That sounds bitter. You shouldn't sound bitter.

LEVY. I'm sorry.

JOAN. I heard Colonel Elwell the other day. You know Colonel Elwell, old Anthony Elwell who owns the mill. He made a speech at the monthly Red Cross banquet and he said that that was the nice thing about this war, it wasn't being fought bitterly by our boys. He said it was just patriotism that kept us going. He's a wonderful speaker, Colonel Elwell; I cried and cried.

LEVY. I remember him.

JOAN. Henry, do you think we're going to win the war?

LEVY. What's the difference?

JOAN. Henry! What a way to talk! I don't know what's come over you. Really, I don't. Why, the papers say that if *they* win the war, they'll burn our churches and tear down our museums and . . . and rape our women. (LEVY *laughs*) Why are you laughing, Henry?

LEVY. I'm dead, Joan.

JOAN. Yes. Then why—why don't you let them bury you?

LEVY. There are a lot of reasons. There were a lot of things I loved on this earth. . . .

JOAN. A dead man can't touch a woman.

LEVY. The women, yes—but more than touching them. I got a great joy just from listening to women, hearing them laugh, watching their skirts blow in the wind, noticing the way their breasts bounced up and down inside their dresses when they walked. It had nothing to do with touching them. I liked to hear the sound of their high heels on pavements at night and the tenderness in their voices when they walked past me arm in arm with a young man. You were so lovely, Joan, with your pale hair and long hands.

JOAN. You always liked my hair. (A pause) No woman will walk arm in arm with you, Henry Levy, while you cheat the grave.

LEVY. No. But there will be the eyes of women to look at and the bright color of their hair and the soft way they swing their hips when they walk before young men. These are the things that mean life and the earth to me, the joy and the pain. These are the things the earth still owes me, now when I am only thirty. Joy and pain—to each man in his own way, a full seventy years, to be ended by an unhurried fate, not by a colored pin on a General's map. What do I care for the colored pins on a General's map?

JOAN. They are not only pins. They mean more. . . .

LEVY. More? To whom? To the Generals—not to me. To me they are colored pins. It is not a fair bargain—this exchange of my life for a small part of a colored pin. . . .

JOAN. Henry, how can you talk like that? You know why this war is being fought.

LEVY. No. Do you?

JOAN. Of course, everybody knows. We must win! We must be prepared to sacrifice our last drop of blood. Anyway, what can you do?

LEVY. Do you remember last summer, Joan? My last leave. We went to Maine. I would like to remember that—the sun and the beach and your soft hands—for a long time.

JOAN. What are you going to do?

LEVY. Walk the world looking at the fine, long-legged girls, seeing in them something deep and true and passionately vital, listening to the sound of their light voices with ears the Generals would have stopped with the grave's solid mud. . . .

JOAN. Henry! Henry! Once you said you loved me. For love of me, Henry, go into the grave. . . .

LEVY. Poor Joan. (*Stretches out his hand tenderly as if to touch her.*)

JOAN (*recoiling*). Don't touch me. (*Pause*) For love of me.

LEVY. Go home, Joan! *Go home!* (*Blackout.*)
(*The spotlight picks out the* THIRD CORPSE, PRIVATE MORGAN, *and* JULIA BLAKE, *he with his back to the audience, standing in the grave, she above and to the right.* JULIA *sobs.*)

MORGAN. Stop crying, Julia. What's the sense in crying?

JULIA. No sense. Only I can't stop crying.

MORGAN. You shouldn't have come.

JULIA. They asked me to come. They said you wouldn't let them bury you—dead and all. . . .

MORGAN. Yes.

JULIA (crying). Why don't they kill me too? I'd let them bury me. I'd be glad to be buried—to get away from all this . . . I—I haven't stopped crying for two weeks now. I used to think I was tough. I never cried. Even when I was a kid. It's a wonder where all the tears can come from. Though I guess there's always room for more tears. I thought I was all cried out when I heard about the way they killed Fred. My kid brother. I used to comb his hair in the morning when he went to school . . . I—I . . . Then they killed you. They did, didn't they?

MORGAN. Yes.

JULIA. It's hard to know like this, I —I know, though. It—it makes it harder, this way, with you like this. I could forget easier if you. . . . But I wasn't going to say that. I was going to listen to you. Oh, my darling, it's been so rotten. I get drunk. I hate it and I get drunk. I sing out loud and everybody laughs. I was going through your things the other day—I'm crazy . . . I go through all your things three times a week, touching your clothes and reading your books. . . . You have the nicest clothes. . . . There was that quatrain you wrote to me that time you were in Boston and . . . First I laughed, then I cried, then . . . It's a lovely poem—you would have been a fine writer. I think you would have been the greatest writer that ever . . . I . . . Did they shoot your hands away, darling?

MORGAN. No.

JULIA. That's good. I couldn't bear it if anything happened to your hands. Was it bad, darling?

MORGAN. Bad enough.

JULIA. But they didn't shoot your hands away. That's something. You learn how to be grateful for the craziest things nowadays. People have to be grateful for something and it's so hard, with the war and all. . . . Oh, darling, I never could think of you dead. Somehow you didn't seem to be made to be dead. I would feel better if you were buried in a fine green field and there were funny little flowers jumping up around the stone that said, "Walter Morgan, Born 1913, Died 1937." I could stop getting drunk at night and singing out loud so that people laugh at me. The worst thing is looking at all the books you piled up home that you didn't read. They wait there, waiting for your hands to come and open them and . . . Oh, let them bury you, let them bury you . . . There's nothing left, only crazy people and clothes that'll never be used hanging in the closets . . . Why not?

MORGAN. There are too many books I haven't read, too many places I haven't seen, too many memories I haven't kept long enough. . . . I won't be cheated of them. . . .

JULIA. And me? Darling, me . . . I hate getting drunk. Your name would look so well on a nice simple chunk of marble in a green field. "Walter Morgan, Beloved of Julia Blake . . ." With poppies and daisies and those little purple flowers all around the bottom, and . . .

(*She is bent over, almost wailing. There is the flash of a gun in her hand, and she totters, falls*) Now they can put my name on the casualty lists, too. . . . What do they call those purple flowers, darling . . . ? (*Blackout.*)

(*The spotlight follows* KATHERINE DRISCOLL *as she makes her way from* CORPSE *to* CORPSE *in the grave, looking at their faces. She looks first at* CORPSE SIX, *shudders, covers her eyes and moves on. She stops at* CORPSE FIVE.)

KATHERINE. I'm Katherine Driscoll. I—I'm looking for my brother. He's dead. Are you my brother?

FIFTH CORPSE. No.
(KATHERINE *goes on to* CORPSE FOUR, *stops, looks, moves on to* CORPSE THREE.)

KATHERINE. I'm looking for my brother. My name is Katherine Driscoll. His name—

THIRD CORPSE. No.
(KATHERINE *goes on, stands irresolutely before* CORPSE TWO.)

KATHERINE. Are you . . . ? (*Realizing it isn't her brother. Goes on to* CORPSE ONE) I'm looking for my brother. My name is Katherine Driscoll. His name—

DRISCOLL. I'm Tom Driscoll.

KATHERINE. Hel—Hello. I don't know you. After fifteen years— And . . .

DRISCOLL. What do you want, Katherine?

KATHERINE. You don't know me either, do you?

DRISCOLL. No.

KATHERINE. It's funny—my coming here to talk to a dead man—to try to get him to do something because once long ago he was my brother. They talked me into it. I don't know how to begin. . . .

DRISCOLL. You'll be wasting your words, Katherine. . . .

KATHERINE. They should have asked someone nearer to you—someone who loved you—only they couldn't find anybody. I was the nearest, they said. . . .

DRISCOLL. That's so. You were the nearest. . . .

KATHERINE. And I fifteen years away. Poor Tom . . . It couldn't have been a sweet life you led these fifteen years.

DRISCOLL. It wasn't.

KATHERINE. You were poor, too?

DRISCOLL. Sometimes I begged for meals. I wasn't lucky. . . .

KATHERINE. And yet you want to go back. Is there no more sense in the dead, Tom, than in the living?

DRISCOLL. Maybe not. Maybe there's no sense in either living or dying, but we can't believe that. I travelled to a lot of places and I saw a lot of things, always from the black side of them, always workin' hard to keep from starvin' and turnin' my collar up to keep the wind out, and they were mean and rotten and sad, but always I saw that they could be better and some day they were going to be better, and that the guys like me who knew that they were rotten and knew that they could be better had to get out and fight to make it that way.

KATHERINE. You're dead. Your fight's over.

DRISCOLL. The fight's never over. I got things to say to people now—to the people who nurse big machines and the people who swing shovels and the people whose babies die with big bellies and rotten bones. I got things to say to the people who leave their lives behind them and pick up guns to fight in somebody else's war. Important things. Big things. Big enough to lift me out of the grave right back onto the earth into the middle of men just because I got the voice to say them. If God could lift Jesus . . .

KATHERINE. Tom! Have you lost religion, too?

DRISCOLL. I got another religion. I got a religion that wants to take heaven out of the clouds and plant it right here on the earth where most of us can get a slice of it. It isn't as pretty a heaven—there aren't any streets of gold and there aren't any angels, and we'd have to worry about sewerage, and railroad schedules in it, and we don't guarantee everybody'd love it, but it'd be right here, stuck in the mud of this earth, and there wouldn't be any entrance requirement, like dying, to get into it. . . . Dead or alive, I see that, and it won't let me rest. I was the first one to get up in this black grave of ours, because that idea wouldn't let me rest. I pulled the others with me—that's my job, pulling the others . . . They only know what they want—I know how they can get it. . . .

KATHERINE. There's still the edge of arrogance on you.

DRISCOLL. I got heaven in my two hands to give to men. There's reason for arrogance. . . .

KATHERINE. I came to ask you to lie down and let them bury you. It seems foolish now. But . . .

DRISCOLL. It's foolish, Katherine. I didn't get up from the dead to go back to the dead. I'm going to the living now. . . .

KATHERINE. Fifteen years. It's a good thing your mother isn't alive. How can you say good-bye to a dead brother, Tom?

DRISCOLL. Wish him an easy grave, Katherine. . . .

KATHERINE. A green and pleasant grave to you, Tom, when, finally . . . finally . . . green and pleasant. (*Blackout.*)
(*The spotlight illuminates* PRIVATE DEAN, *the* SIXTH CORPSE, *where he stands with his back to the audience, listening to his mother, a thin, shabby, red-eyed woman of about forty-five, sitting above and to the right, in the full glare of the spotlight.* DEAN *is in shadow.*)

MRS. DEAN. Let me see your face, son . . .

DEAN. You don't want to see it, mom . . .

MRS. DEAN. My baby's face. Once, before you . . .

DEAN. You don't want to see it, mom. I know. Didn't they tell you what happened to me?

MRS. DEAN. I asked the doctor. He said a piece of shell hit the side of your head—but even so. . . .

DEAN. Don't ask to see it, mom.

MRS. DEAN. How are you, son? (DEAN *laughs a little—bitterly*) Oh, I forgot. I asked you that question so many times while you were growing up, Jimmy. Let me see your face, Jimmy—just once. . . .

DEAN. How did Alice take it when she heard . . . ?

MRS. DEAN. She put a gold star in her window. She tells everybody you were going to be married. Is that so?

DEAN. Maybe. I liked Alice.

MRS. DEAN. She came over on your birthday. That was before this—this happened. She brought flowers. Big chrysanthemums. Yellow. A lot of them. We had to put them in two vases. I baked a cake. I don't know why. It's hard to get eggs and fine flour nowadays. My baby, twenty years old . . . Let me see your face, Jimmy, boy. . . .

DEAN. Go home, mom. . . . It's not doing you any good staying here.

MRS. DEAN. I want you to let them bury you, Baby. It's done now and over. It would be better for you that way. . . .

DEAN. There's no better to it, mom —and no worse. It happened that way, that's all.

MRS. DEAN. Let me see your face, Jimmy. You had such a fine face. Like a good baby's. It hurt me when you started to shave. Somehow, I almost forget what you looked like, Baby. I remember what you looked like when you were five, when you were ten—you were chubby and fair and your cheeks felt like little silk cushions when I put my hand on them. But I don't remember how you looked when you went away with that uniform on you and that helmet over your face. . . . Baby, let me see your face, once. . . .

DEAN. Don't ask me . . . You don't want to see. You'll feel worse—forever . . . if you see . . .

MRS. DEAN. I'm not afraid. I can look at my baby's face. Do you think mothers can be frightened by their children's . . .

DEAN. No, mom . . .

MRS. DEAN. Baby, listen to me, I'm your mother. . . . Let them bury you. There's something peaceful and done about a grave. After a while you forget the death and you remember only the life before it. But this way—you never forget . . . it's a wound walking around forever, without peace. For your sake and mine and your father's . . . Baby . . .

DEAN. I was only twenty, mom. I hadn't done anything. I hadn't seen anything. I never even had a girl. I spent twenty years practising to be a man and then they killed me. Being a kid's no good, mom. You try to get over it as soon as you can. You don't really live while you're a kid. You mark time, waiting. I waited, mom—but then I got cheated. They made a speech and played a trumpet and dressed me in a uniform and then they killed me.

MRS. DEAN. Oh, Baby, Baby, there's no peace this way. Please, let them . . .

DEAN. No, mom . . .

MRS. DEAN. Then once, now, so that I can remember—let me see your face, my baby's face . . .

DEAN. Mom, the shell hit close to me. You don't want to look at a man when a shell hits close to him.

MRS. DEAN. Let me see your face, Jimmy . . .

DEAN. All right, mom . . . Look! (*He turns his face to her. The audience can't see his face, but immediately a spotlight, white and sharp, shoots down from directly above and hits* DEAN's *head.* MRS. DEAN *leans forward, staring. Another spotlight shoots down immediately after from the extreme right, then one from the left, then two more, from above. They hit with the impact of blows and* MRS. DEAN *shudders a little as they come, as though she were watching her son being beaten. There is absolute silence for a moment. Then* MRS. DEAN *starts to moan, low, painfully. The lights remain fixed and* MRS. DEAN's *moans rise to a wail, then to a scream. She leans back, covering her eyes with her hands, screaming. Blackout. The scream persists, fading, like a siren fading in the distance, until it is finally stilled.*)
(*The spotlight on* CORPSE THREE, PRIVATE WEBSTER, *and his wife, a dumpy, sad little woman.*)

MARTHA WEBSTER. Say something.

WEBSTER. What do you want me to say?

MARTHA. Something—anything. Only talk. You give me the shivers standing there like that—looking like that. . . .

WEBSTER. Even now—after this—there's nothing that we can talk to each other about.

MARTHA. Don't talk like that. You talked like that enough when you were alive— It's not my fault that you're dead. . . .

WEBSTER. No.

MARTHA. It was bad enough when you were alive—and you didn't talk to me and you looked at me as though I was always in your way.

WEBSTER. Martha, Martha, what's the difference now?

MARTHA. I just wanted to let you know. Now I suppose you're going to come back and sit around and ruin my life altogether?

WEBSTER. No. I'm not going to come back.

MARTHA. Then what . . . ?

WEBSTER. I couldn't explain it to you, Martha. . . .

MARTHA. No! Oh, no—you couldn't explain it to your wife. But you could explain it to that dirty bunch of loafers down at that damned garage of yours and you could explain it to those bums in the saloon on F Street. . . .

WEBSTER. I guess I could. (*Musing*) Things seemed to be clearer when I was talking to the boys while I worked over a job. And I managed to talk so people could get to understand what I meant down at the saloon on F Street. It was nice, standing there of a Saturday night, with a beer in front of you and a man or two that understood your own language next to you, talking —oh, about Babe Ruth or the new oiling system Ford was putting out or the chances of us gettin' into the war. . . .

MARTHA. It's different if you were rich and had a fine beautiful life you wanted to go back to. Then I could understand. But you were poor . . . you always had dirt under your finger nails, you never ate enough, you hated me, your wife, you couldn't stand being in the same room with me. . . . Don't shake your head, I know. Out of your whole life, all you could remember that's good is a beer on Saturday night that you drank in company with a couple of bums. . . .

WEBSTER. That's enough. I didn't think about it then . . . but I guess I was happy those times.

MARTHA. You were happy those times . . . but you weren't happy in your own home! I know, even if you don't say it! Well, I wasn't happy either! Living in three damned rooms that the sun didn't hit five times a year! Watching the roaches make picnics on the walls! Happy!

WEBSTER. I did my best.

MARTHA. Eighteen-fifty a week! Your best! Eighteen-fifty, condensed milk, a two-dollar pair of shoes once a year, five hundred dollars' insurance, chopped meat. God, how I hate chopped meat!

Eighteen-fifty, being afraid of everything—of the landlord, the gas company, scared stiff every month that I was goin' to have a baby! Why shouldn't I have a baby? Who says I shouldn't have a baby? Eighteen-fifty, no baby!

WEBSTER. I woulda liked a kid.

MARTHA. Would you? You never said anything.

WEBSTER. It's good to have a kid. A kid's somebody to talk to.

MARTHA. At first . . . In the beginning . . . I thought we'd have a kid some day.

WEBSTER. Yeah, me too. I used to go out on Sundays and watch men wheel their kids through the park.

MARTHA. There were so many things you didn't tell me. Why did you keep quiet?

WEBSTER. I was ashamed to talk to you. I couldn't give you anything.

MARTHA. I'm sorry.

WEBSTER. In the beginning it looked so fine. I used to smile to myself when I walked beside you in the street and other men looked at you.

MARTHA. That was a long time ago.

WEBSTER. A kid would've helped.

MARTHA. No, it wouldn't. Don't fool yourself, Webster. The Clarks downstairs have four and it doesn't help them. Old man Clark comes home drunk every Saturday night and beats 'em with his shaving strap and throws plates at the old lady. Kids don't help the poor. Nothing helps the poor! I'm too smart to have sick, dirty kids on eighteen-fifty. . . .

WEBSTER. That's it. . . .

MARTHA. A house should have a baby. But it should be a clean house with a full icebox. Why shouldn't I have a baby? Other people have babies. Even now, with the war, other people have babies. They don't have to feel their skin curl every time they tear a page off the calendar. They go off to beautiful hospitals in lovely ambulances and have babies between colored sheets! What's there about them that God likes that He makes it so easy for *them* to have babies?

WEBSTER. They're not married to mechanics.

MARTHA. No! It's not eighteen-fifty for them. And now . . . now it's worse. Your twenty dollars a month. You hire yourself out to be killed and I get twenty dollars a month. I wait on line all day to get a loaf of bread. I've forgotten what butter tastes like. I wait on line with the rain soaking through my shoes for a pound of rotten meat once a week. At night I go home. Nobody to talk to, just sitting, watching the bugs, with one little light because the Government's got to save electricity. You had to go off and leave me to that! What's the war to me that I have to sit at night with nobody to talk to? What's the war to you that you had to go off and . . . ?

WEBSTER. That's why I'm standing up now, Martha.

MARTHA. What took you so long, then? Why now? Why not a month

ago, a year ago, ten years ago? Why didn't you stand up then? Why wait until you're dead? You live on eighteen-fifty a week, with the roaches, not saying a word, and then when they kill you, you stand up! You fool!

WEBSTER. I didn't see it before.

MARTHA. Just like you! Wait until it's too late! There's plenty for live men to stand up for! All right, stand up! It's about time you talked back. It's about time all you poor miserable eighteen-fifty bastards stood up for themselves and their wives and the children they can't have. Tell 'em *all* to stand up! Tell 'em! *Tell 'em!* (She shrieks. Blackout.)
(A spotlight picks out the FIRST GENERAL. He has his hands to his lips.)

FIRST GENERAL. It didn't work. But keep it quiet. For God's sake, keep it quiet. . . . (Blackout.)
(A spotlight picks out the newspaper office, the REPORTER and the EDITOR.)

REPORTER (in harsh triumph). It didn't work! Now, you've got to put it in! I knew it wouldn't work! Smear it over the headlines! It didn't work!

EDITOR. Put it in the headlines. . . . They won't be buried! (Blackout— Voices call. . . .)

VOICE (NEWSBOY spotted). It didn't work! Extra! It didn't work!

VOICE (in dark. Hoarse whisper). It didn't work! They're still standing. . . . Somebody do something. . . .

VOICE (*spotted, a clubwoman type*). Somebody do something. . . .

VOICE (NEWSBOY *spotted*). Extra! They're still standing. . . .

VOICE (CLUBWOMAN). Don't let them back into the country. . . .

REPORTER (*spotted. Triumphantly*). They're standing. From now on they'll always stand! You can't bury soldiers any more. . . . (*Spotted, a group, owners of the next four voices.*)

VOICE. They stink. Bury them!

VOICE. What are we going to do about them?

VOICE. What'll happen to our war? We can't let anything happen to our war. . . .

VOICE (A PRIEST, *facing the three men*). Pray! Pray! God must help us! Down on your knees, all of you and pray with your hearts and your guts and the marrow of your bones.

VOICE (REPORTER *spotted, facing them all*). It will take more than prayers. What are prayers to a dead man? They're standing! Mankind is standing up and climbing out of its grave. . . . (*Blackout.*)

VOICE (*in dark*). Have you heard . . . ? It didn't work. . . .

VOICE (*in dark*). Extra! Extra! It didn't work! They're still standing! (*Spotted,* MRS. DEAN, MRS. SCHELLING, JULIA BLAKE.)

MRS. DEAN. My baby. . . .

MRS. SCHELLING. My husband. . . .

JULIA BLAKE. My lover. . . . (*Blackout.*)

VOICE (*in dark*). Bury them! They stink!
(*The next set of characters walks through a stationary spotlight.*)

VOICE (*a* FARMER). Plant a new crop! The old crop has worn out the earth. Plant something besides lives in the old and weary earth. . . .

VOICE (*a* NEWSBOY, *running*). Extra! It didn't work!

VOICE (*a* BANKER. *Frantic*). Somebody do something! Dupont's passed a dividend!

VOICE (*a* PRIEST). The Day of Judgment is at hand. . . .

VOICE (*the* FIRST WHORE). Where is Christ? (*Blackout.*)

VOICE (*in dark*). File 'em away in alphabetical order. . . .
(*Spotlight on a man in academic robes, reading aloud from behind a table, after he adjusts his glasses.*)

VOICE. We don't believe it. It is against the dictates of science.
(*Blackout—Spot on* SECOND GENERAL.)

SECOND GENERAL. Keep it quiet!
(MRS. SCHELLING *walks in front of him. The others follow.*)

BESS SCHELLING. My husband. . . .

JULIA BLAKE. My lover. . . .

MRS. DEAN. My baby. . . . (*Blackout.*)

VOICE (*a child*). What have they done with my father?
(*Spot on* BANKER *at telephone.*)

BANKER (*into phone*). Somebody do something. Call up the War Department! Call up Congress! Call up the Roman Catholic Church! Somebody do something!

VOICE. We've got to put them down!

REPORTER (*spotted*). Never! Never! Never! You can't put them down. Put one down and ten will spring up like weeds in an old garden. . . . (*Spots at various parts of the stage.*)

VOICE (*the* THIRD GENERAL). Use lead on them, lead! Lead put 'em down once, lead'll do it again! Lead!

VOICE. Put down the sword and hang the armor on the wall to rust with the years. The killed have arisen.

VOICE. Bury them! Bury the dead!

VOICE. The old demons have come back to possess the earth. We are lost. . . .

VOICE. The dead have arisen, now let the living rise, singing. . . .

VOICE. Do something, for the love of God, do something. . . .

VOICE. Extra! They're still standing.

VOICE. Do something!

VOICE (*in dark*). We will do something. . . .

VOICE. Who are you?

VOICE (PRIEST *in spot*). We are the Church and the voice of God. The State has tried its ways, now let the Church use the ways of God. These corpses are possessed by the devil, who plagues the lives of men. The Church will exorcise the devil from these men, according to its ancient rite, and they will lie down in their graves like children to a pleasant sleep, rising no more to trouble the world of living men. The Church which is the Voice of God upon this earth, amen. . . . (*Blackout.*)

CHORUS OF VOICES. Alleluia, alleluia, sing. . . . (*The scream of the bereft mother fades in, reaches its height, then dies off as the holy procession of priests moves solemnly on with bell, book and candle. A* PRIEST *sprinkles the* CORPSES *with holy water, makes the sign of the cross over them and begins in the solemn Latin of the service. At the end he goes into English—his voice rising in ritualistic passion.*)

PRIEST. I exorcise thee, unclean spirit, in the name of Jesus Christ; tremble, O Satan, thou enemy of the faith, thou foe of mankind, who hast brought death in to the world, who hast deprived men of life, and hast rebelled against justice, thou seducer of mankind, thou root of evil, thou source of avarice, discord, and envy.
(*Silence. Then the* CORPSES *begin to laugh, lightly, horribly. There is a sign from the living men present, and the priestly procession goes off, its bell tinkling. The laughter goes on. Blackout. The* VOICES *call again.* . . .)

VOICE. No. . . .

VOICE. NO!

VOICE. It didn't work. . . .

VOICE. We are deserted by God for our evil ways. It is the new flood, without rain. . . .

NEWSBOY. They're licked.

VOICE. This isn't 1918! This is to-day!

VOICE. See what happens tomor-row!

VOICE. Anything can happen now! Anything!

VOICE. They're coming. We must stop them!

VOICE. We must find ways, find means!

VOICE (*the* REPORTER, *exulting*). They're coming! There will be no ways, no means!

SEMI-CHORUS (*mocking*). What are you going to do?

CHORUS. *What are you going to do?* (*They laugh sardonically.*)

THIRD GENERAL. Let me have a ma-chine gun! Sergeant! A machine gun!
(*A bolt of light comes down to a machine gun set to the left of the grave, midway between the edge of the grave and the wings. The* GENERALS *are clustered around it.*)

THIRD GENERAL. I'll show them! This is what they've needed!

FIRST GENERAL. All right, all right. Get it over with! Hurry! But keep it quiet!

THIRD GENERAL. I want a crew to man this gun. (*Pointing to* FIRST SOLDIER) You! Come over here! And you! You know what to do. I'll give the command to fire. . . .

FIRST SOLDIER. Not to me, you won't. . . . This is over me. I won't touch that gun. None of us will! We didn't hire out to be no butcher of dead men. Do your own chopping.

THIRD GENERAL. You'll be court-martialed! You'll be dead by tomor-row morning. . . .

FIRST SOLDIER. Be careful, General! I may take a notion to come up like these guys. That's the smartest thing I've seen in this army. I like it. . . . (*To* DRISCOLL) What d'ye say, Buddy?

DRISCOLL. It's about time. . . .
(*The* THIRD GENERAL *draws his gun, but the other* GENERALS *hold his arm.*)

FIRST GENERAL. Stop it! It's bad enough as it is! Let him alone! Do it yourself! Go ahead, do it!

THIRD GENERAL (*whispers*). Oh, my God. . . . (*He looks down at gun, then slowly gets down on one knee behind it. The other* GENERALS *slide out behind him. The* CORPSES *come together in the middle of the grave, all facing the gun.* THIRD GENERAL *fumbles with the gun.* VOICES *call.*)

REPORTER. Never, never, never!

JULIA. Walter Morgan, Beloved of Julia Blake, Born 1913, Died 1937.

MRS. DEAN. Let me see your face, Baby?

MARTHA WEBSTER. All you remember is a glass of beer with a couple of bums on Saturday night.

KATHERINE DRISCOLL. A green and pleasant grave . . .

BESS SCHELLING. Did it hurt much, John? His hair is blond and he weighs twenty-eight pounds.

JOAN. You loved me best, didn't you, Henry? . . . best . . .

VOICE. Four yards of bloody mud . . .

VOICE. I understand how they feel, Charlie. I wouldn't like to be underground . . . now . . .

REPORTER. Never, never!

VOICE. Never!

MARTHA WEBSTER. Tell 'em all to stand up! Tell 'em! *Tell 'em!*
(*The* CORPSES *begin to walk toward the left end of the grave, not marching, but walking together, silently. The* THIRD GENERAL *stiffens, then starts to laugh hysterically. As the* CORPSES *reach the edge of the grave and take their first step out, he starts* firing, laughing wildly, the gun shaking his shoulders violently. Calmly, in the face of the chattering gun, the* CORPSES *gather on the brink of the grave, then walk soberly, in a little bunch, toward the* THIRD GENERAL. *For a moment they obscure him as they pass him. In that moment the gun stops. There is absolute silence. The* CORPSES *pass on, going off the stage, like men who have leisurely business that must be attended to in the not too pressing future. As they pass the gun, they reveal the* THIRD GENERAL, *slumped forward, still, over the still gun. There is no movement on the stage for a fraction of a second. Then, slowly, the* FOUR SOLDIERS *of the burial detail break ranks. Slowly they walk, exactly as the* CORPSES *have walked, off toward the left, past the* THIRD GENERAL. *The last* SOLDIER, *as he passes the* THIRD GENERAL, *deliberately, but without malice, flicks a cigarette butt at him, then follows the other* SOLDIERS *off the stage. The* THIRD GENERAL *is the last thing we see, huddled over his quiet gun, pointed at the empty grave, as the light dims —in the silence.*)

CURTAIN

LIST OF CONTRIBUTORS

ANATOLE FRANCE (1844-1924)
AUGUST STRINDBERG (1849-1912)
OSCAR WILDE (1856-1900)
LADY GREGORY, ISABELLA AUGUST
    PERSSE (1859-1932)
ANTON CHEKHOV (1860-1904)
JAMES M. BARRIE (1860-1937)
ARTHUR SCHNITZLER (1862-1931)
MAURICE MAETERLINCK (1862-1949)
W.W. JACOBS (1863-1943)
JOHN GALSWORTHY (1867-1933)
JOHN M. SYNGE (1871-1909)
SERAFIN QUINTERO (1871-1919)
    & JOAQUIN QUINTERO (1873-1944)
LORD DUNSANY, EDWARD JOHN MORETON
    DRAX PLUNKETT (1878-1957)
WILLIAM STANLEY HOUGHTON (1881-1913)
AUSTIN STRONG (1881-1952)
PHILIP MOELLER (1880-1958)
SUSAN GLASPELL (1882-1948)
KENNETH SAWYER GOODMAN (1883-1918)
RUPERT BROOKE (1887-1915)
HOLWORTHY HALL (PSEUDONYM),
    HAROLD E. PORTER (1887-1936)
EUGENE O'NEILL (1888-1953)
GEORGE S. KAUFMAN (1889-1961)
LAWRENCE LANGNER (1880-1962)
LEWIS BEACH (1891-1947)
EDNA ST. VINCENT MILLAY (1892-1950)
ALICE GERSTENBERG (1893-1972)
NOEL COWARD (1899-1973)
CLIFFORD ODETS (1906-1963)
WILLIAM SAROYAN (1909-   )
IRWIN SHAW (1914-   )